CONVEYANCING
LAW & PRACTICE

Michael Harwood BA, LLB (Cantab), Solicitor
Senior Lecturer in Law
Leeds Metropolitan University

Cavendish
Publishing
Limited

CONVEYANCING
LAW & PRACTICE

Cavendish
Publishing
Limited

First published in Great Britain 1993 by Cavendish Publishing Limited, 23A Countess Road, London NW5 2XH.
Telephone: 071-485 0303   Facsimile: 071-485 0304

British Library Cataloguing in Publication Data

Harwood, Michael
Conveyancing Law & Practice (Law & Practice Series)
I Title II Series
344.206438

ISBN 1-874241-78-3

Printed and bound in Great Britain

To Alex and all those who proceed without conveyance.

They should inherit the earth.

CONTENTS

CONTENTS

TABLE OF STATUTES

TABLE OF CASES

INTRODUCTION

The scenario

Do not assume everything (or indeed anything) said, done or advised by Timothy Trippit to be correct. He is, imagine, a trainee solicitor during the first six months of his articles with Jarndyce & Jarndyce. He may be a nephew of one of the partners; or wear a recognisable tie; or just have a mental block when it comes to conveyancing. You may think that he is not as well supervised as professional practice rules (see Rule 13 of the Solicitors' Practice Rules 1990) and a proper trainee solicitor contract require. Never mind! You are to learn (hopefully) from his mistakes; by spotting his mistakes.

Miss Pinky and Mr Perky, who were jointly running the conveyancing department, have just 'run off' together leaving, between them, two partners, five children and numerous uncompleted conveyancing transactions. This may show that there *is* romance in conveyancing; but it has left a very inexperienced Timothy in charge. Fortunately, the house market, and with it conveyancing work, is at present very slack. And, fear not. Pinky and Perky may return (para.16.1).

'Old Jarndyce', as he is known throughout town, will on the other hand materialise to give the (hopefully) correct view of law and practice. He may be imagined perhaps with very white hair; something between an oft-retiring partner and the spirit incarnate of better conveyancing yet to come.

The aims of this book

Conveyancing law and practice is founded in land (and contract) law. I spent a good deal of time at college studying the ancient law of strict settlements but never saw the facsimile of a simple conveyance, far less a real deed. Until I began to work in a solicitor's office, I never fully grasped that Blackacre and Whiteacre were real bits of land, bricks and mortar and corner shops in real streets and real countryside; that by simply drafting deeds, you could make land law do things; and turn ideas into private property.

To the untutored, conveyancing may seem like a series of blank forms to be completed, ready-made precedents to be copied, a checklist of 'things to do before completion'. But all the ready-made forms, precedents and procedures can only be used and adapted to produce effective conveyancing if the land law which gave them birth is fully understood. A good conveyancing practitioner must be a good conveyancing lawyer; and a good conveyancing lawyer is a good land lawyer. If you have not embraced a proper understanding of land law, you should probably not be embarking on a conveyancing course.

This book focuses on residential conveyancing. In the detail that space permits, it describes the forms and procedures used in this area. It shows Timothy handling (and more frequently mishandling) the various stages of typical transactions. It shows, generally through the mouth of Old Jarndyce, how they should be handled and attempts to expand and discuss the law which determines the forms and procedures. Hopefully, the reader will be helped to learn, not only how to do what she is doing, but why she is doing it and how, in the interests of a particular client in a particular transaction or of all clients, creatively to adapt and modify what she is doing. Further, it focuses on freehold conveyancing, with a chapter at the end on leasehold and residential conveyancing, pointing out where the two differ.

Hopefully, too, this book will provide the sufficiently detailed exposition of the law necessary to support the workbooks produced for individual legal practice courses and to support other students studying conveyancing.

Knowledge of the law and practice is no more than a tool. As already suggested, the good practitioner must be able to adapt the tool to the needs of a particular client or circumstance. But, in addition, she needs the skills actually to use the tool – not, as it were, clumsily to stick it into the nervous client. It is beyond the scope of this book to teach the skills – negotiating, interviewing, drafting, researching, etc. Indeed, adequate teaching of at least some of them is beyond the scope of any written text. They can only be learnt by constant performance and correction. I have, however, endeavoured, where possible in the course of describing transactions, to focus attention on the importance and use of these skills, especially research and drafting.

Timothy's transactions

The text picks up, from time to time, four transactions being handled (or mishandled) by Timothy. None of them is followed step by step throughout. They are intended to give some idea of the law in practice; the use of forms, etc. Brief details of these transactions and where they are dealt with in the text are given in Appendix 2.

Appendix 1 contains a checklist of the main steps likely to be followed in the typical sale and purchase transactions. It is designed in part to present a framework within which to view these transactions. It is important to have a checklist for a transaction – unless you have an infallible memory for what you should do today rather than for what you should have done yesterday. In practice, you need to devise your own system of keeping track of a transaction to ensure that steps are taken at the right time and nothing is overlooked.

Further reading and research

I have included a short bibliography at the end of the book (Appendix 8). This includes standard texts on land, contract, trust law, etc. with which the reader should in any case be familiar.

More importantly, it also includes conveyancing practitioners' works on the substantive law and published precedents useful to conveyancing lawyers. Interspersed in the text are questions – frequently asking the reader to identify Timothy's latest error and correct it. Answers to these questions are not provided. In practice, there are no answers at the end of the book. You form a view and take a decision; and end up with either a satisfied customer or a process server at the door. The questions should be considered after reading the relevant parts of this text, those in the bibliography and doing any other necessary research.

It might be a good idea to collect your answers in a file; and review them as your knowledge of conveyancing and the law increases.

You should read both the text and the questions critically. A relatively short, general text cannot deal with every possible set of facts and circumstances. As you read you should constantly be asking yourself: 'What would be the position if the facts were like this instead of as stated; if this had happened instead of what is said to have happened?'; that is, constantly to be asking 'Yes, but what if ...?' questions.

I have not 'overloaded' the text with citation of cases and articles. A book of this size and range could not discuss in detail all the difficult points that might arise on any day in practice. Such points can only dealt with (other than by checking one's negligence policy) by referring to the detailed, specialist practitioners' works where all the necessary references will be found.

Usages in the text

Where another text is referred to frequently, I have used an abbreviated citation as indicated in the bibliography.

I have set out only one solicitor's letter in full, with addresses, heading, etc. (see Document 1.6.2); for the rest, for reasons of space, I have merely indicated the identities of the writer and recipient.

The text refers throughout to the Standard Conditions of Sale (Second Edition) (identified in the text as the 'Standard Conditions'). More specifically, reference is to the printed form of Agreement published jointly by the Law Society and the Solicitors' Law Stationery Society which incorporates the Standard Conditions. This set of standard conditions, produced jointly by the Law Society and the Solicitors' Law Stationery Society plc, was intended to replace the Law Society

Conditions (1984 revision) and the National Conditions of Sale (20th edition) – two of the most commonly used sets of standard conditions. The Standard Conditions provide illustration of a typical set of standardised contract conditions used in practice. A copy of the Standard Conditions is contained in Appendix 3.

In general, where the text does not make a distinction between registered and unregistered conveyancing law or practice, it can be assumed that they are the same.

After toying uncomfortably with the (s)he, his/her format, I have used the female gender throughout where either would be possible and the male traditional. If I had been a feminist I would probably have done this without mentioning the fact; it may therefore be taken as a 'gesture' to post-feminism!

Many thanks to my brother who produced the plans to go with the various transactions.

I gratefully acknowledge the permission of the Law Society to reproduce the Standard Conditions of Sale, the formulae for exchanging contracts by telephone or telex, their code for completion by post and parts of the TransAction Protocol documentation. I also gratefully acknowledge the permission of the Solicitors' Law Stationery Society to reproduce the Standard Conditions of Sale; the part of the Local Land Charges search form and Additional Enquiries of the local authority; the draft Land Registry form of transfer; and the applications for official searches in the Land Charges Registry and the Land Registry.

Finally, I have endeavoured to deal with the law as at 1 October, 1993.

Michael Harwood

CHAPTER 1

TAKING INSTRUCTIONS

TIMOTHY AT WORK. THE FIRST MORNING

Monday, 1 February, 10 am. Timothy is sitting there, coffee in one hand, the *Times* crossword (with two clues completed) in the other. He has been sitting there since 9 am. The conveyancing market is slack. At last! His phone goes and reception tells him that a Miss Fancy French would like to see him.

Full of confidence, Timothy asks for her to be shown up. Maybe his first real conveyancing transaction; not one of those make-believe fantasies dreamt up by the tutors at law school, which Timothy could never take seriously. ('If only you had,' an off-stage Jarndyce might be heard to interject.)

Miss French enters.

Some minutes later - 65 to be precise - Miss French has departed together with her yapping three year old daughter, Debbie, and snivelling dog. Timothy has copious notes outlining in some detail Miss French's previous marital career (blessed by Debbie) and the supposed physical and cerebral prowess of her new 'friend', Sam Saunders. Timothy's scribbled jottings do reveal (at least to those who can read his scribble) that Sam has moved into her flat; that they have decided to buy a house together; and that Sam has just put down the deposit on the ideal place - 'Just opposite the Abbey - lovely for the dog in summer - and Debbie of course'; she wants Timothy to act for her and Sam. There is a great deal that Timothy has not learnt - for example, where Miss French lives, works or can be contacted!

OLD JARNDYCE COMMENTS

'This,' says Jarndyce, with his penchant for understatement, 'is not altogether a good start.'

When taking instructions, as at all stages of a conveyancing transaction, certain fundamental principles need to form the bedrock of your work.

1.1

1.2

CLIENT CARE

1.3   Efficiency. You do not want to waste your own (i.e. your firm's money-making) or your client's time. You do not want to have to keep going back to the client for information which could have been obtained at an earlier interview. As far as possible, get from the client at the first interview all the information necessary to proceed with the transaction; or the source where the information can be obtained. Whether the client is garrulous, like Miss French, or taciturn, it is your job politely and tactfully to elucidate all the necessary information. If you have to ask the client to discover further information, make sure she knows exactly what is required. Write it down if necessary.

At the same time, as a matter of courtesy and good solicitor-client relations (which will ultimately appear in the balance sheet as goodwill), you do not want the client to feel that she has been treated brusquely or not listened to sympathetically.

You also need, throughout the transaction, to keep the client fully informed of progress; to be satisfied that you are acting with her authority (below, para.1.9.1); and that you are properly advising on the implications of all aspects of the transaction.

Rule 15 of the Solicitors' Practice Rules 1990, on client care, provides:

'(1) Every principal in private practice shall operate a complaints handling procedure which shall, *inter alia*, ensure that clients are informed whom to approach in the event of any problem with the service provided.

(2) Every solicitor in private practice shall, unless it is inappropriate in the circumstances:

(a) ensure that clients know the name and status of the person responsible for the day to day conduct of the matter and the principal responsible for its overall supervision;

(b) ensure that clients know whom to approach in the event of any problems with the service provided; and

(c) ensure that clients are at all relevant times given any appropriate information as to the issues raised and the progress of the matter.' (*Guide*, p.16; and see *Guide*, Chapter 13).[1]

The commentary in the *Guide* includes the following which may be particularly relevant in a conveyancing transaction (para.13.03):

---

[1]   For evidence that Rule 15 is being flouted by a significant proportion of the profession, see the research of the Solicitors Complaints Bureau, reported in the Law Society Gazette, 21 March 1993, p.6.

On Rule 15(2)(c):

'1. One of the objects of this rule is to ensure that clients who are unfamiliar with the law and lawyers receive the information they need to make the legal process more comprehensible. This will reduce the area of potential conflict and complaint. Different levels of information may be appropriate for different clients.

2. Clients should normally be told in appropriate language at the outset of a matter or as soon as possible thereafter the issues in the case and how they will be dealt with. In particular, the immediate steps to be taken must be clearly explained. It may be helpful to give an explanatory leaflet to the client.

3. Solicitors should keep clients informed both of the progress of matters and of the reason for any serious delay which occurs.

5. Solicitors should normally explain to clients the effect of any important and relevant documents. At the end of the matter solicitors should normally write to clients confirming that it has been completed and summarising any future action to be taken by the client or the solicitor.

6. Solicitors should consider whether it is appropriate to confirm the advice given and the instructions received in writing. Confirmation in writing of key points will both reduce the risk of misunderstanding by clients and assist colleagues who may have to deal with the matter.'

The Council of the Law Society's Written Professional Standards: Information On Costs For Clients (revised, 1 February, 1991 - *Guide*, p.280) includes the following:

'(a) <u>On taking instructions</u>

On taking instructions the solicitor should:

(i) give clients the best information possible about the likely cost of the matter. If no fee has been agreed or estimate given, the solicitor should tell clients how the fee will be calculated, e.g. whether on the basis of an hourly rate plus mark up, a percentage of the value of the transaction, or a combination of both, or any other proposed basis.

(b) <u>On confirming instructions</u>

When confirming clients' instructions in writing the solicitor should:

(i) record whether a fee has been agreed and, if so, what it is and what it covers and whether it includes VAT and disbursements;

(ii) tell clients what other reasonably foreseeable payments they may have to make either to the solicitor or to a third party and the stages at which they are likely to be required; and

(iii) confirm oral estimates - the final amount payable should not vary substantially from the estimate unless clients have been informed of the changed circumstances in writing.'

As to giving information as to costs, the *Guide* comments (p.283):

'(4) When giving estimates, solicitors should take care to ensure that they are not binding themselves to an agreed fee unless this is their intention. Clear and appropriate words should be used to indicate the nature of the estimate.'

A conveyancing transaction is normally a relatively short-lived, standardised matter. It is common to charge a fixed fee. The letter confirming instructions should state the amount, make it clear whether or not it includes VAT; and give an estimate of disbursements. Most conveyancing disbursements - stamp duty, Land Registry fees, search fees, etc. are fixed or fixed in relation to the consideration; and so a fairly accurate estimate is possible once the purchase/sale price is known.

The First Annual Report of the Solicitors' Complaint Bureau commented on the effects of the lack of effective communication between solicitors and clients.

'Many of the complaints we get can be traced to a breakdown in communications between solicitor and client. About 90% of complaints are resolved immediately once the client understands what has been going on. Some of the complaints would never have been made if the solicitor had explained to his client what was happening or the client had asked him.'

'Informal complaints are also damaging: research has shown that dissatisfied customers are likely to tell far more people of their dissatisfaction than satisfied customers are of their satisfaction.'[2]

BACK TO TIMOTHY

1.4   Meanwhile, Timothy, realising that the interview has not been entirely satisfactory, goes to reception to get a telephone directory, hoping to find listed an unmistakable F. French or S. Saunders.

To his immense relief, Miss French is still there, telling the receptionist all about Sam. He asks her to spare a few more moments. 'We might as well take down a few details while you are here.'

By now, he has found in his desk two of the firm's standard blank forms - 'Instructions on Purchase' and 'Instructions on Sale'. With a nice, new-found blend of efficiency and charm, he soon has the first one completed as follows:

---

[2]   See *Client Care: A Guide*, Law Society, 1991, p.1.

Document 1.4.1 French/Saunders Purchase: Instructions

Jarndyce & Jarndyce
Instructions on Purchase
Client: *M/s French, Mr S. Saunders*

Date	1st February 1993
Full name and address of client 1	Fancy French, 22 Backup Lane, Ledchester LR5
Full name and address of client 2	Samuel Saunders, as above
Full names and address of sellers	Michel and Marie Melanie Rocard, 8 Longfellow Road, Ledchester
Name and address of sellers' solicitors	Copperfields, Ledchester
Name and address of estate agents	Dream Homes, Abbey Road branch
Details of property	
Address	24 De Lucy Mount, Ledchester
Tenure	Freehold
Price	£75,000
Whole or part	Whole
Deposit paid	£1,000 paid to Dream Homes [See para. 2.3.1.]
Chattels to be bought	
Price	To sort out with vendors
Fixtures to be taken by vendor	As above
Related sale	N/A Living in rented accommodation. Assured shorthold.
Synchronise exchange	N/A
Completion date	a.s.a.p. Not yet agreed. Seller happy with early date. Property empty.
Mortgage	Ledchester and Bongley,
Lender	Commercial Road branch.
Amount	£65,000
Joint purchasers: beneficial interest	To be instructed. Sam will go along with a joint tenancy. Advised joint tenancy.
Additional information	Would like keys on exchange to get on with redecoration. Seller has agreed
Local authority	Ledchester
Signed	TT

OLD JARNDYCE COMMENTS

1.5 The Instructions on Sale form will be quite similar.

Question Draft a suitable blank form for taking instructions on sale. Consider the importance and significance of each item of information included. *After* your attempt, compare it with the one in para.5.1.3. As your knowledge progresses review your draft. Should you add to or amend it?

The events just related emphasise the importance of using a set of checklists to reduce the danger of missing vital information or not taking necessary action at the right time. Develop a system of procedures that suits you and helps efficiency. It is useful to have a checklist for the whole transaction, on which each step can be ticked off as it is taken and a note made of anything outstanding so that it is not overlooked. However, remember that as much as conveyancing may be standardised or simplified, it is not a mass production-line process. No two transactions and the needs of no two clients are exactly the same. Proper skill involves the ability to spot, appreciate and deal with the uncommon feature, the pitfall in any transaction.

Question Fancy has said that the property is empty. Might the length of time for which it has been empty have any legal significance? Suppose that the property is vandalised or squatted (a) before exchange of contracts; or, (b) between contract and completion. Explain the possible legal implications. See Chapter 4.

Question Suppose Fancy tells you that the flat she and Sam are at present living in, is on a 12 months' assured shorthold, with about six months left to run. She asks you whether, assuming the purchase can be completed, she can save rent by giving notice and leaving before the 12 months expires. Advise her. Note the Housing Act 1988; and see Bibliography (Appendix 8).

TIMOTHY PONDERS

1.6 Feeling fairly pleased with himself, Timothy ponders his next step. He dictates the following three letters:

Document 1.6.1 French/Saunders Purchase: Letter to Dream Homes

Jarndyce & Jarndyce

Solicitors

24, The Strand, Ledchester LR2 3JF Tel: (2350) 002244 Fax: (2350) 123765 Dx: Ledchester Park Square 14709

Our ref: TT/MH

To: Messrs Dream Homes
Estate Agents
Abbey Road,
Ledchester
1 February 1993

Dear Sirs,

24 De Lucy Mount, Ledchester
Subject to contract

We are instructed that our clients, M/s F. French and Mr S.
Saunders, have agreed to purchase the above property for
£75,000 through your agency.
We understand that they have paid you a preliminary deposit
of £1,000.
Will you please kindly confirm and let us have a copy of your
particulars of sale.

Yours faithfully,

Jarndyce & Jarndyce

Jarndyce & Jarndyce

Partners: J.J. Jarndyce, Thomas Trippit, Trevor Trippit, Barry Bopper, Henry Oxbridge. **Consultant:** Edward Trippit

Note: For the statutes and rules governing the content of a solicitor's
notepaper, see the Solicitors' Publicity Code, 1990 (*Guide*, p.223); also,
Solicitors' Investment Business Rules 1990, Rule 8 (*Guide*, p.528)

Document 1.6.2 French/Saunders Purchase: Letter to Vendor's Solicitor

Jarndyce & Jarndyce

Solicitors

24, The Strand, Ledchester LR2 3JF Tel: (2350) 002244 Fax: (2350) 123765 Dx: Ledchester Park Square 14709

To: D. Copperfield & Co.
Solicitors
Bank Street, Ledchester LR2 6JT

1 February 1993

Dear Sirs,

24 De Lucy Mount, Ledchester
Your client: Mr & Mrs Rocard
Subject to Contract
Our ref: TT/MH1

We have today been instructed by Ms F. French and Mr S.
Saunders on the purchase of the above property for £75,000.
We understand that no completion date has been agreed; though
the property is now vacant and your client is happy to
exchange and complete as soon as possible.
We understand that your clients have agreed to let our
clients have the keys immediately on exchange to start redecoration.
We assume that, in accordance with your usual practice, you
do not wish to follow the Transaction Protocol [para. 7.12.]; and
we await receipt of draft contract at your earliest convenience.

Yours faithfully,

Jarndyce & Jarndyce

Jarndyce & Jarndyce

Partners: J.J. Jarndyce, Thomas Trippit, Trevor Trippit, Barry Bopper, Henry Oxbridge. **Consultant:** Edward Trippit

Document 1.6.3 French/Saunders Purchase: Client Care Letter

Jarndyce & Jarndyce

Solicitors

24, The Strand, Ledchester LR2 3JF Tel: (2350) 002244 Fax: (2350) 123765 Dx: Ledchester Park Square 14709

To: Ms French,
22 Backup Lane,
Ledchester LR6 3TE

1st February 1993

Dear Ms French,

<u>24 De Lucy Mount, Ledchester</u>

Further to your visit today re the purchase of the above, we confirm we are pleased to act for you and Mr Saunders on the charge discussed not including disbursements; and will you please to let us have a note of chattels agreed to be bought as soon as possible.

Yours faithfully,

Jarndyce & Jarndyce

Jarndyce and Jarndyce

Partners: J.J. Jarndyce, Thomas Trippit, Trevor Trippit, Barry Bopper, Henry Oxbridge. **Consultant:** Edward Trippit

OLD JARNDYCE COMMENTS

1.7   **Question** The letter to Ms French is not satisfactory in either style or content. In the light of para.1.3. above what matters should the letter deal with?[3] Draft a more suitable and more intelligible letter confirming instructions. Should it be addressed to M/s French alone? It is important that your client understands exactly what you are saying. To this end, two of the most important principles may be:

(a) To avoid legal jargon and long words wherever possible.

(b) To avoid long, involved sentences. Many a client has been lost in a forest of sub-clauses.

We will now look at some of the points that arise from these instructions.

1.8   STEPS FOLLOWING INSTRUCTIONS

The vendor's solicitor

1.8.1   At the time of instructing a solicitor, the vendor may or may not have found a prospective purchaser; or,indeed, may not yet have put the house on the market. The immediate steps to be taken and the urgency depend on what stage the vendor has reached in selling the property and the date for exchange and for completion which is being contemplated. They may also depend on whether TransAction Protocol is to be followed (para.7.12). This in turn depends upon the purchaser's solicitor agreeing to use it. The main significance, at this stage, of following TransAction Protocol is that the vendor's solicitor will makepre-contract searches and enquiries and supply them to the purchaser with the draft contract. Under traditional conveyancing practice, the purchaser's solicitor would be left to do these for herself.

The following steps will normally be necessary upon receipt of instructions from the vendor:

(a) Write to the client confirming instructions. See above as to what this letter should contain. The client might at the same time be sent a leaflet, either one produced by the firm or by the Law Society, explaining the steps which will have to be taken in the transaction.

(b) Write to the vendor's estate agents informing them that you have been instructed and to obtain a copy of the agent's particulars of sale.

---

3   And see, generally, *Client Care: A Guide*, The Law Society, 1991.

(c) Write to the prospective purchaser's solicitor. Depending on the stage that the matter has reached it may simply be to confirm that you are acting and will be sending a draft contract. If you are in a position to do so, the draft contract and documents to accompany it can be sent. You should establish at once with the purchaser's solicitor whether or not TransAction Protocol is to be used.

(d) Obtain the title documents.

One of the main functions of the vendor's solicitor is to draft the contract of sale. This determines what property, for what estate, with what rights and subject to what incumbrances, the vendor will be obliged to convey to the purchaser. When the contract has been formed and as part of the contractual obligation, the vendor will have to prove her title to the purchaser; that is to prove in the way required by conveyancing law that she does own what she has agreed to sell.

It follows that the vendor's solicitor needs to investigate the vendor's title and be satisfied what title she has and can prove before sitting down to draft the contract. The contract must be framed to offer only the title which the vendor has and can prove. These matters are dealt with in more detail in subsequent chapters. But it does mean that the vendor's solicitor will need to get the title documents as soon as instructions have been received.

In the case of unregistered title this means the title deeds. If the land is not mortgaged, the vendor will be able to produce them; or give written authority to the solicitor to obtain release of them from the bank or whoever else is holding them for the vendor. If the land is subject to an outstanding mortgage, the deeds will be held by the mortgagee. Most institutional lenders are prepared to release the deeds to a solicitor in return for a professional undertaking to hold them to the mortgagee's order and to either return them or redeem the mortgage (paras.5.1.1 and 5.13). For this purpose, the vendor-borrower's mortgage account number may be needed. If, for any reason, the mortgagee will not hand over the deeds, arrangements will have to be made to obtain copies from the mortgagee. Under s.96 of the Law of Property Act 1925, a mortgagor is entitled to inspect and have copies of the title deeds held by the mortgagee.

Similar principles apply if the title is registered. In this case, if there is no outstanding mortgage the vendor, as proprietor, will have a land certificate. This is the official copy of the register issued by the Land Registry (para.7.8(c)). If the land is mortgaged the land certificate is held at the Registry and a charge certificate issued to the chargee (mortgagee). The vendor's solicitor will obtain this in the same way as the title deeds in the case of unregistered land.

However, neither the land nor charge certificate necessarily reflects the current state of the register - and it is the register itself that determines the state of the vendor's title.

The vendor will therefore need to apply for an office copy of the register and title plan (para.13.12). Application is made on printed form 109 (para.11.2.1).

When writing to the mortgagee a redemption figure as at the date of estimated completion should also be asked for. This may be necessary to advise the purchaser on the financial aspects of the transaction.

(e) Pre-contract investigations on behalf of the purchaser. Under traditional conveyancing procedure, the purchaser's solicitor will make a number of pre-contract searches and investigations relating to the property. These are listed and dealt with in Chapter 4. Where TransAction Protocol is being followed, these will be made by the vendor's solicitor and supplied to the purchaser with the draft contract (Appendix 6). If the Protocol is being followed these should be put in hand on receipt of instructions.

The documents to be provided by the vendor's solicitor under TransAction Protocol include the Seller's Property Information Form containing a standard set of questions to be answered in part by the vendor and in part by her solicitor. The vendor's solicitor should get these answered by the vendor when taking instructions; or give the vendor the form to take away to complete. Similarly, a completed Fixtures, Fittings and Contents Form has to be supplied to the purchaser's solicitor detailing what chattels and fixtures are and what are not included in the sale. Filling this in should be attended to on taking instructions.

Even where the Protocol is not being followed, the following points should be noted:

(i) It may be followed in part. For example, the purchaser's solicitor may agree to take over (and pay for) a Local Land Charges Registry search done by the vendor's solicitor (para.4.5).

(ii) As already stated, the vendor's solicitor must satisfy herself as to the vendor's title before drafting the contract. For example, there may be some query whether the property is subject to restrictive covenants. If it is, they will have to be disclosed in the contract. Or the vendor may be uncertain whether or not she has signed papers, to finance central heating for example, creating a second mortgage on the property. Information on this will be needed to advise the client on the financial implications of the sale. It may be necessary to resolve such doubts by a search in the Central Land Charges Register; or, in the case of registered title, by checking the office copy entries on the register.

Thus, the vendor's solicitor may have to make some of these pre-contract searches to check any doubt as to the title which needs to be resolved before drafting the contract.

Question The vendor's spouse is claiming an equitable interest in the (unregistered) property and also threatening to register a right of occupation under the Matrimonial Homes Act 1983. Would a clear search in the Central Land Charges Register make it safe for the vendor's solicitor to advise her to ignore the claims of the spouse and proceed with the contract?

(iii) The purchaser's solicitor will be delivering a set of Enquiries before Contract similar to the Property Information Form. It may save time to get the standard enquiries answered by the vendor when taking instructions. Similarly, the parties will in any case need to agree on what fixtures and chattels are being excluded from or included in the sale. Again, it may be possible to get information on this when taking instructions; or at least direct the client to sort it out with the purchaser and produce the details.

The purchaser's solicitor

Here the following steps may be necessary: **1.8.2**

(a) Letter to the client confirming instructions; and dealing with the matters already mentioned.

(b) Letter to vendor's solicitors informing them that she is acting for the purchaser; and stating whether she wishes to use TransAction Protocol.

(c) If TransAction Protocol is not being followed it may be necessary to get the pre-contract investigations started, especially the Local Land Charges Search and Additional Enquiries of the local authority, (which can take the authority a substantial time to deal with). If enough detail has been supplied on taking instructions it may be possible to do this even before receipt of the draft contract. The urgency of taking these steps, depends on the time scale of the transaction.

Giving advice. Professional and legal obligation to the client

When taking instructions and as the transaction progresses, there will   **1.8.3**
be a number of matters on which the client may need to be advised.

A vendor will commonly need advice on the following matters:

(a) Finance, including your costs;

(b) Taxation, particularly capital gains tax;

(c) The implications, where this is the situation, of selling part of a property.

A purchaser will commonly need advice on the following:

(a) Finance, including advice on mortgages and your costs;

(b) Having the property surveyed;

(c) The implications of a joint purchase;

(d) Insurance.

Each of the above will be dealt with in the course of this book. Since much of the advice will be relevant and common to a great number of vendors and purchasers, it is useful if a firm produces a booklet called, say, 'Buying and Selling A Home' containing advice on these matters. This can be handed to each client with an indication that further, more specific and individual advice can be given as necessary.

The particular circumstances may immediately suggest that the client needs advice on some particular aspect of the transaction.

It is important to keep a file note of advice given.

Giving bad advice or failing to give advice when it should be given has a number of possible consequences (apart from loss of reputation and goodwill). These consequences may equally follow from any incompetence in handling a transaction.

A client's dissatisfaction, if it is not such as can be resolved by the firm's internal complaints handling procedures, may lead to action by the Law Society for inadequate professional service or, in a more serious case, professional misconduct; and/or to action by the client in the civil courts.

(a) Complaint to the Solicitors Complaints Bureau. A client can make a complaint to the Solicitor's Complaints Bureau of the Law Society in respect of inadequate professional services[4] – that is where 'the professional services provided by a solicitor in connection with any matter in which he or his firm had been instructed by a client were in any respect not of the quality that could reasonably have been expected of him as a solicitor ...' 'Inadequate professional service includes organisational as well as professional incompetence.' It might include, for example, unreasonable delay by a solicitor in dealing with the matter overall or in taking a particular step; failure by the solicitor to seek instructions; failure to following instructions; failure by the solicitor to account to the client or to account in time or making significant accounting errors; failure by the solicitor to advise the client or keep the client fully informed, or other lack of communication; and general incompetence or inefficiency (including organisational incompetence) that does not give rise to a specific legal cause of action in negligence.' (*Guide*, para.30.11).

---

[4]   Solicitors Act 1974, s.44A as amended by Administration of Justice Act 1985, s.1.

If there is found to have been inadequate professional services the Complaints Bureau may take the following steps:

(i)   Disallow all or part of the solicitor's costs;

(ii)   Direct the solicitor to rectify the error;

(iii)   Direct the solicitor to pay compensation to the client;

(iv)   Direct the solicitor to take at his or her expense such other action in the interests of the client as the SCB may direct. (*Guide*, para.30.13).

In a more serious case a client's complaint may lead to proceedings before the Solicitors Disciplinary Tribunal for unbefitting conduct or breaches of the rules relating to professional practice, conduct and discipline under the Solicitors Act 1974 as amended. In such event more or less serious sanctions from rebuke to being struck off may follow.[5]

(b) A claim in the civil courts in contract, or possibly tort, for negligence.[6]

The implied obligation of a solicitor to his client has been described as follows:[7]

> 'At common law a solicitor contracts to be skilful and careful, for a professional man gives an implied undertaking to bring to the exercise of his profession a reasonable degree of care and skill. It follows that this undertaking is not fulfilled by a solicitor either who does not possess the requisite skill or does not exercise it.
>
> 'A solicitor's duty is to use reasonable care and skill in giving such advice and taking such action as the facts of the particular case demand.
>
> 'The standard of care is that of the reasonably competent solicitor, and the duty is directly related to the confines of the retainer. It has been said that the court should beware of imposing on solicitors duties going beyond the scope of what they are requested and undertake to do. There is no such thing as a general retainer imposing on the solicitor a duty, whenever consulted, to consider all aspects of the client's interest generally.
>
> 'Although a solicitor is not liable for a mistake as to the construction of a doubtful statute, difficult to interpret or unexplained by decisions, he may be liable if he fails to realise that the statute presents difficulties of interpretation.
>
> 'A solicitor must pass on to his client and use all information material to his client's business regardless of the source of that information.'

---

5   See, generally, *Guide*, Part VII.

6   As to whether a claim can be brought in tort as well as contract, see *Midland Bank Trust Co. Ltd. v. Hett, Stubbs and Kemp* [1979] Ch. 374; and *Banque Keyser S.A. v. Skandia (U.K.) Insurance* [1989] 3 W.L.R 25, at p.106.

7   *Cordery's Law Relating to Solicitors* (8th ed.,1988), p.137 *et seq.*, footnotes omitted.

As always in negligence, each case depends on its facts and the view of the court as to what a reasonably competent solicitor would do in the situation. But, to give a few examples (taken from the same text, at p.144):

> 'A solicitor is liable for failing to inform a purchaser for whom he is acting that the rents of the property being purchased are in excess of the standard rents permitted by the Rent Acts and that the excess will have to be refunded if claimed by the tenants; for failing to inform his client of the risk of undertaking repairs in the absence of a signed contract and to obtain the signed contract at once; for failing to inform a purchaser that a local land charge search revealed that the plans of the building on the land being purchased had not been approved by the local authority; for not inquiring for title deeds when his client is advancing money on mortgage; for not making proper searches in bankruptcy on a purchase or mortgage, unless the position of the vendor or mortgagor is well known; for careless inquiry into the vendor's title, as where he was content with a partial copy and thereby overlooked a clause against alienation in a will; or where he failed to ascertain that the vendor to his client who purported to convey as beneficial owner was in fact a trustee and had purchased the property in breach of trust so that when the purchaser came to sell a year later he found the title was defective; or where an abstract was carelessly compared with the deeds so that a bad title was accepted.'

In conveyancing, there is a standard, recognised practice in most situations. Adherence to such practice is likely (though not invariably) to satisfy a court.[8] Conversely, where loss is caused as a result of departing from the general practice, a finding of negligence is likely to follow.

At the same time, even in what might be thought of as the humble field of residential conveyancing, the client's very best interest may require something beyond competence. There may be situations in which a bold departure from general practice is indicated, or in which there is no general practice to follow. If practice is governed only by the avoidance negligence writs, it may well become the practice of defensive law and of mediocrity; hardly the highest accolade for the aspiring young lawyer.

In addition to common law liability, the Supply of Goods and Services Act 1982 implies a term that a person such as a solicitor supplying a service in the course of business will act with reasonable care and skill, within a reasonable time (where no specific time has been agreed) and for a reasonable charge (ss.11–15).

Any attempt by a solicitor to limit such statutory or common law liability for negligence is subject to the Unfair Contract Terms Act 1977, s.2. which only allows it in so far as it is 'reasonable' as defined in the Act.

---

[8] See *Simmons v. Pennington* [1955] 1 W.L.R. 183. Contrast *Edward Wong Finance Co. Ltd. v. Johnson, Stokes and Master* [1984] A.C. 296, below, para.14.11(c); and *G.& K. Ladenbau (U.K.) Ltd. v. Crawley & De Reya* [1978] 1 W.L.R. 266, below, para.4.10.1.

JOINT PURCHASE AND CONFLICT OF INTEREST

Probably the large majority of home purchases are by partners, married or unmarried. In the absence of unusual circumstances, the same solicitor is likely to be acting for both partners and, indeed, also for the institutional lender providing the purchase loan. The same applies when the couple come to sell.

1.9

Fancy and Sam are, according to Fancy, purchasing jointly. Sam, we are told, has put down a deposit. This raises a number of issues to be considered.

Does Timothy have the authority to act for both?

So far Timothy has seen only Fancy. He has only her word that Sam is in agreement with the project. He has addressed the letter to her alone – both impolite and unwise.

1.9.1

Assuming that it is proper to act for both (below) it is important to be satisfied that your actions are authorised by both and that both are fully informed and advised. It is probably wise to see both before exchange to be sure that both are in agreement. Timothy might have made a note on the note of instructions that Sam was not present.

'A solicitor's authority springs from the retainer given to him by his client. His authority to act is limited by any special condition imposed, and supplemented by any special authority conferred, by the retainer.'[9]

Briefly, the authority of an agent can arise in the following ways.

(a) Actual authority, which may be express or implied. Implied authority is the authority to do acts which are reasonably incidental to the execution of the express authority. The scope of implied authority depends on the cirumstances of each case.

(b) Authority arising by operation of law; that is authority which has not actually been authorised. This may be:

(i) Apparent authority. This exists where there has been a representation of authority made by the principal to the third party with whom the agent has purported to act on behalf of the principal.

(ii) Usual authority. This term is sometimes used to mean implied or apparent authority. As a distinct type of authority, if it is, it means acts which are within the class of acts usually confided to an agent of that character.

---

[9]   Cordery, p.76.

(iii) Authority of necessity.

(iv) Authority arising by ratification of an initially unauthorised act.

If a solicitor, or anyone else, acts without authority, the supposed principal will not be bound. The agent herself may be liable for breach of warranty of authority.

The respective interests in law and equity

1.9.2   It is not, in general, your job to make decisions for your clients. It is your job to advise (in this case both of) them so that they can make a properly informed decision; and then to give legal effect to that decision.

In the case of a joint purchase - wherever you know that more than one person is contributing financially to or participating in the purchase - it is necessary to advise and take instructions on allocation of both the legal and equitable ownership of the property.

Normally, one would expect joint purchasers to take the legal title jointly and be registered as joint proprietors (a conveyance on sale of all unregistered freehold land now giving rise to compulsory registration of title). This will mean that neither can deal with the property without the consent of the other (or a court order under s.30 of the Law of Property Act 1925). If only one person is registered as proprietor, that person can sell and deal with the property without consent of anyone else, unless a restriction has been entered on the register preventing any disposition giving rise to capital money by a sole proprietor from being registered (para.7.7(c)). Even with a restriction, it would in principle be open to the proprietor to appoint a second trustee and so overreach the equitable interest of any beneficiary.

As to the equitable ownership, a number of principles should be kept in mind.

First, in equity the parties can be joint tenants or tenants in common; and, if tenants in common, either in equal shares or in some other shares. The significant feature of a joint tenancy is the right of survivorship; though a joint tenancy in equity can be severed unilaterally, *inter vivos*, by any one of the joint tenants.

Secondly, the equitable interests should be expressly declared in the conveyance or (in the case of registered land) transfer, or in some other written form, by those contributing to the purchase price[10] and signed by

---

[10] The declaration must be made by those contributing the purchase money. In *City of London Building Society v. Flegg* [1988] A.C. 54. their was a declaration of trust for themselves by the son-in-law and daughter. This could not effect the beneficial entitlement of the parents who had contributed to the purchase money. And, although the interests of the parents were overreached by the mortgage, this did not affect their claim to a share in the money received.

all of them to satisfy the Law of Property Act 1925, s.53(1)(b). Such an express declaration will normally be decisive regardless of the actual contribution of each party; and will only be set aside by the court in the event of fraud, misrepresentation or undue influence.[11]

On a transfer of registered title to joint purchasers, the printed form of transfer provides for a statement by the transferees as to whether the survivor can give a valid receipt for capital money arising on a disposition of the land. This might be thought enough in itself to indicate a beneficial joint tenancy. The courts have decided otherwise; and it should be seen as no more than an indication of whether the Registrar is required to enter a restriction, as mentioned above, on the register. It is intended to determine whether a purchaser can safely deal with a sole, surviving proprietor. It is always important, in conveyancing, to distinguish between what interest a person has in property and whether a purchaser will be affected by that interest.

Probably contrary to what was a common belief and commonly acted on, the courts have decided that a statement that the survivor of joint tenants can give a valid receipt for capital money, will not in itself be taken to indicate an intention to create a joint tenancy. Such a statement could also be made where the joint proprietors hold in trust for one other adult person absolutely. In such a case, the 1925 legislation does not impose a trust for sale; so a sole trustee can deal with the land and, in this situation, this statement would be made to reflect this fact.[12]

In *Re Gorman*[13] the facts were slightly different. The transfer, in addition to containing the statement that a survivor could give a receipt for capital money, contained a declaration that 'The transferees are entitled to the land for their own benefit'. This - not a model of the specific - did not state whether they were to be joint tenants or tenants in common in equity. But it did, so the court in *Huntingford* analysed, rule out the possibility that they held for some sole, third person.[14] The statement that a survivor could give a receipt could therefore only be referring to a beneficial joint tenancy.

The above cases demonstrate the importance with a transfer of registered land, as with a conveyance of unregistered, of making an express declaration of the beneficial interest, whether a joint tenancy or a

---

[11] See *Goodman v. Gallant* [1986] 2 W.L.R. 236; *Bank of Montreal v. Jane Jaques Stuart* [1911] A.C. 120.

[12] *Huntingford v. Hobbs* [1992] F.L.R. 437; applied in *Skelding v. Hanson* and *Evans v. Hayward*, (both 1992, Lexis Transcripts).

[13] [1990] 1 W.L.R. 616.

[14] In fact it did not. If X provides the purchase money and the property is conveyed to A and B, no declaration by A and B alone can affect X's equitable, sole entitlement to the whole property. See footnote 10 above.

tenancy in common is intended; and if the latter, the respective shares to be held. If this declaration is made, as is normal, in the transfer itself, a copy of the transfer certified as accurate by the solicitor should be kept with the title deeds; for the transfer itself is retained in the Registry and not normally released.

Thirdly, where there is no effective, express declaration of the beneficial interests, the courts will apply the presumptions and principles of equity (with which the reader should be fully familiar and which should not need iteration here) to determine those interests. The starting point is that if a person has contributed to the purchase price the courts will presume a resulting trust in favour of that person of a share in proportion to the contribution.[15]

Fourthly, it is particularly important to ascertain and evidence in proper written form the intention as to beneficial entitlement in the case of purchasers who are not married (whether or not co-habitees). In the absence of marriage (when the Matrimonial Causes Act 1973 gives the court wide discretion to adjust property rights), once fixed, entitlement to the property can only be varied by agreement.

Fifthly, where legal title is to be held by a purchaser who has a spouse, that spouse (whether or not she has an equitable interest) is likely to have a statutory right of occupation under the Matrimonial Homes Act 1983, which can be protected on the register and cannot be overreached; though it cannot be overriding.

Timothy appears to have advised a joint tenancy without any enquiry as to the respective contributions of Fancy and Sam, and without even seeing Sam to learn his views on the matter.

Question In the light of the above, and any further necessary research, draft a short (maybe 500 words) section on joint purchasing that might go into a firm's leaflet of advice to clients purchasing a house.

Question You are asked to advise A on the following facts; A and B (then co-habiting) purchased a large house with registered title 10 years ago. A contributed 60% of the purchase price; B 10%. The rest was raised by a building society mortgage-loan. Until six months ago A paid the mortgage instalments while B paid the other household expenses out of their respective wages. The transfer contained a statement that 'The survivor of them can give a valid receipt for capital money arising on a disposition of the land'. They were subsequently registered as joint proprietors and no restriction was (or has been) placed on the register.

---

15 For these principles see Cheshire & Burn, Chapter 10.

Six months ago, A and B split up and B is living elsewhere with a new partner. At the moment A is living with her mother and the house is unoccupied. She has just heard from a common friend that B has entered into a contract to sell the house to C, forging A's signature on the contract and on the form of transfer. Completion is due next week; and B is planning to go abroad with his new partner and the entire proceeds of sale.

Advise A as to her equitable interest, if any, in the property.

Advise A on what steps, if any, can be taken immediately to protect her position. Would the position be affected if C had already received a clear certificate of search from the Land Registry in readiness for completion?

On what facts might A have a claim for negligence against the solicitor who acted on the original purchase? Note: *Ahmed v. Kendrick*.[16]

Conflict of interest

Fancy and Sam are joint purchasers. It is extremely common to act for   1.9.3
joint purchasers (as well as their institutional mortgagee) or joint vendors; and the question of conflict does not usually arise. Nevertheless it is a situation in which the solicitor should be conscious that it can arise; and consideration of it in this context is a convenient reminder that acting for both vendor and purchaser is not the only conflict of interest situation.

Rule 6 of the Solicitors' Practice Rules 1990 provides:

(1) Without prejudice to the general principle of professional conduct that a solicitor shall not accept instructions to act for two or more clients where there is a conflict between the interests of those clients, a solicitor or two or more solicitors acting in partnership or association shall not act for both seller and buyer on a transfer of land for value at arm's length, or for both lessor and lessee on the grant of a lease for value at arms's length, or for both lender and borrower in a private mortgage at arm's length.

(2) Provided no conflict of interest appears, and provided the seller or lessor is not a builder or developer selling or leasing as such, and provided the solicitor or any solicitor practising in partnership or association with that solicitor is not instructed to negotiate the sale of the property concerned, the rule set out in paragraph (1) of this rule shall not apply if:

(a) the parties are associated companies; or

(b) the parties are related by blood, adoption or marriage; or

(c) both parties are established clients (which expression shall include persons related by blood, adoption or marriage to established clients); or

---

[16] (1988) 56 P. & C. R. 120.

(d) on a transfer of land, the consideration is less than £5,000; or

(e) there is no other solicitor or other qualified conveyancer in the vicinity whom either party can reasonably be expected to consult; or

(f) two associated firms or two offices of the same firm are respectively acting for the parties provided that:

> (i) the respective firms or offices are in different localities; and

> (ii) neither party was referred to the firm or office acting for him or her from an associated firm or from another office of the same firm; and

> (iii) the transaction is dealt with or supervised by a different solicitor in regular attendance at each firm or office.

(3) In this rule:

(b) "private mortgage' means any mortgage other than one provided by an institution which provides mortgages in the normal course of its activities.'

Where these exceptions do not apply, the solicitor cannot act regardless of whether there is a conflict of interest. If one of the exceptions does apply she can act provided there is no conflict.

The fact that a transaction is at market value does not necessarily mean that it is at arm's length for the purpose of the rule. Whether a transaction is at arm's length must be determined by reference to the proximity and relationship between the parties. Thus, for example, it would be possible (subject to there being no conflict of interest) for a solicitor to act for personal representatives and a beneficiary or the settlor of a trust and the trustees (*Guide*, para.24.01).

Even where the case falls within Rule 6(2) a solicitor should not, save in the most exceptional circumstances, act for both seller and a buyer where there is a contract race (para.4.13).

A conflict of interest or a significant risk of conflict may exist before instructions are accepted, in which case they should not be accepted. Alternatively, it may arise during the course of the transaction. In this case, the solicitor should in general cease to act for both clients (*Guide*, para.15.03).

Fancy and Sam are of course joint purchasers; so the only question which arises is whether there is a conflict of interest or a significant risk of one.

There does not seem to be much judicial guidance on what amounts to a conflict of interest. Sam may be contributing the bulk of the difference between the mortgage loan and the purchase price; it may be the intention that he will be paying the mortgage instalments. One might expect this to be reflected in him having the bulk of the equitable interest. They may in fact have agreed to hold as beneficial joint tenants. It is not for a solicitor to tell her client not to make a gift to another; though it is her duty to advise of the implications. The following principles may be of guidance in deciding whether a conflict exists. If acting for both clients would involve a contravention or of any of them there is a conflict.

(i) With certain exceptions, a solicitor must disclose to a client and use all information relevant to her situation, whatever the source (*Guide*, para.16.07).

(ii) She must keep confidential a client's business until the client permits disclosure (*Guide*, para.16.03).

In an obvious illustration, if Fancy is seeking to keep some aspect of the matter secret from Sam - for example that she could afford to contribute to the purchase price - there would be a conflict situation.

(iii) If there is anything to suggest that a transaction between A and B to the advantage of B might be set aside for undue influence, then a solicitor should not be acting for both of them;[17] and should be insisting that at least one of them takes independent legal advice.

(iv) It is one thing to advise parties of the implication of the options open to them, and to give effect to their common, agreed course. It is another matter, and to be avoided in this context, to go beyond that and become involved in negotiating which option is to be adopted. You cannot, as it were, effectively negotiate with yourself. If there is any serious lack of agreement as to any aspect of the transaction, you should not be acting for both.

There is one final matter to mention in this context. Your client may need the consent of some other person to proceed with the transaction. For example, a vendor-wife may need the consent of the husband to release his rights under the Matrimonial Homes Act 1983. You are not acting for the husband. But in writing to seek his consent on behalf of your client you must again beware of the possibility of undue influence in such a situation/relationship and of the consent subsequently being set aside; and should at least advise the other person of the desirability of taking independent legal advice. This is not an issue of conflict but of duty to your own client to protect her transactions from subsequent avoidance.

In *Cresswell v. Potter*[18] the husband's solicitor gave a document in which the wife released to the husband her interest in the matrimonial

---

17 See *Bank of Montreal v. Jane Jacques Stuart* [1911] A.C. 120.

18 [1978] 1 W.L.R. 255; and see *Barclays Bank plc. v. O'Brien* [1992] 3 W.L.R. 593 (noted at [1992] Conv. 443, M.P. Thompson) which appears to put the onus on the benefitting party (the mortgagee bank in this case) to ensure that the co-owner fully understood the nature of the transaction. And for rejection of appeal in House of Lords, see [1993] 4 All E.R. 417.

home to an enquiry agent who persuaded the wife to sign. The result was that the release was subsequently set aside by the court. As Megarry J. put it:

> 'It would not have been very difficult to send to the plaintiff [the wife] a short covering letter which explained that by signing the release, the plaintiff would be giving up her half-share in Slate Hall to the defendant in return for nothing except an agreement by him that she would never have to pay anything under the mortgage, adding that she ought to consider getting independent advice before signing the document. If in the teeth of that information the plaintiff had executed the release without obtaining such advice, I think that the requirement that there should be independent advice might well have been discharged.'

OTHER RULES OF CONDUCT RELATING TO CONVEYANCING

1.10   (a) A solicitor acting for the seller of property should not prepare a form of contract which he or she knows or ought to know will be placed before a prospective buyer for signature before that party has obtained or has had a proper opportunity to obtain legal advice (*Guide*, para.24.03).

(b) A solicitor who conducts general insurance business should do so only as an independent intermediary and not as a tied agent (*Guide*, para.24.06).

(c) In relation to mortgages and life policies, a solicitor must comply with the Council statement on the Financial Services Act 1986: life policies and tied agents (*Guide*, para.24.07).

(d) It is not unprofessional for a solicitor to retain title deeds belonging to his or her client pending payment of professional costs owed by that client where the retention is a proper exercise of a solicitor's lien (*Guide*, para.24.11).

Other conduct principles are considered later, where appropriate.

LICENSED CONVEYANCERS

1.11   Section 22 of the Solicitors Act 1974, the foundation of solicitors' monopoly – or one should now really say former monopoly – of conveyancing, provides that any:

> 'unqualified person who directly or indirectly –
>
> > (a) draws or prepares any instrument of transfer or charge for the purposes of the Land Registration Act 1925, or makes any application or lodges any document for registration under that Act at the registry, or

(b) draws or prepares any other instrument relating to real or personal estate, or any legal proceeding,

shall, unless he proves that the act was not done for or in expectation of any fee, gain or reward, be guilty of an offence.'

To be 'qualified' a solicitor must not only have been admitted and be on the roll, but must also hold a current practising certificate.

That monopoly has been breached by s.11 of the Administration of Justice Act 1985 which allows licensed conveyancers to provide 'conveyancing services' as defined by s.11(3).

It has been further, and more fundamentally, breached by s.36 of the Courts and Legal Services Act 1990 which sets up the machinery for allowing building societies and other 'authorised practitioners' to provide conveyancing services.

According to the Council For Licensed Conveyancers, which controls the profession in the way that the Law Society controls the solicitors' profession, there are about 800 licensed conveyancers with about 1,500 students. Licensed conveyancers, in very much the same way as solicitors, are subject to a code of professional conduct; and have the backing of a professional indemnity insurance and a compensation fund.

The Law Society Council's statement on dealing with licensed conveyancers states, *inter alia* (*Guide*, p.447):

'In so far as dealings with licensed conveyancers are concerned, it should normally be possible to proceed as if the conveyancer was a solicitor and was bound by the same professional obligations as a solicitor. For example, if it is agreed to use the Law Society's code for the exchange of contracts by telephone, it is understood that any failure to respect the code would expose the licensed conveyancer to disciplinary proceedings of the same kind to which a solicitor would be exposed in similar circumstances: the same comment applies to the Law Society's code for completion by post, the use of client account cheques at completion and reliance on undertakings. In view of the fact that licensed conveyancers may practice in partnership or association with others, subject to approval by the Council for Licensed Conveyancers, it is however important to make sure that the person you are dealing with is a licensed conveyancer, or a person working immediately under his or her supervision.'

The identity of firms of licensed conveyancers can be checked in the Directory of Solicitors and Barristers.

Traditionally, conveyancing has been the bread and butter work of the conventional solicitors' practice. At present this situation is under serious threat. But so is the quality of the conveyancing service available to the public; whether from solicitors or licensed conveyancers; whether from conveyancers or the other professionals needed by the home mover.

'The real problem is that there has been an increase in the number of solicitors and others who offer conveyancing services as well as significant increases in capacity brought about by modern technology. This means that, apart from market extremes such as occurred in 1988, the capacity to do conveyancing work exceeds, and will probably continue to exceed, the amount of work available despite the growth in home ownership.

This, coupled with price advertising and a 'cheapest is best' mentality by the home-buying public, has resulted in a dramatic fall in conveyancing prices. This has made it difficult for firms to provide conveyancing services.'[19]

This book is an attempt to describe the legal aspects of a proper conveyancing service, whether provided by solicitors or licensed conveyancers. If it had been intended to explain how to provide such a service and make a profit, it probably would not and could not have been written.

---

[19] Paul Marsh, Chairman of the Law Society's property and commercial services committee; 'Low Cost Conveyancing', (*Law Society's Gazette*, 12 May 1993, p.2.

CHAPTER 2

FINANCE

TIMOTHY IS CONFUSED AGAIN

Timothy is at his most reassuring and least informative.

Miss Obebe is worried about the cost of buying and selling. Her boyfriend was going to help with the deposit on the purchase but he has just been made redundant. She is expecting a legacy from her father's estate – he died last month. That is what prompted her to move; but the step-mother is claiming a share of the estate – under the Family Provision Act or something – she was separated from Olive's dad and he left her nothing in the will. She does not know when the money will come through. She is a nurse but there are rumours that the hospital is going to close. She has had an offer from the building society and they seem happy about lending her 85% of the price; but they want her to take out an endowment mortgage – whatever that is – and there is payment for something called an called an excess guarantee policy. She is beginning to think of giving up the idea of moving and staying where she is.

Timothy, perhaps motivated by something less than a proper professional attitude, sees one of his first conveyancing transactions about to disappear; and tells her that there is really nothing to worry about. 'Don't worry,' he says, 'You can easily raise the deposit by a bridging loan. We will give an undertaking to cover that. And the excess policy is just in case you die. Don't worry about our costs; they are never as much as clients expect; and we can reduce stamp duty by allocating more of the purchase price to the carpets you are buying (Document 4.1.2). 'And by the way,' he adds, 'if you have not fixed things up with the building society yet, I can arrange an endowment policy on very good terms through my brother who works for one of the big life companies.'

Question After reading this chapter and doing any further necessary research, comment on Timothy's advice; particularly in relation to a bridging loan, giving an undertaking, the excess guarantee policy, the legal costs, arranging an endowment mortgage and the adjustment of the purchase price.

List the further information you would need to advise Miss Obebe properly on her finances.

OLD JARNDYCE IS LESS REASSURING

2.2   The average client is on a tight budget when changing homes. The client should be asked, when you are taking instructions, to detail how she proposes to finance the transaction; advised of all the possible costs and expenses with actual (where possible) or approximate amounts; and warned not to exchange if there is any risk of not being able to meet the commitment.

From a financial perspective there are three stages to a purchase transaction. Before exchanging the client should be satisfied that she will have the necessary financial resources at each stage. Money will be needed at the following three stages:

(i)   Payment of the deposit and any other pre-completion expenditure.

(ii) The balance of the purchase price and other payments to be made on completion.

(iii) Post-acquisition. Mortgage instalments and the other recurrent costs of home ownership.

Nothing further need be said about (iii). Taking the first two in turn:

THE DEPOSIT

2.3   A deposit is a part payment of the purchase price made to the vendor on exchange of contracts. But it is more than this: it is security for performance of the contract. If the purchaser wrongfully fails to complete (see Chapter 16) the vendor will in principle be entitled to forfeit (i.e. retain) the deposit - regardless of her actual loss - subject to the overriding discretion of the court under s.49(2) of the Law of Property Act 1925 to order its return.[1]

Under an open contract there is no obligation to pay any deposit. Invariably the contract will require one.

Standard Condition 2.2.1. provides:

'The buyer is to pay or send a deposit of 10% of the purchase price no later than the date of the contract. Except on a sale by auction, payment is to be made by banker's draft or by a cheque drawn on a solicitors' clearing bank account.'

10% is the conventional amount; but the parties can agree some smaller or larger deposit.

---

1   See *Faruqi v. English Real Estates Ltd.* [1979] 1 W.L.R. 963; below, para.10.5.1.

A banker's draft is in effect a cheque drawn by a bank on itself payable at its head office or another branch office or on another bank; so it is not liable to be stopped or dishonoured. The deposit money will be transferred by the purchaser's solicitor into the bank's own name and the bank will provide the draft in favour of the vendor's solicitor.

Normally, in a sale by private treaty (i.e. not by auction) the vendor's solicitor will not and should not exchange without either receiving payment of the deposit or a solicitor's undertaking to pay it (as is likely in the case of exchange by telephone).

If for any reason - as might happen for example on a sale by auction - a contract is made and the deposit deliberately not paid, the vendor can (under both an open contract and the Standard Conditions) immediately treat the contract as discharged and sue for damages. These will be treated as at least the amount of the deposit regardless of actual loss.

Where Standard Condition 2.2.4. applies and the vendor takes a cheque which is subsequently dishonoured, for the deposit, the vendor must give seven working days notice before electing to treat the contract as discharged. The vendor does not of course have to treat the contract as discharged; and can instead treat it as still subsisting and seek to enforce payment of the deposit and the contract as a whole.

Preliminary deposits

A deposit should be distinguished from what is sometimes called a preliminary deposit - that is a sum paid (generally to the vendor's estate agent) when an agreement to buy subject to contract is made.

2.3.1

Such a payment is not in law a deposit at all; it is simply an indication of the prospective purchaser's serious intent. In relation to the contract, its effect is psychological, not legal. The prospective purchaser remains absolutely free to withdraw for whatever reason and recover the deposit.[2] Similarly it does not obligate the vendor to sell. If the negotiations do mature into a binding contract, the payment unless agreed otherwise will become part of the deposit proper and subject to the principles outlined below.

An estate or other agent does not have the implied or ostensible authority of the vendor to receive such a preliminary deposit; and the vendor's knowledge that it is being taken does not by itself amount to such authority.[3] It follows that the agent does not hold the money as

---

[2] Unless the payment can be shown in fact to be the consideration for a separate binding contract - e.g. a payment for an option to purchase the property; which would be subject to the Law of Property (Miscellaneous Provisions) Act 1989.

[3] *Sorrell v. Finch* [1977] A.C. 728; in which five prospective purchasers each paid a deposit of £550 to the agent before he disappeared.

agent for the vendor (nor as stakeholder); that if the contract does not materialise the purchaser will normally have to look to the agent to recover the deposit; and will have no right to recover it from the vendor.

Recovery of such a preliminary deposit is now substantially protected at least in the case of reputable agents belonging to one of the recognised professional bodies. Section 13 of the Estate Agents Act 1979 provides that client's (i.e. the prospective purchaser here) money is held on trust for the client, thus protecting it in the event of the agent's bankruptcy. Section 14 requires such money to be paid into a separate client account under the Estate Agents (Accounts) Regulations 1981.[4] Section 16 which requires an estate agent to have authorised insurance cover for clients' money against non-repayment by the agent, has not yet been brought into force; though the recognised professional bodies do in fact have bonding schemes to serve this purpose.

From every point of view, if a purchaser is persuaded to pay a preliminary deposit it should be for as small an amount as possible.

Position of payee of deposit

2.3.2   The deposit proper may be paid direct to the vendor. More usually it will be paid to the vendor's agent; generally her solicitor; or maybe the auctioneer in the case of a sale by auction.

Such a payee may hold the deposit as either agent for the vendor or (although in other respects agent for the vendor) as stakeholder.

A stakeholder is under an obligation not to release the deposit to either party (nor to anyone else) until that party becomes entitled to it. In *Rockeagle Ltd. v. Alsop Wilkinson*[5], a deposit of £35,000 was paid to the vendors' solicitor to be held by him as stakeholder. The vendors went into receivership, owing the solicitor £10,000. The plaintiffs took over the contract from the vendors, and they and the purchaser instructed the solicitor to transfer the deposit to a new stakeholder. The solicitor refused and on completion of the sale claimed to be entitled to retain the £10,000 out of the deposit. It was held that as a stakeholder the solicitor was obliged to transfer the deposit on the instructions of both parties; so was not entitled to retain the money due to him.

---

4   S.I. 1981/1520; and under para.7 of these regulations if more than £500 is paid the prospective purchaser may be entitled to interest on it.
5   [1991] 3 W.L.R. 573.

Question What would the position be if the vendor owed the solicitor a sum of money; the solicitor was *not* instructed to transfer the deposit held as stakeholder before completion; and completion took place. Would the solicitor in that case be entitled to retain the money due from the vendor out of the deposit? Note: consider the rules relating to a solicitor's lien.

If the transaction proceeds normally to completion, the vendor will become entitled to the deposit. The stakeholder will be personally liable if she hands it over to the wrong person; so if there is any possibility of dispute as to entitlement, it should not be handed over to one party without the authority of the other (para.14.8.1(b))

Money held by a person as agent for the vendor, on the other hand, must be handed over to the vendor at any time on demand, leaving the vendor free to do what she likes with it; though, of course, she may become liable to repay it to the purchaser if, for example, the purchaser lawfully rescinds. This means that the purchaser is not protected against the insolvency or fraud of the vendor; though she would have a lien on the property agreed to be bought to secure its return. Such a lien is registrable as a class CIII land charge in the case of unregistered land; by notice or caution in the case of registered title.

In the absence of contractual provision to the contrary, the vendor's solicitor or estate agent will hold any deposit as agent for the vendor; an auctioneer will hold as stakeholder.

Standard Conditions 2.2.2. and 2.2.3. provide:

'2.2.2. If before completion date the seller agrees to buy another property in England and Wales for his residence, he may use all or any part of the deposit as a deposit in that transaction to be held on terms to the same effect as this condition and condition 2.2.3.

2.2.3. Any deposit or part of a deposit not being used in accordance with condition 2.2.2. is to be held by the seller's solicitor as stakeholder on terms that on completion it is to be paid to the seller with accrued interest.'

'Accrued interest' is defined in Standard Condition 1.1.1(a).

This provision is designed to enable a deposit to be 'passed up the line' in the case of a chain of transactions. The first purchaser in the chain (likely to be a first-time buyer and financially the least secure) will have to find the deposit; her vendor will be able to use this deposit, supplementing it if buying a more expensive property with a larger deposit, as the deposit on her own purchase; and so on up to the top of the chain where the final deposit should be held by a solicitor as stakeholder. The advantage of this is that the same fund can be used towards the deposit on a number of transactions; and so smooth the operation of the chain. A disadvantage is that a purchaser may not know who is holding her deposit. If a purchaser in the chain becomes entitled to recover her deposit (on rescission) her vendor may no longer hold the deposit, have no right to recover it from her vendor, and be unable to repay it.

In practice, where a chain of contracts are all exchanged at more or less the same time, the deposit is likely to be sent, by mutual agreement, directly to the solicitor to the vendor at the top of the chain.

Clearly, a purchaser is more secure if the deposit is held by her own vendor's solicitor as stakeholder. Whether Standard Condition 2.2.2. and 2.2.3. ought to be amended by special condition to this effect is a matter of negotiation and whether the client herself wants to take advantage of it.

Question Draft such a special condition to override Standard Condition 2.2.2. and 2.2.3. Note: it can be done by a single short sentence.

Deposit money (like any other money) held by a solicitor as agent for the vendor will be subject to the Solicitors' Accounts Rules 1991, Part III (*Guide*, p.647) under which the vendor may be entitled to receive interest. Similarly, and subject to any agreement in writing, where the solicitor holds as stakeholder, interest (if payable under these Rules) must be paid to the person to whom the stake is paid (Rule 24). (Compare Standard Conditions 2.2.3. and 7.2(a).)

Under the Estate Agents (Accounts) Rules 1981 (S.I. 1981/1520) similar rules apply where the deposit is held by an estate agent or auctioneer as agent for the vendor. Where it is held by such a person as stakeholder any interest can be retained by the stakeholder.

Where Standard Condition 2.2.3 applies any preliminary or other deposit held by an agent or auctioneer should on exchange of contracts be transferred to the vendor's solicitor or the Standard Condition amended. In practice, neither is usually done. The agent is likely to be allowed to retain the money and eventually on completion deduct her commission from it.

If a purchaser becomes entitled to recover the deposit and it is held by an agent for the vendor, she must look to and can only look to the vendor for recovery and has a lien on the contract land to secure its recovery. The vendor will be liable whether or not she has actually received the money from the agent. If, in this situation, it is held by a stakeholder, the money is recoverable by the purchaser from the stakeholder; but if the stakeholder is insolvent or otherwise unable to repay, it can be recovered from the vendor who will thus bear the loss.

Financing the deposit

The purchaser will not receive any mortgage loan until completion of   **2.3.3**
the purchase; nor will she normally have received the proceeds of any
property she is selling before then. She will therefore have to find the
cash for the deposit from another source.

She may have her own available cash; but if a large percentage of the
purchase price is being borrowed on mortgage loan this may not be the
case. Other possibilities are:

(a) To negotiate a reduced deposit, or indeed non-payment of a
deposit, with the vendor. In this situation it should be noted that if
the vendor serves notice to complete (para.16.8) then under Standard
Condition 6.8.4. the full deposit becomes immediately payable. In
such a situation the purchaser is not likely to comply. The significance
is that whatever her actual loss the vendor will then become entitled
to the full amount of the deposit from the defaulting purchaser.

(b) The use of the deposit received on her own sale under Standard
Condition 2.2.2. This will by itself be less than the amount needed if
10% of a lower selling price.

(c) A short term bridging loan from a bank or other lenders. The
disadvantage is that the interest rate is likely to be high; and should
not normally be taken at least until contracts have been exchanged on
any sale which is going to finance the purchase.

(d) Use of a deposit guarantee scheme. This is arranged through an
insurer. The insurer will guarantee to pay the deposit to the vendor if
the purchaser fails to complete (and will then seek to recover it from
the purchaser). The disadvantage to the purchaser is that a premium
has to be paid to obtain such insurance.

Whatever method is resorted to, it should be stressed that the
purchaser should not proceed to exchange unless satisfied that at
completion she will have sufficient funds on an acceptable, long term
basis to finance the total purchase including the deposit.

In addition to the deposit, there may be other expenditure which has
to be met before any money becomes available at completion. For
example, there may be a survey or at least a lender's valuation fee.

FINANCING COMPLETION OF THE PURCHASE: AVAILABLE CAPITAL

A purchaser needs, before exchange of contracts, the information and   **2.4**
advice to enable her to calculate accurately how much capital she will
have available at completion; and how much she will need. She can then

decide whether she can afford to proceed. This is particularly important where, as so often is the case today, the client is borrowing a high proportion of the price on mortgage loan and has little capital of her own.

The available capital is likely to be derived from one of three sources.

(a) Personal savings and resources. By personal resources I mean money lent or given generally by a member of the client's family, quite possibly without security. Where capital is being provided by such a source, especially say a cohabitee, it may be desirable to make clear in a written document or note the exact terms on which it is being provided; whether as a gift or loan; if as a loan, on what terms and whether or not with security; and particularly important, whether the contributor is intended to acquire an interest in the property in return for the contribution. In this context, if there is any request for you to act also for the contributor whether or not a private mortgage security is involved, the professional rules relating to conflict of interest will need careful consideration (para.1.9.3).

(b) Proceeds of sale of the existing home. The client will need to know what capital proceeds will be available on completing the sale after meeting the related costs (below, para.2.6) and paying off any outstanding mortgages.

If you are not also acting on the sale you will have to get a net figure from the solicitors who are acting or the client herself.

If you are acting you will need to check what debts are secured on the property and get estimated redemption figures as at the expected date of completion from the creditors or the client herself. If the sale is to be completed later than the purchase, finance will have to be found (by bridging loan or otherwise) to cover the intervening period. It should be remembered that it is likely to be a condition of any mortgage advance that any existing loan is paid off before the new money is advanced.

It should also be remembered that work may have been done on the property being sold - for example, the installation of central heating - which is still being paid for by instalments. Such a credit arrangement may be secured by a charge on the property or (in the case of any chattels included in the sale) subject to a hire-purchase contract. In either case the purchaser will want to be satisfied that outstanding amounts will be paid off before completion. The client should be asked for details of any such agreement relating to anything the benefit of which is going to pass to the purchaser. Consideration may need to be given to whether anyone other than the client has a claim to part of the proceeds of sale - such as a contributor to the original purchase price. Finally, possible liability to capital gains tax may need to be considered (below, para.2.7.1).

(c) Mortgage loans. These merit a section to themselves.

MORTGAGE LOANS

Normally, the purchaser will be raising a substantial part of the price   **2.5**
by a mortgage loan from a building society or one of the other major
mortgage-lending institutions. Whether it is a repayment, endowment or
some other type of mortgage loan, the essence is that the borrower
(mortgagor) will execute a mortgage of the property to the lender
(mortgagee) as security for the loan and interest.

Types of mortgage

Today the lending institutions offer many different types of loan on a   **2.5.1**
variety of terms. The real difference between them all lies in the method
and terms for repayment of capital and interest; and to some extent in the
security required. Normally, mortgages are divided into two categories.

(a) Repayment mortgages

Here the property (the house) is mortgaged to the lending institution.
The loan is to be repaid over an initially agreed mortgage period
(commonly 20 or 25 years) by, generally monthly, instalments with
interest on the amount of loan outstanding from time to time. The initial
instalments are calculated by the lender so that on the basis of the then
rate of interest, at the end of the mortgage period the loan and all interest
will have been repaid and the mortgage be redeemed. Normally, the
borrower will agree to pay a fluctuating rate of interest which can be
varied up or down from time to time by the lender to reflect national
interest rate movements. Many institutions, in an attempt to attract
custom, agree to peg the interest rate for a specified period (fixed rate
mortgages); or offer a lower than usual rate of interest rate for an initial
period (low start mortgages) though the difference may be recouped later
in the life of the mortgage. If the interest rate is varied, the monthly
instalments will normally be varied; though sometimes an increase in
interest rates is accommodated by maintaining the same instalments and
extending the mortgage period. Each instalment will comprise in part a
repayment of capital (initially an extremely small part) and in part the
interest due. As time goes by and the outstanding loan is reduced the
amount of interest payable will reduce and consequently the element of
capital repayment in the instalment increase.

As with any institutional, domestic mortgage the borrower will be
entitled to repay the loan at any time (on giving any notice required by
the mortgage terms). Indeed, any limitation on this right in any mortgage
runs the risk of being held void as a clog on the equity of redemption. If

the borrower changes homes the existing mortgage will be redeemed out of the proceeds of sale; and a new loan secured on the new property. If the value of the property decreases and especially if a high proportion of its initial value has been borrowed, it is possible that the price realisable on sale will not be sufficient to pay off the outstanding mortgage debt. This 'negative equity' situation has become a familiar one in recent years with a falling property market.

The main disadvantage with a repayment mortgage by itself is that if the borrower dies during the mortgage period the outstanding loan will still have to be paid off. This is of particular importance where the property is the family home and the borrower's income needed to pay the instalments. The borrower can insure against this by taking out what is commonly called a mortgage protection policy, generally arranged with an insurance company through the lending institution. This is a life policy under which, in return for a regular fixed premium during the mortgage period, a capital sum is paid on death of the insured during the mortgage period. This amount payable decreases each year in line with the amount expected to be outstanding on the mortgage.

(b) Endowment mortgages

As with a repayment mortgage the land (the house) is mortgaged to the lender as security. The borrower pays interest (which again is normally liable to fluctuate) on the loan by usually monthly instalments for the agreed mortgage period. But here the borrower does not make any repayment of the loan capital during the mortgage period. At the end of the period the full amount of the loan is still outstanding; and interest has to be paid on this amount throughout the life of the mortgage.

In addition to the mortgage of the land, the borrower is required to take out an endowment insurance policy fixed to mature at the end of the mortgage period (or on earlier death). This will normally be arranged through the lending institution with an insurance company, the lending institution retaining any agency commission paid by the insurance company. The borrower will pay the regular, generally fixed, premiums on the policy. In return the policy will pay out the assured sum either on the death of the insured or at the end of the mortgage period whichever is the earlier. This capital will be available to pay off the mortgage loan. Whether it is sufficient depends on the terms of the policy. It may guarantee payment of a fixed sum with perhaps the possibility of a bonus depending on the success of the insurance company's investments. If the guaranteed sum is less than the loan – sometimes called a 'low-cost endowment' – with the difference depending on the bonus, the borrower may end up with insufficient to pay off the loan. One of the disadvantages is that there may be less scope to make adjustments to payments to deal with temporary financial difficulties of the borrower; and if the security is enforced by the lender the policy will have a very low surrender value in relation to premiums paid.

The endowment policy used as security may be a new policy taken out for the purpose; or it may be an existing policy already held by the borrower.

If the house is sold the loan will be paid off out of the proceeds of sale and the mortgage of both house and policy discharged. The policy can then be used to support an endowment mortgage on the new home. However, another disadvantage, if a more expensive property is bought with a larger loan an additional endowment policy will have to be taken out to cover the difference (unless the difference is lent simply on repayment terms).

The endowment policy will be mortgaged to the lender in addition to the land as an additional (collateral) part of its security. Each of the major lending institutions has its own standard documentation and requirements in relation to the policy. The solicitor acting for the lender must ascertain what these are and see that they are used and complied with. If the policy is an existing one, she should check with the insurance company that there is no outstanding mortgage of the policy.

The duty of the borrower's solicitor (likely to be the same person) to the client is to make sure that the endowment policy is in force and adequate to the client's needs and the insurers at risk when the money is released; and to be able to explain its financial and legal implications to the client.

From a legal point of view, as with land, a legal or equitable mortgage of an endowment policy is possible.

(i) A legal mortgage is created by an assignment of the policy in writing to the lender with a proviso for reassignment on redemption. To complete the assignment and enable the lender to sue on the policy in its own name express notice in writing of the assignment must be given by the lender to the insurers.[6] This notice should be sent in duplicate for one of the copies to be returned receipted by the insurers and placed with the deeds together with the policy and assignment, to be held by the lender.

On redemption of the mortgage before maturity – if the house is sold – a reassignment in writing should be signed by the lender. Commonly it is endorsed on the assignment; or included in the vacating receipt on the mortgage of the land itself.

---

[6]   Law of Property Act 1925, s.136.

The same process of assignment, notice and reassignment will be repeated for any new endowment mortgage.

(ii) Most lending institutions no longer require a legal mortgage of the policy and rely on an equitable one. No particular form is necessary for an equitable mortgage if the intention is present. A deposit of the policy with the lender is normally sufficient; though there will normally be written evidence of the purpose of the deposit either included in the mortgage of the land or some other document. This may also contain provision, by the borrower giving the lender irrevocable power of attorney, for the lender to be able to acquire legal title to the policy and so realise its value on default by the borrower without the intervention of the court.

Notice to the insurers is not essential to the validity of an equitable mortgage of the policy; but is desirable to preserve the priority of the lender against possible later mortgages of the same policy and to prevent the insurance monies being paid out to the borrower.

When a legal or an equitable mortgage of a policy is redeemed, notice of its discharge should be given to the insurers. When a policy matures or a claim is made on it on death, the insurers may require evidence of discharge of any mortgage, legal or equitable, of the policy that has been created at any time. Therefore, all assignments and reassignments should be preserved with the policy in safe custody so that they can be produced to the insurers if necessary. Where a reassignment is included in the lender's receipt endorsed on the mortgage of the land, the receipted mortgage will have to be sent to the Land Registry for the discharge of the land mortgage to be entered on the register. The Registry should be requested to return the receipted mortgage to the borrower so that it can be put with the policy.

(c) Other mortgages

Other types of mortgage are encountered. For example, index linked, where the capital repayable is linked to the index of inflation and is therefore liable to increase in line with inflation. These are unusual in the field of institutional lending on homes.[7] A pension linked mortgage is similar to an endowment mortgage save that the capital sum payable under the policy on retirement is used to pay off the capital loan.

Whatever type of mortgage is being considered, the important thing is to be able to understand the terms of the offer and advise, in particular, on the financial terms of repayment and what security is required.

---

[7]   See *Multiservice Bookbinding Ltd. v. Marden* [1979] Ch. 84; and *Nationwide Building Society v. Registrar of Friendly Societies* [1983] 3 All E.R. 296.

The mortgage offer and conditions

Where part of the purchase price is being financed by a mortgage   2.5.2
loan, contracts should not be exchanged on the purchase until a
satisfactory offer of a mortgage advance has been received and accepted
by the client.

The offer will contain the financial details of the proposed mortgage;
and both standard general conditions common to all loans by that lender
and probably a number of special conditions applicable in the particular
case. It should be remembered that on an institutional mortgage the
solicitor will probably be acting for both lender and borrower; and will
owe a legal and professional duty to both to see that the conditions of
making the loan are satisfied. It should also be remembered that while
acting for both there is always the possibility of a conflict of interest arising.

'Solicitors acting contemporaneously for a buyer and lender should
consider their position very carefully if there is any change in the
purchase price, or if the solicitors become aware of any other
information which they would reasonably expect the lender to consider
important in deciding whether, or on what terms, it would make the
mortgage advance available. In such circumstances the solicitor's duty to
act in the best interests of the lender would require them to pass on such
information to the lender.

Solicitors have a duty of confidentiality to clients, but this does not affect
their duty to act in the best interests of each client. If the buyer will not
agree to the information being given to the lender, then there will be a
conflict between the solicitor's duty of confidentiality to the buyer and
the duty to act in the best interests of the lender. Solicitors must
therefore cease acting for the lender and must consider carefully whether
they are able to continue acting for the buyer.' (Council's Standards and
Guidance Committee: 'Guidance - Mortgage Fraud.' (*Guide*, p.471).

A few examples of likely general conditions, taken from a leading
building society's offer of advance, are as follows:

'12. The applicant is liable for the Society's legal costs and disbursements
which may be deducted from the advance.

13. The solicitor must establish the name(s) of all persons of full age at
the time of the mortgage who are or will also be occupying the property.
Except in Scotland the Society requires that each such person should sign
a Consent on the Society's standard form before completion. Where
details of proposed occupiers have been provided by the Applicant this
information is supplied herewith.

14. The Society must have a first charge on the property.

15. Repayment mortgages - life cover.

The Solicitor should ensure that any desired life assurance cover is in
place before completion. A quotation will normally be provided by the
Society in connection with the Offer of Advance.

16. Endowment and Level Term Policies

Before completion, the policy or formal notice of acceptance must be inspected and the Solicitor should ensure that:

(a) the risk has been accepted, age admitted and the first or current premium paid;

(b) the Applicant must execute the Society's form of Deed of Assignment. Acknowledgement that the Society's interest is noted must be obtained from the insurance company;

(c) a separate Deed should be used for each policy assigned;

(d) the policy, Deed and Acknowledgement must be enclosed with the Title Deeds.

17. No alteration should be made to the Society's standard forms without the prior consent of the Society.

18. Roads and Sewers.

The Solicitor must notify the Society prior to exchange of contracts:

(a) if there is any outstanding liability against the property for road charges and/or

(b) if the sewers have not been adopted or there are no satisfactory arrangements for their subsequent adoption.

Any retention will be released to the Applicant unless his prior authority for release to the Solicitor has been obtained.'

Question Assuming a purchasing client of average intelligence, explain the purpose and significance of condition 13. Draft the form that you think the Consent referred to in this condition might aptly take.

Of the possible special conditions that are commonly attached to offers, the following three are worth noting:

(a) Retentions for repairs. As a result of its valuation report the lender may retain a specified amount of the advance until specified works are carried out to the satisfaction of the lender. This means that unless arrangements can be made for access and the work done prior to completion, that amount will not then be available. This amount will have to be financed by a bridging loan or from some other source until the work is done. And the client should be warned that the work may in fact cost more than the retention. Depending on the seriousness of the required work, the lender may be prepared simply to accept an undertaking to do it after completion without making any retention.

(b) If more than a certain percentage (commonly 80%) of society's valuation (not the purchase price which may be higher) is being lent, the lender may require insurance for this excess to be paid for either by a single premium to be taken out of the advance, or by additions to the instalments for a specified period of time.

(c) The lender will normally require any outstanding mortgage on the existing property to be redeemed before the new advance is paid. This can of course create problems where the client has to move to a new home before getting a buyer for the existing one; a situation which may in any case have serious financial implications.

CALCULATING THE COST OF COMPLETION

In addition to the purchase price itself the purchaser will have to find **2.6** the related legal costs and disbursements. The solicitor will need to be satisfied that the client will have sufficient capital resources and that there will be enough money coming into the client account to complete the transaction. (As to accounting to the client, see para.14.8.2).

A simple balance sheet can be prepared in two columns putting all the expected receipts on one side and the expected expenditure on the other side.

On the usual sale and purchase transaction, the client's debits may include the following:

Purchase price (including deposit already paid).

Additional price for chattels.

Retention and other deductions from mortgage advance (para.2.5.2).

Solicitor's costs for acting on the sale and redemption of existing mortgages plus VAT (value added tax)

Solicitor's costs for acting for purchaser on purchase and new mortgage loan plus VAT.

Solicitor's costs for acting for lender on new mortgage (payable by client as borrower) plus VAT.

Solicitor's costs for giving investment advice plus VAT.

Solicitor's disbursements, including:

Stamp duty on purchase (para.10.7.1).

Land registry fees.

Other search fees.

All the above are likely to pass through the solicitor's hands. In addition, the client should consider the possible need to find:

Interest on bridging loan or other costs of financing deposit.

Estate agent's fees.

Survey or valuation fee (payable before exchange) (para.3.4).

Capital gains tax payable on sale.

Removal costs.

Further the client is likely to be faced with a possibly hefty first payment soon after completion being the first instalment on the mortgage, premium on any endowment policy, premium on house and contents insurance, etc; and needs to be advised to calculate the total regular outgoings that ownership of the property is likely to entail, and whether these can be afforded.

If, on comparing the two sides of such a balance sheet, there is a shortfall, the client will have to consider how if at all the deficit can be met. Possibilities are: additional personal savings and resources; negotiating a lower purchase price; persuading the mortgagee to lend more on the first mortgage; borrowing an additional sum on second mortgage from another financier. Here the client needs to be warned of the dangers of getting into the clutches of loan sharks and high, if not exorbitant, rates of interest.

Question Prepare an estimate, as accurate and detailed as possible, of how much it is going to cost Fancy French and Sam Saunders to buy 24 De Lucy Mount. (See Document 1.4 for instructions). Do research if necessary, e.g. to find out current fees for searches; by ringing a building society to find out the costs of the alternative possible valuations/surveys on the price of the house; by finding out from solicitors how much the professional fee would be likely to be on this sort of transaction. Where an amount is not discoverable make the best estimate possible.

TAXATION

2.7   Three forms of taxation are likely to be relevant in a domestic conveyancing transaction:

(a) Stamp duty on purchase. (para.10.7.1).

(b) Capital gains tax on sale.

(c) Income tax relief on mortgage loans.

Capital gains tax

2.7.1   Under the Taxation of Chargeable Gains Act 1992 (TCGA), the vendor may be liable to pay capital gains tax. As will be explained, any gain made on the sale of one's home is normally exempt.

The general aim of this tax is to tax any increase in the capital value of an asset between its acquisition and subsequent disposal by the taxpayer. It is payable on a chargeable gain accruing in the year of assessment on the disposal of a chargeable asset (TCGA, s.1(1)). The taxpayer is liable for any year of assessment during any part of which she is resident or ordinarily resident in the U.K. (TCGA, s.2(1)).

Normally tax will be calculated on the money consideration received on the disposal provided the disposal is by bargain at arm's length; Otherwise, e.g. in the case of a gift, it will be on the then market value of the asset.

To arrive at the taxable gain, there will be deducted from this ((TCGA, s.38)):

(a) The price of acquiring the asset - the initial cost. If the asset was acquired before March 31, 1982, its initial cost will normally be its market value on that date.

(b) The incidental costs of acquiring the asset 'including fees, commission or remuneration paid for the professional services of any surveyor or valuer, or auctioneer or accountant, or agent or legal adviser and costs of transfer or conveyance (including stamp duty) and advertising.'

(c) Any expenditure incurred to enhance the value of the asset (if reflected in its value on disposal); and any expenditure incurred to establish, preserve or defend title to the asset.

The initial cost and other expenditure under (a) to (c) will be increased (thus reducing the taxable gain) by the indexation allowance - that is the rise in the retail prices index between the dates of expenditure and disposal.

(d) The incidental costs of disposal.

Before fixing the taxable amount, any chargeable gain in any year of assessment will be reduced by (TCGA, s.2(2)):

(a) Any allowable loss in the current year of assessment. Allowable losses are in general calculated in the same way as gains.

(b) Any allowable loss from a previous year of assessment which has not already been set off against a gain. Thus, in general, losses can be carried forward but not back (apart from those in the year of assessment in which the taxpayer dies).

(c) The taxpayer's annual personal relief which at present is £5,500 (TCGA, s.3(1)).

The taxpayer is charged to tax on the amount thus calculated at her marginal rate of income tax - at the higher rate which she is paying, 40% or 25% at present.

Private residence exemption

2.7.1(a)   The sale of a private residence together with up to half a hectare of land occupied and enjoyed with the dwelling[8] may be exempt from capital gains tax. The residence must have been the taxpayer's only or main residence at some time during her period of ownership.

If this condition has been satisfied throughout the period of ownership the gain will be completely exempt. In calculating the period of residence any non-residence during the 36 months prior to disposal can be ignored. Certain other periods of absence can also be treated as period of qualifying residence, including:

(i) Any period of absence not exceeding three years in total;

(ii) any period of absence in employment abroad;

(iii) up to four years' absence due to the needs of employment.

Where there are periods of absence which cannot be counted as residence under the above, the gain will be apportioned by multiplying it by the period of residence as a fraction of the total period of ownership. Similarly, there will be an apportionment if part of the dwelling has been used *exclusively* for the purpose of a trade, business, profession or vocation, the part so used not being exempt from the tax.

If the taxpayer has more than one residence during any period, she can conclusively determine which is to be treated as her only or main residence for any part of such period by giving written notice to the inspector of taxes within two years of the start of any period for which the election is made. But an election can only be made for a period when it can properly be said that both dwellings were the residence of the taxpayer. Most obviously, if one of two houses is occupied by a third party under a lease or exclusive licence no election is possible. If occupation by the taxpayer has been sporadic and intermittent it might be difficult to argue that it was her residence.[9] If an election is not made when it could be, the matter will be decided by the inspector of taxes.

In general, a disposal of assets between spouses *inter vivos* or on death is treated as a disposal giving rise to neither gain nor loss; so that taxation on the gain (or loss) is deferred until the acquiring spouse disposes of the asset to a third party. Spouses may only have one main residence for so long as they are living together and any notice of election must be given by them both. Where an owning spouse transfers her interest in the main residence to the other while they are still living together, and it is

---

[8]   Thus if part of the land is sold first the house being retained, the gain on the sale may be exempt; but if the house is sold first, a subsequent sale of part of its former garden will not be exempt.

[9]   See 'Tax planning: the second family home', M. Hutton (S.J. 22 May, 1992, p.491).

subsequently disposed of by the acquiring spouse, the acquiring spouse will be able to treat the previous period of qualifying ownership by the other as exempt. Where an owning spouse leaves the matrimonial home on separation, and it is subsequently transferred to the other spouse (still residing there) as part of the divorce settlement, the transferring spouse will on the transfer be allowed (by concession) to treat the period after leaving as an exempt period.

Death

There is no disposal of assets on a person's death and so no charge to capital gains tax (though there may be liability to inheritance tax). If the asset is transferred to a beneficiary, the beneficiary is deemed to acquire it at the market value as at the date of death.   **2.7.1(b)**

Income tax relief

Under the Income and Corporation Tax Act 1988, s.354, within certain limits tax relief is available on the interest element of mortgage payments. It is not available on any capital element; nor on the premiums on the life assurance associated with an endowment mortgage.   **2.7.2**

It is available to the owner of an interest in the land where the loan is used to purchase the interest or to build a new home on the land. The land must be used as the only or main residence of the taxpayer. Temporary absences of up to one year are in practice ignored. If a taxpayer with a qualifying loan has to move, either abroad or at home, by reason of employment, she can continue to claim the relief, provided the absence is not expected to last more than four years and the property can reasonably be expected to be used as the only, or main, residence on return.

Relief is only available in respect of home improvement loans if the loan was made before 6 April 1988 (Finance Act 1988, s.43).

For loans made since 1 August 1988, relief is available on the interest paid on a loan or loans of up to £30,000 on one property. If more than £30,000 is borrowed relief will be given on the interest on the first £30,000. On loans made before that date it was possible for two or more individuals (not being spouses) each to borrow towards the purchase price and each to claim the tax relief up to £30,000. This is now only possible where the same loan has been continued since before 1 August 1988 (ICTA 1988, s.356A). Thus if the property is sold, relief will be reduced to the limit of £30,000 on the loan on the new home. In general terms, where now there are two or more unmarried purchasers, relief up the £30,000 limit will be apportioned between them in proportion to their contributions to the interest payments.

Where a second loan is taken to purchase a new home before the existing home has been sold, relief continues to be available on the old loan (as well as the new one) for up to 12 months provided the new home is in fact occupied (ICTA, s.354(5)).

From 1990-91 a husband and wife who are living together can elect that qualifying interest paid by one be treated as paid by the other.

Relief is actually granted through MIRAS, that is mortgage interest relief at source. (ICTA 1988, s.369-379). Income tax is paid in full on income without reference to the mortgage loan; but tax at the basic rate is deducted from the interest element of mortgage payments. The amount of deduction to be made and the net instalment to be paid will be provided by the lending institution. From 1991-92 higher rate relief on such loans has been abolished. Relief cannot be claimed except through the MIRAS system. If a temporary, qualifying bridging loan is being taken to finance the deposit or pending the sale of the existing home, the relief will only be available if the loan is made on a separate loan account rather than an overdraft on current account.

FINANCIAL ADVICE AND PROFESSIONAL CONDUCT

2.8   In dealing with the financial aspects of a transaction, and particularly when required to guide the client through the choice of mortgage and the arrangement of any necessary endowment policy, the solicitor needs to heed the Financial Services Act 1988 and the relevant professional conduct rules. A person taking out an endowment policy is in effect making an investment through the medium of the insurers. It is usual for insurance companies to have tied agents (who cannot to that extent be independent) and offer substantial commissions for the introduction. Clearly in this context careful thought may have to be given to questions of conflict of interest, the duty to remain independent and to act in the best interests of the client.

Any person must have authorisation under the Financial Services Act 1988 to carry on investment business. The very wide definition of investment business contained in Part II of Schedule I of the Act includes arranging deals in investments (including making arrangements for a client to take out a life policy in connection with a house purchase) and giving investment advice (which itself includes giving advice on a particular investment but not generic advice; advising, for example, that one endowment policy is better than another, but not that an endowment mortgage is better than a repayment one).

For solicitors, authorisation in the form of an investment business certificate is normally obtained through the Law Society acting as a Recognised Professional Body (*Guide*, para.26.07).

The Solicitors' Investment Business Rules 1990 apply to all firms which hold a certificate (*Guide*, p.528). *Inter alia*, these require that the firm must state in all its business letters, notices and other publications which relate to its discrete investment business that it is regulated by the Society in the conduct of investment business or that it is authorised by the society to conduct investment business.

In addition to these rules, the Solicitors' Practice Rules themselves may be relevant; particularly Rule 1 which is fundamental to the relationship which exists between a solicitor and her client; and Rule 3 which concerns the making and acceptance of referrals of business to or from another person. This in turn requires adherence to the Solicitors' Introduction and Referrals Code 1990 (*Guide*, p.232), and, the Council Statement on the Financial Services Act - life policies and tied agents.(*Guide*, p.443). This Statement includes the following:

'A solicitor's independence, and thus his ability to give impartial and disinterested advice, is a fundamental element of his relationship with his clients. In relation therefore to clients who need, or are likely to need, life insurance, solicitors should either act as independent intermediaries themselves and assess the client's requirements, survey the market, recommend the best policy available, and arrange for the transaction, or they should introduce the client to another independent intermediary who will do the same. The solicitor's duty to give his client independent advice would not be discharged by referring such a client to an adviser who is not an independent intermediary, for example, a bank, building society or estate agent or insurance agent which is an appointed representative, i.e. a tied agent. If, however, a solicitor has assessed a client's need for life assurance, identified the client's requirements, surveyed the market and selected a life office on appropriate criteria, then the solicitor may either arrange the taking out of the policy or may introduce the client to the life office or its representative so that this can be done. This work would need authorisation and would be 'discrete investment business' under the Solicitors' Investment Business Rules 1990. Alternatively the solicitor who does not profess expertise in life insurance can always refer the client to an independent intermediary.

'Building society agencies

Rule 12 of the Solicitors' Practice Rules 1990 prohibits solicitors from being 'appointed representatives' or tied agents for investment business, and the agency arrangements solicitors may have with building societies which themselves are tied agents clearly must be confined to non-investment business otherwise the solicitor-agent might be in breach of the rule.

'Insurance company agencies

So far as investment business is concerned, insurance companies have cancelled their existing agency agreements and arranged for those solicitors who will themselves be giving independent advice to register with the companies for the purpose of the payment of commissions.

However, it will still be possible for solicitors to have agencies with insurance companies for business other than investment business, e.g. buildings insurance (although a solicitor must not enter into any arrangement under which he will be constrained to refer business to a particular company).'

It should finally be noted that Rule 10 of the Solicitors' Practice Rules requires that a solicitor account to the client for any commission received of more than £10 unless, having been informed of the amount, the client agrees to its retention by the solicitor.

CHAPTER 3

PHYSICAL CONDITION OF THE PROPERTY

'TRUST TIMOTHY!'

'Trust me,' Timothy is heard to say as he shows Miss French out.　　**3.1**

Fancy had been in to see Timothy, yet again. The snivelling child had been left at Granny's. The dog had not; and immediately began to make amorous advances to Timothy's leg; which hardly helped his already limited powers of concentration.

Miss French was in this wine bar last night with her friend – 'No, not Sam'. He had all these horror stories about house buying. 'Have you insured?', said the friend. 'You should have done. Mark my words, as soon as you sign the contract the house will be burnt down. I've seen it happen. And you will still have to pay. Once the contract is signed, vendors don't care. They will move out if it suits them and squatters will move in. And all this earth warming that's happening. I've been reading about it. The earth is drying out and houses that have stood for years are just collapsing.'

Miss French is worried.

Timothy is reassuring. 'Don't worry,' he says. 'The new Standard Conditions deal with all that. The vendor will be responsible if there is anything wrong with the property. *Caveat emptor* doesn't apply any longer. And the vendor has to insure. In any case you are getting a mortgage loan from the Ledchester and Bongley. Their surveyor will make sure the property is all right; no need for you to have a survey done. Save yourself a lot of money. And they will look after insurance.'

Miss French is reassured; and arranges for her and Sam to come in later to sign the contract (although Timothy has not yet even sent off an application for a local search! – para.4.1.9).

OLD JARNDYCE COMMENTS

As usual, Timothy has cooked the law into a tangle of something　　**3.2**
softer than *al dente* spaghetti.

In relation to the physical condition of the property, a purchasing client may need proper advice on the following matters before signing the contract:

(a) The obligations of the vendor as to the physical condition of the property.

(b) Surveys and valuations.

(c) Insurance.

(d) Fixtures and fittings.

(e) The identity of the property and boundaries.

As to (d), see para.4.4.2. As to (e) see paras.5.4. and 7.11. I will take a look at each of the others in turn. What follows applies equally to unregistered and registered title.

Question After reading what follows (and doing any further necessary research) examine Timothy's advice. Explain where he has got the law wrong. Write a short note of advice to a client explaining what she needs to know in relation to these matters.

THE OBLIGATIONS OF THE VENDOR

3.3   In general, it has been said, there is no law against letting a tumbledown house.[1] Similarly, there is no general law against selling one; and no obligation to tell the purchaser that it is a tumbledown house.

Under an open contract the rule is caveat emptor. The purchaser must take the property in whatever physical state it is in at the date of contract. The Standard Conditions do not alter this rule.

Of course, if the vendor does make any false, pre-contract statement about the condition of the property, she may be liable for misrepresentation (para.4.4.1). If the contract itself contains any express, false statement or guarantee as to the condition of the property, there may be liability for breach of contract. (For the position of builder-vendors, see below, para.3.6).

Position between contract and completion

3.3.1   Under an *open* contract the rule is that upon exchange of contracts the risk passes to the purchaser. If the property is damaged by fire, flood, vandals or in any other way, the purchaser will still be obliged to complete and pay the full purchase price. This principle is qualified in one, or possibly two, ways:

---

1   *Robbins v. Jones* (1863) 15 C.B.N.S. 221.

(a) The vendor is under a duty to take reasonable care to keep the property in a reasonable state of preservation and as it was at the time of contract. Thus in *Smith v. Gorman*[2] the vendor contracted to sell a house to the purchaser with completion agreed for 31 January, 1978. On 6 January the vendor let the purchaser have a key to enable her mortgagee's valuer to gain access. On 24 January the vendor moved out without telling the purchaser and without turning off the water supply. The pipes froze and burst causing severe damage. It was held that the purchaser had not been let into occupation or possession; that the vendor was in breach of duty in vacating the property in the middle of winter without turning off the water; and so was liable to pay damages to the purchaser.

(b) Frustration. Traditionally, it was considered that the doctrine of frustration could not apply to a land transaction. 'The subject matter of the contract is simply a specified piece of land described in the contract and nothing more.'[3] Whatever happens on the surface, the estate in the land can still be transferred to the purchaser; and the land will still be there because notionally its ownership extends down to the centre of the earth and up to the sky - *ad coelum et ad inferos*. It has now been accepted by the courts that the doctrine can apply to put an end to a lease, though the circumstances will have to be unusual.[4] Once this is accepted there is no logical reason why the doctrine should not be applicable to a contract to grant or sell a lease; or to sell the freehold. But the circumstances probably would have to be very unusual and unforseen.[5] Where, as with Standard Condition 5.1.1., the Standard Conditions expressly deal with the passing of risk, it is particularly unlikely that the doctrine will be applied.

The Standard Conditions

These do significantly alter the open contract position after exchange. They provide:

3.3.2

'5. PENDING COMPLETION.

5.1. Responsibility for the property.

---

[2] (1981) (Lexis transcript).

[3] *Amalgamated Investment and Property Co. Ltd. v. John Walker & Sons Ltd.* [1976] 3 All E.R. 509, at p.519 (Sir John Pennycuick); the court did not rule out the possibility of frustration operating.

[4] *National Carriers Ltd. v. Panalpina (Northern) Ltd.* [1981] A.C. 675. And see *Hussein v. Mehlman* [1992] 32 E.G. 59 deciding that a lease can be repudiated and the repudiation accepted by the tenant handing in the keys - reflecting perhaps an increasing willingness of the courts to focus on the contractual element of land transactions.

[5] See M.P. Thompson, [1984] Conv. 43.

5.1.1. The seller will transfer the property in the same physical state as it was at the date of the contract (except for fair wear and tear), which means that the seller retains the risk until completion.

5.1.2. If at any time before completion the physical state of the property makes it unusable for its purpose at the date of the contract:

(a) the buyer may rescind the contract

(b) the seller may rescind the contract where the property has become unusable for that purpose as a result of damage against which the seller could not reasonably have insured, or which it is not legally possible for the seller to make good.

5.1.3. The seller is under no obligation to the buyer to insure the property.

5.1.4. Section 47 of the Law of Property Act 1925 does not apply.'

If the situation comes within Standard Condition 5.1.2 the purchaser or vendor, as the case may be, will be able to rescind; but this probably would not relieve the vendor of liability to pay damages for breach of Standard Condition 5.1.1. (As to the meaning of rescission, see para.16.2.).

Where the purchaser is let into occupation before completion, the obligation to keep in repair and the risk are transferred to the purchaser (Standard Condition 5.2.2(f), 5.2.3.).

The above Standard Condition principles apply equally to the sale of freehold and leasehold. (On leasehold see, further, para.17.3.2.)

SURVEYS AND VALUATIONS

3.4   It follows from the above that a purchaser needs to be satisfied as to the physical condition of the property before exchanging contracts; and should be advised on the possible need to have a survey done. There are two main possibilities to look at:

(a) The purchaser may choose to rely on a valuation done by her mortgagee. Before deciding to lend, a building society is under a statutory duty[6] to have 'a written report on the value of the land and any factors likely materially to affect its value made by a person who is competent to value.'

Similarly, in practice, any institutional lender is likely to have a professional valuation done before committing itself.

Such a valuation is commissioned by the lender; though paid for by the borrower. Nevertheless, it has been established by the courts that

---

6   Building Societies Act 1986, s.13.

such a professional, at least in the case of the average house purchase, is expected to realise that the borrower may well rely on the valuation report; and therefore owes a duty of care not only to the instructing lender but also to the borrower who does in fact rely on the report. In practice, most institutional lenders do make a copy of the report available to the borrower; though their literature is generally framed to discourage reliance on it! A number of points are worth noting:

(i) The duty will normally exist even where the borrower has been advised to have her own independent survey done. But the duty is not normally owed to anyone other than the lender and that particular mortgage applicant. Thus if the latter makes the report available to a subsequent purchaser there will be no duty; and the person handing it on should make it clear that she too does not accept any responsibility for its accuracy.

(ii) If the valuer is a staff employee of the lender, the lender too may be vicariously liable for the negligence of the valuer.

(iii) Any attempt to limit or exclude the liability of the valuer or her employer will be subject to the test of reasonableness under s.2 of the Unfair Contract Terms Act 1977; and, at least in the case of the average, modest house purchase, is likely to be held ineffective for that reason.[7]

(iv) However, the courts have made a distinction between a valuation for mortgage purposes and a structural survey.[8] A less detailed investigation of the property, so it is said, is required in the former case. The duty of the mortgage valuer has been put as follows:[9]

'The valuer, in my opinion, must be a professional person, typically a chartered surveyor in general practice, who, by training and experience and exercising reasonable skill and care, will recognise defects and be able to assess value. The valuer will value the house after taking into consideration major defects which are, or ought to be obvious to him, in the course of a visual inspection of so much of the exterior and interior of the house as may be accessible to him without undue difficulty.'

The point is that a valuation is an appraisal based on a limited investigation; but it is an appraisal by a supposedly competent surveyor who should recognise the significance of what is visible.

[7] See, generally, *Smith v. Eric S. Bush* [1989] 2 All E.R. 514.
[8] See M.Harwood, 'A Structural Survey of Negligent Reports' (1987) 50 M.L.R. 588.
[9] *Smith v. Eric S. Bush* (note 7 above), *per* Lord Templeman, p.525.

In *Beaton v. Nationwide Building Society*[10] the valuer carelessly (so held) concluded that relatively extensive, repointed step-cracking in the exterior brickwork and further, unrepaired cracking, pointed only to structural movement in the past which was many years old, and not to any continuing movement.

(b) A purchaser may decide to have her own, independent survey done, whether or not she is also paying for her mortgagee's valuation.

Clearly, this is advisable where the property is in any way out of the ordinary, by reason of price, history, location, age, etc.

In such a case the purchaser will have a contract directly with the chosen surveyor. The surveyor will owe a contractual duty of care and face potential liability for professional negligence.[11] The following points should be noted:

(i) Even a structural survey does not guarantee the state of the property. There may be hidden defects (most seriously, for example, in the foundations) which even a competent structural survey would not be expected to discover.

(ii) The surveyor will only be liable for doing negligently what she has contracted to do. And only within these limits will the Unfair Contract Terms Act 1977 apply to any attempt to exclude or limit liability.

Most building societies urge their loan applicants to have, as an addition to their own valuation, either a homebuyer's (or similarly named) report or a 'full' structural survey. In either case, it is important for the purchaser to read the terms of engagement (which will generally be in standard form) to discover exactly what the surveyor is agreeing to investigate.

The homebuyer's report is normally done for an additional fee by the lender's valuer at the same time as the mortgage valuation. Its scope is likely to be particularly limited. The conditions attached to the one offered by one building society, typically, includes the following:

'The surveyor will inspect as much of the surface areas as is practicable, and will lift loose floorboards and trap doors where accessible, but will be under no obligation to raise fixed floorboards or to inspect those areas of the property that are covered, unexposed or are not readily accessible. Inspection will therefore exclude both the roof space, if there is no or no reasonably accessible roof hatch, and the outer surfaces of the roof if they cannot be readily seen ... except where the contrary is stated parts of the structure and of the woodwork which are covered, unexposed or inaccessible, will not be inspected.'

---

10   (1991) (Lexis transcript).

11   Note Supply of Goods and Services Act 1982, ss.12-16.

In addition, this report excludes the testing of services and defects of no structural significance or of a minor nature. It will point out any further investigation which may be called for; but will not provide such further investigation without a further fee.

Such a homebuyer's report may give reassurance. It is doubtful whether it gives any greater protection than reliance on the lender's valuation.[12]

The cost and extent of investigation of a full structural survey will depend on negotiation between the surveyor and the person instructing the survey (though in practice a standard form contract will be offered). Even such a survey does not guarantee the state of the property in every respect. There may still, for example, be inaccessible parts of the structure.

(iii) Even where a purchaser successfully establishes a claim for professional negligence, it should be remembered that damages awarded may not cover the total loss. The measure of damages in such cases, whether against the mortgagee's valuer or an independently-commissioned surveyor, is in general the difference between the price paid for the house and the market price in its actual condition (i.e. taking into account the undiscovered defects). In particular, if the necessary repairs are carried out and cost more than this difference, the extra will not, it seems, be recoverable.[13] Further, the amount recoverable for resulting distress and inconvenience may be severely limited.[14]

INSURANCE

A client should be advised to read any insurance policy that she takes out with great care. Policies vary a great deal in what damage and events they do and do not cover.   **3.5**

The usual house policy will not normally provide cover against events which have occurred and defects already existing before the policy was taken out. In other words insurance will not normally mitigate the

---

[12] And may simply reflect a move by institutional lenders to shift the cost implications of cases such as *Smith v. Eric S. Bush* directly onto the borrower.

[13] See *Watts v. Morrow* [1991] 4 All E.R.937; suggesting (at p.950) that to allow the full cost of repairs would be to 'put the plaintiff in the position of recovering damages for breach of warranty that the condition of the house was correctly described by the surveyor and, in the ordinary case, as here, no such warranty has been given.' This is hard to understand. The essential obligation of a surveyor *is* precisely to give a correct description of the property in so far as a competent survey can do so; and the plaintiff is not claiming for defects which a competent survey would not have discovered.

[14] *Watts v. Morrow* (note 13 above). See, generally, L.S.G., 20 March 1991, p.18 (S.Migdal and A.Holmes); N.L.J., May 8, 1992, p.632 (E.Macdonald); S.J., 2 October 1992, p.962 (C.Boxer).

effect of the caveat emptor rule; or relieve the purchaser of the need to be satisfied as to the physical condition of the property before exchanging contracts.

Insurance between contract and completion

3.5.1 Under an open contract (where risk passes to the purchaser on exchange) the vendor does not need to maintain her insurance after contract; though in practice it is not likely to be cancelled. If she does not cancel it and the purchaser also insures, there is likely to be the problem of double insurance mentioned below.

The Standard Conditions

3.5.2 Although the risk remains with the vendor, Standard Condition 5.1.3. expressly excludes any obligation on her to insure. Unless Standard Condition 5.1.1. has been amended and the incidence of risk passed to the purchaser, the vendor should be advised of the need to keep her insurance in force until completion. If the property is damaged or destroyed between contract and completion, the vendor will be liable and get either a reduced purchase price or (if the purchaser or vendor herself exercises a Standard Condition 5.1.2. right to rescind) no money at all. Clearly the vendor needs to be insured against this risk of loss.

A purchaser, upon exchange of contracts, has an insurable interest in the property and is entitled to insure. If, however, she does, this may give rise to a double insurance situation. One leading policy provides:

> 'If at the time of any loss, destruction, damage or liability arising under this policy there is any other insurance covering the loss, destruction, damage or liability or any part of it, the Insurer will not pay more than its rateable proportion.'

If the purchaser does insure and the vendor's policy contains such a clause, the vendor will not be fully compensated for any loss. The price paid by the purchaser will be reduced by the amount of the loss; and the vendor will only receive part of the balance from her insurance company.[15]

The purchaser faces little risk whether or not the property is insured during this period. She still holds the purchase price (less deposit paid); and can retain enough of this to compensate for the damage to the property. She will only have a problem if she rescinds and, for whatever

---

[15] The purchaser will not receive anything since, having paid a reduced price, she will not have suffered any loss.

reason, there is difficulty in recovering the deposit from the vendor; or if the value of the damage to the property and any other recoverable, incidental costs (such as alternative accommodation pending reinstatement) recoverable under Standard Condition 5.1.1. together exceed the balance of the purchase price.[16]

It follows from the above that the best procedure may be for a special condition to be added to the contract

(a) obliging the vendor to keep the property insured to its full value until completion; and to produce on exchange the receipt for the current premium covering the period between contract and completion; and

(b) obliging the purchaser *not* to insure the property before completion.

In addition the purchaser's solicitor should require a copy of the vendor's policy to be supplied to the purchaser before exchange. The purchaser needs to be satisfied that the policy does cover the property adequately in the period between contract and completion. To give a simple example, most policies provide no or reduced cover if the property is vacant or unfurnished for longer than a specified period. This may be important if the vendor is planning to vacate before completion.[17] Similarly, the vendor should herself be advised by her solicitor to examine the terms of her policy carefully at the time of sale to check whether cover will be affected in any way.

In practice it seems that institutional lenders commonly insure the property from exchange as a matter of course. If the above approach is adopted, they should be instructed not to insure on behalf of the purchaser until completion. The lenders do not need to insure in their own interest before completion as they will not hand over the loan until then. And they can protect their position by requiring solicitors acting for them to check that the above provisions have been made.

If the purchaser is let into occupation before completion she is under a duty to insure (Standard Condition 5.2.2(g)). This reflects the passing of the risk to the purchaser in this situation. In this situation, the sort of clause suggested above could be used in the contract with the obligations of the vendor and purchaser being transposed.

---

[16] And this is a risk faced by a purchaser whenever she lawfully rescinds for any breach by the vendor - for example, failure to prove title. It is not confined to rescission on the happening of an insurable event.

[17] See, further, M.Harwood, S.J. 1 May 1992, p.408; 6 November 1992, p.1110.

NEW BUILDINGS

3.6   In general, the above principles apply whether the house is newly-built or a hundred or more years old. But in the case of a new house, the purchaser (whether the immediate purchaser from the builder/developer or a subsequent purchaser) may have important additional protection in relation to the physical condition of the property.

(a) Contract. Today, most builders are speculative in that they acquire the land, build what and how they think best, and attempt to sell the completed property. In this case, the purchaser will just have a contract to buy the land and house.

On the other hand, a builder may undertake by contract to build a house for a particular person; either on land owned by the builder which will then have to be conveyed to the purchaser, or on the person's own land. In the former case, there are likely to be two separate contracts - a building contract and the contract to sell the land. In the latter case there will only be the building contract. In either case what is to be built and how it is to be built will be determined by the express and implied terms of the building contract (whether or not separate from any contract for sale of the land). The agreement to build will be subject at the least to the Supply of Goods and Services Act 1982 as to care and skill.

An examination of building contracts is beyond the scope of this book. Understanding them requires a good deal of expertise; but a solicitor should be able to advise a client when necessary on their legal implications and on the need for architectural or other technical, professional support to ensure that the work is done satisfactorily and in accordance with the client's specified requirements.

(b) Tort. In the absence of any relevant contract, there may possibly be an action in tort in respect of faulty workmanship or materials. However, after a flowering period of enthusiasm, the courts have retreated from the notion of giving common law compensation in tort for economic loss ('pure economic loss') caused by faulty building work. One cannot do better perhaps than quote part of the headnote from the report of the House of Lords' decision in *Murphy v. Brentwood District Council*[18]:

> '... while the principle in *Donoghue v. Stevenson* applied to impose a duty on the builder of a house to take reasonable care to avoid injury or damage, through defects in its construction, to the persons or property of those whom he ought to have in

---

[18] [1991] 1 A.C. 399.

contemplation as likely to suffer such injury or damage, that principle as stated applied only to latent defects; that, where a defect was discovered before any injury to person or health or damage to property other than the defective house itself had been done, the expense incurred by a subsequent purchaser of the house in putting the defect right was pure economic loss; and that to hold that a local authority in supervising compliance with the building regulations or byelaws, was under a common law duty to take reasonable care to avoid putting a purchaser of a house in a position in which he would be obliged to incur such economic loss was an extension of principle that should not, as a matter of policy, be affirmed.'[19]

Section 1(1) of the Defective Premises Act does give a statutory remedy:

'A person taking on work for or in connection with the provision of a dwelling (whether the dwelling is provided by the erection or by the conversion or enlargement of a building) owes a duty:

(a) if the dwelling is provided to the order of any person, to that person; and

(b) without prejudice to paragraph (a) above, to every person who acquires an interest (whether legal or equitable) in the dwelling;

to see that the work which he takes on is done in a workmanlike or, as the case may be, professional manner, with proper materials and so that as regards that work the dwelling will be fit for habitation when completed.'

There is a six year limitation period which runs from when the dwelling is completed, whenever the defect is discovered.

In fact, the s.1 duty is of little importance in practice. This is because s.2 provides that it is not to apply where the building is covered by an approved scheme.

The only approved scheme at present is the 'combined warranty and protection' scheme operated by the National House-Building Council (NHBC) known as Buildmark.[20] The purchaser of a new house (or indeed one less than ten years old) is not likely to get a mortgage from a respectable, institutional lender unless it is protected by this, or a similar, recognised, scheme; or is backed by an architect's certificate.[21]

The builder will have to be, as the vast majority of builders are, registered with the NHBC. In brief the scheme operates like this:

---

[19] Compare *Lonrho v. Tebbit* [1991] 4 All E.R. 973; and *Targett v. Torfaen B.C.* (1991) 24 H.L.R. 164.

[20] See P.J.Palmer, L.S.G., 4 October, 1989, p.17.

[21] There is a scheme, known as Foundation 15 marketed by Zurich International, which is a similar, insurance backed scheme. An architect's certificate is also backed by insurance.

(a) The original purchaser:

The scheme operates by bringing into existence a contract between the builder and the NHBC and the original purchaser. This contract does not affect any other common law or statutory rights of the purchaser (except under s.1 of the 1972 Act). It is only available to purchasers who are acquiring the freehold or a leasehold of at least 21 years of the home; and are acquiring it for use as a residence by themselves, their tenants or licensees.

In brief, it gives the purchaser the following rights:

(i) The builder warrants that the home has been, or will be, built in accordance with NHBC requirements and in an efficient and workmanlike manner and of proper materials and so as to be fit for human habitation.

(ii) The builder agrees to put right any 'defect or damage' reported during the initial guarantee period. This is normally two years from the issue of the 10 year notice certificate. 'Defect or damage' does not include wear and tear, deterioration caused by neglect, normal dampness, condensation or shrinkage and, more significantly, 'anything which [the purchaser] knew about, or should reasonably have known about, when [she] acquired the home'. The NHBC guarantees performance of these obligations by the builder - for example, if the builder becomes insolvent.

(iii) For the rest of the 10 year period from the issue of the 10 year notice (the structural guarantee period) the NHBC, backed by insurance, agrees to put right any 'major damage' reported during this period which is due to structural defect or caused by subsidence, settlement or heaving affecting the structure, and any defect in the drainage system. There are limitations and exclusions which it is not possible to detail here.

The purchaser will receive the offer of cover (form BM1) and sign and return to NHBC the acceptance of cover (form BM2). The purchaser's solicitor is required to certify to the NHBC that she has handed over to the purchaser the offer of cover and the NHBC Buildmark booklet (which contains the terms of the scheme). The home will then, upon completion, be inspected by an NHBC inspector and, if this is satisfactory, the NHBC will issue the 10 year notice. If the builder has failed to comply with NHBC requirements she will be in breach of the Buildmark contract; and if the failure is due to the fraud or insolvency of the builder, NHBC undertake to provide compensation to the purchaser. The scheme is also designed to cover the common parts of flats and maisonettes.

The purchaser's solicitor should check in enquiries before contract that the vendor-builder is a member of the scheme and that the building will be covered by Buildmark. The documentation is normally handed over in a package by the builder's solicitor on exchange of contracts. Since the NHBC makes its offer of cover expressly on behalf of itself and the builder which therefore binds them both when the acceptance form is posted, there is no need for any special condition in the contract of sale obliging the builder to provide the Buildmark cover.

The ten year notice should be placed with the title deeds for safe-keeping.

(b) Subsequent purchasers:

The Buildmark contract is expressed to be made not just with the original purchaser but also with any subsequent purchaser and a mortgagee in possession. Although such a subsequent purchaser is not in fact a party to the contract, there can be little doubt that this is effective[22] to give the benefit to a subsequent purchaser without the need for express assignment. To be on the safe side, a special condition can be put into the contract of sale by the original purchaser agreeing that the new purchaser will have the benefit of the Buildmark contract (and similarly when this purchaser sells). This will in itself be sufficient in equity to transfer the benefit. The vendor's solicitor should in any case supply a copy of the 10 year notice with the draft contract; and on completion, the original together with the Buildmark booklet.

Under the Buildmark contract any defect must be reported 'as soon as possible after its appearance'. The claim of a subsequent purchaser may be defeated by the failure of the vendor to report a defect in time. Where a property is being bought with the benefit of Buildmark, pre-contract investigations should seek to check that there are no unreported defects. This is one reason why, even where the property is sold with the benefit of Buildmark, a pre-contract survey of some sort may be necessary.

---

[22]   Either by estoppel, under s.78 of the Law of Property Act 1925 or novation.

CHAPTER 4

PRE-CONTRACT INVESTIGATIONS

THURSDAY, 18 FEBRUARY.
TIMOTHY THINKS ABOUT FORMS

There is a letter for Timothy this morning from Moriarties **4.1**
(reproduced overleaf).

Question Is the proffered Local Search acceptable? (See para.4.5)
Draft a letter to Moriarties in reply to their letter, stating that you will
deal with the title in due course (see Chapter 11 and the Questions in
para.11.3.5); and dealing with the offer of the Local Search.

Document 4.1.1 Obebe Purchase: Letter from Vendor's Solicitor

---

MORIARTY & Co.
_____ Solicitors _____

17 February 1993

Dear Sirs,

Mixford to Obebe
16 Winchester Avenue, Ledchester
Your ref: PP/MH
Subject to contract

We thank you for your letter of 29 January last and note that
you are acting for the buyer, Miss Obebe on her purchase from
our client.
We enclose herewith draft contract together with office copy
entries in the register and title plan.
Please note that we will not be following National Protocol;
but we do enclose Local Search Certificate and Additional
Enquiries dated 15 June last when our client originally put
the house on the market, which you may wish to take over on
reimbursing us the fees.
We also enclose Property Information Form and Fixtures and
Fittings list completed by our client.
Please also note that on the instructions of our client we
have also sent out today a draft contract and the above documentation to another prospective purchaser. Our client has
received two firm offers for the property and feels that the
fair course is to send draft contracts to both prospective
buyers. However, Miss Mixford is in no way committing herself
to exchanging with the sender of the first signed contract or
otherwise.
You will note from the office copy entries that the registered proprietors are Norman and Nora Mixford, Miss Mixford's
uncle and aunt. Our client inherited from her uncle who sur-
vived his wife by a few hours in a car crash; she being his
executrix and sole beneficiary. No doubt you will let us
know your title requirements in this respect in due course.

Yours faithfully,

Moriarty & Co.

Moriarty & Co.

The special conditions are as follows:

Document 4.1.2 Obebe Purchase: Draft Contract

AGREEMENT

(Incorporating the Standard Conditions of Sale (Second Edition))

Agreement Date	:	
Seller	:	Nancy Mixford of 16 Winchester Avenue, Ledchester, Yorkshire
Buyer	:	Olive Obebe of 14 Hardcastle Drive, Ledchester, Yorkshire
Property (freehold/leasehold)	:	Freehold property known as 16 Winchester Avenue, Ledchester, registered at H.M. Land Registry with absolute title.
Root of Title/Title Number:		WYK 787260
Incumbrances on the Property:		The covenants shown or referred to in the charges register of the above title an office copy of which title is annexed hereto and incorporated herein; and the buyer shall be deemed to purchase with full knowledge thereof
Seller sells as	:	Beneficial Owner
Completion date	:	19 March 1993
Contract date	:	
Purchase Price	:	£88,500
Deposit	:	£ 8,850
Amount payable for chattels:	:	£ 1,500
Balance	:	£81,150

The Seller will sell and the Buyer will buy the Property for the Purchase Price.
The Agreement continues on the back page.

WARNING	Signed
This is a formal document, designed to create legal rights and legal obligations. Take advice before using it.	Seller/Buyer

---

SPECIAL CONDITIONS

1.This agreement incorporates the Standard Conditions of Sale (Second Edition). Where there is a conflict between those conditions and this agreement, this agreement prevails.

2. Terms used in this agreement have the same meaning as in those conditions.

3. The property is sold subject to the Incumbrances on the Property and the Buyer will raise no requisitions on them.

4. The property is sold with vacant possession on completion

or 4. The Property is sold subject to the following leases or tenancies:.

5. The sale includes the fitted carpets in the sitting room and two largest bedrooms for which an additional £1,500 will be paid. Other fixtures fittings and chattels are included or excluded from the sale without increase or reduction in the sale price as shown on the attached list of Fixtures, Fittings and Contents.

Seller's solicitors: Moriarty & Co., Tumbledown House, The Bedrow, Ledchester

Buyer's solicitors: Jarndyce & Jarndyce, 24 The Strand, Ledchester

Note: For the Standard Conditions of Sale, see Appendix 3.

Document 4.1.3 Obebe Purchase: Office Copy Entries on Register and Title Plan

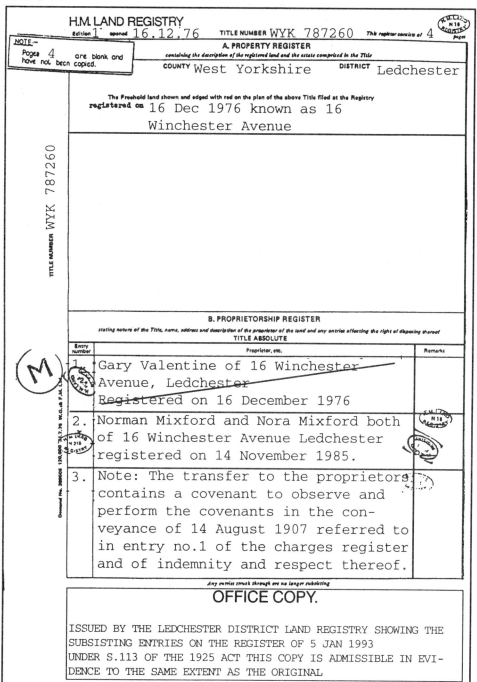

H.M. LAND REGISTRY

Edition 1 opened 16.12.76   TITLE NUMBER WYK 787260   This register consists of 4 pages

NOTE:–
Pages 4 are blank and have not been copied.

A. PROPERTY REGISTER
containing the description of the registered land and the estate comprised in the Title

COUNTY West Yorkshire   DISTRICT Ledchester

TITLE NUMBER WYK 787260

The Freehold land shown and edged with red on the plan of the above Title filed at the Registry registered on 16 Dec 1976 known as 16 Winchester Avenue

B. PROPRIETORSHIP REGISTER
stating nature of the Title, name, address and description of the proprietor of the land and any entries affecting the right of disposing thereof
TITLE ABSOLUTE

Entry number	Proprietor, etc.	Remarks
1.	Gary Valentine of 16 Winchester Avenue, Ledchester Registered on 16 December 1976	
2.	Norman Mixford and Nora Mixford both of 16 Winchester Avenue Ledchester registered on 14 November 1985.	
3.	Note: The transfer to the proprietors contains a covenant to observe and perform the covenants in the conveyance of 14 August 1907 referred to in entry no.1 of the charges register and of indemnity and respect thereof.	

Any entries struck through are no longer subsisting

OFFICE COPY.

ISSUED BY THE LEDCHESTER DISTRICT LAND REGISTRY SHOWING THE SUBSISTING ENTRIES ON THE REGISTER OF 5 JAN 1993 UNDER S.113 OF THE 1925 ACT THIS COPY IS ADMISSIBLE IN EVIDENCE TO THE SAME EXTENT AS THE ORIGINAL

Page 2.

TITLE NUMBER WYK 787260

C. CHARGES REGISTER

containing charges, incumbrances etc., adversely affecting the land and registered dealings therewith

Entry number	The date at the beginning of each entry is the date on which the entry was made on this edition of the register	Remarks
1.	16 December 1976 - A conveyance of the land in this title and other land dated 14 August 1907 made between (1) Arthur Eddison and William Exley and (2) William Bower contains covenants particulars of which are set out in the schedule annexed.	
2.	16 December 1976 - A conveyance of the land in this title dated 11 July 1919 made between (1) Samuel Redhead Meredith and Edward Thomas Clark (Mortgagees) (2) William Bower (Vendor) and (3) Harry Bulmer (Purchaser) contains covenants particulars of which are set out in the schedule annexed.	
3.	16 December 1976 - CHARGE dated 10 December 1976 registered on 16 December 1976 to secure the moneys including the further advances therein mentioned.	
4.	PROPRIETOR - NATIONWIDE BUILDING SOCIETY of New Oxford House, High Holbon, London, WC1V 6PW, registered on 16 December 1976.	
5.	14 November 1985 - CHARGE dated 10 November 1985 to include the moneys including the further advances therein mentioned.	
6.	PROPRIETOR - LEDCHESTER AND BONGLEY BUILDING SOCIETY of Society House, The Bedrow, Ledchester, registered on 14 November 1985.	

Any entries struck through are no longer subsisting

OFFICE COPY.

ISSUED BY THE LEDCHESTER DISTRICT LAND REGISTRY SHOWING THE SUBSISTING ENTRIES ON THE REGISTER OF 5 JAN 1993
UNDER S.113 OF THE 1925 ACT THIS COPY IS ADMISSIBLE IN EVIDENCE TO THE SAME EXTENT AS THE ORIGINAL

TITLE WYK 787260	Page 3
C. CHARGES REGISTER — continued.	
Schedule of restrictive covenants	Remarks
The following are particulars of the covenants contained in the Conveyance, dated 14 August 1907 referred to in the Charges Register. TO THE INTENT nevertheless that eighteen feet in width part of and to be taken from the North side of the said plot of land thereby conveyed and seven feet six inches in width part of and to be taken from the South side thereof for the whole extent of such sides respectively together with the like quantities in width added or to be added thereto by the owners for the time being of the land opposite or next to such sides respectively and forming together the said street called Winchester Avenue and the said back road should for ever thereafter remain open and unbuilt upon and be used as foot, horse and carriage roads as well by said Arthur Eddison and William Exley or other the owners or owner for the time being of the said remaining hereditaments and their or his present or future grantees as by said William Bower his heirs and assigns AND that no clay should be gotten from the said plot of land except so far as was necessary for excavating for buildings nor should any bricks be made or burnt upon any part of the said plot of land AND ALSO that the materials used in facing all buildings fronting to Winchester Avenue aforesaid should be stone or the best pressed bricks. . . . . COVENANT by the said William Bower that he would at all times thereafter duly observe perform fulfil and keep the several intents subject to which the said plot of land thereby conveyed and was thereinbefore expressed to be thereby conveyed.	
The following are particulars of the covenants contained in the Conveyance, dated 11 July 1919 referred to in the Charges Register. The purchaser with the object and intent of affording the Vendor a full and sufficient indemnity but not further or otherwise did thereby covenant with the Vendor that he would at all times thereafter observe and perform such and so many of the covenants stipulations and conditions set forth or referred to in the said Indenture of the 14th August 1907 as related to and affected and as were or ought to be observed and performed by the owner for the time being of the premises thereby conveyed. And would at all times thereafter keep indemnified the Vendor his heirs executors and administrators and against all losses costs damages and expenses which he or they or any of them should be put unto bear or sustain for or by reason or in consequence of the future none observance or non-performance thereof. AND FURTHER that no building or other erection should at any time be placed beyond the frontage lines of the buildings then erected thereon AND that the said dwellinghouse and premises thereby conveyed should not at any time thereafter be used for any other purpose than as a private dwelling-house.	

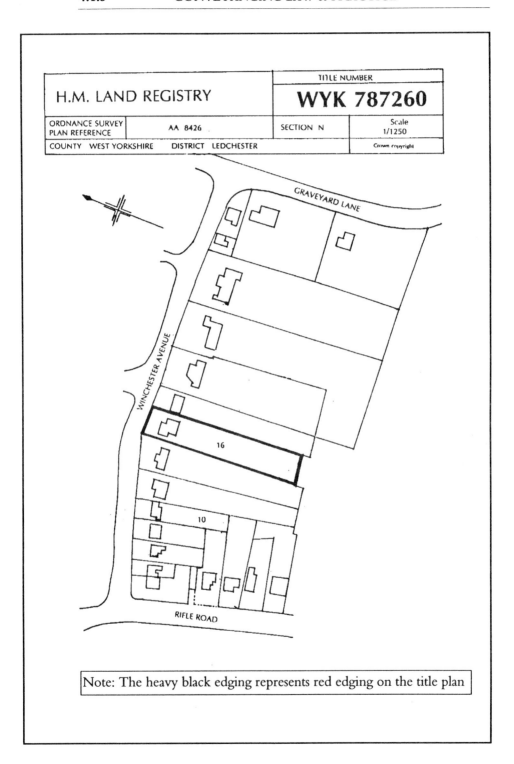

	TITLE NUMBER
H.M. LAND REGISTRY	**WYK 787260**

ORDNANCE SURVEY PLAN REFERENCE	AA 8426	SECTION N	Scale 1/1250
COUNTY WEST YORKSHIRE DISTRICT LEDCHESTER			Crown copyright

GRAVEYARD LANE

WINCHESTER AVENUE

16

10

RIFLE ROAD

Note: The heavy black edging represents red edging on the title plan

Document 4.1.4. Obebe Purchase: Seller's Property Information Form with Replies

SELLER'S PROPERTY INFORMATION FORM

Address of the Property: *16 WINCHESTER AVENUE*

LEDCHESTER

MIXFORD TO OBEBE

IMPORTANT NOTE TO SELLERS

* Please complete this form carefully. It will be sent to the buyer's solicitor and may be seen by the buyer.

* Incorrect information may mean you have to pay compensation to the buyer. For many of the questions you need only tick the correct answer. Where necessary, please give more detailed answers on a separate sheet of paper. Then send all the replies to your solicitor so that the information can be passed to the buyer's solicitor.

* The answers should be those of the person whose name is on the deeds. If there is more than one of you, you should prepare the answers together.

* It is very important that your answers are correct because the buyer will rely on them in deciding whether to go ahead.

* It does not matter if you do not know the answer to any question so long as you say so.

* Do not tell the buyer anything about the property unless you are willing to accept legal liability for what you say. This applies to this questionnaire and to anything else you tell him, even in casual conversation.

* The buyer will be told by his solicitor that he takes the property as it is. If he wants more information about it, he should get it from his own advisers, not from you.

* If anything changes after you fill in this questionnaire but before the sale is completed, tell your solicitor immediately. This is as important as giving the right answers in the first place.

* Please pass to your solicitor immediately any notices you have received which affect the property. The same goes for notices which arrive at any time before completion.

* If you have a tenant, tell your solicitor immediately there is any change in the arrangements but do nothing without asking your solicitor first.

* You should let your solicitor have any letters, agreements or other documents which help answer the questions. If you know of any which you are not supplying with these answers, please tell your solicitor about them.

* Please complete and return the separate Fixtures, Fittings and Contents Form. It is an important document which will form part of the contract between you and the buyer. Unless you mark clearly on it the items which you wish to remove, they will be included in the sale and you will not be able to take them with you when you move.

This form comprises 8 pages. Please ensure you complete all sections on all pages.   Please turn over to next page. TA3/1

IF YOU ARE NOT SURE ABOUT ANYTHING, ASK YOUR SOLICITOR

FOR OFFICE
USE ONLY
PIF
PARA NO

Part I – to be completed by the seller

1 Boundaries

"Boundaries" mean any fence, wall, hedge or ditch which marks the edge of your property.

1.1 Looking towards the house from the road, who either owns or accepts responsibility for the boundary:

Please tick the right answer

(a) on the left?

| WE DO ✓ | NEXT DOOR | SHARED | WE DON'T KNOW | 1.1 & 1.3 |

(b) on the right?

| WE DO | NEXT DOOR ✓ | SHARED | WE DON'T KNOW | 1.1 & 1.3 |

(c) at the back?

| WE DO ✓ | NEXT DOOR | SHARED | WE DON'T KNOW | 1.1 & 1.3 |

1.2 If you have answered "we don't know", which boundaries have you actually repaired or maintained?

(Please give details) _____ 1.2

1.3 Do you know of any boundary being moved in the last 20 years?

(Please give details) *no* _____ 1.4

2 Disputes

2.1 Do you know of any disputes about this or any neighbouring property?

| NO ✓ | YES: (PLEASE GIVE DETAILS) | 2.1 & 2.2 |

2.2 Have you received any complaints about anything you have, or have not, done as owners?

| NO ✓ | YES: (PLEASE GIVE DETAILS) | 2.1 & 2.2 |

TA3 2

2.3 Have you made any such complaints to any neighbour about what the neighbour has or has not done?

Please tick the right answer

NO ✓	YES: (PLEASE GIVE DETAILS)

21 & 22

3 | Notices

3.1 Have you either sent or received any letters or notices which affect your property or the neighbouring property in any way (for example, from or to neighbours, the council or a government department)?

NO	YES ✓	COPY ENCLOSED	TO FOLLOW	LOST

3.2 Have you had any negotiations or discussions with any neighbour or any local or other authority which affect the property in any way?

31, 32 & 33

NO ✓	YES: (PLEASE GIVE DETAILS)

RE TREE PRESERVATION ORDER ON CHESTNUT IN GARDEN

4 | Guarantees

4.1 Are there any guarantees or insurance policies of the following types:

(a) NHBC or Foundation 15 (for houses less than 15 years old)?

NO ✓	YES	COPIES ARE ENCLOSED	WITH DEEDS	LOST

(b) Damp course?

NO	YES ✓	COPIES ARE ENCLOSED	WITH DEEDS ✓	LOST

(c) Double glazing?

NO ✓	YES	COPIES ARE ENCLOSED	WITH DEEDS	LOST

(d) Electrical work?

NO ✓	YES	COPIES ARE ENCLOSED	WITH DEEDS	LOST

(e) Roofing?

NO ✓	YES	COPIES ARE ENCLOSED	WITH DEEDS	LOST

(f) Rot or infestation?

NO	YES ✓	COPIES ARE ENCLOSED	WITH DEEDS	LOST

(g) Central heating?

NO ✓	YES	COPIES ARE ENCLOSED	WITH DEEDS	LOST

(h) Anything similar? (e.g. cavity wall insulation)

NO ✓	YES	COPIES ARE ENCLOSED	WITH DEEDS	LOST

(i) Do you have written details of the work done to obtain any of these guarantees?

NO	YES ✓	COPIES ARE ENCLOSED	WITH DEEDS	LOST

41

ESTIMATES WITH DEEDS

Please turn over to next page. TA3/3

CONVEYANCING LAW & PRACTICE

4.2 Have you made or considered making claims under any of these?

Please tick the right answer

| NO ✓ | YES (PLEASE GIVE DETAILS) | 4 2 |

_____

_____

5 | Services

(This section applies to gas, electrical and water supplies, sewerage disposal and telephone cables.)

5.1 Please tick which services are connected to the property.

| GAS ✓ | ELEC ✓ | WATER ✓ | DRAINS ✓ | TEL ✓ | CABLE T.V. |

5.2 Do any drains, pipes or wires for these cross any neighbour's property?

| NOT AS FAR AS WE KNOW ✓ | YES: (PLEASE GIVE DETAILS) | 5 1 |

_____

_____

5.3 Do any drains, pipes or wires leading to any neighbour's property cross your property?

| NOT AS FAR AS WE KNOW ✓ | YES: (PLEASE GIVE DETAILS) | 5 2 |

_____

_____

5.4 Are you aware of any agreement which is not with the deeds about any of these services?

| NOT AS FAR AS WE KNOW ✓ | YES: (PLEASE GIVE DETAILS) | 5 3 |

_____

_____

6 | Sharing with the neighbours

6.1 Do you and a neighbour share the cost of anything used jointly, such as the repair of a shared drive, boundary or drain?

| YES (PLEASE GIVE DETAILS) | NO ✓ |

_____

_____

TA3/4

FOR OFFICE
USE ONLY
PH·
PARA NO

6.2 Do you contribute to the cost of repair of anything used by the neighbourhood, such as the maintenance of a private road?

Please tick the right answer

YES	NO ✓

6.1

6.3 If so, who is responsible for organising the work and collection of contributions?

6.2

6.4 Please give details of all such sums paid or owing, and explain if they are paid on a regular basis or merely as and when work is required.

6.3 & 6.4

6.5 Do you need to go next door if you have to repair or decorate your building or maintain any of the boundaries?

YES ✓	NO

6.5

CUTTING HEDGE

6.6 If "Yes", have you always been able to do so without objection by the neighbours?

YES ✓	NO: PLEASE GIVE DETAILS OF ANY OBJECTION UNDER THE ANSWER TO QUESTION 2 (DISPUTES)

6.5

6.7 Do any of your neighbours need to come onto your land to repair or decorate their building or maintain the boundaries?

YES ✓	NO

6.5

TO REPAIR FENCE

6.8 If so, have you ever objected?

NO ✓	YES: PLEASE GIVE DETAILS OF ANY OBJECTION UNDER THE ANSWER TO QUESTION 2 (DISPUTES)

2.1

7 Arrangements and rights

Are there any other formal or informal arrangements which give someone else rights over your property?

NO ✓	YES: (PLEASE GIVE DETAILS)

7.2

8 Occupiers

8.1 Does anyone other than you live in the property?
If "No" go to question 9.1.
If "Yes" please give their full names and (if under 18) their ages.

YES	NO ✓

8.1

8.1

	USE ONLY
	PH
	PARA NO

8.2(a)(i) Do any of them have any right to stay on the property without your permission?

NO:	YES: (PLEASE GIVE DETAILS)

(These rights may have arisen without you realising, e.g. if they have paid for improvements or if they helped you buy the house).

8.2(a)(ii) Are any of them tenants or lodgers?

NO	YES: (PLEASE GIVE DETAILS AND A COPY OF ANY TENANCY AGREEMENT)	8.2(a)

8.2(b) Have they all agreed to sign the contract for sale agreeing to leave with you (or earlier)?

NO	YES: (PLEASE GIVE DETAILS)	8.2(b)

9 | Restrictions

If you have changed the use of the property or carried out any building work on it, please read the note below and answer these questions. If you have not, please go on to Question 10.

Note   The title deeds of some properties include clauses which are called "restrictive covenants". For example, these may forbid the owner of the house to carry out any building work or to use it for the purpose of a business—unless someone else (often the builder of the house) gives his consent.

9.1 (a) Do you know of any "restrictive covenant" which applies to your house or land?

✓ NO	YES	9.1

(b) If "Yes", did you ask for consent?

NO	YES: (PLEASE GIVE DETAILS AND A COPY OF ANY CONSENT)	9.1

9.2 If consent was needed but not obtained, please explain why not.

	9.2

TA3 6

9.3 If the reply to 9.1(a) is "Yes", please give the name
and address of the person from whom consent has to be
obtained.

10 Planning

10.1 Is the property used only as a private home?

Please tick the right answer

YES	NO: (PLEASE GIVE DETAILS)
✓	

10.1

10.2 (a) Is the property a listed building or in a
conservation area?

YES	NO	DON'T KNOW
		✓

10.2(a)

(b) If "Yes", what work has been carried out since
it was listed or the area became a conservation area?

10.2(b)

10.3 Has there been any building work on the property
in the last four years?

NO	YES: (PLEASE GIVE DETAILS)

10.3

DAMP PROOF COURSE
WOODWORM TREATMENT

10.4 Have you applied for planning permission,
building regulation approval or listed building consent
at any time?

NO	YES:	COPIES ENCLOSED	TO FOLLOW	LOST
✓				

10.4

10.5 If "Yes", has any of the work been carried out?

NO	YES: (PLEASE GIVE DETAILS)

Please turn over to next page. TA3·7

81

11 Fixtures

Please tick right answer

11.1 If you have sold through an estate agent, are all the items listed in its particulars included in the sale?

✓ YES	NO

11.1

If "No" you should instruct the estate agent to write to everyone concerned correcting this error.

11.2 Do you own outright everything included in the sale?

YES	NO: (PLEASE GIVE DETAILS)

(You must give details of anything which may not be yours to sell, for example, anything rented or on H.P.)

12 Expenses

Have you ever had to pay anything for the use of the property?

✓ NO	YES: (PLEASE GIVE DETAILS)

12.1

(Ignore rates, water rates, community charge and gas, electricity and phone bills. Include anything else: examples are the clearance of cess pool or septic tank, drainage rate, rent charge.)

13 General

Is there any other information which you think the buyer may have a right to know?

✓ NO	YES: (PLEASE GIVE DETAILS)

Signature(s) *Nancy Mixford*

Date *16 July 1992*

![crest]

THE LAW SOCIETY

This form is part of The Law Society's TransAction scheme. · The Law Society 1992
The Law Society is the professional body for solicitors in England and Wales
February 1992

TA3/8

SELLER'S PROPERTY INFORMATION FORM

Part II – to be completed by the seller's solicitor and to be sent with Part I

A Boundaries

Does the information in the deeds agree with the seller's reply to 1.1 in Part I?

Please tick the right answer

✓ YES	NO (PLEASE GIVE DETAILS)

SEE OFFICE COPY AND TITLE PLAN ENCLOSED

B Relevant Documents

(i) Are you aware of any correspondence, notices, consents or other documents other than those disclosed in Questions 3 or 4 of Part I?

(ii) If "Yes", please supply copies of all relevant documents.

YES	✓ NO

C Guarantees

If appropriate, have notices of assignment of any guarantees been given in the past?

YES	NO

N/A

D Services

Please give full details of all legal rights enjoyed to ensure the benefit of uninterrupted services, e.g. easements, wayleaves, licences, etc.

NOT AWARE OF ANY

E Adverse Interests

Please give full details of all overriding interests affecting the property as defined by the Land Registration Act 1925. s. 70 (1).

NOT AWARE OF ANY PLEASE RELY ON SEARCHES AND INSPECTION.

F Restrictions

Who has the benefit of any restrictive covenants? If known, please provide the name and address of the person or company having such benefit or the name and address of his or its solicitors.

NOT KNOWN. ONLY INFORMATION IS IN REGISTER OF TITLE

G Mechanics of Sale

(a) Is this sale dependent on the seller buying another property?

Please tick the right answer

YES	NO ✓

(b) If "Yes", what stage have the negotiations reached?

N/A

(c) Does the seller require a mortgage?

YES	NO	*N/A*

(d) If "Yes", has an offer been received and/ or accepted or a mortgage certificate obtained?

Seller's Solicitor *Moriarty & Co.*

Date *17 February 1993*

Reminder

1. The Fixtures, Fittings and Contents Form should be supplied in addition to the information above.

2. If the property is leasehold, also complete the Additional Property Information Form.

THE LAW SOCIETY

This form is part of The Law Society's TransAction scheme   The Law Society 1992
The Law Society is the professional body for solicitors in England and Wales
February 1992

Document 4.1.5 Obebe Purchase: Extract from Fixtures, Fittings & Content List

FIXTURES FITTINGS AND CONTENTS (2ND EDITION)

Address of the Property: *16 WINCHESTER AVENUE*

MIXFORD TO OBEBE

1. Place a tick in one of these three columns against every item.

2. The second column ("excluded from the sale") is for items on the list which you are proposing to take with you when you move. If you are prepared to sell any of these to the buyer, please write the price you wish to be paid beside the name of the item and the buyer can then decide whether or not to accept your offer to sell.

	INCLUDED IN SALE	EXCLUDED FROM SALE	NONE AT PROPERTY
TV Aerial/Satellite Dish	✓		
Radio Aerial			✗
Immersion Heater	✓		
Hot Water Cylinder Jacket	✓		
Roof Insulation	✓		
Wall Heaters			
Night Storage Heater			✓
Gas/Electric Fires		✗	
Light Fittings:			
Ceiling Lights	✓	☐	☐
Wall Lights	✓	☐	☐
Lamp Shades	☐	✓	☐
N.B. If these are to be removed, it is assumed that they will be replaced by ceiling rose and socket, flex, bulb holder and bulb.			
Switches	✓		
Electric Points	✓		
Dimmer Switches			✓

Document 4.1.6 Obebe Purchase: Extract From Local Land Charges Search Form

---

(Local Land Charges Rules 1977 Schedule 1, Form C)

Official Number **90/23832**
(To be completed by the registering authority)

The duplicate of this form must also be completed:
a carbon copy will suffice

For directions, notes and fees see overleaf

Insert name and address of registering authority in space below

LEDCHESTER CITY COUNCIL
LOCAL LAND CHARGES
SECTION,
CIVIC HALL,
LEDCHESTER LR2 4YC

Register of local land charges

Requisition for search and official certificate of search

Requisition for search
(A separate requisition must be made in respect of each parcel of land except as explained overleaf)

An official search is required in Part(s) of
the register of local land charges kept by the above-named
registering authority for subsisting registrations against the land
[defined in the attached plan and]² described below.

Description of land sufficient to enable it to be identified

16 WINCHESTER AVENUE, LEDCHESTER

Name and address to which certificate is to be sent

MORIARTY & CO.
SOLICITORS
TUMBLEDOWN HOUSE
THE BEDROW
LEDCHESTER LR2 6PQ

Signature of applicant *(or his solicitor)*
Moriarty & Co.

Date
3 JUNE 1992

Telephone number
390088

Reference
HH/AC/MIXFORD

Enclosure
Cheque/Money Order/Postal Order/Giro *£27.50*

Official certificate of search

To be completed by authorised officer

It is hereby certified that the search requested above reveals
no subsisting registrations¹
or the *ONE* registrations described in the Schedule
hereto³ up to and including the date of this certificate.

Signed *Jane Rogerson*

On behalf of *Ledchester City Council*

Date
15 June 1992

---

1 Delete if inappropriate. Otherwise insert Part(s) in which search is required.

2 Delete if inappropriate. (A plan should be furnished in duplicate if it is desired that a copy should be returned.)

3 Delete inapplicable words. (The Parts of the Schedule should be securely attached to the certificate and the number of registrations disclosed should be inserted in the space provided. Only Parts which disclose subsisting registrations should be sent.)

4 Insert name of registering authority.

Document 4.1.7 Obebe Purchase: Additional Enquiries of Local Authority

CON. 29 (1991)
To be submitted in duplicate

Search No......................

ENQUIRIES OF
LOCAL AUTHORITY
(1991 EDITION)

Please type or use BLOCK LETTERS

A.
To *Ledchester City Council*
Local Land Charges Section
Civic Hall
Ledchester LR2 4YC

A. Enter name and address of District or Borough Council for the area. If the property is near a Local Authority boundary, consider raising certain Enquiries (e.g. road schemes) with the adjoining Council.

B. Enter address and description of the property. A plan in duplicate must be attached wherever possible, and may be insisted upon by some Councils. Without a plan, replies may be inaccurate or incomplete. A plan is essential if Optional Enquiry 18 is raised.

B.
Property
16 Winchester Avenue, Ledchester

[Note: Plan, not reproduced, is as on Office Copy, Document 4.1.3.]

C. Enter name and/or location (and mark on plan, if possible) any other roadways, footpaths and footways (in addition to those entered in Box B) to which Enquiries 3 and (if raised) 19 are to apply.

C.
Other roadways, footpaths and footways

Back Winchester Avenue
(Edged green in enclosed plan)

D. Answer every question Any additional Enquiries must be attached on a separate sheet in duplicate, and an additional fee will be charged for any which the Council is willing to answer.

E. Details of fees can be obtained from the Council or from the Association of District Councils, 26 Chapter Street, London SW1P 4ND.

D.
A plan in duplicate is attached　　　　YES/NO

Optional Enquiries are to be answered (see Box G)　YES/NO

Additional Enquiries are attached in duplicate on a separate sheet　　　　YES/NO

F. Enter name and address of person or firm lodging this form.

G. Tick the Optional Enquiries to be answered.

E.
Fees of £　*£75*　　　are enclosed.

Signed:　*Moriarty & Co*

Date:　*3 June 1992*

Reference:　*M/AC/MIXFORD*

Tel. No.:　*390088*

Please read the Notes on page 4.

G.　Optional Enquiries

17	21	25	29	33
18	22	26 ✓	30	
19	23	27	31	
20	24	28	32	

F.
Reply to
Moriarty & Co., Solicitors,
Tumbledown House
The Bedrow
Ledchester LR2 6PQ

OYEZ The Solicitors' Law Stationery Society Limited, Oyez House, 7 Spa Road, London SE16 3QQ
Conveyancing 29(1991)

LAW SOCIETY COPYRIGHT
8.92 F23006 [5033379]

PART I—STANDARD ENQUIRIES
(APPLICABLE IN EVERY CASE)

DEVELOPMENT PLANS PROVISIONS
Structure Plan
1.1.1 What structure plan is in force?

1.1.2 Have any proposals been made public for the alteration of the structure plan?

Local Plans
1.2 What local plans (including action area plans) are adopted or in the course of preparation?

Old Style Development Plan
1.3 What old style development plan is in force?

Unitary Plan([1])
1.4.1 What stage has been reached in the preparation of a unitary development plan?

1.4.2 Have any proposals been made public for the alteration or replacement of a unitary development plan?

Non-Statutory Plan
1.5.1 Have the Council made public any proposals for the preparation or modification of a non-statutory plan?

1.5.2 If so, what stage has been reached?

Primary Use and Provisions for the Property
1.6 In any of the above plans or proposals:
  (a) what primary use is indicated for the area?
  (b) what provisions are included for the property?

Land required for Public Purposes
1.7 Is the property included in any of the categories of land specified in Schedule 13 paras 5 and 6 of the T&CP Act 1990?

DRAINAGE
Foul Drainage
2.1.1 To the Council's knowledge, does foul drainage from the property drain to a public sewer?([2])

2.1.2 If so, is the connection to the public sewer effected by:
  (a) drain and private sewer, or
  (b) drain alone?

Surface Water Drainage
2.2.1 Does surface water from the property drain to a public sewer?

2.2.2 Does surface water from the property drain to a highway drain or sewer which is the subject of an agreement under s.21(1)(a) of the Public Health Act 1936?

2.2.3 If the reply to either 2.2.1 or 2.2.2 is "Yes", is the connection to that sewer or highway drain effected by:
  (a) drain and private sewer, or
  (b) drain alone?

Combined Private Sewer
2.3 Is there in force in relation to any part of the drainage of the property an agreement under s.22 of the Building Act 1984?

Adoption Agreement
2.4.1 To the Council's knowledge, is any sewer serving, or which is proposed to serve, the property the subject of an agreement under s.18 of the Public Health Act 1936?([3])

2.4.2 If so, is such an agreement supported by a bond or other financial security?([4])

Potential Compulsory Drainage Connection
2.5 If the Reply to either Enquiry 2.1.1 or 2.2.1 is "No", to the Council's knowledge is there a foul or surface water sewer (as appropriate) within 100 feet of the property and at a level which makes it reasonably practicable to construct a drain from the property to that sewer?([5])

Sewerage Undertaker
2.6 Please state the name and address of the sewerage undertaker.

MAINTENANCE OF ROADS ETC.
Publicly Maintained
3.1 Are all the roadways, footpaths and footways referred to in Boxes B and C on page 1 maintainable at the public expense within the meaning of the Highways Act 1980?

Resolutions to make up or adopt
3.2 If not, have the Council passed any resolution to:
  (a) make up any of those roadways, footpaths or footways at the cost of the frontagers, or
  (b) adopt any of them without cost to the frontagers?
If so, please specify.

Adoption Agreements
3.3.1 Have the Council entered into any outstanding agreement relating to the adoption of any of those roadways, footpaths or footways? If so, please specify.

3.3.2 Is any such agreement supported by a bond or other financial security?([4])

ROAD SCHEMES
Trunk and Special Roads
4.1.1 What orders, draft orders or schemes have been notified to the Council by the appropriate Secretary of State for the construction of a new trunk or special road, the centre line of which is within 200 metres of the property?

4.1.2 What proposals have been notified to the Council by the appropriate Secretary of State for the alteration or improvement of an existing road, involving the construction, whether or not within existing highway limits, of a subway, underpass, flyover, footbridge, elevated road or dual carriageway, the centre line of which is within 200 metres of the property?

Other Roads
4.2 What proposals of their own([6]) have the Council approved for any of the following, the limits of construction of which are within 200 metres of the property:
  (a) the construction of a new road, or
  (b) the alteration or improvement of an existing road, involving the construction, whether or not within existing highway limits, of a subway, underpass, flyover, footbridge, elevated road or dual carriageway?

Road Proposals Involving Acquisition
4.3 What proposals have the Council approved, or have been notified to the Council by the appropriate Secretary of State, for highway construction or improvement that involve the acquisition of the property?

Road Proposals at Consultation Stage
4.4 What proposals have either the Secretary of State or the Council published for public consultation relating to the construction of a new road indicating a possible route the centre line of which would be likely to be within 200 metres of the property?

OUTSTANDING NOTICES
5. What outstanding statutory notices or informal notices have been issued by the Council under the Public Health Acts, Housing Acts or Highways Acts?
(This enquiry does not cover notices shown in the Official Certificate of Search or notices relating to matters covered by Enquiry 13.)

BUILDING REGULATIONS
6. What proceedings have the Council authorised in respect of an infringement of the Building Regulations?

---

(1) This enquiry relates only to London Boroughs and other metropolitan authorities.
(2) Any reply will be based on information supplied to the Council by the sewerage undertakers.
(3) The enquirer should also make similar enquiries of the sewerage undertaker even if the Council reply to this enquiry.
(4) The enquirer should satisfy himself as to the adequacy of any bond or other financial security.
(5) If the Council cannot reply in the affirmative, the enquirer must make his own survey.
(6) This enquiry refers to the Council's own proposals and not those of other bodies or companies.

PLANNING APPLICATIONS AND PERMISSIONS

Applications and Decisions

7.1 Please list:
(a) any entries in the Register of planning applications and permissions,
(b) any applications and decisions in respect of listed building consent, and
(c) any applications and decisions in respect of conservation area consent.

Inspection and Copies

7.2 If there are any entries:
(a) how can copies be obtained?
(b) where can the Register be inspected?

NOTICES UNDER PLANNING ACTS

Enforcement and Stop Notices

8.1.1 Please list any entries in the Register of enforcement notices and stop notices.

8.1.2 If there are any entries:
(a) how can copies be obtained?
(b) where can that Register be inspected?

Proposed Enforcement or Stop Notice

8.2 Except as shown in the Official Certificate of Search, or in reply to Enquiry 8.1.1, has any enforcement notice, listed building enforcement notice, or stop notice been authorised by the Council for issue or service (other than notices which have been withdrawn or quashed)?

Compliance with Enforcement Notices

8.3 If an enforcement notice or listed building enforcement notice has been served or issued, has it been complied with to the satisfaction of the Council?

Other Contravention Notices etc.

8.4 Have the Council served, or resolved to serve, any other notice or proceedings relating to a contravention of planning control?

Listed Building Repairs Notices, etc.

8.5.1 To the knowledge of the Council, has the service of a repairs notice been authorised?

8.5.2 If the Council have authorised the making of an order for the compulsory acquisition of a listed building, is a "minimum compensation" provision included, or to be included, in the order?

8.5.3 Have the Council authorised the service of a building preservation notice?([7])

DIRECTIONS RESTRICTING PERMITTED DEVELOPMENT

9. Except as shown in the Official Certificate of Search, have the Council resolved to make a direction to restrict permitted development?

ORDERS UNDER PLANNING ACTS

Revocation Orders etc.

10.1 Except as shown in the Official Certificate of Search, have the Council resolved to make any Orders revoking or modifying any planning permission or discontinuing an existing planning use?

Tree Preservation Order

10.2 Except as shown in the Official Certificate of Search, have the Council resolved to make any Tree Preservation Orders?

COMPENSATION FOR PLANNING DECISIONS

11. What compensation has been paid by the Council under s.114 of the T&CP Act 1990 for planning decisions restricting development other than new development?

PRE-REGISTRATION CONSERVATION AREA

12. Except as shown in the Official Certificate of Search, is the area a conservation area?

COMPULSORY PURCHASE

13. Except as shown in the Official Certificate of Search, have the Council made any order (whether or not confirmed by the appropriate Secretary of State) or passed any resolution for compulsory acquisition which is still capable of being implemented?([8])

AREAS DESIGNATED UNDER HOUSING ACTS ETC.

Clearance

14.1 Has any programme of clearance for the area been —
(a) submitted to the Department of the Environment, or
(b) resolved to be submitted, or
(c) otherwise adopted by resolution of the Council?

Housing

14.2 Except as shown in the Official Certificate of Search, have the Council resolved to define the area as designated for a purpose under the Housing Acts? If so, please specify the purpose.

SMOKE CONTROL ORDER

15. Except as shown in the Official Certificate of Search, have the Council made a smoke control order or resolved to make or vary a smoke control order for the area?

CONTAMINATED LAND

16.1 Is the property included in the Register of contaminated land?
16.2 If so:
(a) how can copies of the entries be obtained?
(b) where can the Register be inspected?

PART II—OPTIONAL ENQUIRIES

(APPLICABLE ONLY AS INDICATED ON PAGE ONE)

RAILWAYS

17. What proposals have been notified to the Council, and what proposals of their own have the Council approved, for the construction of a railway (including light railway or monorail) the centre line of which is within 200 metres of the property?

PUBLIC PATHS OR BYWAYS

18. Has any public path, bridleway or road used as a public path or byway which abuts on or crosses the property been shown in a definitive map or revised definitive map prepared under Part IV of the National Parks and Access to the Countryside Act 1949 or Part III of the Wildlife and Countryside Act 1981? If so, please mark its approximate route on the attached plan.

PERMANENT ROAD CLOSURE

19. What proposals have the Council approved for permanently stopping up or diverting any of the roads or footpaths referred to in Boxes B and C on page 1?

TRAFFIC SCHEMES

20. In respect of any of the roads referred to in Boxes B and C on page 1, what proposals have the Council approved, but have not yet put into operation, for:
(a) waiting restrictions,
(b) one-way streets,
(c) prohibition of driving,
(d) pedestrianisation, or
(e) vehicle width or weight restrictions?

ADVERTISEMENTS

Entries in Register

21.1.1 Please list any entries in the Register of applications, directions and decisions relating to consent for the display of advertisements.

21.1.2 If there are any entries, where can that Register be inspected?

Notices, Proceedings and Orders

21.2 Except as shown in the Official Certificate of Search:
(a) has any notice been given by the Secretary of State or served in respect of a direction or proposed direction restricting deemed consent for any class of advertisement?
(b) have the Council resolved to serve a notice requiring the display of any advertisement to be discontinued?
(c) if a discontinuance notice has been served, has it been complied with to the satisfaction of the Council?
(d) have the Council resolved to serve any other notice or proceedings relating to a contravention of the control of advertisements?
(e) have the Council resolved to make an order for the special control of advertisements for the area?

COMPLETION NOTICES

22. Which of the planning permissions in force have the Council resolved to terminate by means of a completion notice under s.94 of the T&CP Act 1990?

---

(7) The Historic Buildings and Monuments Commission also have power to issue this type of notice for buildings in London Boroughs, and separate enquiry should be made of them if appropriate.

(8) This enquiry refers to the Council's own compulsory purchase powers and not those of other bodies.

PARKS AND COUNTRYSIDE

Areas of Outstanding Natural Beauty

23.1 Has any order under s.87 of the National Parks and Access to the Countryside Act 1949 been made?

National Parks

23.2 Is the property within a National Park designated under s.7 of the National Parks and Access to the Countryside Act 1949?

PIPELINES

24. Has a map been deposited under s.35 of the Pipelines Act 1962, or Schedule 7 of the Gas Act 1986, showing a pipeline within 100 feet of the property?

HOUSES IN MULTIPLE OCCUPATION

25. Is the property included in a registration of houses scheme (houses in multiple occupation) under s.346 of the Housing Act 1985, containing control provisions as authorised by s.347 of that Act?

NOISE ABATEMENT

Noise Abatement Zone

26.1 Have the Council made, or resolved to make, any noise abatement zone order under s.63 of the Control of Pollution Act 1974 for the area?

Entries in Register

26.2.1 Has any entry been recorded in the Noise Level Register kept pursuant to s.64 of the Control of Pollution Act 1974?

26.2.2 If there is an entry, how can copies be obtained and where can that Register be inspected?

URBAN DEVELOPMENT AREAS

27.1 Is the area an urban development area designated under Part XVI of the Local Government Planning and Land Act 1980?

27.2 If so, please state the name of the urban development corporation and the address of its principal office.

ENTERPRISE ZONES

28. Is the area an enterprise zone designated under Part XVIII of the Local Government Planning and Land Act 1980?

INNER URBAN IMPROVEMENT AREAS

29. Have the Council resolved to define the area as an improvement area under s.4 of the Inner Urban Areas Act 1978?

SIMPLIFIED PLANNING ZONES

30.1 Is the area a simplified planning zone adopted or approved pursuant to s.83 of the T&CP Act 1990?

30.2 Have the Council approved any proposal for designating the area as a simplified planning zone?

LAND MAINTENANCE NOTICES

31. Have the Council authorised the service of a maintenance notice under s.215 of the T&CP Act 1990?

MINERAL CONSULTATION AREAS

32. Is the area a mineral consultation area notified by the county planning authority under Schedule 1 para 7 of the T&CP Act 1990?

HAZARDOUS SUBSTANCE CONSENTS

33.1 Please list any entries in the Register kept pursuant to s.28 of the Planning (Hazardous Substances) Act 1990.

33.2 If there are any entries:
(a) how can copies of the entries be obtained?
(b) where can the Register be inspected?

GENERAL NOTES

(A) Unless otherwise indicated, all these enquiries relate to the property as described in Box B on page 1, and any part of that property, and "the area" means any area in which the property is located.

(B) These enquiries will not necessarily reveal (i) matters relating to properties other than the Property specified in Box B on page 1, or (ii) matters relating to land outside the area of the Council to whom these enquiries are sent, or (iii) matters which are outside the functions of that Council (although, under arrangements made between District Councils and County Councils, the replies given to certain enquiries addressed to District Councils cover knowledge and actions of both the District Council and the County Council).

(C) References to "the Council" include references to a predecessor Council and to a Committee or Sub-Committee of the Council acting under delegated powers, and to any other body or person taking action under powers delegated by the Council or a predecessor Council.

(D) References to an Act, Regulation or Order include reference to (i) any statutory provision which it replaces and (ii) any amendment or re-enactment of it.

(E) References to any Town and Country Planning Act, Order or Regulation are abbreviated, eg "T&CP Act 1990".

(F) The replies will be given after the appropriate enquiries and in the belief that they are in accordance with the information at present available to the officers of the replying Council(s), but on the distinct understanding that none of the Councils, nor any Council officer, is legally responsible for them, except for negligence. Any liability for negligence shall extend for the benefit of not only the person by or for whom these Enquiries are made but also a person (being a purchaser for the purposes of s.10(3) of the Local Land Charges Act 1975) who or whose agent had knowledge, before the relevant time (as defined in that section), of the replies to these Enquiries.

(G) This form of Enquiries is approved by the Law Society, the Association of County Councils, the Association of District Councils and the Association of Metropolitan Authorities and is published by their authority.

The Replies are given on the attached sheet(s)

Signed ....
               Proper Officer

Date..

Note: The replies, being on a separate sheet, have not been reproduced here.

There is also a letter from Copperfields as follows:

Document 4.1.8 French/Saunders Purchase: Letter from Vendor's Solicitor

D. Copperfield & Co.

17 February 1993

Dear Sirs,

Rocard to French and Saunders
24 De Lucy Mount, Ledchester
Your ref: TT/MH

We beg to remind you that we sent you the draft
contract in this matter by letter dated 2 February
last crossing yours of 1 February confirming your
instructions to act.
We remind you that our clients are anxious to
exchange and have already stressed the urgency of
the matter as they are anxious to make arrangements
to take up occupation of their retirement home in
Eldorado.
Please kindly inform us of the situation without
delay.

Yours faithfully,

D. Copperfield & Co.

D. Copperfield & Co.

Timothy thinks

4.1.9   His daily attempt to get beyond answering two clues in the *Times* crossword (poor Timothy - this is already something of an office joke) will have to be postponed. Both letters hint, even to Timothy's untrained sense, at urgency. There is work to be done. But what? Timothy looks both helplessly and hopefully towards Old Jarndyce who maintains his ethereal silence.

'Ah!' says Timothy, thrown back on his own meagre resources. 'The Obebe contract. Registered title. Everything is on the register. They have sent me local searches and a property information form - part of Transaction - whatever that is (Timothy was skiing in Austria when Transaction was being taught). Not sure why - no need for any of those pre-contract searches and enquiries that you have to do with unregistered title. Better get the contract signed.' He dictates a short letter to Miss Obebe asking her to come in and sign the contract on her purchase (forgetting - just for a moment of course! - that he has not yet even drafted the contract on her sale (para.7.1)). He adds a note that there is a contract race; and if she hurries up and gets the contract signed, she will win the race and be guaranteed to get the property.

Timothy then rummages on his desk for the French/Saunders file. (If genius is the infinite capacity to take pains; there must be a place for a proper filing system and a tidy desk in the spectrum of competence.) He knows it is there because Miss French has been ringing him daily - always with the yapping dog in the background - with a stream of questions. Timothy has been exhorted to find out whether dogs can be taken into the Abbey Grounds, how much traffic there is on the main road, whether she can have a 'proper' dog kennel built in the back garden for Piddles; what schools there are in the neighbourhood for, as Timothy now calls her, the little sniveller; does the roof need attention and if it does, how much is it likely to cost; how much does the central heating cost to run; and so on, endlessly. Timothy's lame response to every such question has been that he would find out. 'That is what enquiries before contract are for' - so he thinks.

Eventually, Timothy finds the file.

He now digs out from Miss Pinky's meticulous system every form of search and enquiry that he can find, completes all the following to be dispatched: Enquiries Before Contract form (to which he adds 37 additional queries, including a request for the local bus timetables for the area, all inspired by Fancy's many questions); Local Land Charges search form; Additional Enquiries of the Local Authority; Commons Search; mining search; Central Land Charges search form. He does not include a public index map search - 'That is for registered title,' he thinks. He even takes two hours off to visit the property, happening to know a rather pleasant hostelry in the area where his cronies are wont to gather at this sort of time; has a long chat with an old man living next door to 24 and makes copious notes about the state of the roads, buses, abbey grounds. He looks over the fence of 24 itself. 'Inspecting the property,' it is called – he remembers from his lecture notes, but is not sure what he is looking for and sees nothing apart from some pretty pink flowers and a cantankerous-looking old lady sitting on the doorstep enjoying the February sunshine (could this conceivably prove to be significant, especially as the property is supposed to be empty? See the Instructions on Purchase, Document 1.4).

Question On the information available, what pre-contract investigations should Timothy have made on behalf of Miss Obebe and on behalf of Miss French and Sam Saunders?

Read through the documentation supplied by Moriarties relating to the Obebe purchase. What matters do you think need further investigation, or raising with the client?

OLD JARNDYCE COMMENTS

(having, as usual, intercepted the unhappy product of Timothy's burst of activity before it can be dispatched into the city like shrapnel of the firm's exploding reputation; and redirected it to the office of Miss Fit, who has not only passed her ILEX conveyancing exam but also knows more about sensible conveyancing practice than anyone else in the office save Old Jarndyce himself.)   4.2

GENERAL PRINCIPLES OF PRE-CONTRACT INVESTIGATIONS

As usual Timothy is displaying the classic symptoms of chronic confusion. With some differences, the principles underlying pre-contract investigations are the same for unregistered and registered conveyancing. The following paragraphs focus on unregistered title; para.4.1.2 then comments on the differences in the case of registered title.   4.3

It is the duty of the purchaser's solicitor to make certain investigations before contract. The purpose is to find out information needed by the purchaser before committing herself to a contract. Some of these investigations will be made as a matter of course in almost every purchase (unless done by the vendor the results being supplied to the purchaser with the draft contract (see para.7.12). The need to make others will have to be judged in the circumstances of the particular case.

Possible investigations can usefully be classified in various ways as follows:

(a) According to the target at which they are directed. In the case of unregistered title the following investigations are relevant (for registered title, see para.4.12):

(i) Preliminary Enquiries of the vendor.

(ii) Search in the Local Land Charges Register.

(iii) Additional Enquiries of the Local Authority.

(iv) Public Index Map search.

(v) Inspection of the property - at least by the purchaser herself.

(vi) Other searches and enquiries depending on the circumstances.

(b) It is also useful to appreciate that the matters being investigated can be put into the following categories:

(i) Matters affecting the title to the property; that is anything which affects the ability of the vendor to convey the legal freehold free from any equitable interest under a trust and free from any incumbrance.

(ii) Matters affecting the physical condition of the property.

(iii) Other matters, operating outside the existing legal and physical boundaries, but which bear upon its environment and present or future enjoyment.

(c) From another perspective these matters can also be classified into:

(i) Those matters which the vendor is under a duty to disclose before contract. It is particularly important in this area to remember that the vendor's duty of disclosure may (and invariably is to some extent) limited by the express terms of the contract. Even if a particular adverse matter ought under the contract to be disclosed by the vendor without prompting, it is often safer, cheaper and more convenient to discover its existence before contract and withdraw, rather than enter the contract in ignorance and rely upon the vagaries of a judicial remedy for breach of contract for non-disclosure.

The vendor's duty of disclosure can be summarised as follows:

Under an open contract (para.5.3.1) it is the duty of the vendor to be in a position at the time due for completion to convey to the purchaser the legal fee simple absolute in possession (the legal freehold) free from any trust and free from any incumbrance. It follows that the vendor is under a duty to disclose to the purchaser before contract any limitation on such a complete title. This applies even if the vendor and her solicitor are not themselves aware of the limitation. The only qualification to this under an open contract is that the vendor need not disclose any irremovable title defect of which the purchaser already knows; and need not disclose patent defects in title (para.4.7). Irremovable defects are those which the owner is not entitled as of right to remove on the payment of money. If a defect is removable the vendor can be required to remove it before completion, whether or not the purchaser knew about it at the time of contract.

This duty of disclosure may be restricted (or indeed extended) by the express terms of the contract. However:

> 'It is a well established rule of equity that, if there is a defect in title or encumbrance of which the vendor is aware, the vendor cannot rely upon conditions such as those in the present case unless full and frank disclosure is made of its existence.[and, in this context] the knowledge of the vendor's solicitor is treated as that of the vendor, and it is no answer for him to say that he has not read the contents of his own conveyancing file.'[1]

Standard Condition 3 provides as follows:

'3.1. Freedom from incumbrances.

3.1.1. The seller is selling the property free from incumbrances, other than those mentioned in condition 3.1.2.

3.1.2. The incumbrances subject to which the property is sold are:

(a) those mentioned in the agreement

(b) those discoverable by inspection of the property before the contract

(c) those the seller does not and could not know about

(d) entries made before the date of the contract in any public register except those maintained by HM Land Registry or its Land Charges Department or by Companies House

(e) public requirements.

3.1.3. The buyer accepts the property in the physical state it is in at the date of the contract, unless the seller is building or converting it.

3.1.4. After the contract is made, the seller is to give the buyer written details without delay of any new public requirement and of anything in writing which he learns about concerning any incumbrances subject to which the property is sold.

3.1.5. The buyer is to bear the cost of complying with any outstanding public requirement and is to indemnify the seller against any liability resulting from a public requirement.'

---

[1] *Rignall Developments Ltd. v. Halil* [1987] 3 W.L.R. 394 at pp.399,400.

'Public requirement' is defined in Standard Condition 1.1.1. as 'any notice, order or proposal given or made (whether before or after the date of the contract) by a body acting on statutory authority'.

(ii) Those matters which the vendor is not under a duty to disclose. Subject to the above duty, the vendor can safely, in law, remain silent. The rule is *caveat emptor*. There is no duty to disclose physical defects in the property itself; nor any one of all those other matters which might affect its use or enjoyment or its environment. But if the vendor does open her mouth and make a misleading statement by words or conduct she runs the risk of incurring liability for breach of contract, misrepresentation or by estoppel.

(d) Finally, the objects of investigations can be classified according to the ways in which enjoyment of the property might be affected, especially:

(i) Planning. Whether there has been any breach of planning law enforceable against the purchaser; and whether planning law will interfere with (or indeed enhance) the client's intended enjoyment of the property or any works she wants to carry out.

(ii) Access. Whether there is adequate and legally secure access to the property.

(iii) Drainage and other services. Whether these are adequate and legally secure.

(iv) Boundaries. Ownership and liability for maintenance.

(v) The physical condition of the property.

(vi) Any easements, covenants or other legal restrictions on the property which might affect its use and enjoyment. Conversely, any which might enhance its enjoyment.

Items (i), (ii), (iii) and (vi) are dealt with in Chapter 6; (v) has been dealt with in Chapter 3. For (iv) see paras.5.4 and 7.11.

Where the property is affected by some adverse interest, two questions should be kept quite distinct.

(i) Does the purchaser have a personal remedy against the vendor for breach of contract, etc? Or possibly against someone else such as a negligent solicitor?

(ii) If the purchaser completes and takes a conveyance of the property, will the owner of the adverse interest be able to enforce it against her? For example, the vendor is under a duty (both under an open contract and the Standard Conditions) to disclose any charge registered in the central Land Charges Registry; and will potentially be liable to the purchaser for failing to do so. On the other hand, the owner of the registered charge will potentially be able to enforce it as a proprietary right against the purchaser, whether or not it has been disclosed and whether or not the purchaser knew about it.

What follows next is a look at some of the specific pre-contract investigations that may be necessary in the case of unregistered title.

PRELIMINARY ENQUIRIES (OF THE VENDOR)

The purchaser can, of course, ask the vendor what questions she likes   **4.4**
before contract either in person or through their respective solicitors. Equally, the vendor can refuse to answer; or answer in such a guarded and qualified way that the answer is not illuminating and cannot be relied upon.

It is customary for the purchaser's solicitor to address a set of questions (generally known as Preliminary Enquiries or Enquiries Before Contract) to the vendor through the latter's solicitor. She will use either one of the published sets (such as the Oyez, Enquiries Before Contract, Form Con.29, Long) or her own firm's standard set, adding or striking out particular questions to suit the particular transaction.

Traditionally, Preliminary Enquiries are sent to the vendor's solicitor by the purchaser's solicitor after receipt of the draft contract; and will include any queries relating to the terms of the draft contract. Increasingly, today, as part of the attempts to speed up the conveyancing process, the vendor's solicitor will send a standard set of enquiries with replies entered with the draft contract. This is the procedure adopted where the Law Society's Transaction Protocol is being followed (para.7.12). Under Transaction Protocol there is a Seller's Property Information Form (Document 4.1.4). In its latest mode, Part I of the form contains questions which are answered by the vendor personally (hopefully with the assistance and advice of her solicitor if necessary). Part II contains questions to be answered by the solicitor and dealing with information more likely to be available to her from the deeds, etc. In addition, there is an Additional Property Information form containing questions specific to leasehold.

Question Your client (of average intelligence) has just put her property on the market. She is worried about how to deal with potential purchasers who come to view; what she can tell them and what she must not tell them. The roof has a bit of a leak in very heavy rain which she does not think it worth bothering with as she is selling. She is also worried that she might say something to a prospective buyer that commits her to sell.

In a few hundred words and language that she should be able to understand, advise her how to handle prospective purchasers. (Before doing this, read the rest of this chapter and Chapter 9.)

Where questions (a set chosen in effect by the vendor's solicitor unless Transaction Protocol is being used) and answers are supplied with the draft contract, there is of course nothing to stop the purchaser's solicitor seeking the answers to additional questions, arising from examination of the draft contract or otherwise. And it remains the duty of the purchaser's solicitor to consider whether the material and information supplied by the vendor is sufficient; and what further is needed.

In general, preliminary enquiries are about non-title matters. Questions of title (whether the title is investigated before or after exchange of contracts (para.10.6.4) are more conventionally raised in requisitions on title. But in practice, where title is investigated before exchange, the two will probably be merged into a single set of queries. Nevertheless, it is best to keep the two distinct in one's mind. Title is today a relatively straightforward matter; it is clearly a matter for the solicitor to investigate; and it is normally easy to pinpoint what questions (requisitions) are legitimate and necessary for the vendor to deal with.

On the other hand information on non-title matters is probably of increasing importance to a purchaser and of increasing complexity. Partly because there is no legal obligation on the vendor to answer any, it is not so easy to say what questions the vendor can properly be expected to answer; or to say which should be asked formally through the solicitors and which should be left to the parties themselves to sort out.

In recent years there have been attempts to move towards a standard, nationally uniform, set of pre-contract questions, to reduce their number, and to discourage the addition of a large number of what are regarded as superfluous additional questions to standard forms of preliminary enquiries. Such a move may oil the wheels of cheap conveyancing. How far it is in the interests of the client is another matter. A sensible/properly advised purchaser will normally want as much accurate information as possible about the property and its environment before committing herself to a contract. Some purchasers are astute and experienced enough to know what they want to know and how to find it out, whether from the vendor or elsewhere. Others may not appreciate, until it is too late, what they need to know. At one time there was a trend for solicitors to add a mushrooming number of supplementary questions to already long standard forms. Today, the trend is probably the other way. Purchasers are likely to want/need to get contracts exchanged as soon as possible; and to be under pressure from their vendors and their own purchasers to do so. Solicitors are under pressure to pump conveyances through the system as quickly as possible. The trend is probably to encourage the purchaser who wants to delve beyond the standard enquiries to do so for herself. It is partly a question of the proper function of a lawyer, beyond the conventional one of investigating title; what she should be doing for the client, what she should be advising the client to do for herself; what she should be ignoring unless raised by the client; and what she can charge for doing or not doing these things.

Even within the framework of the questions which are now conventionally asked, the present system is to some extent a charade. The reliability of the replies depends on the extent and reliability of the vendor's knowledge. It is by no means unknown, at least where the latest Transaction Protocol Property Information form is not being used, for the vendor's solicitor to answer the enquiries without consulting the client; and, indeed, for the replies not to be communicated and explained to the purchaser by her solicitor. The central legal principle that the vendor does not have to answer, but that any false answer may give a remedy for misrepresentation, is a recipe for vague and non-committal answers and as few answers as possible – 'So far as the vendor is aware'; 'Please rely upon inspection of the property' etc (compare the answers to the Property Information Form (Document 4.1.4). Indeed, for the intelligent purchaser it is probably much better to ask most of the questions directly of the vendor and make a note of the answers, rather than indirectly through the solicitors.

Certain principles as to what questions can properly be asked by the purchaser's solicitors may be suggested.

Questions should only be asked about those matters which are particularly within the knowledge of the owner of the property; not on matters in respect of which more reliable information is readily obtainable elsewhere – for example, by local authority searches.

It is generally considered that questions should not be asked about the physical condition of the property – though they are asked about the availability of guarantees for works done. If such questions are asked, the answer is likely to be that the purchaser should rely on her own survey and investigations; in spite of the fact that this is a matter on which the vendor is most likely to have information.

In general there is no need for solicitors to raise questions the answers to which do not call for legal interpretation or advice. These can be left to the parties to sort out between themselves. Clearly, Timothy has allowed himself to be pushed by Mrs French into asking a host of totally unnecessary questions.

Liability of the vendor for misleading statements

The purchaser who feels that she has been misled by the vendor's replies to enquiries, or any other statement or conduct of the vendor, may have a remedy under three main heads:

4.4.1

(a) For breach of contract; where the replies have been incorporated into the main contract or can be construed as part of a collateral contract (para.9.5.3). In normal circumstances, unless replies have been expressly incorporated into the main contract, they are not likely to be held to have contractual effect.

It is important in practice that proper instructions are taken; and that whatever the parties want to be an enforceable part of their agreement has been properly incorporated by express provision into the contract. It should be remembered that if any matter expressly agreed between them is not incorporated, the whole contract might fail under s.2 of the Law of Property (Miscellaneous Provisions) Act 1989 (Chapter 9).

(b) For fraudulent, negligent or innocent misrepresentation. A misrepresentation is a false statement of fact made by one party to the contract to the other party (generally the vendor to the purchaser) which is one of the factors inducing that other to enter into the contract. A misrepresentation does not have to be in writing to give rise to liability; though it is quite common to find a contractual term seeking to exclude liability for oral statements.

Although damages and/or rescission may be available for both breach of contract and misrepresentation, the remedies for the two are by no means identical; and as shown by *Hamp* (below) it is important to distinguish between the two.

(c) Proprietary estoppel. The principle of proprietary estoppel has developed in recent years as a broad equitable principle; and it is difficult to give a simple statement of its requirements. It can perhaps be said that if the vendor (as it will normally be) has by statement, conduct or even acquiescence encouraged the purchaser to act to her detriment in reliance on a belief that she is to get some interest in property, the vendor may be estopped from denying that interest to the purchaser. Such estoppel does not depend on the existence of a contract and does not have to be put into writing; indeed, it may enable an agreement avoided by s.2 of the Law of Property (Miscellaneous Provisions) Act 1989 to be enforced (para.9.5.3).

Hamp v. Bygrave[2] illustrates some of these principles. The plaintiffs contracted to buy a large house in Sussex with over seven acres of gardens and paddock. They were suing the vendors for removing certain garden ornaments which had been in the gardens when they viewed and at the time of contract. The items included eight patio lights fixed to the walls, five stone urns, a stone statue and a lead trough. The estate agents' particulars expressly incorporated the items in their description of the property. At one stage of the negotiations

---

2   (1982) Lexis Transcript.

the vendors suggested excluding these items as a way of reducing the price. This suggestion was dropped and eventually a sale agreed subject to contract without mention of the items. Preliminary Enquiries sent by the plaintiffs' solicitors included the following standard, common-form ones relating to fixtures and fittings:

'(a) Does the sale include all the following items now on the property: trees, shrubs, plants, flowers and garden produce; greenhouses, garden sheds and garden ornaments;?

(b) What fixtures and fittings affixed to the property are not included in the sale?'

The replies were, respectively, 'Yes' to (a) and 'None' to (b).

After exchange of contracts one of the requisitions on title was the common-form one: 'If the enquiries before contract replied to on behalf of the vendor were repeated herein, would the replies now be the same as those previously given? If not please give full particulars of any variation.' The answer given - again in common-form - was: 'Yes, save as varied by subsequent correspondence, if any'. In fact, by this time some of the ornaments had been removed by the vendors.

Boreham J. decided as follows:

(i) Contrary to an argument by the vendors, there was on the evidence no oral agreement between the parties to exclude the items from the sale.

Question On the assumption that s.2 of the Law of Property (Miscellaneous Provisions) Act 1989 was then in force, what should the decision have been if there had been such an agreement? Would it have made any difference whether the items were fixtures or chattels? (See *Ram Narayan v. Rishad Hussain Shah.*[3])

(ii) The statements in the estate agents' particulars and the Replies to Preliminary Enquiries were not actionable as misrepresentations (and this was not in fact pleaded). In so far as they were statements of fact about the property they were true - the ornaments were on the property. What the plaintiffs were trying to show was that the statement of *intention* to include them in the sale was binding.

(iii) The Replies to Preliminary Enquiries were not part of the contract of sale. Boreham J. said:

'Whether or not an assertion or representation is to have contractual effect as a warranty must depend on the intention of the parties, such intention being a matter of inference from all the relevant circumstances.'

---

3   [1979] 1 W.L.R. 1349.

Here, in particular, the words prefaced to the Replies: 'These replies are believed to be correct, but the accuracy is not guaranteed and they do not obviate the need to make appropriate searches, enquiries and inspections' negatived any contractual intention. And the request for their confirmation in the requisitions would have been otiose if they had already become part of the contract. In any case, the replies, said Boreham J.:

'were not intended to create a warranty ... they were not of themselves intended to create any contract, their purpose was to enable a proper contract of sale to be drawn up.'

Question If they had been intended to be part of the contract, and on the assumption that the Law of Property (Miscellaneous Provisions) Act 1989, s.2 was in operation, what would have been the effect?

(iv) The items in dispute were fixtures and so passed to the purchasers under the contract as part of the land without express mention. Their removal by the vendors was therefore wrongful. This aspect of the decision (other than in the case of the patio lights) may be open to criticism. Boreham J. seems to have interpreted the purpose of annexation test to mean the subjective classification of an item as a chattel or a fixture by the person bringing it onto the land. But if you build a house it does not become a chattel because you call it a chattel.

(v) Further, the vendors were estopped from denying that the items were included in the sale. Their 'references to those items were calculated to induce the plaintiffs to act in the belief and on the basis that they were all included in the sale ... [and] the plaintiffs did act on that understanding and so paid more than they would otherwise have done.'

Fixtures and chattels

4.4.2   It is convenient to interpolate here something about fixtures and chattels.

Fixtures present at the time of contract pass under a contract for the disposition of land unless expressly excluded. Chattels do not pass unless expressly included. There may be no argument about the photograph of granny on the mantelpiece, but in practice, especially in the residential situation, it is extremely difficult to say with certainty whether a great many items from fitted carpets to light bulbs are fixtures or chattels. It is important therefore that the contract deals with the matter and preferably deals with all items about which dispute might arise. The special conditions should stipulate which items are included in and which are excluded from the sale. If this is done on a separate list, the list should be properly incorporated into the contract. If any separate price has been agreed for specified chattels, such chattels and the price should be identified in the contract. If the price of the land can be reduced, and stamp duty saved, by an honest apportionment of the total price between the land (including fixtures) and chattels, the client should be so advised (para.10.7.1).

Under Transaction Protocol, the vendor is required to complete and supply to the purchaser with the draft contract a detailed Fixtures, Fittings and Contents Form. This covers items from immersion heaters to curtains, carpets and dustbins; and provides for the vendor to tick whether they are included in the sale, excluded or not at the property. It might be necessary to add to the list. This completed form should be attached to the contract and incorporated by express provision. The printed special conditions of the Standard Conditions provide: 'The chattels on the property and set out on any attached list are included in the sale.' This is not really adequate; especially if, as is commonly the practice, the list is not actually attached. And the Transaction Protocol form deals both with the inclusion of items which may be chattels and the exclusion of items which may be fixtures, the latter not being mentioned in Standard Condition 3.1.3.

Question Draft a suitable standard contract clause to incorporate the Transaction Protocol form.

Question Timothy has just had a phone call from Miss Obebe's mother. She had promised to buy her daughter a complete set of curtains for the new house and went round yesterday to Winchester Avenue to measure up. She says that when she first viewed the house with her daughter there was a large, almost new shed in the garden. Her daughter explained to Miss Mixford that she hoped to use the shed to make the hand-thrown pottery which she sells in Ledchester market in her spare time. The mother tells Timothy that she noticed yesterday that the shed had gone. She did not mention it to Miss Mixford for fear of upsetting the sale; but her daughter is annoyed. Timothy says that he is in the middle of an interview (he is not) but will ring back as soon as he is free. He puts down the phone and digs out the Obebe file. The Fixtures and Fittings list shows the shed to be included in the sale. Timothy rushes off to the firm's library, where he tries to find an entry for 'sheds' in the index to *Emmett on Title*.

What advice should Timothy give Mrs Obebe? What advice should he give if the shed were not mentioned in the Fixtures and Fittings list and were removed by Miss Mixford *after* exchange of contracts?

Where chattels are included in the sale, Standard Condition 9.2. applies:

'9.2. Whether or not a separate price is to be paid for the chattels, the contract takes effect as a contract for the sale of goods.

9.3. Ownership of the chattels passes to the buyer on actual completion.'

The effect of this is that s.12 of the Sale of Goods Act 1979 applies giving the purchaser the benefit of an implied condition that when title is to pass the vendor will have the right to sell the goods free from any charge or incumbrance (such as an outstanding hire-purchase agreement; and the client should be advised to be sure that there are none such). Since, under Standard Condition 9.3. title is to pass only on completion, s.18 of the 1979 Act will not apply. This means that, as with the land itself under Standard Condition 5.1.1. (para.3.3.1), the risk remains with the vendor until completion; and, for her own protection, the vendor should keep the items insured until then.

Position of solicitors and other agents in relation to preliminary enquiries

4.4.3   The purchaser's solicitor is under a legal and professional duty to pursue proper enquiries on behalf of the client. (This of course applies not just to Preliminary Enquiries of the vendor but any other pre-contract searches and investigations which should be made in the circumstances.)

Computastaff Ltd. v. Ingledew Brown Bennison and Garnett and others[4], although decided on rather special facts and possibly open to criticism for imposing too high a duty on solicitors, does show the need to think beyond sending off a standard form of Preliminary Enquiries and filing away the replies.

In this case the replies to preliminary enquiries showed the rateable value of the business premises to be leased to the plaintiffs as £8,305. The plaintiffs' own estate agents, having got the figure from the landlord's letting agent, had stated it as £3,305. The plaintiffs' solicitor spotted this discrepancy in the information received, pointed it out to the plaintiffs, and asked the plaintiffs' estate agents which figure was correct. They in turn checked with the letting agents and as a result confirmed the lower figure; and, on this understanding, the plaintiffs took the lease, discovered that the higher figure was the correct one and suffered loss. The plaintiffs' solicitor was held liable for negligence (as were their estate agents) mainly on the basis it seems that he should have pursued the further inquiry with the landlord's solicitor.

---

[4]   (1983, Lexis Transcript).

The case does show that a solicitor must always make a careful judgment as to the proper place to seek any particular information.

The purchaser's solicitor must communicate any relevant information to the client; and the purchaser will be deemed to have knowledge of information communicated to the solicitor in that transaction.

> 'In this as in all other normal conveyancing transactions, after there has been a subject to contract agreement, the parties hand the matter over to their solicitors who become the normal channel for communication between the vendor and purchaser in all matters relating to the transaction. In doing so, in my judgement the parties impliedly give actual authority to those solicitors to receive on their behalf all relevant information from the other party relating to the transaction. The solicitors are under an obligation to communicate that relevant information to their own clients. At the very least, the solicitors are held out as having ostensible authority to receive such information. ... In my judgement such knowledge should be imputed to the principal.'[5]

In the case just quoted, the vendors had initially misrepresented that the drainage was to the mains rather than to a cesspool. This misinformation was repeated in the replies to enquiries before contract, and by the surveyor employed by the purchasers to survey the property for them (he having simply asked the vendors as to the drains - a procedure, rather surprisingly perhaps, held by the court to show sufficient professional competence). The information had been corrected by a letter from the vendors' estate agents to the purchasers' solicitor which was not communicated to the purchasers (and indeed disappeared from the file) who purchased in ignorance of the truth.[6]

The vendor's solicitor, like the purchaser's solicitor, is taken to know what is on the file; and the vendor is taken to know what her solicitor knows. Thus, in *Rignall Developments Ltd. v. Halil,*[7] the plaintiff contracted at auction to purchase a house from the defendant without first doing a local land charges search (para.4.5). The contract contained a provision that the property was sold subject to any matter which would be disclosed by searches and inquiries of the local authority; and that the purchaser would not raise any requisition or objection in relation to such matter. In fact there was, as the search done after contract showed, an adverse entry in the local land charges register. This recorded a condition attached to an improvement grant made for the property that the house had to be available for letting for a specified period. Breach of this condition, binding on the owner for the time being of the property, would make the grant repayable. In replies to a requisition on title

---

5   *Strover v. Harrington* [1988] 2 W.L.R. 572, p.586 (Browne-Wilkinson V.-C.).

6   The case was also decided on the basis that the purchasers had not suffered any actual loss.

7   [1987] 3 W.L.R. 394.

(para.10.6.2) as to whether any improvement grant had been made, the defendant's solicitor - whilst claiming to answer without obligation and maintaining the contractual rights - did produce a local search which had been with the deeds all the time and revealed the important improvement grant. It was held that the potential liability to repay the grant was an incumbrance since it was binding on the owner for the time being of the property; that the vendor had not made full and frank disclosure of an incumbrance which she knew about (through the agency of her solicitor) and could not therefore rely on the special condition. She had not therefore shown good title at the time due for completion. It was further held, in arriving at this decision, that s.198 of the Law of Property Act 1925, deeming registration of a local land charge to be '*notice*' to all the world, did not fix the purchaser with knowledge of the incumbrance so as to relieve the vendor of this duty of disclosure.

This case underlines how important it is for the vendor's solicitor to check the title before drafting the contract; and Standard Condition 3.1.2(d) and 3.1.5. must be read subject to it.

A vendor's solicitor or estate agent has the ostensible authority of the vendor to make statements about the property to prospective purchasers. If false, such statements may therefore give rise to action for misrepresentation against the *vendor*. This authority may be negatived by notice to the recipient of the statement, in which case the vendor herself will not be liable - though the agent herself may be personally liable in tort for negligent misrepresentation. Such exclusion of authority is not caught by s.3 of the Misrepresentation Act 1967 (para.4.4.4).

A solicitor or other agent faces potential personal liability in tort for negligent statement or advice to someone other than her own client and in the absence of any contract with that person. The basis of this liability is commonly referred to as the principle in *Hedley Byrne & Co. Ltd. v. Heller & Partners Ltd.*[8] In the *Computastaff* case (above), the plaintiffs' estate agents had got the wrong information as to rateable value from the landlord's letting agent. The latter was held liable under the Civil Liability Contribution Act 1978 to contribute to the damages payable by the former to the plaintiffs.[9]

But the trend of recent judicial opinion is to limit the circumstances in which a duty of care and therefore potential liability will be held to exist under *Hedley Byrne v. Heller.*[10] It is certainly unlikely that the client

---

[8]   [1964] A.C. 465.

[9]   Compare *Ross v. Caunters* [1980] Ch. 297, approved in *White v. Jones* (1993, Lexis transcript) - solicitor held liable to intended beneficiary for negligently failing to carry out instructions to draw up a will.

[10]   Compare *Ross v. Caunters* [1980] Ch. 297 and *Clarke v. Bruce Lance & Co.* [1988] 1 W.L.R. 881.

of one solicitor will be able to establish such a duty owed to her by the *other* side's solicitor.

In *Gran Gelato Ltd. v. Richcliff (Group) Ltd.*[11] an enquiry before the grant of a sub-lease asked whether there were any rights affecting the superior lease which would in any way inhibit the enjoyment of the proposed underlease. The intending lessor's (i.e. the sub-lessor) solicitor replied, 'Not to the lessor's knowledge'. There was in fact such an adverse right. The lessor was liable for misrepresentation. As stated by Nicholls V.-C. (p.875):

> 'The seller will be as much liable for any carelessness of his solicitor as he would be for his own personal carelessness. He will be so liable, because in the ordinary way the solicitor has implied authority for the seller to answer on his behalf the traditional inquiries before contract made on behalf of the buyer. Some of the inquiries will raise questions of fact. Others will raise legal, conveyancing points which the client cannot answer himself. The client leaves all these matters to the solicitor to handle for him, after seeking instructions where appropriate from the client on any particular points.'

But the court refused to find a duty of care owed to the purchaser (i.e. sub-lessee) by the vendor's (i.e. sub-lessor's) solicitor who was therefore not liable.

Limiting liability for misleading statements

Any provision in the contract of sale which seeks to exclude or limit **4.4.4** the liability of the vendor to the purchaser (or vice versa) for misrepresentation will be subject to the test of reasonableness under s.3 of the Misrepresentation Act 1967[12] The courts have taken a tough view of such clauses. In *Walker v. Boyle*[13] the purchaser was seeking to rescind for misrepresentation in spite of Standard Condition 17 of the National Conditions of Sale (one of the predecessors of the Standard Conditions) which was incorporated into the contract and provided:

> 'No error, mis-statement or omission in any preliminary answer concerning the property shall annul the sale, nor (save where the error, mis-statement or omission is in a written answer and relates to a matter materially affecting the description or value of the property) shall any damages be payable, or compensation allowed by either party, in respect thereof.'

---

[11] [1992] 2 W.L.R. 867. For a criticism of the case, see M. Whincup, 'Taking a Solicitor's Word,' (1992) 142 N.L.J. 820.

[12] As substituted by s.8 of the Unfair Contract Terms Act 1977.

[13] [1982] 1 All E.R. 634.

The clause did not protect a vendor who incorrectly (and knowing the truth) represented to the purchaser that there were no disputes regarding the boundaries of the property. It was held, on the principle mentioned above, that failure to give full and frank disclosure about this possible defect in title prevented the vendor from relying on condition 17. Further, the condition was ineffective under s.3 of the 1967 Act. It is notable that Dillon J. took this view in spite of the fact that condition had been a common, standard one in sale contracts for many generations (though its effect circumscribed by the courts) and that there were solicitors acting for both parties who would presumably understand and be able to advise on the effect of the condition. Dillon J. said:

> 'It is , of course, the duty of a solicitor to advise his client about any abnormal or unusual term in a contract, but I think it is perfectly normal and proper for a solicitor to use standard forms of conditions of sale such as the National Conditions of Sale. I do not think he is called on to go through the small print of those somewhat lengthy conditions with a tooth-comb every time he is advising a purchaser or to draw the purchaser's attention to every problem which on a careful reading of the conditions might in some circumstance or other conceivably arise. I cannot believe that purchasers of house property throughout the land would be overjoyed at having such lengthy explanations of the National Conditions of Sale ritually foisted upon them.'

In other words, a purchaser should be able to act on the assumption that the terms of her contract are reasonable and fair. But a solicitor should understand and be able to explain the terms when the circumstances require it.

Question Consider how Standard Condition 7 (Appendix 3) differs from condition 17 of the National Conditions of Sale. After researching if necessary, the remedies for misrepresentation, explain how Standard Condition 7 seeks to modify those remedies. Acting for a vendor, can you suggest any modification that you might make to Standard Condition 7 without running foul of s.3?

Disclaimers of the vendor's liability are often found in estate agents' particulars and in the replies to preliminary enquiries. Since the particulars and the replies will not normally have contractual force (see above) neither can the disclaimer. Therefore, without need to resort to s.3, it cannot bind a purchaser suing the vendor for misrepresentation contained in the particulars or replies. At most, such a disclaimer might support evidence that the purchaser did not rely on the statement.

Such disclaimers often seek to extend their protection to the solicitor or other agent. The agent cannot be personally liable for misrepresentation since she is not a party to the contract; and so s.3 has no application. Where the solicitor or agent is potentially liable in tort for negligent statement or advice, s.2 of the Unfair Contract Terms Act 1977 would probably apply and, again, subject the disclaimer to the test of reasonableness (and see para.3.4).

Local Authority Searches

Under the Local Land Charges Act 1975 each district and London **4.5** borough council (and the Common Council of the City of London) keeps a register of local land charges. The registers of local land charges are quite distinct from and should never be confused with the central Land Charges Registry at Plymouth.

Local land charges comprise a very extensive array of burdens generally of a public nature (rather than private property interests) enforceable by local authorities, the Crown, government departments and other public bodies and utilities. In general they represent financial charges (i.e. monies recoverable from the owner of the land) and restrictions on the use or enjoyment of the land. The list of possible charges is so long and varied that it is not possible here to deal with it in detail. Nevertheless, the great importance of these charges must not be underestimated. A solicitor must have a sufficient understanding of the possible charges (and the matters revealed by replies to additional enquiries of the local authority - below, para.4.6) to spot anything which may have implications for the client's pocket or enjoyment of the property; and to be able to advise a landowner of her right and obligations as such. A number of reference works on local charges are included in the bibliography (Appendix 8).

What follows is a few examples of the different types of charge that might affect a property.

(a) A financial charge to recover the cost of works incurred by the local authority under the private street works code (para.6.7).

(b) A range of charges to secure the recovery of money expended by the local authority on work which it was the primary obligation of the landowner to do. For example, under the Highways Act 1980, s.146, the landowner is under an obligation to maintain stiles across footpaths passing through her land. On default, the highway authority can, after giving 14 days notice do the work and recover the cost as a land charge from the owner. Similarly, under the Environmental Protection Act 1990, s.81, a local authority has powers to abate a statutory nuisance and recover the cost from the defaulting owner as a land charge.

(c) A great number of charges restrict the use or enjoyment of land under planning and environmental law (see also, para.6.5). For example:

(i) Designation of an area as a conservation area. A conservation area is one of special architectural or historic interest the character or appearance of which it is desirable to preserve or enhance, designated under the Planning (Listed Buildings and Conservation Areas) Act 1990. The main significance of designation is that planning permission is more likely to be refused and there are narrower limits on development automatically permitted under the General Development Order.

(ii) Designation as a listed building under the same Act. The list is of buildings designated by the government as being of special architectural or historic interest. Any work for the alteration or extension of such a building which affects its character as such a building needs listed building consent whether or not the work also constitutes development and needs planning permission. In 1972 the painting of a front door yellow in the Georgian Royal Crescent in Bath was held by the Secretary of State to require consent.

Also registrable as charges are conditions attached to listed building consents; and listed building enforcement notices - i.e. notices designed to enforce compliance with listed building controls.

Building preservation notices are also registrable. These give temporary protection to an unlisted building pending a decision whether to list it or not.

(iii) Tree preservation orders.

(iv) Cases where public money has been granted to the landowner and is repayable in certain circumstances.

(v) Compulsory purchase orders where notice to treat has been served.

(vi) Enforcement notices and stop notices under the Town and Country Planning Act 1990. These are the chief mechanisms for enforcing planning control (para.6.5.2).

(vii) Conditions attached to the grant of planning permissions. Applications for permission, unconditional grant of permissions and refusals are not registrable as land charges; but a separate public register of applications is kept by the authority and one of the additional enquiries (para.4.1.7) asks whether there is any relevant entry.

Search procedure

4.5.1   The register consists of 12 parts. A search can be made in one or more individual parts; but it is not easy to say which parts might produce relevant information in any case, and the fee for searching in the whole is cheaper than searching in three or more individual parts. Invariably, then, the whole register is searched.

Charges are registered against the land (unlike the central Land Charges Register where entries are against the name of the estate owner at the time of registration - para.13.6). It is therefore important when requisitioning an official search by post to be sure that it is sent to the authority for the area in which the land lies.

A personal search can be made or an official one requisitioned. In either case the necessary fee has to be paid.

A personal search of the register can be made by attending at the authority's office. This is not to be recommended, unless urgency makes it the only course. It is time consuming, easy to miss relevant entries and somewhat greater protection is given by an official search. From the solicitor's point of view, a personal search does not give the protection of s.13 of the 1975 Act. This exempts a solicitor from any liability for an error in an official certificate of search. This immunity does not of course cover a solicitor's negligence in reading or interpreting the results of the search. A solicitor making a personal search for the client is subject to the ordinary law of negligence.

The procedure for making an official search is utterly simple. There is a printed form of application (LLC1) which complies with the requirements of the Local Land Charges Rules 1977 and which includes detailed instructions. This must be completed and sent in duplicate to the relevant local authority. The application must identify the property either by giving the postal address or, if this is not sufficient to enable the property to be identified, by a scale plan, also to be sent in duplicate. The second part of the form contains the form of official certificate of search which will be completed by the authority either indicating 'no subsisting registrations', or referring to attached schedules identifying any registered charges.

The legal effect of charges and searches

Any local land charge, whether or not it has been registered, is binding   **4.5.2**
on successive owners of the land.[14] In this sense at least they are incumbrances on the title. An outstanding local land charge will therefore bind a purchaser (like any other owner of the land) whenever it was created and whether or not registered. Further, it is enforceable even if not revealed by a search, either because it not registered at the time or because of an error in the search. An official certificate gives no immunity.

---

[14]   Local Land Charges Act 1975, s.1.

However, s.10 of the 1975 Act, does give a *purchaser* a right to compensation from the local authority for loss suffered as a consequence in the following cases:

(i) in the case of a personal search, where the charge was in existence but not registered at the time of the search;

(ii) in the case of an official search, if the charge was either not registered or not shown by the certificate of search.

Where, as in the normal sale and purchase transaction, there is a contract (other than a qualified liability contract - that is one which is made conditional on the results of local searches) prior to completion and conveyance of the property, the search must have been made before the time of the contract (the 'relevant time'). In any other case - e.g. in the case of a lease where often negotiations lead straight to the grant of the lease without any preceding contract - the relevant time is the acquisition of the interest (in the case of a registered title transaction this means completion rather than the subsequent registration).

The search can have been made by the purchaser herself or her agent. But the purchaser can also claim if the search was by someone else provided the purchaser or her agent had knowledge of it before the relevant time. This latter provision is particularly intended to cover the case where (as under Transaction Protocol and increasingly even when the Protocol is not being used) the vendor's solicitor makes a local search and Additional Enquiries of the local authority and supplies them to the purchaser with the draft contract. The same principle will give the right to compensation to the purchaser's mortgagee.[15]

Position between vendor and purchaser

4.5.3   Under an open contract the vendor would be under a duty to disclose all local land charges existing at the date of the contract.

Standard Conditions 3.1.2(d) and 3.1.5. follow the traditional conveyancing practice of selling the property subject to any such charges, thus putting the onus on the purchaser to discover any for herself before contract. This tradition is also reflected in the compensation provisions of s.10 of the Local Land Charges Act 1975 which entitles only a 'purchaser' to claim compensation and does not envisage the vendor suffering loss.[16]

---

[15] In the case of a mortgage, the offer of a loan is likely to be made before searches are done, though subject to title being proved satisfactory. Presumably this makes the loan agreement a qualified liability agreement.

[16] I.e. if a vendor, due to an incorrect certificate, failed to disclose a subsisting local land charge in the contract.

However, when taking instructions and drafting the contract, the vendor's solicitor needs to remember that she must have an accurate picture of what title subject to what incumbrances and defects the vendor has to sell; that a limiting clause such as 3.1.2(d) will not protect against non–disclosure of title defects known to the vendor and that any factually incorrect replies to the purchaser's enquiries may constitute actionable misrepresentation.

In practice a vendor is likely to have knowledge of local land charges affecting the property either from search certificates held with the deeds or as a result of some kind of notification from the imposing authority. It follows that a vendor's solicitor may find it necessary to check the position as to local land charges by doing a search. Where Transaction Protocol is being followed, and increasingly where it is not, the vendor's solicitor does make the local search and additional enquiries and supply them to the purchaser's solicitor with the draft contract.

An official search gives no period of protection against charges created or registered after the date of the search (compare central Land Charges searches, para.13.6). It follows that a purchaser needs a search made as close to the date of contract as possible.Practitioners will normally rely on a search which is not more than about two months old. A search is more likely to be out of date where it has been done by the vendor. To enable less than fresh searches to be used, the Law Society has set up a search validation scheme. This provides insurance cover against any reduction in the market value of the property caused by new adverse local land charges or a change in replies to additional enquiries arising between the date of the search done and the date of contract. The purchaser has to pay a fixed premium for this cover. It can be used by solicitors whether or not TransAction Protocol is being followed. The solicitor wanting cover will complete the form and send it with the premium to the insurers; and on completion the validation scheme certificate will be placed with the title deeds. The scheme can only be used for a search and additional enquiries which are not more than six months old.

It is duty of the purchaser's solicitor, even where TransAction Protocol is being used, to check that the local search and replies to Additional Enquiries are satisfactory in all respects - including date. If they are more than about two months old, either the validation scheme should be used or a new search and additional enquiries made. If they are older than six months new ones will have to be done. The search supplied by Moriarties in the Obebe purchase (Document 4.1.1) was more than six months old; clearly Timothy should have sent it back and done his own fresh search and additional enquiries.

Charges arising after exchange

4.5.4   Under an open contract the general principle is that the risk passes to
the purchaser on exchange (para.3.3.1). This means that the purchaser
takes the benefit of any increases in the value in the property and bears
any decrease - e.g. due to fire damage - if this is not caused by the
vendor's default or neglect. It seems that this extends to the risk of a
central or local authority imposing burdens on the property[17]; or indeed
compulsorily acquiring it. As Lawton L.J. said in *Amalgamated Investment*[18]:

> 'Anybody who buys property knows, and certainly those who buy
> property as property developers know, that there are all kinds of hazards
> which have to be taken into consideration. There is the obvious hazard
> of planning permission. There is the hazard of fiscal and legislative
> change. There is the hazard of existing legislation being applied to the
> property under consideration -compulsory purchase for example.'

On the other hand there is also a principle that the vendor is under a
duty to give vacant possession at completion (para.14.6). This principle
has been applied to relieve a purchaser where the property was
requisitioned by the government between contract and completion.[19]
The cases seem to suggest that in some situations there may be a conflict
between these two principles which has not been judicially resolved.

The Standard Conditions quoted above put the risk and burden of all
such matters arising between contract and completion on the purchaser.[20]

ADDITIONAL ENQUIRIES OF THE LOCAL AUTHORITY

4.6   It has been indicated that even under an open contract the vendor's
duty of disclosure is limited to matters of title. It is for the purchaser,
before committing herself to a contract, to satisfy herself as to the physical
state of the property and any other matters which might affect her use
and enjoyment of the property and its environment.

The standard form of Additional Enquiries which is sent to the local
authority in addition to the requisition for a search of the register is aimed

---

17   *Hillingdon Estates Co. v. Stonefield Estates Ltd.* [1952] 1 Ch. 627; *Amalgamated Investment and Property Co. Ltd. v. John Walker & Sons Ltd.* [1976] 3 All E.R. 509.

18   See previous note, at p.518.

19   *James Macara Ltd. v. Barclay* [1945] 1 K.B. 148 (exercise of power to take possession under the Defence (General) Regulations 1939 -though possession not actually taken); compare *Korogluyan v. Matheou* (1975) 30 P. & C.R. 309; in which *Hillingdon* was distinguished *(obiter)* on the very artificial ground that in the latter case notice to treat but not a subsequent notice to enter had been served.

20   See *Korogluyan v. Matheou*, (note 19 above).

at getting information on what might be called public matters particularly within the knowledge of the local authority.

Some such matters are not registrable as local land charges; some may operate outside the boundaries of the property but nevertheless affect its enjoyment. For example, new roads in the neighbourhood may affect traffic flow and pollution levels. Further, there may be matters as yet only at the drawing board stage (or not yet even thought of) which will at some time in the future affect the property.

There has to be a limit to the type of information which a purchaser's solicitor can be expected to seek; and to both the area and the time span over which she can be expected to make enquiries. Beyond this the purchaser must seek what information she wants herself.

The printed form of Enquiries of Local Authorities (commonly referred to as Additional Enquiries) agreed between the Law Society and the various local authority associations, is Form Con 29 (1991) (Document 4.1.7).[21] This is for use with all local authorities, both district councils and London boroughs. The form must be submitted in duplicate with the appropriate fee. The fee is now at the discretion of the local authority. In Ledchester it is £75 to include the standard cost of the local search. The notes on the form indicate that a plan of the property in duplicate should be attached whenever possible and may be insisted upon by some councils; and that without a plan replies may be inaccurate or incomplete.

The form contains two sets of questions. Part I contains those standard enquiries which are applicable in every case. Part II contains additional, optional enquiries. The applicant has to indicate which if any of these optional ones she wants answering. As with the local search the use of a compulsory, standard form simplifies matters; but again it is important to understand the significance of the questions and possible replies; to know which if any of the optional enquiries need to be asked; to be able to spot those matters which need to be drawn to the attention of the client and those which require further investigation. The standard questions relate for example to the status of existing roads and proposals for new roads; the status of the foul and surface water drainage; planning matters including planning proposals and decisions which might affect the future use or enjoyment of the property; miscellaneous matters such as smoke control orders and entry in the register of contaminated land. The optional enquiries include, for example, a question whether any public footpath or bridleway crosses the property.

---

[21] For a note on discussions between the Law Society and the various local authority associations on the wording of some of the questions and the layout of the form, see Law Society's Guardian Gazette, Vol. 89, 27 May 1992, p.14.

Liability for incorrect replies

4.6.1   The form contains the following statement:

'The replies will be given after the appropriate enquiries and in the belief that they are in accordance with the information at present available to the officers of the replying Council(s), but on the distinct understanding that none of the Councils, nor any Council officer, is legally responsible for them except for negligence. Any liability for negligence shall extend for the benefit of not only the person by or for whom these Enquiries are made but also a person (being a purchaser for the purposes of s.10(3) of the Local Land Charges Act 1975) who or whose agent had knowledge, before the relevant time (as defined in that section), of the replies to these Enquiries.'

As between the authority and the person making the Enquiries, whether the vendor or purchaser, this creates contractual liability. Where the vendor makes the Enquiries and hands them over to the purchaser before contract, the authority expressly assumes a duty of care and will potentially be liable in tort.[22] Where enquiries are made of a local authority outside the standard form, liability will be governed by the ordinary principles of negligent misstatement.

INSPECTION OF THE PROPERTY

4.7   There are three main reasons for inspecting the property before contract:

(a) to check its physical condition (para.3.4).

(b) to check the physical identity. The vendor is under an obligation to show good title to and convey the property as identified in the contract. But the purchaser needs to be satisfied that the boundaries of the property in the contract tally with those on the ground - that she is buying what she thinks she is buying.

(c) to check for patent, title defects. As explained above under an open contract the vendor is under no obligation to disclose patent title defects. A patent defect is a defect of title which is discoverable by reasonable care on an inspection of the property. These might include, for example, an easement of light to a neighbour's window; or if title to part of the property had been acquired by a stranger by adverse possession - with a consequent shift in the patent boundary features.

Standard Condition 3.1.2(b) makes the sale subject to the incumbrances 'discoverable by inspection of the property before

---

[22] See *Coats Patons (Retail) Ltd. v. Binningham Corporation* (1971) 69 L.G.R. 356; *JGF Properties Ltd. v. Lambeth LBC* [1986] 1 E.G.L.R. 179.

contract'. Presumably, though not limited to those *reasonably* discoverable, this would be held to have the same effect as the open contract principle.

Whether or not the rights of persons, other than the vendor, residing in the property are patent or 'discoverable' has not been clearly decided. It has to be remembered that what we are concerned with here is the duty of the vendor to the purchaser; not the distinct question of whether any such rights will bind a purchaser who completes. If there is no duty to disclose the purchaser will have no remedy once contracts are exchanged. If there is such a duty the purchaser can, in law, ignore the possibility until after exchange, and refuse to complete until satisfied that there are none that would bind her after completion.

It is submitted that the principle of *caveat emptor* should not be pushed in the direction of holding such rights to be patent (or 'discoverable'). The vendor is in a position to know who else has any interest in the property; such rights are only discoverable on making enquiries, rather than inspection; and the prospective purchaser cannot be expected to start delving into the family history and relationships of the vendor at this stage. For this reason the question of adverse rights of residents other than the vendor is dealt with later (paras.13.10, 13.15).

The Property Information Form and most standard forms of preliminary enquiries of the vendor do include questions about other occupants of the property; and it is of course better to discover such rights before contract if possible.

It must be rare for the purchaser's solicitor herself to inspect the property, unless there is evidence of some particular problem which needs investigation. But, at least, the solicitor should be able to advise the client of what matters to look out for when viewing the property.[23]

INDEX MAP SEARCH

Contrary to Timothy's notion, this is a search which should always be done in the case of unregistered title; and will *not* be done in the case of an already registered title.

4.8

The search is an official one of the Index Map and Parcels Index made by the district Land Registry for the area which includes the property; and should be addressed on printed form 96 together with the appropriate fee. A plan is not necessary if the registry can identify the property from the postal description.

---

[23] See *McManus Developments Ltd. v. Barbridge Properties Ltd.* (1992), Lexis Transcript.

The search will reveal whether any title (freehold or leasehold) to the property is registered; and, if not registered, whether any caution against first registration has been registered. It is possible, though unlikely, that the whole or part of the property being sold has in fact been registered in a previous purchaser's name. If it has, the registered title will, in principle, prevail, though subject to the possibility of rectification of the register. This possibility and the danger of not making the search (and more generally the importance of checking the identity of the property shown in the title offered by the vendor is illustrated by the case of *Epps v. Esso Petroleum Ltd.*[24] A house, 4 Darland Avenue, and the adjoining garage were originally owned by the same person. The dispute related to an 11 foot strip of land lying between the two properties though on the garage's side of the physical, dividing wall. In 1959 the personal representatives of the common owner sold and conveyed the garage including the strip to a Julian Ball who, the area having become one of compulsory registration, was registered as first proprietor. However, earlier, in 1955, the house (again including the strip) had been sold by the personal representatives to a Mrs Jones. In 1968 her personal representatives sold and conveyed the house with strip to the plaintiffs. On seeking to register, the plaintiffs were not able to register the strip (now registered together with the garage in the name of the defendants who had bought from Ball in 1964). The plaintiffs were seeking (and failed to get) rectification of the register in relation to the strip.

A number of points are worth making:

(a) The sale to Mrs Jones was a sale of part (i.e. part of the land in the single title of the common owner. In such a situation the title deeds will be retained by the vendor; though the purchaser will get in her conveyance an acknowledgement for their production (para.12.4.3). As a matter of good conveyancing practice the purchaser should get the vendor to endorse a memorandum of the sale of part on the last title deed of the common owner. In fact in *Epps* a memorandum of the 1955 sale was endorsed on the Probate of the common owner; though it only noted a sale of 4 Darland Avenue and was, as noted by Templeman J. 'uninformative and in retrospect misleading' in that it did not indicate that a new strip had been added beyond the existing wall boundary of the property. A solicitor acting for the purchaser of the land in such a title should spot such a memorandum (and it should be abstracted by the vendor when deducing title); and should check what was included in the earlier sale of part and that it did not include any part of what is now being bought. In *Epps* if the defendants' title had not become registered, the plaintiffs would have had an

---

[24] [1973] 1 W.L.R. 1071.

unanswerable case. They had obtained the earlier legal title which would have been good against all the world and prevailed over the later conveyance to Ball. This in turn illustrates how registration can (subject to the possibility of rectification) cure a defective title and destroy a good one.

If Ball's solicitors had called for a copy of the conveyance to Mrs Jones they would have seen that the strip had been included in the sale to her. This was not it seems put forward in the case as a ground for allowing rectification. And it has to be said that the problem arose (and this was partly why rectification was refused under s.82(1)(c) of the Land Registration Act 1925) because Mrs Jones had failed when she bought, although having covenanted to do so, to move her boundary to enclose the strip. When Ball purchased there was nothing on the ground to indicate that the strip was not still part of the garage property.

(b) The solicitors acting for the plaintiffs when they bought in 1968 should have done a public index map search. This would have revealed that the strip was already registered in the defendants' name. This was another reason why rectification in favour of the plaintiffs was refused.

(c) The plaintiffs clearly thought that their purchase was to include the disputed strip. It is probably fair to say that when viewing the property before contract, even though not lawyers, they should have appreciated that the obvious, physical boundary of the property did not tally with what they were expecting to buy; and should have got the matter resolved at that stage. It is also worth adding that the solicitor acting for them on the purchase did not after completion and registration notice the discrepancy between the title plan received from the Land Registry (excluding the strip) and what had been conveyed to them.

This aspect of the case perhaps at least underlines the need for a solicitor to warn a purchasing client to check that the physical boundaries on the ground match the expected purchase.

(d) For completeness, it should be added that if the strip had been actually occupied by Mrs Jones in 1959 at the time of the conveyance to Ball, the title would have been protected against the registration of Ball as an overriding interest under s.70(1)(g) of the Land Registration Act 1925. In fact all that could be shown was an occasional parking of a car on the strip.

To return to the index map search. A caution against first registration is the method by which the owner of an interest in unregistered land can make sure that her interest is brought to the attention of the registry prior to first registration. She will then have the chance to show her interest and have it protected on the title register. Normally, where the interest is shown in the title deeds of the property which will be produced to the registry on first registration, this will not be necessary. The trouble in *Epps* was that there was nothing on the title deeds of the retained land (the garage) to show that the extra strip had been sold off.

In practice the index map search is made before contract. Under the Standard Conditions this is necessary because of Standard Condition 3.1.2(d).

CENTRAL LAND CHARGES REGISTER SEARCH

4.9   Text books on conveyancing commonly state that a search in the central Land Charges Register is not necessary before contract; but go on to suggest that in some circumstances it may be a good idea to do one at least against the vendor, particularly mentioning the case of the 'haunting' spouse of the vendor who might at any time materialise and register a class F right of occupation under the Matrimonial Homes Act 1983.

For the reasons which follow, I suggest that this notion is misconceived and that there really is no need to search until the pre-completion search (para.13.6).

The central Land Charges Register is a national, public register maintained at Plymouth under what is now the Land Charges Act 1972. It should not be confused with the registers of Local Land Charges, already discussed. Even more important, it should not be confused with the registers of title to registered land kept by the various district Land Registries.

Charges are registered against the name of the estate owner at the time of registration.

It is assumed that the reader, having assiduously pursued if not enjoyed her study of land law, will be familiar with the principles and the different classes of charge, A - F.

Any registered charge is an incumbrance on the title. Under an open contract it is the duty of the vendor to disclose it, unless of course it is to be removed on completion - for example, a *puisne* mortgage which is to be redeemed. Similarly, there is a duty of disclosure under the Standard Conditions (see Standard Condition 3.1.2(d)).

Until the Law of Property Act 1969, s.24, it was thought[25] that s.198 of the Law of Property Act 1925 relieved the vendor of the duty of

---

[25] This thought stemmed from the decision of Eve J. in *Re Forsey & Hollebone's Contract* [1927] 2 Ch. 379.

disclose and made it necessary to search before contract. This provides that the registration 'shall be deemed to constitute actual notice to all persons and for all purposes connected with the land affected'. Such a search could in any case only be done if the names of all previous estate owners on the title were first obtained from the vendor.

Section 24(1) of the 1969 Act provides that on a contract for the sale or disposition of land, the question of whether a purchaser had knowledge of a registered charge 'shall be determined by reference to his actual knowledge and without regard to the provisions of section 198 of the Law of Property Act 1925'. Under sub-section 2 of s.24, the vendor cannot contract out of the duty of disclosure which thus arises. Section 24 does not, of course, affect the question of whether a purchaser who completes will be bound by any registered charge. Hence, a search must be done pre-completion.

The common justification for making such a search pre-contract is that it is better for a purchaser to discover these matters before contract and back out (no doubt paying some legal costs to her solicitor) rather than rely upon the possible expense and uncertainty of a post-contract remedy. And it is fair to say that registration of a class F land charge, unlike most other central land charges, is outside the control of the vending spouse. She may have chosen to marry; but in the present context the charge will probably have been registered without her consent or indeed knowledge.

However, the following points should be noted. First, land charges can be registered so as to affect a purchaser at any time up to completion (or, at least, up to the protection period given by the purchaser's pre-completion official search - para.13.6(c))[26] A pre-contract search gives no idea of what may be brewing in the mind of the vendor's spouse.

More fundamentally, in my view, the clear philosophy of conveyancing should be that the vendor is selling something, should state clearly in the contract exactly what she is offering for sale (and if deserted husbands and equity-owning grannies go with the property this should be stated!), and the purchaser should be able and expected to rely on what is set out in the contract. The vendor is in a position to know who may have registrable or other claims to the property and should sort these out before putting the property on the market.

Where TransAction Protocol is being followed, the vendor's solicitor is required to do a Land Charges search against the vendor and 'any other appropriate name' and supply it to the purchaser with the draft contract and other documents. For reasons given above, this really is unnecessary.

---

[26] See *Wroth v. Tyler* [1974] Ch. 30.

Of course, it should be stressed that the vendor's solicitor should be satisfied (by doing a search if necessary) as to the actual and potential (in the case of uncooperative spouses, grannies, etc) incumbrances when drafting the contract and advising the client.

SEARCH IN THE COMMONS REGISTER

4.10   If there is any possibility that the property includes common land (which under the 1965 Act includes waste land of a manor), a town or village green or is subject to rights of common land, an official search should be made in the public registers maintained by county, metropolitan district and London Borough councils under the Commons Registration Act 1965. Each of these authorities maintains two registers; one for town or village greens and one for common land; but a single official search covers both.

The application for a search is made in duplicate on prescribed form CR21 with the appropriate fee and two copies of a plan clearly identifying the land in question.

Final (as opposed to provisional) registration of the land as a common or village or town green, or of common rights, is conclusive as at the date of registration. Common land or village or town green land which was not registered by 30 July 1970 ceased to be such; similarly, common rights which had not been registered by then ceased to be exercisable unless protected on the register of title at the land registry. Although the registers may indicate the identity of the owner, there is no guarantee that this is accurate.

There is limited provision for the register to be amended from time to time (ss.13,14) where, for example. land ceases to be or becomes common land.[27]

The significance of registration, from the purchaser's and landowner's point of view, is that it is almost certain to prevent any development of the land.

(i) If there are common rights these cannot of course be interfered with.

(ii) There is likely, though not necessarily, to be a public right of access under s.193 of the Law of Property Act 1925 or other legislation.

(iii) The land is likely to be protected by s.194 of the same Act. This makes it unlawful to erect any building or fence or construct any other works whereby access to the land is prevented or impeded without the

---

[27] And note the Common Land (Rectification of Registers) Act 1989, which allowed three years for any land with dwelling houses erected on it continuously from 1945 to be removed from the registers.

consent of the Secretary of State. The Secretary of State, in deciding whether to give consent (which is most unlikely) must, *inter alia*, have regard to the health and comfort and convenience of the local inhabitants in relation to the use of the common as an open space.

When a search should be made

Under the Standard Conditions, by virtue of Standard Condition 3.1.2(d), the search should be made before contract. Registered matters will of course bind a purchaser on completion.   **4.10.1**

If there is any doubt whether to make a search, one should be made. A search should be made (unless the status of the particular land is known) whenever any part of the land (even a small part if its use is significant for the purchaser, and whether in town or country) appears never to have been built on, especially if the public appears to have access; and especially if other available information rings an alarm bell.

In *G&K Ladenbau (UK) Ltd. v. Crawley & de Reya*[28] the purchaser's solicitor was held liable in negligence for failing to make a search which would have revealed registration. The land consisted of once marshy land beside a river which had been reclaimed by the deposit of waste from a nearby motorway construction. Before exchange, he had received a deed which showed that the mineral rights had previously belonged to the lord of the manor. This was an alarm bell warning that the land might have been manorial waste.

The fact that planning permission has been granted for development does not affect registered common rights.

OTHER POSSIBLE SEARCHES AND ENQUIRIES

There may be other pre-contract investigations about the property which circumstances indicate to be necessary.   **4.11**

First, it should be stressed that the responses to the investigations already discussed should be studied carefully; and may require further investigation.

It is not possible here to list all the other possible investigations which may be necessary. Some may arise from the location of the property; some from physical features impinging on it; or from the particular use intended by the purchaser. (For relevant texts, see the bibliography, Appendix 8).

---

[28]   [1978] 1 All E.R. 682.

To give a few examples: If the property lies within a coal, tin, or limestone mining or a clay quarrying or brine extraction area, investigation may be necessary particularly in relation to any danger of subsidence and the possibility of compensation if there is subsidence.

It may be necessary to check the routes of pipe-lines and cables under the property - especially if a client is proposing to develop.

If the property is crossed or bounded by existing or disused railways or rivers enquiries of the appropriate authority may be necessary in relation to location of the boundary and liability for boundary fences and banks.

REGISTERED TITLE

4.12   Timothy (para.4.1.9) is as confused about this as most other things. His notion that pre-contract searches and enquiries are not necessary in the case of registered land is *totally* misconceived. The general principles governing pre-contract investigations are the same for bother unregistered and registered title. There are some differences in the particular investigations necessary.

Preliminary Enquiries of the vendor; search in the Register of Local Land Charges; Additional Enquiries of the local authority

4.12.1   These will be invariably necessary in the case of registered title and for the same reasons; and the same standard forms will be used.

Inspection of the property

4.12.2   Property should at least be inspected by the purchaser herself. This again is necessary for the same reasons. As already stressed, although it may be uncommon for the solicitor herself to inspect, she should at least feel satisfied that the purchaser herself knows what to look for, particularly in relation to patent defects and the correspondence between the identity of the property on the ground and in the draft contract.

It should also be stressed again that what the purchaser is concerned with is patent defects in title, a concept common to registered and unregistered title. Subject to what has been said above (para.4.7) she is not concerned at this stage with the rights of those in actual occupation. The wording of some forms of Enquiries Before Contract (e.g. Oyez, Con 29 (Long)) which refers to overriding interests and persons in actual occupation is strictly inapt; unless of course the contract itself uses the same language when stating expressly the burdens subject to which the property is to be taken.[29]

Index Map

A search here is not relevant and not necessary when the title is already registered. Any interest protected by a caution against first registration will have been dealt with on first registration; and either given protection on the register of title or adjudged invalid.

4.12.3

Central Land Charges register

Again, a search here is not relevant and not necessary. All burdens on the title will be protected on the register, overriding or not enforceable against a purchaser.

As to bankruptcy only searches pre-completion, see para.13.14).

4.12.4

Land Registry search

A pre-contract search here is not necessary. As already stressed under an open contract it is the vendor's duty to prove her title, subject only to defects disclosed in the contract and any permissible limits on the duty contained in the contract. The contract will have to disclose any defects/incumbrances contained in the register of title. Today this is usually done by incorporating a copy (office copy under the Standard Conditions) of the register in the contract and sending it to the purchaser with the draft contract.

Standard Condition 3.1.2(d) confirms this principle by making it clear that the purchaser is not expected to search in the Land Registry before contract.

4.12.5

Other possible searches and enquiries

What has been said in relation to unregistered title applies equally here.

4.12.6

---

[29] Compare the first edition of the Standard Conditions, s.c. 3.1.2(d), which makes the sale subject to 'if the title is registered, overriding interests'.

CONTRACT RACES

4.13   Moriarties have instituted a contract race on the sale by Miss Mixford (Document 4.1.1).

A contract race exists where, on the instructions of the client, a draft contract for a property is sent to more than one prospective purchaser at the same time. It does not necessarily involve a legal obligation to sell to the first prospective purchaser willing to exchange unless there is a separate contract to that effect.

In *Daulia Ltd. v. Four Millbanks Nominees Ltd.*[30] there was no contract race; but the prospective vendors (the defendants) orally promised the plaintiffs that if the latter attended the defendants' offices the following morning before 10 o'clock with a banker's draft for the deposit and their part of the contract signed, they (the defendants) would exchange. The plaintiffs complied with the requirements but the defendants, having meanwhile received a higher offer, refused to exchange. It was held, on an application by the defendants to strike out, that the facts if proved gave rise to a valid, unilateral contract - i.e. complying with the above requirements constituted acceptance of the offer to exchange on the main contract. However, this preliminary contract was itself one for the sale of land and so caught by s.40 of the Law of Property Act 1925; and not being evidenced in writing was not enforceable. Further, the required acts done by the plaintiffs did not amount to a sufficient act of part performance within s.40(2) of the Act.

Timothy has got it wrong. He has simply misread Moriarties' letter excluding any obligation to exchange with the first prospective purchaser to produce a signed contract.

Any such preliminary contract will now be within s.2 of the Law of Property (Miscellaneous Provisions) Act 1989; and will itself have to satisfy the requirements of that section.

Question V sends out a draft contract for the sale of Blackacre each to P1 and P2 with a covering letter saying that she will exchange with the first of them to return the draft signed. Two weeks later, after doing her local searches, and before P2, P1 signs and returns the draft to V. V refuses to sign her part. Advise P1. With particular reference to s.2, what procedures and what forms of wording would you recommend to make an offer such as V's legally binding and irrevocable, so that V would have to sign her part

---

[30]   [1978] 2 All E.R. 537.

and complete the exchange? Could the doctrine of proprietary estoppel be relied upon if necessary? (See para.9.8 on options and s.2.)

The Law Society's Directives

There is nothing illegal in sending out more than one draft contract at **4.13.1** the same time. The basis of English conveyancing is that until there is a binding contract at exchange each side accepts the risk of the other backing out for whatever reason and thus wasting any pre-contract costs already incurred. Indeed, the ordinary sale by auction is really a kind of contract race, the prize going to the highest rather than the fastest bidder.

Nevertheless, there is commonly a feeling that in morality (at least by the one to suffer from the other's 'immorality') that once a preliminary bargain has been struck with agreement subject to contract, neither party should back out without exceptional reason; and that neither should start negotiating with someone else behind the other's back.

The Law Society has, in this case at least, made its members the guardians of morality. The Council's Direction, as revised in January 1993, provides (*Guide*, p.435):

> 'The Council recognise that a solicitor acting for a vendor may sometimes be instructed by his client to deal with more than one prospective purchaser at the same time.
>
> The Council have accordingly directed that where a vendor instructs his solicitor to submit (whether simultaneously or otherwise) forms of contract to more than one prospective purchaser, the following steps by the solicitor are obligatory:
>
> (A) Where the solicitor is acting for the vendor.
>
> The solicitor (with his client's authority) must at once disclose the vendor's decision direct to the solicitor acting for each prospective purchaser or (where no solicitor is acting) to the prospective purchaser(s) in person and such disclosure, if made orally, must at once be confirmed in writing. If the vendor refuses to authorise disclosure, the solicitor must cease acting for the vendor forthwith.'

Non-compliance is a matter of professional conduct with the possibility of disciplinary proceedings.

The Directive goes on to say that, because of the danger of a conflict of interest, only in the most exceptional circumstances should a solicitor act for one of the prospective purchasers as well as the prospective vendor when a contract race situation exists. Of course, unless one of situations listed in Rule 6(2) of the Solicitors' Practice Rules 1990 is present, (para.1.9.3), the solicitor is in any case not allowed to act for both.

The Directive prohibits altogether acting for more than one prospective purchaser in a contract race situation.

The *Guide*, in its note, (para.24.04) emphasises that it is the decision to deal with more than one prospective purchaser that must be notified, not the actual submission of two or more contracts. It also warns that care should be taken where a first, draft contract has previously been sent out and nothing heard from that prospective purchaser. The Directive will apply if it is decided to send out a contract to another unless and until the first has been withdrawn.

CHAPTER 5

DRAFTING THE CONTRACT: UNREGISTERED TITLE

TIMOTHY TRIES HIS HAND

Friday morning, 19th February. There is a bundle on Timothy's desk when he arrives at work. The deeds of Fell View from the Ledchester & Bongley Building Society (the Goldberg Sale). In spite of some years (we diplomatically omit to mention how many) struggling with a law degree followed by the Law Society Finals, this is the first time that Timothy has seen a real deed of conveyance. He is disappointed. Expecting something like a medieval, illuminated manuscript on finest parchment heavy with wax seal, he finds documents typed on ordinary (though of rather better quality than Basildon Bond) paper and the seals no more than red circles of paper stuck on (one of which becomes detached and floats gently to earth as he looks at the document).

5.1

The magic and awe of conveyancing immediately dissolves in Timothy's mind; buying and selling land is really no different from buying and selling shares (about which his father has taught him much); so he begins to think. Confidence ('Over-confidence!' Old Jarndyce is heard to mutter) in himself as a fine conveyancing lawyer is boosted. There is nothing to it.

Timothy takes the bundle of documents and methodically starts to put them all in chronological order. The first one to come to hand is a conveyance on sale dated 24 June 1974. 'Ah!' says Timothy, intoning old lecture notes from memory, 'Under an open contract, a good root of title is a document which is at least 15 years old, deals on the face of it with the whole legal and equitable interest in the property, contains an adequate description of the property and contains nothing to cast doubt on the title. A conveyance on sale or a mortgage is likely to provide a good root.' (It has to be said that Timothy has got this right.) He is happy; this is a conveyance on sale. It is nearly 20 years old. He puts the documents back in a bundle with a note for the secretary to photocopy the 1974 conveyance and all the later ones and do an epitome (para.10.6.1). 'Now to draft the contract,' he thinks.

Timothy takes out the Goldberg file. There is a copy of the letter and undertaking sent to the manager of the local branch of the Ledchester & Bongley in the following terms (see *Guide*, Form 2, p.455).

Document 5.1.1 Goldberg Sale: Letter to Vendors' Building Society

---

Jarndyce & Jarndyce
Solicitors

24, The Strand, Ledchester LR2 3JF Tel: (2350) 002244 Fax: (2350) 123765 Dx: Ledchester Park Square 14709

The Manager,
Ledchester & Bongley Building Society,
Commercial Road,
Ledchester

29 January 1993

Dear Sirs,

Mr and Mrs Goldberg.
Sale part Fell View, Koppax

We are acting for Mr & Mrs Goldberg of Fell View, Wensleydale
Avenue, Koppax which is subject to a first mortgage to your
society. They have agreed subject to contract to sell part of
the garden with the benefit of planning permission to a Mr & Mrs
Singh.
We understand that our clients have discussed the matter with
you and that you are prepared to release the part of the garden
sold from the mortgage; and that in return they have agreed that
the net proceeds of sale will be paid by us direct to you in
reduction of the mortgage debt.
We are on your panel of solicitors and should be grateful if you
would forward the deeds to us so that we can prepare the draft
contract.
In return for the deeds we undertake to hold them on your behalf
and to return them to you on demand in the same condition in
which they now are, pending completion of the sale.
If the sale is completed we undertake to pay to you the net proceeds of sale after deduction of the estate agent's commission
and our usual costs and disbursements relating to the transaction; and to return the title deeds to you suitably endorsed.
The number of our clients' mortgage account is BB 125894642.
The price agreed for the plot subject to contract is £10,000. We
envisage that our fees and disbursements will not exceed £800.

Yours faithfully,

Jarndyce & Jarndyce

Jarndyce & Jarndyce

Partners: J.J. Jarndyce, Thomas Trippit, Trevor Trippit, Barry Bopper, Henry Oxbridge. Consultant: Edward Trippit

---

Note: As to professional undertakings, see para.5.13; Guide Chapter 19.
As to endorsement of sale on deeds, see para.14.10.

5.1.2   In addition, Timothy finds on the file a note signed by both the Goldbergs giving their irrevocable authority to Jarndyce & Jarndyce to pay the proceeds of sale on completion to the building society.

Question Explain how this undertaking satisifies (assuming that it does!) the essential requirements of a solicitor's professional undertaking (para.5.13). Note that the specific authority of the clients is not really needed in this situation; any more than it is to discharge any mortgage out of the proceeds of sale. The building society holds the title deeds in its own right as mortgagee. The deeds can only be obtained and the property sold free of the mortgage in accordance with the clients instructions if the money is paid over to the society. It would be different if there were a surplus of proceeds after total discharge of the mortgage. It is different where an undertaking to pay over the proceeds is given, for example, to a bank to secure a bridging loan. The bank, not being a mortgagee of the property, has no right to the property or the proceeds of its sale without the clear authority of the vendor.

Nevertheless, it is always important that the client does clearly understand and authorise what is being done on her behalf.

The letter from the Ledchester & Bongley accompanying the title deeds confirms their willingness to release the part being sold on the above terms.

There is also a plan of the property showing the portion to be sold off (Document 5.1.4).

There is also on the file a completed form of Instructions on Sale completed by Mr Perky before his flight to love. Where this form indicates that it is a sale of part, Mr Perky has noted: 'See attached sheet for details of easements and covenants, etc'. This sheet appears to have become detached. Timothy rummages for it in the file without success However, his new found confidence in his conveyancing skills tells him 'Not to worry. It won't make any difference. The Standard Conditions already cover sales of parts.' (A noise off suggests that Old Jarndyce may at this point be worrying.)

The Instructions on Sale are as follows:

Document 5.1.3 Goldberg Sale: Instructions on Sale

Jarndyce & Jarndyce: Instructions On Sale

<u>Client:</u> *Mr. & Mrs. Goldberg*   <u>Date:</u> *29 January 1993*

Full names and addresses and phone number of clients	*Larry and Lolita Goldberg, Fell View, Wensleydale Avenue, Koppax. Koppax 246777*
Full names and addresses of purchasers	*Jinder and Balraj Singh, 222 Upper Wharfedale Road, Ledchester 6.*
Name and address of purchasers' solicitors	*Moriarties*
Name and address of estate agents	*n/a*
Details of property Address Freehold/leasehold Registered or unregistered Sale of whole/part Location of deeds	*Part garden at Fell View - Freehold - unregistered. See file for plan produced by client and details of easements, etc.* *Mortgagees*
Price	*£10,000*
Deposit paid	*no*
Chattels to be sold. Fixtures to be excluded	*n/a*
Related purchase	*n/a*
Synchronise exchange	*n/a*
Completion date	*asap*
Outstanding mortgages. Lenders; amount outstanding; account number	*Ledchester and Bongley, Ledchester branch. approx. £12,000 outstanding - a/c BB 125894642.*
Other persons whose consent to sale needed	*No. Held jointly by Goldbergs.*
Additional information	*Being sold with benefit of outline permission for one house - 20 June 1992. - on file. Footpath along river used by public occasionally. G's never tried to stop them. G's not interested in retaining right to use septic tank at Pit Mansion - have mains drainage now.*

5.1.4   The plan on the file, prepared by a surveying friend of Mrs Goldberg's and based on the plan from the 1970 conveyance (Document 5.2(a)) is as follows:

Document 5.1.4 The Goldberg Sale Plan

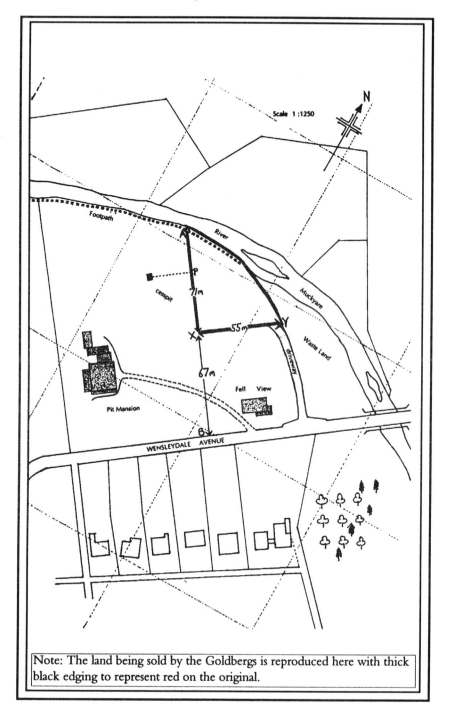

Note: The land being sold by the Goldbergs is reproduced here with thick black edging to represent red on the original.

5.1.5   Timothy has decided that the golden rule in any conveyancing transaction is to 'Find an appropriate blank form and fill it in. ' A few words with the secretary reassures him that all he has to do is to 'Fill in the blank contract form. I'll print it out.'

He soon finds a blank contract form in a drawer. It is entitled 'AGREEMENT (incorporating the Standard Conditions of Sale (First Edition)'. He is innocent of the fact (and the secretary assumes him to be much too wise to be told) that the first edition has been replaced by a second edition which makes substantial and significant changes to the first edition of the Standard Conditions. Luck is with him. The form has been scribbled on (no doubt by one of Miss Pinky's offspring). Delving into the drawer, he finds another copy which happens to be the second edition.

Wasting little time (and less thought) and using the information from the file and what he remembers from the deeds (now with the secretary and too much trouble to fetch), he has soon completed the front page of the form as follows:

Document 5.1.6 Goldberg Sale: Draft Contract

AGREEMENT
(Incorporating the Standard Conditions of Sale (Second Edition))

Agreement Date   :

Seller   : *Larry & Lolita Goldberg, both of Fell View, Wensleydale Avenue, Koppax, Yorkshire*

Buyer   : *Jinder and Balraj Singh, both of 222 Upper Wharfedale Road, Ledchester 6*

Property   : *All that freehold plot of land being part*
(freehold/leasehold)   *of Fell View aforesaid and more particu-larly delineated on the plan annexed hereto and thereon edged in red.*

Root of Title/Title Number: *A conveyance on sale dated 24 June 1974 and made between Sedgewick Smiler of the one part and Lolita Goldberg og the other part.*

Incumbrances on the
Property   : *The covenants and easements referred to in the said conveyance.*

Seller sells as   : *Beneficial Owner.*

Completion date   :
Contract date   :
Purchase Price   : *£10,000*
Deposit   : *£ 1,000*
Amount payable for
chattels   :
Balance   : *£9,000*

The Seller will sell and the Buyer will buy the Property for the Purchase Price.
The Agreement continues on the back page.

WARNING	Signed
This is a formal document, designed to create legal rights and legal obligations. Take advice before using it.	**Seller/Buyer**

Note: The inside two pages of the form contain the Standard Conditions Of Sale (Appendix 3).
The plan intended is the one produced by the Goldbergs; above, Document 5.1.4.

SPECIAL CONDITIONS

1. (a) This Agreement incorporates the Standard Conditions of Sale (Second Edition). Where there is a conflict between those Conditions and this Agreement, this Agreement prevails.

(b) Terms used or defined in this Agreement have the same meaning when used in the Conditions.

2. The Property is sold subject to the Incumbrances on the Property and the Buyer will raise no requisitions on them.

3. The chattels on the Property and set out on any attached list are included in the sale.

4. The Property is sold with vacant possession on completion.

or 4. The Property is sold subject to the following leases or tenancies:

Seller's Solicitors : *Jarndyce & Jarndyce, 24 The Strand Ledchester*

Buyer's Solicitors: *Moriarty & Co. Tumbledown House, The Bedrow, Ledchester.*

Timothy can think of nothing to add and is about to leave it as it is.   **5.1.7**
The words 'indemnity covenant' do suddenly float into his mind. 'You
always need an indemnity covenant,' he thinks. So he adds a special
condition 5: 'The Purchaser will in the conveyance enter into the usual
indemnity covenant.' 'Usual' is a word frequently resorted to by
Timothy, whether in a pub or a contract, when he is not quite sure what
he is asking for.

Timothy fails to express any choice between the alternative versions
of special printed condition 4.

Question Is Timothy's identification of the 1974 conveyance
accurate? (See below, Documents 5.2(a) and (b)).

Having drafted his first contract and feeling highly satisfied with
himself Timothy leaves the room to give it to the secretary and goes to
get himself a cup of coffee.

Old Jarndyce, who is never far away, steps, as it were, front stage.

OLD JARNDYCE COMMENTS – THE TITLE TO FELL VIEW

Once again Timothy seems to be showing more enthusiasm to learn   **5.2**
about the law of negligence than conveyancing.

Before proceeding it might be useful to explain briefly the history of
the property and rescue the text of the 1970 and 1974 Conveyances from
the secretary.

Pit Mansion originally belonged to the family that owned the local
coal-pit; subsequently to a high-ranking official of the National Coal
Board. It was then bought by Bonnie and Clyde Smith (who between
them controlled Bonnie & Clyde Smith Ltd.). In 1970 (the first
conveyance shown below) they sold part of the garden to Sedgewick
Smiler. Sedgewick intended to build a house for himself on part of the
land; and a house to be sold off on the other part. He built Fell View but
died before completing the rest of his plan. His son and executor, John
Sedgewick Smiler, sold the whole to the Goldbergs in 1974 (the second
conveyance shown below). The Goldbergs are now selling off this other
part with the benefit of planning permission to the Singhs who are
planning to build the second house.

Document 5.2(a) Goldberg Sale: The 1970 Conveyance

THIS CONVEYANCE is made the first day of June 1970 Between
Bonnie and Clyde Smith Ltd whose registered office is situate at Pit
Mansion, Wensleydale Avenue, Koppax Yorkshire (hereinafter called
"the Vendor") of the one part AND Sedgewick Smiler of 15 Pit Walk
Koppax Yorkshire (hereinafter called "the Purchaser") of the other
part
WHEREAS the Vendor is seised of the property hereinafter described
and hereby conveyed together with other adjoining property (not the
subject of this conveyance) for an estate in fee simple free from
incumbrances
AND WHEREAS the Vendor has agreed to sell the part of the property
hereby conveyed to the Purchaser at the price of five thousand pounds
NOW THIS DEED WITNESSETH as follows:
1. In consideration of the sum of five thousand pounds (receipt
whereof the Vendor hereby acknowledges) the Vendor as Beneficial
Owner HEREBY CONVEYS unto the Purchaser ALL THAT parcel of land
(hereinafter referred to as "the Property") being part of the gardens
of the said Pit Mansion and being more particularly delineated on the
plan annexed hereto and thereon edged in red TOGETHER WITH the
rights contained in the first schedule hereto To Hold the same unto
the Purchaser in fee simple.
2. The Purchaser Hereby Covenants to observe and perform the restrictive covenants contained in the second schedule hereto with the
intent that the said covenants shall run with and bind each and every
part of the Property and that the benefit of the said covenants shall
be annexed to and run with each and every part of the adjoining land
(hereinafter referred to as the "Retained Land") retained by the
Vendor which retained land is known as Pit Mansion aforesaid and is
more particularly delineated on the said plan annexed hereto and
thereon edged in blue.
3. The Purchaser covenants with the Vendor that the Purchaser and his
successors in title will within six months from the date hereof erect
and thereafter maintain in good condition and of at least four feet
in height a stone wall wooden fence or substantial hedge on and along
the Purchaser's side of the boundary line between the points marked
"A" and "B" on the said plan annexed hereto.
4. The Vendor hereby acknowledges the right of the Purchaser to the
production of the deeds and documents specified in the third schedule
hereto and to delivery of copies thereof and undertakes with the
Purchaser for the safe custody thereof.
5. It is hereby certified that the transaction hereby effected does
not form part of a larger transaction or of a series of transactions
in respect of which the amount or value or the aggregate amount or
value of the consideration exceeds five thousand five hundred pounds.

IN WITNESS whereof the vendor has caused its common seal to be hereunto affixed and the purchaser has hereunto set his hand and seal
the day and year first above mentioned.

FIRST SCHEDULE

The right for the Purchaser and his successors in title to
the Property or any part thereof to drain water and soil from the
Property through a pipe to be constructed within ten years from the
date hereof approximately along a straight line from the point marked
"P" on the said plan to discharge into the cesspit identified as such
on the said plan Together with the right to enter on so much as may
be necessary of the Retained Land for the purpose of constructing
and thereafter inspecting repairing maintaining cleansing emptying
renewing the said pipe or cesspit doing as little damage as reasonably possible to the Retained Land and making good any damage so
done.

SECOND SCHEDULE

1. Not to erect any building or construction on the Property other
than two detached dwelling houses and any buildings reasonably considered to be ancillary thereto.
2. Not to carry on any business trade or profession on the Property
other than that of dental surgeon medical practitioner or solicitor
and Not to use any such dwelling-house (save as aforesaid) other than
for residence by a single family.

THIRD SCHEDULE

1960	Conveyance	(1) B. Butterfield
		(2) B. & C. Smith
1962	Conveyance	(1) B. & C. Smith
		(2) Bonnie & Clyde Smith Ltd

The common seal of the said Bonnie & Clyde Ltd
was hereunto affixed in the presence of:

Director *Bonnie Smith*
Secretary *Clyde Smith*

Signed sealed and delivered by
the said Sedgewick Smiler in the
presence of *Alexandra Kollontai*   *Sedgewick Smiler*
ALEXANDRA KOLLENTAI,
LECTURER
17 RED HILL LEDCHESTER

Note: The plan referred to, not reproduced here, is the same as document 5.1.4. save that it shows all the land between the wasteland and the
line A-B edged red].

Document 5.2(b) Goldberg sale: The 1974 Conveyance

THIS CONVEYANCE is made the 24 day of June 1974 Between John Sedgewick Smiler 20 Miners' Walk Koppax Yorkshire (hereinafter called "the Vendor") of the one part AND Larry and Lolita Goldberg both of 92 Longacre Castlebridge Yorkshire (hereinafter called "the Purchasers") of the other part.

WHEREAS at the date of his death Sedgewick Smiler was seised of the property hereby conveyed for an estate in fee simple subject as hereinafter mentioned but otherwise free from incumbrances

AND WHEREAS the said Sedgewick Smiler died on the 25th day of December 1973 having by his will dated the 10th day of June 1973 appointed the Vendor to be his Executor and Trustee

AND WHEREAS Probate of the said will was granted to the Vendor on the 15th day of January 1974 out of the Ledchester District Probate Registry

AND WHEREAS the Vendor has not previously given or made any assent or conveyance in respect of the said property AND has agreed to sell the said property to the Purchasers at the price of fifteen thousand pounds

NOW THIS DEED WITNESSETH as follows:-

1. In consideration of the sum of fifteen thousand pounds (receipt of which sum the Vendor hereby acknowledges) the Vendor as Personal Representative HEREBY CONVEYS unto the Purchasers ALL THAT parcel of land together with the dwelling-house erected thereon known as Fell View Wensleydale Avenue Koppax Yorkshire All which property is more particularly delineated on the plan annexed to a conveyance dated the 1st day of June 1970 and made between Bonnie & Clyde Ltd of the one part and the said Sedgewick Smiler of the other part and thereon edged in red TOGETHER WITH the right of drainage contained in the said conveyance TO HOLD the same unto the Purchasers in fee simple as joint tenants SUBJECT TO the covenants contained in the said conveyance so far as the same are still subsisting and capable of taking effect and affect the property hereby conveyed but otherwise free from incumbrances.

2. The Purchasers (with the object of affording to the Vendor a full indemnity in respect of any breach of the said covenants but not further or otherwise) hereby jointly and severally covenant with the Vendor that the Purchasers and the persons deriving title under them will at all times hereafter perform and observe the said covenants and keep the Vendor and his successors in title as personal representative of the said Sedgewick Smiler indemnified against all actions claims demands and liabilities in respect thereof in so far as the same are still subsisting and capable of taking effect and affect the property hereby conveyed.

3. It Is Hereby Declared and Agreed that:

    (a) the Purchasers hold the said property the net proceeds of sale from it and the net income until sale upon trust for themselves as tenants in common in equal shares.

    (b) the Purchasers shall have the powers to deal with the property equal to those of a sole beneficial owner.

4. The Vendor hereby acknowledges the right of the Purchasers to the production of the said Probate to the will of the said Sedgewick Smiler and to delivery of copies thereof.

5. It is hereby certified that the transaction hereby effected does not form part of a larger transaction or of a series of transactions in respect of which the amount or value of the consideration or the aggregate amount or value of the consideration exceeds fifteen thousand pounds.

IN WITNESS whereof the parties hereto have hereunto set their hands and seals the day and year first above mentioned.

Signed sealed and delivered by
the said Sedgewick Smiler   *Sedgewick Smiler*
in the presence of:

    Alexandra Kollentai
    ALEXANDRA KOLLENTAI,
    LECTURER. 17 RED HILL,
    LEDCHESTER

Signed sealed and delivered by
the said Larry Goldberg
in the presence of: *Larry Goldberg*

    Henrietta Pudden
    HENRIETTA PUDDEN,
    21 CLUB STREET,
    WILTON

Signed sealed and delivered by
the said Lolita Goldberg   *Lolita Goldberg*
in the presence of:

    Henrietta Pudden
    AS ABOVE

Question If you were acting for the Singhs, and in the light of all the information supplied, what particular investigations would you make and what matters would you check on before advising exchange of contracts?

The Singhs want to know whether they will be able to stop the public using the path along the riverside. What will determine the answer to this question? And where will you find the answer? (Note para.6.7).

Should the existence of this footpath have been disclosed in the contract, under the Standard Conditions of Sale? Would this answer be the same if it were an open contract?

To appreciate the importance of care in drafting the contract, it is necessary to have a clear picture of the legal effect of exchanging contracts; and of the elements of such a contract; a matter which we will now look at.

5.2.1

THE LEGAL EFFECT OF A CONTRACT

Broadly speaking, from a legal point of view, the two most crucial points, the conveyancing Rubicons of no return in a sale transaction, are exchange of contracts, as it is commonly called (i.e. the creation of a binding contract) and completion. Completion is the stage at which (in final performance of the contract) the title to the property is finally transferred to the purchaser (subject to registration in the case of registered title) and in return the purchaser hands over the balance of the purchase money. This is dealt with later (see Chapter 14). We are concerned here with exchange.

5.3

In accordance with ordinary contract law, until there is a binding contract neither prospective vendor nor prospective purchaser is legally bound to the other. Either side can withdraw for any reason whatsoever without penalty or liability.[1] If a prospective purchaser has paid what is commonly called a preliminary deposit (para.2.3.1) she can recover it.

The moment a binding contract does come into existence, both parties are legally bound. Each party becomes liable to complete the contract and, wrongfully failing to do so, will be liable for breach of contract. From this moment their respective rights and obligations are determined by the terms of the contract; and cannot unilaterally be altered.

---

[1]   But note that financial liability may have been incurred for work done to the solicitors, estate agents, valuers, etc.

It is therefore important to be able to identify the contract terms; to understand them and be able to advise the client in simple English on their implications; and to be able to negotiate and draft any necessary amendments.

The content of a sale contract

5.3.1   The terms of the contract, like indeed the terms of any contract, are derived from two sources:

(a) Express terms. The express terms are those which have been expressly agreed between the parties and written into the contract. In general, the parties can agree to whatever terms they like – for example, that completion will take place on a certain date. As will be seen, this freedom of contract is limited in a few respects by statute and equity.

In principle, and occasionally in practice, the parties may form a contract which contains no more than the parties (who is selling to whom), the identity of the property and the price. This gives the basic minimum certainty to constitute a valid contract. Such a contract is commonly referred to as an open contract. In contrast to a sale of goods contract, in the absence of agreement on price, the courts will not imply a reasonable price and there will be no contract.

(b) Implied terms. A moment's thought, even to a Timothy brain, will indicate that a sale of land transaction involves a whole galaxy of other matters which must, or may have to, be decided – for example, on what date must completion take place; what is to happen if the building is destroyed by fire before completion; is the purchaser required to pay a deposit; what if the vendor's husband suddenly claims an interest in the property and refuses to move out? However, failure to deal expressly in the contract with any or all of these points does not leave the parties in a contractual vacuum. Provided there is a valid contract, the law contains, enmeshed in past decisions and statute, what can be seen as a reserve storehouse of principles and terms which will be applied to resolve any matter not settled by the expressly agreed terms. These implied terms are commonly referred to as the terms implied under an open contract (and lawyers talk of 'the open contract position').

If a contract is a contract by correspondence[2] and in so far as it is not governed by its own express terms, it will be governed by what are generally known as the statutory conditions of sale. This is a set of

---

2   See *Steam v. Twitchell* [1985] 1 All E.R. 631; *Pips (Leisure Productions) Ltd. v. Walton* (1982) 43 P. & C.R. 415.

conditions drawn up by the Lord Chancellor under s.46 of the Law of Property Act 1925 to govern such contracts.[3] Parties to any contract can use these conditions if they wish by express incorporation as a set of standard conditions; but they deal only with the very basic matters and are not resorted to in practice.

In practice, parties would be foolish to leave all matters to be decided by these implied terms; and will incorporate a full set of express terms into their contract dealing with more or less all issues that might arise.

The practice is for the vendor's solicitor to draft the contract for the purchaser's solicitor to approve or suggest amendments. The terms as finally negotiated will then be incorporated into the final form of the contract ready for exchange (Chapter 9).

If a solicitor sat down, with a blank sheet, and attempted to draft a full set of express terms every time she acted on a sale, she would soon find herself using substantially the same clauses time and time again. She would, in effect, be creating her own standard form of contract.

All sale of land transactions have a great deal in common. It is therefore possible and desirable to have available a single, standard set of terms which can be used in whole or part in any sale of land contract. Indeed, as will be seen, conveyancing solicitors use standard forms and precedents as the basis for most stages in any transaction.

Use of such a standard set of contract terms is advantageous for a number of reasons: (i) It saves time and money; (ii) A lot of thought *should* have gone into the drafting of a set of standard terms. This means that, hopefully, it will deal with all points that may arise in a comprehensible and suitable manner, reasonably fair to both sides. Without their use, it would be all too easy to overlook (or not deal fully) with important issues - and typically, the issue not dealt with would be the one to give rise to a dispute; (iii) Such standard terms are likely to have come before the courts at some time; their meaning is likely to have acquired the certainty of a judicially binding construction.

Sets of standard terms (commonly described as standard conditions - though of course they are made up of both conditions and warranties) have been published. The one most commonly used by lawyers today for residential conveyancing is probably that produced jointly by the Law Society and the Solicitors' Law Stationery Society Ltd., known as 'The Standard Conditions of Sale (Second Edition)'. These Standard Conditions have been incorporated into a printed form of contract, published by the same two bodies, and used as the basis for illustration throughout this book.

---

[3]   S.R.& O. 1925, No. 779.

Alternatively, a firm may draft and use its own set of standard conditions. Or a solicitor may think it desirable to make her own standard amendments (to be incorporated as a matter of course in each transaction) to a published set.

There are, of course, matters which will necessarily need to be changed from transaction to transaction - most obviously, the identity of the parties, the property and the price; and the date for completion; on a sale of part the restrictive covenants that may need to be imposed on the purchaser's land and so on. Any term which is put in to add to or amend the standard conditions is commonly referred to as a special condition (though, again, it may of course itself be a condition or a warranty).

At this point, a caveat needs to be entered. No set of standard conditions is perfect; or necessarily reflects what both sides want and are prepared to negotiate for. And no two transactions are exactly alike. Timothy's attitude that there is a standard form for everything which only needs filling in is a dangerous one. For every transaction it is important to consider whether there is any feature of that transaction or of the client's requirements which necessitates amendment of whatever standard conditions are being used.

Void conditions

5.3.2   A number of contractual conditions are made void by statute. For example, the overreaching machinery is fundamental to the philosophy of the 1925 legislation; that is that buying and selling land is about buying and selling the legal estate. The legislation is designed to keep equitable, trust interests off the title, to guarantee that a purchaser will take free of any such without having to investigate them.

Section 42(1) of the Law of Property Act 1925 accordingly provides that any stipulation requiring a purchaser to take a title made with the concurrence of a person entitled to an equitable interest, if it can be made without such concurrence (that is by operating the overreaching machinery) will be void. To deter avoidance of this rule, s.42(2),(3) and (8) provide that any stipulation requiring the purchaser to pay towards the cost of operating the overreaching machinery or of getting in any outstanding legal estate will be void.[4]

---

[4]   Compare s.110(1) and (5) of the Land Registration Act 1925, designed to prevent the sanctity of the register as the basis of conveyancing of registered land from being undermined.

The section does not insist that the overreaching machinery must be used; merely that the vendor cannot insist on it not being used. In practice, it is common to have a person (such as a person who has originally contributed to the purchase price) with a certain or a possible equitable, trust interest in the property to join in the contract or otherwise sign a consent to release her interest.

Under s.48 of the Act any term which might restrict a purchaser in the selection of a solicitor to act for her will be void; including one that the conveyance or registration of title is to be carried out by a vendor-appointed solicitor at the purchaser's expense.

The section does not prevent the vendor stipulating the form (i.e. the wording) of the conveyance and charging a reasonable sum for doing so. And this is commonly done by estate developers for the sake of preserving uniform conveyancing on the estate and avoiding negotiation over the wording of each individual conveyance.

Equally, it does not prevent the customary practice whereby, on the grant of a lease, the lease is prepared by the lessor's solicitor at the cost of the lessee (subject to the Costs of Leases Act 1958 (para.17.2.3)).

As to conditions requiring the purchaser to cure stamping defects, see para.10.7.1.

Drafting the contract: general points

In addition to what has been said, a few basic objectives should be kept in mind when drafting the contract.

5.3.3

(a) You must draft the contract so as to reflect accurately your client's instructions and authority. This of course also involves, where necessary, drawing the client's attention to and explaining the points on which her instructions are necessary.

(b) You must be very careful to create in the contract only obligations which your client is capable of fulfilling. The objective is *not* to draft your client into court for breach of contract. This applies particularly in deciding what title can be offered to the purchaser.

Since the abolition of the rule in *Bain v. Fothergill* a vendor will be liable to pay substantial damages for loss of bargain and not just the purchaser's legal costs, if there is a defect in title which is not dealt with in the contract (para.10.6.4).

Timothy has failed miserably to pursue either of these objectives. He has lost a crucial part of the instructions; he has drafted the contract without checking what if any title to the land the Goldbergs have. His laxity is not unique.

In *Errington v. Martell-Wilson*[5] Latey J. opened his judgment as follows:

'From first to last this has been an unhappy action, punctuated by a series of mistakes and errors of judgment. This went on until the eve of the hearing when the Plaintiff's solicitors included in the large bundle of documents for the use of the judge a letter from the Defendant's solicitors, informing the Plaintiff's solicitors of the amount of a payment into court.'

Mrs Martell-Wilson was an old lady of 82 in 1977. The plaintiff's solicitor approached her with a view to buying a piece of land which his client wanted to develop. Eventually, a letter came from her solicitors to the plaintiff's solicitors:

'all we have been able to extract from her as yet in relation to the property - she appears for the time being to have mislaid the title deeds of which we have on our file a schedule receipted by her - is a copy of a plan, referred to by her as 'the deeds', comprising in our opinion considerably more land, although it includes the sites of Nos 1 to 10 Walton Terrace that is now the subject of this transaction. In the meantime we have been able to prepare from the papers in our file a draft contract and this we are enclosing, together with a duplicate, with a view to getting this matter moving at least. Although we cannot be certain, we do not believe that the copy plan herewith is the same as the one referred to in the draft contract.'

Note, in passing, the importance if you part with deeds which you hold of getting a receipted schedule signed by the person to whom they are passed.

The matter did move - without the deeds! - and the next thing we read in the report is that 'a contract was signed dated the 28th March 1972. Within a few days the Plaintiff discovered that [Mrs Martell-Wilson] had no title to the property.' She had in fact forgotten, being old, that she had sold it five years earlier. Needless to say (the defence of mental incapacity and unconscionable bargain having been rejected on the facts - see *Cresswell v. Potter*[6]), the plaintiff was held entitled to damages - in fact for misrepresentation (para.4.4.1).

I will now turn to consider some of the special conditions which need to be drafted, following the sequence of the form used by Timothy.

---

5   (1980) Lexis Transcript.
6   [1978] 1 W.L.R. 255.

IDENTITY OF THE PROPERTY AND BOUNDARIES

The contract must contain an accurate legal and physical description   **5.4**
of the property.

The legal description will state whether the land is freehold or
leasehold; and, if leasehold, whether a lease or a sub-lease. (See Chapter
17 for leases.) Unless the contract provides otherwise it is implied that the
freehold will be proved and conveyed.

As to physical description: The vendor's solicitor needs to be satisfied
that the description of the property in the contract is accurate and clear
and that it corresponds with (i) what she wants to sell; and (ii) what she is
able to prove title to.

The purchaser's solicitor will need to be satisfied that the property as
defined in the contract matches what the client wants to buy.

The property can be described verbally, or verbally with reference to
an attached plan. Where the boundary features are long established it may
not be felt necessary to have a plan prepared. Frequently the verbal
description and a plan can be adopted from a previous conveyance of the
whole property; but care should be taken that it is accurate and
sufficiently definite. The parcels clauses (as they are known) in old
conveyances tend to be prolix, written in what is now archaic legal
language and often not very illuminating in relation to the property on
the ground. 'All that piece or parcel of land now in the occupation of
John Thomas as tenant' may at best lead you to a plot of land in some
churchyard!

Where only part of the land in the existing title is being sold, a plan
will invariably be desirable.

Particular care is needed on behalf of both vendor and purchaser
where there is anything to suggest that the boundary line may not be
clear and undisputed on the ground and correspond with available plans.
In *McManus Developments Ltd. v. Barbridge Properties Ltd.*[7] the plaintiff
purchasers were claiming, *inter alia,* against their solicitor for negligence.
Although a sale of registered title, the same principles apply.

The property was described in the contract as 'Garden House, rear of
33 Hartswood Road, London W12. (Registered at H.M. Land Registry
under absolute title no. NGL 436091)'. The problem was that a fence
supposedly marking the northern boundary on the ground was between
three and four metres to the north of the true boundary line shown on
the title plan of the registered title (of which the plaintiffs' solicitor had a
copy). When the discrepancy was discovered by the plaintiffs after

---

[7]   (1992) Lexis Transcript.

completion they had to buy in the extra strip in order to carry out their intended development. The plaintiffs did have a copy of the estate agent's location plan which, like the filed plan, showed the correct position of the boundary and their solicitor had orally advised them before contract to check the boundaries.

The basis of the finding of negligence was that one day before completion the plaintiffs had discovered that the fence had been moved by the neighbours to what in fact was the true boundary. They immediately informed their solicitor who treated it simply as a matter of unlawful encroachment by the neighbour, wrote to the vendor's solicitors requiring them to get the fence put back to its former position and this was in fact done. The plaintiffs' solicitor thereupon completed the purchase. In fact, unknown to the plaintiffs or their solicitor, a dispute was seething over the boundary between the vendor and the neighbour. In the view of the court the information that the fence had been moved 'was calculated to set alarm bells ringing in a solicitor's mind'. A competent solicitor would at that point have made a proper investigation as to why the fence had been moved and whether there was any dispute as to ownership of the boundary. Indeed, if the solicitor had checked the boundary on the ground with the filed plan, the true position would immediately have become obvious.[8]

Hopefully, the verbal description will tally with any plan annexed. If, in any document, there is a discrepancy the court will have to decide which prevails. If the property is referred to as 'more particularly delineated on the plan annexed' (or words to that effect) the plan will normally prevail. If the plan is referred to as being 'for the purposes of identification only' (or words to that effect), the verbal description will normally prevail.

Land Registry plans

5.4.1   (See also para.11.2.3). It should be remembered when drafting or perusing a draft contract that any conveyance of unregistered title on sale will now have to be registered by the purchaser.

> 'One of the distinguishing features of registered conveyancing is that the land is described by reference to an official plan based upon the ordnance survey map, revised up to date. Consequently, an applicant for first registration must give the registry sufficient information by plan or verbal description to enable his land to be identified with precision on the ordnance survey map of the Land Registry general map.'

---

8   See also *Jackson v. Bishop* (1979) 48 P. & C.R. 57; below para.5.7.

The same authors also say:

'More than one in eight of the plans which are brought into the registry on first registration, or in connection with transfers of part of the land in a registered title, contain errors and inaccuracies which are too serious to be ignored.'[9]

The best plan for submission to the Registry is likely to be one based on the ordnance survey map,[10] though copyright permission is needed to use these maps. The Law Society has an arrangement with the Ordnance Survey Department under which solicitors can obtain a general licence to use their material.

Ownership of boundaries

Who owns the privet hedge? Where exactly is the line dividing me from my neighbour? There are probably many running battles and little final certainty in this area. It is uncommon for the title deeds (except perhaps on new developments and when part of the property has been sold off) to delineate the mathematically exact line of boundaries and the consequent ownership of boundary features. Where ownership of boundary features such as fences and walls is shown on plans it is conventional to do it by means of a 'T' facing inwards from the boundary. The significance of the 'T' should be incorporated into the verbal description.

5.4.2

In usual conveyancing practice the need to show and prove the exact line of boundaries is avoided by what can be called the general boundaries rule. Standard Conditions 4.3.1. (iterating this open contract principle) and 4.3.2. provide:

'4.3.1. The seller need not:

(a) prove the exact boundaries of the property;

(b) prove who owns fences, ditches, hedges or walls.

4.3.2. The buyer may, if it is reasonable, require the seller to make or obtain, pay for and hand over a statutory declaration about facts relevant to the matters mentioned in condition 4.3.1. The form of declaration is to be agreed by the buyer, who must not unreasonably withhold his agreement.'

This principle allows the vendor a measure of latitude in proving the exact limits of the property; but failure to show the boundary line to a significant degree would not be protected by the condition.

---

[9] Ruoff & Pryer, pp.18, 22.

[10] Except, for example, where there are overlapping floors when proper architectural plans may be advisable.

The Land Registry normally adopts the same general boundary principle on its filed plans; which again means that if any dispute arises between neighbours it will have to be resolved as a question of fact in the light of all the evidence and common law presumptions as to the limit of boundaries. If the relevant deeds sent on registration of the title do mark boundaries with a 'T' which is referred to in the verbal description, this will be replicated on the title plan and noted on the property register.

ROOT OF TITLE

5.5

(See also Chapter 10). In principle, the vendor must prove her title; that is prove that she owns the legal estate which she has agreed to sell (the legal freehold or leasehold) free from any trust and free from any incumbrances other than those to which the contract declares the land to be subject and any which are patent at the time of the contract.

The contract determines, by its express and implied terms, how that title must be proved, that is what evidence of title must be offered.

In traditional conveyancing practice at least, the actual proof takes place after formation of contract.

How can V(endor) prove her ownership of the legal estate being sold? She can show that the title was transferred to her in one of the ways stipulated by law for the effective transfer of the legal estate -for example, a deed of conveyance, a written assent to her as a testamentary beneficiary of a deceased relative – and in most cases some deed or legal document is needed for the transfer of the legal estate. But what if the person (W) transferring it to her did not own it, was a squatter for example? If W did not own it, any transfer to V would be ineffective. The ownership of the real owner of the legal estate (that is someone with a better right than W), being legal and good against all the world, can be asserted against W and V V is driven to go yet another stage further back and show how the land was transferred effectively from say X to W; and so on.

In fact, the law puts a limit on how far back the vendor has to go; and is so designed that a title proved over this period will run very little risk of challenge.

Section 23 of the Law of Property Act 1969, provides that under an open contract 15 years is 'the period of commencement of title' which a purchaser of land may require. The proof of title for this period must start with a good root of title. Here, Timothy has got something right. His definition of a good root of title is correct. His application of the rule is less happy (below). The vendor will then have to prove title by tracing and proving the legal history of the land in an unbroken chain from the root to her own ownership.

The Standard Conditions do not alter this open contract rule as to the age and quality of a good root. It is usual, as Timothy has drafted, for the contract to stipulate what root is being offered. Unless, as for example under TransAction Protocol, title is deduced with the draft contract, the contract is not accompanied by copy of the root document or the subsequent documents constituting the chain of title. These are provided by way of deducing title after contract.

Whenever one document is referred to in another (as here when stipulating the root document in the contract) it should be identified by stating its nature, its date and the parties to it. Timothy has not even managed this correctly. More seriously, he has identified the wrong document.

Where the document specified as the root of title is not a good root, the vendor (to avoid being in breach of contract) should put in a special condition stipulating the defect and requiring the purchaser not to object; alternatively she should provide (if there is one) an earlier document which is a good root. The document stipulated by Timothy, with such careless abandon (the 1974 Conveyance) is unsatisfactory. It identifies the property only by reference to the plan on an earlier conveyance (the 1970 conveyance). If the contract were left like this, the purchaser would probably be entitled to reject the 1974 conveyance as a satisfactory root. In any case, under s.45(1) of the Law of Property Act 1925 (para.10.5.2) she would be entitled to requisition production of the earlier conveyance. It follows that Timothy should have used the 1970 conveyance as the root of title. If for any reason (e.g. if it had been lost) it were not possible to produce this, the 1974 conveyance should be used and a special term put in the contract stating the absence of the earlier document and consequent deficiency in the title and requiring the purchaser to accept title subject and without objecting to this deficiency.

Question John Keats is instructing you on the sale of his house and market garden of 10 acres, Nightingfield, at Koppax. There is a problem. The title deeds have been lost. John, as the only child, took over the property when his father, William, died about seven years ago and continued to work the market garden. His father, by then a widower, had always kept the deeds in a box under his bed; but on his death neither the box nor the deeds could be found. John had worked the garden with his father for many years; and so when William died John just carried on without any formal papers being signed.

(a) How can you check whether the land has been registered, either in William's name or in the name of someone else?

(b) Suppose it has been registered in William's name. What steps will you advise John to take now?

(c) Suppose that for the last five years, part of the garden – a part on the boundary, not cultivated by John because of pollution from a nearby stream – has been registered with possessory title in the name of neighbour, Pablo Neruda. Advise John.

(d) Assume that no part of the property has been registered, and that you are drafting the contract of sale. What evidence of title can John not offer? What evidence can he offer? Draft a suitable special condition to put in the contract. Research a suitable form and draft the document to be incorporated into the contract containing this evidence. (See para.7.11(b) and 10.4.1).

APPURTENANT RIGHTS AND INCUMBRANCES ALREADY AFFECTING THE PROPERTY

5.6   When drafting both the contract and the conveyance for a sale of part of the vendor's land (as in the Goldberg transaction), it is important to distinguish between:

(a) Those rights and obligations affecting the land which are already in existence at the time of the contract. These may exist whether the vendor is selling only part or the whole of her land. Existing rights and obligations affecting the land will be for the benefit of or a burden on adjoining land owned by someone other than the vendor. As such, the vendor cannot modify them in any way; and can only pass on the benefit or burden as it exists.

(b) New rights and obligations which the parties have agreed to create; designed to benefit or burden the land being retained by the vendor. (As to these see Chapter 6).

Appurtenant rights

5.6.1   Any benefits already attached to the property being sold (easements or covenants) may be set out or incorporated by reference in the contract in the description of the property preceded by the words 'Together With ...' They will then be set out in the conveyance in the same way (in the parcels clause – see para.12.4.2). The benefit will then pass to the purchaser as part of the estate being purchased (the fee simple, if the freehold is being purchased).

In fact rights which are appurtenant (that is the benefit of which is attached to so as to run with the dominant property) will pass automatically to the purchaser on a conveyance without express mention in the contract or conveyance. Section 62 of the Law of Property Act 1925, implies an all estates clause, as it is called, into a conveyance of the land. It provides:

'A conveyance of land shall be deemed to include and shall by virtue of this Act operate to convey, with the land, all buildings, erections, fixtures, commons, hedges, ditches, fences, ways, waters, watercourses, liberties, privileges, easements, rights and advantages whatsoever appertaining or reputed to appertain to the land or any part thereof, or, at the time of conveyance, demised, occupied, or enjoyed with, or reputed or known as part or parcel of or appurtenant to the land or any part thereof.'

Note that the section operates to pass existing rights (as now being discussed); but it has also been held to operate on a sale of part of the land to convert quasi-easements into new, actual easements in favour of the part purchased.

Where existing appurtenant easements or covenants are expressly set out in the contract description as part of what is being sold, it should be remembered that the vendor is thereby obligating herself to convey them just as much as the land itself. The vendor must therefore be in a position to prove title to the rights just as to the land. If she is not able to do this a special condition should be put in the contract barring the right to raise requisitions or objections in respect of the title to the easement or covenant.

The purchaser of land with the benefit of easements or covenants needs to be satisfied that the right was created by a landowner with title (i.e. to the servient land) to create it ; that it was properly annexed to the dominant and servient properties (which will be shown by the original wording of the easement or covenant); registered against the servient owner if necessary; and that title has passed down to the present vendor.

Even if the easement or covenant was intended to run with the whole land of the vendor it will not necessarily run with the part of that land being sold. It is generally a question of the proper construction of the words used on the creation of the right. For example, in the case of a restrictive covenant the benefit will only run with part if, when created, it was expressed to be for the benefit of 'each and every part' of the covenantee's land (or words to the same effect). If a restrictive covenant was not expressly annexed to the dominant property, its benefit can still be expressly assigned on a conveyance of the land.

In practice, proving title to appurtenant easements and covenants does not normally present a problem. The easement or covenant will usually have been created earlier in the title when the property was sold off as part by the common owner of the intended dominant and servient properties. Title to the easement or covenant will be shown in the deeds to have passed down from them along with the title to the dominant land and, assuming that there is no evidence that the easement has been extinguished, proof of title to the land will embrace proof of title to the easement or covenant.

The 1970 conveyance granted a drainage easement in favour of the property being purchased then by the Goldbergs.

The grant of the drainage easement in the 1970 conveyance makes it clear that it could be enjoyed by the owner of any part of the dominant property. In fact, as the Instructions on Sale note, the Goldbergs are no longer interested. A special condition could be put into the contract agreeing a Declaration (to be put in the ensuing conveyance) under which they would (effectively at least in favour of the Singhs and their successors in title) release any right for the owners of the retained Fell View to exercise the easement. On the facts, this is not really necessary. Any such drain has to enter Pit Mansion at point P on the plan; this is inside the part being sold to the Singhs. The courts would not imply into the conveyance to the Singhs the reservation of an easement in favour of Fell View to lay a drain across the Singhs' property to point P (but see next Question).

Question Assuming that such a Declaration is to be put into the conveyance, draft it. If Standard Condition 3.3. of the contract were not modified (as to which see, para.6.4.4) and no special condition were put in the contract as to the drainage right, would the Goldbergs be able to assert a right to use it after conveyance?

For the transfer and registration of appurtenant rights in the case of registered land, see para.7.9.

Incumbrances

The 1970 conveyance contains a number of restrictive covenants imposed on the land purchased by the Goldbergs. These are clearly and expressly intended to bind each and every part of the property; and will (subject to having been registered) bind the Singhs as subsequent purchasers of part. The contract drafted by Timothy does not set out the actual wording of the obligations imposed by the earlier conveyance. As with benefits a contract should disclose not only the existence of but set out the actual wording of any burdens attached to the property. Especially in the light of special condition 2 of the Standard Conditions of sale (barring requisitions on the incumbrances), the prospective purchaser's solicitor should insist on this before exchange of contracts.

It is common simply to include with the contract a copy of the wording of the relevant clauses in the deed creating the benefit or burden of easements and covenants. But the prospective purchaser's solicitor should consider the need to see the whole deed. For example, in the case of a restrictive covenant burdening the property it may be necessary to see the whole deed to ascertain the identity of the dominant property and whether the covenant is likely to be still enforceable.

Positive covenants and indemnity covenants

Finally, the 1970 conveyance contains a positive obligation to erect a fence along the boundary with Pit Mansion. This is a positive obligation. As such the burden is not capable in itself of running with the covenantor's land and will only be directly enforceable by the owners[11] of the benefitted land against the original covenantor personally and his estate.[12] It should be noted that as it is worded it will continue to bind the covenantor and his estate even after parting with the land. Consequently it is usual for the covenantor when selling to require an indemnity covenant by the purchaser to be included in the conveyance. This is a covenant by the purchaser (who will now be in control of the land affected) with the vendor to perform the terms of the covenant and to indemnify the vendor if, on failing to do so, the vendor is sued by the original covenantee (or person with the benefit of the covenant) in contract on the positive covenant. The 1974 conveyance contains such an indemnity covenant by the Goldbergs; and they in turn will want a similar one from the Singhs in respect of the part of the Pit Mansion boundary to the property which they are buying. In this way, a chain of indemnity covenants is built up as the title changes hands; so that, in principle at least, if there is a breach and the original covenantor sued liability can be passed down the line to the actual wrongdoer.

The existence of the indemnity covenant in the 1974 conveyance should be shown in the contract. But Timothy is wasting ink in putting in a special condition requiring an indemnity covenant from the Singhs. Standard Condition 4.5.3. already provides for the purchaser to give one (and the court would order one even without such a condition). Note that an indemnity covenant is only necessary, and under the Standard Conditions will only be given, where the vendor will continue to be liable. If there is a break in the chain of covenants on the title, a covenant will not be required.

An indemnity covenant will be required in the case of both positive and restrictive covenants; though in the case of the latter, since direct enforcement (by injunction or damages in lieu, in equity) against the

5.6.3

---

11   The words used would probably be sufficient to annex the *benefit* of the covenant to the retained land by virtue of s.78 of the Law of Property Act 1925.

12   As to the possibility of an obligation to fence existing as an easement, see *Crow v. Wood* [1971] 1 Q.B. 77; but this case concerned only the passing of the benefit of the obligation under s.62 and so establishes very little.

present owner is normally possible, action against the original covenantor to the restrictive covenant is not likely. In the case of restrictive covenants a distinction should be noted between imposing the proprietary burden on the land and the personal burden on the covenantor. For the burden of a restrictive covenant to run the covenantor will have to show an intention to bind subsequent owners of the land. This may be done, for example, by expressing the covenant to be made on behalf of herself and successors in title to the land. But at the same time the covenant may make it clear that the covenantor is only intended to be personally liable while she retains some interest in the land. In this case, she will not be under any liability after parting with the land; and neither she nor any subsequent owner of the land will be entitled to (or indeed need) an indemnity covenant.

If there has been a break in the chain of indemnity covenants, there will be no liability and no right to take one. For example, a personal representative may have neglected to include an indemnity covenant in an assent to a beneficiary (as she would have been entitled to under the Administration of Estates Act 1925, s.36 (10)).

CAPACITY OF THE VENDOR: COVENANTS FOR TITLE

5.7   In describing the capacity of the Goldbergs as beneficial owner rather than trustees, Timothy has (unwittingly one might guess) adopted the common conveyancing practice. He has not considered that this practice might be faulty.

The capacity of the vendor stated in the contract is the capacity in which she will have to convey it (para.12.4.2). In turn, the capacity in which she conveys determines what covenants for title are implied into the conveyance by virtue of s.76 of the Law of Property Act 1925.

The general principle of conveyancing law is that until completion the parties are bound by the contract and can sue for any breach. However, upon completion the contract is said to merge with the conveyance. In other words, with certain exceptions the contract comes to an end at that point and is replaced by the conveyance. If, after that, the purchaser discovers any defect in the title - for example a binding but hitherto undiscovered restrictive covenant - her only possible remedy is to sue for breach of the covenants for title contained expressly or by the statutory implication in the conveyance.

Merger will not occur when, on a proper construction of the contract, it can be said that the obligation was intended to persist after conveyance. The intention may have to be inferred from the nature of the obligation. For example, an obligation in the contract of sale to erect a house on the land will persist after completion of the purchase with the house not yet finished. The obligation to give vacant possession will not merge (para.14.6). In *Mason v. Schuppisser*[13] a term in the contract giving the vendor a right to re-purchase was held to persist.

To avoid subsequent dispute, the intention that any specified terms should persist after completion should be expressed in the contract, the term incorporated into the conveyance, or initially made part of a separate contract.

Standard Condition 7.4. provides: 'Completion does not cancel liability to perform any outstanding obligation under the contract.' Presumably this means that the principle of merger is not to apply at all to a contract subject to the Standard Conditions.[14]

The doctrine of merger applies equally to registered land; and, it is generally assumed, operates on transfer rather than registration.

The parties are free to negotiate what guarantees of title they wish and provide in the contract for these to be incorporated in the conveyance. Almost invariably in practice the contract and conveyance will simply state the capacity of the vendor and allow this to determine the covenants for title in accordance with s.76.

The covenants to be implied by s.76 in relation to freehold dealings (for leasehold, see para.17.3.2 and 17.5(d)) depend on whether the person 'conveys and is expressed to convey':

(a) as beneficial owner in a conveyance (other than a mortgage) for valuable consideration (which expression does not include marriage);

(b) as beneficial owner in a mortgage of the property;[15]

(c) as settlor in a settlement; or

(d) as trustee, mortgagee or personal representative.

The effect of the covenants

The four covenants (though they are described in the section and sometimes regarded as one covenant) are set out in Schedule 2, Part I; and can be listed as follows: full power to convey; quiet enjoyment; freedom from incumbrances; for further assurance.

These covenants provide a limited guarantee of the purchaser's title and that the vendor will (at the purchaser's expense) do anything further

---

[13]   (1899) 81 L.T. 147.

[14]   Though arguably a distinction might be made between outstanding obligations (yet to be performed) which would not merge, and liability for obligations already broken which would not be covered by s.c. 7.4. and would still merge.

[15]   For title covenants in relation to mortgages, see para.8.3.1(g).

necessary to perfect a title which is found to be imperfect. Two points should be noted. First, it is the basic duty of the purchaser's solicitor properly to investigate the title being offered *before* conveyance. Especially today, when (though the student may find it hard to believe) title is so much a simpler matter, any significant defect coming to light after completion is likely to be a result of careless conveyancing. Secondly, the covenant is in any case not an absolute guarantee of the purchaser's title. The covenantor is only liable for the acts or omissions of herself and her predecessors in title back to the last purchase for value; and the lawful acts and omissions of those who have acquired a derivative interest from the covenantor.

The matter is best explained by an illustration. Suppose A sells and conveys to B who, in turn, sells and conveys to C. In both cases the vendor conveys as beneficial owner. After completion C discovers that the land is subject to a hitherto undiscovered, but enforceable, mortgage. If the mortgage was created by A, then C can in principle sue A on the covenant given to B. The benefit of the title covenants runs with the land. But C cannot sue her own vendor, B, in this case; the defect was created behind the last conveyance for value (from A to B). If the mortgage was created by B, then C can sue B on the covenant in the B to C conveyance.

Potentially, therefore, the person suffering as a result of the defect should have a claim against someone back in the chain of ownership. But that person, or her personal representatives may not be traceable, may not be worth suing, or, if a company, may have gone into liquidation. The right of action may have been barred under the Limitation Act 1980. On all but the covenant for quiet enjoyment, the time limit of 12 years starts to run from the date of the conveyance containing the covenant being sued on. In the case of quiet enjoyment it is 12 years from disturbance of the enjoyment. There may be no beneficial owner covenant to rely on. Suppose that A, having created the mortgage, had died and the land passed to PR her personal representative; and suppose that PR had sold and conveyed it to B. The only statutory covenant implied on a conveyance by a personal representative, mortgagee or trustee is that the person conveying has not herself 'done or knowingly suffered ' anything to be done to incumber the title. In this case no-one would be liable to C.

There is a further possible weakness. There is judicial opinion which suggests, because s.76 only implies the covenants where a person 'conveys and is expressed to convey', that the beneficial owner (for example) covenants only apply where the vendor is both stated in the conveyance to be and is in fact beneficial owner of the property. If this view does find judicial favour it is a serious limit on the utility of the covenants. One of the most common post-completion title problems is probably the discovery that there has been a double conveyance. S sells and conveys land to B which, it is discovered, has already been conveyed to A. B can have no title, at least in unregistered conveyancing.[16] A's title is legal and good against all the world. If the above mentioned view is correct, B cannot sue S on the title covenant, because S was not in fact beneficial owner (or any sort of owner) of the land at the time of the conveyance to B. Without delving here into the arguments it is submitted that the broader view is correct.

In *Jackson v. Bishop*[17] a residential estate, Hummicks Estate, was being developed by the second defendants. The first defendants bought plot 6; the plaintiffs then bought plot 7. Dispute arose between them as to the correct position of the dividing boundary. The identical plan on each conveyance was copied directly from the site plan, purported to be drawn to a given scale; and gave the purported measurements of the boundaries. The dividing boundary on each conveyance plan was shown in the same position. No room for dispute here one might think. But there was. Both parties were claiming a small triangle of land.

Examination of the plan showed internal inconsistency. Two of the boundaries were marked in figures as 209 feet and 70 feet; but when these boundary lines were measured on the plan and scaled up they emerged as respectively 195 and 83 feet. Further inconsistency emerged when an attempt was made to match up the plan to the reality on the ground.

> 'the plan showed an inspection cover giving access to certain oil pipe lines as being adjacent to and immediately outside the south-eastern boundary of plot number 6, and only a short distance, some 17 or 18 feet from the southernmost corner of that plot, whereas if one applied to those fixed features on the ground which could be determined without hesitation, the plot as indicated by the scale and the boundaries drawn to scale, that oil inspection cover would have fallen well within the plot.'[18]

Using this position of the inspection cover as the base line gave the disputed triangle to plot 6; using the alternative gave it to plot 7.

The necessary logic of the Court of Appeal's decision (though they denied this) seems to be that both interpretations were correct. For they decided that the disputed plot had been conveyed to plot 6; and then subsequently (and therefore ineffectively) to the plaintiffs with plot 7 - a double conveyance. The plaintiffs were therefore held entitled to damages from the developers for breach of the covenants for title. No

---

[16] In registered conveyancing registration might cure B's title at the expense of A.

[17] (1979) 48 P. & C.R. 57; [1982] Conv, 324; and see *Conodate Investments Ltd. v. Bentley Quarry Engineering Co. Ltd.* [1970] E.G.D. 902.

[18] Per Bridge L.J., at p.61.

mention was made of s.76 or its correct interpretation; by inference it supports the view preferred above.[19]

The case is also noteworthy because it illustrates the importance of accurate identification of the property in contract and conveyance.

The danger of the courts taking a narrow view of 'conveys and is expressed to convey' in s.76 can be avoided by using a standardised, special condition. Section 76(7) recognises that the statutory implied covenants may be varied or extended and still operate in the same way.

In fact very few solicitors do this. A special condition might be in something like the following terms:

'The vendor will convey as beneficial owner and the conveyance will contain the following clause: "The covenants contained in Schedule 2, Part I of the Law of Property Act 1925 shall be implied herein and operate in the manner provided by s.76 of that Act whether or not the vendor is in fact beneficial owner of the property".'

There is a related problem, perhaps of more practical importance, in the common case of a sale by legal joint tenants who between them in fact own the whole equitable interest, either as joint tenants or tenants in common. They will be either express or statutory (by virtue of ss.34–36 of the Law of Property Act 1925) trustees (for sale). *Prima facie* there correct contracting and conveyancing capacity is as trustees (not, note, as trustees for sale). It increasingly seems to be the practice for vendor's solicitor (without prompting from the purchaser's solicitor) to designate them as beneficial owner in the contract, with a view to giving the purchaser the full set of beneficial owner covenants for title.

It is submitted that this is not good practice. Apart from the possible doubt mentioned above as to the application of s.76 where the vendor's real capacity is not what the conveyance states that it is, s.76(1) does say that the covenants are deemed to be made 'by the person or by each person who conveys ...' The vendors may (or may not) between them hold the whole beneficial interest; but each one alone manifestly does not. Further, the whole pattern of conveyancing under the 1925 legislation is based on the principle that on a sale by trustees the purchaser is not concerned with ownership of the beneficial, equitable interest.

In the light of what has been said earlier, with modern title, it is unlikely that a purchaser will be affected by defects created before acquisition by the vendor. If she is, she may have a remedy on that earlier owner's previous covenant; and no remedy against the vendor because the defect arose before the last conveyance for value.

In short, the limited trustees covenant is perfectly adequate.

---

[19] The developers were also held liable in negligence; see [1982] Conv. 324.

NEW RIGHTS AND OBLIGATIONS NEEDED ON A SALE OF PART

These are dealt with in Chapter 6.   **5.8**

THE COMPLETION DATE

This is the date agreed by the parties for completion when title will be   **5.9**
transferred to the purchaser by conveyance or (in the case of registered
land) transfer (subject to registration), when she will be given vacant
possession (if the sale is with vacant possession), the balance of the
purchase price paid to the vendor and any other outstanding matters dealt
with. (See Chapter 16 for the consequences of late or non-completion.)

The contractual completion date should not be confused with the
agreement date. The latter will be inserted at the time the agreement is
made to show when it was made.

Fixing of the date for completion is a good example of the
relationship between implied terms, standard conditions and special
conditions. (para.5.3.1). The open contract position (i.e. the implied
term) is that completion must take place within a reasonable time. What
is reasonable is a question of fact in each case depending on what has to
be done by way of proving title, drafting documents, etc. Standard
Conditions 6.1.1. and 6.1.2. provide:

'6.1.1.Completion date is twenty working days after the date of
the contract but time is not of the essence unless a notice to
complete has been served.

6.1.2. If the money due on completion is received after 2.00 pm,
completion is to be treated, for the purposes only of conditions
6.3. and 7.3., as taking place on the next working day.'

Question Explain the consequences for the purchaser if completion
takes place at 4.00 pm on the agreed completion date as a result of the
purchaser's solicitor having been held up by another appointment. What
would you put into the contract by way of amendment or addition if
both parties wanted completion to take place at 4.00 pm on that date.

Normally the parties want to agree their own specific completion date
which will be inserted as a special condition. Under special printed
condition 1(a) of the printed form being used by Timothy this will then
prevail over the standard condition.

CONTRACT RATE

5.10   Standard Condition 1.1.1(g) provides: 'Contract rate', unless defined in
the agreement, is the Law Society's interest rate from time to time in force.'

This is the rate of interest used as the measure of compensation under
Standard Condition 7.3.2. where either party is liable for late completion
(para.16.6). It is usual to set it at something like 4% above the base rate of a
specified one of the big clearing banks; or, under the Standard Conditions,
to leave it as that fixed for this purpose by the Law Society and published
weekly in the *Law Society Gazette* (fixed at 4% above the base rate of
Barclays Bank plc). Since it may become payable by either party it is not
usually in the interests of either party to set it at a punitive rate.

THE DEPOSIT

5.11   This is dealt with in Chapter 2.

CHATTELS AND FIXTURES

5.12   These are dealt with in para.4.4.2.

PROFESSIONAL UNDERTAKINGS

5.13   The Ledchester and Bongley sent the title deeds to Jarndyce &
Jarndyce in return for their undertaking (Document 5.1.1).

Solicitors are often asked to give undertakings. In conveyancing
transactions the most common occasions are:

(a) An undertaking given by the vendor's solicitor to a mortgagee to
obtain the title deeds so that the draft contract can be prepared. The
mortgagee will normally want a guarantee that the deeds will be held
to its order and, in particular, not handed over to the borrower; and
either get the deeds back or, if completion takes place, the money to
discharge the mortgage. In the Goldberg case they will want on
completion (in accordance with their agreement), the return of the
deeds (which will not be handed over to the Singhs as they relate also
to the retained part of Fell View) and the net proceeds of sale.

In the case of registered land, the mortgagee would be holding a charge
certificate (with the land certificate held at the Land Registry) or the
Land Certificate itself in the case of an informal mortgage. The land or

charge certificate will not necessarily be up to date with all current entries on the register. The proper procedure for the vendor's solicitor is therefore to obtain up to date office copies of the entries on the register (para.11.2.1) and use these as the basis for drafting the contract. Copies (office copies under the Standard Conditions) will in any case have to be supplied to the purchaser either with the draft contract or immediately after exchange of contract in order to prove title.

(b) An undertaking given to a bank or other financier by the purchaser's solicitor to secure a bridging loan to the client, generally either to enable her to pay the deposit on exchange (para.2.3.3) or to finance the full purchase price pending the sale of an existing property.

(c) An undertaking by the vendor's to the purchaser's solicitor on completion to guarantee that an outstanding mortgage will be discharged out of the proceeds of sale (para.15.3.1).

In some cases forms of undertaking have been agreed or recommended for general use. For example, forms of undertaking have been agreed with banks; and there is a recommended form of undertaking to discharge a building society mortgage (See *Guide*, p.454).

The *Guide* defines an undertaking as follows (para.19.01):

'An undertaking is an unequivocal declaration of intention addressed to someone who reasonably places reliance on it and made by:

(a) a solicitor or a member of staff in the course of practice; or

(b) a solicitor as 'solicitor', but not in the course of practice whereby the solicitor becomes personally bound.'

Such a professional undertaking is normally acceptable because it is enforceable in the following ways:

(a) Failure to honour it is *prima facie* serious professional misconduct likely to give rise to disciplinary proceedings.

(b) The court, by virtue of its inherent jurisdiction over its own officers, has power to enforce performance of a solicitor's professional undertaking.

It follows that, in giving any professional undertaking, a solicitor should adhere to the following principles:

(i) She should have any necessary authority of the client in writing and signed. For example, when a bridging loan is being made to finance the purchase deposit, the express, irrevocable authority of the client will be needed for an undertaking to pay the proceeds of the related sale to the lender.

(ii) She should undertake only what she is sure that she will be able to honour. Thus on undertaking to pay the proceeds of sale to a lender of bridging finance, the undertaking should be expressly limited to the

fail to complete; or the client may change solicitors. Similarly, the undertaking should be confined to the net proceeds of sale after deduction of legal costs, disbursements, etc. And if the money likely to be available is not likely to be sufficient to cover the loan this must be made clear to the lender.

(iii) Since an undertaking given by a partner will bind other partners in the firm, and since a solicitor employer is responsible for the undertakings given by a member of her staff, whether or not admitted, there should be clear rules within a firm as to who has authority to give undertakings.

CHAPTER 6

SALE OF PART

TIMOTHY'S INSTRUCTIONS COME TO LIGHT

The lost, additional instructions relating to the Goldberg sale **6.1** (para.5.1.2) have come to light in the Obebe file. Timothy glances through them. Having already decided that the Standard Conditions must say all that needs to be said about a sale of part, he decides to stick to that view (Timothy was famous at law school for stubbornly defending an untenable position with untenable arguments).

A few moments later, as Timothy leaves to do a little shopping in town, the hand of Old Jarndyce (shaking a little with age or despair?) is seen rescuing a now crumpled sheet of paper from the waste bin. This is what it contains. (Note: For the initial instructions and plan, see Documents 5.1.3 and 5.1.4).

Document 6.2 Additional Instructions on Goldberg Sale

Re: Mr and Mrs Goldberg
Sale, part Fell View

Singhs to build and maintain a fence along the new boundary — at least four feet high. Must get it done before the building work starts.

G's have given Singhs papers relating to planning permission.

Singhs to have access from road along the driveway. Their services to be laid along driveway. G's service pipes come straight in from road — not along driveway. Singhs to pay half cost of repairs to drive.

Have talked to Singhs about G's making new access opening at side of present one into driveway bay with new drive to Fell View; then transferring present driveway to Singhs outright apart from access bay.

Not to hold up sale for this.

We will advise G's on planning implications.

Make sure that Singhs can only build one house. Mrs Singh a doctor. G's don't mind a surgery, but nothing else. Otherwise just one-family house.

Singhs to have sole use of cesspit. G's have main drainage now.

Question (a) Can the Singhs take the benefit of the planning permission granted to the Goldbergs?

(b) What are the planning implications of the suggestion for a new access? Consider Town and Country Planning Act 1990, s.336(1); Town and Country Planning General Development Order 1988, Schedule 2, Part 2, Class A; Case notes at 1981 J.P.L. 380 and 1988 J.P.L. 787; and Encyclopedia of Planning Law and Practice, p.38106.

If there is any doubt whether they need planning permission, what is the easiest way to get a ruling? See Town and Country Planning Act 1990, s.192.

(c) What would the implications be if Timothy's course were adopted, and none of the matters mentioned in the above additional instructions were dealt with expressly in the contract? For example, would the Singhs nevertheless acquire a right of access along the driveway? If the Goldbergs had in the past been wont to walk down to the river and along the footpath to Lower Koppax, would they be able to go on doing so?

Note: As to the footpath, see further, Question after Document 5.2(b).

(d) Is the instruction that Singhs are to 'pay half cost of repairs to drive' sufficiently clear and specific? Is it clear whether it relates to the cost of making good the drive after work on the service pipes or to the routine maintenance of the surface of the drive? Do both need to be dealt with?

(e) Suppose the Goldberg's service pipes and cables do at present pass along the driveway. Would the contract need to be amended to take account of this? If so, in what way? Would the Goldbergs need to reserve easements?

Question After reading the rest of this chapter, draft the parts of the contract on the Goldberg sale not dealt with by Timothy in Document 5.1.6.

OLD JARNDYCE COMMENTS

6.3   Unless indicated otherwise what is said applies equally to unregistered and registered title.

A sale of part occurs where the owner sells part of the land in a single title (whether unregistered or registered) retaining the rest.[1] On the ground it means that she will be selling off part of her land and retaining

---

1   The property being sold could, of course, be held under a separate title from the retained land.

adjacent land. In residential conveyancing, a sale-off is likely to be seen to fall into one of two categories, although legally the same:

First, where the builder/developer acquires a site, builds houses and sells off each plot with house to an individual purchaser. Secondly, where, as in the case of the Goldbergs, the owner of a single property sells off a piece - maybe to a neighbour for use as extra garden or maybe as a plot for erection of a new house.

In the first case the client-purchaser will be buying a standardised product, with a standardised title. The developer's solicitor is likely to supply the individual plot purchaser's solicitor with a bundle of documents including (where the title is registered):

- Draft contract with plan.

- Standard form of transfer. The contract will normally contain a provision that the transfer is to be in the form supplied by the vendor.

- Copy of the planning permission and building regulation approval.

- Copies of the agreements and bonds relating to the drains and roads.

- The NHBC documentation.

- Local searches and Additional Enquiries of the local authority.

- Office copies of entries on the register. As to title plan, see para.7.11(b)(i).

Another situation which should be mentioned, with its own features, is the sale-off of flats by a developer, either purpose built or converted out of a larger, older building. Such flats will undoubtedly be sold off on long leases rather than freehold. The title aspects of leasehold are looked at in Chapter 17. Apart form that, most of what is said below is equally applicable.

The residential estate development is likely to have the following features of significance to the conveyancer. Each of them is equally capable of applying to an isolated sale-off such as that of the Goldbergs:

(a) The creation of a new road, drainage, power and water supply systems, laid over what is, initially at least, the private land of the developer. Each plot owner needs the guarantee of access to this system by suitable public or private rights.

(b) The imposition of a common set of restrictions (restrictive covenants) on the purchaser of each plot, dictating to a greater or lesser extent the limits of behaviour of each plot owner. In law this may involve the creation of a building scheme - a common set of restrictions enforceable by each plot owner against the owner of each other plot.

(c) The erection of new houses by the developer and a concern for guarantees as to workmanship and materials.

(d) The need to comply with planning law.

(e) Matters due to the severance of the legal title; namely

(i)   The retention of the title documents by the vendor (para.14.9.2).

(ii)   The creation of easements by implied grant or reservation.

(iii)   The demarcation of boundaries and the ownership and maintenance of boundary features.

(iv)   The need to provide an accurate plan based description which can be transposed to identify on the ground the property sold and that retained. (On this see paras.5.4 and 7.11(b)).

(v)   The release of the part sold from subsisting mortgages.

This Chapter focuses on a sale of part. But many of the principles discussed are of more general application.

Whenever acting for a purchaser of a property which has been divided from a larger property in the recent past or which is part of a recently developed estate, it may be necessary to check that the sale-off transaction was handled correctly by the then purchaser's solicitor, not leaving matters adverse to the interests of your client. Indeed, on any purchase, any of the above matters may be of relevance in the particular circumstances and need special attention. For example, if the house being purchased was recently built it will be necessary to check for planning and building regulation approval and NHBC guarantee etc. Again, wherever the house being purchased does not have access directly onto a public highway with services leading directly into the highway, it will be necessary that the property has the benefit of all the necessary easements. If your client wants to change the use of the property from, say, residence to a shop, you will have to be prepared to advise on planning law and check the title for restrictive covenants adverse to such a change. And so on.

It seems convenient to deal with the above matters under the following heads:

CREATION OF NEW EASEMENTS AND COVENANTS

6.4   It is important to distinguish between:

(a) existing rights which may be appurtenant to or a burden on the property before sale. Here, in the contract and conveyance, it is simply a question of passing on to the purchaser the benefit or burden of the already existing right. There is no scope for altering the content of them. (See paras.5.6, 7.11(c)).

(b) The creation of new rights. The effect of a sale of part is to bring into existence two separately owned properties with the opportunity to create new easements and covenants between vendor and purchaser as owners respectively of the retained land and the part sold.

Taking instructions

You do not want to discuss the subtleties of Thesiger L.J.'s judgment in *Wheeldon v. Burrows*[2] with the client; nor tell jokes about pleasure grounds in Weston-super-Mare.[3] What you must do is to get clear instructions from her as to what rights she has agreed to grant the purchaser and what to reserve to herself; prompting her if necessary about matters that she may not have thought of.

6.4.1

Possible rights

Attention should be paid to the following principles:

6.4.2

(a) New easements and covenants may consist of burdens imposed on the part sold for the benefit of the part retained; or burdens on the part retained for the benefit of the part sold.

(b) It may be possible to give effect to the intentions of the parties by the creation of one or more of the following proprietary rights - that is rights capable of binding successors to the burdened land and enforceable by successors to the benefited land: easements, profits, restrictive covenants, proprietary estoppel, rentcharges and leases.

A lease is different from the others in that it gives possession of the owner's property to the lessee for a longer or shorter period. Leases are dealt with in Chapter 17.

Profits - the right to take some part of the produce of the soil or of the soil itself from a person's land - are probably not often encountered in practice today; except perhaps in the context of fishing and other sporting rights. Even here one is more likely to be creating pure contract, rather than property, rights. One feature of profits to note is that (unlike easements) they can exist in gross, that is belonging to a person and her assigns and not appurtenant to any dominant property.

Rentcharges. The only type of rentcharge (a periodic payment charged on freehold and not to be confused with rent service), relevant in the present context, which can still be created is the 'estate

---

2   (1879) 12 Ch.D.31.
3   See *Re Ellenborough Park* [1956] 1 Ch. 131, for the case without the jokes.

rentcharge' - that is, one intended to secure the performance of positive covenants or one intended to contribute to the cost of services and repairs to a property. In practice the estate rentcharge is not used to support the few positive covenants encountered on the sale of freehold houses. These are dealt with in different ways (see below). Flats, where the enforcement of positive covenants is crucial, are normally dealt with as leasehold where the problem does not arise. Rentcharges will not therefore be dealt with further.

Proprietary estoppel is not often used as a formal conveyancing device - though it could be and it is important in the context of informal arrangements relating to land where formal requirements have not been satisfied.

Positive covenants are in the nature of bastard, proprietary rights. The benefit can be made to run provided certain conditions are satisfied (that it touches and concerns the land intended to be benefited, etc). The burden cannot be made to run as such; though various devices are available to conveyancers to more or less achieve the same result (below).

Easements and restrictive covenants are dealt with below.

Any other obligation agreed between the parties in relation to the use of land can only be created in contract as a matter of personal obligation, that is as a licence, not enforceable by or against successive owners of their respective properties (though the benefit of a contractual obligation can normally be expressly assigned). Personal, contractual or non-contractual (bare licence) obligations may arise between the parties either because they did not want to create property rights or because their agreement does not fulfil the law's requirements to create an easement, restrictive covenant or other proprietary right. If the parties only intend to create personal rights (licences) this intention should be made clear. For example:

> 'The vendor hereby gives the purchaser a personal licence to park her car in the driveway of the vendor's retained land paying therefore £1 per week, such licence to be enforceable only between the vendor and purchaser personally and to be terminable by the vendor or purchaser on giving one month's notice.'

Such an agreement does not affect the title in any way; and it is generally best to have it in a separate agreement, outside the contract of sale of the property.

In drafting the contract of sale, the point to bear in mind is that without care proprietary obligations may be created when only personal ones were intended; and only personal ones when proprietary ones were intended.

Question Suppose that V sells part (a greengrocer's shop) of her property to P. The conveyance contains a provision as follows:

> 'V so as to bind the retained land and the owners for the time being thereof grants to P and the owners for the time being of the land hereby conveyed the right to use the access across the retained land for all purposes connected with the business carried on on the land hereby conveyed subject to the exigencies of the business carried on on the retained land.'

Would this, or could it if modified, create an easement in favour of P's land? Note: Consider *Green v. Ashco Horticulturist Ltd.*[4]

Question Suppose V is selling a freehold farm cottage to P. V has agreed that P and subsequent owners of the cottage shall be allowed to park in the farmyard.

Could this right be granted as an easement? Note: *Newman v. Jones* (1982) unreported; see Maudsley & Burns, *Land Law: Cases and Materials* (5th ed.), 573. Draw an imaginary plan of the scenario. Draft a suitable easement, if you think such possible; if not, draft a suitable licence agreement. What further instructions might you need from the vendor-client before drafting?

What follows next is more specifically directed at easements and covenants.

Drafting easements

The contract determines what goes into the conveyance. Preferably, the contract should include the exact wording which is to be drafted into the conveyance. Particular care should be taken with the following matters:

(a) Identifying both the dominant and servient properties.

(b) Making clear the intention that the easements are intended to be attached to and run with both the servient and dominant properties.

(c) Making clear the ambit of the intended right.

Taking each of these in turn:

(a) The identity of the property. The retained land, like the land sold, must be properly identified in the contract (and consequentially the conveyance/transfer) for example by being referred to in the contract as 'shown edged in green on the annexed plan'. If the easement affects less than the whole land sold or retained, the land affected must be clearly

6.4.3

---

4   [1966] 1 W.L.R. 889.

identified; for example, the exact boundaries of any right of way granted across the retained land.

The courts may be able to gather the identity of the land intended to be benefitted by construing the conveyance in the light of the circumstances surrounding it at the time of execution – the factual matrix.[5] With proper drafting this sort of thing should not be necessary.

In *Scott v. Martin*[6] the issue was the width of a private road over which the plaintiff had been granted an express right of way (i.e. the extent of the servient land over which the easement was exercisable). The conveyance contained the following parcels clause (i.e. description of the property being conveyed in fee simple):

> 'All that piece of land situate in and having a frontage on the west to a private road called Allerton Garth at Alwalton in the County of Huntingdon which said property forms part of Ordnance Survey Number 38 and is for the sake of more particular identification only and not of limitation delineated on the plan annexed hereto and thereon edged red Together With a right of way at all times and for all purposes over and along the said private road leading into Church Lane.'

The plaintiff contended that the road in this description meant and the right of way extended to include the three feet wide verges on either side of the carriageway. The defendant as owner of the soil had sold and conveyed part of one of the verges to the second defendant who had enclosed it. The verbal description of the road (given above) did not refer to the delineation of the road on the plan. The plan did in fact show the road edged with two continuous black lines with two broken black lines about three feet (when scaled up) inside these. The court held that the plan, although for the purposes of identification only, was part of the conveyance and could be referred to clear up any ambiguity in the verbal description; though not to contradict the verbal description. It further held that the road in the verbal description meant the same as the road shown on the plan; that this included the verges; that therefore the right of way extended to include the verges as claimed by the plaintiff. The court also held that the planning permission for the development could be referred to as part of the matrix existing at the time the conveyance was executed. The documentation accompanying this permission supported the decision reached.

Question Re-draft the above clause, using a plan if necessary, to eliminate the ambiguity.

---

5   See *Johnstone v. Holdway* [1963] 1 Q.B. 601; it is not clear whether the judge was applying this recognised aid to the construction of documents or was looking totally outside the conveyance to discover the identity of the dominant property. The distinction is in any case a blurred one.

6   [1987] 1 W.L.R. 841.

(b) Intention that the easements should run as proprietary rights. A new easement to be granted in favour of the purchaser might be drafted into the contract as follows:

> 'The Property [which will have been described elsewhere in the contract] is sold Together with a right for the purchaser and her successors in title and those authorised by her to pass and repass with or without vehicles at all reasonable times over and along the part of the driveway coloured yellow on the plan annexed hereto for the purpose of gaining access to the property hereby agreed to be sold the purchaser and her successors in title contributing one half of the costs of maintenance of the said driveway.'[7]

If the same right were being created in favour of the vendor's retained land, the clause might be modified as follows:

> 'There will be excepted and reserved to the vendor out of the property hereby agreed to be sold a right for the vendor and her successors in title and those authorised by her to pass and repass with or without vehicles at all reasonable times over and along the part of the driveway coloured yellow on the plan annexed hereto for the purpose of gaining access to the property to be retained by the vendor and edged in green on the said plan the vendor and her successors in title contributing one half of the costs of maintenance of the said driveway.'

The following points should be noted.

First, the precedents give the exact wording to be incorporated into the conveyance. Secondly, they clearly create easements not licences (and the right being created fulfils all the legal requirements for it to be capable of existing as an easement). The inclusion of the right as being sold 'Together With' the property shows that it is part of what is to be conveyed in fee simple. Similarly, the formula 'Excepting and Reserving' the right shows that the right is being kept back from the fee simple that is to be conveyed as part of the fee simple retained by the vendor. The intention to create a fee simple easement is further indicated by granting it to 'the Purchaser and her successors in title', i.e. to the successive owners of the dominant land.

Thirdly, this precedent is an example of the common case where the parties want to impose positive obligations permanently binding on the owner of one of the properties – i.e. here, to contribute to the cost of repair and maintenance of the subject matter of the right, in this case the driveway. It has been done here, and this is the standard way of doing it, by relying on the principle in *Halsall v. Brizell*[8] – that is that the person who enjoys the benefit of a right (here the easement of way) must

---

[7]   See Encyclopedia of Forms and Precedents, vol.35, para.587; Form 61.

[8]   [1957] Ch.169.

comply with the obligation (here to contribute to the cost of maintenace) which is made a condition of its enjoyment.

(c) The ambit of the right. The above precedent shows the need to spell out the precise ambit of the right being created in accordance with the particular wishes of the parties. In this context thought may have to be given to a possible change of use of the dominant property. What if Mrs Singh does open a doctor's surgery? Is it envisaged that the access up the drive will embrace the consequential increase in the amount of traffic? As always, where the parties have not made a matter express and clear, where there is a dispute, the courts will have to construe whatever terms have been put in the document creating the right.

In *Rosling v. Pinnegar*[9] the appellant bought a house and land with the benefit of a right of way (an easement) along a private lane to the house, expressly created in an earlier conveyance, 'at all times and for all purposes' 'in common with the Purchaser and all other persons entitled thereto'. The house was derelict when purchased by the appellant. He renovated it and opened it to the public causing a substantial increase in traffic flow along the lane. It was held that the change in use of the house, in that it had been opened to the public causing increased traffic, did not amount to breach of the grant; but that the provision that its use was to be enjoyed with others 'entitled thereto' implied that user should not be such as to interfere with that user by others. On this basis the user was excessive and restrained by injunction.

The following are some of the matters that may need to be agreed and drafted into the contract and conveyance on, by way of example, the grant of a new easement of drainage. They may be dealt with in defining the easement, as ancillary rights attached to it, or as conditions of its exercise:

- Defining the exact route of the drain on the plan, especially if it is a new one to be constructed by the purchaser.

- If it is a new drain, the right to enter the servient land to construct as well as the right thereafter to use the drain.

- Whether use is to be exclusive or shared with, e.g. the dominant owner.

- Who is to be liable to maintain or contribute to the cost of maintenance and repair?

- Right of access onto the servient property to inspect and maintain, doing as little damage as possible and making good any damage done. Whether such right of access should be restricted in any way, e.g. to certain times except in emergency.

---

9   (1986) 54 P.& C.R. 124.

- If it is a new drain, whether it should be required to be constructed within a certain period of time.

Implied easements

On a sale of part, easements may arise by implied grant in favour of the purchaser's land under the rule in *Wheeldon v. Burrows*, under s.62 of the Law of Property Act 1925, as easements of necessity or as intended easements. They may, unusually, arise by implied reservation in favour of the vendor's retained land as easements of necessity or intended easements.

6.4.4

If the contract is silent on the matter the above rules will apply. This is not normally sensible. If disputes subsequently arise they will have to be resolved by evidence, from outside the deed, of events which become increasingly remote in time and ambivalent.

The Standard Conditions (Standard Condition 3.3.) provide:

'3.3.2. The buyer will have no right of light or air over the retained land, but otherwise the seller and the buyer will each have the rights over the land of the other which they would have had if they were two separate buyers to whom the seller had made simultaneous transfers of the property and the retained land.'

The effect of this is that the purchaser will get no implied easement of light or air; but subject to that, both vendor and purchaser will be able to claim under any of the heads of implied easements. This may be fairer to the vendor; and it may be useful where the parties have not addressed their minds to the issue. But it really just compounds the problem of proof and uncertainty. And it should be added that such easements would not be identified by entry on the register of title when the title is registered.

There are two main alternatives. First, special conditions could be drafted to create expressly agreed easements, leaving Standard Condition 3.3. as a long-stop to govern anything which has not been expressly provided for. Secondly, and perhaps preferably, the creation of implied easements could be excluded altogether; so that both vendor and purchaser could get only those easements expressly agreed in the contract. Note that this second course requires a special condition both excluding Standard Condition 3.3. and providing for a declaration in the conveyance negativing the creation of any implied easements in favour of either vendor or purchaser. It is not enough just to exclude Standard Condition 3.3. This would simply restore the common law position.

Question Draft such a special condition.

Drafting restrictive covenants

6.4.5   Whereas easements (and profits) are granted together with the fee simple or reserved out of the fee simple conveyed, restrictive covenants arise out of a covenant – that is an agreement by deed – between the parties. This agreement, if it satisfies the necessary legal requirements, is then recognised as having the same proprietorial effect as an easement; and the benefit and burden will run with both properties.

It is therefore necessary that the conveyance/transfer expresses the covenant in the form of an agreement between the vendor and purchaser, distinct from the parcels clause.

In general, what has been said about drafting easements applies equally here. The dominant and servient properties must be clearly identified; subject to ss.78 and 79 of the Law of Property Act 1925 (below), the intention to annex the benefit and burden to the dominant and servient properties respectively must be shown; and the precise content of the obligation clearly defined. Again, it is preferable if the contract contains the exact formulation to be used in the conveyance. As with easements, it may be convenient, especially if a number of covenants or easements are being created, to place them at the end of the document in schedules which will be incorporated into the body of the document by reference. It should be remembered (from the study of land law) that the covenant should be annexed to the whole and every part of the dominant property. If this is not done it will not normally be enforceable by a subsequent purchaser of only part of it.

A standard introductory clause might be as follows:

'The Purchaser shall in the transfer [or conveyance] enter into the following covenant with the Vendor:

"The Purchaser covenants with the Vendor to the intent that the burden of the covenant will run with the land and bind the Property hereby transferred [or conveyed] and every part of it and that the benefit of the covenant will be annexed to and run with the Retained land more particularly identified on the said plan annexed hereto and thereon edged green and every part of it to observe and perform the stipulations set out in the second schedule hereto." '

The restrictive stipulations can then be set out in the schedule in accordance with the parties' agreement. For example:

'1. Not more than one house shall be built on the property hereby conveyed, such house to be used as a private dwelling house in the occupation of one family only or as the professional residence for a one doctor of medicine.'

Even if the intention to annex the benefit to the land of the covenantee and the burden to that of the covenantor is not expressed, it may be implied under ss.78 and 79 of the Law of Property Act 1925. Section 79 provides that a covenant relating to land of the covenantor shall, unless a contrary intention is expressed, be deemed to be made by the covenantor on behalf of himself, his successors in title and the persons deriving title under him or them. Successors in title is stated to include, in the case of restrictive covenants, the owners and occupiers for the time being of the land of the covenantor.

Section 78 applies the same principle to the benefit of the covenant.

Nevertheless, these sections can only help if the dominant and servient properties - to which the covenant relates - are identified as such in the documents.[10] It is difficult not to identify the servient property when drafting a covenant restricting its use; it is quite easy to omit all mention of the dominant property. In spite of ss.78 and 79, it is unwise not to use express words of annexation and in doing so identify the dominant property.[11]

The difficulty of framing covenants to cover all eventualities is illustrated by the case of *C. & G. Homes Ltd. v. Secretary of State for Health*[12]: The district health authority, acting on behalf of the Secretary of State, acquired two houses to provide, in the words of Nourse L.J. (struggling for an expression other than 'private dwelling house'), 'small NHS homes for people who have suffered from mental disability'.

Each house was subject to the following covenants whereby the Secretary of State was:

'not to cause or permit or suffer to be done in or upon the property any act or thing which may be or become a nuisance, annoyance, danger or detriment to the [plaintiff] or owners or occupiers for the time being of other parts of the estate' and 'not at any time within 10 years of the date [of the transfer] to carry on or from the property any trade business or manufacture whatsoever with the exception of [certain specified professions] and not to use the dwelling house for any purpose or purposes other than those incidental to the enjoyment of a private dwelling house.'

---

[10] See *Federated Homes Ltd. v. Mill Lodge Properties Ltd.* [1980] 1 W.L.R. 594. If the annexation fails for this reason, it may still be possible for the covenantee expressly to assign the benefit to a purchaser when she comes to sell the land; see *Newton Abbott Co-operative Society Ltd. v. Williams and Treadgold Ltd.* [1952] Ch. 286.

[11] Especially as there is still a view that even if s.78 does effect statutory annexation of the benefit, s.79 (which is not worded exactly the same) does not.

[12] [1991] 2 W.L.R. 715.

The issue was whether the use mentioned above was in breach of this covenant. It was held by the Court of Appeal, first, that this use was not use as a 'private dwelling house'. (Perhaps 'less-than-public dwelling house' would have been the occupants' natural choice of expression to define their position!) It was therefore in breach of the covenant.

Secondly, the court decided, even more surprisingly perhaps, that the effect of the use on the marketability of the plaintiff company's neighbouring property was not a 'detriment' within the meaning of the covenant, since it was a financial loss suffered in the exploitation of the retained land, but dissociated from the enjoyment of it.[13] Surprising, because one of the central purposes of restrictive covenants has always been to maintain the amenities and thereby the financial value of the dominant property.

The point about the covenant in the present context is that it shows that even the most detailed drafting can leave areas of uncertainty of meaning and application.

PLANNING

6.5   Planning law is a major and important topic. It may affect the client whether buying a new house on a residential estate or just building an extension to a house already owned.

It is not possible here to give more than a brief outline. Details of the standard works are included in the Bibliography (Appendix 8).

A prospective purchaser may be concerned with two main questions:

(a) Has there been any building, change of use or other work on the property which will render the purchaser liable to enforcement proceedings under planning law?

(b) Will planning law interfere with purchaser's intended use of the property or any building work that she may wish to carry out?

The starting point, in relation to both these questions, is that any development requires express planning permission. 'Development' is defined as 'the carrying out of building, engineering, mining or other operations in, on, over or under land, or the making of any material change in the use of any buildings or other land'.[14]

This definition contains two basic elements which should not be confused: building and other operations; and material change of use.

---

[13] *Per* Nourse L.J., p.724.

[14] Town and Country Planning Act 1990, s.55.

The definition is extremely wide. 'Building operations' is expressed to include, *inter alia*, demolition of buildings, and also 'other operations normally undertaken by a person carrying on business as a builder'.[15] If it were not for the General Development Order (below) and other exemptions, even building a garden wall would require express application for planning permission (and in some circumstances it does).

Some activities are manifestly development: building a house; changing a house into a shop. Whether a change of use is material is a question of fact and degree. Thus, in one case, the installation of an egg-vending machine on farmland adjacent to a lay-by on the public road was held to be a material change of use.[16] It is expressly provided that changing the use of a single dwelling house to two or more is development and so does require express permission.

Some activities do not need express permission, either because they are exempt or deemed by statute not to constitute development. The most important in the present case are:

(a) Permitted development. The Town and Country Planning General Development Order 1988 (S.I. 1988 No. 1813.) (commonly referred to as the GDO) specifies various classes of development which may be undertaken on land without the need to apply to the local planning authority for express permission. Such development is known as permitted development. Schedule 2 to the Order is divided into 28 Parts each containing a number of classes of permitted development which must comply with the conditions stated in that Class. The most important Parts in the present context are Part 1 ('Development within the curtilage of a dwelling-house) and Part 2 ('Minor operations'). It is worth setting these out in full:

---

[15] Ibid, s.55 (1A).
[16] *Hidderley v. Warwickshire C.C.* (1963) 14 P.& C.R. 134.

SCHEDULE 2

PART 1

DEVELOPMENT WITHIN THE CURTILAGE OF A
DWELLINGHOUSE

CLASS A

Permitted
Development

A. The enlargement, improvement or other
alteration of a dwellinghouse.

Development
Not
Permitted

A.1 Development is not permitted by Class A if –

(a) the cubic content of the resulting building
would exceed the cubic content of the
original dwellinghouse –

(i) in the case of a terrace house or in the
case of a dwellinghouse on article 1(5) land,
by more than 50 cubic metres or 10%,
whichever is the greater;

(ii) in any other case, by more than 70
cubic metres or 15%, whichever is the
greater;

(iii) in any case, by more than 115 cubic
metres;

[(b) the part of the building enlarged,
improved or altered would exceed in height
the height part of the roof of the original
dwellinghouse;]

[(c) the part of the building enlarged,
improved or altered would be nearer to any
highway which bounds the curtilage of the
dwellinghouse than –

(i) the part of the original dwellinghouse
nearest to that highway; or

(ii) 20 metres,

whichever is nearest to that highway;]

[(d) the part of the building enlarged,
improved or altered would be within 2 metres
of the boundary of the curtilage of the
dwellinghouse and would exceed 4 metres in
height;]

(e) the total area of ground covered by
buildings within the curtilage (other than the
original dwellinghouse) would exceed 50% of
the total area of the curtilage (excluding the
ground area of the original dwellinghouse);

(f) it would consist of or include the
installation, alteration or replacement of a
satellite antenna;

(g) it would consist of or include an erection
of a building within the curtilage of a listed

building; or

(h) it would consist of or include an alteration to any part of the roof.

A.2 In the case of a dwellinghouse on any article 1(5) land, development is not permitted by Class A if it would consist of or include the cladding of any part of the exterior with stone, artificial stone, timber, plastic or tiles to an existing external surface.

Interpretation of Class A

A.3 For the purposes of Class A −

(a) the erection within the curtilage of a dwellinghouse of any building with a cubic content greater than 10 cubic metres shall be treated as the enlargement of the dwellinghouse for all purposes including calculating content where −

(i) the dwellinghouse is on article 1(5) land, or

(ii) in any other case, any part of that building [would be] within 5 metres of any part of the dwellinghouse;

(b) where any part of the dwellinghouse would be within 5 metres of an existing building within the same curtilage, that building shall be treated as forming part of the resulting building for the purposes of calculating the cubic content.

CLASS B

Permitted Development

B. The enlargement of a dwellinghouse consisting of an addition or alteration to its roof.

Development Not Permitted

B.1 Development is not permitted by Class B if −

(a) any part of the dwellinghouse would, as a result of the works, exceed the height of the highest part of the existing roof;

(b) any part of the dwellinghouse would, as a result of the works, extend beyond the plane of any existing roof slope which fronts any highway;

(c) it would increase the cubic content of the dwellinghouse by more than 40 cubic metres, in the case of a terrace house, or 50 cubic metres in any other case;

(d) the cubic content of the resulting

building would exceed the cubic content of the original dwellinghouse –

> (i) in the case of a terrace house by more than 50 cubic metres or 10%, whichever is the greater;
>
> (ii) in any other case, by more than 70 [cubic] metres or 15%, whichever is the greater, or
>
> (iii) in any case, by more than 115 cubic metres; or

[(e) the dwellinghouse is on article 1(5) land.

CLASS C

Permitted Development

C. Any other alteration to the roof of a dwellinghouse.

Development Not Permitted

C.1 Development is not permitted by Class C if it would result in a material alteration to the shape of the dwellinghouse.

CLASS D

Permitted Development

D. The erection or construction of a porch outside any external door of a dwellinghouse.

Development Not Permitted

D.1 Development is not permitted by Class D if –

(a) the ground area (measured externally) of the structure would exceed 3 square metres;

(b) any part of the structure would be more than 3 metres above ground level;

(c) any part of the structure would be within 2 metres of any boundary of the curtilage of the dwellinghouse with a highway.

CLASS E

Permitted Development

E. The provision with a curtilage of a dwellinghouse of any building or enclosure, swimming or other pool required for a purpose incidental to the enjoyment of the dwellinghouse [as such], or the maintenance, improvement or other alteration of such a building or enclosure.

Development Not Permitted

E.1 Development is not permitted by Class E if –

(a) it relates to a dwelling or satellite antenna;

(b) any part of the building or enclosure to be constructed or provided would be nearer to any highway which bounds the curtilage than –

(i) the part of the original dwellinghouse nearest to that highway, or

(ii) 20 metres,

[(c) where the building to be constructed or provided would have a cubic content greater than 10 cubic metres, any part of it would be within 5 metres of any part of the dwellinghouse;

(d) the height of that building or enclosure would exceed –

(i) 4 metres, in the case of a building with a ridged roof; or

(ii) 3 metres, in any other case;

[(e) the total area of the ground covered by buildings or enclosures within the curtilage (other than the original dwellinghouse) would exceed 50% of the total area of the curtilage (excluding the ground area of the original dwellinghouse); or

(f) in the case of any article 1(5) land or land within the curtilage of a listed building, it would consist of the provision, alteration or improvement of a building with a cubic content greater than 10 cubic metres.

Interpretation of Class E	E.2 For the purpose of Class E "purpose incidental to the enjoyment of the dwellinghouse (as such)" includes the keeping of poultry, bees, pet animals, birds or other livestock for the domestic needs or personal enjoyment of the occupants of the dwellinghouse.
CLASS F Permitted Development	F. The provision within the curtilage of a dwellinghouse of a hard surface for any purpose incidental to the enjoyment of the dwellinghouse [as such].
CLASS G Permitted Development	G. The erection or provision within the curtilage of a dwellinghouse of a container for the storage of oil for domestic heating.
Development Not Permitted	G.1 Development is not permitted by Class G if – (a) the capacity of the container would exceed 3500 litres; (b) any part of the container would be more than 3 metres above ground level; or (c) an part of the container would be nearer to any highway that bounds the curtilage than –

(i) the part of the building nearest to that highway, or

(ii) 20 metres,

whichever is nearer to the highway.

CLASS H
Permitted Development

H. The installation, alteration or replacement of a satellite antenna on a dwellinghouse or within the curtilage of a dwellinghouse.

Development Not Permitted

[H.1 Development is not permitted by Class H if—

(a) the size of the antenna (excluding any projecting feed element, reinforcing rim, mounting and brackets) when measured in any dimension would exceed —

(i) 45 centimetres in the case of an antenna to be installed on the chimney;

(ii) 90 centimetres in the case of an antenna to be installed on or within the curtilage on article 1(7) land other than on a chimney;

(iii) 70 centimetres in any other case;

(b) the highest part of an antenna to be installed on a roof or a chimney would, when installed, exceed in height —

(i) in the case of an antenna to be installed on a roof, the highest part of the roof;

(ii) in the case of an antenna to be installed on a chimney, the highest part of the chimney;

(c) there is any other satellite antenna on the dwellinghouse or within its curtilage;

(d) in the case of article 1(5) land, it would consist of the installation of an antenna —

(i) on a chimney;

(ii) on a building which exceeds 15 metres in height;

(iii) on a wall or roof slope which fronts a waterway in the Broads or a highway elsewhere.]

[Condition H.2 Development is permitted by Class H subject to the following conditions —

(a) an antenna installed on a building shall, so far as practicable, be sited so as to minimise its effect on the external appearance to the building;

(b) an antenna no longer needed for the reception or transmission of microwave radio energy shall be removed as soon as reasonably practicable.]

Interpretation
of Part I

I. For the purposes of Part I –

"resulting building" means the dwellinghouse as enlarged, improved or altered, taking into account any enlargement, improvement or alteration to the original dwellinghouse, whether permitted by this Part or not.

PART 2

MINOR OPERATIONS

CLASS A

Permitted
Development

A. The erection, construction, maintenance, improvement or alteration of a gate, fence or wall or other means of enclosure.

Development
Not
Permitted

A.1 Development is not permitted by Class A if –

(a) the height of any gate, fence, wall, or means of enclosure erected or constructed adjacent to a highway used by vehicular traffic would, after the carrying out of the development, exceed one metre above ground level;

(b) the height of any other gate, fence, wall or means of enclosure erected or constructed would exceed two metres above ground level;

(c) the height of any gate, fence, wall or other means of enclosure maintained, improved or altered would, as a result of the development, exceed its former height or the height referred to in sub-paragraph (a) or (b) as the height appropriate to it if erected or constructed, which is the greater; or

(d) it would involve development within the curtilage of, or to a gate, fence, wall or other means of enclosure, surrounding, a listed building.

CLASS B

Permitted
Development

B. The formation, laying out and construction of a means of access to a highway which is not a trunk road or a classified road, where that access is required in connection with development permitted by any class in this Schedule (other than by Class A of this Part).

CLASS C

Permitted
Development

C. The painting of the exterior of any building or
work.

Development
Not
Permitted

C.1 Development is not permitted by Class C
where the painting is for the purpose of
advertisement, announcement, or direction.

Interpretation

C.2 In Class C "painting" includes any
application of colour.

Article 1(5) land, that is the areas defined in Article 1(5) of the Order, includes the National Parks, areas of outstanding natural beauty, the Broads and conservation areas. In these areas the development permitted under Schedule 2 of the Order is in some cases restricted.

Under Article 4 of the Order, if either the Secretary of State or the local planning authority is satisfied that it is not expedient that development in Schedule 2 should be carried out without express permission, she or it can give a direction (known as an Article 4 Direction) excluding the operation of the Order for the specified area. Orders are particularly likely to be made in conservation areas.

(b) Change of use within the same use class. The Town and Country (Use Classes) Order 1987 made under what is now the Town and Country Planning Act 1990, ss.55(2)(f) and 333(3) (S.I. 1987 No. 764). specifies 15 different classes of use. A change of use within one of the classes is deemed not to be development and so does not require permission. For example, the following are in the same class: the use of premises to provide (a) financial services, or (b) professional services (other than health or medical services) or (c) any other service (including use as a betting shop) appropriate to a shopping area provided, in all three cases, the services are provided principally to visiting members of the public. Thus an accountant could become a bookmaker; but not a barrister without having to get new planning permission for the change of use of the premises!

(c) By s.55(2) of the 1990 Act 'the use of any building or other land within the curtilage of a dwelling-house for any purpose incidental to the enjoyment of the dwelling-house as such' is deemed not to be development. Note that this exemption relates only to use; not to any building work which would have to be considered separately. Thus, by way of example, an existing outhouse could be converted into extra sleeping accommodation for the family. But to park a commercial vehicle used for business purposes in the house drive would not be within the exemption, unless the change could be said to be not material. Again, it is a question of fact and degree whether a hobby carried out at home (whether or not involving a commercial element) comes within the provision - i.e. is incidental to the enjoyment of the dwelling-house as such. Thus, the use of outbuildings to breed dogs and the use of a kitchen to prepare sandwiches and salads for local firms have been held not to be within the exemption.

(d) By s.55(2)(a) of the 1990 Act, the carrying out of works for the maintenance, improvement or alteration of a building which either only affect the interior or do not materially affect the external appearance, are deemed not to be development and so do not require permission.

(e) Simplified planning zones: A simplified planning zone is an area designated as such by the local planning authority and made subject to a scheme. The scheme will specify types of development within the area which can be carried out without express permission. The sort of area envisaged for the scheme is the disused industrial estate or where a specific area has been designated in the development plan as a new industrial estate.

Where there is doubt whether express permission is needed for a particular proposal, an application can be made to the local planning authority under s.192 of the 1990 Act for a certificate of lawfulness.

Planning permission

The London Boroughs and metropolitan district councils are the planning authorities for their areas. Outside these areas planning control is normally exercised by the district council with a few matters being reserved to the county council; though all applications are addressed to the district council in the first place.

6.5.1

The Lake District has a Special Planning Board, and the Peak District a Joint Planning Board, exercising control in those areas.

In certain cities Urban Development Corporations have taken over from the local authorities as the planning authorities.

Application for permission has to be made to the relevant authority. Application may be made for full permission in the first place; or for outline permission which commits the authority to allow the development but subject to final approval of specified, reserved matters such as road access, landscaping.

If full permission is granted, the development must, unless it states otherwise, be commenced within five years. In the case of outline permission, application for full permission must be made within three years of the outline permission; and the development itself must begin within five years of the outline permission, or, if later, within two years of the full permission. These time limits are important. Development not complying with them will be unauthorised.

Permission may be granted unconditionally (very unusual), subject to conditions or refused. Any failure to comply with a condition makes the development liable to enforcement proceedings.

There is a right of appeal against refusal or the imposition of conditions to the Secretary of State. The appeal is in effect a reconsideration of the application. Subject to this, a decision can only be challenged, in court, on the limited grounds of *ultra vires* - i.e. that the minister or the local planning authority has not taken into account all the relevant factors or has taken irrelevant factors into account or has been in breach of the rules of natural justice.

Whether or not express permission will be granted for any particular proposal cannot be said with certainty until an application has been made and decided. A guide to the likely outcome of any proposal can be gained from the development plan and from informal approach to the planning officers of the authority. Since 1947 local planning authorities have been under a duty to prepare development plans for their areas. These are the formalisation of their policies for the future development of the area. In general a development plan consists of two elements: First, a structure plan, being essentially a written statement. In effect this is intended as the strategic policy for the area taking into account its physical, demographic and economic characteristics. Secondly, a local plan. This sets out within the framework of the structure plan, the detailed policies for an area showing how the overall strategy is intended to be implemented on the ground.

Thus a local plan should indicate whether the area of a particular proposal is intended for business, residential use, etc.

A development plan may be 'old style' prepared under provisions contained originally in the Town and Country Planning Act 1947; or 'new style' prepared under provisions contained originally in the 1968 Town and Country Planing Act. In the case of metropolitan districts and the London Boroughs there may be a unitary plan prepared under the Local Government Act 1985. The unitary plan is intended to replace and combine the functions of the structure and the local plans.

In addition the local planning authority may have prepared non-statutory planning and development proposals for the area.

It has to be stressed that all such plans, statutory or otherwise, can be altered; and even without alteration there is no guarantee that permission will be granted merely because the proposal is in accord with the relevant plans.

Initial information on relevant development plans will be given in replies to Additional Enquiries of the local authority.

Enforcement of planning law

6.5.2   Any development without necessary planning permission or in breach of condition attached to a permission is a contravention of planning law.

Where the local planning authority suspects that there may have been a breach, it can serve a planning contravention notice under ss.171 (C) and

(D) of the 1990 Act [17] on the owner or occupier, requiring information which will enable it to decide whether there has been a breach.

Where it decides that there has been a breach it can serve an enforcement notice on the owners and occupiers of the land. The notice will detail the breach considered to have occurred; the steps required to remedy it; and the time within which those steps must be taken. Under s.172 of the 1990 Act, the local planning authority will only issue a notice where it is expedient to do so having regard to the provisions of the development plan and any other material considerations.

An appeal against an enforcement notice is possible to the Secretary of State on the grounds, *inter alia*, that planning permission ought to be granted. The development can thus be authorised retrospectively.

The authority can, if it considers it expedient, issue a stop notice under s.183 of the 1990 Act, with or after service of the enforcement notice. The purpose of a stop notice is to bring the allegedly unlawful activity to a halt during the period until the enforcement notice takes effect. Without this the developer could continue building and, by appealing, etc. delay the taking effect of the enforcement notice, hoping that retrospective permission would ultimately be given.

Where the breach consists solely of non-compliance with a condition attached to a permission, the authority can, under s.187A of the 1990 Act[18], issue a breach of condition notice specifying the steps required to comply with the breached condition. There is no appeal against such a notice.

Failure to comply with a planning contravention notice, an enforcement notice, a breach of condition notice or a stop notice is a criminal offence.

Where the breach consists of carrying out building, engineering, mining or other operations without permission, enforcement action can only be taken within four years from the completion of the operation. The same time limit applies where the breach is the change of use of any building to use as a single dwelling. In the case of any other breach enforcement action must be taken within 10 years of the date of the breach.

Where there has been any sort of building work on the property (whether a new house or the extension of the dog kennel!) or change of use, the purchaser will need to be satisfied that either the development was in accordance with planning law (by production of the permission); or that planning permission was not needed; or that the time limit for

---

[17]   Inserted by s.1. of the Planning and Compensation Act 1991.

[18]   Introduced by the Planning and Compensation Act 1991.

enforcement has expired. It should be remembered that not every breach (for example, where it has gone officially undetected) will be revealed by local authority searches and additional enquiries.

BUILDING REGULATIONS

6.6   Planning permission and building regulation compliance are two separate requirements. Even if building work does not require planning permission, it must comply with any building regulations relevant to the work.

The Building Regulations 1991 (S.I. 1991 No. 2768), made under the Building Act 1984, are designed to ensure compliance with standards of health and safety in building work. Under Regulation 11 of the Regulations, any person who intends to carry out building work or make a material change of use (as defined in regulations 3 and 5) must deposit plans with specified details with the local authority. The authority must pass the plans unless they are defective or show that the proposed work would contravene the building regulations in which case they will be rejected. If the work does not commence within three years of deposit of the plans, the local authority can decide to treat the deposit as of no effect. The work itself must comply with the Regulations and be inspected at various stages.

Any breach of the Regulations is (generally) a criminal offence; and under s.36 of the Act the authority can within one year of completion of the work take enforcement proceedings against the owner of the building.

The authority can be requested to - and in some cases, must - issue a certificate when the work is complete. If the authority is satisfied, after taking all reasonable steps, that such is the case, the certificate will state that the regulations specified in the certificate have been complied with. Such a certificate is evidence, though not conclusive evidence, that they have been complied with.

The purchaser of a new building should be satisfied that the plans have been approved by production of the local authority's notice passing them; and that the work itself complies with the building regulations. Where the building is covered by the NHBC guarantee (para.3.6) this will in effect guarantee that the building work is in accordance with the regulations.

An action in tort against the authority or inspector for pure economic loss caused by negligence in carrying out the duties under the Regulations is not likely to succeed; see *Murphy v. Brentwood D.C.*[19]

---

[19]   [1991] A.C. 399 (para.3.6).

The standard form of Additional Enquiries of the local authority asks whether proceedings have been initiated in respect of breach of the regulations. As with planning law, it should be remembered that there may be breaches undetected by the authority.

ROADS AND ACCESS

A purchaser will need to be satisfied on two matters: **6.7**

(a) That she will have any necessary right of access to the property, whether by public right of way or easement.

(b) As to responsibility for maintaining the access roads, and any potential liability for their maintenance that may be imposed on her.

In this context access routes, whether roads or paths, can be classified into three main categories.

(a) Highways maintainable at the public expense. A highway is a route along which the public have a right of a passage. A highway may be a public footpath along which the public have a right of way on foot; a public bridleway (normally referred to simply as a bridleway) along which the public have a right of way on foot and horseback; or any other highway (a public carriageway) along which the right of passage extends to vehicular traffic.

A highway maintainable at the public expense is one which the highway authority is under a duty to maintain out of public funds. Each highway authority is under an obligation to keep, available for public inspection, a list of the highways in its area which are maintainable at the public expense.

(b) A highway not maintainable at the public expense is one which there is no such public duty to maintain. These are not common. If, for example, a landowner dedicated a way across her land to the public (making it a highway on acceptance of the dedication by the public, evidenced by user) the way would not be maintainable at the public expense unless and until adopted by the highway authority.

(c) Private streets or ways. Any way which is not a highway must be a private one over which there is no public right of way. A right of passage over such a way may be created as an easement the benefit of which will be attached to and confined to the dominant property or properties; and the burden of which will be annexed to the land over which it passes. As explained above, the permitted use of an easement may be more or less restricted as to the time, mode of enjoyment, etc. A right of passage over private land may also exist (occasionally) as a customary right; or as a licence (para.6.4.2).

A highway authority has various statutory powers under which it can make up private ways prior to adopting them (that is turning them into highways maintainable at the public expense) and charging the cost of doing so to the frontagers. For example, where a street is not sewered, levelled, paved, flagged,channelled and lighted the authority may execute street works under the private street works code and apportion the cost between the premises frontaging the street. The street can then be declared a highway maintainable at the public expense.

New roads

6.7.1   Where a new residential estate is being developed normally new roads will be constructed. Like the rest of the development these need planning permission. But this itself does not guarantee that the roads will be adopted. It is possible and usual therefore for the developer to enter into an agreement with the highway authority under s.38 of the Highways Act 1980 under which the developer will agree to build and make up the roads to a specified standard, whereupon, on a specified date, they will become maintainable at the public expense. Such an agreement should be supported by a bond – that is an insurance guarantee that if the developer goes into liquidation the road works will be completed. If there is no such agreement and bond, the purchaser of a plot fronting onto the road faces the likelihood that the highway authority will do the work under the private street works code and charge the cost to herself and other frontagers.

Finally, it should be noted that highway authorities have wide, statutory powers to improve, widen and build roads (in the case of trunk and special roads, the authority being the Secretary of State).

Procedure on purchase

6.7.2   There is no obligation on a vendor under an open contract to show any right of access to the property; or to prove title to anything beyond the property being sold. It is therefore necessary for the purchaser's solicitor to check. The local land charges search should indicate whether there is any outstanding charge on the property for street works. The Replies to Additional Enquiries of the authority should indicate which of the access roads indicated by the enquirer on the front of the form are maintainable at the public expense; which are subject to a s.38 agreement and whether any such agreement is supported by a bond; and any information held by the authority on proposals to make up roads, improve existing roads or build new ones within 200 metres of the property. The enquirer would need to satisfy herself that any bond was for a sufficient amount to cover the possible works. The distance of 200 metres is an arbitrary figure, without legal significance, being chosen as the sort of distance within which any road changes are likely to have a major impact on the property. If a client were worried about roads beyond this limit she could be directed to the highway authority to seek information.

Insofar as access roads are not highways maintainable at the public expense, the purchaser's solicitor needs to check that satisfactory easements of access are available; and this includes roads subject to s.38 agreements until they have been adopted (para.6.4). It is important to remember that whether, under the terms of the contract, a purchaser is to get the benefit of existing easements or to have new ones created in her favour, the vendor must prove title to the easement. She must be able to show, in the case of an existing easement, that the easement was lawfully granted; in the case of a new easement, that she has title to the intended servient property and so title to grant the easement.

DRAINS AND SEWERS

Under what is now the Water Industry Act 1991, powers in relation to water supply and foul and surface water disposal are vested in water undertakers and sewerage undertakers. These consist of the old statutory water companies and the new water companies as successors to the old water authorities.

6.8

A drain, whether foul or surface water, is one that drains one building or buildings in the same curtilage. A sewer is one that drains more than one. A public sewer is one that is vested in a sewerage undertaker.

Under s.102 of the 1991 Act, a sewerage undertaker has power (but is not obliged) to adopt private sewers, that is to vest them in itself as public sewers.

Like roads, sewers can be built (subject to planning approval) but will only become public and so maintainable by the sewerage undertaker if adopted under s.102 or other statutory authority. Until this happens, the property owner will be concerned, again as with roads, where any private drain or sewer serving the property crosses other property, that the necessary easements exist or will be created by the owner of the servient property.

The owner of a drain is responsible for the cost of maintaining her own drains. If drainage is by private sewer, that is with shared use, she will need to be satisfied that there is a satisfactory arrangement with the others as to the cost of maintenance either by agreement or by condition attached to the easement.

Under s.106 of the 1991 Act, the owner of a drain or sewer has, with certain exceptions, the right to connect up to the public sewer. The connection will normally be made by the undertaker and the cost recovered from those requiring the connection.

Under the Building Act 1984, ss.59 and 21, the local authority can require work to be done on private drains and sewers to bring them up to standard and can require a drain to be connected to a public or private (if there is a right of connection) sewer if there is one available within 100 feet of the building at a level that makes connection practicable and there is a right to pass the drain through any adjoining land.

Under s.21 of the same Act, connection can similarly be required in the case of a new building.

Under s.104 of the 1991 Act, a sewerage undertaker can enter into an agreement with a developer (or anyone else) that if a proposed sewer is constructed in accordance with the terms of the agreement, the undertaker will on a specified date or completion of the work or other specified time declare the sewer to be vested in the undertaker – that is to become a public sewer. Where the sewerage system on a new estate has not yet been vested in the undertaker, a purchaser's solicitor should check that such an agreement (which, by s.104(5), is enforceable by the purchaser against the undertaker) has been made. If the developer has not already fulfilled her side of the agreement by constructing the sewerage system, etc, it should be a term of the sale agreement that it will be fulfilled; and there should be a bond of sufficient value lest the developer should become insolvent before it is.

In so far as any part of the property's drainage system has not yet been or will not be vested in the undertaker, the purchaser needs to check for satisfactory drainage easements.

On purchase of an established property, the purchaser will need to know whether the property drains into a public sewer without crossing other property. If its private drains do cross other property, a check will have to be made as to necessary easements. If it is not connected to a public sewer, she will need to know whether there is a public sewer (or a private one with a liability to connection) within one hundred feet of the property. Most of the above information should be revealed by replies to the Additional Enquiries of the local authority, though in some cases the replies advise further enquiries of the sewerage undertaker. The line of drains may have to be discovered by survey or enquiry of the vendor.

WATER SUPPLY

The purchaser will need to check that the water supply is connected   **6.9**
to the mains and working satisfactorily.

A water undertaker can be required to provide a mains water supply;
to connect that supply to the individual premises' service pipe; and to
supply water for domestic purposes. The person requiring the mains
supply or the connection to the mains will have to meet the cost.

Since the water mains belong to the undertaker from the beginning
there is no problem (as there are with roads and sewers) of any period
prior to adoption by the undertaker.

The service pipe from the water mains to the premises generally
belongs to, and is the responsibility of, the individual owner; or, in the
case of common service pipes, the common owners. Where there is a
common service pipe, the arrangements for repair should be investigated.
Where the service pipe reaches the property across other private land, it is
necessary to check that satisfactory easements exist.

The undertakers have wide statutory powers under the Water
Industry Act 1991 to lay and maintain pipes; but, in general, they only
have power to lay service pipes in private land if there is already a service
pipe laid there.

Where the water supply is from a private source, such as a well, any
necessary easements of supply and access need to be considered. Under
s.80 of the Water Industry Act 1991, a local authority can require
remedial steps to be taken if satisfied that the water supply is not
wholesome - including requiring the owner to obtain connection to the
mains.

POWER SUPPLY

Under the Electricity Act 1989, s.10 and Schedule 10, mains   **6.10**
electricity suppliers have power, in the absence of agreement,
compulsorily to acquire wayleaves across private land for cables.

As with the mains water pipes, the cables to the premises will be
vested in the supplier from the beginning.

In the case of gas, under the Gas Act 1986, Schedule 3, in the absence
of licence or easement by agreement, the mains gas suppliers have
statutory powers to compulsorily acquire land for laying pipes; and to
enter land for the purpose of maintaining them. As with water and
electricity, the pipes will be vested in the supplier from the beginning.

CHAPTER 7

DRAFTING THE CONTRACT:
REGISTERED TITLE

TIMOTHY FINDS ANOTHER FILE

It is still the 19th. When taking out the Goldberg file, Timothy has **7.1**
found that another file has slipped inside it: the Obebe sale file. He is
reminded that the time has come (if not passed!) to prepare the contract
on this one.

In fact, in fairness to Timothy, he has not been idle on the Obebe sale
– prompted no doubt by the benign immanence of Old Jarndyce. He has
sent off a requisition for a search in the Local Land Charges Register and
Additional Enquiries. He has sent off to the district Land Registry, and
received, office copy of the entries on the register of title and title plan.
There is already on the file, obtained by Miss Pinky before her
increasingly lamented departure, a completed Instructions on Sale form;
copies of the Property Information Form and the Fixtures Fittings and
Contents List both completed by Miss Obebe. These are headed
TransAction Protocol; so Timothy has decided to use TransAction
Protocol (para.7.12). He is not quite sure what it is; but he is quite sure
that it will mark him as a modern conveyancer. No one has told him (or
rather no one has told him twice!) that it can only be used if the other
side agrees. Secretly, he suspects that it is just an advertising agency's
presentation of the same old conveyancing procedures.

Question Is there any truth in this thought? (See para.7.12).

The Instructions on Sale form is as follows: **7.2**

Document 7.2 Obebe Sale: Instructions On Sale

Jarndyce & Jarndyce: Instructions On Sale

Client: _M/s Obebe_   Date: _29 January 1993_

Full names and addresses and phone number of clients	_Olive Obebe, 14 Hardcastle Drive, Ledchester. Ledchester 278456._
Full names and addresses of purchasers	_Harry and Hilary Headcase, Flat 10B, Chapelville Road, Ledchester._
Name and address of purchasers' solicitors	_Havishams. Miss Havisham._
Name and address of estate agents	_Dream Homes, Chapel St Mary Branch._
Details of property Address Freehold/leasehold Registered or unregistered Sale of whole/part	_14 Hardcastle Drive, Ledchester. Freehold, Registered, Sale of whole._
Location of deeds	_Deeds with building society._
Price	_£62,500._
Deposit paid	_£100 paid to Dream Homes._
Chattels to be sold. Fixtures to be excluded	_See Fixtures and Fittings list. All curtains and carpets included._
Related purchase	_16 Winchester Avenue, Ledchester. See file._
Synchronise exchange	_YES_
Completion date	_To be arranged Provisionally 19 March._
Outstanding mortgages. Lenders; amount outstanding; account number	_Ledchester and Bongley, Commercial Road Branch. £55,000 believed outstanding. Account no. AB 724862154._
Other persons whose consent to sale needed	_Boyfriend lives with her but not claiming any interest. Not interested in owning property. Has done a lot of improvements. He is going to help with deposit on the new house._
Additional information	_Bought newly built from Starrabs, the developers, last year. Will bring in NHBC papers._

Question What letters do you think should have been written immediately on receiving the above instructions? Write them.

Question Advise Miss Obebe on the basis of the above information (and see para.1.9.2) what rights her boyfriend might be able to claim if he suddenly did get a taste for property ownership. Would it make any difference if they were married? You are also acting for the Ledchester and Bongley in relation to the mortgage loan on her purchase. What if any duty would you owe to them in relation to the boyfriend? What steps, if any, might be taken in relation to the purchase to protect the interests of Miss Obebe and the building society?

What steps, if any, would you recommend in relation to the contract of sale of the existing house, or otherwise as part of the sale transaction, in relation to the boyfriend, which would protect the interests of Miss Obebe, and probably be satisfactory to the purchaser? (See paras.1.9.2 and 13.10). Draft any necessary clauses or documents.

7.3   The office copy entries on the register and title plan are as follows:

Document 7.3 Obebe sale: Office Copy Entries on Register and Title Plan for 14 Hardcastle Drive

H.M. LAND REGISTRY

Edition 1 opened 15.2.92   TITLE NUMBER WYK 543210   This register consists of 4 pages

NOTE:—
Pages 4 are blank and have not been copied.

A. PROPERTY REGISTER
containing the description of the registered land and the estate comprised in the Title

COUNTY WEST YORKSHIRE   DISTRICT LEDCHESTER

The Freehold land shown and edged with red on the plan of the above Title filed at the Registry
registered on 15 Feb 1992 known as 14 Hardcastle Drive

The land in this title has the benefit of the following rights granted by a transfer dated 5 February 1992 by Starrabs Ltd (Transferor) to Olive Obebe over the land tinted pink and brown on the title plan:
1. The right (in common with the transferor and all other persons entitled thereto) of free passage of running water soil gas and electricity through such sewers drains pipes watercourses cables and wires which may now or at any time within the perpetuity period be laid or constructed in on under or through the land tinted pink and brown TOGETHER with the right (upon due notice being given) to enter upon such parts of the land tinted pink and brown as may be necessary for the purpose of maintaining or repairing such sewers drains pipes watercourses cables and wires making good forthwith any damage caused by such entry to the reasonable satisfaction of the owner or owners for the time being of the land tinted pink and brown and any part thereof as may be affected by the exercise of such right. 2. A right to enter upon such parts of the land tinted pink and brown as may be necessary for the purpose of maintaining the land in this title making good nevertheless any damage occasioned thereby. 3. A right of way on foot and by vehicles over and along the land tinted brown for the purpose of access to and egress from the land in this title and each and every part thereof.

B. PROPRIETORSHIP REGISTER
stating nature of the Title, name, address and description of the proprietor of the land and any entries affecting the right of disposing thereof
TITLE ABSOLUTE

Entry number	Proprietor, etc.	Remarks
1.	Olive Obebe of 14 Hardcastle Drive Ledchester, registered on 15 February 1992.	
2.	RESTRICTION registered on 15 February 1992 EXCEPT under an order of the registrar no disposition by the proprietor of the land of this title to be registered without the consent of the proprietor for the time being of Charge No.3.	

OFFICE COPY.

ISSUED BY THE LEDCHESTER DISTRICT LAND REGISTRY SHOWING THE SUBSISTING ENTRIES ON THE REGISTER OF 15 FEB 1993. UNDER S.113 OF THE 1925 ACT THIS COPY IS ADMISSIBLE IN EVIDENCE TO THE SAME EXTENT AS THE ORIGINAL.

Note: As to the right of access to a neighbour's property to repair one's own, see Access to Neighbouring Land Act 1992.

Page 2.

TITLE NUMBER WYK 543210

C. CHARGES REGISTER

containing charges, incumbrances etc., adversely affecting the land and registered dealings therewith

Entry number	The date at the beginning of each entry is the date on which the entry was made on this edition of the register	Remarks
1.	A transfer of the land in this title dated 5 February 1992 made by Starrabs Ltd to Olive Obebe contains the covenants particulars of which are set out in the Schedule annexed.	
2.	The land in this title is subject to the following rights for the benefit of the land tinted pink and brown on the title plan: For the benefit of each and every part of the land tinted brown: (a) The right of free passage and running of water soil gas and electricity through the sewers drains pipes and watercourses cables and wires situate and running at the date hereof or at any time within the said perpetuity period in on under over or through the land in this title. (b) The right (at the cost of the person or persons exercising such right) within the said perpetuity period to connect any sewers drains pipes water-courses cables and wires that may now or within the said perpetuity period run in on under over or through the land in this title PROVIDED THAT the same shall not thereby be overloaded or their capacity exceeded and subject to the consent of the appropriate authorities. (c) The right (at the cost of the person or persons exercising such right) within the said perpetuity period to lay sewers drains pipes watercourses cables and wires in on under over or through the land in this title (whether in addition to or in substitution for the then existing sewers drains pipes watercourses cables and wires).	
3.	15 February 1992 - CHARGE dated 5 February 1992 registered on 15 February 1992 to secure the moneys including the further advances therein mentioned. PROPRIETOR - Ledchester and Bongley Building Society of Society House The Bedrow Ledchester registered 15 February 1992.	

Any entries struck through are no longer subsisting

OFFICE COPY.

ISSUED BY THE LEDCHESTER DISTRICT LAND REGISTRY SHOWING THE SUBSISTING ENTRIES ON THE REGISTER OF 15 FEB 1993
UNDER S.113 OF THE 1925 ACT THIS COPY IS ADMISSIBLE IN EVIDENCE TO THE SAME EXTENT AS THE ORIGINAL

TITLE WYK 543210	Page 3
C. CHARGES REGISTER — continued.	
Schedule of restrictive covenants	Remarks

The following are the particulars of the covenants contained in a Transfer dated 5 February 1992 referred to in the Charges Register.

The purchaser doth hereby for himself and his assigns and with intent to bind all persons in whom the hereditaments and premises hereby conveyed shall for the time being be vested for any Estate or interest therein covenant with the Vendors their heirs and assigns the owner or owners for the time being of the other hereditaments forming part of the Hardcastle Estate aforesaid that he the Purchaser his heirs and assigns owners and occupiers of the premises hereby conveyed will at all times hereafter observe and perform the conditions and stipulations in relation to the premises hereby conveyed which are contained in the said first schedule hereto.

THE FIRST SCHEDULE above referred to

1. FENCES Each purchaser shall within three months of the date of the purchase erect (if not already erected) and afterwards maintain in good condition a good and sufficient open pale or other approved fence or hedge on the side or sides of the Plot marked "T" on the plan within the boundary.

2. NOT to keep any animals upon the property in such manner as to cause a nuisance or annoyance to the owners and occupiers of the adjoining and neighouring properties.

3. NOT to hang out any washing in the front garden of the property.

4. NOT to cover up or interfere with any manhole or inspection cover on the property.

5. NOT to erect a place a building shed or other erection of any kind whether temporary or permanent on the Property or any part thereof nor to park place or put any caravan mobile home or similar vehicle or thing on the Property or any part thereof nor to make any addition to or structural alterations in the elevation of the exterior of any building from time to time upon the Property unless the plans drawings and elevations thereof shall have been previoulsy submitted to and approved in writing by the Transferor or its Surveyor for the time being and a fee of Thirty Pounds (£30) or such other higher fee as may from time to time be recoverable plus Value Added Tax paid for the examining of such plans.

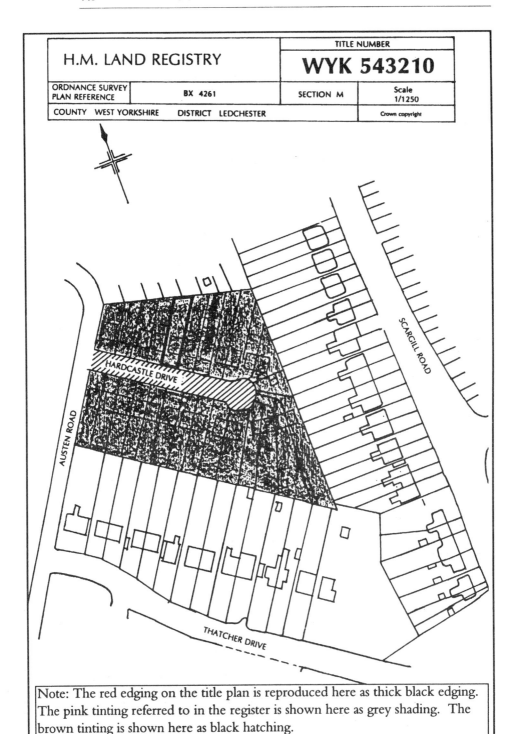

TITLE NUMBER	
H.M. LAND REGISTRY	**WYK 543210**

ORDNANCE SURVEY PLAN REFERENCE	BX 4261	SECTION M	Scale 1/1250
COUNTY WEST YORKSHIRE DISTRICT LEDCHESTER			Crown copyright

Note: The red edging on the title plan is reproduced here as thick black edging. The pink tinting referred to in the register is shown here as grey shading. The brown tinting is shown here as black hatching.

OLD JARNDYCE ON THE FUNDAMENTALS OF
REGISTERED CONVEYANCING

Before looking at the drafting of a contract for the sale of a registered **7.4**
title, it is worth reviewing a few of the fundamental principles and the
essential way in which registered title differs from unregistered.

A comparison of unregistered and registered conveyancing

(a) The same proprietary interests can be created in registered as in **7.4.1**
unregistered land – beneficial freehold and leasehold ownership, trusts,
easements, restrictive covenants, etc. And, generally, they can be
created in the same way.

(b) What is an incumbrance in the one is equally an incumbrance in
the other; and so in relation to a contract the vendor's duty of
disclosure is essentially the same.

(c) The rules which govern the formation of a valid contract and the
rules which determine the rights and obligations of the parties under
the contract are generally the same.

Question Read through the Standard Conditions. Point out where
they do distinguish between registered and unregistered title. Explain the
reason for any such distinction.

(d) The two systems are fundamentally different in the following
ways:

(i) In the way ownership of land (freehold or leasehold)
incumbrances and other interests can be protected so as to be
enforceable against a purchaser or other transferee of the land.

(ii) In unregistered title legal ownership is determined by the deeds
and documents of title. Assuming that V is the legal, freehold
owner of Blackacre a deed of conveyance will be needed and will
be sufficient to transfer that ownership to P. In the case of
registered title, ownership depends in principle on the state of the
register. If V is the registered proprietor of Blackacre (and the fact
that she is so registered will in itself mean that she *is* the legal
owner) a deed of transfer – i.e. roughly the equivalent to a deed of
conveyance in unregistered conveyancing – will be necessary to
transfer ownership to P; but it is not enough and in itself will only
transfer equitable title (a minor interest). P will only become
proprietor (legal owner) when she is registered as proprietor in
place of V at the appropriate district Land Registry.

(i), (ii) and (iii) in turn lead to a difference in the method by which the vendor fulfils her contractual duty to prove title to what she is selling. And it means that the terms of the contract dealing with proof of title will be drafted differently in the two cases.

To understand this difference it is necessary to understand the way in which proprietary interests in the two types of title are classified for the purpose of determining their enforceability against transferees or anyone else with a contrary interest.

Question It has been said that the policy of registration of title in this country is to 'simplify the machinery of conveyancing without altering the substantive rules of law'. The same authors also say that it is to 'substitute a single, established title, guaranteed by the state, in place of the traditional title which must be separately investigated on every purchase at the purchaser's own risk'.[1] Again, it has been said that 'today, proof of title, whether registered or unregistered, is a relatively simple matter. The real problems facing a purchaser and her lawyer lie outside the realm of title and are the same in both registered and unregistered conveyancing'.

As you pursue the practice of the practice of conveyancing, consider the truth of these various statements.

Classification of interests

7.4.2   In the case of unregistered title any proprietary interest will fall into one of the following categories; and this categorisation will determine any steps needed to protect the interest and its enforceability against a transferee or other contrary interest:

(a) Legal estates and interests which are not registrable under the Land Charges Act 1972. Such an estate or interest will be good against all the world and enforceable against anyone with a subsequent contrary claim. The legal freehold ownership itself, and similarly any legal lease, come into this category. So do legal easements and legal mortgages protected by the deposit of title deeds.[2]

(b) Those legal and equitable interests that are registrable under the Land Charges Act 1972. Such interests will, if properly registered, be

---

1   Megarry & Wade, pp.195,194.

2   Though such a legal mortgage can lose priority to a subsequent mortgage by gross negligence.

binding on any subsequent, contrary claim; but void against the purchaser[3] of an adverse interest if not registered.

(c) Equitable interests which are not registrable. Such interests - e.g. the interest arising by proprietary estoppel - are enforceable against any subsequent adverse claimant except a bona fide purchaser for value of a legal estate without notice of the interest. Equitable interests arising under a trust come in this category - for example, the interest under a resulting trust for sale of a contributor to the purchase price of land. However, such trust interests may be overreached if the correct conveyancing mechanisms are employed (for example, sale by at least two trustees in the case of a trust for sale). In this event notice becomes irrelevant.

In general, in all these categories, the crucial time for determining enforceability of the interest is the moment that the legal estate is conveyed to the purchaser.[4]

In the case of registered title, the above categories are totally irrelevant. Any proprietary interest in registered land will fall into one of the following categories:

(i) Interests which are substantively registrable - i.e. with their own individual titles. The most important registrable interests are the legal freehold and legal leases granted for more than 21 years - that is the legal ownership of the land - legal mortgages and legal easements.

Correctly speaking, it is titles to land that are registered, not the land itself. Two registered titles may, and commonly do, exist in relation to the same piece of land at the same time. For example, the registered freehold proprietor may grant a 99 year lease to T. T's lease will need to be registered with its own, new register and title number and T will be shown on this register as proprietor of the leasehold interest. (It will also have to be noted on the charges register of the freehold title so as to bind transferees of the freehold title).

Registered mortgages (known as registered charges) do not have their own title registers. They are registered on the charges register of the title mortgaged - i.e. the freehold or leasehold as the case may be. Similarly, an easement will not (since it can only exist as a burden on a servient property and a benefit to a dominant property) have its own register of title. It will normally, if created expressly, be substantively registered on the property register of the title to the dominant land and noted in the charges register of the servient property.

---

[3]   Either for value of any interest or of a legal estate for money or money's worth, depending on the class of land charge.

[4]   In the case of registrable land charges, if a purchaser takes her conveyance within the protection period of an official search certificate, the crucial date will be the date of the search (para.13.6).

Unless and until a registrable interest is substantively registered, it will fall into the category of either a minor or an overriding interest.

(ii) Overriding interests An overriding interest is any incumbrance, interest right or power not entered on the register but subject to which any registered disposition takes effect.[5] Thus an overriding interest will bind a purchaser or other transferee of the registered title even though there is no mention of it on the register and whether or not she has notice or knows of it. Indeed, it should be stressed that the doctrine of notice is not (with one or two minor, exceptions) relevant to registered conveyancing.

The list of overriding interests is contained in s.70(1) of the Land Registration Act 1925 as amended by the Land Registration Act 1986. The most important are as follows (the lettering following that in the Act):

'(a) Rights of common, drainage rights, customary rights (until extinguished), public rights, profits a prendre, rights of sheepwalk, rights of way, watercourses, rights of water, and other easements not being equitable easements required to be protected by notice on the register.'

Basically, this category includes public and customary rights, profits and legal (and possibly equitable) easements.

'(f) Subject to the provisions of this Act rights acquired or in course of being acquired under the Limitation Acts.

(g) The rights of every person in actual occupation of the land or in receipts of the rents and profits thereof, save where enquiry is made of such person and the rights are not disclosed.

(h) In the case of possessory, qualified or good leasehold title, all estates, rights, interests and powers excepted from the effect of registration.

(i) Rights under local land charges unless and until registered or protected on the register in the prescribed manner ...

(k) Leases granted for a term not exceeding twenty-one years.'

If an interest is overriding it will not be a minor interest (Land Registration Act 1925, s.3(xv)).

(iii) Minor interests Any interest in registered land which has not been or cannot be substantively registered and is not overriding will necessarily be a minor interest. Minor interests require protection by an appropriate entry on the register of the title affected.

---

5   Land Registration Act 1925, s.3(xvi).

FIRST AND SUBSEQUENT REGISTRATION   **7.5**

First registration

Before the introduction of the system of registration of title in this   **7.5.1**
country[6] all title was unregistered. Since then, under the Land
Registration Act 1925, registration of title has been made compulsory in
an increasing number of areas. The programme is that ultimately all
freehold and long leasehold titles will be registered; and registered
conveyancing will be the only system.

Under the Registration of Title Order 1989 (S.I. 1989 No.1347)
compulsory registration of title was finally extended to the whole of
England and Wales as from 1 December, 1990.

Compulsory registration means that first registration of (a previously
unregistered) title must be applied for on:

(i) A conveyance on sale of the freehold.

(ii) The grant of a term of years absolute for more than 21 years from
the date of the grant.

(iii) The assignment on sale of a leasehold held for a term of years
absolute having more than 21 years to run from the date of the
assignment (Land Registration Act 1925 as amended by the Land
Registration Act 1986).

Conveyances and assignments not on sale do not attract compulsory
registration – for example, an assent by personal representatives, a legal
mortgage by the existing owner, a vesting deed executed by a local
authority on compulsory purchase or an exchange of land where no
equality money is paid.[7] The pace at which all freehold land and existing
long leases are converted to registered title depends therefore on the pace
at which such titles change hands on sale. In the Chief Registrar's Annual
Report for 1991–92 it was stated that by the year 2011, 19 million
properties should be registered. This would leave about 2 million
unregistered including those passed down rather than sold and those
belonging to public authorities and corporate institutions.[8]

A transaction which gives rise to first registration will be conducted
and take effect in all respects according to the rules of unregistered land
conveyancing. However, in addition, and within two months of

---

[6] Registration of title was in fact introduced on a voluntary (and little used) basis by the Land
Registry Act 1862 and the Land Transfer Act 1875.

[7] See Ruoff & Pryer, p.56.

[8] See [1993] Conv. 101.

completion (i.e of legal title vesting) the purchaser, assignee or grantee, as the case may be, must apply to the appropriate District Registry for first registration of the title acquired. This means that the newly acquired title will have to be proved to the satisfaction of the Registrar in the same way that it was (hopefully) proved to the purchaser, assignee or grantee herself.

When the Registrar has investigated the title, the unregistered title will be converted into a registered title with absolute, qualified, possessory or good leasehold whichever is found to be appropriate (below). For the use of Land Registry forms see below, para.7.5.3. For the procedure on applying for first registration, see para.15.4.2.

Registration is compulsory in the sense that if the title is not registered within the two month period the legal estate will revert to the vendor, assignor or grantor as the case may be who will hold it on trust for the purchaser, assignee or grantee. Consequently, the latter will have only an (equitable) minor interest which, if coupled with actual occupation will become an overriding interest under Land Registration Act 1925, s.70(1)(g).

The Registrar has a discretion to accept late applications and this will cure the defect. Where a defaulter lodges her application out of time, she must satisfy the Registrar (with appeal to the court) that the application for registration could not have been made within the prescribed period of two months; or could only have been made within that period by incurring unreasonable expense; or that it was not made in time because of some accident or other sufficient cause.

Failing such acceptance a new deed would have to be executed by the original vendor, assignor, grantor or whomsoever the legal title had then passed to (if for example the vendor had died); and, although there would be a right to have such a conveyance under the principle in *Saunders v. Vautier*[9] such a person might be difficult to trace.

The consequences of first registration

7.5.2   Sections 5 and 6 of the Land Registration Act 1925 establish the position at the opening of play as it were. It is commonly said that registration gives a title guaranteed by the state. This is by no means completely true.

Registration of a person as first proprietor of a freehold estate with absolute title vests the legal fee simple absolute in possession in that person 'together with all rights, privileges and appurtenances belonging or appurtenant thereto' (s.5).

---

[9]   (1841) Cr. & Ph. 240.

But the title is limited in a number of important ways:

(i) It is subject to any minor interest appearing on the register. These will of course be revealed when the register is searched by a purchaser and so present no difficulty.

(ii) Any overriding interests affecting the registered land. These do present one of the major dangers to the purchaser of registered land, since they will not appear on the register and inspection of the land will not necessarily reveal them.

(iii) Where the first proprietor is a trustee she will hold subject to minor interests of which she has notice even if these are not protected by any entry on the register. Thus if the proprietor is a trustee for sale she will be subject to the interests of any beneficiaries of which she has notice.

(iv) Quite separately, but equally important, under s.82 of the Land Registration Act, the court or Registrar (with appeal to the court) has jurisdiction to rectify the register in certain circumstances. To this extent a proprietor can be deprived of her registered title. Under s.83 there may be a right to compensation from public funds in such a circumstance; but this does not necessarily follow.[10]

For other matters which may not be revealed by the register, or not revealed in adequate detail, see below para.7.10.

Dealing with the land prior to first registration

Under Rule 72 of the Land Registration Rules 1925 a person having the right to apply for registration as first proprietor can deal with the land in any of the ways permitted by the Act. *Pinekerry v. Needs (Contractors)*[11] is a neat illustration of this principle and the consequences of not applying for first registration in time. R had bought the land some months earlier; but had not applied for registration within the two months period nor for an extension of time in which to apply in accordance with s.123 of the Land Registration Act 1925 and the Land Registration Rules. Thus when R did apply for registration he had no 'right' to be registered as proprietor. R agreed to sell to A who was obtaining a mortgage from M. A, in accordance with M's requirements, required a legal title from R and refused to complete until R had in fact been registered as proprietor. R was claiming interest for this consequential period of delay in completing. It was held that he was not entitled to it. A purchaser is, subject to the terms of the contract, entitled to the legal title. At the time due for completion R did not have the legal title since he had not been

---

[10] See, e.g. *Epps v. Esso Petroleum Co. Ltd*. [1973] 1 W.L.R. 1071; para.4.8.

[11] [1992] NPC 15, (C.A.).

registered; nor had he applied for registration within the two months or an official extension granted by the Registry, which would have brought him within Rule 72. Although the Registry did in fact process his application out of time, R had no right to insist on this.

Registration of subsequent dispositions

7.5.3   The proprietor of a registered title can, in effect, do anything that the owner of the equivalent unregistered title can do; and in general according to the same substantive rules of land law. There are two important qualifications to this:

(a) The transaction must be carried out in the manner and using the forms, if any, prescribed by the Land Registration Acts 1925 to 1988 and Rules. What follows in relation to use of forms applies equally to any transaction involving the Land Registry.

Rule 74 of the Land Registration Rules 1925 as amended provides:

'The forms in the Schedule hereto shall be used in all matters to which they refer, or are capable of being applied or adapted, with such alterations and additions, if any, as are necessary or desired and the Registrar allows.'

Rule 75 of these Rules provides:

'Instruments for which no form is prescribed or to which the scheduled forms cannot conveniently be adapted, shall be in such form as the Registrar shall direct or allow, the scheduled forms being followed as nearly as circumstances will permit.'

Individual Rules prescribe specific forms for particular transactions. Thus, for example, Rule 98 provides that a transfer of the land comprised in a freehold title shall be made by an instrument in Forms 19 or 20 (19 is for a transfer of the whole of the land in a title; 20 for transfer of part of the land). Form 56, prescribed by Rule 170, is for an assent to a devisee of land or for the purposes of an appropriation.

Some of the statutory forms have been modified by the Registrar under the above powers, in some cases two or more statutory forms being hatched out of one original version.

In addition to the statutory forms, modified or not, s.127 of the Land Registration Act provides:

'Subject to the provisions of this Act the Chief Land Registrar shall conduct the whole business of registration under this Act, and shall frame and cause to be printed circulated or otherwise promulgated such forms and directions as he may deem requisite or expedient for facilitating proceedings under this Act.'

A number of forms have been promulgated by the Registrar under these powers.

All these forms statutory or promulgated can be described as prescribed forms; and they must be used whenever appropriate. However, this system of prescribed forms for registered title is by no means inflexible; and the Registrar has wide discretion to allow variations. 'Alterations and additions to the prescribed forms are permitted so long as no document other than that produced has to be perused and the general principles on which the registers are kept are not violated.'[12]

Most of the prescribed forms, statutory and promulgated, have been printed by HMSO and law stationers, each with its own individual form number which, if it is a statutory form, generally corresponds to the number in the Schedule to the Land Registration Rules. Where a needed form has not been printed its wording has to be copied from the Schedule or the wording published by the Land Registry.

In general, there is no legal obligation to use the printed version of forms; a document using the necessary form of wording can be typewritten or printed from a machine (or indeed handwritten) on stout A4 size paper with a sufficient margin on the left hand side to allow for stitching into the land certificate if necessary.

Printed forms can be obtained from HMSO shops and law stationers. A list of the available printed forms can be obtained from HMSO - itself a printed list! – Land Registry Sectional List, No 43.

A list of the more commonly used printed forms is included in Appendix 7.

A number of practice guidance leaflets are published by the Land Registry and are available from district registries.

There is no prescribed form of wording for leases or mortgages. In practice the same forms and precedents are used for these as in unregistered conveyancing. Institutional lenders use a single printed form for mortgages of registered and unregistered title. But with both leases and mortgages the property must be clearly identified by reference to the title number.

For further comment on the drafting of registered title documents, see below, Chapter 12.

(b) The disposition of a registered title will not be effective at law to create a registered interest until registered. This is one of the central distinctions between registered and unregistered conveyancing.

Section 19(1) of the Land Registration Act 1925 provides that any transfer of a registered estate or part of it shall be completed by registration of the transferee as the new proprietor. Similarly, s.19(2) provides that any other disposition by the registered proprietor

---

[12]   Ruoff & Pryer, p.64.

transferring or creating an interest must be completed by registration of the proprietor of the interest. Thus not only transfers of the whole or part of the land in a freehold or leasehold title but also, for example, the grant of registrable leases, creation of mortgages and legal easements, constitute dispositions and require to be completed by registration.

Registration is deemed to have taken place on the day when the application is delivered to the appropriate district Land Registry. An up to date list of district registries and the areas which they cover can be obtained from any district Registry. An application which is delivered after 9.30 am on one day is deemed to have been delivered on the following day. If the order of delivery of two documents by different applicants on the same day is crucial the matter can be decided by the court or Registrar with appeal to the court. (See Land Registration Rules 1925, as amended, Rules 83–85).

The effect of registration of a disposition

By s.20 of the Land Registration Act 1925, in the case of freehold, the registration of any such disposition for valuable consideration of or out of an absolute title confers on the transferee or grantee the legal estate subject only to:

(i) Minor interests protected on the register.

(ii) Overriding interests.

(iii) As in the case of first registration, the possibility of rectification under s.82.

It should also be added that, very unusually, a transferee, may be fixed with a constructive trust in favour of someone with a claim to an adverse interest in the property even though that claim is not protected on the register or overriding. But such a trust will be a new one imposed on the transferee, rather than a previously existing one subject to which she has taken the land.[13]

Where the disposition is not for valuable consideration, the transferee or grantee will in addition take subject to minor interests even if not protected on the register.

If a disposition is not registered it is not void, but it remains a minor interest (and equitable) unless and until it is registered and does not have the above protection; though if the transferee or grantee is in actual occupation the interest may be protected as an overriding one.

---

[13] See *Peffer v. Rigg* [1978] 3 All E.R. 745, using s.59(6) of the Land Registration Act 1925; and *Lyus v. Prowsa Developments Ltd.* [1982] 2 All E.R. 953. But today such a constructive trust will have to survive very close scrutiny of the circumstances by the court; see *Ashburn Anstalt v. Arnold* [1989] Ch. 1; and *Burr v. Copp* [1983] CLY 2057.

CLASSES OF REGISTERED TITLE

The proprietorship register of the title register will specify whether the title is absolute, possessory or qualified or (applicable only to leasehold) good leasehold.

7.6

Subject to the possibility of conversion to a better class of title, the class of title depends on how satisfied the Registrar is with the title on application for first registration.

The classes of leasehold title are dealt with in Chapter 17.

(a) Absolute title

If the Registrar approves the title, as will generally be the case, it will be registered as absolute, with the effect described above (para.7.5.2) giving the best class of title. Even if the unregistered title contains technical flaws the Registrar has power at the time of first registration

'to turn a Nelson's eye upon them and grant absolute title, provided the flaws are not likely to lead to the landowner being deprived of his estate. This he can do even if the landowner has only asked for possessory title.'[14]

The effect of s.20 of the Land Registration Act 1925 is that such registration cures any then defect in the title (subject again to the possibility of rectification). *Argyll Building Society v. Hammond*[15] is illustrative of the strength and weakness of registration of title. The appellant was registered as proprietor with absolute freehold title of a house in north London. The facts, as assumed for the purpose of this appeal on a preliminary point, were that his sister and brother-in-law had forged a transfer of the property to themselves while he was in America, and on the same day executed a charge to the building society. The sister and brother-in-law and the society were registered as proprietors of the freehold and the charge respectively. When the building society sought to obtain possession, the appellant materialised and claimed rectification.

It was held that registration of the sister and brother-in-law as proprietors gave them a valid title in spite of the (assumed) forgery and enabled them to create a valid mortgage. Nevertheless, there was discretionary power in the court under s.82 of the Land Registration Act 1925 to order rectification even against an interest such as the society's innocently acquired and properly protected on the register. The exercise of the discretion was left to the court hearing the trial of the action. The

---

[14] Ruoff & Pryer, p.23; and see Land Registration Act 1925, s.13.
[15] (1984) 49 P. & C.R. 148.

advantage to the society of its rather fleeting appearance on the register was that it might have a claim to compensation from public funds. In unregistered conveyancing, the mortgage would have been *void ab initio*; and the only claim would have been against the sister and brother-in-law.

(b) Possessory title

Registration with possessory title has the same effect and is subject to the same limits as absolute, except that it is additionally subject to one other and fundamental limitation: It is subject to any adverse interest existing at the time of first registration. And if such an adverse interest is given recognition by rectification of the register, there will be no compensation for the possessory proprietor. However, the title is guaranteed in respect of events subsequent to the first registration in the same way as absolute title.

Most commonly, possessory title is granted on the application of an adverse possessor. This means that the right of the real owner to recover the property will not be affected. However, as time passes without challenge, the possessory title will become more and more secure. The rights of the real owner will after, normally, 12 years from the start of the adverse possession, be barred under the Limitation Act 1980. Possessory title is also likely to be granted where the applicant for first registration cannot produce the title deeds - for example, if they have been lost; and occasionally where there is a documentary title but it is a weak one.

Under s.77 of the Land Registration Act 1925 as amended and Rule 48 of the Land Registration Rules 1925 as amended, once a possessory title has been registered for 12 years (15 if first registered before 1 January, 1987) the proprietor if in possession has a right to have it converted to absolute freehold; and the Registrar must convert earlier if satisfied as to the title. The latter might happen for example if the missing title deeds were found.

A possessory title is by no means necessarily unmarketable. Its practical security depends on how long it has been so registered and all the surrounding circumstances; and whether a purchaser's or lender's solicitor feels able to recommend that it is marketable and acceptable with or without title insurance.

(c) Qualified title

This is rare in practice; and can only be granted on an application for such a title (though the Registrar may recommend this course). It means (Land Registration Act 1925, s.7.) that the title is found to be subject to some specific defect which will be entered on the register excluding the defect from the effect of registration - for example, that the rights of the beneficiaries under a particular trust are preserved because the title shows the land to have been purchased by one of the trustees from the co-trustees.

The effect of qualified title is as for absolute, except that it is subject to the specified defect.

Qualified title can be converted to absolute if the Registrar can be satisfied as to the title - i.e. that the defect no longer exists.

PROTECTING MINOR INTERESTS

Section 101 (1) of the Land Registration Act 1925 provides: **7.7**

'Any person, whether being the proprietor or not, having a sufficient interest or power in or over registered land, may dispose of or deal with the same, and create any rights or interests therein which are permissible in like manner and by the like modes of assurance in all respects as if the land were not registered, but subject as provided by this section.'

If a transaction relating to registered land is not a registrable disposition, it can only create a minor interest (which may of course gain protection by becoming overriding if, for example, coupled with actual occupation). Such a minor interest, to be enforceable against a transferee for value of the registered title or against other adverse minor interests, must be protected by entry of a notice, caution, restriction or inhibition as appropriate on the register of the title affected. In general, the Land Registration Acts 1925-1988 and the Land Registration Rules 1925 as amended specify which method of protection is appropriate.

(a) Notice

A notice is entered on the charges register of the title. The process of entering a notice is commonly referred to a 'noting' the interest.

Entry of a notice is the normal method of protecting restrictive covenants, easements, leases (unless overriding) and other land charges and incumbrances (apart from mortgages).

In general a notice can only be entered with the consent of the registered proprietor who must produce the land certificate to the Registry. If the land is subject to a registered charge, the chargee will have a charge certificate and the land certificate will be held at the Registry. If an existing chargee is to be bound by the interest noted, she too will have to give consent in the same way and produce the charge certificate to the Registry. However, in the case of a spouse's right of occupation under the Matrimonial Homes Act 1983, neither consent nor production of the land certificate is necessary; and here the application is made on printed form 99 with no fee payable. For other applications, printed form A4 is available.

A separate application for the entry of notices is not necessary on first registration, when the Registrar will automatically note whatever interests burdening the land are shown by the title produced.

Similarly, when an application is made for registration of a transfer of part, any incumbrances created by the transfer will be entered on the registers of the existing and new title as necessary without separate application (though of course they will have to be included in the transfer and drafted as they would be for unregistered title).

On the other hand, where such incumbrances are created independently of any transfer - for example, if a proprietor grants her neighbour an easement or restrictive covenant - a separate application will be necessary by the grantee with the consent of the grantor and production of the land certificate.

Section 52(1) of the Land Registration Act 1925 provides:

'A disposition by the proprietor shall take effect subject to all estates, rights and claims which are protected by way of notice on the register at the date of registration or entry of notice of the disposition, but only if and so far as such estates, rights and claims may be valid and are not (independently of this Act) overridden by the disposition.'

Thus, in general, a purchaser, chargee or other disponee will be bound by any interest protected by notice on the register. A date against each entry in the charges register shows when the interest was noted.

A notice is the most effective method for the protection of incumbrances; but it does not make enforceable an interest which is not enforceable under the general law. Thus, for example, a restrictive covenant will not bind a purchaser of the servient land if it is not noted (or otherwise protected) on the register; but the dominant owner seeking to enforce will still have to show that the requirements of *Tulk v. Moxhay* are satisfied (and this will not be shown or guaranteed by the noting on the register). Similarly, the noting of an estate contract will not make it enforceable if the requirements of s.2 of the Law of Property (Miscellaneous Provisions) Act 1989 have not been satisfied.[15a]

(b) Caution

Entry of a caution against dealings under s.54 of the Land Registration Act 1925 is a device enabling anyone claiming an interest in the registered property to ensure that she is notified of any proposed disposition (referred to as a 'dealing' in s.54) of the land.

[15a] And see *Mortgage Corporation Ltd. v. Nationwide Credit Corporated Ltd.* [1993] 3 W.L.R. 769 deciding that a charge protected by notice can be overridden by an earlier charge not protected on the register.

The application must be made in printed form 63; but the land certificate does not have to be with the Registry so the consent of the proprietor is not necessary. In this sense it is commonly thought of and commonly is a 'hostile' entry made where the landowner is not prepared to co-operate. The application must be supported by a statutory declaration in prescribed form (the basic form being included on the back of form 63) stating the nature of the interest to be protected. Thus, a claim to be entitled to the benefit of an option or ordinary contract to purchase the land, or to have a lease of the land, or to be entitled as a beneficiary under a trust for sale to a share in the proceeds of sale, could all be protected by entry of a caution; though in the last case the claim could be overreached by two joint vendors in the ordinary way.

A caution is entered in the proprietorship register with the date of entry. The entry gives no indication of the claim sought to be protected. A person lodging a caution without reasonable cause is liable to pay such compensation as may be just to any person who suffers damage as a result.

Where there is a caution on the register which is preventing an intended disposition, it can be dealt with in one of three ways:

(i) The cautioner may agree to withdraw it (because for example her claim has been satisfied in some way).

(ii) The registered proprietor may apply by letter to the Registrar for a warning-off notice to be sent to the cautioner.

(iii) A warning-off notice will be sent on its own initiative by the Registry whenever a disposition by the registered proprietor is lodged for registration.

In the case of (ii) and (iii), if the cautioner does nothing in the period specified in the notice (usually 14 days) or agrees to removal, the caution will be cancelled. Alternatively, the cautioner may object to the proposed dealing in which case she will be given the opportunity at a judicial hearing before the Registrar (with appeal to the court) to show why the caution should be continued or the proposed disposition not be registered. If not able to show such cause the caution will be cancelled.

A caution can be entered against both the freehold or leasehold title and against any charge already on the register. The last will prevent any disposition by the chargee - e.g. a sale in the exercise of the power of sale to enforce the security - which would automatically override any interest protected only by a caution against the freehold or leasehold title. If the cautioner claims for some reason to have priority over the registered charge the caution should be registered against the charge as well as against the freehold/leasehold title itself.

Neither a notice nor a caution validates an interest which is not valid under the general law. A caution is inferior in that the cautioner may be called on at any time at short notice to establish and defend her interest.

Further, a caution does not give priority to an interest; it merely preserves any priority which it otherwise has under the general law. A notice does give priority to a (valid) interest. For example, Proprietor P contracts to sell to A who puts no entry on the register; then contracts to sell to B who gets the contract noted on the register. B gains priority over A. If A had entered a caution, this would have preserved her priority. But if A put no entry on the register, and B entered only a caution, A's interest would prevail.[16]

Under s.53 of the Land Registration Act 1925 a caution against first registration can be made in the same way; and will be revealed on a search of the index map (para.4.8).

(c) Restriction

A restriction is designed to enforce any limit on the power of the registered proprietor of the land or a charge to deal with the land or the charge as the case may be. It should be remembered that a central principle of registered title is that a proprietor can dispose of or deal with the land in any way permitted by law, subject only to what is on the register (and overriding interests). Thus, for example, a purchaser buying from a sole proprietor is only concerned with any trust if it is protected in some way on the register.

A restriction will prevent a specified transaction from being registered unless a specified procedure is complied with.

The application for a restriction may be endorsed on a transfer of the title or other document to be sent for registration; or it may be applied for separately on form 75. Application can be made by the proprietor of the registered land (freehold or leasehold) or of a registered charge. As with a notice, entry requires the land certificate to be at the Registry.

In certain cases the Registrar is under a duty to enter a restriction. For example, under the Land Registration Act 1925, s.58(3) and Land Registration Rules 1925, Rule 213 (as amended) a restriction in Form 62 must be entered on the registration of joint proprietors of the land or charge unless it is shown to the satisfaction of the Registrar that the survivor of them will have the power to give a valid receipt for capital on a disposition of the land or charge. This restriction is in the following form:

> 'No disposition by a sole proprietor of the land (not being a trust corporation) under which capital money arises is to be registered except with an order of the Registrar or of the court.'

Thus, it is essential for joint applicants for registration to supply the information necessary to decide whether this restriction is needed; and all printed forms for first registration and registration of dealings by joint

---

[16] See *Barclays Bank Ltd. v. Taylor* [1974] Ch. 137.

proprietors contain the necessary question to be answered by the applicants' solicitor.

Other cases in which a restriction may need to be applied for include:

(i) To protect the beneficial interest where a nominee is registered as proprietor: 'Except under an order of the Registrar no disposition or dealing other than a transfer to [nominator] is to be registered without her consent.'

(ii) To protect shares in partnership property where the partners are registered as joint proprietors: 'Except under an order of the Registrar no disposition by the proprietors of the land is to be registered after the death of either [any] of them without the consent of the personal representative of the deceased proprietor.'

(iii) By a chargee to prevent dealings with the equity of redemption without the chargee's consent (a condition commonly found in mortgages): 'Except under an order of the Registrar no disposition by the proprietor of the land is to be registered without the consent of the proprietor for the time being of charge no ...' Without such a restriction the borrower could sell or lease the land, though of course only subject to the mortgage.

The Registrar can refuse to enter any restriction which is unreasonable or likely to cause inconvenience.

(d) Inhibitions

Apart from bankruptcy (para.13.12.4) inhibitions are rare. They are used to prohibit totally or partially the exercise of unfettered powers of disposition of the proprietor. In practice a restriction will usually be more appropriate.

THE DOCUMENTATION ASSOCIATED WITH REGISTERED TITLE

(a) The register of title

The register means primarily the official record kept at the appropriate district Land Registry of one estate owner's title to a particular piece of land, freehold or leasehold, with its own title number. The expression is also sometimes taken to include the Registry's filed plan of that title (the title plan).

7.8

Each register consists of three parts, each part also being referred to as a register:

(i) The property register. This contains a verbal description of the property and identifies it by reference to a title plan. (As to title plans see para.11.2.3). It also states whether the land is freehold or leasehold. In the case of leasehold it will give short particulars of the lease (not all the terms of the lease which will be returned to the lessee - and remains an essential part of the title to be kept safe with the land or charge certificate, as the counterpart lease will be for the reversioner). The property register will state, if such be the case, that the lease contains a prohibition against assignment without licence. Thus the Registry does not concern itself with or investigate whether any such consent has been obtained; and it is essential to preserve consents with the title documents.

The property register may also contain information about easements or (occasionally) covenants which are appurtenant to (i.e. benefit) the land (below).

(ii) The proprietorship register. This states the class of title (absolute, etc); the name and address of the registered proprietor; and any restrictions, cautions, creditors' notices or bankruptcy inhibitions.

(iii) The charges register. This contains all the subsisting burdens and incumbrances on the title protected by notice, including a note of registered leases to which the title is subject - the lease will, of course, also have its own register - adverse restrictive covenants and other land charges and adverse easements; also any notice of deposit of the land certificate. In addition, charges are registered here together with the name and address of the proprietor of the charge.

(b) Office copies of the register and title plan

These are copies actually issued by the Registry of the entries on the register. They should be distinguished from photocopies of the office copies and can be identified by the presence of the Land Registry watermark in the paper. Office copies of the register and title plan and of documents filed at the Registry are admissible in evidence in judicial proceedings.

(c) The land certificate and charge certificate

A land certificate is prepared by the Registry for each registered freehold and leasehold title. It is a document bearing the seal of the registry and contains office copies of entries on the register and of the title plan (and possibly certified copies or originals of other documents (see below).

It is issued to the registered proprietor; but if there is a registered charge against the title, the land certificate is held at the Registry and in its place, while the charge continues, a charge certificate is issued to the proprietor of the charge. The charge certificate is similar to the land certificate, containing office copies of the entries on the register and of the title plan and also containing, bound into it, the original mortgage deed.

In general, with exceptions such as in the case of cautions, the land certificate must be produced to the Registry on any dealing with the land and if any entry or alteration is to be made to the register. Similarly, the charge certificate must be produced when any entry affecting the charge is to be made on the register – for example on the discharge of the charge. Whenever it is produced at the Registry the land or charge certificate will always be updated to make it correspond with the register. There is also a panel inside the certificate for Registry date stamps to show when it was last updated. Since, however, some entries on the register can be made without its production, there is no guarantee that the certificate does so correspond at any particular time. It is for this reason that on sale and other transactions, investigation of title is based on office copies and official searches of the register itself (see Chapter 13).

The land certificate is admissible in evidence of what it contains and can be said to be the equivalent of the title deed in the case of unregistered title; while the holding of the charge certificate is the equivalent of the deposit of the title deeds with a first mortgagee. But it must be stressed that title itself is constituted by the entries on the register. This is demonstrated by the fact that a lost or destroyed certificate can and will be replaced by the Registry.

EASEMENTS AND COVENANTS ON THE REGISTER

(a) Easements

Legal easements are overriding interests. It has been held that equitable easements are as well.[17] If this is correct all adverse easements will bind a purchaser of the servient property whether or not shown on the register.

In considering both easements and restrictive covenants it is important to keep in mind the distinction between their benefit (and the dominant property to which they are appurtenant) and their burden (and the servient property on which they are incumbrances).

Legal easements existing at the time of first registration are overriding. On first registration of the dominant property the Registry will enter any shown to exist on the property register as appurtenant to the registered title; and this will give them the same guaranteed validity as the registered title to the land itself. On first registration of the servient property, any easements shown to exist will be noted on the charges register of the new title.

7.9

---

[17] *Celsteel Ltd. v. Alston House Holdings Ltd.* [1985] 2 All E.R. 562.

Any easement expressly created by the registered proprietor is a
'disposition' within s.19 of the Land Registration Act 1925 and to be
legal must be completed by registration. Until this is done it will only be
a equitable interest though, as noted above, even as such it may be
overriding. Where the easement is expressly created by grant or
reservation on a transfer of part of the land in a title (the usual situation in
which they arise) the Registrar will automatically enter easements on the
property register of the dominant title and note them against the charges
register of the servient title.

If an easement is created by separate grant – for example, if one
neighbour grants another a right of way over her land – application for
registration will have to be made and provision for the servient owner
(the grantor) to deposit her land certificate at the Registry so that the new
easement can be noted.

On a sale or other transfer of registered land the benefit of any
easement shown on the property register as appurtenant to the title will
pass automatically to the transferee.[18] They are part of the registered title
which is being sold and, on the assumption that office copies of the
register are supplied with the draft contract, do not need to be mentioned
separately in the contract. On a sale of the servient title, the burden of
easements noted on the charges register are of course incumbrances
which will bind the transferee and which there is a duty to disclose; and
the contract should expressly state that the sale is subject to them and
disclose their content either by setting them out or, usually, by
incorporating a copy of the register into the contract. Not all easements
are shown on the title register of either the dominant or servient
property. Implied easements can arise under s.62 of the Law of Property
Act 1925 and *Wheeldon v. Burrows* just as in the case of unregistered title.
They will be legal and overriding without mention on the register
provided they arose out of a registered disposition of part of the land.
Similarly, easements in the course of or having arisen by prescription are
legal and overriding without registration. Both implied and prescriptive
easements can be registered on the property register of the dominant
property and noted against the servient title and registration will give
them the guarantee of validity that goes with registration.[19] But this is not
bound to happen any more than such easements will appear on the title
deeds of an unregistered title.

On a sale of the servient property the duty of disclosure extends
(subject to the terms of the contract) to all adverse easements unless they

[18] See Land Registration Act 1925,s.20(1); and Law of Property Act 1925, s.62; and Land
Registration Rules 1925, as amended, rule 256.
[19] See Land Registration Rules 1925, as amended, Rules 250-258.

are patent. On a sale of the dominant property the benefit of any already existing implied or prescriptive appurtenant easements will pass automatically to the purchaser without mention; and there is no need to mention them in the contract. Indeed, if they are mentioned care should be taken. The contract should state that no requisitions or objections are to be made on them; otherwise, the vendor will be under a duty to prove the title to their benefit as to the rest of the property being sold (and see para.5.6).

(b) Restrictive covenants

Restrictive covenants can only arise by express agreement. Any shown to exist at the time of first registration of the servient property will be noted in the charges register. Similarly, any created subsequently will need to be noted in the charges register of the servient property to be binding on a transferee.

Where practicable the text of the covenants is set out in full in (or in a schedule incorporated into and part of) the charges register with the identity of the deed creating them. If this is not practicable they will be noted in the charges register and the original document creating them or a certified copy stitched into or issued with the land or charge certificate with the original filed at the Land Registry.

On a sale of the land the burden of any existing restrictive covenants affecting the land must be disclosed in the same way as the burden of easements.

As to the benefit of restrictive covenants, appurtenant covenants are not normally included in the property register of the dominant title. Even if, on special request being made, they are shown the form of wording will be that a specified transfer contains covenants expressed to be for the benefit of the land in the title. In other words there is no guarantee that the covenant is enforceable by the dominant proprietor.

As with easements, on a sale of the registered title the benefit of any existing, appurtenant restrictive covenants (whether or not shown on the property register) will pass automatically by the transfer without mention in the contract or transfer. If appurtenant, existing covenants are included in the contract description of the property (whether by incorporation of the property register or by specific mention) the vendor should be able to prove title to the benefit or should exclude requisitions or objections on them. For example:

> 'The property is sold with the benefit of the rights contained or referred to in the property register of the said title and the Purchaser having been supplied with a copy thereof shall raise no objection or requisition in relation thereto.'

(c) Positive and indemnity covenants

If positive covenants are created after first registration, the burden will be noted on the proprietorship register of the title. This does not make the burden of such covenants run with the land; it is intended by the Registry to help remind a vendor's solicitor that an indemnity covenant will be needed in the transfer.

As to indemnity covenants, see para.12.9(g). They are required in the same circumstances as on the sale of unregistered title; and Standard Condition 4.5.3. is equally applicable.

IS THE REGISTER SELF-CONTAINED?

7.10   The underlying philosophy of registered title is that the register presents a complete, self-contained picture of the ownership of the freehold or leasehold estate, its appurtenant rights and its burdens. Apart from overriding interests, there are other cases where it may be necessary to look beyond the four corners of the register to get a complete picture. For example:

(i) The actual covenants and terms contained in a registered lease are not recorded in the register. The original lease, after registration, should be retained in safe custody with the land or charge certificate of the leasehold title; the counterpart with the land or charge certificate of the reversionary title.

(ii) The original mortgage deed creating a registered charge of the property will be included with the charge certificate; details of its terms will not normally be available from the Registry. Under s.96(1) of the Law of Property Act 1925 a borrower has a right (at her own cost) to inspect and have copies of the mortgage. For convenience of information a borrower should preserve a copy of the mortgage.

(iii) If a registered lease contains a qualified covenant against assignment this will be noted on the property register; but the register does not guarantee that necessary consents to assignments have been obtained (the absence of which consent might make the lease liable to forfeiture). Consents to assignments need to be kept with the land or charge certificate. The same principle applies to an obligation in the lease to give notice to the lessor of assignment or charging of the lease.

(iv) The benefit of implied and prescriptive easements appurtenant to the land is not likely to be evidenced on the title register of the dominant property (nor the burden on the register of the servient property); similarly with the benefit of restrictive covenants.

Documentary evidence of such rights where available should be kept with the land or charge certificates.

(v) The benefit of restrictive covenants relating to the land is not usually shown on the register.

DRAFTING THE CONTRACT

It follows from what has been said that there are three crucial stages to the normal sale of registered title transaction: **7.11**

(a) Formation of contract (exchange of contracts).

(b) Transfer to the purchaser.

(c) Registration of the transfer at the Registry.

The three are linked together. The terms of the transfer are governed by and give effect to the terms of the contract. In turn, the transfer must be acceptable to the Registry in form and content so as to give rise to the required registration.

The contract is the base line of this structure and its drafting requires careful thought. What follows is based on the format of the Law Society's printed form of contract, incorporating the Standard Conditions, as used in the Goldberg sale (Document 5.1.6). It focuses on the points of departure from a contract for the sale of unregistered title.

Agreement date; seller and buyer

'No problem; these are the same as for unregistered title,' says Timothy. 'Timothy has got something right,' says Old Jarndyce.   **7.11.1**

The property

It is essential that the description of the property states whether it is freehold or leasehold, gives the title number and the class of title and a brief description of the property as given in the property register. (See the draft contract on the Obebe purchase, Document 4.1.2). Where as is now usual a copy of the register and title plan is provided with and incorporated into the contract there is no need for anything further by way of description of the property; and, as already mentioned, there is no need to mention any appurtenant easements or covenants referred to in the property register. As with unregistered title, if any existing appurtenant rights are expressly set out in the contract description of the property, the vendor should either be in a position to prove title to them or should expressly exclude any requisitions or objections in relation to them.   **7.11.2**

Thus for example, the description might be:

'The freehold property known as ... registered at H.M. Land Registry with title absolute under title no...'

Sale of part

7.11.2(a)   On a sale of part of the land in a title, the property description should in addition to the above make it clear that this is the case and include a plan identifying what is being sold. Thus, you would expect something like the following:

'All that plot of freehold land more particularly shown on the plan attached hereto and thereon edged in red being part of the property known as ... comprised in title number ... and registered at H.M. Land Registry with absolute title.'

As to the plan in such a case:

'It is desirable that this plan [which will also be needed for the transfer] should be an extract from, or based upon, the vendor's filed plan. If the land is unfenced or otherwise undefined, except by surveyor's pegs on the ground, it is essential that the boundaries on the plan to the transfer [and therefore the contract also] should be tied by means of accurate measurements to permanent features such a road junctions or existing walls or fences.'[20]

See, further, para.5.4.

The land certificate will have to be produced to the Land Registry to register the new title to the part purchased and amend the register of the existing title to show what has been removed from the title. In this situation, the land certificate can be deposited by the vendor at the Registry using form A.15. A special condition will need to be put into the contract requiring the vendor to place the certificate on deposit at the Registry and to supply the purchaser with the deposit number prior to completion.

Where a new, residential estate of more than 20 plots is being developed, a procedure has been agreed by the Registry to simplify the identification of the property. This is described in Practice Leaflets 7 and 14. A detailed, accurate, large-scale lay-out plan is filed at the Registry, with a copy officially stamped by the Registry being returned to the developer. The contract and rest of the transaction for each plot can then proceed without use of the title plan for the whole estate (which may be very large). The contract can then identify the plot being sold by annexing an extract from the approved layout plan and its plot number. An identical copy of the plan will be used annexed to the transfer.

---

[20]   Ruoff & Pryer, p.85.

The purchaser's solicitor will need to be satisfied that the client's plot on the ground is as shown on the plan. The vendor will supply office copies of entries on the register; but not of the title plan. Instead the purchaser's solicitor will apply to the Registry on form 109 for a certificate of official inspection of the title plan. The certificate, on form 102, will confirm (hopefully) that the plot is part of the vendor's title and that it is not affected by any colouring on the title plan relating to adverse entries on the register (or, if it is, give details).

Immediately prior to completion, the purchaser will do a standard pre-completion search on form 94B (para.13.12) which can identify the plot simply by reference to its plot number on the approved plan. This will confirm (again, hopefully) that no adverse entries have been made in the register or the title plan since the date of the office copy.

Thus the contract description may be something like this:

'All that plot of freehold land comprised in title number ... and registered with absolute title which is shown as plot number ... on the accompanying plan, being a true copy or an extract from the plan of the vendor's said ... estate which plan was officially approved by the ... district land registry on ... Together with the dwelling house erected thereon And Together With the easements described in the First Schedule to the draft transfer annexed hereto but Excepting and Reserving to the Vendor the easements described in the Second Schedule thereto.'

In addition there will be a condition in something like the following terms:

'The vendor shall be under no obligation to supply to the Purchaser a copy or extract of the title plan of the above-mentioned title but arrangements have been made with the ... district land registry for the Purchaser (on his applying on printed form 109 for an official certificate of inspection of the title plan) to be informed whether the land sold to the Purchaser is within the Vendor's said title and whether or not it is affected by any colour or other references shown on the title plan of such title.'

On such a development, and contrary to the usual conveyancing practice, the transfer will be drafted in a standard form by the vendor and supplied as part of the contract with a special condition that it is to be the one used on the transfer. Thus, one might expect something like the following:

'The draft form of transfer attached hereto the form of which has been approved by the ... district land registry for general use in connection with the vendor's ... estate comprised within the above mentioned title shall be used without alteration (save only for such variations as may be necessary for defining the powers of joint or corporate purchasers) for the transfer to the purchaser and in particular the purchaser shall in the transfer to him covenant with the vendor in the terms set out in clause [2] of the draft to observe and perform the stipulations contained in the [Third Schedule].'[21]

This form of transfer will probably have been approved by the Registry with a written guarantee that the easements granted by it will be registered, thus saving the need for the vendor to prove her title to grant the easements on the sale of each plot.

Each transfer will have to incorporate a separate plan, normally based on an extract from the approved lay-out plan. This plan must contain sufficient detail to identify the property and its dimensions in relation to nearby recognisable features. A plan 'for the purpose of identification only' will not be accepted by the Registry.

Less than absolute title

7.11.2(b)   Under an open contract and the Standard Conditions, in the absence of provision to the contrary, it is implied that absolute title will be proved and conveyed. It follows that if the title is less than absolute (for example, possessory), this must be stated clearly in the contract. But, even if the possessory title is correctly described as such in the contract, s.110(2) of the Land Registration Act 1925 provides:

'The vendor shall, subject to any stipulation to the contrary, at his own expense furnish the purchaser with such copies, abstracts and evidence (if any) in respect of any subsisting rights and interests appurtenant to the registered land as to which the register is not conclusive, and of any matters excepted from the effect of registration as the purchaser would have been entitled to if the land had not been registered.'

Standard Condition 4.2.1. provides:

'The evidence of registered title is office copies of the items required to be furnished by s.110(1) of the Land Registration Act 1925 and the copies, abstracts and evidence referred to in section 110(2).'

In the absence of special condition, the vendor will have to deduce and prove the title to the freehold prior to the first registration in accordance with the rules of unregistered conveyancing. Since the reason for the title only being possessory will invariably be that this was not possible at the time of first registration, the vendor's solicitor will probably have to insert a special condition into the contract barring investigation of and objections to this title and possibly offering whatever evidence of title the vendor does have - for example a statutory declaration of actual possession (i.e. adverse possession) for whatever period possible.

---

[21]   See Ruoff & Pryer, p.211.

A purchaser who then contracts on this basis will have decided to take the risk.

Thus, for example, one might find:

'1. Title to the Property is registered at H.M. Land Registry with possessory title under the title number ... and title shall be deduced in accordance with the Land Registration Act 1925 Section 110 save that copies of the entries on the register title plan and any documents referred to on the register shall be office copies.

2. The Purchaser shall not require the Vendor to supply any evidence of title prior to first registration.'

Or one might find:

'2. The title prior first registration to the property coloured green on the Plan shall consist of a statutory declaration made by the Vendor in the form of the draft annexed to this agreement.'

Here the declaration would state, for example, that the vendor had been in uninterrupted possession of the property for a specified period without acknowledging the right of any other person to possession or to the rents and profits of the property in question. (See Encyclopedia, Volume 36, p.249; and paras.5.5 and 10.4.1).

Question   After researching the matter, explain whether a statutory declaration (as opposed to a simple statement) is obligatory in this situation; and the advantage of the former over the latter.

Explain why uninterrupted possession is evidence of title; and the significance of saying that there has been no acknowledgement of the right of any other person during the period of possession.

Incumbrances

Under an open contract the vendor's duty of disclosure is the same in the case of registered as unregistered title. Subject to the terms of the contract, the vendor must disclose any incumbrances other than those which are patent or already known to the purchaser (and those which are to be removed before completion).   **7.11.3**

The Standard Conditions (3.1.) do not differentiate between registered and unregistered title in this respect.

Disclosure of incumbrances is done in the contract by reference to the state of the register a copy being supplied as part of the contract. For example:

'Incumbrances on the property. The matters referred to in entries nos ... on the charges register of the said title a copy of which is incorporated herein.'

Printed special condition 2 of the Law Society's form of contract excludes the right to raise requisitions or objections on the incumbrances: 'The property is sold subject to the Incumbrances and the Buyer will raise no requisitions on them.' Incumbrances that are to be removed - such as mortgages - will not be mentioned in the contract.

If there is any caution or inhibition on the register which is not to be cleared off, this too must be made clear in the contract.

The same duty of disclosure extends to overriding interests. Subject to Standard Condition 3.1. these too must be disclosed (para.4.3).

Capacity of the vendor

7.11.4
The capacity of the vendor will be stated in the contract in the same way as for unregistered title. As indicated in Chapter 5, in unregistered title the main significance of the capacity relates to the covenants for title to be implied and the extent of the acknowledgement in relation to retained title deeds. Acknowledgement in the case of registered title is dealt with later (para.12.9).

Covenants for title

Rule 76 of the Land Registration Rules 1925 provides for the vendor's capacity to be stated and the covenants for title to be implied in a registered transfer in the same way as in an unregistered conveyance. What has been said in Chapter 5 is therefore equally relevant here, particularly as to the limitations on the protection given by the covenants.

However, the likely utility of the covenants may be even more limited (though not to be ignored) in the case of registered title. The implied covenants only relate to the subject matter *expressed* to be conveyed. The practice in registered conveyancing (in both the contract and the transfer) is to describe the property by reference to the title register and not to set out the details of the incumbrances shown on the register. Rule 77(1) of the Land Registration Rules 1925 provides that the title covenants shall take effect as though the disposition was expressly made subject to:

'(a) all charges and other interests appearing or protected on the register at the time of the execution of the disposition and affecting the title of the covenantor...'

This simply means that the covenants will not guarantee the property free of any adverse interest shown on the register. But equally it would seem to mean that, where only a possessory or qualified title is being sold, the covenants will not extend the limited guarantee implicit in such a title - i.e. in the case of possessory title, will not guarantee the pre-registration title in any way. Under Rule 77, the conveyance is expressly subject to any pre-registration defect.

In the case of the sale of an absolute title, the assumption might be, as the title is guaranteed by the state once it is on the register (subject to entries on the register and overriding interests), that there is no part for the covenants to play. The covenants might however be relevant in two situations (which justifies their retention):

(i) Where the title is rectified against the covenantee under s.82 of the Land Registration Act 1925 and either public fund compensation is not available under s.83 or a larger sum is potentially recoverable by suing the covenantor on the title covenant.[22]

(ii) Where the transfer to the covenantee has not been (or because of the defect cannot be) registered. The case of *A.J. Dunning & Sons (Shopfitters Ltd. v. Sykes & Son (Poole) Ltd.*[23] illustrates such a situation. This was another case of a double conveyance by developers. The defendants, the developers, sold land including the small piece in issue referred to as the yellow land to purchasers who were registered as proprietors. Unfortunately, the purchasers had not included the yellow land in the fencing with which they enclosed their purchase. Subsequently, the defendants sold and transferred land including this yellow land to the plaintiffs. Consequently, the Registry refused to register title of the plaintiffs to the yellow land. The defendants were held liable for breach of the title covenants.

The main point of law decided in the case was that the term 'register' in Rule 77 (quoted above) meant only the register of the transferor's title not the global register encompassing all registered land nor the register of adjoining land. The register of the adjoining property of the original purchasers did show their interest as proprietors of the yellow land. The defendants' title did not show any charge or interest in the yellow land; it simply excluded it from the title.[24]

It should be stressed that *Dunning* was an unusual case, though by no means unique. Reliance on the covenants was only possible because it was the defendants who had done the act or omission giving rise to the defect (by previously selling the same land to the first purchasers).

There is a further limit on the ambit of the covenants in the case of registered title (and an isolated introduction of the concept of notice into registered conveyancing). Rule 77(1)(b) excludes reliance on the covenants in relation to overriding interests of which the purchaser had notice. In unregistered conveyancing a claim is not, it seems, barred even

---

[22] For an, unsuccessful, claim on this basis see *Meek v. Clarke* (1982), Lexis transcript; which also illustrates how the covenants do not protect against title paramount.

[23] [1987] Ch. 287.

[24] Though, if the plaintiffs' solicitor had properly compared the transfer plan he was using with the title plan on the defendants' register the discrepancy should have been noticed.

if the covenantee had knowledge of the defect at the time of conveyance.[25] This makes it even more important to discover overriding interests before completion.

Title number

7.11.5   This must of course be given, either here or in the description of the property.

Completion date; contract rate; chattels and fixtures

7.11.6   What has been said in relation to unregistered title contracts applies equally here.

Question In the light of the above and using the same format, draft the contract for the Obebe sale. See Documents 7.2 and 7.3 for Instructions on Sale and the office copy entries on the title. Include any special conditions you think necessary (not implying that any are) relating to insurance (para.3.5), fixtures and fittings (para.4.4.2), and the NHBC agreement (para.3.6).

Question You are drafting a contract of sale for Silencia Ramsbotham the title to whose large house and two hectare garden is registered with absolute title. When taking instructions you have learnt the following facts: The next door property is a college for theology students. The students hold noisy barbecue-parties into the early-morning hours every weekend; and are constantly throwing rubbish into Silencia's garden. Constant complaining to the college authorities has produced no result - this is one of the reasons why Silencia wants to move. For a long time she has been in dispute with the neighbour on the other side over ownership of the dividing fence (which both claim); There are two outstanding mortgages on the property which will be paid off out of the proceeds of sale. The local rambling club is claiming a right of way (which, they say, has been a right of way since medieval times) along her drive. The property register of Silencia's title shows that her property has the benefit of a right of way across the grounds of the theology college to the village shops.

How, if at all, should the above matters be dealt with in the draft contract? Draft any necessary clauses. Insofar as they do not have to be

---

[25] *Great Western Railway v. Fisher* [1905] 1 Ch. 316; though it is difficult to see why in principle the vendor should not be able to get rectification to make the conveyance expressly subject to a defect of which the purchaser's knowledge before contract excluded the vendor's duty of disclosure.

shown in the contract, would Silencia have to disclose them to a purchaser in dealing with the purchaser's enquiries before contract?

TRANSACTION PROTOCOL

In 1990 the Law Society introduced (with a great deal of media 'hype') a recommended conveyancing procedure for use in domestic conveyancing transactions, to be known as TransAction Protocol (more formally known as the National Conveyancing Protocol). A second edition was published in 1992; and the Protocol is due to be relaunched in 1994.

7.12

There is no legal or professional duty on solicitors to use or not to use it. In using it a solicitor is not giving a professional undertaking to comply with its requirements; its use is subject to the overriding professional duty of the solicitor to her client. It does not change the law of conveyancing or in general the duty of a solicitor in relation to the transaction. Where it is used it does to some extent change traditional conveyancing practice.

The Council statement which introduced the Protocol stated its purpose to be to streamline conveyancing; to speed up pre-contract formalities; and to improve communication between solicitors and their clients.

The Protocol (and modern domestic conveyancing practice in general) has to be seen as just part of the response to the development of owner-occupied housing as an increasingly mass-produced, consumer article, serving a relatively mobile, job-chasing population, and spreading to the lower socio-economic groups. These factors demand - and the necessary profit margins of solicitors reflect this demand - cheaper, speedier and (hopefully) more efficient conveyancing procedures.

It has been said that:

'There is little in it which is either new or controversial. It represents the kind of routine and standard practice which has been carried out for the past five or ten years or so. As a statement of preferred practice, the protocol is quite capable of working satisfactorily.'[26]

The terms of the Protocol are reproduced in Appendix 6 as it is a useful statement of most (though not all) the steps likely to be necessary in an ordinary, domestic conveyancing transaction; and can usefully be compared with the steps based on more tranditional procedure in Appendix 1.

---

[26] F. Silverman, 'Problems with the Protocol' Law Society's Guardian Gazette, 25 September 1990, p.22; and see Conveyancer's Notebook, [1990] Conv. 137.

To highlight a few of its specific points:

(a) The respective solicitors should agree at the outset whether or not they are going to use the Protocol. If they use it any decision to depart from its procedures should be notified to the other side.

(b) It involves the use of the Standard Conditions of Sale and certain standardised, Protocol forms: namely, the Seller's Property Information Form (Document 4.1.4) and Additional Property Information Form - the latter for use on sale of leasehold (para.17.3.1); and a Fixture, Fittings and Contents List (Document 4.1.5).

(c) Subject to the overriding duty of client confidentiality, it requires the solicitor to keep the other side informed of progress in the client's related purchase/sale.

(d) The main departure from traditional practice (if not from general modern trends) is that the vendor's solicitor will supply the purchaser's solicitor with a package with the draft contract. This will include a local search and additional enquiries of the local authority; completed Property Information form and Fixtures, Fittings and Contents form; and the evidence of title. Traditionally, the purchaser's solicitor would do local and other pre-contract searches for herself after receiving the draft contract; and would have to take the initiative in sending any enquiries before contract which she wanted the vendor to answer; and traditionally, evidence of title would be supplied by the vendor after exchange of contract.

CHAPTER 8

MORTGAGES

TIMOTHY HAS NOT RETURNED

Timothy has not yet deigned to return from the wine bar. Old **8.1**
Jarndyce is secretly rather hoping that he has drowned in a butt of sack;
but suspects that they would not sell Falstaff's favourite tipple at
Timothy's favourite wine bar. Meanwhile, Old Jarndyce will collect
together a few thoughts on mortgages.

It is assumed that the reader is familiar with the general law governing
mortgages of both unregistered and registered land. This chapter gathers
together some of those aspects relating to conveyancing transactions.

OUTSTANDING MORTGAGES

The vendor's property is likely to be subject to one or more **8.2**
mortgages at the time of sale. Her solicitor should consider the following
points:

(a) Prior to drafting the contract and giving the client any necessary
financial advice, the vendor's solicitor will need to know what
mortgages are outstanding on the property and how much is needed
to redeem them. This may involve a search in the Land Charges
Register, in the case of unregistered title, for possible second or
subsequent mortgages. In the case of registered title they will be
revealed by entries on the register of title.

(b) In the case of unregistered title, the deeds will have to be obtained
from the mortgagee in order to prepare the draft contract. In the case
of registered title, the office copy entries should be used to draft the
contract. (See paras.1.8.1, 5.11 and 5.13).

(c) Any outstanding mortgage will have to be cleared off the title
(except in the unusual case where the property is being expressly sold
subject to the mortgage). There are three ways in which this can
happen:

(i) The usual course is for the mortgage to be redeemed either
before completion or after completion in accordance with the
vendor's solicitor's undertaking given to the purchaser's solicitor
(para.14.9.3).

(ii) On a sale of part of the vendor's land, the mortgagee may agree to release the part being sold (paras.12.4(c) and 14.9.3).

(iii) The mortgagee may sell in exercise of the power of sale (below).

The purchaser's solicitor and outstanding mortgages

8.2.1   The purchaser's solicitor will need to check that any mortgage has been cleared off the title in one of the above ways.

In the case of discharge it is important to check that there is a proper receipt, properly executed, operating as a discharge and not a transfer of the mortgage (para.14.9.3).

The unregistered title to 24 De Lucy Mount, being purchased by Fancy French and Sam Saunders shows a mortgage of 4 July 1985 and a subsequent sale by the building society (Documents 10.2.4 and 10.2.5).

In the case of unregistered title, a purchaser buying from a mortgagee (and the same principles apply when investigating a sale by a mortgagee earlier in the title) needs to check that the statutory power of sale given by s.101 of the Law of Property Act 1925 has arisen - that is, that the mortgage money 'has become due'. Subject to this, the title of a purchaser in good faith will be protected even if the statutory power was 'improperly or irregularly' exercised (Law of Property Act 1925, s.104(2)). Although a mortgage can contain an express power of sale, mortgagees normally rely on the statutory power, which gives the purchaser the protection of s.104(2)[1] Thus, the purchaser does not have to investigate whether the power of sale is being properly exercised; and will be protected so long as she does not have actual knowledge of irregularity or of facts suggesting irregularity. Any claim which the mortgagor may have for irregularity in the sale will have to be made against the mortgagee.

The purchaser will take the legal estate of the mortgagor free of all subsequent mortgages (even if protected on the register), free of the borrower's equity of redemption and free of any interests derived out of that equity[2]; but subject to any mortgages or other interests having priority to that of the mortgagee selling. In practice, a second or subsequent mortgagee selling will arrange to redeem any earlier mortgages out of the proceeds of sale (and there is a right to redeem them) so that the property can be sold unincumbered.

---

[1]   And a sale is deemed to be in exercise of the statutory power unless the contrary intention appears (s.104(3).

[2]   *Duke v. Robson* [1973] 1 All E.R. 481; *Lyus v. Prowsa Developments Ltd.* [1982] 2 All E.R.

As indicated above, the purchaser does need to check that the mortgage money was due at the time of sale. Traditionally, mortgage deeds made the money due (the legal date of redemption) six months after the date of the mortgage; even though neither party expected the money to be repaid on that date. In the absence of such provision in the mortgage deed (which is not always included in modern, institutional, instalment mortgages) the purchaser should require evidence that the money (i.e. repayment of the loan) was due at the time of sale. In the case of an instalment mortgage it has been held that the mortgage money is due (for the purpose of allowing sale) when any instalment is in arrear.[3] This must be subject to any contrary intention in the mortgage.

The abstracted mortgage (Document 10.2.4) merely states that the mortgage contains the 'usual mortgage clauses'. A requisition should be raised for a copy of these clauses and a check made that the power of sale had arisen.

In the case of registered land, the purchaser is only concerned where she herself is buying from a mortgagee. By s.34(1) of the Land Registration Act 1925, the proprietor of a registered charge has all the powers of a legal mortgagee. In effect, ss.101 and 104, described above, apply to a registered charge as they do to a mortgage of unregistered land.

The transfer by the proprietor of the registered charge must be in form 31 and on application for registration will have to be accompanied by the charge certificate. As with unregistered title, the purchaser should check that the mortgage money has become due; although the Registrar will make no enquiries as to whether a case has arisen to authorise the sale or whether the best price has been obtained.[4]

The Registrar will serve notice on the proprietors of subsequent charges (which will be overreached by the sale) requesting lodgement of their charge certificates. The purchaser will of course take subject to any prior registered charges (and other entries on the register or overriding interests) which are binding on the chargee selling.

CREATION OF A NEW MORTGAGE

Two situations should be distinguished: 8.3

(a) Where the purchaser is buying with the aid of a mortgage.

(b) Where an existing owner is raising money (for whatever purpose) by a mortgage loan - i.e. a loan that is not being used to finance the purchase.

---

[3]   *Payne v. Cardiff R.D.C.* [1932] 1 K.B. 241.

[4]   See Ruoff & Roper, para.24-12.

In general the same principles apply in relation to the mortgage but, in particular, the distinction, may affect what adverse interests are capable of binding the mortgagee and therefore the steps to be taken by the mortgagee's solicitor (paras.13.10, 13.15).

The purchase-linked mortgage

8.3.1   The purchaser/borrower's solicitor may also be acting for the lender. This is possible in the case of an institutional lender provided there is no conflict of interest. In the case of a private mortgagee, it is only possible if one of the exceptions stated in Rule 6 applies *and* there is no conflict of interest (para.1.9.3).

The mortgage transaction closely parallels the purchase transaction with, in effect, the borrower in the position of a vendor, having to show good title to the land and convey it (in this case by way of mortgage) to the lender; the lender in the position of a purchaser (taking a mortgage of the land in return for the money (in this case the loan).

The following points should be noted (bearing in mind that the purchaser/borrower's solicitor may be the same person as the lender's):

(a) The borrower may need advice in relation to the available types of mortgage loan; and in relation to the lender's valuation/survey requirements (paras.2.5 and 3.4).

(b) The lender will make an offer of a mortgage loan which may be accepted by the borrower. This offer will be accompanied by and subject to conditions. Some of these will be addressed to the borrower herself (e.g. as to any retention of part of the advance pending repairs); others directly to the lender's solicitor (e.g. as to the lender's particular requirements as to title) (para.2.5.2).

(c) As to title, it should be appreciated that a title acceptable to a purchaser/borrower may properly be rejected by the lender; and the making of the loan will be conditional on a proper title to the property being proved. The purchaser's solicitor should bear this in mind when advising the purchaser whether to exchange contracts. The lender is not bound by the contract of purchase. If it does contain onerous terms as to title, etc. these must be acceptable to the lender as well as the purchaser. The same applies to the outcome of all pre-contract investigations (Chapter 4). The lender as well as the borrower needs to be satisfied before contracts to purchase are exchanged. If a separate solicitor is acting for the lender, approval of the results of pre-contract investigations should be sought before contracts are exchanged. On the need to satisfy the lender as to title see *Pinekerry v. Needs (Contractors)* (para.7.5.2) and *Luck v. White* (para.10.6.6).

(d) Pre-completion steps, relating to investigation of title, will need to be done on behalf of the lender as they are done on behalf of the purchaser/borrower. If a separate solicitor is acting for the lender, the proof of title will have to be forwarded by the purchaser's solicitor to the lender's solicitor. As to who will do pre-completion searches, in whose name, see paras.13.6 (unregistered title) and 13.12.3 (registered title).

It has to be remembered that the lender is concerned not just with the title of the vendor; but also with the intervening title of the purchaser/borrower; but for the unlikelihood of the purchaser encumbering the title so as adversely to affect the lender, see paras.13.10, 13.15.

(e) In the case of an endowment mortgage, the borrower's solicitor will have to take the necessary steps required by the lender to prepare and complete the mortgage of the endowment policy (paras.2.5.1(b) and 15.3.2).

(f) In principle, the mortgage deed is drafted by the lender to be approved by the borrower, engrossed by the lender when agreed and forwarded to the borrower's solicitor for execution by the borrower. There is rarely any need for execution by the lender. In practice, institutional lenders have standard, printed mortgage deed forms, which simply have to be completed and executed by the borrower.

It is important to remember that the borrower is undertaking a serious commitment and should appreciate the financial and legal implications. Though it has to be said that with the standardised mortgage practices of the large institutional lenders there is little scope for negotiation or departure from their imposed practice; which is probably why there is not seen to be much risk of conflict of interest!

(g) A mortgagor who mortgages as beneficial owner, is bound by the four beneficial owner covenants; but in this case they are absolute and not limited to defects arising since the last transaction for value.[5]

(h) The lender's solicitor will have to report on title to the lender; and if satisfactory receive the advance cheque in preparation for completion (para.14.2).

(i) After completion registration of the purchase and mortgage will have to be attended to by the lender's solicitor (paras.15.4.2, 15.5.2). The charge certificate and other documents of title will be sent to the mortgagee (para.7.8(c)).

---

[5] Law of Property Act 1925, s.76(1)(C) and Schedule 2, Part III.

CHAPTER 9

FORMATION OF CONTRACT

MONDAY, 1ST MARCH.
TRAINEE TIMOTHY BACK AT WORK

Timothy walks into the office having just been entrusted to file a   **9.1**
request for the issue of an originating application in the local County
Court under Order 24 (Summary proceedings for the recovery of land).
Timothy does rather enjoy the part (small though it may be - and we will
not reproduce here his drafting of the affidavit in support) he is
occasionally allowed to play in the eviction of squatters. Timothy has
rather strongly coloured views on lager louts, gypsies, social security
scroungers and anyone else who would not be admitted to his favourite
wine bar. It is fair perhaps to note in passing, that the present target of
Order 24 is short haired, the legitimate husband of a legitimate wife with
2.5 legitimate children, a highly skilled (though redundant) computer
programmer and the victim of a vast negative equity in a once proudly
owned home.

Reflecting on the merits of Order 24 and the promise of an evening
in the wine bar with his favourite Fiona, he absent-mindedly puts the
file in the filing drawer marked 'Completed Transactions' and looks at
his diary.

'Got to exchange on the Goldberg sale this afternoon; And on
Obebe.' He gets out the Goldberg file and finds a copy of the contract
signed by his clients, Mr and Mrs Goldberg, together with a copy signed
by the purchasers and the following letter from Moriarty & Co. (For the
Instructions on Sale, see Document 5.1.3).

Document 9.2(a) Goldberg Sale: Letter from Purchasers' Solicitor

MORIARTY & Co.
——— Solicitors ———

To: Messrs Jarndyce & Jarndyce
24 The Strand
Ledchester LR2 3JF
22 February 1993

Dear Sirs,

Garden at Fell View, Koppax
Subject to contract
Our ref: MEC/HP/561
Your ref: TT/MH

Our clients are now ready to exchange contracts and we
enclose copy contract signed by them together with our cheque
for the deposit of £1,000 to hold both to our order pending
exchange of contracts.
We have entered 14 March next as the completion date as
agreed between our respective clients.
Please note that our clients have agreed to exchange on the
condition that your clients let them have occupation immediately so that building work can commence. Such occupation is
on the understanding that if completion takes place after the
agreed completion date for any reason whatsoever, any liability of our clients will be limited to that provided for in
Standard Condition 7; and that accordingly Standard Condition
5.2.6. shall not apply.
This agreement is intended to be and is hereby expressly
incorporated into the contract.
We hope to speak to you on the phone on Monday to exchange
according to Formula A.

Yours faithfully

Moriarty & Co.

Moriarty & Co.

Note: The instruction by Moriarties to hold the 'cheque' to their order means that, if taken literally, Jarndyces could not cash the cheque until exchange. This would pose problems if the deposit money were needed by the vendor for the deposit on a simultaneous, related purchase (unless the cheque were simply endorsed over in favour of the vendor's own vendor - in which case solicitors endorsing it would become liable on the cheque). An alternative would be to require the deposit money to be held to order. The cheque could then be paid into the bank immediately.

Timothy gets on the phone and manages to contact Mary Moriarty Junior who is handling the matter. After a few pleasantries, they exchange using formula A. Putting down the phone, Timothy dictates a letter to Moriarties enclosing the part contract signed by Mr and Mrs Goldberg with instructions for it to be sent first class; and a letter to Mr & Mrs Goldberg stating that exchange has taken place and that the purchasers can now be allowed onto the property. He sends the deposit cheque to accounts and completes a memorandum of exchange form in the following terms:

Document 9.2(b) Goldberg Sale: Memorandum of Exchange

Jarndyce & Jarndyce
Memorandum of Exchange By Telephone

Property	*Part garden at Fell View, Wensleydale Avenue, Koppax*
Sellers	*Mr & Mrs Goldberg*
Buyer	*Jinder & Balraj Singh*
Persons exchanging	*TT / Mary Moriarty Junior*
Date and time	*1 March 1993. 2.05 pm*
Formula	*A*
Deposit	*£1,000 - Moriarty cheque*
Completion date	*14 March 1993*
When note made	*2.20 pm*
Signed	*TT*

Question What does Standard Condition 6.1. have to say about the time of day for completion? What would the position be if on the 14 March, Moriarties did not produce the money until after 2 pm; or, if they were ready with the money but there was no one available at Jarndyce's to complete until after 2 pm?

Note: Standard Condition 6.1.1. will invariably be amended, by implication, by the insertion in the special conditions of a specific date for completion. It may be necessary to amend Standard Conditions 6.1.2. and 6.1.3. to match your client's requirements. For example, a purchaser may not be able to complete until after 2 pm when she has received the proceeds from her sale; a vendor may need to complete by a particular time to provide the money necessary for her purchase. The purchaser should not complete until certain that the vendor is leaving the property (and not leaving it full of unwanted junk and rubble); and the vendor should not complete until assured that she is going to get the balance of the money. In other words, ideally, the keys should be handed over at completion when a draft for the balance of the purchase price is handed over.

Question Suppose that you act for a purchaser who will not have funds available for completion until after 3pm on completion date; but would like to have the keys to start moving in at 12 noon on that date. The vendor is agreeable to this arrangement. Draft any special condition you think necessary to amend/replace Standard Conditions 5.2., 6.1.2., 6.1.3. (See below, para.9.4.1, as to Standard Condition 5.2.2).

Of course, in practice, the client's removal arrangements will often not be known until after contract and nearer the date of completion. A mutually satisfactory arrangement will have to be agreed then with the other party's solicitor.

In reality, practice on completion may be more 'relaxed' than suggested by the above; with a degree of trust entering into the final stages. The vendor is likely to hand over the keys to the purchaser arriving with her pantechnicon at more or less the time that the solicitors are completing the transaction.[1] But care should be taken before advising a selling client to hand over the keys, and before handing over the purchase money for a buying client.[2]

---

[1] For a case where the courts had to try and ascertain the exact moment of completion in relation to the buyer moving in, and the difficulty of doing so with modern completion practice, see *Abbey National Building Society v. Cann*, [1990] 2 W.L.R. 832.

[2] For the relevant provision (para8.3) of TransAction Protocol, see Appendix 6.

TIMOTHY BACK AT WORK

Timothy then takes out the Obebe file and finds a note saying that the **9.3** other solicitors on both the sale and purchase will be available to exchange this afternoon. He checks and finds that he has his client's part of the contract on both the sale and purchase signed by Miss Obebe. A glance at his check list suggests that there is no outstanding matter to be attended to prior to exchange. Conscious of the dangers of not synchronising exchange, he first rings Havishams and is told by Miss Havisham that she is ready to exchange on the sale according to formula B and will be in the office for the next hour. He then rings Moriarties and exchanges with Mr Moriarty on Miss Obebe's purchase using formula B, makes a file note of the exchange, and then again rings Havishams. Miss Havisham is not available. Thirty minutes later she rings Timothy. After an embarrassed hmming and haaing, she confesses that her clients have just been on the phone and told her to withdraw as they have found a cheaper property.

Timothy puts the phone down with one hand, reaching with the other into his drawer for a small flask of whisky which he keeps there, and begins to wish that he had taken his father's advice and gone to work on the family pig farm. If only Fiona had liked pigs!

After a moment, realising that the problem will not go away, he gets on the phone to Miss Obebe at work. Before he is able to break the news to her that she now has two properties, Miss Obebe says 'Oh, I'm so glad I've got hold of you. Is it too late to cancel the sale? My sister would like to buy it; and she is talking of a higher price than the Headcases were offering. She can afford it. Her husband's a law lecturer. And she wants you to act for her as well which will save a bit more money won't it? Can we come and see you tomorrow and you can help get her to agree a price?'

Timothy, hoping that she does not notice the sound of relief in his voice, says that he should be able to arrange that. And, thinking to himself, 'Professional conduct rules - conflict of interest - two sisters related by blood; no problem here', he arranges an appointment with the two sisters for the following afternoon. He puts down the phone, makes a note of the new instructions, and finishes off the flask of whisky.

Question Will the Headcases be able to recover their preliminary deposit paid to Dream Homes? (see Document 7.2); and, if so, from whom? (para.2.3.1).

Question Can Timothy properly act for Miss Obebe and her sister as suggested? (See para.1.9.3)

OLD JARNDYCE COMMENTS

Occupation before completion

9.4.1   Maybe, in a conveyancer's paradise, the purchaser's solicitor would
always hand over the money with one hand and receive the keys giving
possession with the other. But conveyancing must adapt to the
convenience of the client, not the other way round.

If the property is already vacant, the purchaser may want possession
before completion. The vendor may be happy to oblige. She can be
earning interest on the purchase money (see Standard Condition
5.2.2(d)); and she can be relieved of the responsibility for the physical
state of an empty property (see Standard Conditions 5.1.1., 5.2.3.).

Standard Condition 5.2. is an attempt to cover this eventuality. A
number of points should be considered.

(a) There is a fairly serious risk to the property owner (one that it
would be very hard to contract out of) in allowing a prospective
purchaser into occupation *before* exchange of contracts. Standard
Condition 5.2. will not of course be applicable; since this can only
have contractual effect when it becomes part of a binding contract. In
the event of dispute, the courts are likely to hold that the occupant
has been given exclusive possession and is therefore a tenant - even if
a written agreement is drawn up indicating that only a licence is
intended.[3] The danger is that, if a contract does not materialise, the
occupant may be able to claim security of tenure as an assured tenant
under s.1 of the Housing Act 1988; only liable to be evicted if one of
the limited grounds specified in the Act can be established. Clearly, an
owner should not get herself into this situation.

(b) If a purchaser is let into occupation *after* and pursuant to a contract
to buy, s.5.2. does apply. In *Street v. Mountford* the House of Lords
recognised that there were exceptional situations in which a person's
exclusive possession could be effectively attributed to some legal
relationship other than that of landlord and tenant; and recognised the
purchaser let into occupation under a contract to purchase as such a
situation.[4] Thus, although you cannot turn a tenancy into a licence by
calling it a licence, it is safe to assume that effect would normally be
given to Standard Condition 5.2.2. Whether a tenant or a licensee,

---

[3]   See *Street v. Mountford*, [1985] A.C. 809; *Bretherton v. Paton* [1986] 1 E.G. 172 (C.A.); and
Bhattacharya v. Raising (1987) (unreported - Lexis transcript).

[4]   [1985] A.C. 809, at p.828, *per* Lord Templeman.

the contracted purchaser will be subject to her obligation to complete; but her status might become important if the contract were found to be void; or if the purchaser had proper grounds for rescinding the purchase contract.

A contract to buy, made with a sitting tenant, does not automatically imply immediate surrender of the tenancy[5]; but, if considered necessary, a term could be put into the sale contract expressly surrendering the tenancy and replacing it with a Standard Condition 5.2. licence. This would presumably be effective, even if the tenant were an assured tenant.

(c) If completion is delayed beyond the contractual completion date, the Standard Conditions make the purchaser potentially liable, in effect, to pay double compensation - twice the contact rate on the purchase price less deposit paid - under Standard Conditions 5.2.2(d) and 7.3. This in effect gives the vendor benefit of the purchase money and of the land at the same time. The term introduced by Moriarties' letter (above) is an attempt to deal with this and align the position to that under open contract rules.

On the other hand, a purchaser in occupation, faced by relatively low payments for delay, may not be in a hurry to complete. If 5.2.2(d) is removed it might be desirable to increase the contract rate of interest.

(d) Standard Condition 5.2.5. enables either side to terminate the licence on giving five working days' notice. This may put the purchaser in a vulnerable position, especially if, as in the Goldberg case, she is going to embark on expensive works on the property. Of course, the vendor will still normally be obliged to complete in accordance with the contract and reinstate the purchaser into possession. But it might be advisable - especially if there is to be some delay between contract and completion - to make the licence terminate only on completion or rescission.[6]

(e) More serious, is the question of whether the purchaser will be able to recover the value of works done on the property (and cost of moving, etc) if the contract is not finally completed for any reason. This is a matter on which the purchaser in particular needs clear advice and warning.

Note that, under Standard Condition 5.2.2(f), the occupying purchaser must not alter the property. Obviously, this will have to be amended where the purpose - as in the Goldberg case - is to do anything other than repair work.

---

5   *Nightingale v. Coutney* [1954] 1 Q.B. 399.

6   For an attempt, in breach of contract, to evict a licensee contractor from a building site, see *Hounslow L.B.C. v. Twickenham Garden Developments Ltd.* [1971] Ch. 233.

If the contract proves to be void for any reason, it seems that the purchaser may be in a position to claim equitable compensation for work done on the property under the principle of proprietary estoppel.[7] Where the contract is terminated as a result of the vendor's breach, the purchaser will be entitled to damages. Damages may include the cost of improving the property if the expenditure was in the contemplation of the parties at the time of contract.[8] On the other hand, if it is the purchaser's breach which brings an end to the contract, she will not get compensation for work done on the property; and, indeed, a suing vendor may claim that changes made to the property have increased the loss.[9]

(f) Acceptance of title. Once the purchaser accepts the vendor's title it is too late to raise further requisitions (see para.10.6.7). If a purchaser goes into occupation under an open contract and exercises acts of ownership (such as making alterations) this is presumed to imply acceptance of title in relation to any irremovable title defects of which she then has notice - e.g. those shown by a delivered abstract. Standard Condition 5.2.7. deals with this issue; and preserves the full right to raise requisitions where the purchaser is let into occupation. But where, as in the Goldberg case, occupation is given to exercise acts of ownership such as doing works, it may not be enough to say that the right (i.e. the open contract right mentioned above) is 'unaffected'. It may be desirable to provide that any works done by the purchaser will not be deemed to be acceptance of title or waiver of any right to raise requisitions.

Question In the light of the above discussion consider and draft what amendments/ additions to Standard Condition 5.2. you think might be reasonable in a case where the intention is to give the purchaser occupation on exchange to carry out major building works.

Note: The above demonstrates a number of points about negotiating and drafting contracts:

(a) Standard, common form, general conditions are clearly essential. You could not (and do not need to) sit down and draft a complete set of terms every time you carry out a conveyancing transaction.

(b) Whether you use the Standard Conditions or some other published set, you should not simply assume that they comprise a perfect

---

[7]   See *Lee-Parker v. Izzet (No. 2)* [1972] 1 W.L.R. 775; Megarry & Wade, p.804.

[8]   See *Lloyd v. Stanbury* [1971] 1 W.L.R. 535, where the expenditure was held not recoverable, partly on this ground.

[9]   See *Maskell v. Ivory* [1970] Ch. 502.

set of conditions. You may think it desirable to produce your own in-house standard variations to be included in any contract.

(c) No set of standard conditions, however well drafted, can cater for all situations. Each time a contract is drafted thought should be given to the possible need to amend your standard form of conditions to cover the exigencies of the particular transaction.

(d) Drafting conditions, whether standard or special, is not a simple matter and needs careful thought. You have to think through all the possible eventualities that you are trying to provide for, how you are going to provide for them; and then articulate your provisions in the clearest, simplest, most unambiguous language possible. (See also para.5.3.1).

Access to do work before completion

Standard Condition 5.2. does not itself determine whether a purchaser is being given occupation or merely rights of access for some purpose such as decoration. Which is intended should be made clear in writing, preferably in the contact itself.[10]

9.4.2

In the case of access only, the permitted works and anything else agreed should also be spelt out; If Standard Condition 5.2.4. applies the rest of Standard Condition 5.2. will not. The purchaser's presence on the property (so long as she keeps to the terms of the agreement) will be as a licensee, since she will not have exclusive possession. The licence can be revoked at any time on giving reasonable notice in the absence of a contract not to revoke it. What has been said about compensation for work done on the property applies equally here. A purchaser's solicitor cannot, of course, give an undertaking to complete in these situations; unless she is sure of being able to fulfil the undertaking (see para.5.13 as to undertakings).

Question Draft an agreement, to be separate from the contract of sale, giving the buyer access to do certain works. Specify the works (which you can invent) with sufficient particularity.

Would such an agreement be caught by s.2 of the Law of Property (Miscellaneous Provisions) Act 1989?

---

[10] See *Desai v. Harris* Independent, 16 February 1987 (C.A.) for a case where a clause in the contract did specify, though the proper construction of the clause was in dispute.

FORMATION OF A BINDING CONTRACT

9.5   A contract for the sale of land is subject to all the rules which govern the formation of any contract.

In addition, s.2 of the Law of Property (Miscellaneous Provisions) Act 1989 must be complied with. Section 2 recognises two, and only two, ways in which a binding contract 'for the sale or other disposition of an interest in land' can be made. 'Interest in land' is defined by s.1(6) to include any interest in the proceeds of sale of land. Thus, in spite of the possible effect of the doctrine of conversion at common law, the interest of a beneficiary under a trust for sale of land is deemed to be an interest in land within the section. The term will not normally apply to a licence; since it seems now to be accepted that a licence by itself does not constitute an interest in land.[11]

If the section is not complied with there is no binding contract; and, subject to what is said below (para.9.5.3), either side is free to withdraw.

The two ways are firstly, by exchange of contracts. Here two copies (commonly referred to as 'parts') of the contract are produced and a binding contract comes into existence when the two copies are exchanged. 'Exchange' means that in a contract between S and B, possession of one copy passes from S to B and possession of the other from B to S.

Each copy must incorporate 'all the terms which the parties have expressly agreed'. A term does not have to be in identical wording in each copy; but, as would be the case with any contract, however expressed, the terms in each copy must have the same meaning[12], otherwise the agreement would be void as a contract for uncertainty of terms. Clearly, it is advisable for the wording of each copy to be identical. An agreed term may be set out in the copy contract itself; or it may be set out in a separate document which the copy contract incorporates by reference.

It is quite common in practice for the signed contract to state that the Standard Conditions of Sale (2nd edition) are incorporated, without referring to any particular document containing those standard conditions. It is arguable (though probably the courts would get round it) that this is not incorporation by reference to some other 'document', and that s.2 is not satisfied. Both for this reason, and so that the client has before her the whole of what she is agreeing to, any standard conditions being used should be fully set out as part of the contract document.

---

[11]   See *Ashburn Anstalt v. W.J. Arnold & Co.* [1989] Ch. 1.

[12]   See *Record v. Bell* [1991] 1 W.L.R. 853.

It is important that the written contract does contain *all* the terms which the parties have agreed and want to include. A party, seeking to use s.2 to avoid liability, might argue that some additional term was in fact agreed (perhaps during an early stage before solicitors became involved), and that s.2 has not been satisfied because this term has not been included in the written contract. You can probably guard against this effectively by including a special condition in the written contract to the effect that: 'This contract is intended to replace any previous agreement and to contain *all* the terms finally agreed between the parties.' This would of course leave anything previously agreed and not properly incorporated without legal effect,[13] unless it could be seen as a separate, valid collateral contract (below).

Each party to the contract or her authorised agent must sign one of the copies. In practice, a party signs the copy to be handed to the other party.

The second way is by the use of a single document constituting the contract. Each party, or her authorised agent, must sign the contract which must incorporate all the expressly agreed terms. Again, the section is satisfied if a term is set out in the contract document itself or in a separate document which is incorporated by reference into the contract document.

In the ordinary sale and purchase transaction where different solicitors are acting (whether from different firms or, in the few cases permitted – see para.1.9.3 – from different offices of the same firm) it is usual to use the exchange procedure. Where (again in the few situations permitted by professional conduct rules) the same solicitor is acting for purchaser and vendor, exchange is not possible. The notion of a person exchanging contracts with herself has been judicially described as an 'artificial nonsense'.[14] To comply with s.2 the one-copy contract (whether or not it incorporates other documents) method *must* be used. Here the contract will normally come into existence when both parties have unconditionally signed.

Side letters and last-minute amendments

It is not uncommon for last-minute amendments/additions to be made to a contract by exchange of solicitors' letters. This practice raises a number of issues one of which is compliance with s.2.

9.5.1

---

[13] Conceivably, the courts might take the view that an incomplete document which declares itself to be complete is still incomplete. But, see *McGrath v. Shah* (1987) 57 P. & C.R. 452 where there was a term that the written contract constituted the entire terms of the contract. This was held effective to prevent representations made before the contract being treated as part of the contract; and, further, this term was held not to be caught by s.8 of the Misrepresentation Act 1967 since it defined what the terms of the contract were rather than seeking to restrict or exclude liability for what were terms.

[14] *Smith v. Mansi* [1962] 3 All E.R. 857, p.861.

In *Record v. Bell*[15] there was a standard form, contract subject to the National Conditions of Sale, by the plaintiffs to sell a house in Smith Square, London, to the defendant. At the time of exchange the plaintiffs' solicitors did not have current copies of the title register; and accordingly sent a covering letter with their clients' part of the contract stating that exchange was conditional on there being none other than certain specified incumbrances on the title. In return, the defendant's solicitor sent their client's part of the contract together with a covering letter which stated: 'This letter is written to be attached to the contract of sale and is part of the contract between the parties. It is agreed that...' and went on to set out in substance (so it was held) the same condition as to title. This letter was 'annexed physically' (presumably, though not stated in the report, pinned or stapled) to the defendant's part of the contract.

It was held that s.2 had not been satisfied (though the court went on to hold that the agreement was enforceable as a collateral contract; see below). On a contract by exchange, as here, any express term must be incorporated into both parts of the contract. It was held that the extra term had been incorporated into the defendant's part - presumably, by being fixed together, the letter and part contract were deemed to have become one document. But the plaintiffs' solicitors had not done this. Their part of the contract (the National Conditions of Sale form) did not contain the new term; and did not contain any reference incorporating the letter. And it must be, so it seems, the 'contract' (here, the National Conditions of Sale form) which incorporates the other document (here the letter).[16] This suggests that practices developed under s.40 of the Law of Property Act 1925 and the old pre-1989 Act law are no longer adequate. Under the old law you could enforce the contract if you could find any document signed by the defendant if this led you back by linking references to other documents; and if these documents together contained all the terms of the contract. Under the old law the documents in *Record v. Bell* would have been sufficient for the plaintiffs to enforce.

Section 2 and 'subject to contract' correspondence

9.5.2   Under the pre-1989 Act law it was the invariable, and necessary, practice to mark all pre-exchange correspondence 'subject to contract'. The effect of s.40 of the Law of Property Act 1925, as interpreted by the courts was that:

---

[15] [1991] 1 W.L.R. 853.

[16] But, see *Tootal Clothing Ltd. v. Guinea Properties Ltd.* (1992) 64 P. & C.R. 452; below, para.9.5.3.

(i) a valid contract for the sale of land could be made orally;

(ii) to be enforceable its terms had to be evidenced by a written memorandum (which could consist of several linked documents (as mentioned above) signed by the defendant or her authorised agent;

(iii) a solicitor does not have implied authority to *make* a contract for her client; but does have implied authority to write letters incidental to the transaction. It followed, so it was held,[17] that a solicitor's letter could (possibly unwittingly) by itself or with linked documents constitute an effective s.40 memorandum of an oral contract previously made by the clients. Prospective purchaser and vendor might have met and shaken hands on a deal, without legal advice and without negotiation on all the details which need to be considered before making such a contract. Such a solicitor's letter might tie them beyond recall to the oral agreement;

(iv) the words 'subject to contract' indicate an intention not to be legally bound (i.e. they negative any intention to create legal relations by what is being said). A letter which denied liability in this way could not, so the courts finally made up their minds,[18] show the necessary acknowledgement of an existing contract to constitute a s.40 memorandum.

What is the position under s.2? It was suggested by the Law Commission, in proposing the new law, that:

'It will still be possible to create contracts by correspondence, so it will still be desirable for the parties to use the formula 'subject to contract' on letters which contain, or which refer to documents containing, the terms of the contract, if the letters are signed by a party to the contract. Use of the phrase, however, would not strictly still be necessary in letters written on behalf of the parties.'[19]

Consider the following points:

(a) Clearly, a client should be advised (if it is not to late!) not to sign anything in writing; and that, if anything has to be put into writing, it should be clearly marked 'subject to contract'.

Question (i) Suppose S signs a letter to B: 'Further to our talk, I am prepared to sell you Blackacre for £100,000.' B signs a reply: 'Thank you for your letter. I am pleased to accept your offer.' Analyze how this would (if it would) satisfy s.2. (ii) How would the position be affected if,

---

[17] See *Daniels v. Trefusis* [1914] 1 Ch. 788.

[18] See *Tiverton Estates Ltd. v. Wearwell Ltd.* [1975] Ch. 146.

[19] Law Commission Report, Transfer of Land, Formalities for Contracts for Sale, etc. of Land, (Law Com. No. 164).

during the talk, B had agreed with S, if the sale went ahead, to 'also take the livestock at valuation'. (Read the rest of this chapter before considering this question).

(b) As stated above, employing a solicitor as a conveyancer does not cloak the solicitor with implied or apparent authority to make a binding contract on behalf of the client. The solicitor may, of course, be given such authority expressly or by ratification; in which case the client will be, and will expect to be, bound. It is true, therefore, that a solicitor will not normally need to protect her client by use of the words 'subject to contract'. Nevertheless, there might be situations in which a court would hold that a solicitor's letter purported to agree to something on behalf of the client and purported to have authority to do so. There is a risk that the solicitor personally (not the client) might be held liable for breach of implied warranty of authority; or there might be facts on which it could be held that the client had held out the solicitor as having authority to sign (para.1.9.1).

It therefore seems wise to continue to head correspondence 'subject to contract' to make it clear that no such authority exists or is being asserted. It will remembered that the Moriarty letter (above Document 9.1(a)) is headed 'subject to contract'. This seems to be a case in which the words should *not* have been used. Ignoring the words, Moriarties clearly *were* intending to create a binding amendment to the contract on behalf of (and presumably with the express authority of) their clients. The use of the words would presumably be held to negative contractual intention; and to prevent the amendment contained in the letter from being part of what the parties had 'expressly agreed'. Presumably, therefore, the unamended contract would be held to satisfy s.2 and be binding; the amendment to have no legal effect.

Enforcement outside s.2

9.5.3   Section 2 of the 1989 Act does not apply to the following contracts:[20]

(a) A contract to grant a legal lease within s.54(2) of the Law of Property Act 1925 - i.e. a lease taking effect in possession for a term not exceeding three years at the best reasonably obtainable without taking a fine (i.e. a lease at a rack rent). Such leases can themselves be created orally. It is logical that a contract for such a lease should be subject to the same rule. In practice, such leases (especially periodic tenancies) are likely to be made without any preliminary contract (and

---

[20] See s.2(5).

commonly without the intervention of solicitors). The first and only legal agreement between the parties will be that contained in the lease itself. This *is* likely (though not necessarily) to be in writing in the form of a 'tenancy agreement' (in law having the same meaning and effect as a 'lease') signed by the landlord; with a duplicate counterpart signed by the tenant for retention by the landlord.[21]

(b) A contract made in the course of a public auction (see below).

(c) A contract regulated under the Financial Services Act 1986.

The above three types of contract are not subject to any formal, writing requirement at all and can now be made orally.[22] Obviously, such contracts still *can* be made in writing; and should, for practical and evidential reasons, be made in writing or (as in the case of auction sales) be reduced into writing as soon as possible.

Where an agreement is made which is subject to, but fails to satisfy, s.2, there is in law no contract; and either side is free to withdraw at any time.

Nevertheless, the facts of the situation may give rise to legal obligation by virtue of other legal principles.[23]

(a) The rules relating to implied, resulting and constructive trusts. Such trusts can be created without a contract; and, even in relation to land, without writing.[24]

(b) Proprietary estoppel.[25] Even in the absence of a contract, A may be able to claim an interest in land or other equitable relief against B under this principle. In general, A will have to show:

(i) that she acted to her detriment (e.g. by spending money on improvements to the land) in reliance on a belief that she was to be granted an interest in the land; and

(ii) that B encouraged or acquiesced in the act of detriment knowing of this reliance.

---

[20] See s.2(5).

[21] Note that if, as is likely to be the case, an assured shorthold is intended, the requirements of the Housing Act 1988 will have to be complied with.

[22] For a suggestion that the wording of the 1989 Act fails to repeal s.40 of the Law of Property Act 1925 in relation to these contracts, see J.A. Greed, 'Is Exchange of Contracts Binding?' N.L.J., 2 March, 1990.

[23] See Law Com. No. 164 (f.n. 19 above); and para.5.1 *et seq*.

[24] See, e.g. *Hodgson v. Marks* [1971] Ch. 892.

[25] See, generally, Megarry & Wade, p.804; in particular, *Crabb v. Arun District Council* [1976] Ch. 179. For the relationship between proprietary estoppel and the doctrine of part performance under the repealed s.40 of the Law of Property Act 1925, see K.G. Nicholson, '*Richard v. Hogben*: Part Performance and the Doctrines of Equitable and Proprietary Estoppel' (1986) 60 Aus.L.J. 345. For a review of the principles, see *Lim Teng Huan v. Ang Swee Chuan* [1992] 1 W.L.R. 113 (P.C.).

Such a doctrine might well apply where the vendor allowed the purchaser to spend money on improving the property before both discovered that non-compliance with s.2 made the contract void.

In *Du Boulay v. Raggett*[26] (decided under s.40 of the Law of Property Act 1925) R agreed orally with DB and T to bid for land at an auction on the terms that the land would then be divided between them. R purchased at the auction, but then failed to carry out the agreement. It was held that he was bound and specific performance ordered. The facts established a fiduciary duty owed by R to DB and T and it would be unconscionable to allow R to rely on the absence of written evidence under s.40. In effect, R held the land as constructive trustee for the others. Alternatively, T's refraining from bidding at the auction constituted an act of part performance under s.40(2). The trustee principle would presumably apply equally after the 1989 Act; and what was seen as an act of part performance could equally be seen as giving rise to a proprietary estoppel.

(c) Rectification. 'If the parties have reached agreement but fail to record all the terms in writing, or record one or more of the terms wrongly, then either party may apply to the court for the written contract to be rectified.[27] The document as rectified will then satisfy s.2.

(d) Collateral contract. This is a contract which is separate and distinct from the main contract but in some way linked to it. Commonly it will consist of a promise or guarantee given by A to B in consideration of which B will enter into the main contract. In the well-known case of *De Lassalle v. Guildford*[28] the plaintiff agreed to and did enter into a lease from the defendant in consideration of a guarantee from the defendant that the drains were in good order. They were not! The plaintiff was held liable for breach of the collateral contract.

The doctrine may be important in the context of last-minute amendments which have not been incorporated into the main, written contract. In *Record v. Bell*[29] the court held that the letter was 'an offer of a warranty by [the vendor's solicitor] to [the purchaser's solicitor] as to the state of the title, and it was done to induce him to exchange contracts given that protection. That offer was accepted by exchanging contracts'. It was on this basis that the plaintiffs' claim for specific performance did in the end succeed.

---

[26] (1989) 58 P. & C.R. 138.
[27] Law Com. No. 164, para.5.6. And see s.2(4) of the 1989 Act.
[28] [1901] 2 K.B. 215.
[29] [1991] 1 W.L.R. 853.

Could this principle be applied to the Moriarty amendment (their letter, Document 9.2(a) above)? There are two difficulties:

(i) The letter does say that their clients have agreed 'to exchange on condition that your clients let them have occupation...' - a classic hallmark of the collateral contract. However, it also goes on to say that the term is intended to be incorporated into the main contract. In *Record v. Bell* Judge Paul Baker decided that such an intention did not exclude the existence of a collateral contract; but it is difficult to see how a term expressly intended to be part of a main contract can yet be held to be part of a separate, collateral contract.

(ii) The collateral contract by itself might be one for the disposition of an interest in land and so also caught by s.2. This was not the case in *Record v. Bell*; but it might be the case with the Moriarty amendment - if, for example, the amendment were held to intend to give the purchasers occupation as tenants rather than licensees (see para.9.4.1 above).

The court might be able to find that there are two separate agreements not collateral in the sense defined above. In *Tootal Clothing Ltd. v. Guinea Properties Ltd.*[30] there were two documents - a 'lease agreement' which did not mention the other document referred to by the court as the 'supplemental agreement' and which stated that 'this agreement sets out the entire agreement between the parties'. Under the supplemental agreement the defendant landlord agreed to pay the plaintiff tenant £30,000 towards the shopfitting works to the demised premises. After the lease had been executed the landlord reneged on this promise.

The landlord argued that the supplemental agreement was not enforceable because it had not been incorporated into the lease agreement. The court decided that it was not caught by s.2. and was enforceable. In effect, although the parties had initially made a single bargain, they had, by 'contractual choice' turned it into two separate contracts. The supplemental agreement was not within s.2; and even if it was it satisfied that section. The lease agreement was not in issue since the lease had been executed. Even if it had been, it would have been enforceable. It did not have to incorporate the supplemental agreement which was a separate contract.

Old Jarndyce advises on amendment procedure

Both Timothy and Moriarties seem to have tied themselves (or rather their clients) in potentially litigious knots. The transaction may well   **9.5.4**

---

[30]   (1992) 64 P. & C.R. 452.

proceed amicably to final completion. But it may not. If dispute does arise, or one side wants to back out, the legal position is far from clear. This is not good conveyancing.

Particularly in the light of s.2, it is important to have a proper procedure for incorporating last-minute amendments/additions into the contract:

(i) Any amendment to the contract should be written into the contract document itself; or, at least, a term should be written into this document identifying and incorporating the letter or other document which does contain the term.

(ii) Where the contract is in two parts to be exchanged, the amendment, in identical terms, should be put into each part.

(iii) Ideally, if feasible, 'clean' copies of the contract should be produced showing the whole text as finally agreed without alterations or obvious additions to existing text. Such final copies should then be signed by the respective clients.

(iv) In general, a signature only authenticates what is there when it is made. Any amendment or addition made to the text should be signed or initialled by the client in the margin opposite. To avoid later argument this should be done even if, in fact, the change was made before the contract was signed.

(v) The client must agree to the whole contract, including any amendments. If the client herself signs, as indicated above, this of course indicates agreement and makes the contract binding within s.2.

(vi) A s.2 contract can be signed by an authorised agent of the party – and presumably this authority can be given orally. As indicated above, a solicitor does not normally have implied or apparent authority to make or sign a contract (as opposed to a pre-1989, s.40 memorandum) on behalf of a client. Failing express authority (or post facto ratification) the client will not be bound; and the solicitor who purports to have authority runs the risk of being sued personally for breach of warranty of authority.

If, therefore, it is not practicable for the client herself to sign any last-minute amendments (or the contract itself), the solicitor should obtain the client's express authority before signing for her. Of course, at times it may be proper to act without prior authority, in the expectation of subsequent ratification. Whether it is proper or wise must, of course, depend on the amendment being made, how well the client and her wishes are known, etc.

Note that the above principles apply to the insertion of the completion date. They do not affect insertion of the date of exchange.

Old Jarndyce comments on the Obebe exchange

The chance of a party backing out at the very last minute, as Miss   **9.5.5**
Obebe's purchaser did, is fairly remote. The fortuitous desire of the other
party to withdraw at the same time is even more unlikely. Timothy had a
bit of bad luck; and a bit of good luck. But luck does not make an
impressive curriculum vitae. Conveyancing procedures should be
designed as far as possible to eliminate error and reliance on luck.

METHODS OF EXCHANGE

Broadly speaking, there are three methods of exchanging contracts: **9.6**

(a) Personal exchange

Here the solicitors for both or all (for example, if there is to be
simultaneous exchange on two or more contracts) parties will meet and
physically exchange contracts; and the buyer's solicitor will hand over
the deposit. Even with only a single contract, this method will not often
be practicable.

(b) By postal or document exchange agency

Each solicitor will post her client's part of the contract to the other.
Normally, the purchaser's solicitor will send her client's part of the
contract with the deposit to the vendor's solicitor; and, on receipt of this,
the vendor's solicitor will post the vendor's part. It is commonly assumed
(though not decided and by no means certain[31]), by analogy with the
common law, postal acceptance rule,[32] that the contract will become
binding when the second part is placed in the post. Standard Condition
2.1.1. iterates this principle; but this condition cannot be contractually
binding until it is found to be part of a contract; so it can hardly be used
to determine whether there is a contract of which it is part.[33]

Document exchange agencies, commonly referred to as DMX, are in
effect private enterprise postal organisations. Thus, for example, solicitor A

---

[31] See the opposing views expressed in *Domb v. Isoz* [1980] Ch. 548. The post office is an agent
to transmit letters not to receive them on behalf of the addressee; whereas the essence of exchange
is the actual or constructive transfer of possession to the other party.

[32] See *Adams v. Lindsell* (1818) 1 B. & Ald. 681.

[33] An offer can stipulate any particular method of acceptance; and acceptance by such method
will be effective. So it could, very artificially, be argued that the buyer's part constitutes such an
offer and Standard Condition 2.1.1. such a stipulation; the seller's part being categorised as
acceptance of this offer.

will have her own numbered box at the local exchange office, which she will normally collect from at least once a day. Another local solicitor, B, wanting to deliver a document to A will place it in A's box. For delivery to C, in a different exchange area. the document will be deposited at the local exchange office which will transmit it to C's box to be collected by C. Members of the exchange are bound by the exchange's rules which will govern, for example, the time when a document sent through the system will be deemed to have been received by the addressee.[34]

It is commonly thought, again by analogy with the postal acceptance rule, that the contract will be binding when the second part is deposited at the sender's document office. And, again, Standard Condition 2.1.1. iterates the same principle.

(c) Exchange by telephone

It was recognised by the court in *Domb v. Isoz*[35] that exchange of contracts could effectively take place by telephone; and this is now, no doubt, the standard way of exchanging for its speed, convenience and utility when synchronised exchange on linked transactions is desired (see below).

From a legal point of view, the essential essence of the matter is this: solicitor S is ready to exchange by telephone with solicitor B. Solicitor S may already hold B's signed part of the contract (previously sent by post or document exchange) to solicitor B's order (i.e. as her agent). On the telephone, solicitor B will release that part so that thenceforth it will be held by solicitor S unconditionally on behalf of her own client, S. If solicitor B still holds B's signed part, she will agree to hold it from that moment unconditionally on behalf of solicitor S (i.e. as agent for solicitor S). At the same time, the same procedure will be adopted in relation to S's signed part of the contract. The matter was put like this by Buckley L.J. in *Domb v. Isoz*[36]:

> 'Exchange of a written contract for sale is in my judgment effected as soon as each part of the contract, signed by the vendor or purchaser as the case may be, is in the actual or constructive possession of the other party or his solicitor. Such possession need not be actual or physical possession; possession by an agent of the party or of his solicitor, in such circumstances that the party or solicitor in question has control over the document and can at any time procure its actual physical possession will, in my opinion, suffice. In such a case the possession of the agent is the possession of the principal. A party's solicitor employed to act in respect

---

[34] See *John Willmott Homes Ltd. v. Read* (1985) 51 P. & C.R. 90.

[35] [1980] 1 Ch. 548.

[36] [1980] 1 Ch. 548, p.557.

of such a contract has, subject to express instructions, implied authority to effect exchange of contracts and so to make the bargain binding upon his client. This he can, in my judgment, do by any method which is effectual to constitute exchange.'

Exchange by telephone does carry risks; though these risks are not all peculiar to telephone exchange: for example, the risk of misunderstandings inherent in any telephone conversation, with possible subsequent dispute as to what was said or agreed; the risk that the two parts are not identical and contain the completion date and all other agreed amendments and additions.

It is to minimise these risks that the Law Society has recommended detailed procedures to be followed. These formulae are set out in Appendix 4. Formula A is for use where one solicitor is holding both parts of the contract; Formula B for where each is still holding her own client's part.

Use of these Formulae, like Formulae C, is not mandatory or legally necessary. But, for the reasons mentioned above, it is desirable to use them or some similar, clear and agreed procedure.

Timothy and the Obebe exchange

Could Timothy have avoided the near fiasco in the Obebe transaction? More often than not a client is simultaneously selling one home and buying another. The mortgage loan on the present house will have to be paid off to allow a new loan on the new home; the proceeds of sale will be needed to help finance the new purchase; there will have to be a new home to move into when the old has to be vacated. The sale and purchase are crucially interdependent.

9.6.1

There is a risk, if steps are not taken, of what happened in the Obebe case; that after contracts have been exchanged on the client's purchase, the client's own prospective purchaser refuses to exchange. The client is left with an unwanted, and probably unaffordable, second home. Conversely, the client may find herself bound to sell but with no contract to purchase – and potentially homeless.

The problem is compounded by the fact that a whole chain of linked transactions, each one dependent on the next, is likely to be involved. Apart from the risk just mentioned, there is here the practical problem that if one person in the chain drops out during the negotiation stage, the whole chain collapses. Like trying to get all the horses in a national hunt race ready for the off at the same time, it is difficult to get everyone in the chain happy with a proposed completion date and ready to sign at the same time. If one person backs out, everything grinds to a halt until a new prospective purchaser steps in to the gap; by which time another person may have dropped out.

Little can be done about the last problem. But Formulae C is designed as a procedure for actual exchange to prevent the client being left with two houses or no house. It does not prevent her being left where she is. Essentially it is a two part procedure. Imagine that A (who is not selling - a first-time purchaser) is buying from B, who is buying from C, who is buying from D (who is not buying - maybe going into an old people's home). First, solicitor A will, by telephone, undertake to solicitor B to exchange with solicitor B if called upon to do so by solicitor B within a specified time; solicitor B will in turn give the same undertaking to solicitor C; and so on up to the top of the chain.

The second stage will be activated by solicitor D at the top of the chain who will contact solicitor C by telephone and require her to exchange in accordance with the undertaking. The actual exchange will be in effect the same as under formulae A or B. Solicitor C will then be able to repeat this process down the line with solicitor B; and so on.[37]

A solicitor has implied authority to exchange; but Formula C requires an undertaking to exchange within a specified time in the future. This is probably not within the implied authority. The client's express, written and irrevocable authority needs therefore to be obtained. (See Appendix 4 for recommended form of wording).

Like Formulae A and B, Formula C is not without its difficulties. It depends, for example, upon someone having to be available to carry out the second stage during the stipulated time. Use of it in the Obebe transaction would, ironically, have defeated Miss Obebe's last minute change of mind; but then she would have been warned when asked to authorise use of the Formula.

The danger of not checking that both parts of the contract are not identical is not peculiar to telephone exchange. The case of *Harrison v. Battye*[38], a case of postal exchange, is worth mentioning if only to show that perhaps any solicitor is capable of 'doing a Timothy'. After one copy of the contract had been sent to the purchasers' solicitors, the parties agreed to amend by reducing the deposit payable. The purchasers' solicitors amended their part and sent it signed to the vendor's solicitors. The latter not only failed to amend their client's part of the contract in the same way, but by mistake sent the purchasers' part back to the purchasers' solicitor by way of exchange with a covering letter saying: 'We enclose part contract signed by our client to complete the exchange.' The court held that as the two parts were not identical, there was no contract. Ironically, and reminiscent of Timothy's experience, the vendor

---

[37] For possible alternatives to Formula C and discussion of exchange by telephone, see L.S.G. 1/6/88; 18/11/87; (1985) 82 L.S.G. 306.

[38] [1974] 3 All E.R. 830.

whose solicitor had made the mistake apparently gained by becoming entitled to the £200 profit for which the house was sold.

Question Could the purchaser not have obtained rectification of the vendor's part? On this, see the judgment of Sir Eric Sachs.

Lord Denning suggested that: 'The clerical error (in sending forward the purchasers' form) would have been overlooked.' Could such a mistake be overlooked? On what principle? Could it be argued that constructive, though not physical, possession of the vendor's part had been transferred by virtue of the letter quoted above?

AUCTION SALES

A distinction has to be drawn between sales by auction and sales by private treaty (that is any sale which is not by auction). **9.7**

The ordinary rules of contract law as applied to auction sales should be familiar enough to the reader.

In relation to the sale of land by auction, the following points should be noted:

(a) The auctioneer is agent for the vendor; though, in the absence of agreement to the contrary, she will receive any deposit as stakeholder. This means that the vendor may incur liability for any misrepresentation in the particulars of sale or at the auction itself.

(b) Under ss.2 and 4 of the Law of Property (Miscellaneous Provisions) Act 1989, 'a contract made in the course of a public auction' can be made orally. There is no requirement at all as to formality. In practice, the property will be sold under the Standard Conditions or some other set of express terms which the purchaser will be expected to sign when the sale is made.

There is no provision in the Standard Conditions as to how the deposit is to be paid on sale by auction. The position where a subsequently dishonoured cheque has been accepted or the deposit not paid, has been mentioned (para.2.3).

Standard Condition 2.3. deals specifically with sales by auction. The provision contained now in Standard Condition 2.3.5. was considered in *Richards v. Phillips*.[39] The Lyric Theatre, Hammersmith, was knocked down to the plaintiff for £26,000, at which point another bidder, D, claimed that he had bid at the same price (and the evidence supported this

---

[39] [1969] 1 Ch. 39.

claim). In the face of D's protests, the auctioneer put the property up for sale again. This time, the bidding went up to £37,500 before it was again knocked down to the plaintiff. The issue, as seen by the court, was really one of fact; whether a dispute had arisen 'respecting a bid' which entitled the auctioneer under the conditions of sale being used to restart the auction. The court held that there was.

One might argue that the conditions of sale were not relevant. The first sale to the plaintiff at £26,000 was not evidenced in writing signed by the vendor under s.40 of the Law of Property Act 1925 which was applicable at that time.[40] The contract, and with it the condition about disputed bids, was therefore not enforceable. It would follow that the auctioneer was legally entitled to ignore the first contract and put the property up for sale again whether or not there was a dispute.

Question Suppose that the above events happened after s.2 of the Law of Property (Miscellaneous Provisions) Act 1989 had come into operation. How would this affect the legal analysis of the facts?

(c) Standard Condition 2.3.4. is intended to prevent any argument for a collateral, unilateral contract (accepted by attending and bidding) to sell to the highest bidder.

(d) Standard Condition 2.3.2. and 2.3.5. are aimed to reflect the statutory requirements contained in the Sale of Land By Auction Act 1867.

The effect of s.5 of this Act is that:

(i) If the sale is subject to a reserve price this must be made clear in the terms of sale. What the reserve price is does not have to be disclosed.

(ii) If the sale is without reserve, it is unlawful for the vendor to employ anyone to bid on her behalf.

(iii) The vendor, or one person on her behalf, can bid provided there is a reserve and provided this right to bid has been expressly reserved in the terms of sale. The right must be exercised strictly in accordance with its terms.

(d) Whether a vendor decides to sell by auction or by private treaty is a matter of weighing up the respective advantages and disadvantages in the particular situation.

---

[40] The court mentioned, but did not seek to answer, the question of whether the auctioneer owed some sort of legal duty to the purchaser to sign a s.40 memorandum on behalf of the vendor.

From a prospective purchaser's point of view, the crucial factor is that if pre-contract investigations are going to be made, they will have to be made before the auction; and if there is a higher bidder they will have been paid for in vain. This can be mitigated to some extent if, as can and does happen, the vendor produces up to date local searches and Additional Enquiries.

OPTIONS

An option is an agreement under which the owner of the property, the grantor of the option, gives the grantee of the option the right to acquire the property within a specified period of time. The option will specify how the option is to be exercised, normally by giving notice to the grantor. The option will lapse if not exercised within the time limit; but until then the grantor cannot retract the option. The grantee of the option is free to exercise it or not. The terms of the contract which will exist when the option is exercised must be certain when the option is created.   **9.8**

Developers, for example, will commonly purchase options on differently owned properties within a possible site, giving themselves the chance to ensure assembly of all the properties and to get planning permission before committing themselves to purchase.

There has been debate as to how s.2 of the Law of Property (Miscellaneous Provisions) Act 1925 applies to options The answer may depend on how the option is analysed. One view is that there is only one contract - the option agreement - which is a conditional contract for the disposition of land and so within s.2. On this view the option agreement must, but its exercise need not, satisfy s.2. An alternative view is that the option agreement itself, which may or may not be within s.2. (another point of debate[41]), creates an irrevocable offer. On this view the exercise of the option is itself the creation of a contract (the acceptance of the irrevocable offer) and so must satisfy s.2. The problem here is that the exercise of the option is normally by means of unilateral notice by the grantee of the option; and not by the exchange of signed documents envisaged by s.2.[42]: 'It is evident that the draftsmen of this section did not take account of options.'[43]

---

[41] See *Daulia Ltd. v. Four Millbanks Nominees Ltd.* [1975] 2 All E.R. 587; and see, above, para.4.13.

[42] See E.W. Christie and T.W. Evans, 'Options & s.2: Cause for Concern?' L.S.G., 25 July 1990, p. 21; J.E. Adams, 'Options & s.2: Some Cause for Concern' L.S.G. 19 September, 1990, p.19.

[43] *Chippenham Golf Club v. North Wilts D.C.* (1991) 64 P. & C.R. 527, p.530 (Scott L.J.).

In *Spiro v. Glencrown Properties Ltd.*[44] Hoffmann J. applied a workmanlike view to the matter in deciding that the agreement creating the option was within s.2 as a contract for the sale or other disposition of an interest in land; but that the exercise of the option was not and did not have to satisfiy s.2:

> 'The exercise of the option is a unilateral act. It would destroy the very purpose of the option if the purchaser had to obtain the vendor's countersignature to the notice by which it was exercised. The only way in which this concept of an option to buy land could survive section 2 would be if the purchaser ensured that the vendor not only signed the agreement by which the option was granted but also at the same time provided him with a countersigned form to use if he decided to exercise it. There seems no conceivable reason why the legislature should have required this additional formality.'

Hoffmann J. took the view that an option is analogous to a conditional contract for the sale of land rather than an irrevocable offer though, looked at strictly, *sui generis*.

In *Chippenham Golf Club v. North Wilts D.C.*[45] the Court of Appeal did not question this decision; though they did stress and decide on the basis that the option agreement is *sui generis*, is not a conditional or any sort of contract for the sale of land; and that therefore the statutory power of the council to 'sell land' did not include the power to grant options.

The conclusion, following these decisions, must be that an option agreement is a contract for the disposition (not sale) of an interest in land; that the exercise of the option is not a separate contract but is simply the exercise of the option.

The spirit of *Spiro* was followed in *Armstrong & Holmes Ltd. v. Holmes*[46] when it was decided in the High Court that the option agreement is an estate contract registrable as a Civ land charge (this was not disputed); but that the agreement resulting from the exercise of the option was not a separate contract which required separate registration. Registration of the original option agreement protected the rights arising from exercise of the option.

Whichever view is eventually preferred and adopted by the judiciary, caution demands that while uncertainty remains steps should be taken to ensure that the option and its exercise do satisfy any possible s.2 requirement. It could perhaps be done on something like the following lines:

---

[44] [1991] Ch. 537. Quotation taken from Lexis Transcript.
[45] (1991) 64 P. & C.R. 527.
[46] (1993) Lexis Transcript; The Times, 23 June 1993.

The option agreement would be in two parts, one part to be signed by each party to the agreement and exchanged immediately.

This agreement would contain a clause stating that on exercise of the option, the sale was to be on the terms of the sale document (containing the conditions of sale) signed by the grantor of the option and incorporated therein and annexed to the grantor's part of the option agreement (thus the grantor would sign in two places); that this sale document was intended to be an irrevocable offer by the grantor for the sale of the land on the terms of the option; and that the offer was open to acceptance by the grantee signing a copy of the sale document and serving it on the grantor in accordance with the terms of the option.

On exchange of the option agreement, the grantee of the option would hold the vendor's signed part of the option agreement incorporating the vendor's signed part of the sale agreement.

If the grantee of the option chose to exercise it she would sign her part of the sale document and serve it on the grantor in accordance with the requirements of the option agreement.

Question Do you consider the above a satisfactory method ensuring that an option transaction is valid under s.2? Can you suggest any alternative procedure?[47] Draft the necessary clauses.

In any event, if the option agreement itself complies with s.2, and the notice exercising the option is properly given, there is no reason why the court should not enforce the option agreement by requiring the grantor to enter into the sale agreement itself.

A right of pre-emption (commonly called a right of first refusal) obliges the grantor of the right, if she decides to sell, to offer it first to the grantee on the agreed terms.

Curiously, to say the least, the courts have held that the right of pre-emption does not constitute an interest in land until the grantor takes some step indicating an intention to sell;[48] at which point it does automatically constitute such an interest.

Clearly, the agreement creating the right should be made to satisfy s.2. If and when the grantor does decide to sell, she is obligated to enter into a s.2 contract to sell to the grantee if the latter so wishes. If the original agreement satisfies s.2. there is no reason why the courts should not specifically enforce the obligation to enter into the sale agreement.

---

[47] Compare P. Jenkins, 'Options and Contracts After the Law of Property (Miscellaneous Provisions) Act 1989' [1993] Conv. 13.

[48] *Pritchard v. Briggs* [1980] Ch. 338.

PROTECTING THE CONTRACT

9.9   A contract for the sale of land is an estate contract. In the case of unregistered land it can be protected by registration as a Civ land charge; and if not registered will be void against a purchaser of a legal estate for money or money's worth.

Registration to be effective must be against the correct name of the current estate owner (in the case of a sub-sale, this means against the name of the head vendor) (para.13.6).

Similarly, in the case of registered land, the contract will be a minor interest, and unenforceable against a transferee for value if not protected on the register.

The situation is not likely to arise. The second purchaser would have to have taken a conveyance/transfer followed by registration (or registered her own contract in time) to defeat the first. If a purchaser did lose her claim to the land in this way for non-registration, she would have a claim for damages for breach of contract against the vendor - if the vendor were worth suing - who would therefore be unlikely to gain by selling the same piece of land twice. But it can happen inadvertently or, indeed, deliberately.[49]

In practice, it is not usual to protect the contract in this way, unless, for example, there is to be a long delay between contract and completion; or circumstances to suggest that the vendor might agree to sell and convey elsewhere.

---

[49]   See *Midland Bank Trust Co. Ltd. v. Green* [1981] A.C. 513.

CHAPTER 10

INVESTIGATION OF TITLE: UNREGISTERED TITLE

TIMOTHY ON TITLE

In his post Timothy finds a letter from Copperfields enclosing the title on the French/Saunders purchase. 'Ah,' says Timothy, 'Requisitions needed. Nothing difficult here. Bound to be a standard form.' **10.1**

He gets out the file and finds the contract signed by the vendors, the Rocards. It incorporates the Standard Conditions and includes the following special conditions:

'Root of title: Conveyance on sale of 4 August 1974 Between J. Sprat (1) and C. & M. Lamb (2).

Incumbrances: The covenants contained or referred to in the said conveyance.'

The printed special conditions, to which Timothy has never bothered to apply his mind, include the following:

'2. The property is sold subject to the Incumbrances on the Property and the Buyer will raise no requisitions on them.'

Timothy rummages among the jumble on his desk and does find a printed form of Requisitions on Title. This includes a number of standard, printed requisitions with an indication to 'Please strike out requisitions which are not applicable'. Timothy decides to leave it to the vendor's solicitor to do the striking out. 'After all, he's selling the property. He should know what's not applicable.'

The form also contains space for additional requisitions specific to the title; and the instruction 'Requisitions founded on the Abstract of Title or Contract must of course be added to the above'.

Timothy feels that honour requires a positive response to this. He works his way painfully through the title with the constant reference to his once best friend's lecture notes (borrowed and never returned – the mysteries of title, like the price of friendship, always were obscure to Timothy). The title sent by Copperfields is as follows:

Document 10.2 French/Saunders Purchase: Epitome of Title

D. Copperfield & Co.   EPITOME OF TITLE

24, DE LUCY MOUNT, LEDCHESTER

No of Document	Date	Desciption Of Document	Evidence now supplied	Original handed over on completion?
1.	4.8.1974	Conveyance J.Sprat (1), C.& M.Lamb(2)	Photocopy	Yes
2.	5.8.1975	Death of C.Lamb		
3.	12.8.1984	Death of M.Lamb		
4.	1.5.1985	Probate of M.Lamb to Marion Lamb	Office copy	No
5.	4.7.1985	Conveyance on sale. M.Lamb(1) B.Blenkin-sop(2)	Photocopy	Yes
6.	4.7.1985	Mortgage B.Blenkin-sop (1), Ledchester and Bongley B.S. (2)	Abstract	Yes
7.	4.4.1991	Conveyance on sale. Ledchester and Bongley B. S. (1) M.& M.M.Rocard (2)	Photocopy	Yes

The epitome is accompanied by the following documents:

Document 10.2.1 French/Saunders Purchase: Photocopy of Conveyance of 4 August 1974

THIS CONVEYANCE is made the *4th* day of August 1974 Between Jack Sprat of Leaning View Halifax in the county of West Yorkshire (hereinafter called "the Vendor") of the one part AND Charles and Mary Lamb both of 17 Elia Road Ledchester Yorkshire (hereinafter called "the Purchasers") of the other part

WHEREAS the Vendor is seised of the property hereinafter described and hereby conveyed for an estate in fee simple in possession subject as hereinafter mentioned but otherwise free from incumbrances

AND WHEREAS the Vendor has agreed to sell the said property to the Purchasers at the price of sixteen thousand pounds

NOW THIS DEED WITNESSETH as follows:

1. In consideration of the sum of sixteen thousand pounds (receipt of which sum the Vendor hereby acknowledges) the Vendor as Beneficial Owner HEREBY CONVEYS unto the Purchaser All That parcel of land together with the dwelling house erected thereon known as 24 De Lucy Mount Kirkstall Ledchester aforesaid TO HOLD the same unto the Purchasers in fee simple as joint tenants Subject only to the covenants contained or referred to in a conveyance dated the 15th day of August 1906 and made between Arthur Eddison of the one part and William Exley of the other part so far as the same are still subsisting and capable of taking effect and affect the property hereby conveyed

2. The Purchasers (with the object of affording to the Vendor a full indemnity in respect of any breach of the said covenants but not further or otherwise) hereby jointly and severally covenant with the Vendor that the Purchasers and the persons deriving title under them will at all times hereafter perform and observe the said covenants and keep the Vendor and his estate and effects indemnified against all actions claims demands and liabilities in respect thereof in so far as the same are still subsisting and capable of taking effect and affect the property hereby conveyed.

3. It is hereby declared that the Purchasers or others the trustees for the time being of this deed shall have full power to mortgage charge lease or otherwise dispose of all or any part of the said property with all the powers in that behalf of an absolute owner.

4. It is hereby certified that the transaction hereby effected does not form part of a larger transaction or of a series of transactions in respect of which the amount or value or the aggregate amount or value of the consideration exceeds £20000.

IN WITNESS whereof the parties hereto have hereunto set their hands and seals the day and year first above mentioned.

Signed sealed and delivered by
the said Jack Sprat in the *Jack Sprat*
presence of: *Mary Hubbard*
MARY HUBBARD,
SOLICITOR,
LEDCHESTER

Signed sealed and delivered by
the said Charles Lamb in the *Charles Lamb*
presence of: *Andre Malraux*
ANDRE MALRAUX, WRITER,
HUESCA ROAD, LEDCHESTER

Signed sealed and delivered by
the said Mary Lamb in the
presence of: *Andre Malraux* *Mary Lamb*
As Above

Document 10.2.2 French/Saunders Purchase: Office Copy of Probate of theWill of Mary Lamb

COPIES OF THIS GRANT ARE NOT VALID UNLESS
THEY BEAR THE IMPRESSED SEAL OF THE COURT

In the High Court of Justice
The District Probate Registry at Ledchester

BE IT KNOWN that Mary Lamb of 24 De Lucy Mount Ledchester

died on   the 12th   day of August   19 84

domiciled in England and Wales

AND BE IT FURTHER KNOWN that at the date hereunder written the last Will and Testament

(a copy whereof is hereunto annexed) of the said deceased was proved and registered in the said Registry of the High Court of Justice

and Administration of all the estate which by law devolves to and vests in the personal representative of the said deceased was granted by the aforesaid Court to

Marion Lamb of 28 Union Road Tolpuddle Dorset DS2 4JF

It is hereby certified that it appears from information supplied on the application for this grant that the gross value of the said estate in the United Kingdom
does not exceed the sum of £ 125,000   and that the net value of such estate
does not exceed the sum of £ XXXXXX 40,000

Dated the 1st   day of May   19 85

District Registrar/Probate Officer

Probate | Extracted by D. Copperfield & Co. | **DR2**
80

Document 10.2.3 French/Saunders Purchase: Photocopy of Conveyance of 4 July 1985

THIS CONVEYANCE made the *4th* day of July 1985 Between Marion Lamb of 28 Union Road Tolpuddle Dorset (hereinafter called "the Vendor") of the one part And Barry Blenkinsop of Mount Parnassus Avenue Ledchester Yorkshire (hereinafter called "the Purchaser") of the other part

WHEREAS by a Conveyance dated the 4th day of August 1974 and made between Jack Sprat of the one part and Charles and Mary Lamb of the other part the property hereby conveyed was conveyed to the said Charles and Mary Lamb as joint tenants in fee simple

AND WHEREAS the said Charles Lamb died on the 5th day of August 1975

AND WHEREAS the said Mary Lamb died on the 12th day of August 1984 having by her will dated the 6th day of June 1974 appointed the Vendor to be sole executrix thereof and probate of the said will was granted to the Vendor out of the Ledchester District Registry on the 1st day of May 1985

AND WHEREAS the said Mary Lamb was at the date of her death the beneficial owner of the said property

AND WHEREAS the Vendor has not previously made or given any assent or conveyance of the said property and has agreed to sell the same to the Purchaser for the sum of £30,000

NOW THIS DEED WITNESSETH as follows:
1. In consideration of the sum of £30,000 (receipt of which sum the Vendor hereby acknowledges) the Vendor as personal representative HEREBY CONVEYS unto the Purchaser all that property known as 24 De Lucy Mount Ledchester West Yorkshire together with the dwelling erected thereon TO HOLD the same unto the Purchaser in fee simple subject to the covenants contained in a conveyance made the 15th day of August 1906 and made between Arthur Eddison of the one part and William Exley of the other part in so far as the same are still subsisting and capable of taking effect and affect the property hereby conveyed.
2. It is hereby certified that the transaction hereby effected does not form part of a larger transaction or of a series of transactions in respect of which the amount or value or the aggregate amount or value of the consideration exceeds thirty thousand pounds

IN WITNESS whereof the parties hereto have hereunto set their hands and seals the day and year first above mentioned.

Signed sealed and delivered by the
said Marion Lamb in the presence of: *Marion Lamb*
Henry Butcher
HENRY BUTCHER, SOLICITOR,
LEDCHESTER.

Signed sealed and delivered by the
said Barry Blenkinsop in the presence of:
George Orwell   *Barry Blenkinsop*
GEORGE ORWELL, WRITER,
WINSTON SMITH COURT,
LEDCHESTER.

Document 10.2.4 French/Saunders Purchase: Abstract of Mortgage of 4 July 1985

4 July 1985	By a mortgage of this date made between Barry Blenkinsop (thereinafter called "the borrower")of the one part and the Ledchester and Bongley Building Society (thereinafter called "the Society") of the other part It was witnessed that in consideration of the sum of £20,000 paid by the Society to the Borrower (receipt of which was thereby acknowledged) the Borrower as beneficial owner thereby charged all that property known as 24 De Lucy Mount Kirkstall Ledchester to the Society by way of legal mortgage.

Usual mortgage clauses

Executed by the Borrower and attested.

Document 10.2.5 French/Saunders Purchase: Photocopy of Conveyance of 4 April 1991

THIS CONVEYANCE made the 4th day of April 1991 BETWEEN the Ledchester and Bongley Building Society whose registered office is situate in The Bedrow Ledchester West Yorkshire (hereinafter called "the Vendor") of the one part AND Michel and Marie Melanie Rocard both of 24 De Lucy Mount Ledchester aforesaid (here-inafter called "the Purchasers") of the other part

WHEREAS by a mortgage dated the 4th July 1985 and made between Barry Blenkinsop of the one part and the Vendor of the other part the property hereby conveyed was charged by way of legal mortgage to the Vendor to secure the sum of £20000 and interest thereon

AND WHEREAS immediately prior to the mortgage the said Barry Blenkinsop was seised of the said property for an estate in fee simple sub-ject as hereinafter mentioned but otherwise free from incumbrances

AND WHEREAS the Vendor in exercise of its statutory power of sale has agreed to sell the said property to the Purchasers for a like estate free from the said mortgage for the sum of £45000

NOW THIS DEED WITNESSETH as follows:
1. In consideration of the sum of forty-five thousand pounds (receipt of which sum the

Vendor hereby acknowledges) the Vendor as mortgagee in exercise of the statutory power of sale HEREBY CONVEYS to the Purchasers All That property known as 24 De Lucy Mount Kirkstall Ledchester together with the dwelling-house erected thereon To Hold the same unto the Purchasers in fee simple as tenants in common in equal shares Subject To the covenants contained or referred to in a conveyance date the 15th day of August 1906 and made between Arthur Eddison of the one part and William Exley of the other part in so far as the same are still subsisting and capable of taking effect and affect the property hereby conveyed But freed and discharged from the said mortgage and all monies and claims under it.

2. The Purchasers (with the object of affording the Vendor a full indemnity in respect of any breach of the said covenants but not further or otherwise) hereby jointly and severally covenant with the Vendor that the Purchasers and the persons deriving title under them will at all times hereafter perform and observe the said covenants and keep the Vendor and its successors in title indemnified against all actions claims and demands and liabilities in respect thereof in so far as the same are still subsisting and capable of taking effect and affect the property hereby conveyed.

3. It is hereby declared that the Purchasers or other trustees for the time being of this deed shall have full power to mortgage charge lease or otherwise dispose of all or any part of the said property with all the powers in that behalf of an absolute owner.

The seal of the Vendor is hereto affixed by order of the Board of Directors in the presence of

John Smith, **DIRECTOR**
Debbie Bellamy, **SECRETARY**

by authority of the Board of Directors.

Signed as a deed and delivered by the said Michel Rocard in the presence of: *Michel Rocard*
Henry Butcher
HENRY BUTCHER, SOLICITOR, LEDCHESTER.

Signed as a deed and delivered by the said Marie Melanie Rocard in the presence of: *Marie Rocard*
Henry Butcher
AS ABOVE

TIMOTHY RAISES REQUISITIONS

10.3   Timothy takes the standard, printed form of requisitions and fills in the address of the property and names of purchasers and vendors with commendable accuracy.

He then dreams up the following ones to be added in by the secretary:

1. Please supply original certificates of search in Local Land Charges Registry against all estate owners shown on the title.

2. The joint purchaser, Mary Lamb, in the 1974 conveyance appears to have changed her name to Marion in the conveyance of 4th July 1985.

[Timothy thinks he has been rather clever spotting this one. We do not!]

Please provide evidence of the change of name.

3. The declaration as to beneficial entitlement of Mary Lamb in the conveyance of 4 July 1985 should have been made by Mary Lamb herself - see Law of Property (Joint Tenants) Act 1964, s.1(1).

[If only Timothy had the stamina to read as far as s.1(2)]

4. Please supply original Probate of Mary Lamb.

5. Please confirm that a s.36 statement was endorsed on the Probate of Mary Lamb.

6. Please supply evidence of the discharge of the mortgage of 4 July 1985.

7. The conveyance of 1974 should not contain both certificate of value and show ad valorem duty paid. Please explain..

8. Please confirm that the usual indemnity covenant will be given in respect of the covenants in the 1907 conveyance - see Standard Condition 4.5.3.

OLD JARNDYCE INTERVENES

10.4   Timothy is just about to send this 'masterpiece' down to the secretary to be processed when Old Jarndyce, beginning to see the firm's reputation as a member of an endangered species, intervenes.

Question After reading the rest of this chapter, and the other relevant paragraphs referred to, explain what is wrong, (if anything!) with each of Timothy's Requisitions.

Explain what is wrong with the title as deduced; and draft the necessary Requisitions. Pay particular attention to the following aspects:

Do the present purchasers need to give an indemnity covenant? Consider in this context the 1985 conveyance. See Standard Condition 4.5.3. and para.5.6.3.

The death of a joint tenant followed by the death of the sole survivor; followed by a sale by the personal representative of the sole survivor. What matters would this lead you to check?

What matters would you check on in relation to the sale by a mortgagee?

Note: See also questions after Document 12.2 below.

Question Refer back to the Goldberg title (para.5.2(a) and (b)). What requisitions would you expect the Singhs' solicitor to raise if only the two conveyances shown were offered as evidence of the title?

SOME GENERAL PRINCIPLES RELATING TO PROOF OF TITLE AND REQUISITIONS

10.5   It is the duty of the vendor to prove title - that is, to prove (in the manner required by conveyancing law) that she is able to convey (or compel someone else to convey) to the purchaser the title which she has undertaken to convey in the contract. In an open contract this means the fee simple absolute in possession free from any trust and free from incumbrances.

This duty may be limited by the terms of the contract in two ways:

(a) The title itself (i.e. the interest being sold) may be limited in some way. In the French/Saunders transaction the property was expressed to be subject to the covenants in the 1907 conveyance (para.10.1 above). Similarly, if the property is expressly sold as leasehold, the purchaser cannot then complain that it is not freehold.

(b) The contract may limit the proof of that title which the purchaser would otherwise be entitled to receive. Thus, special condition 2 (para.10.1) is intended to restrict the right of the purchaser to raise requisitions in respect of the 1907 covenants.

In a more extreme case, in a sale of unregistered land, the vendor may for example have lost all or some of the title deeds; but she may in fact have held and occupied the property for, say, 20 years. A special condition will have to be put into the contract stating that the purchaser will accept as proof of title a statutory declaration by the vendor to this effect. Or suppose that the vendor purchased from someone whose only available title was by adverse possession. A special condition something like the following might be found:

'The property was conveyed to the vendor by a conveyance dated the 4th day of June 1986 made between William Williams and the Vendor.

The said William Williams was in undisturbed possession of the Property in his own right for a period of more than 15 years immediately preceding the date of the conveyance to the vendor without at any time giving any acknowledgement of any right of any other person to either the possession or to the rents and profits of the Property.

A statutory declaration made by the said William Williams and which confirms the said possession of the property will be handed over on completion.

A copy of the conveyance and the said statutory declaration has been supplied to the Purchaser who shall raise no objection or requisition in relation to them.' (Encyclopedia, Form 159) (And see para.7.11).

Question What is the significance of the phrase 'without at any time giving any acknowledgement of any right of any other person to either the possession or to the rents and profits of the Property'?

Question Consider the implications of such a title when first registration is applied for. What title would the Registry be likely to grant? And what would be the disadvantage of being registered with such a title? Is registration with such a title any better than not being registered at all? (See paras.5.5 and 7.11).

The purchaser will have to decide before exchanging contracts whether to take the risk of accepting such a limited proof of the vendor's title. It should be stressed that such a title will by no means necessarily be unacceptable. A judgment has to be made of the risks in all the circumstances of the particular case and the client purchaser (and mortgagees if also acting for them) advised accordingly.

The obligation of the vendor

10.5.1   As already explained (para.5.3.3) the vendor's solicitor should have carefully investigated the title before drafting the contract; and checked that either she could prove the title to be offered, or put suitable special conditions in the contract limiting the vendor's obligations as to proof.

Quite apart from any such express limitations in the contract, the vendor does not have to produce absolute proof that she owns the title being sold. Indeed, such absolute proof of ownership is not possible; at least in the case of unregistered title (and see para.5.5).

Suppose you are buying from S. S might be in possession; but she might be in possession as a squatter and liable to be evicted by the real 'owner'.[1] She can, however, produce the conveyance by which she acquired the land five years ago from R. If R owned the land then so does S. The deed of conveyance is the proper method for transferring legal title to unregistered land. But what if R did not own it? *Nemo dat quod non habet.* It is a basic proposition of English law that you cannot transfer title in what you do not own. But S can also produce the conveyance by which R acquired the land 20 years ago from Q. But what if ... and so on; back, in theory, to the original partition of the Garden of Eden, Lockean contract, or whatever other past mythical event you prefer to explain and justify the origins of private property.

Conveyancing law limits any such absolute obligation on the vendor in two ways:

(a) It stipulates what evidence of title the vendor must (subject to the terms of the contract) produce and the purchaser must accept. The most obvious example is that the vendor only has to produce proof of title going back at least fifteen years. It is convenient to explain this requirement here.

The vendor of unregistered title must produce a good root of title. This is a document at least 15 years old which on the face of it:

(i) deals with the whole legal and equitable ownership;

(ii) contains a proper description identifying the property; and,

(iii) contains nothing to cast doubt on the title.

Starting with this the vendor must produce proper evidence of the whole subsequent legal history of the property, leading from one transaction or event to another, down to her own ownership. If the title is good, this chain (as it can be pictured) will be demonstrably unbroken and undamaged.

---

[1]   Of course, the real owner would have to prove her title if she tried to evict S; though, English unregistered title being relative, she would only have to prove that her title was better than, superior to, S's.

Conveyancing law as developed by the courts and statute is so designed that if the purchaser receives a title proved in all respects as laid down by the law, she will have a title which is normally secure against any adverse claims. Suppose that the root provided is a conveyance on sale from S1 to P1. Suppose that in fact S1 did not own the property, that the real owner was X, and that S1 was a squatter. This scenario is itself unlikely. The root is a conveyance on sale. Therefore, when P1 bought it can be assumed that S1's title was examined a further 15 years[2] back. In any case, X's title is almost certainly barred under s.1 of the Limitation Act 1980. This requires that, normally, any action to recover land must be brought by the person entitled or her successors within twelve years from when the right to recover arose.

Of course title defects which bind the purchaser can and do materialise after completion even where all the proper rules for investigation of title have been complied with. (This can and does also happen due to the negligence of conveyancing lawyers.) At least in unregistered conveyancing (see para.7.5.2 as to registered title) there is no such thing as a 100% guaranteed title. For example, the vendor may have previously mortgaged the property by legal mortgage protected by deposit of title deeds; she may then have somehow persuaded the mortgagee to let her have the title deeds back and sold the property without disclosing the existence of the mortgage to an innocent purchaser. The purchaser would probably acquire the property subject to the mortgage; and her only remedy if any would be on the covenants for title (para.5.7).

The contract should state what document is to be provided as the root of title; and make clear the nature of that document - e.g. whether it is a conveyance on sale or by way of gift. Normally, the root offered will be a conveyance on sale. This is probably the best possible root of title, for the reason outlined above, and is clearly acceptable. If any other root is offered in the draft contract, the purchaser's solicitor must decide whether it is acceptable. For example, the contract might stipulate that 'Title shall commence with a voluntary conveyance dated the 4th July 1976 made between William Williams(1) and the Vendor (2) and the Purchaser shall assume without requiring any further evidence that the donor under that conveyance was solvent at the date of the conveyance'.

---

2   Or 30 years if the sale was before the Law of Property Act 1969, s.23.

Question Explain in your own words (and words that the average client could understand) the importance of the donor being solvent in such a situation (see para.13.7).

If a purchaser accepts a title shorter than the 15 years, she will be deemed to have notice of any interests which investigation for the full period would have revealed; will be bound by any land charges registered against estate owners over the full period (and earlier -para.13.6(a)); and will not be entitled to compensation under s.25 of the Law of Property Act 1969 in respect of any such charges (para.13.6(a)).

(b) If the evidence produced by the vendor shows what is sometimes called a good marketable title, the purchaser will be required to accept it even if containing some technical defect.

If investigation of title does not reveal any defects, then the vendor has shown good title and the purchaser will be in breach if she fails to complete. Conversely, if some defect does emerge (other than one disclosed or properly dealt with in the contract the vendor will have failed in her duty to prove title and will be in breach.

Somewhere in between these two extremes, at the end of investigation of title there may remain some point of doubt as to whether the title is good or bad. This is likely, for example, where the proper construction of a document or the existence of a fact on which the title depends is undecided. Here the title is doubtful. In general, the courts will not force (by specific performance) a doubtful title on an unwilling purchaser. In principle it is for the vendor (if wanting to enforce the contract for the full contract price) to get the doubt resolved by litigation if necessary. However, if the court decides that there is in reality no serious threat to the title from the matter in doubt, it may force the purchaser to complete and accept whatever risk there may be. As Megarry J. put it in *Darvell v. Basildon Development Corporation*[3] ' nothing which could be called a substantial or reasonable probability of litigation. Instead there was mere conjecture of an attack by what would be idle litigation'. In such a situation, the vendor can be said to have shown a good, marketable title.

In that case the plaintiff entered into a contract (so it was held) by correspondence to sell to the defendant corporation. The corporation refused to complete and resisted the plaintiff's claim to specific performance on the ground that the title was doubtful and not marketable.

---

[3]   [1969] E.G.D. 605.

The plaintiff had bought the property from a Mr Rand. The plaintiff's father had acted as Mr Rand's estate agent (and therefore in a fiduciary relationship) on the sale; and had suggested the sale to his own daughter. Shortly after the contract had been made the plaintiff's father, had persuaded Mr Rand's father (who was being cantankerous about moving out) to leave on terms advantageous to his daughter, the plaintiff in the present case. It followed that, conceivably, Mr Rand junior might have a claim to have the contract with the plaintiff set aside in equity because of the involvement of the fiduciary. Briefly, the law here is as follows:

The self-dealing rule

(i) If trustees or personal representatives sell any part of the trust property (or estate) to one or more of their own number, the beneficiaries have an absolute right to have the contract set aside even if it was a fair and honest transaction. The transaction will only be saved if authorised by court order, by the trust instrument, by all the beneficiaries (being *sui juris*), or (in the case of a personal representative) if she was acquiring the property under a contract made with the deceased. The transaction will equally be voidable against anyone who subsequently acquires the property from the trustee except a bona fide purchaser for value without notice.

Where investigation by a purchaser's solicitor shows such a self-dealing anywhere on the title, the vendor must be requisitioned to show that it was authorised in one of the ways mentioned; or to provide such authorization

The fair dealing rule

(ii) Where a trustee purchases the interest of a beneficiary under the trust from that beneficiary, the fair dealing rule applies. The court has a discretion to set the transaction aside unless satisfied that there was no impropriety. Such a transaction will not normally concern a purchaser of the property since the equitable interests will in any case be overreached, and the matter will only concern the trustee and beneficiary.

Principal and fiduciary

(iii) A principle similar to that in (ii) applies where a fiduciary (such as a person's solicitor, estate agent - as in the present case - or banker) profits from a transaction with the principal. This quite clearly applies where the transaction is directly between the fiduciary and the principal. The court will set aside the transaction if vitiated by undue influence or is otherwise unconscionable (see para.1.9.3). If, for example, a solicitor purchases property from her client (when there is a presumption of undue influence) the transaction will be set aside unless she can show that the transaction was fair, and that the client was fully informed and understood the nature of the transaction. The equity to set aside the transaction will bind a transferee of the property unless a bona fide purchaser for value of a legal estate without notice. It follows, as in (i) above, that if investigation of title reveals any such transaction affecting the property, the purchaser's solicitor needs satisfactory evidence that it is not liable to be set aside.

In *Darvell's* case, Megarry J. recognised that the principle stated in (iii) potentially applied to a transaction between the principal and a relation of the fiduciary; i.e. to the transaction between Mr Rand and the plaintiff.

To return to the facts of this case. Megarry J. was not in a position to decide whether the transaction would or would not be set aside so as to bind Mr Rand who would be the person, if any, entitled to have it set aside; since Mr Rand was not a party to the action between the plaintiff and the Corporation. And, of course, if he did sue and get it set aside the Corporation which would have acquired with notice of the possibility would be bound. However, he did decide that the prospect of such an attack was so remote - there clearly had been full disclosure by the estate agent, he was not using his daughter, the plaintiff, as a cloak behind which to buy the property himself, and Mr Rand had as a witness in court expressed himself happy with the transaction - that it should be dismissed. The Corporation was therefore obliged to complete and accept whatever notional risk there might be.[4]

In contrast is the case of *Faruqi v. English Real Estates*[5] the court declared the contract not to be specifically enforceable when the property was found to be subject to restrictive covenants and the deed which would have disclosed what those covenants were could not be produced. It was not possible to say how bad or doubtful the title was.

The property, which was registered with absolute title, had been purchased by the plaintiff purchaser at auction. The plaintiff was bringing a vendor-purchaser summons (para.10.6.6) for a declaration that the defendant vendor had not shown good title. The contract provided that 'The properties will be sold subject to ... (b) the entries on the registers of title'. It then proceeded to include some particularly repressive conditions as to incumbrances affecting the title as follows:

'Where by the special conditions of sale any property is sold subject to any lease, covenant, restriction or other matter a copy of the said lease covenant restriction or other matter may unless

---

[4] See also *MEPC Ltd. v. Christian-Edwards* [1981] A.C. 205.
[5] [1979] 1 W.L.R. 963.

otherwise provided in the said special conditions be inspected at the said offices of the solicitors for the vendor at any time during normal office hours and the purchaser shall be deemed to purchase with full notice and knowledge of such matters whether or not he shall have availed himself of the opportunity of such inspection and shall raise no objection or inquiry or requisition thereon.

The purchaser shall raise no objection, requisition or inquiry in respect of any rights, covenants, obligations, easements, quasi-easements, privileges, licences subsisting, acquired or being acquired over under or in respect of the properties whether or not the same are disclosed to the purchaser. Neither the vendor nor the auctioneers shall be under any liability to disclose the same whether or not the same are known to them.'

Clearly the purchaser, whether or not on the advice of his lawyer, was taking a risk in accepting a contract with such a condition without further investigation before making a contract.

The vendor did not provide the purchaser with copies of the entries on the register before contract. In fact the charges register, a copy of which the purchaser's received after contract, contained a note that the title was subject to restrictive covenants contained in a deed of 1883 and that neither the deed nor a certified copy had been produced on first registration. When the purchaser's solicitors then requisitioned the vendor's solicitors for a copy of the deed they were told that it could not be produced.

In deciding the case the court applied the following principles:

(i) The purchaser had by contract agreed to take the property subject to any entries that there might on the register and any other incumbrances; excluded his right to raise requisitions about any that might exist; and relieved the vendor of any duty to disclose any incumbrances whether or not he knew about them. At common law, so decided Walton J. these terms were binding on the purchaser (although a copy of the covenant noted on the charges register was not in fact available for inspection as promised by the condition).

(ii) In equity, there is a principle that a vendor can only rely on a clause excluding or limiting the right to raise objections or requisitions on the title if there has been full and frank disclosure of what the vendor does know (and see para.4.4.3). As it was put by Fry J. *In Re Marsh and Earl Granville* (1883):[6]

'a vendor who desires to limit the rights of a purchaser must do so by explicit and plain conditions, and he must tell the truth, and all the truth, which is relevant to the matter in hand.'

---

[6]   24 Ch.D.11, at p.17, cited by Walton J. at p.967.

In the present case the vendor had not complied with this principle. They had known about the lack of any information about the covenants mentioned on the charges register. Indeed, when the vendor itself had bought there was a perfectly proper and acceptable term in that contract as follows:

> 'The property is sold subject to the covenants restrictions and agreements contained or referred to in a deed dated May 17, 1883, and expressed to be made between the several persons whose names and seals are subscribed and set out in the second schedule thereto of the first part and the United Land Co of the second part. The vendors are unable to discover the whereabouts of this deed or any copy thereof but the purchaser shall be deemed to purchase with full knowledge thereof and shall make no inquiry objection or requisition with respect thereto.'

The result in the present case was that the plaintiff was entitled to a declaration that specific performance would not be ordered. Further, the court, exercising the discretionary power to do so given by s.49(2) of the Law of Property Act 1925, ordered the deposit (held by a stakeholder) to be repaid to the plaintiff.

(iii) The defendant was not of course seeking damages at common law for breach of contract, as it was a vendor and purchaser summons brought by the purchaser. Walton J. did however suggest in passing (and following the view of Megarry J. in *Schindler v. Pigault*[7]) that the effect of a court order for return of the deposit under s.49(2) was to put an end to the contract at common law. The vendor would not therefore be able to sue for damages at common law (though the purchaser would not herself be able to claim her costs of investigating title or damages since she could not have terminated the contract at common law for any breach by the vendor.[8]

The emergence of any such unresolved doubt as to the title during investigation may pose a problem for the purchaser's (and indeed the vendor's) solicitor. Is she to advise the purchaser (and the mortgagees if also acting for them) that the title should be accepted together with the doubt? In practice, more or less technical defects on the title are quite common. In most cases the purchaser and vendor will be anxious to get the matter completed on schedule. The solicitor has to make a judgment

---

[7]　(1975) 30 P. & C.R. 328.

[8]　The point was not raised in the case but s.110 of the Land Registration Act 1925 requires a vendor 'notwithstanding any stipulation to the contrary' to provide the purchaser with a copy of any documents affecting the land 'noted on the register'. It would seem that the vendor who was not able to produce copies of the covenants, was in breach of this provision despite the express conditions in the contract; and so was in fact in breach of contract at common law.

in the light of knowledge of the cases and her conveyancing experience. Would a court order the purchaser to complete? Can, maybe, a reduction of the purchase price be negotiated on account of the doubt? Is insurance against the title risk necessary?

In the French/Saunders transaction, (para.10.1 above), as far as we are told, only the existence but not the content of the covenants referred to in the 1974 root conveyance (and actually contained in the pre-root 1907 conveyance) appears to have been disclosed to the purchaser before exchange of contracts. What is the position in the light of the special conditions quoted? Timothy was obviously foolish to allow the exchange to take place without finding out what the covenants were. Since the vendor has not disclosed the details of the covenants the position would probably be as in *Faruqi* – at least if the covenants did impose any limit on use not to be expected for the type of property, the sort which did in any way affect the value of the property adversely (see *Faruqi*, at p.968). The vendor's solicitor should properly have incorporated a copy of the actual wording of the covenants into the contract; or an explanation of their non-availability.[9]

Further principles, relevant in the present context, should be noted:

If Fanny and Sam did complete the purchase they would be bound by the covenants. They are pre- 1925 covenants and so not registrable as land charges; they are therefore subject to the doctrine of notice. Fanny and Sam, either actually or imputedly (through their solicitors) have notice of their existence at the time of acquiring the legal estate and would take subject to them.

Question   Would they have any remedy under the covenants for title? (See para.5.7).

Pre-root investigation

When investigating title Timothy would, at least in the absence of the   **10.5.2** special condition 2, quoted in para.10.1 above, be entitled to requisition a copy of the covenants and raise other relevant requisitions about them. The actual covenants are contained in a pre-root document. Under the Law of Property Act 1925, s.45(1) the general principle is that a purchaser is not entitled to raise requisitions relating to pre-root documents or title. However, this is subject to two qualifications:

---

[9]   A standardised condition barring requisitions on any incumbrances is perhaps not good practice. Either there is nothing, as it were, to hide; or the problem should be disclosed in the contract.

(i) If a serious pre-root defect in title does in fact come to light, the court will not order specific performance against the purchaser and may order return of the deposit under s.49(2) with the consequences discussed above.

(ii) Under s.45(1) The purchaser is entitled to requisition production of pre-root documents in three cases.

First, if any document on the title was executed under a power of attorney created before the root, the purchaser is entitled to a copy or abstract of the document creating the power. This right cannot be excluded by the contract (para.12.4.4(e)).

Secondly, any document 'creating or disposing of an interest, power or obligation which is not shown to have ceased or expired, and subject to which any part of the property is disposed of by an abstracted document'. Thus, if the title produced suggests that the property is still affected by any matter dealt with in a pre-root document, a copy or abstract of that document should be requisitioned. Common examples are as follows: The root document describes the property by reference to a plan in an earlier pre-root conveyance; the property appears to be subject to restrictive covenants or easements shown to have been created by a pre-root conveyance. In any such case, an abstract or copy of the whole pre-root document should be requisitioned; not just the plan or clause containing the easements or covenants. The whole will normally be necessary to identify the dominant property and determine the full effect of the clause.

Thirdly, any pre-root document creating a trust subject to which the property has been disposed of during the title period. The basis of modern conveyancing is to keep trusts off the title through the mechanism of overreaching. Property (that is the legal estate) is sold free of any trusts which will be transferred to the proceeds of sale. This category is therefore not likely to arise in practice. Of course, quite apart from this provision and what is shown by the documentary evidence of title, there may be evidence that the property is subject to a trust which has not been cleared off the title and which the purchaser's solicitor will need to investigate. Suppose that V is selling to P. The root (or any other document) on the title is a sale by A to B; and there is significant evidence that in fact X contributed to the purchase price. A subsequent sale by B alone to V raises the possibility that the property is still subject to the trust. P's solicitor will need to raise requisitions and either be satisfied that X does not have any claim or insist on the appointment of a second trustee to overreach any claim that she does have.

In the second and third cases above the right to pre-root documents may be modified by express term in the contract.

STEPS IN PROVING TITLE

The following description is based on the provisions of the Standard Conditions. If other standard conditions are used their relevant terms will have to be studied. In the absence of relevant express terms the open contract rules will govern.

10.6

Delivery of abstract or epitome and copies by vendor

This is sometimes referred to as deducing title. Under Standard Condition 4.1.1. immediately after exchange of contracts the vendor must send the purchaser evidence of title (or, to state it more accurately, an abstract or epitome and copies of the evidence of title which the vendor will be able to produce). In the case of unregistered title this evidence must consist of either an abstract of title or an epitome with photocopies of the relevant documents. (Standard Condition 4.2.2.)

10.6.1

Before the days of photocopies an abstract was the method used. This was typed on brief paper (approximately A3) and consisted of, in general, a copy of the exact wording of each document and statement of each event affecting the title which had to be proved. It was written in narrative form using the past tense and passive voice. The date of each document or event was normally put in the left hand margin together with a note of any stamping. Conventional abbreviations for a great number of common terms were used, so that 'vendor' became 'vdr', 'purchaser' became 'pr' and 'other' became 'or'. Standard clauses might not be set out in full. For example, the testimonium and execution of a deed might simply be recorded as 'Executed by both parties and attested'. Similarly, clauses more or less standard to most mortgages would be rendered as 'Usual mortgage clauses' (see the mortgage on the French/Saunders title above, Document 10.2.4).

With the universal use of photocopiers the art of writing abstracts hardly needs to be learnt. It is necessary to be able to read and understand one. A vendor's solicitor may only have an examined abstract and not the original documents in relation to part of the title – for example, where the title has previously been split off from a larger title and the originals retained by the owners of the whole. She will supply a photocopy of this; or, more probably, send the examined abstract itself to the purchaser's solicitor with instructions to hold it to her order pending completion.

An epitome is a schedule of documents and events which constitute the title and should be accompanied by photocopies of the documents including any necessary to prove the scheduled events (see Document 10.2).

Whether evidence is to be provided by abstract or epitome and copies, certain principles should be appreciated:

(a) The vendor must supply evidence of all documents and matters which affect and are therefore necessary to prove the title which she has agreed to sell. The vendor should have checked the title before drafting the contract. The evidence supplied should be complete. Any burdens or defects on the title should either have been removed (or arrangements made for their removal - as in the case of mortgages which are to be discharged out of the proceeds of sale); or they should be dealt with in the contract. If this has been done it should not be necessary for the purchaser's solicitor to raise other than standard requisitions.

(b) Any document or event dealing with or affecting the legal estate must be deduced. This obviously includes conveyances and assents. It also includes legal mortgages even if previously discharged since the purchaser is entitled to be satisfied that they have been properly discharged. In practice previously discharged equitable mortgages of the legal estate are not deduced - unless any registration on the land charges register has not yet been cancelled.

Equally, any death, marriage or change of name affecting the legal title will have to be deduced and proved in the appropriate way. Marriages and deaths can be proved by the original or an official copy of the certificate. Death can also be proved by production of the original or an office copy of the grant. A change of name can be proved by a deed poll - that is a deed made by a single person - in this case changing her name. But a person can change her name without formality; and other evidence may be satisfactory - for example, a statutory declaration by the person herself or someone who knows or knew her.

It is customary and proper practice to deduce any official certificates of land charge searches against any estate owners on the title that are available; though there is apparently no duty to do so.

Copies of any relevant memoranda endorsed on any of the title documents should be included. Where the absence of any endorsed memorandum is significant (e.g. of any previous assent on a probate) this should be stated.

Any transaction creating or relating to easements, restrictive covenants or other incumbrances should be included. For example, if the vendor has previously sold off another part of her property, that sale may have created easements or restrictive covenants either over or in favour of the property now being sold. If this is the case the previous conveyance should be deduced. The part sold off may have been held under the same title as the part now being sold. In this case the purchaser's solicitor may need to be satisfied that no part of what is now being purchased was included in the earlier sale; and, in this case, a memorandum of the earlier sale should have been endorsed on the last conveyance of the common title; here, the memorandum as well as the earlier conveyance should be deduced.

In general, equitable interests existing behind a trust of the legal estate (or behind the title of personal representatives) do not need to be and should not be deduced. The principle of modern conveyancing is that such interests are cleared off the title by the overreaching mechanism and do not concern a purchaser.[10] Where the legal title or evidence from elsewhere discloses the existence of such interests, the purchaser is entitled to be satisfied that they have been (or will be on conveyance to her) cleared off the title by adoption of the correct procedures; but will not be entitled to investigate details of those interests. For example, suppose an estate owner on the title has died and the legal estate passed to her executrix. The personal representative has sold and conveyed the property or assented it to a beneficiary. A purchaser will not be entitled to investigate the terms of the will or the entitlement of the beneficiary (para.14.7.1). Similarly, if the title (or information discovered elsewhere) shows that the legal estate was held on trust for sale, the purchaser will not be entitled to investigate the nature of the beneficial interests under that trust provided the property was then conveyed by all of the trustees being at least two in number or a trust corporation. Where such interests are capable of being cleared off the title by overreaching, the purchaser can insist (but does not have to), on this procedure being adopted.[11]

On the other hand, there may be situations where the overreaching machinery cannot or has not operated. Here the vendor is under a duty to disclose and the purchaser entitled to investigate the equitable interests if necessary to be satisfied that they do not any longer burden the title. For example, if investigation of title reveals a sale by trustees to one of their own number, the purchaser would be entitled, subject to the terms of the contract (unless, for example, a court order authorising the sale could be produced), to investigate the equitable interests to be satisfied who the beneficiaries were under the trust, that they were *sui juris* and that they consented (or now consent retrospectively) to the affected sale (para.10.5.1(ii) above). Of course, as with any defect in title, the vendor should have disclosed this defect in title in the contract; and either provided for it to be cured in the way just described, or added a proviso excluding the right of the purchaser to object to the defect.

Again, suppose that S, the vendor, is found to be holding in trust for one other adult person, X. In this case the 1925 legislation does not automatically impose a trust for sale and there might not be one. In the

---

[10] See Law of Property Act 1925, s.10.

[11] Law of Property Act 1925, s.42(1).

absence of such a trust for sale, even the appointment of a second trustee would not overreach X's interest. As before, subject to the terms of the contract, the purchaser would be entitled to investigate X's interest and (on being satisfied that she was in fact the sole equitable beneficiary, insist on her concurrence in the sale.

(c) It is important to be clear about the distinction between, first, the documents which are sent to the purchaser by way of deducing title; secondly, the documents which have to be produced for inspection; and, thirdly, the documents which have to be handed over to the purchaser at completion.

First, at the present stage of deducing title, the purchaser is only entitled to and normally will only receive abstracts or copies, not the originals, of deed and documents. It would generally be imprudent of the vendor's solicitor to let the originals out her control prior to completion and receipt of the purchase money. In any case, commonly the property will be mortgaged and the vendor's solicitor will be holding the deeds as agent for and to the order of the mortgagees. She will therefore not be entitled to deliver them to the purchaser's solicitor. If originals or examined abstracts are sent it should be on the basis that they are held to the order of the vendor's solicitor pending completion. What the purchaser is concerned with at this stage is to be satisfied that, on the assumption that the originals are as shown in the abstract/copies supplied, the title is a good one.

Secondly, before completing, the purchaser's solicitor will need to be satisfied that the abstract/copies do in fact match the originals. For this purpose the vendor's solicitor must produce the originals for examination. Standard Condition 4.2.3. provides:

> 'Where the title to the property is unregistered, the seller is to produce to the buyer (without cost to the buyer):
>
> (a) the original of every relevant document, or
>
> (b) an abstract, epitome or copy with an original marking by a solicitor of examination either against the original or against an examined abstract or against an examined copy.'

For convenience this examination normally takes place at completion. Obviously, if a significant discrepancy between the abstract/copies and the originals is found completion will have to be held up until it is sorted out.

Thirdly, there is the question of which of the original documents will be handed over to the purchaser at completion. This is dealt with later (para.14.9.2).

When preparing the epitome, the vendor's solicitor should indicate clearly for each document or event what evidence is being supplied with the epitome, and whether or not the original will be handed over at completion. Where she will not be able to satisfy Standard Condition

4.2.2. or 4.2.3. a special condition will be needed in the contract relieving the vendor of liability to that extent. For example:

'The seller only has in her possession an unmarked abstract of the conveyance designated herein as the root of title. A photocopy of the said abstract is annexed hereto and the purchaser shall assume without objection or requisition that the abstract is a true abstract of the original conveyance.'

Under s.183 of the Law of Property Act 1925, it is a criminal offence and a statutory tort to conceal from the purchaser any instrument or incumbrance material to the title or to falsify any pedigree on which the title depends.

Perusing title and requisitions

It is the duty of the purchaser's solicitor to peruse (i.e. examine) the evidence of title supplied; and to satisfy herself that (subject to the terms of the contract) the vendor can prove title, in the proper manner, to what she has agreed to sell. Note that this involves showing title not only to the property being sold but also to any easements or restrictive covenants existing or to be granted over adjoining property. It must be shown that the person who granted or will grant the easement or covenant was or is the owner of the adjoining property. Thus, if the vendor is selling part of her land and granting an easement to the purchaser over the land retained, she will have to show title to the retained land as well as that being sold (para.5.6.1).

10.6.2

After perusing the title the purchaser's solicitor will raise requisitions (i.e. address requisitions to the vendor's solicitor) on the evidence of title supplied by the vendor. Each requisition should indicate clearly the defect which is being queried; and state if possible the action which is expected of the vendor's solicitor to deal with it, or alternatively ask how she proposes to deal with it.

For example:

'There is no evidence of an assent by the personal representative of Annie Walker in her own favour prior to selling as beneficial owner in the conveyance of 6 September 1980. Please confirm that such an assent was executed, supply a copy and confirm that the original will be handed over on completion.'

Standard Condition 4.1.1. provides that the time limit for raising written requisitions is 'six working days after either the date of the contract or the date of delivery of the seller's evidence of title on which the requisitions are raised whichever is the later'. It further provides that:

'The time limit on the purchaser's right to raise requisitions applies even where the seller supplies incomplete evidence of his title, but the buyer may, within six working days from delivery of any further evidence, raise further requisitions resulting from that evidence. On the expiry of the relevant time limit the buyer loses his right to raise requisitions or make observations'.

This last sentence is the same in effect as standard clauses making time for raising requisitions 'of the essence'.

Where the time between contract and agreed completion date is less than 15 working days, Standard Condition 4.1.4. stipulates a shorter period for raising requisitions and dealing with them; and for preparing the conveyance or transfer.

If the vendor has not at first supplied all the evidence of title which she should have done the purchaser must still make any requisitions on the evidence which has been supplied; but will have a further six working days from delivery of the further evidence in which to raise requisitions on the further evidence. Thus, different periods may apply to different parts of the evidence of title.

Once the time limits have elapsed, it will be too late to raise requisitions relating to the vendor's evidence of title; and to that extent the purchaser will be deemed to have accepted title and waived any objection not already made. If a vendor's solicitor does choose as a matter of courtesy to answer out of time requisitions, she should make it clear that they are being dealt with as a matter of courtesy; and that the vendor's rights (i.e. to insist on completion at the agreed date) are not to be affected.

There are important exceptions to these contractual time limits on raising requisitions.

First, it is said that if any objection goes to the root of title it can be made even after expiry of the time limit. It is by no means clear what defects will be held to come within this category. Obviously such objections should, in any case, normally be made within the time limits. In *Rosenberg v. Cook*[12] the vendor had bought the land from a railway company. It was clear that in the circumstances the railway company had no power to sell, making the conveyance to the vendor void. Nevertheless, it was held that this defect did not entitle the purchaser to object out of time, rescind and recover his deposit. The court applied a fundamental principle of English property law; though its application in this context might be questioned. The principle is that, at least unregistered, title to land is based on possession, not ownership. What you have and what you sell is your right to possession. And possession (like that of an adverse possessor) in itself constitutes a right to possession,

---

[12]   (1881) 8 Q.B.D. 162.

good against all except someone who comes along able to show a superior right to possession. The vendor could therefore transfer what he had agreed to transfer - his right to possession. But a right to possession derived immediately from a void conveyance is clearly a very different thing from one shown to be derived from a full length legitimate chain of title going back to a good root. If this is good law it is hard to imagine what defect would let in out of time objections.[13]

Secondly, and most important in practice, the contractual time limit does not govern requisitions relating to defects not discoverable from the face of the vendor's evidence; for example, those appearing from pre-completion searches and inspection of the property. Requisitions on such defects must be made within a reasonable time of their discovery. In *Re Cox & Neve's Contract*[14] the purchaser objected to the title on the grounds that there was a restrictive covenant restricting the right of building on part of the property which would bind him if he completed. The root of title stipulated by the vendor was a mortgage of 1852, giving the purchaser a title two years shorter than he would have been entitled to under an open contract (at that time 40 years; for acceptance of a title shorter than the statutory one, see para.10.5.2 above). The restrictive covenant was contained in a deed of 1847. The purchaser discovered its existence not from the vendor but from a third party when making enquiries about a different matter. His objection was made after expiry of the contractual time limit for requisitions. It was held that the purchaser was not too late to object as the defect had not been contained in the vendor's evidence of title; that the vendor had failed to prove the title agreed to be sold; and that the purchaser was therefore no longer bound by the contract.

Thirdly, a purchaser is entitled to raise what are known as matters of conveyance as opposed to matters of title, even after expiry of the time limits. A matter of conveyance is a defect (albeit it is a defect of title) which the vendor herself has a right to remove without the concurrence of any other person. The commonest example is where there is an outstanding mortgage on the property (unless of course it has been sold expressly subject to the mortgage). The vendor can be required to discharge the mortgage prior to completion. Similarly, where the property is subject to a trust for sale, a sole vendor who is in a position to do so, can be required to appoint a second trustee to overreach the beneficial interests.

---

[13] The purchaser would probably have failed even on the basis of in-time objections since the contract expressly excluded the right to raise requisitions in relation to the conveyance from the railway company.

[14] [1891] 2 Ch. 109.

Standard form Requisitions

10.6.3   Printed, standard form Requisitions are available for example, the Oyez printed form. These contain printed requisitions which are likely to be raised in most transactions. For example:

'1. If the enquiries before contract replied to on behalf of the Seller were repeated here, would the replies now be the same as those previously given? If not, please give full particulars of any variation.

4(A) All subsisting mortgages or charges must be discharged on or before completion.

(B) In respect of each subsisting mortgage or charge;

(i) Will a vacating receipt, discharge of registered charge or consent to dealing, entitling the buyer to take the property freed from it, be handed over on completion?

(ii) If not, will the Seller's solicitor give a written undertaking on completion to hand one over later?

(iii) If an undertaking is proposed, what are the suggested terms of it?'

(As to this requisition, see para.10.6.3 below.)

This Form concludes with:

'The right is reserved to make further requisitions which may arise on the replies to the above, the usual searches and enquiries before completion, or otherwise.'

A common form reply to this last is: 'Noted, subject to contract.'

Any requisitions specific to the particular title have to be added to the above printed ones; and any of the printed ones which are not needed should be struck out.

Pre-contract deduction and investigation of title

10.6.4   It is increasingly the practice, especially with registered title, for the vendor's solicitor to send her evidence of title with the draft contract; and indeed for the purchaser's solicitor to investigate and satisfy herself as to this aspect of title before exchange.

Both the legal and practical aspects of this practice, which reflects a significant change in the nature of conveyancing, merit some discussion.

Historically, before the reforms now encompassed in the 1925 legislation, land title was a complex matter with a high potential for defects. Even in 1914, some 90% of residential accommodation was in (commonly weekly) tenancies. Freehold ownership was vested in a relatively small number of the landed families and entrepreneurial classes. Their titles were complicated because the land was subject to highly complex family settlements; and because the common law did not contain the present day mechanisms such as overreaching keeping the beneficial interests under such settlements off the title. Much of conveyancing was about the drafting of these settlements and transferring the settled land from one generation to the next. Where conveyancing in today's usual sense of buying, selling and mortgaging freehold did take place, the central focus of attention, the most expensive, time-consuming and problem provoking part of the process was investigation and proof of title. It was natural for this process to take place after exchange of contracts. Without this guarantee the purchaser would not want to incur the expense of investigating title. The vendor, then as now, was under a duty to disclose any defects or limitations on the title in the contract and then prove that title. But the complexities and difficulty of proving of title were recognised by two rules in particular. First, under the rule in *Bain v. Fothergill* if the purchaser rescinded the contract on discovering an undisclosed defect in title, she was only entitled to recover her deposit with interest and the legal costs of investigating title; not damages for loss of bargain. Secondly, for a long time it has been customary to include a standard term in the contract giving the vendor a right to rescind (with no liability other than to return the purchaser's deposit) on being unable or unwilling on reasonable grounds to deal with a requisition on title.

Today, partly because of social changes and partly because of reform of unregistered conveyancing law and the introduction of registered title, conveyancing is very different.

Over 60% of housing is now owner-occupied, by which is meant not a family estate but a terraced, semi-detached or detached house with, maybe, a bigger or smaller garden. Together with vastly increased social mobility, this has increased the pressure for speed and cheapness in conveyancing. Today, it is a matter of having to sell a house in London to buy one to go with a new job in Leeds all, hopefully, in the space of a month or two. The client is likely to focus on the exchange of contracts as the secure foundation on which to commit herself to future plans. If one contract is upset on discovery of a defect in title, a whole chain of dependent contracts is likely to become entangled. If a client's sale is rescinded because of a title defect, she is still likely to be committed on her purchase with possibly disastrous financial consequences. As far as possible the client wants to be able to rely upon the contract, once made, being completed.

At the same time, and in response to these changing pressures, even unregistered title has been vastly simplified. In the common case it is likely to consist of one or two previous conveyances with a one or two standard building society or bank mortgages and maybe a death and probate in the family. Indeed, today it is perhaps doubtful whether unregistered conveyancing is more complicated or less secure than registered.

This has been reflected in the abolition of the rule in *Bain v. Fothergill*. And now the second edition of the Standard Conditions omits any right for the vendor to rescind without penalty on not being able to deal with requisitions on title. All this means that the vendor needs to be, and with relative ease can be, sure of her title before committing herself to a contract. It also makes it desirable, and practically possible, for the purchaser's investigation of the vendor's evidence of title to take place before contract.

Another rather different response to the above factors has been discussed from time to time; that is to make the initial agreement between purchaser and vendor (maybe made in an estate agent's office and before either side has consulted a lawyer) binding; subject to a right to back out in certain circumstances. Indeed, as far as proof of title is concerned such a scheme could easily be devised at least for registered title. Lawyers could be by-passed. The vendor could be required to produce an office copy of entries on the register; a contract in a form approved by a consumer protection group could be signed.

In my view (says Old Jarndyce) any such development would not be desirable. As suggested above, title is no longer usually complicated or a problem. What has happened is that the threat to the purchaser living happily ever after in her new home comes today from matters other than title. These are matters which were not generally a threat or did not exist in earlier days of conveyancing. They are matters on which a purchaser does need skilled advice before committing herself to a contract. They are matters to which the law schools and domestic conveyancers have not devoted enough serious attention. I refer to such things as planning including threats to the physical environment from development beyond the boundary walls; the physical condition of the property itself; ownership of boundaries which can be more crucial to the owner of a terraced house rather than of a large, landed estate; insurance and financial advice; advice where co-habitees are buying.

All these things are matters which a purchaser needs to be happy about before signing any sort of contract. In short, in my view, the emphasis of conveyancing has, or should have, shifted from the post contract to the pre-contract stage.

The legal implications of pre-contract investigation

The basic duty of the vendor is still to prove and convey the property as agreed in the contract. If the vendor does deliver her evidence of title with the draft contract, the purchaser is not (subject to the terms of the contract for example limiting or excluding the right to raise requisitions) obliged to investigate it at that stage. Standard Condition 4.1.1. envisages this situation and gives six working days from the date of the contract in which to raise the requisitions. However, there are two rules which in this situation the purchaser's solicitor should bear in mind.

First, the vendor does not have disclose and the purchaser will have to take subject to any incumbrances of which she has knowledge at the time of contract. This means that if the purchaser's solicitor does investigate the vendor's evidence of title before contract and discovers defects not mentioned in the contract, they will bind the purchaser. But the key word is knowledge, not notice. It does not put any obligation on the purchaser to investigate title before contract and discover defects.

Secondly, where evidence of title has been supplied and investigated before contract, the act of exchanging contracts might be deemed to be acceptance of title and waiver of objections. (see para.10.6.7). The Standard Conditions do not deal with this situation.

In summary: where evidence of title is supplied before contract, the purchaser's solicitor should either investigate it and be satisfied with it before exchanging; or, if choosing not to investigate it or not being fully satisfied with it, should make it clear in writing to the other side before exchanging that the right is retained to raise requisitions (or further requisitions) after and in accordance with the terms of the contract.

Replies to requisitions

Standard Condition 4.1.1. requires the vendor 'to reply in writing to any requisitions raised' within four working days after receiving the requisitions. The purpose of replies is to deal satisfactorily with the purchaser's legitimate requisitions and objections on title; that is to provide the proper evidence of title which has been omitted from the evidence originally supplied; or cure a defect which has been pointed out. It follows that, although the standard conditions refer to 'any' requisitions, the vendor need only deal substantively with legitimate ones. If the vendor's solicitor considers that any requisition is not a proper one – because for example it is out of time – the reply should state why it is not being dealt with. **10.6.5**

If as a matter of courtesy out of time requisitions are answered, the reply should make it clear that this is the case and that it is without prejudice to the vendor's rights; otherwise the vendor may be taken to have waived the right to insist on the time limits. (see *Luck v. White* below).

Requisitions should be addressed to a specific point; there is no obligation to answer general ones.

If the vendor fails to reply within the stipulated time limits, that will be a breach of contract; and, if for example it contributes to a delay in completion may give the purchaser a right to compensation under Standard Condition 7.3.

Care should be taken when replying to requisitions, that a reply does not inadvertently constitute a professional undertaking which it may not be possible to honour. Requisitions will commonly ask for confirmation that outstanding mortgages will be discharged before completion or the usual undertaking given (see para.5.13 as to undertakings; and para.14.9.3 as to discharge of mortgages). A simple affirmative given by a solicitor in response to this will constitute a professional undertaking to do one or the other. Before giving such a reply the solicitor should be satisfied that there will be sufficient monies available to her from the sale to honour the obligation; and that there are no unknown charges that might be embraced by it.

Observations on replies

10.6.6   Under Standard Condition 4.1.1. the purchaser has three working days after receiving replies in which to make written observations on the replies. Failure to make any such observations will (although not stated in the standard conditions) be likely to constitute acceptance of title by the purchaser; and waiver of any right to pursue further requisitions already raised. It follows that if the purchaser's solicitor is not satisfied with any of the replies to requisitions, she should make this clear in observations within the above time limit.

There is no provision in the Standard Conditions for response to the observations or further stages. These, if there are any, must be taken within a reasonable time as under an open contract.

In practice, by this stage one of two things will have happened. The purchaser may be satisfied with the title as evidenced by the vendor and accept it (below, para.10.6.7). Alternatively, the parties will be in dispute as to whether the vendor has fulfilled her obligations to prove title in accordance with the contract. For example, the vendor may be refusing to answer a requisition which she considers improper; the purchaser may consider evidence offered not to be adequate. If the dispute cannot be resolved, as obviously it ought to be, wherever possible, by negotiation, it will have to be resolved by litigation. And each side's solicitor will have to make a judgment on the strength of her client's case and advise on steps accordingly. In general terms, either side may feel entitled to:

(a) treat the contract as discharged for a breach of condition by the other side;

(b) serve notice to complete and treat the contract as discharged on non-compliance.; or

(c) seek specific performance.

Courses (a) and (b) are risky where the rights of the matter are not clear. If a contract is wrongly treated as discharged this is in itself a breach giving the other side a right to treat it as discharged.

The vendor and purchaser summons is a summary procedure available for deciding disputes as to title. It is a procedure little used today, showing perhaps that title does not usually give rise to dispute.

Luff v. Raymond[15] is an interesting case in that it concerns the sale not of land as such but of a mortgage. A mortgage is as much an interest in land as beneficial freehold ownership, entitling the mortgagee to recover the loan and interest and any other sums secured under the mortgage and to enforce the other terms of the mortgage. The reason for selling a mortgage is likely to be to raise an immediate capital sum; in return the purchaser will get a (presumably) larger sum paid over a longer period. Such a mortgage can be sold and transferred in the same way as ordinary freehold or leasehold ownership. The case is also interesting in showing the path that such a dispute might take.

The special conditions in the contract provided that if (but only if) completion took place on the contractual completion date, 26 August, the purchaser would be entitled to the August instalment of £210 due under the mortgage. The mortgage itself contained a provision that the borrower would keep the buildings insured with an insurer approved by the lender and produce the policy and receipts for payment of premiums to the lender if required. After exchange of contracts, and within time, the purchaser raised the following requisition: 'Please give full details of the fire insurance maintained under clause 1 of the mortgage and confirm that the policy will be handed over on completion.' The vendor's solicitors failed to reply to this requisition. In consequence, the purchaser who considered this requisition to be fundamental, refused to complete on 26 August. The vendors did, on 5 September, supply the requested insurance details. But now the argument shifted to whether or not the purchaser was entitled to receive the £210 on completing late. If the requisition was a proper one, the vendor was wrong in not answering it in time for completion on the agreed date and wrong not to complete in accordance with the notice to complete; and the purchaser would be entitled to the £210 and damages for breach of contract. If it was not a proper one, the purchaser was at fault in failing to complete on the agreed date and forfeited the £210. On 9 September the purchaser served notice to complete on the vendor, that is to complete with the purchaser having the benefit of the £210. The vendor, disputing the claim to the £210, failed to complete in accordance with the notice. In these situations the

---

15   (1982) Lexis transcript.

vendor at least has the advantage of holding on to the deposit and forcing the purchaser to take action if she wants to recover it. Here the purchaser was suing for specific performance (to include payment of the £210) and/or damages.

Was the requisition a proper one? Dillon J. put the matter like this:

'It is normal practice on any transaction in respect of land for a large number of questions to be asked either by way of preliminary inquiry or by way of requisition. Very often they are questions which it is reasonable for a purchaser or his advisers to ask in order to get information at some stage about the property that is being bought and solicitors for the purchaser might well be negligent if they failed to ask many of such questions, but it is quite plain that they cannot all be questions which would entitle a purchaser to refuse to complete, notwithstanding that contracts have been exchanged, until an answer was forthcoming. The primary duty of a vendor, once contracts have been exchanged, is to deduce title to the property as described in the contract of sale, or as represented on behalf of the vendor, in accordance with the terms of the contract for sale. The requisitions are normally directed to that or to the form of the conveyance of the property to the purchaser. I am not suggesting that the requisitions which a purchaser is entitled to insist on having answered before he completes must inevitably and in all cases be limited to requisitions which fall within that general description; there may be other cases, but I cannot think that it can go so far as is suggested in the passage I have read from Emmett.'

The passage in Emmett was suggesting that the purchaser should answer to the best of his ability all specific questions put to him in respect of the property or the title thereto.

Dillon J. dealt with the facts of the case before him by making three points:

'The first is that the vendor does not in the contract of sale in any way warrant or represent that the borrowers have observed all the covenants in the mortgage. He does not warrant that the property is in the state of repair required by the mortgage. He does not warrant that the property is insured in accordance with the mortgage or that the sum for which insurance, if there is insurance, is effected is the full insurable value of the property.

The second point is that, as between vendor and purchaser, the risk of destruction of the property by fire or other peril passes to the purchaser on the contract being made and not on completion, and therefore, it is too late for the purchaser to start exploring matters of insurance after contract.

The third point is that the purchaser, having contracted to purchase the mortgage, has an insurable interest in the property, which she could protect without serious practical difficulty, in my judgment, at her own expense over an interim period until satisfied as to the particulars of the borrower's insurance if she has failed to make inquiries about insurance before exchanging contracts.'

It followed that the purchaser was in breach; and the vendor was entitled to specific performance – that is, in return for a transfer of the mortgage, to payment of the purchase price with interest during the period of delay and with the vendor retaining the disputed £210.

Question   In the light of the principles enunciated in this case, consider the propriety of the requisition made in this case if made today on a sale of freehold under the Standard Conditions. Consider particularly the significance of Standard Condition 5.1. (para.3.5.2).

Of course, reasonable requisitions should be answered if possible whether or not technically legitimate, the vendor's legal position being expressly reserved if necessary.

Luck v. White[16] provides a useful warning for solicitors acting for a purchaser where the purchase price is being raised in part by mortgage, especially where other solicitors are acting for the mortgagee. The mortgagees will have to be satisfied with the title before releasing the money needed to complete the purchase. The purchaser's solicitor will have to prove title to the mortgagee's solicitors; and their view of title may be more stringent.

The case also illustrates the serious attention that needs to be given to any step in a conveyancing transaction and its possible implications. The dispute was over a contract to buy a house in 1971 for £5,200 which was not finally resolved until the order for specific performance in March 1973.

The standard conditions in use provided for requisitions to be raised within 14 days of delivery of the abstract; and completion was fixed for 14 May 1971, 124 days after exchange of contracts. In fact the abstract had been delivered and the title investigated by the purchaser's solicitor before exchange. The purchaser had been let into possession immediately on exchange. The trouble arose because the abstract was not sent by the purchaser's solicitors to the building society's solicitors until 13 May; and they sent requisitions on 24 May . Completion had to be delayed until the building society was satisfied as to title. On 27 May the purchaser's solicitors sent on the building society's requisitions to the vendor's solicitors seeking 'their assistance' to be able to answer them. The vendor's solicitors dealt with these requisitions by letter the following day without reserving the contractual rights relating to time for delivering

---

[16]   (1973) Lexis transcript.

requisitions. In June, the vendor's solicitors, having failed to get a firm date for completion from the purchaser and the purchaser having refused to vacate, served notice to complete expiring on 6 September. After this the vendor's solicitors continued to press the purchaser's solicitors to complete. By November, the building society had been satisfied and a completion date was fixed, 16 November . But now the dispute shifted to liability for interest on the unpaid purchase money from the contractual date for completion. Consequently, completion did not take place; and the purchaser issued a writ seeking specific performance.

The first issue was this: had the vendor done all that was required of him under the contract by way of proving title. *Prima facie* he had, because he had satisfactorily answered all requisitions raised within the fourteen days allowed by the contract; and those raised on 27 May were out of time and there was no obligation to deal with them. Indeed, Goulding J. found that the purchaser's solicitors had accepted title before exchange of contracts. Goulding J. did find on construing the contract that it did allow further requisitions to be raised within 14 days after exchange on certain aspects of title. But of course none had been delivered in that time.

However, Goulding J. did state the following principle of law:

'... a vendor who receives and deals with requisitions out of time, without making any allusion to his rights under the contract, may be held to have waived the stipulation imposing a time limit. But it is necessary to look at the facts of the particular case to see whether that proposition is applicable.'

Goulding J. went on to hold that, since the purchaser's solicitors had made it clear that they were simply 'seeking assistance' to deal with their mortgagee's requisitions, the vendor's solicitors in replying were not waiving their contractual rights and were therefore entitled to serve a notice to complete.

The other and decisive issue was whether the vendor's solicitors had waived the effect of their notice to complete - i.e. to give them the right to treat the contract as discharged on non-compliance. It was held that they had, by continuing to treat the contract as still subsisting after expiry of the notice. Goulding J. stated:

'It would have been easy for the vendors to reserve their rights in express terms. They might, for example, have extended the period for compliance with the notice to a specified day, time to be of the essence in that regard. Indeed, the mere extension of the period to a new fixed date would on the authorities have preserved the position that time was of the essence, without fresh stipulation to that effect. The vendors however, did nothing of the kind. They encouraged the purchaser to try to complete notwithstanding the expiry of the notice, and there was nothing to tell him at what moment the axe would fall. If the party who is in the right allows the defaulting party to try to remedy his default after an essential date has passed, he cannot then call the bargain off without first warning the defaulting party by fixing a fresh limit, reasonable in the circumstances.'

Finally, Goulding J. held that the failure of the purchaser to complete on 16 November did not in itself entitle the vendor to treat the contract as discharged. That date, as he had already held, was not subject to an effective completion notice. The refusal by the purchaser at that time to pay interest on the purchase price for the delay did not in itself show an intention no longer to perform the contract; an intention which would be necessary to discharge the contract in the absence of time having been made of the essence by the terms of the contract or a completion notice.

Question   Write a clear statement (drafting any necessary document/notice) of what the vendor's solicitors should have done at each stage of the above events to preserve the position of the vendor, so that the vendor would have been in a position to treat the contract as discharged and retain the deposit on non-completion on 16 November.

Acceptance of title

Acceptance of title means that the purchaser has indicated her   **10.6.7** satisfaction with the title offered; or at least waived the right to make or pursue any further objections. Acceptance can be express; invariably in practice it is determined by the contract or to be inferred from the circumstances.

Really, there are normally two stages to acceptance. First, there is acceptance of the title as evidenced by the abstract/epitome and copies supplied by the vendor under the contract. As has been seen, under the contract, there will be deemed to be acceptance to the extent that the time limit in Standard Condition 4.1.1. for making objections on this evidence has expired, and the purchaser has not preserved her right to pursue further unsatisfactory replies to any already made.

Acceptance of the title evidenced by the vendor may also be inferred from other steps taken by the purchaser from which it can be inferred that she has accepted the title. However, Standard Condition 4.5.1. confirms what is probably the open contract position that acceptance will not be inferred from submission of a draft conveyance for approval. Similarly, Standard Condition 5.2.7. provides that entry into occupation by the purchaser before completion will not affect the right to raise requisitions.

Acceptance in the above (what might be called the first stage sense) does not bar the purchaser from objecting to defects discovered elsewhere;

or to conveyancing defects. Acceptance in this total sense will in practice only occur with completion itself when the purchaser has made her pre-completion searches, inspected the property and examined the title deeds and not discovered anything adverse not dealt with in the contract.

SPECIFIC POINTS ON TITLE

10.7   Most of the specific matters likely to arise on a title are dealt with elsewhere. What follows points to the appropriate paragraphs and deals with a few others. These principles apply both to every previous transaction on the title; and to the immediate transaction in hand between the present vendor and purchaser.

Stamping

10.7.1   In the case of unregistered title, there are two aspects of stamping to consider:

(a) Stamping defects on the title documents;

(b) Stamping of the purchase document.

It is convenient to deal with both here.

(a) Stamping defects

When perusing title the purchaser's solicitor should check that every document that requires stamping has been properly stamped and raise a requisition pointing out any defect and requiring it to be rectified. It is the obligation of the vendor to cure any stamping defect by having the document stamped and paying any penalty for late stamping. Under the Stamp Act 1891, s.117, any provision in the contract which attempts to preclude the purchaser from objecting to a stamping defect or to shift the burden of late stamping onto her is void.

Stamp duty is payable on documents rather than transactions. A document which is not properly stamped is not admissible in evidence in court, unless a solicitor undertakes to the court to rectify the defect and pay any penalty. The court will of its own volition take notice of any stamping defect. A document which is not properly stamped will not be accepted by the Land Registry.

In general, documents can be stamped late on payment of the duty with interest, plus a penalty equal to the amount of the unpaid duty and a further £10. The fact that a document is impressed with an *ad valorem* stamp is not conclusive that it has been correctly stamped; though unless the contrary is known, it can be assumed that it has.

There are three types of stamping to consider:

(a) *Ad valorem* duty stamp. This is impressed on the face of the document by the stamp office to which it will have to be delivered; and shows the amount of duty paid on that document.

The amount of duty payable may depend on the class of document, when it was executed and the consideration or value of the property. It is therefore necessary to know the position at the date of execution of any document you are looking at. The position of the documents most likely to be encountered is as follows:

(i) Conveyance or transfer on sale. Here, *ad valorem* stamp duty has been payable since before the Stamp Act 1891. The duty depends on the consideration (*ad valorem*) for that conveyance (unless it is part of a larger transaction or series of transactions, in which case duty will be based on the total consideration). The rate of duty has varied at various periods. Printed tables showing these different rates are available from law stationers to be used when checking previous conveyances in a title. Where the consideration does not exceed a specified amount – the amount again depending on the date of the conveyance – it is exempt from duty. If it exceeds the amount, duty is payable on the full consideration, not just the excess. Until the Finance Act 1984, where the consideration did not exceed another specified amount, a reduced rate of duty was payable.

To qualify for either total exemption or the reduced rate, the conveyance must contain a certificate of value as specified in s.34(4) of the Finance Act 1958, and as illustrated in the two conveyances reproduced above in the French/Saunders title Documents 10.2.1 and 10.2.3. Contrary to Timothy's notion it has therefore been possible to have a conveyance which contains both a certificate of value and shows duty to have been paid. In fact, both these conveyances have been correctly stamped and certificated.

At present a conveyance or transfer on sale is exempt if the consideration does not exceed £60,000 and the conveyance/transfer contains a certificate of value. Otherwise duty is payable at the rate of £1 per £100 (50p if the consideration does not exceed £500).

(ii) Deeds of gift. *Ad valorem* duty on gifts was abolished by s.82 of the Finance Act 1985. And the deed does not have to be adjudicated (as formerly it did) or pay a fixed deed duty of 50p provided that it is certified under s.87 of the 1985 Act; that is that it has a certificate stating that it belongs to one (and stating which one) of the categories specified in the Stamp Duty (Exempt Instruments) Regulations 1987 (S.I. 1987 No. 516).

(iii) Assents. Prior to the 1985 Act, if made by deed, these bore a fixed deed duty of 50p. The 1985 Act abolished this provided again that the assent was certified under s.87. Under s.36 of the Administration of Estates Act 1925 assents need only be in writing and in practice a deed is not used.

(iv) Deeds appointing new trustees. The only duty, the fixed deed duty of 50p was abolished by the 1985 Act. The deed must be certified as above if it vests the trust property in the new trustees or, on the retirement of a trustee, in the continuing trustees.

(v) Powers of Attorney and Acknowledgements for the production of deeds. The only duty, the fixed 50p duty, was abolished by s.85 of the 1985 Act; and certification is not required.

(b) Adjudication. The stamp office can be asked to adjudicate a document; that is to decide what duty is payable. The instrument will be stamped with an adjudication stamp and the correct duty will then be deemed to have been paid (s.12 of the Stamp Act 1891). Voluntary dispositions required adjudication before stamp duty on them was abolished (above). Now a document will only be sent for adjudication when there is some doubt as to the correct duty payable.

(c) Particulars delivered stamping. Certain documents must be produced to the stamp office (who provide a printed form) even though no duty is payable, together with a statement containing certain particulars. The document will then be stamped with a particulars delivered stamp (commonly referred to as a PD stamp).

PD stamping is required for a transfer on sale of the fee simple; and the grant or transfer on sale of any lease initially of seven years or more.

(b) Stamping of the purchase deed

As explained above the vendor must cure any stamping defect found on the existing title. On the other hand it is the responsibility of the purchaser to stamp the conveyance to her. This requirement applies equally to a conveyance of unregistered title and a transfer of registered title.

The deed must be presented to the stamp office (whose address will be found under Inland Revenue in the telephone directory) within thirty days of execution (i.e. of completion); otherwise the penalties mentioned above may have to be paid, although the stamp office has discretion to waive or mitigate the penalties. A purchase deed executed from 16 March 1993 (if not stamped before 23 March 1993) is exempt if the consideration is not more than £60,000 and it contains a certificate of value at that amount.[17]

---

[17] Finance Act 1993, s.201.

Where the purchase deed has to be registered (either on first registration or on a subsequent dealing) and requires only PD stamping (coming within the *ad valorem* exemption limit) it can be sent direct to the district Land Registry with the statement of particulars when application is made for registration. The Registry will then attend to having it PD stamped.

Under s.5 of the Stamp Act 1891, it is an offence to execute or to be concerned in the preparation of an instrument which does not fully and truly set forth all the facts and circumstances affecting the liability to or amount of duty payable. It is important to bear this in mind (and warn the client) when, for example, part of the total purchase price is being allocated to chattels included in the sale, the title to which passes by delivery without any duty being payable. There might be an offence by both client and solicitor if the price of the chattels is inflated just to reduce stamp duty. It might amount to professional misconduct by the solicitor; and the court would probably refuse to enforce the contract[18] because of the illegality.

Execution of documents

The purchaser's solicitor should check that all necessary persons are party to each document on the title; and that each document, including the conveyance to the purchaser herself, has been properly executed by all whose execution is required (para.12.4.4).   **10.7.2**

Mortgages

If there is any mortgage on the title, a check should be made that it has been (or will be) cleared off the title by discharge or release by the mortgagee or by a sale by the mortgagee (para.14.9.3).   **10.7.3**

Disposition by the sole survivor of joint tenants

A check is needed to show that the survivor was able to give good title either by reliance on the Law of Property (Joint Tenants) Act 1964, the appointment of a second trustee, or otherwise (para.14.7.2).   **10.7.4**

---

[18] *Saunders v. Edwards* [1987] 2 All E.R. 651; where the court did exceptionally allow an action against the vendor to succeed in tort for fraudulent misrepresentation that a terrace roof was included with the property.

Death of a sole owner

10.7.5   Here it is necessary to check that title passed properly to and from the personal representative(s). In particular, thought should be given to the title of the personal representatives as shown by the grant, the possible need for an assent and memorandum of assent on the grant, the presence of any necessary s.36 statement and absence of any adverse memorandum on the grant, and the provision of an acknowledgement for production of the grant (para.14.7.1).

The identity of the property

10.7.6   Care should be taken that the property to which the title proves ownership is exactly the property which the client has agreed to purchase. The identification of the property in each document on the title should therefore be checked; that identification should be checked with the contract and both should be seen to correspond with the boundaries of the property on the ground.

Incumbrances

10.7.7   A check should be made that there are no incumbrances revealed by the title which have not been disclosed in the contract.

Acknowledgements for title deeds

10.7.8   A check should be made that there is a satisfactory acknowledgement for the production of any of the title documents which are not to be handed over on completion, (see para.12.4.2).

Minors

10.7.9   As from 1 January 1970 the age of majority has been 18.

A contract by a minor for the acquisition or disposition of an interest in land is binding on the minor unless repudiated by her before or within a reasonable time of reaching majority. On repudiation a minor can only recover any deposit paid if there has been a total failure of consideration. If a minor-vendor repudiates, the court can order her to repay any purchase money paid if it is just and equitable to do so.

A minor cannot hold a legal estate in land; but can hold any equitable interest (e.g. under a trust).

In the case of unregistered land, an attempt to convey a legal estate to an minor alone operates as a contract for valuable consideration to create a settlement in proper form (under the Settled Land Act 1925) for the benefit of the infant. A conveyance to a minor jointly with one or more adults vests the legal estate in the adult(s) on a statutory trust for sale for the benefit of those entitled in equity (including the minor).

Under s.15 of the Law of Property Act 1925, there is a rebuttable presumption that the parties to a deed are of full age. This means that the purchaser can assume that parties to deeds on the title were not and the vendor herself is not a minor unless there is evidence to suggest the contrary. The presumption does not affect the legal consequences described above if there is a minority as a party.

The same principles apply to registered title. A minor will not be registered as proprietor. If, under the above or other principles, the minor is entitled in equity, the proprietor will hold in trust for the infant with appropriate restrictions being put on the register. Should a minor be registered as proprietor by accident, it is assumed that the minor will technically become the proprietor; but the register would be subject to rectification under s.82 of the Land Registration Act 1925 to correct the position.

In the case of both unregistered and registered title, if it is desired to give a minor the benefit of an interest in land, the proper course is to create a trust for sale with adult trustees or (an unlikely choice today) use the Settled Land Act 1925 machinery.

CHAPTER 11

INVESTIGATION OF TITLE: REGISTERED TITLE

OLD JARNDYCE CONTINUES

Blackacre passes from A to B to C to V. Each in turn is registered as **11.1** proprietor. V is selling to P. The premise of registered title is that the register is V's title; and is proof and guarantee of that title. The premise of unregistered conveyancing is that you can only be sure (relatively) of V's title if you are sure of C's title and that there has been a proper conveyance from C to V; that you can only be sure of C's title if you are sure of B's title and a proper conveyance from B to C; and so on.

In principle a purchaser of registered land does not need to and cannot look behind the register to the legal history of previous transactions.

To that extent at least, title to registered land is a simpler matter; requisitions on title in the sense of investigating the previous legal history of the property should not be necessary; and much of the text book discussion tends to focus on showing what rules of unregistered title do *not* apply.

Nevertheless, to get herself registered as a proprietor in place of V, free of any unwanted adverse interests, P does have to satisfy the Registry that title has properly passed from V to herself. And the rules governing the transmission from V to P, parallel the rules governing the transmission from A to B, from B to C, from D to V and from V to P in the case of unregistered title. To a great extent it is the same process, but it is only concerned with one transaction instead of several stretching back.

The starting point, as with unregistered title, is that a purchaser of freehold (and similarly with leasehold) wants, and is entitled to proof of, the freehold free from adverse trusts or incumbrances save those agreed to in the contract.

To be satisfied of this the purchaser is concerned with three matters:

(a) proof of the state of the register;

(b) proof relating to those matters as to which the register gives no guarantee;

(c) the execution of a valid transfer to herself.

THE REGISTER

Office copies

The purchaser needs to be satisfied as to the state of the register at the time that she lodges her application to register. It is that moment which determines her priority in relation to other entries and other applications.

Section 110(1) of the Land Registration Act 1925 provides that on a sale or other disposition of registered land to a purchaser, the vendor shall, generally at her own expense and notwithstanding any stipulation to the contrary in the contract, if required, furnish the purchaser with:

(a) a copy of the subsisting entries on the register;

(b) a copy of any filed plans noted on the register which affects the land being dealt with;

(c) a copy or abstract of any other document noted on the register.

A copy (as opposed to an office copy) does not prove the state of the register.

Section 113 of the Land Registration Act 1925, as amended, provides that office copies of, and extracts from, the register and of and from documents filed in the registry 'shall be admissible in evidence in all actions and matters ... to the same extent as the originals would be admissible'.

Office copies can be obtained (now by anyone) under the Land Registration (Open Register) Rules 1991 by application on Form 109.

An office copy of the register and the title plan (below) is contained in the Land or Charge Certificate. An office copy will show the state of the register at the time it was issued (shown on the copy). The Land or Charge Certificate will show the state of the register when the Certificate was last brought up to date with the register. This date is stamped in the Certificate.

Under Standard Condition 4.2.1:

'The evidence of registered title is office copies of the items required to be furnished by section 110(1) of the Land Registration Act 1925 and the copies, abstracts and evidence referred to in section 110(2).'

Thus, under the Standard Conditions the purchaser will have satisfactory evidence of the state of the register as at the date of the office copy supplied. The office copy of the title plan will enable her to check that the identity of the property on the ground which she thinks she is buying corresponds with that described in the contract; and that both correspond with what is in fact included in the legal title being offered. The office copy of the register will show – as at its date – whether the vendor is registered as proprietor, with what class of title, whether freehold or leasehold, with the benefit of what registered appurtenances, and what adverse minor interests are protected on the register.

Having an office copy of the register and title plan is most convenient to the purchaser. A purchaser will need to make an official search of the register prior to completion. The official certificate of search will show what entries, if any, have been made on the register since either the Land Certificate was brought up to date, or the date of an office copy, whichever the purchaser asks for. If the purchaser does an official search from the date of the office copy at a time which allows her to complete and submit her application for registration within the protection period given by the search, she can be satisfied that what she acquires as the new proprietor will tally with what she contracted for.

If not provided with office copies (if contracting under different conditions of sale) the purchaser would have to obtain her own; or obtain the date when the Land certificate was last brought up to date, use that as the date for her search and then, before actually completing, check the entries in the Land Certificate itself against her non-office copy.

Copies of other documents noted on the register

> 'Whereas the Land Registry endeavours to produce a register of title complete in itself, there are cases in which, for example, the complicated nature of a grant of easements by reference to large scale plans, or the length of restrictive covenants, renders it necessary that notice of the document should be entered on the register, but without producing its terms thereon verbatim and that the document itself or a certified copy of it should be filed for reference. As between vendor and purchaser the filed documents are deemed to be complete and correct and if they prove to be otherwise, anyone suffering loss is entitled to compensation from the Land Registry.'[1]

11.2.2

Such documents are thus part of the register of title, equally accessible, and a purchaser will need proof of them (by office copy) to complete her picture of the registered title.

The title plan

There may be some confusion between the different maps and plans kept at the Registry; and between the terms 'filed plan' and 'title plan'. In a general sense, any map or plan kept at the Registry can be said to be filed there.

11.2.3

---

[1]   Ruoff & Roper, para.17.04.

The Registry keeps what is known as a Public Index Map (though the whole register of title is now open to public inspection). This is in fact a collection of maps based on Ordnance Survey maps. Each of these maps may be a section of the Ordnance Survey map itself, or a special map for a particular area based on the Ordnance survey map and known as the General Map. Coupled with the Index Map is a Parcels Index. Between them the Index Map and Parcels Index show whether or not any parcel of land is registered; and, if so, whether freehold or leasehold (or both); and, if not registered, whether there is any caution against first registration.

Distinct from this system, each registered title has its own title plan as part of its register of title.

A 'filed plan' is a plan prepared for that particular title alone on which the extent of the registered property is shown edged in red (and any land sold out of the title shown in green).

With older registrations the plan for that particular property may consist of an extract taken from the General Map with the particular property for which it has been extracted shown tinted pink.

The title plan to a property thus means either the filed plan or the portion of the General Map referred to in the register of that title.[2]

MATTERS SHOWN BY THE REGISTER

11.3   The entries on the register, encompassing the register itself, the title plan and any documents referred to on the register, may reveal a number of matters of importance to a purchaser.

The class of title

11.3.1   The different classes of title have been described. The vendor must be able to convey with the class of title stated in the contract. In the absence of express provision, the vendor's obligation is to transfer with absolute freehold title. If this is what the register shows the title to be there is no problem.

If the title is less than absolute, for example possessory, the purchaser will be concerned with the element of the title not guaranteed by the registration – in the case of possessory, the title prior to first registration; and if the purchaser's right is not barred by special condition the vendor will need to prove that title according to the rules of unregistered conveyancing (see, further, para.7.11.2(b)).

---

[2] See Ruoff & Roper, para4.06 to 4.14; and Land Registration (Open Register) Rules 1991, r.1(2).

\entries on the register

The property may, in the contract, have been sold expressly subject to   **11.3.2**
incumbrances protected on the register, for example, restrictive covenants
or easements over the property. These will have been expected by the
purchaser and give no problem.

The entries may protect incumbrances which the vendor can and is
expecting to remove before completion. The common case is where
there are subsisting charges which the vendor will redeem either before
completion or after completion in pursuance of a professional
undertaking (para.14.9.3).

Another case would be on a sale by a sole surviving trustee, with a
restriction on the register against paying capital money to less than two
trustees or a trust corporation. Here, a new trustee could be appointed
and the restriction complied with.

Where an interest protected on the register is not dealt with in the
contract and cannot be removed by the vendor, the vendor will be in
breach of contract, having failed to produce a good title, and the
purchaser will be entitled to treat the contract as discharged and/or
claim damages.

Sale by a person other than the proprietor

The register may show that the vendor is not the proprietor.   **11.3.3**
Section.110(5) of the Land Registration Act 1925 provides:

> 'Where the vendor is not himself registered as proprietor of the
> land or the charge giving power of sale over the land, he shall, at
> the request of the purchaser and at his own expense, and
> notwithstanding any stipulation to the contrary, either procure the
> registration of himself as proprietor of the land or the charge, as
> the case may be, or procure a disposition from the proprietor to
> the purchaser.'

In practice, it is quite common and convenient for a person who is
entitled to be registered to deal with the land without first getting herself
registered. Section 37(1) of the Act provides:

> 'Where a person on whom the right to be registered as proprietor
> of registered land or of a registered charge has devolved by reason
> of the death of the proprietor, or has been conferred by a
> disposition or charge, in accordance with this Act, desires to
> dispose of or charge the land or to deal with the charge before he
> is himself registered as proprietor, he may do so in the prescribed
> manner, and subject to the prescribed conditions.'

The crucial principle is that the purchaser must be satisfied that she
will obtain whatever evidence is required by the Registry, showing the

devolution of title from the proprietor to the vendor, so as to enable her (the purchaser) to obtain her own registration.

The Registry will require the same evidence of the devolution whether it is produced by the vendor or the purchaser. A number of situations where this might happen will be discussed next.

Disposition by the personal representative of a sole proprietor

11.3.4   If a joint proprietor dies, title passes automatically to the survivor (as in the case of unregistered land (below)). If a sole proprietor dies, title is transmitted to her personal representative(s) as in the case of unregistered title by grant of probate or letters of administration.

If the personal representatives want to get themselves registered in place of the deceased proprietor, they will have to produce evidence of the grant. The Registry is not concerned with the possibility of any memoranda endorsed on the grant, nor with the terms of the will. It is only concerned that all the personal representatives named in the grant (and no one else) are applying for registration. For this reason the Registry accepts an office copy of the grant (or even a certified photocopy). If the personal representatives are registered, they will be identified as such in the proprietorship register.

Alternatively, under Rule 170 of the Land Registration Rules 1925, they can sell[3] without first having themselves registered; and the purchaser will need the same evidence to be able to produce to the Registry. Although, under Rule 170(4) of the these Rules, production of the original grant is required, the Registry is not concerned with the contents of the will, and will assume the personal representative to have acted properly. It accepts an office or certified other copy of the grant; and there is therefore no need for an acknowledgement for production of the original grant to be included in the transfer.

The transfer by the personal representative will be in the usual form (printed Form 19 or 20) and the personal representative will transfer as such.

An assent of registered land must be made in Form 56. An assentee, who may be the personal representative herself, will be registered as proprietor on production of the evidence of the grant (as above) and the assent in Form 56. The Registry is not concerned with whether the assent has been made to the right person. If an assentee fails to protect her title by registration, she will be in the same position as anyone else who has failed to protect an interest in registered land on the register. In

---

3   As in the case of unregistered title a sole personal representative can deal with the land.

the absence of such protection (and subject to any adverse actual occupation by the assentee[4]) a purchaser is not concerned with any possible previous assent.

It follows that s.36(6) and (7) of the Administration of Estates Act 1925 have no application to registered land; a purchaser is not concerned with the possibility of memoranda endorsed on the grant; and does not need a s.36 statement of no previous disposition from the vending personal representative (on s.36, see para.14.7.1).

Joint proprietors

If one of two or more joint proprietors dies, title will pass by survivorship to the survivor(s). The Registry will require either an official copy of the death certificate or the original or certified copy of the grant as proof of the death, together with the Land Certificate; and will then remove the name of the deceased from the register.   **11.3.5**

Whether or not a purchaser can deal with a sole survivor depends simply on whether there is any restriction on the register (subject always to the possibility of adverse interests protected by actual occupation). If there is, either a new trustee will have to be appointed, the property transferred to the new and existing trustee jointly and the name of the new trustee added to the register as a proprietor, or the existing and new trustee can dispose of the property to a purchaser providing the purchaser with the evidence of appointment and transfer to be presented to the Registry.

Where a sole survivor wishes to have such a restriction removed, she will have to satisfy the Registry as to her sole entitlement to the equitable interest by statutory declaration or otherwise.

If the sole survivor dies, title will pass, as on the death of any sole proprietor, to her executrix or executrices. What has been said above (para.11.3.4) applies equally here, even if there is only one executrix. On application for registration by the executrix herself as such or an assentee or transferee from the executrix, the Registry will remove any joint tenancy restriction from the register.

It follows from the above that the Law of Property (Joint Tenants) Act 1964 has no application to registered land.

---

[4]   The title of an assentee may, it has been suggested, be destroyed under general law by failure to have a memorandum put on the grant as against a purchaser who takes a statement under s.36(6) of the Land Registration Act 1925 of no previous disposition; in which case there would be no right to protect by actual occupation.

Questions

(a) Refer back to the letter from Moriarties on Miss Obebe's purchase and the draft contract and office copy entries (Documents 4.1.1., 4.1.2. and 4.1.3.). Draft a letter to Miss Obebe's solicitor, stating what your requirements are as to proof of title. Note that Nancy Mixford is selling as beneficial owner and not as personal representative.

(b) What would the position be if Nora and Norman had died together there being no evidence as to who died first?

(c) Would your letter be different in (a) (Nora having died first) if there were a restriction on the register as follows:

'No disposition by one proprietor of the land (being the survivor of joint proprietors and not being a trust corporation) under which capital money arises is to be registered except under an order of the Registrar or of the court.'

Re-sales and sub-sales

11.3.6   The vendor may sell to a purchaser who immediately re-sells to another purchaser. There may be a transfer from the vendor to the purchaser followed by a transfer by the purchaser to the sub-purchaser. Commonly, it is convenient to have a single transfer from the vendor to the sub-purchaser. Subject to any provision in the contract, a purchaser can require a conveyance to someone other than herself. The only provision in the Standard Conditions (Standard Condition 8.2.5.) relates to the grant of a new lease. It may be desirable for the purchaser to join in such a direct transfer to give a receipt for any excess of the sub-purchase price over the initial purchase price; and, being expressed to join in as beneficial owner, to give the implied covenants for title.

Question Consider how stamp duty would be calculated in such a case of a single transfer direct from the vendor to the sub-purchaser. The rule is the same for registered and unregistered title. See Stamp Act 1891, ss.58, 59.

Showing the registered title in such a case gives no difficulty. The title searched will show the vendor as proprietor. If the purchaser has already taken a transfer to herself and lodged it for registration, the sub-purchaser's official search (para.13.12) will reveal the application. The sub-purchaser will then be able, within her priority period to lodge the transfer to herself for registration.

Where the vendor has sold part of her land to the purchaser, who is re-selling the part to the sub-purchaser, similar principles apply. In this case, a new register of title will be needed for the part sold, and at the time of the re-sale may not yet have been created. Again, title to the vendor's whole will be shown. The sub-purchaser's search against this title will show the application to register the transfer of the part (if it has already been lodged), and any incumbrances imposed on the part by that transfer. The purchaser can then complete on the transfer to herself and lodge that for registration, in due course to be registered as the proprietor of the part.

Sale by mortgagee

The chargee of a registered charge has the same power of sale as the legal mortgagee of unregistered land.   **11.3.7**

The purchaser will have to be satisfied by examination of the charge contained in the charge certificate held by the chargee that the power of sale has arisen in accordance with general land law rules. She will also have to be satisfied by examination of the register that the chargee/vendor has priority over any other charges on the register if the sale is intended to be free of them; and that there is no entry on the register affecting the right of sale. Under s.29 of the Land Registration Act 1925, subject to any contrary entry on the register, priority between registered charges is governed by the date of registration (which is shown on the register).

The transfer will overreach the interests not only of subsequent mortgagees, but also that of the proprietor/borrower and in general any interests created by the borrower out of her equity.[5] The transfer must be in Form 31; and will be lodged at the Registry with the charge certificate.

MATTERS OFF THE REGISTER

The register of title is not conclusive of all the matters that might affect the title. Subject to the terms of the contract the vendor is under a duty to transfer the property free from incumbrances (para.4.3). This includes matters not on the register which would bind a purchaser. In particular, a purchaser needs to be satisfied that the property is not subject to any overriding interests that will bind her. Particularly important in practice are the rights of persons in actual occupation of the property (para.13.15) and legal easements which, if implied or prescriptive, will not be registered.   **11.4**

---

5   See *Lyus v. Prowsa Developments Ltd*. [1982] 2 All E.R. 953.

Finally, there may be rights appurtenant to the land, title to which is not guaranteed by the register. This in particular applies to the benefit of appurtenant covenants. If the sale has been expressed to be with the benefit of any such rights, the vendor will (subject to the terms of the contract) be obliged to prove title to them under the general law.

CHAPTER 12

DRAFTING THE DEED

NOW WHAT HAS HE GOT WRONG?

It is 8 pm. There is a light on in Timothy's office. He was on the **12.1**
point of leaving at 4 o'clock when one of the legal executives just
happened to ask if he had drafted the conveyances for French/Saunders
and the Obebe purchase. She was sure, of course, that he had. Just could
not remember seeing them. Only they were due for completion in nine
days time.

He had not. Taking his coat off, muttering that he was just about to
do them, and 'just checking to see that this coat still fits', he returned to
his office.

Question Standard Condition 4.1.2. provides that 'The buyer is to
send the seller a draft transfer at least 12 working days before completion
date'.

If Timothy's delay causes delay in completion explain what the legal
consequences might be both for Miss Obebe and for Jarndyce &
Jarndyce? (See Chapter 16.) Remember that if Timothy causes delay in
completing on Miss Obebe's purchase, she will probably also have to
delay completion of her sale. Consequently, both her vendor and her
purchaser may be forced in turn to delay linked transactions. A whole
chain of linked transactions could be brought to a grinding halt. How if
at all would this affect legal remedies?

By 8 pm Timothy has produced the following draft (for the title, see
Documents 10.2 to 10.3):

Document 12.2 French/Saunders Purchase: Draft Conveyance

Draft conveyance. French/Saunders of Rocard.
24 De Lucy Mount, Ledchester.

THIS CONVEYANCE made the ..... day of ..... 1993 BETWEEN
Michel and Marie Rocard both of 8 Longfellow Road Kirkstall
Ledchester in the County of West Yorkshire (hereinafter
called "the Vendors") of the one part And Fancy French and
Samuel Saunders both of 22 Backup Lane Ledchester aforesaid
(hereinafter called "the Purchasers") of the other part

WHEREAS the Vendors are seised of the property hereby conveyed for an estate in fee simple in possession subject as
hereinafter mentioned but otherwise free from incumbrances

AND WHEREAS the Vendors have agreed to sell the said property
to the Purchasers at the price of £75000

NOW THIS DEED WITNESSETH as follows:-
1. In consideration of the sum of seventy-five thousand
pounds (receipt of which sum the vendors hereby acknowledge
the Vendors as beneficial owner HEREBY CONVEY unto the
Purchasers All That property known as 24 De Lucy Mount
Ledchester aforesaid together with the dwelling erected
thereon TO HOLD the same unto the Purchasers in fee simple as
beneficial joint tenants Subject to the covenants contained
in a conveyance made the 14th day of August 1907 between
Arthur Eddison of the one part and William Exley of the other
part in so far as the same are still subsisting and capable
of taking effect and affect the property hereby conveyed.
2. It is hereby certified that the transaction hereby effected does not form part of a larger transaction or of a series
of transactions in respect of which the amount or value or
the aggregate amount or value of the consideration exceeds
seventy five thousand pounds.

IN WITNESS whereof the parties hereto have signed this document as a deed the day and year first above written.

Signed by the said Michel Rocard
as a deed in the presence of:
Signed by the said Marie Rocard
as a deed in the presence of:
Signed by the said Fancy French
as a deed in the presence of:
Signed by the said Samuel Saunders
as a deed in the presence of:

Questions

1. What has Timothy done wrong here? (Note the Instructions on purchase, para.1.4 and see also para.10.4)

2. What of leaving out Marie Rocard's middle name? (See Document 10.2.5. Could this have serious consequences? (Consider for example para.13.6(b)).

3. Should there be a certificate of value, either as worded or at all? Note para.10.7.1. What stamping will be needed on the conveyance?

4. If Fancy is bitten by her dog and dies a year after purchasing, what will determine whether Sam will be able to sell without appointing a new trustee? Bear in mind that the purchase will be subject to compulsory registration.

5. Explain the significance and legal effect of the phrase 'as beneficial joint tenants'.

6. This precedent, whether or not drafted correctly, is a straightforward conveyance on sale. Any particular conveyance may have special features to incorporate. To deal with any such feature you should (other than running for the nearest book of precedents – though it is quite proper to use precedents so long as you understand what you are using) first research the law. What are the rules which govern the end which is being sought? You should then be able to produce a draft that complies with the law and achieves the desired end.

The unregistered freehold of Horseacre, Fetlock Lane, Stableshire, was owned by Jill Black and John Beauty (her co-habitee) upon trust for themselves as tenants in common in equal shares. Jill was recently killed in a riding accident having made a will leaving her share in Horseacre to Jennifer Oates. John and Jennifer have agreed to sell the property to Molly Codel and her husband Jacob for £50,000 (Jacob providing £30,000, the rest being raised by a mortgage loan). Molly and Jacob want to hold as beneficial joint tenants. Horseacre was previously owned by Harvie Smith who purchased under a conveyance dated 24 June 1956 from Maggie Smith (no relation). This conveyance contained certain restrictive covenants entered into by Harvie for the benefit of land retained out of the title by Maggie. The covenant was created in the following terms:

> 'For the benefit and protection of the Vendor's retained land and each and every part thereof and so as to bind the property hereby purchased and each and every part thereof into whosoever hands the same may come but so that the Purchaser shall not be personally liable on the said covenants after he shall have parted with all interest in the said property the Purchaser hereby covenants on behalf of himself and the person deriving title under him to observe the restrictions set out in the second Schedule hereto.'

Harvie died in 1970 whereupon the property was sold and conveyed by his personal representative to Jill and John. The title is still unregistered.

Draft the conveyance of the property to Molly and Jacob. Invent any further details that you think necessary. Pay particular attention to the conveyancing and drafting implications of: stamp duty requirements; the fact that Jill has died leaving her share to Jennifer (Can John alone as survivor convey a good title? If not what steps must be taken? Can any such necessary steps be incorporated into the conveyance to Molly and Jacob?); the fact that Molly and Jacob want to hold as beneficial joint tenants; the need, if there is one, for an indemnity covenant in respect of the restrictive covenants created in the conveyance to Harvie Smith. Read the wording of the covenant carefully and bear in mind what entitles a vendor to such an indemnity covenant. Compare the wording of the covenant in clause 5 of the precedent set out in para.12.3.1 below.

7. Refer to Document 4.1.8. Suppose that Mrs Rocard has departed for Eldorado. Before leaving she executed a general power of attorney under s.10 of the Powers of Attorney Act 1971. Does this enable Mr Rocard to execute the conveyance on her behalf? If not, what steps should have been taken before she left? Draft any necessary document (below, para.12.4.4(e)).

OLD JARNDYCE COMMENTS – CONVEYANCE OF UNREGISTERED LAND   12.3

Rule 72 transfers

Where, as will now always be the case with a conveyance on sale of   12.3.1
the freehold, application for first registration will have to be made by the purchaser, it is possible to use a conveyance in traditional form as above; or it is possible to use what is known as a Rule 72 Transfer. This is a Land Registry form of transfer adapted to the circumstance that the land is not in fact registered. Such a Transfer is acceptable to the Land Registry on the basis of rule 72 of the Land Registry Rules 1925 which allows a 'person having the right to apply for registration as first proprietor ... to deal with the land in any way permitted by the Act before he himself is registered as proprietor'. This is a dubious use of rule 72 since until completion the purchaser does not have such a right.

There is a printed form, Form 19 (Rule 72) for the conveyance of the whole of a title under this provision. This is a very slightly modified version of Form 19 (the transfer of the whole of an already registered title). It may be a sentimental attachment to the delightful(?) prolixity of traditional conveyancing language with its 'aforesaid' and 'heretobefores' but in my view (says Old Jarndyce) unregistered land is unregistered and should be contracted, requisitioned and conveyed as unregistered land until it is safely delivered as such to the land registry to be turned into registered land.

The title which has to be proved to the Land Registry is an unregistered title; the use of Rule 72 merely leads to sloppy (or sloppier) conveyancing.

There are published, conveyancing precedents in the traditional format but using a leaner, more easily comprehensible style. Parker's Modern Conveyancing Precedents (2nd edition, 1989) suggests, with justification, in its Preface that 'The publication of Modern Conveyancing Precedents in 1964 was the first serious attempt to use plain English when drafting legal documents'.

The skeleton precedent which it offers (p.12) for a 'Conveyance of land comprising part of the garden of the vendor's house subject to existing covenants and creating new ones' is as follows (Parker's sidenotes omitted in part):

'This Conveyance dated ... is made between

    (1) the Vendor

    (2) the Purchaser

1. The Vendor acknowledges receipt from the Purchaser of £... the purchase price of the land described in the first schedule ('the Property').

2. The Vendor as beneficial owner conveys to the Purchaser the fee simple estate in the Property.

3 The Property is subject to such covenants and restrictions contained in a conveyance dated ... etc as are still effective and relate to the Property.

4. The Purchaser covenants with the Vendor:

    (a) to perform and observe the covenants and restrictions referred to in clause 3 so far as they relate to the Property and to indemnify the Vendor against any liability resulting from any future breach or non-observance;

    (b) to perform the covenants set out in the second schedule.

5. The Purchaser also covenants with the Vendor for the benefit of the whole and every part of the land shown edged blue on the attached plan[1] ('the Retained Premises') and so as to bind the

---

[1] 'The covenants would almost certainly enure to the benefit of every part of the land without the addition of the words 'of the whole and every part of'; see *Federated Homes Ltd. v. Mill Lodge Properties Ltd.* [1980] 1 All E.R. 371, but it was held in *Roake v. Chadha* [1983] 3 All E.R. 503 that there may be exceptional cases that depend on the construction of the covenant as a whole' (Parker's sidenote); and see para.6.4.5. above.

whole and every part of the Property that he will observe the restrictive covenants set out in the third schedule [but the Purchaser shall be under no liability for any breach occurring after he has parted with all his interest in the Property].

6. The Vendor covenants with the Purchaser to indemnify the Purchaser against liability resulting from any breach or non-observance of the covenants referred to in clause 3 so far as they relate to the Retained Premises.

7. The parties declare that no rights over the Retained Premises shall vest in the Purchaser by implication as a result of both the Property and the Retained Premises being owned by the Vendor prior to the execution of this deed.

8. The Vendor undertakes to keep safe the documents listed in the fourth schedule and acknowledges the right of the Purchaser to their production and to the supply of copies.

[Add any appropriate standard clauses. Certificate of value if applicable]

First Schedule.

The land shown edged red on the attached plan.

The following rights are included in this Conveyance.

[Set out easements, etc. to be granted]

The following rights are excepted from this Conveyance.

[Set out rights to be excepted]

Second Schedule.

[Set out positive covenants]

Third Schedule.

[Set out restrictive covenants]

Fourth Schedule.

[List documents to which acknowledgement relates].'

Question Using this precedent as a basis and the information provided in the text, and after reading this chapter, draft the conveyance on the Goldberg sale. For the details of the transaction, see Documents 5.1.3, 5.1.4, 5.1.6 and 6.2. If you consider further information necessary invent it to fit in with the facts that are given.

A note on punctuation, etc

Legal draftsmen traditionally tend to be fond of capital letters and totally averse to the use of punctuation marks. There is no legal magic in the use of capital letters or bold type. It is largely a matter of the presentation and appearance of the document.

12.3.2

It has been said that

'The system of punctuation of legal documents has become entirely confused ... the refusal to use a comma has reached such fantastic lengths that we often read this sort of thing:

"By a Conveyance dated ... and made between John Williams Vaughan Jones Richards and Thomas Richards of the one part and Ivan Williams Jones Thomas Hughes Richard Vernon and Richard Simpson of the other part ..." '[2]

The underlying reason for not using commas is the sensible one that a large number of clauses strung together can lead to ambiguity – just as can the absence of commas.

One of the surest ways of avoiding ambiguity is to avoid long sentences. 'Jack built a house.' is not ambiguous – that is, as long as you know who Jack is and what a house is!

Procedure on drafting

12.3.3   The Standard Conditions of sale (Standard Conditions 4.1.2. to 4.1.4.), reflecting the open contract position, require the purchaser's solicitor to draft the conveyance. The vendor's solicitor is to approve or revise it. If the draft is not approved amendments will have to be negotiated and agreed; though the Standard Conditions do not provide a time schedule for this process. When agreed, the draft itself can, if suitable, be used as the engrossment (i.e. the final, fair copy). Otherwise, the purchaser's solicitor will have to engross the conveyance in accordance with the agreed draft, have it executed by the purchaser if necessary, and send it to the vendor's solicitor to be executed by the vendor in preparation for completion. Subject to what has just been said, the Standard Conditions stipulate time limits within which these steps must be taken.

THE PARTS OF A CONVEYANCE

12.4   Broadly speaking a conveyance can be divided into four main parts (although all are equally part of the conveyance):

(a) The introductory part consisting of the commencement, date, parties and recitals.

(b) The testatum or operative part, which defines and actually transfers the property.

---

2   Parker, p.3.

(c) Additional clauses including covenants, declarations, etc to suit the particular circumstances.

(d) The conclusion, consisting of the testimonium, execution and attestation.

Introductory part   **12.4.1**

(a) The Commencement

The opening words simply tell what the deed is: 'This Conveyance ...'; or (in the case of the sale of a lease): 'This Assignment ...' In view of s.1 of the Law of Property (Miscellaneous Provisions) Act 1989 (below, para.12.4.4(b)) it is useful to indicate immediately that a deed is intended by saying 'This deed of Conveyance ...' etc.

(b) The date

The date will normally be inserted upon and as the date of completion itself. A deed takes effect on delivery, which may be prior to completion (below, para.12.4.4); but there is a presumption that the date shown on the deed is the date of delivery. The date is not crucial in that the deed will take effect (on delivery) if it contains no date or an impossible date. Nothing is gained by backdating the deed in an attempt to come within the protection of a Central Land Charges search which is governed by the date of completion of the purchase.

(c) Parties

This states who the parties to the deed are. The vendor and purchaser will be parties. In addition, anyone else whose consent is necessary to transfer the legal estate; or who is required to enter into any obligation. For example, on a sale of part, a mortgagee of the whole may be joined to release the part sold from the mortgage. Another case would be where someone with an equitable interest in the property is joining in to release that interest; though this could be done by a separate, written and signed release.

The address of each party should be given. In the case of a company, building society or other corporation, this will be its registered office.

Where the same person or object is to be referred to several times throughout the conveyance, it is usual, to reduce prolixity, to identify her or it by a brief label on first giving a full description and then to identify it by the label in the rest of the document.

(d) Recitals

In a traditional, unregistered conveyance, each recital begins with the word 'Whereas ...'. They explain how the vendor came to own the property (when not conveyed to her by the previous owner - for example, where the vendor is the personal representative of a deceased owner); and the reason for the present conveyance (for example, that the vendor is a mortgagee selling in exercise of the power of sale). They are not an operative part of the conveyance but their significance is that:

(i) a recital in a deed 20 years old is sufficient evidence of the fact recited;

(ii) a recital (being part of the deed) can be resorted to in order to resolve any ambiguity in the operative part of the deed;

(iii) a statement in a recital may constitute an estoppel against the party making it (so that she cannot then make an allegation in conflict with the recital).[3]

It follows that, today, recitals in existing deeds may assist a vendor in proving her title; and in showing a title acceptable to the Land Registry. Since a sale of freehold will now lead to first registration, there is less justification for drafting recitals into the new conveyance. They may still be useful to spell out the descent of the title to the present vendor. Further, on a sale by a personal representative, the statement under s.36(6) of the Administration of Estates Act 1925 (para.14.7.1) might still be put in the form of a recital.

Operative part or Testatum

12.4.2   This is traditionally introduced by the words, 'This Deed Witnesseth as follows:-' followed by numbered paragraphs containing the operative clauses of the deed.

(a) Consideration and receipt clause

Under s.5 of the Stamp Act 1891, an instrument must set out the facts affecting its liability to duty (para.10.7.1).

A receipt clause is included for three reasons:

(i) Under s.67 of the Law of Property Act 1925, if a receipt clause is contained in the body of a deed there is no need for any further receipt for the consideration (the purchase price). Where the price is

---

[3] See *Cumberland Court (Brighton) Ltd. v. Taylor* [1964] Ch. 29. Compare *T.C.B. Ltd. v. Gray* [1986] Ch. 621; statement in testimonium creating estoppel.

paid to someone other than the vendor - for example, a mortgagee joining in to release the part sold - the consideration clause will normally state this and the receipt clause be modified accordingly.[4]

(ii) Under s.68 of the Law of Property Act 1925, a subsequent purchaser can rely upon the receipt in the deed as proof that the money was paid. This means that if in spite of the receipt clause, the vendor retains a lien on the property for actually unpaid money, she will have to protect it by retention of the title deeds or registration as a land charge.

(iii) By s.69 of the same Act, the receipt in the conveyance is sufficient authority to the purchaser to pay the money to the vendor's solicitor producing the deed, without further proof of authority. Payment to an unauthorised person would not discharge the debt.

(b) Capacity of the vendor

This may have legal significance in three ways:

(i) It will determine the covenants for title to be implied into the conveyance (para.5.7).

(ii) It will (where title deeds are being retained) determine whether or not an undertaking for safe custody as well as acknowledgement for production is given (below, para.12.4.3(c)).

(iii) Conveyance as beneficial owner or a statement that the vendor is so interested is necessary to take advantage of the Law of Property (Joint Tenants) Act 1964 (para.14.7.2).

(c) The operative words of conveyance

These words, usually beginning 'Hereby Conveys', the very essence of what the conveyance is doing, transfer legal title to the purchaser. There is no magic formula; any words that show the necessary intention will be effective.

In the case of a mortgagee joining in to release, there will be a statement to the effect that 'The vendor hereby conveys and the mortgagee hereby releases the property from the mortgage'.

(d) The parcels clause

This describes and defines the physical limits of the property being conveyed (see para.5.4).

---

4 Compare Parker, Precedent 99.

(e) Rights benefitting the property

This clause, introduced by the words 'Together with', includes (generally by reference to the earlier conveyance creating them) the existing rights already appurtenant to the property being sold. In fact, any rights already appurtenant to the land will pass automatically without express mention by virtue of s.62 of the Law of Property Act 1925. On sale of part it will also include within the same formula new rights (generally easements) being granted to the purchaser over the retained land.

(f) Exceptions and reservations

On a sale of part, the vendor may reserve rights over the land sold.[5] Any part of the land itself being excluded from the sale (for example, the minerals) and any new rights over the land sold being created in favour of the retained land (for example, new easements) will be set out here.

With both the grant and reservation of new rights, as with restrictive covenants, unless they are few and simple, it is often better to set out the details in schedules incorporated into this part of the deed by reference. The drafting of new easements will have to follow the terms of the contract. This has been dealt with in Chapter 6 (particularly, para.6.4.3).

(g) Habendum

This is the part of the conveyance which defines the estate which is being granted to the purchaser. On a sale of freehold this will necessarily be the fee simple (absolute in possession – though these words are not stated) since that is the only legal estate now possible. These words of limitation are not essential in that under the Law of Property Act 1925, ss.60 and 63, the whole estate of the vendor will pass unless a contrary intention appears; but if they are not expressed it is possible that the statutory, implied covenants for title will not operate since the vendor is in effect only purporting to transfer whatever he happens to have.

(h) Existing incumbrances

After the Habendum a clause commencing 'Subject to' sets out the existing incumbrances subject to which the property is sold. Commonly, rather than setting them out in full they are identified by reference to the earlier conveyance which contains or refers to them.

This operative part, with its additions and subtractions, gives the measure of what is being conveyed to the purchaser.

---

5   For the technical meaning of the terms 'exception' and 'reservation' see Megarry & Wade, p.857.

Additional clauses   12.4.3

Further clauses may be necessary depending on the particular circumstances. Some of those most commonly needed are as follows (the order is not important):

(a) Indemnity covenant

See para. 5.6.3.

(b) Certificate of value

See para. 10.7.1.

(c) Acknowledgement and Undertaking

(And see para.14.9.2).Where the vendor is properly retaining any of the title deeds (generally, on a sale of part; or on a sale by a personal representative who will retain the original grant) the purchaser's solicitor should obtain copies or abstracts of the originals marked as examined against the originals. But the purchaser will also want a guarantee that she can, at any time in the future, have the originals produced if necessary to defend her title.

Standard Condition 4.5.4. of the Standard Conditions provides:

'The seller is to arrange at his expense that, in relation to every document of title which the buyer does not receive on completion, the buyer is to have the benefit of:

(a) a written acknowledgement of his right to its production; and

(b) a written undertaking for its safe custody (except while it is held by a mortgagee or by someone in a fiduciary capacity).'

The acknowledgement will be in something like the following terms:

'The vendor acknowledges the right of the purchaser to production of the documents specified in the schedule (the possession of which is retained by the vendor) and to delivery of copies of them and undertakes with the purchaser for the safe custody of them.'

The clause, reflecting the Standard Conditions, consists of two parts – an acknowledgement of the right to production; and the undertaking as to safe custody. Where the acknowledgement is given, its effect is governed by s.64 of the Law of Property Act 1925. This obligates the covenantor, if required, to produce the specified documents for the purposes of inspection, for judicial proceedings, and to supply true copies of them. If, when they are required, the documents are still available the court can order their production in accordance with the acknowledgement. But it does not impose any obligation on the covenantor to take care of the deeds or pay damages if they are lost.

It is customary practice, therefore, to stipulate in the contract (as in Standard Condition 4.5.4(b)) for an undertaking for their safe custody. This, under s.64(9) imposes an obligation to keep the documents safe, whole, uncancelled and undefaced unless prevented from doing so by fire or other inevitable accident. If the undertaking is breached damages will be recoverable.

The benefit and burden of both acknowledgement and undertaking run with the land and the deeds respectively. So a subsequent purchaser of the part would be able to enforce against a subsequent purchaser of the retained land.

To be effective the acknowledgement must be given by the person who has the legal possession of the deeds which may be, for example, a mortgagee and not the vendor. In such a case, under Standard Condition 4.5.4. the vendor must arrange the necessary acknowledgement and undertaking. But it is customary practice, followed in Standard Condition 4.5.4., that a fiduciary, such as a personal representative and including a mortgagee, only gives the acknowledgement without the undertaking. Normally the mortgagee will be a party to the conveyance (to release the part sold) and will give the acknowledgement there. Standard Condition 4.5.4. means, presumably, that the vendor will be under an obligation to provide the undertaking when the deeds are recovered from the mortgagee or other fiduciary. It is commonly said that a special condition in the contract should provide for this obligation to be spelt out in the conveyance. Since, on a sale of freehold, first registration should follow more or less immediately this last point does not seem to be of much importance.

When the sale is by joint tenants (even if they are themselves beneficially entitled) they are technically trustees. There should be a special condition in the contract stipulating that they will give the undertaking as well as the acknowledgement. Again, in the view of the imminent registration, the point does not seem to be of the greatest importance.

Title deeds may have been retained on a previous transfer of the land. When investigating title the purchaser's solicitor should check that on every such occasion a valid acknowledgment was given of which the present purchaser will have the benefit. Thus, if A sold part of Blackacre to B who subsequently sold part of the part to C who is now selling that part to P, A will have retained the title deeds to the whole; B should have received the conveyance to her incorporating an acknowledgement and undertaking; C should have received the conveyance to her incorporating an acknowledgement and undertaking in respect of the conveyance to B. Upon purchase, P will take the benefit of both acknowledgements and undertakings.

If the purchaser will not obtain this benefit in respect of all title deeds not to be handed over, it is a title defect which should be raised in requisitions; and which the vendor should cure by obtaining the missing acknowledgement from the person who now holds the deeds in question. If the vendor has spotted the defect, as she should have done, when drafting the contract, it will no doubt be covered by a special condition barring requisitions or objections on the point; and normally the vendor will at least be able to produce an examined copy or abstract of the unacknowledged deeds.

(d) Implied easements

On a sale of part and depending on the terms of the contract, it may be necessary to have a clause dealing with implied easements. This will usually be in the form beginning 'It is hereby agreed and declared ...'.

The conveyance will be drafted to reflect what has been agreed expressly or by implication in the contract. If the contract contains no express term as to implied easements, it is not usual to mention them in the conveyance; the parties would then be entitled to whatever had arisen by implied grant or reservation, for example under *Wheeldon v. Burrows*, s.62 of the Law of Property Act 1925. If s.62 operated on the conveyance to give the purchaser an easement to which she was not entitled under the contract, the vendor would, in principle, be entitled to claim rectification of the conveyance to match the entitlement under the contract.[6] Where the contract does modify the open contract position in any way, the conveyance must be drafted with a declaration to show this. For example, if Standard Condition 3.3.2. has not been modified by special condition in the contract, there should be a declaration in the conveyance incorporating the Standard Condition 3.3.2. provision. (See further, para.6.4.4.)

It is quite common to have a term in the contract (as an alternative to one like Standard Condition 3.3.2.) simply excluding any right of light or air (or, possibly, way) to the purchaser of part, leaving the rest to be governed by the common law rules of implied creation. It might then be formulated and then drafted into the conveyance/transfer in something like the following terms:

'It is hereby agreed and declared that the Purchaser is not to have any easement of light or air which would or might interfere with or restrict the free use of the Vendor's retained land for building or any other purpose.'

---

[6]   See Megarry & Wade, p.869.

Conversely, a right of light, for example, might be expressly agreed in the contract and transposed into the conveyance/ transfer in the parcels clause in the following terms:

'Together with the right for the Purchaser and her successors in title to enjoy unimpeded access of light to through and for the existing windows [and solar heating apparatus] now existing or to be erected] on the Property.'

(e) Restrictive and positive covenants

These, again, will have to be drafted into the conveyance to reflect what has been expressly agreed in the contract (para.6.4.5).

(f) Joint purchase clauses

Where there are two or more persons involved in the purchase, their solicitor should have taken instructions as to how they intend to hold the legal estate and the equitable interest. The terms on which the purchasers hold the property is their concern and not the concern of the vendor; but it is convenient to deal with it in the conveyance.

The conveyance may contain express provision on three matters:

(i) An express declaration of a trust for sale. It is now generally accepted that whenever the beneficial (equitable) interest is held by two or more persons (as a result of an express declaration of interest or of a resulting trust) a statutory trust for sale of the legal estate to give effect to those interests will be imposed by the Law of Property Act 1925, s.34 - 36 in the absence of an express trust for sale.[7]

In practice, today, it seems to be usual to leave the trust for sale to be imposed by statute in this way rather than to set it out expressly in the conveyance, at least in the case of a beneficial joint tenancy.

(ii) The conveyance should (if it is not done in a separate document) state the beneficial interests – that is whether they are to be joint tenants or tenants in common in equity; and if tenants in common whether in equal or other specified shares.

This is equally important where anyone other than the purchasers (i.e. those taking the legal estate) is to have an interest in equity.[8]

---

[7] These sections do not literally cover all possible situations of equitable co-ownership - e.g. where Blackacre is conveyed to A and B without more and the evidence shows unequal contributions to the purchase price; see K. Gray, *Elements of Land Law* (1987) p.361.

[8] Bearing in mind that the interest of any such person, who is not joint owner of the legal estate, can be overreached.

In all these cases, a purchaser of unregistered land will not be concerned with any such trust or statement of the equitable interests contained in a conveyance to the vendors so long as the overreaching machinery is complied with; but it is important as evidence in the event of dispute as to the equitable entitlement to the property or the proceeds of sale. For the position in the case of registered title, see para.1.9.2, and below, para.12.9(e)).

(iii) The conveyance may contain provision giving the trustees of the legal estate all the powers of dealing with the land of an absolute owner.

The point is that trustees for sale do not as such have the unlimited powers of an absolute owner. For example, they cannot give the land away; nor can they mortgage it other than for specified purposes.

From a purchaser's point of view, there is not generally a problem because:

(i) Normally, the trustees of the legal estate will, in fact, between them own the whole equitable interest (e.g. in the ordinary case of a purchase by spouses who hold as beneficial joint tenants).

(ii) In any case, the transaction is likely to be within the statutory powers of trustees for sale. In particular, under s.28 of the Law of Property Act 1925, they have power to sell the land for the best consideration in money that can reasonably be obtained. Again, by s.17 of the Trustee Act 1925, a mortgagee lending money to trustees is not concerned 'to see that such money is wanted, or that no more than is wanted is raised, or otherwise to the application thereof.' Thus, a purchaser will not be affected by notice of a breach of trust and the overreaching machinery will operate.

However, where the trustees are in fact between them beneficial owners of the equitable interest, it is common to insert a clause in the conveyance extending the powers of the trustees to those of a sole, beneficial owner. Of course, where the trustees are trustees for others, such a clause would not be appropriate; for example, where land is conveyed to A and B to hold in trust for an infant.[9]

---

[9] And in such a case it would be necessary for the person conveying the land for the benefit of the infant to create the trust for sale expressly; otherwise the Settled Land Act 1925 machinery would operate (see s.1 of that Act).

The following is the sort of clause that might be found in a conveyance to joint owners buying for themselves:

'The Purchasers [A and B] agree that:

1. They hold the Property the net proceeds of sale from it and the net income until sale upon trust for themselves as tenants in common as to 20% for A and as to 80% for B.

2. The trustees for sale of the property shall have the powers to deal with it equal to those of a sole beneficial owner.'[10]

12.4.4   Testimonium, attestation and execution

(a) Testimonium

The testimonium is the clause that links the attestation and execution to the body of the deed. In the case of parties who are all individuals it might be: 'In Witness whereof the parties hereto have hereunto signed this conveyance as a deed the day and year first above written.'

In general, it has no legal effect and today is commonly omitted.[11]

(b) Execution and attestation

The purchaser's solicitor should check that all documents on the title have been (and the conveyance to her client is) properly executed in the correct manner by all necessary parties. The vendor and any other party whose participation is necessary to transfer the interest as agreed or who is entering into obligations must execute. The purchaser does not have to execute simply to obtain the title to the property and under s.65 of the Law of Property Act 1925, execution by the purchaser is not necessary to give effect to the reservation of easements or profits by the vendor.[12] It will be necessary if the purchaser is entering into any covenants or declarations of agreement and, in the case of joint purchasers, to give effect to any declaration of their beneficial interest.

It is usual to have an attestation clause for each signatory. The clause is a statement of the fact and intention of the execution and witnessing. It is not in general essential but is evidence that the deed has been properly executed. However, by s.1(2) of the Law of Property (Miscellaneous Provisions) Act 1989, any instrument, to be valid as a deed, must make it

---

10   See Parker, Form 82.

11   But see *TCB Ltd. v. Gray* [1986] Ch.621.

12   See Megarry & Wade, 858.

clear on its face that it is intended by the parties to be a deed (and must be attested). This intention is commonly expressed in the attestation clauses – though it is probably also shown elsewhere in the deed as well.

(c) Execution by individuals

Prior to 31 July 1990, when s.1 of the Law of Property (Miscellaneous Provisions) Act 1989 came into operation, to be effective as a deed, a document had to be signed sealed and delivered. By s.73 of the Law of Property Act 1925 a person can place her mark (usually in the form of a cross) instead of signing.

The standard practice in modern times was to seal by affixing a small circle of red, adhesive paper to the document opposite the intended place of signature, in place of the earlier practice when a person impressed her crest or initials in molten wax on the document.

The courts developed a benign approach to the sealing requirement. What was required by the later decisions was that there should be some evidence of something on the document that could be said to be intended as a seal.[13]

Delivery was (and is) the final and vital formality that actually triggered off the effectiveness of the document as a deed. The moment of delivery, in spite of its importance, may be difficult to pinpoint, since it connotes an act showing an intention to be bound by the deed, rather than (though this is likely to be present) the physical handing over of it.

A deed may be delivered in escrow, that is subject to a condition (which may be implied from the circumstances) that it is not to be effective until the happening of some event. If and when the event occurs, the deed becomes effective (by the principle of relation back) as from the date of delivery in escrow.

In ordinary conveyancing practice, the document would (if necessary) be signed and sealed by the purchaser and then sent to the vendor's solicitor. The vendor would then sign and seal and hand it back to her solicitor in preparation for completion. This could, according to the principles of delivery, be seen as delivery by the vendor with the unsatisfactory result of transferring legal title to the purchaser before completion and before receipt of the purchase money. To avoid this inference, it would have been sensible to analyse the situation by saying

---

[13] See *First National Securities Ltd. v. Jones* [1978] Ch. 109; *Stromdale & Ball Ltd. v. Burden* [1952] Ch. 223; and *T.C.B. Ltd. v. Gray* [1986] Ch. 621, where there was no such mark at all and so the document was held not to be sealed; but a statement in the testimonium that it has been sealed was held to create an estoppel.

that the vendor was signing and sealing the deed and handing it to her solicitor to deliver at completion in return for the purchase money. This could not be said because a solicitor, like anyone else, would need a power of attorney - itself by deed - to have the authority to deliver as agent for the vendor.[14] In practice, this was never done. The analysis used was that the vendor delivered to her solicitor in escrow, the condition being the payment of the balance of the purchase money. This meant, incidentally, that conveyances (being dated as at completion) were invariably wrongly dated!

Prior to 31 July 1990, attestation by a witness was not a legal requirement for a deed by an individual; though invariably conveyances were witnessed.

The position for conveyances by individuals after 30 July 1990 is as follows:

(a) The conveyance must of course still be by deed; except for the exceptional cases where a deed is not required to transfer the legal estate.

(b) By s.1 of the Law of Property (Miscellaneous Provisions) Act 1989, coming into effect from the above date, a document must satisfy the following requirements to be effective as a deed executed by an individual (sealing is *not* now necessary):

(i) It must make it clear on the face of it that it is intended to be a deed.

(ii) It must be signed by the individual executing it in the presence of an attesting witness or signed 'at his direction and in his presence and the presence of two witnesses who each attest the signature';[15] and

(iii) it must be delivered as a deed by him or a person authorised to do so on his behalf.

(c) As before, signature can be by mark.

Section 1(1)(c) provides that a deed is not necessary to give another person authority to deliver a deed on one's behalf. Further, s.1(5) provides that where a solicitor or his agent or employee:

'... in the course of, or in connection with, a transaction involving the disposition or creation of an interest in land, purports to

---

14   In *Longman v. Viscount Chelsea* (1989) 58 P. & C.R. 189, p.195, Nourse L.J. appears to have overlooked this point. In that case there was held to be no delivery on signing and sealing because the agreement for the lease in question was still subject to contract, the intention to deliver thus being negatived.

15   As to the attestation requirement, see Conveyancer's notebook, [1990] Conv. 321. As to the delivery of deeds and the effect of the 1989 Act, see D.N. Clarke, 'Delivery of a Deed: Recent Cases, New Statutes and Altered Practice' [1990] Conv. 85.

deliver an instrument as a deed on behalf of a party to the instrument, it shall be conclusively presumed in favour of a purchaser that he is authorised so to deliver the instrument.'

This means that the escrow fiction is not now necessary, and, in the ordinary case, delivery will take place in law and the deed operate from actual completion.

The form of attestation clause likely now to be found is:

'Signed as a deed by ... in the presence of [signature, name and address of witness].'

This shows the required intention to execute as a deed; delivery will take place subsequently as described above.

(d) Execution by corporations

Again the law has been changed, in this case by s.130 of the Companies Act 1989.

In principle a deed must be sealed and executed by a corporation in accordance with the authority and procedure contained in its constitution.

Prior to the 1989 Act, a purchaser could rely on s.74 of the Law of Property Act 1925. This provides that the deed of a corporation aggregate (as opposed to a corporation sole) will be deemed to have been duly executed if its seal is affixed in the presence of and attested by its clerk or other permanent official or his deputy and a member of the board of directors, council or other governing body. Further, by this section, not only is the authority of those attesting presumed, they are presumed to be who the deed purports them to be.

Delivery is presumed from the fact of sealing.

This section applies to companies, building societies, local authorities and other corporations aggregate. Any other form of attestation of the seal would have to be shown to be authorised by the constitution of the company.

A common attestation clause would be:

'The common seal of the above named company was affixed and the same was delivered in the presence of:

[Signature] ... Director of the above company.

[Signature] ... Secretary of the above named company.'

As a result of s.36A of the Companies Act 1985, added by s.130 of the Companies Act 1989 (coming into force on 31 July 1990) the old procedure, just described, can still be used. But now, as an alternative, use of a seal is not obligatory. A company no longer has to have a common seal.

A deed will be properly executed by a company if the following conditions are satisfied:

(a) it must make it clear on its face that it is intended to be a deed;

(b) it can be executed either

(i), as before, using the common seal; or

(ii) by the signature of a director and secretary or two of its directors;

(c) it must be delivered.

Delivery is presumed to take place on execution unless a contrary intention is shown. A form of attestation clause, under this provision, might be:

'Signed as a deed and delivered by X Ltd. acting by

AB Director ... and

CD Secretary ...'.

The word 'delivered' is not essential. The Law of Property (Miscellaneous Provisions) Act 19189, 1(5) applies to companies. The deed could therefore contain a provision that it is not to be delivered until completion, thus showing a 'contrary intention', and the deed delivered by the solicitor at completion.

Delivery by a company can be unconditional or as an escrow.

By s.36A(6) in favour of a purchaser, if the documents purports to have been signed by a director and the secretary or two directors and to be a deed, it will be deemed to have been duly executed by the company and to have been delivered on execution. A purchaser means a purchaser (including a lessee or mortgagee) in good faith for value of an interest in property.

(e) Execution under a power of attorney

Where an agent is given a power to execute a deed, that power itself must normally be contained in a deed.[16] The deed creating the power is known as a power of attorney.

Thus, if a conveyance is to be executed by someone other than a party herself, the authority of that other person must be established by an effective power of attorney.

---

[16] The authority to deliver a document as a deed does not now have to be given by deed; Law of Property (Miscellaneous Provisions) Act 1989, s.1(1)(c).

(i) General and special powers

The power may be general authorising the donee to do any act which the donor herself could do; or special (limited) giving the donee power to do only specified acts - e.g. to execute a particular deed on behalf of the donor.

The basis of the present law is contained in the Powers of Attorney Act 1971 and the Enduring Powers of Attorney Act 1985. Section 10 and Schedule 1 of the 1971 Act provide a statutory form which can be used for the creation of a general power, as follows:

'This general Power of Attorney is made this ... day of ... 19 ... By AB of ...

I Appoint CD of ... [or CD and EF of ... jointly] [or CD of ... and EF of ... jointly and severally] to be my attorney(s) in accordance with section 10 of the Powers of Attorney Act 1971.

This Power of Attorney has been executed by me as a deed the day and year first above written.

Signed as a deed by the said AB

in the presence of: ...'

A form to 'the like effect' can be used if expressed to be made under the Act. This general power does not extend to functions which the donor has as trustee or personal representative.

As an example of a special power:

'This Power of Attorney is given on the ... day of ... 19 ... By me AB (Donor) of ...

WITNESSES as follows:

1. I Appoint CD (Attorney) of ... to be my Attorney with authority to sell any freehold or leasehold property on my behalf and execute such deeds and documents and employ such professional advisers as may be necessary for that purpose.

This Power of Attorney has been executed by me as a deed.

Signed as a deed and delivered by the above named AB in the presence of ...'

Whether general or special, the power must be by deed to authorise the execution of a deed and its execution must comply with s.1 of the Law of Property (Miscellaneous Provisions) Act 1989 or the rules for execution by corporations.

(ii) Proof of power to a purchaser

As with any other document relevant to the title the purchaser's solicitor will require a copy to be supplied when title is deduced. And if a document on the title is executed under a power of attorney a copy must be produced even if created before the root of title. By s.125 of the Law of Property Act 1925, this right to a copy cannot be excluded.

The vendor must then produce the original or a copy complying with s.3(1) of the 1971 Act (as amended by the Courts and Legal Services Act 1990, s.125, Schedule 17, para.4). This must be a facsimile copy and be certified by the donor, a solicitor, stockbroker or certificated notary public at the end of each page that it is a true copy of the original (or that page of the original as the case may be).

On completion the purchaser will be entitled to receive either the original power (if it relates only to that transaction) or a copy certified as above. If the purchaser subsequently sells, she can if necessary produce a certified (as above) copy of a certified copy as proof of the power (s.3(2) of the 1971 Act).

(iii) Appointment by a trustee

The starting principle is that a trustee cannot delegate her functions in the absence of specific statutory authority.

Under what is now s.9 of the 1971 Act, a trustee can appoint an attorney to carry out her trust functions, subject to the following provisions:

(i) The delegation must be for a period not exceeding 12 months.

(ii) A trustee cannot (under s.9 or any part of the 1971 Act) delegate to a sole co-trustee. Most significantly in the present context this means that one of two joint tenants cannot appoint the other as her attorney. It may also be the case under s.9 (and so should not be risked), that two joint trustees cannot appoint the same person to be attorney for both of them, as this would breach the rule requiring payment of capital money to at least two trustees to activate the overreaching machinery.

(iii) The s.10 (of the 1971 Act) general power cannot be used to delegate trust functions. This is so even if the trustee delegating is in fact beneficial owner. The proper course is to comply with s.9 of the 1971 Act (remembering that even under s.9 a sole co-trustee cannot be appointed).

In *Walia v. Michael Naughton Ltd*.[17] the vendor had herself purchased the registered property from three joint proprietors, A, B and C. The transfer had been executed by B and C, B executing both for himself and for A under a general power of attorney under s.10 of the 1971 Act. This was held to be a defect in title with the result that the notice

---

[17] [1985] 3 All E.R. 673.

to complete served by V was of no effect (para.16.8). The court inferred that they must be trustees, although of course this was not stated on the register, because there was more than one proprietor on the register (as with unregistered title, the existence of two or more joint owners necessarily gave rise to a trust).

(iv) Non-revocation

In principle, a power of attorney can be revoked expressly by the donor, or automatically by the donor's death, bankruptcy or mental incapacity; and any act done by the attorney after such revocation will be void. A purchaser is given certain protection against this possibility. Under s.5(2) of the 1971 Act any person dealing with the attorney will get good title provided she did not know of the revocation. In this context knowledge of the event (such as the death of the donor) giving rise to the revocation is deemed to be knowledge of the revocation (s.5(5)).

What if this initial purchaser subsequently sells? Suppose that Donee of the power (D) transfers to T. T then sells to P. T's title is governed by s.5(2) above. But P's title in turn depends on whether T satisfied s.5(2), i.e. did not have knowledge of any revocation – a negative state of mind which it is difficult to prove.

P's position is governed by s.5(4) of the 1971 Act. This provides that in favour of a purchaser it will conclusively be presumed that T (in the above example) did not know of the revocation, provided either the transfer to T was within 12 months of the creation of the power, or T makes a statutory declaration before or within three months after the sale to P that she (T) did not know of any revocation.

Where a power is expressed to be irrevocable and given to secure a proprietary interest of the donee, then so long as the donee has that interest, the power cannot be expressly revoked by the donor (without the donee's consent) and will not be revoked by her death, bankruptcy or incapacity. Such an irrevocable power is likely to be found in an equitable mortgage putting the donee/mortgagee in a position to enforce the security if need be without the co-operation of the borrower.

(v) Method of execution by the attorney

Under s.7 of the 1971 Act (as amended by the Law of Property (Miscellaneous Provisions) Act 1989) the attorney can (in exercise of the power) execute a deed in her own name; in which case the attestation clause will be to the effect: 'Signed as a deed by AB as attorney on behalf of CD.' Alternatively (and in a few cases this is required by statute), she can sign in the name of the donor; in which case the attestation clause will be to the effect: 'Signed as a deed by CD by her attorney AB.'

If the donor of the power is a company, the attorney can execute in the manner permitted under s.74(3) of the Law of Property Act 1925 – which allows her to execute by signing in the corporation's name in the presence of a witness and affixing her own seal. Alternatively, under s.7 of the 1971 Act as amended by the 1989 Act she can execute as for an individual using her own signature.

A purchaser should check any document on the title (including the conveyance/transfer to herself) which has been executed under a power of attorney to see that all the above requirements have been satisfied.

The Land Registry will require the power or a copy certified as described above; and, if the transaction to be registered has not occurred within 12 months of the creation of the power, the statutory declaration mentioned above. These will be retained at the Registry.

(vi) Enduring powers of attorney

The Enduring Powers of Attorney Act 1985 was passed to enable the creation of a power of attorney which would not be revoked by the subsequent mental incapacity of the donor of the power. An Enduring Power must be created in accordance with the requirements of the Act. If mental incapacity of the donor does occur an application must be made to the Court of Protection for registration of the power; and pending registration the authority of the attorney is limited to maintaining the donor and preventing loss to her estate. Once registered, the attorney resumes her full authority under the power.

Provided the formal creation requirements of the Act are complied with, an Enduring Power can be used by anyone. It is not limited to those who are likely to become mentally incapacitated. In this context it has a number of advantages (from a conveyancing point of view).[18] Like an ordinary power it can be general or special. Unlike an ordinary power it can be used to appoint a sole co-trustee as attorney to exercise the donor's trust functions and such a sole co-trustee if appointed can give a valid receipt for capital money arising on the disposition of land. Thus, in the common case of H and W, joint beneficial owners of the home, H can appoint W attorney under an Enduring Power; and W can (if within the authority given by the power) by herself sell the home and execute the conveyance without the concurrence of anyone else.[19] Further, the power is not limited to the twelve month period imposed on a power under s.9 of the 1971 Act.

---

[18]   For criticism of the Act, see R.T. Oerton, 'A Legislative Blunder' ((1986) 130 S.J. 23).

[19]   W should execute both in her personal capacity and as attorney for H.

Until application is made to the Court of Protection the protection of a person dealing with the attorney and of a subsequent purchaser from that person, is the same as that contained in s.5 of the 1971 Act (above). Thus, a subsequent purchaser should check that the disposition by the attorney was made within twelve months of the creation of the power or require the statutory declaration by the person dealing with the attorney. If there is any reason to suspect that an application has been made at the time of the disposition by the attorney, there should probably be a search at that time in the Court of Protection.

As with an ordinary power of attorney, to register a disposition by the attorney, the Land Registry will require the original or certified copy of the power and, if applicable, the statutory declaration.

The 1985 Act creates a very complicated scheme; and, unless it is being used for its intended purpose - that is to provide against the possible onset of mental incapacity - its use is hardly to be recommended simply as a conveyancing device to enable a sole co-trustee to be appointed attorney. It is probably much easier and just as satisfactory in most cases to appoint a third person to act.

REGISTERED LAND TRANSFERS

The following is the draft prepared by Timothy on the Obebe   **12.5** purchase. For the draft contract (assume it to be the final version) and office copy entries, see Documents 4.1.2 and 4.1.3.

Document 12.6 Obebe Purchase: Draft Transfer

Transfer of Whole to Joint Proprietors[1]	**HM Land Registry** Land Registration Acts 1925 to 1986

Form 19(JP)
(Rules 98 or 115, Land Registration Rules, 1925)

Stamp pursuant to section 28 of the Finance Act 1931 to be impressed here.	When the transfer attracts Inland Revenue Duty, the stamps should be impressed here before lodging the transfer for registration.

(1) For a transfer to a sole proprietor use printed form 19.

County and district } (or London borough } Title number(s)   Ledchester, West Yorkshire
WYK 787260

Property   16 Winchester Avenue

Date _____ 19 ___ In consideration of **Eighty-eight thousand five hundred**

(2) Delete the words in italics if not required.

pounds (£ **88,500**) *the receipt of which is hereby acknowledged* [2]

(3) In BLOCK LETTERS enter the full name(s), postal address(es) (including postcode) and occupation(s) of the proprietor(s) of the land.

I/~We~ [3]   NANCY MIXFORD OF
16 WINCHESTER AVENUE, LEDCHESTER,
WEST YORKSHIRE

(4) If desired or otherwise as the case may be (see rules 76 and 77).

_____ *as beneficial owner(s) hereby transfer to* [4]

(5) In BLOCK LETTERS enter the full name(s), postal address(es) in the United Kingdom (including postcode) and occupation(s) of the transferee(s) for entry in the register.

[5] OLIVE OBEBE of 14 HARDCASTLE
DRIVE, LEDCHESTER, WEST YORKSHIRE

(6) Enter any special clause here.

the land comprised in the title(s) above mentioned [6] [7]

(7) A transfer for charitable purposes should follow form 36 in the schedule to the Land Registration Rules, 1925 (see rules 121 and 122).

(continued overleaf)

(8) Delete the inappropriate alternative.

The transferees declare that the survivor of them (8) ~~can~~ ~~cannot~~ give a valid receipt for capital money arising on a disposition of the land.

(9) If a certificate of value for the purpose of the Stamp Act, 1891 and amending Acts is not required, delete this paragraph.

~~(9) It is hereby certified that the transaction hereby effected does not form part of a larger transaction or series of transactions in respect of which the amount or value or aggregate amount or value of the consideration exceeds £~~ ....

(10) This transfer must be executed by the transferee(s) as well as the transferor(s).

(10) Signed as a deed by

Nancy Mixford

....

in the presence of

Signature of witness

Name

Address

Occupation

(10) Signed as a deed by

Olive Obebe

....

in the presence of

Signature of witness

Name

Address

Occupation

(10) Signed as a deed by

....

in the presence of

Signature of witness

Name

Address

Occupation

(10) Signed as a deed by

....

in the presence of

Signature of witness

Name

Address

Occupation

OYEZ The Solicitors' Law Stationery Society Ltd, Oyez House, 7 Spa Road, London SE16 3QQ

1993 Edition 3.93 F24386 5061122 ★ ★ ★ ★

Questions Timothy has used printed form 19(JP). Which one should he have used? What difference, if any, does it make? Was he correct to strike out the certificate of value? Should he have included an indemnity covenant in the draft? (See para.5.6.3.) On the information available, could the chain of covenants have been broken at any stage? Does the transfer need to be executed by Miss Obebe?

OLD JARNDYCE COMMENTS   12.7

Procedure

Standard Conditions 4.1.2. to 4.1.4. govern the drafting of the transfer   **12.7.1** as they do the drafting of an unregistered conveyance.

The transfer must be in the form, if any, prescribed by the Land Registration Acts 1925 to 1988 and Rules (see further, para.7.5.3).

The commonly used printed forms available for transfers of freehold (and in practice also frequently used for leasehold) are:

- Form 19: The transfer of whole of land in the title.
- Form 19(Co): Transfer of whole by a company or corporation.
- Form 19(JP): Transfer of whole to joint proprietors.
- Form 20: Transfer of part not imposing restrictive covenants.
- Form 43: Transfer of part imposing restrictive covenants.

In general, any prescribed statutory form must be followed although a published, printed form does not have to be used.

> 'The Chief Land Registrar has a discretion to accept modifications or adaptations of statutory forms, where this is appropriate or, where no form is available, to accept forms which follow the statutory forms as nearly as circumstances permit. Anyone who is in doubt may seek approval for the form of a draft document so as to ensure that, when it has been executed, it will be accepted for registration.'[20]

In general, when drafting documents dealing with the title to registered land the following principles should be followed: Recitals should be avoided (see below). In general references to trusts should be avoided; though it may sometimes be necessary, for example in the case of a transfer, to give effect to the appointment of a new trustee. An instrument should stand on its own, without reference to documents other

---

[20] Ruoff & Roper, para.15–10.

than those appearing on the title itself. In general acknowledgements are not necessary (see below).[21]

For ordinary straightforward sales it is common to draft the transfer on the printed form and, assuming it is approved by the vendor's solicitor as drafted, use the draft as the engrossment as well.

The transfer which must be by deed is an essential part of the process of transferring legal title from the vendor to the purchaser. It is roughly the equivalent to the conveyance in an unregistered transaction; and legally, for the purposes of the Law of Property Act for example, it seems that it is classified as a conveyance[22]and will transfer an equitable interest to the purchaser. But it is crucially different in that the purchaser will not get legal title until, on the basis of a transfer, she has been registered as the new proprietor.

12.8 THE PARTS OF THE TRANSFER

12.8.1 Heading

The transfer, like any other Land Registry form, must be headed by a statement of the county and district in which the property is situate (or London borough), the title number (which is the crucial reference), and a short description of the property. This is followed by the date.

12.8.2 Consideration and receipt clause

This is not in fact required by the prescribed statutory form; but it is required and must be included for the reasons given in relation to unregistered title.

12.8.3 Name and address of transferor

The vendor will not necessarily be the person registered as proprietor. This indeed is the case on the Obebe purchase and has been dealt with.

Where part of the land in a title is being sold and a chargee is to release the part sold, the proper course is not for the chargee to join in the transfer, but for her to execute a discharge of that part in Form 53 (see further, para.14.9.3(b)).

---

21 See Ruoff & Roper, para.15.09.

22 *Ahmed v. Kendrick* (1988) 56 P. & C. R. 120.

Capacity and operative words   12.8.4

The operative word normally used is 'transfer'. The capacity will be as specified in the contract. The function of statement of the vendor's capacity in implying covenants for title has been considered (para.7.11.4).

Parcels clause   12.8.5

On a sale of the whole property in a title, it is identified in the heading by its short description and title number. The transferor is then expressed, in the operative part, to transfer the 'land in the title above referred to'.

There is no need at all to mention expressly those appurtenant rights and incumbrances which are shown on the register, as these pass as part of the title transferred.

The benefit of restrictive covenants and other appurtenant rights which are not shown on the register will a pass automatically under s.62 of the Law of Property Act 1925 and s.20(1) of the Land Registration Act 1925 without express mention; though it may be advisable to mention them as one would in an unregistered conveyance to preserve evidence of their existence.

The benefit of other rights which are to be transferred under the contract and which are not appurtenant to the property - such as the benefit of an option to purchase neighbouring land, or of covenants which have not been annexed on creation - will need to be expressly assigned in the transfer. On a sale of part of the title, the transfer will need to identify the title number of the whole and the fact that it is a transfer of part identified by an annexed plan.

Name and address of transferee   12.8.6

The position of joint purchasers is dealt with below.

Execution and attestation   12.8.7

The execution of deeds dealing with registered land is governed by the Land Registration (Execution of Deeds) Rules 1990 (S.I.1990 No.1010). In effect, they should be attested and executed in the same way as for unregistered land. A plan is not necessary when the whole of the property in a title is being sold. It is necessary on a sale of part (above). The plan must be signed by the transferor and by or on behalf of the transferee.

12.9   OTHER MATTERS TO CONSIDER IN RELATION TO
                     DRAFTING THE TRANSFER

Recitals

Recitals are *not* necessary and are frowned on by the Registry.

Certificate of value

This will be needed in the same circumstances as in a conveyance of unregistered title.

Sale of part

New positive and restrictive covenants will have to be included, to reflect what has been agreed in the contract, as they would in a conveyance of unregistered land. Implied easements can arise on a sale of part of a registered title as on a sale of part of unregistered title. Such easements arising in this way will be overriding and will not be mentioned on the register of title. If any declaration is necessary to give effect to a term in the contract dealing with implied easements (for example, negativing the creation of any right of light or air in favour of the purchaser), this should be included in the transfer.

Acknowledgement and undertaking

On a sale of part an acknowledgement for production is *not* normally necessary. The purchaser will acquire a new, registered title. There should be a special condition in the contract requiring the vendor to place the land certificate on deposit at the Registry, if it is not already there. The part will be shown on the title plan of the existing title to have been removed from that title; and the new title for the part will be produced and stand on its own. No further production of the old title will be necessary.

On a sale by a personal representative, acknowledgement for production of the probate is not necessary, even where the personal representative has sold without first getting herself registered as proprietor. The Registry will accept a certified copy of the grant as proof of the title of the personal representative.

An acknowledgement for production may be necessary in two situations. First, on a sale of part of the land where the title purchased is not absolute – for example, where it is a possessory or a good leasehold. Here, an acknowledgement will be needed in respect of any deeds retained by the vendor relating to the part of the title not protected by registration. Secondly, on the sale of part of the land contained in a leasehold title, an acknowledgement will be needed in respect of the lease itself. A new leasehold title to the part purchased will be registered. But, as with all leases (Chapter 17), the lease itself will not be kept at the Registry nor will its terms be shown on the register of title. The purchaser will therefore need an acknowledgment from the vendor who will retain the lease; and a copy should be kept with the title documents of the part.

Joint purchase

The Registry is not interested in the trusts on which the legal title is held. It only wants to know whether a sole survivor of joint proprietors can give a valid receipt for capital money on a subsequent disposition of the land; and whether therefore a restriction should be put on the register. Printed Form 19(JP) contains a declaration to be completed by the purchasers stating whether or not this is the case. A negative answer will lead to a restriction being entered. In the absence of any restriction a purchaser will not be concerned with any limit on the powers of joint proprietors or a sole survivor of them to deal with the land.

Nevertheless as between themselves, those entitled in equity are concerned with the allocation beneficial interests and (if they are not the same persons as the proprietors) the powers of the trustees. The transfer should therefore clearly show as in the case of an unregistered conveyance (unless a separate trust document is to be prepared) whether the transferees are to be joint tenants in equity or tenants in common; and, if tenants in common, the size of their respective shares. (See, further, para.1.9.2). If the powers of the trustee/proprietors are to be enlarged to those of an absolute owner, this too should be shown. A copy of the transfer, marked as examined against the original, should then be kept with the title documents for reference by those entitled under the trust. The transfer is retained at the Registry and in general there is no right to obtain copies.

Sale by personal representative

On a sale by a personal representative neither an acknowledgement for production of the grant nor a statement by the personal representative that there has been no previous assent or transfer is necessary (see further, Chapter 11).

Indemnity covenant

The vendor of registered land will need an indemnity covenant in the same circumstances that a vendor of unregistered land would. Where appropriate an indemnity covenant should be drafted into the transfer.

In unregistered conveyancing any indemnity covenant would be included in the conveyance and so drawn to the attention of vendor and purchaser on a subsequent sale, reminding the vendor to take a similar covenant from the purchaser. But, an indemnity covenant is a personal covenant and, as such, is not seen as part of the title which is registered. The danger is that on a sale the vendor will not be reminded of its existence and to take one from the purchaser. The Land Registry has therefore adopted the practice of entering details of indemnity covenants on the proprietorship register of the title. It does not do this in the case of such a covenant contained in a conveyance giving rise to first registration since the title deeds will be returned to and retained by the first proprietor. On a sale by the first registered proprietor it will therefore be necessary to check back to the title deeds to see whether the covenant is required in the transfer to the purchaser.

Question Refer back to the Instructions on the Obebe sale and office copy entries (Documents 7.2 and 7.3). Draft the transfer to Olive's sister (Herminone Obebe). See para.9.3 and assume that the sale to the sister is on the same terms as agreed with the Headcases.

CHAPTER 13

PRE-COMPLETION STEPS BY PURCHASER

TIMOTHY SEARCHES IN VAIN

Timothy is preparing for completion on the Obebe sale and purchase; **13.1** and on the French/Saunders purchase. He has by now at least got some notion of the distinction between registered and unregistered procedures - or he thinks he has. He collects an armful of forms and fills in one or two that seem to apply to be sent off. On the French/Saunders purchase he completes a Form K 15 (Document 13.2).

Document 13.2 French/Saunders Purchase: Application for Official Search in Land Charges Register

Form K15		Land Charges Act 1972	Payment of fee
	APPLICATION FOR AN OFFICIAL SEARCH NOT APPLICABLE TO REGISTERED LAND Application is hereby made for an official search in the index to the registers kept pursuant to the Land Charges Act 1972 for any subsisting entries in respect of the under-mentioned particulars.		Insert a cross (X) in this box if the fee is to be paid through a credit account (see Note 3 overleaf) [X]

IMPORTANT: Please read the notes overleaf before completing this form

For Official Use only		NAMES TO BE SEARCHED (Please use block letters and see Note 4 overleaf)	PERIOD OF YEARS (see Note 5 overleaf)	
STX			From	To
	Forename(s)	MARIE	1992	1993
	SURNAME	ROCARD		
	Forename(s)	MICHEL	1992	1993
	SURNAME	ROCARD		
	Forename(s)	SAM	1993	
	SURNAME	FRENCH		
	Forename(s)	FANCY	1993	
	SURNAME	SAUNDERS		
	Forename(s)			
	SURNAME			
	Forename(s)			
	SURNAME			

COUNTY (see Note 6 overleaf)	WEST YORKSHIRE
FORMER COUNTY	
DESCRIPTION OF LAND (see Note 7 overleaf)	
FORMER DESCRIPTION	

Particulars of Applicant (see Notes 8, 9 and 10 overleaf)		Name and Address (including postcode) for despatch of certificate (Leave blank if certificate is to be returned to applicant's address)
KEY NUMBER	Name and address (including postcode)	
	JARNDYCE & JARNDYCE SOLICITORS 24 THE STRAND LEDCHESTER	

Applicant's reference:				Date	FOR OFFICIAL USE ONLY
I	I	/	M H	10 MARCH 1993	

Note: The space for entry of 'Key number' on Land Charges Registry and Land Registry forms is for entry of the number under which an applicant solicitor is registered at the Registry. Its use means that the solicitor's name and address does not need to be entered. Jarndyce & Jarndyce no doubt have a key number. Timothy has no doubt not bothered to look on the reverse of the form to discover what it means.

Question What is wrong with Timothy's search? Explain the possible consequences of his errors and omissions. On the assumption that the vendor's solicitor has not produced any searches, list the persons against whom and the years for which a K 15 search should have been made (See chapter 10 for the title).

Question Explain why a search against the purchasers is necessary.

On the Obebe purchase Timothy completes an application for a official Land Registry search against the title and a Bankruptcy Only search (Documents 13.3 and 13.4).

Document 13.3 Obebe purchase: Application for Official Search in Land Registry (Form 94A)

Application by **Purchaser**[a] **for Official Search with priority in respect of the whole of the land in either a registered title or in a pending first registration**	HM Land Registry Form

Small raised letters in **bold** type refer to explanatory notes overleaf.

PRIORITY STAMP

94A

(Land Registration (Official Searches) Rules 1990)

Ledchester _____ District Land Registry[b]

For official use

Please complete the numbered panels.

1 County and District or London Borough:-
Ledchester, West Yorkshire

2 Title number (one only per form) of the registered property or that allotted to the pending first registration:-
WYK 787260

3 Full names of the registered proprietor(s) of the land[c] or of the person applying for registration of the property specified below:-
Norman Mixford/Nora Mixford

4 Full name(s) of applicant(s) (ie. purchaser, lessee or chargee):-
Ledchester & Bongley Building Society

5 I certify that the applicant(s) intend(s) to:-
[P] purchase [L] take a lease of [X C] land money on the security of a registered charge on
[X] the whole of the land in the above registered title or
[ ] the whole of the land in the pending first registration application referred to above

6 Address including postcode or short description of property:-
16, Winchester Avenue, Ledchester

10 Key number[e]   Complete this panel using BLOCK LETTERS and insert the name and address (including postcode) of the person to whom the official certificate of result of search is to be sent.
Jarndyce & Jarndyce Solicitors
24 The Strand
Ledchester
Reference[f] TT/MH

7 If search is against the whole of the land in a registered title enter below the date on which an office copy of the subsisting entries in the register was issued or the last date on which the land or charge certificate was officially examined with the register:-
17 February 1993

8 Enter X in box as appropriate:-
[X] Application is made to ascertain whether any adverse entry[d] has been made in the register or day list since the date shown in 7 above.
OR
[ ] Application is made to ascertain whether any adverse entry has been made in the day list since the date of the pending first registration application.

9 Signed *Jarndyce & Jarndyce*
Date 10 March 1993
Telephone No. Ledchester 002244

Official Certificate of Result of Search
It is hereby certified that the official search applied for has been made with the following result:
[ ] **A** Result of search against the whole of the land in a registered title:-
Since _____ 19____

[ ] No adverse entries have been made.

[ ] Entries have been made. Details of these and of pending applications (if any) are annexed to and form part of this result.

[ ] No adverse entries have been made but there are pending applications details of which are annexed to and form part of this result.

[ ] **B** Result of search against the whole of the land in a pending first registration application:- The property specified is the subject of a pending first registration application. Details are annexed to and form part of this result.

Note:
To obtain priority, the application for registration in respect of which this search is made must be delivered to the proper office at the latest by 9.30 am on the date when priority expires: see priority stamp at the head of this form.

Document 13.4 Obebe Purchase: Application for Bankruptcy Only Search in Land Charges Register

---

Form K16

Land Charges Act 1972 | **Payment of Fee**

Insert a cross (X) in this box if the fee is to be debited to your credit account.

[X]

APPLICATION FOR AN OFFICIAL SEARCH
(BANKRUPTCY ONLY)

(See Note 2 overleaf)

Application is hereby made for an official search in the index to the registers kept pursuant to the Land Charges Act 1972 in respect of the under-mentioned names for any subsisting entries of:
(i) petitions in bankruptcy in the register of pending actions
(ii) receiving orders in bankruptcy and bankruptcy orders in the register of writs and orders
(iii) deeds of arrangement in the register of deeds of arrangement

For Official Use only

#

IMPORTANT: Please read the notes overleaf before completing the form.

NAMES TO BE SEARCHED
(Please use block letters and see Note 3 overleaf)

Forename(s)	*NANCY*
SURNAME	*MIXFORD*
Forename(s)	
SURNAME	
Forename(s)	
SURNAME	
Forename(s)	
SURNAME	
Forename(s)	
SURNAME	
Forename(s)	
SURNAME	

Particulars of Applicant
(see Notes 4, 5 and 6 overleaf)

KEY NUMBER | Name and address (including postcode)

Name and address (including postcode) for despatch of certificate
(Leave blank if certificate is to be returned to applicant's address)

JARNDYCE & JARNDYCE SOLICITORS 24 THE STRAND LEDCHESTER

Applicant's reference: | Date

10 MARCH 1993

FOR OFFICIAL USE ONLY

T T / M H

Question Timothy has made a bankruptcy search against Miss Mixford. Is this correct?

Question On the Land Registry search Timothy appears to have put the date of Moriarties' letter (Document 4.1.1) instead of the date of the office copy in entry 7. Explain the implications of this error.

OLD JARNDYCE COMMENTS

13.5   After exchange of contracts, completion is the next most important step in a conveyancing transaction. It is the point at which the parties complete performance of their obligations under the contract. On a conveyance of unregistered land it is the point at which legal title is transferred to the purchaser. On a transfer of registered land, it is the essential step prior to the purchaser acquiring the legal title by registration. In both cases, it is the point at which the purchaser obtains vacant possession (or, if the property is being sold subject to a lease, possession of the rents). In return the purchaser hands over the balance of the purchase price. At the same time, where the property is being bought with the aid of a mortgage loan, the mortgage will be completed in return for the mortgage loan.

Clearly, before parting with her money (or the mortgagee's money which she will be repaying for many years to come) the purchaser will want to be satisfied that she is getting everything to which she is entitled under the contract. Further, the general principle is, subject to some exceptions, that the contract merges with the conveyance; that is the contract ceases to exist and can no longer be sued on once the conveyance has taken effect (para.5.7).

The vendor, for her part, will be happy if she gets her money; but to get it, and to get it at the agreed completion date, she will have to have performed all her own obligations under the contract.

The steps taken between contract and completion are therefore designed to ensure that each side is in a position to complete in accordance with the terms of the contract.

Check list of steps to be taken

13.5.1   It may be useful here to list the main matters that may have to be attended to by the purchaser's solicitor between contract and completion:

(a) Peruse the title deduced by the vendor's solicitor and raise any necessary requisitions.

(b) When requisitions have been dealt with satisfactorily, accept title subject to pre-completion searches, examination of the title documents and any other outstanding matters.

(c) Draft the conveyance/transfer, send to vendor's solicitor for approval and negotiate any amendments.

(d) Engross conveyance/transfer; get it signed by purchaser if necessary.

(e) Send signed engrossment to vendor's solicitor for execution by vendor in readiness for completion.

(f) Pre-completion searches.

(g) Pre-completion inspection of property, at least by purchaser.

(h) Examination of title documents (in practice done at the time of completion).

(i) Arrange details of completion with vendor's solicitor.

(j) Obtain funds for completion.

(k) Other matters.

The above should be read in conjunction with the more detailed treatment of the various steps in, particularly, Chapters 10, 11, 13 and 14. What follows is concerned with the pre-completion searches and inspection of the property by the purchaser's solicitor. These are part of the process of investigating title and the final checks necessary to ensure that there are no undisclosed incumbrances on the property which will adversely affect the purchaser after completion.

Part A below deals with unregistered title; Part B with registered.

Acting on a purchase-linked mortgage

The purchaser's solicitor will commonly be acting for both the purchaser/borrower and the lending institution. It should therefore be remembered that the solicitor will be performing the steps listed above on behalf of and with a legal and professional duty to both.   **13.5.2**

Where this is the situation the following additional steps will be involved:

(l) Prepare the mortgage deed; and have it signed by the borrower ready for completion of the purchase and mortgage.

(m) Report on title to the lender and (if the title is satisfactory) obtain the mortgage advance.

(n) If an endowment mortgage, ensure that endowment policy is in effect (i.e. the insurance company at risk); prepare assignment of policy to the lender (if required) and have it signed by borrower; prepare notice of assignment in duplicate to be sent to insurance company (para.2.5.1(b)).

Where the mortgagee is separately represented, the purchaser/ borrower's solicitor will in effect be in the same position as a vendor's solicitor, in relation to proving title, etc; and the lender's solicitor will be in the same position as a purchaser's solicitor, providing the advance instead of the purchase price in return for a satisfactory title and a valid mortgage instead of a conveyance/transfer.

A UNREGISTERED TITLE

In the case of unregistered title the following pre-completion steps may be necessary:

(a) Search in the central Land Charges Register.

(b) Search in the Companies Register.

(c) Further search in the Register of Local Land Charges.

(d) Inspection of the property.

CENTRAL LAND CHARGES REGISTER SEARCH

13.6 A search will always need to be made in the central Register of Land Charges kept at Plymouth under the Land Charges Act 1972. The purpose is to check that at the moment when the legal estate is conveyed to the purchaser there will be no undisclosed, registered charges that will bind the purchaser after completion.

(a) Whom to search against

Land charges are (or should be) registered against the name of the estate owner - that is the owner of the legal estate whose estate is intended to be affected - at the time of registration.[1] They are not, in contrast to the register of title at the Land Registry, registered against the land.

It follows that a clear search is needed against every person (including companies) who is or has been an estate owner during the title period starting with the root of title document. This includes not just beneficial freehold owners but, for example, personal representatives, assentees, mortgagees (up to the time when the mortgage is discharged).

---

[1] See Land Charges Act 1972, s.3(1); but note the decision in *Sharp v. Coats* [1949] 1 K.B. 285; J.E. Adams, 'A Fly In the Ointment: Estate Contracts and the Land Charges Computer' (1971) 35 Conv 155. Compare *Barrett v. Hilton Developments Ltd.* [1975] 1 Ch. 237.

It is not necessary to search against persons who were but ceased to be estate owners before the 15 year root of title period. Indeed, it is not normally possible since the purchaser is not entitled to investigate the earlier title (para.10.5.1). If any land charge is registered (and still valid) against such a pre-root owner, it will bind the purchaser. However, by s.25 of the Law of Property Act 1969, the purchaser will normally be entitled to compensation from public funds for any loss suffered as a result. There will be no right to compensation if the purchaser has actual knowledge of the incumbrance (and this includes the knowledge of her lawyer acquired in the course of the same transaction). If the purchaser has agreed in the contract to accept less than the statutory 15 years' title, there will be no compensation for charges which investigation for the full period would have discovered.

Normally, searches will have been done on the occasion of some of the previous transactions on the title. It is customary, though not obligatory, for the vendor to include in the abstract or epitome and copies any such searches that are available. In relation to any such search, the purchaser's solicitor should check (and requisition for further information if necessary), that it was an official search and that:

(i) it was against the correct name;

(ii) for the correct period of ownership;

(iii) that a search against a then owner was followed by a conveyance to a purchaser within the protection period given by the search (see below as to these matters).

In addition the present purchaser's solicitor will, as with all the documents of title, need to see the original or a sufficiently detailed, marked abstract.

In so far as there is not such a satisfactory search against any previous estate owner, the purchaser's solicitor will have to do one. Any such searches against previous estate owners could be done at any time between contract and completion. In practice they will be done together with the pre-completion search against the vendor.

A pre-completion search will always be needed against the vendor (and any other current estate owner - for example, on a sub-purchase, a search should be made against the superior vendor who will in fact be the estate owner)[2] since the vendor will remain the estate owner until completion and so liable until then to have effective charges registered against her.

---

[2] See *Barrett v. Hilton Developments Ltd.* [1975] 1 Ch. 237.

Where the solicitor is also acting for the mortgagee who is providing a loan to finance the purchase, a full search (not just a bankruptcy search – see below, para.13.14) should be done against the purchaser/borrower. It is true that the purchaser does not become estate owner until completion and that until then a land charge cannot be registered against her; and that effectively at the same moment the mortgage to the lender will take effect making it impossible to register charges binding on the lender. But it is possible for a charge to be protected by registration of a priority notice before the completion. In practice this is likely to happen where the purchaser of part assumes the burden of restrictive covenants for the benefit of the vendor's retained land. Under the priority notice procedure contained in s.11 of the Land Charges Act 1972, a person intending to register a land charge can give priority notice of the intention on Form K 6 to the registry. This must be done at least 15 working days before completion of the purchase. This means that it will be revealed in the mortgagee's pre-completion official search (which must be done within 15 working days of completion). Application to register the charge covered by the priority notice must be made within 30 working days of the priority notice (and of course after completion of the purchase). Under s.11(3) registration is then deemed to have taken effect at the moment of creation of the charge (i.e at the moment of purchase) and so binds the mortgagee.

A mortgagee (having seen the contract of purchase) would know of such restrictive covenants and would expect to be bound by them. But the same principle could apply if the purchaser created other charges (for example, a contract of sub-sale) without informing the mortgagee. A full search should therefore be made on behalf of the mortgagee against the purchaser. And, as a purchaser for money or money's worth the mortgagee will not be bound by any charge not registered.[3]

It should be noted that, where as will now be the case on any sale of the freehold, conveyance is followed by first registration any new permanent land charges of this sort (such as new restrictive covenants) will have to be protected on the new title at the Land Registry, not on the central Land Charges Register (para.15.4.2(c)).

(b) Procedure on searching

The search should be made on Form K 15. Care is needed in a number or respects.

(i) The name to search against. In law, one's name is a matter of usage. A person does not have a legally correct name; and so may be known by and have two or more equally correct names. Getting the name of

---

3   But see *Abbey National Building Society v. Cann* [1991] AC 57, below para.10.

the owner right is important both when registering a charge and when doing a search.

A search should be done against the form (or each of the forms if more than one) of the name shown on the title. The Registry computer is programmed to search against a few, but not many, variations of any given name. In *Standard Property Investment plc v. British Plastics Federation*[4] the house was conveyed into the names of the purchasers shown as Roger Caudrelier and Hilary Caudrelier in the conveyance. A first mortgage by them to the Abbey National Building Society was not in dispute. A second mortgage to the plaintiff was registered under the Land Charges Act 1972 against the same names. The couple entered into a third mortgage to the defendant who before completion did an official search against Roger Denis Caudrelier and Hilary Claire Caudrelier, a search which failed to reveal the second mortgage.

It was held that the registration of the second mortgage was against the correct names and so effective. The search by the third mortgagee was not against the correct names (i.e. those shown on the conveyance to the Caudreliers); so the second mortgage had priority over the third when the property had to be sold to enforce repayment of the loans. If a correct search had been made it would, in the absence of error by the Registry, have revealed the second mortgage and so warned the defendant.

Section 10(4) of the Land Charges Act 1972 provides that in favour of a purchaser or an intending purchaser, an official certificate of search, 'according to its tenor, shall be conclusive, affirmatively or negatively, as the case may be'. Thus, if an entry is not revealed by an official search against the correct name, the purchaser (and presumably her successors in title) take free of the registered charge. A search against an incorrect version of the name will not give this protection even where the undisclosed charge was itself registered against an incorrect version.[5] The owner of a charge who is deprived of her charge by an incorrect certificate has no claim to compensation from any public fund. She may have a claim in negligence against the Registry's officers.

Officers of the Registry will not be liable if there is a discrepancy between the details on the search application and the search certificate. The solicitor receiving the search should check that the two do correspond - e.g. that the names on the certificate are the same as those against whom the search was requested.

(ii) Period covered by the search. The search should cover all the years for which the title shows the person searched against to have

---

4   (1985) 53 P.& C.R. 25; and see *Oak Co-Operative Building Society v. Blackburn* [1968] Ch. 730.

5   *Oak Co-Operative Building Society v. Blackburn* [1968] Ch. 730.

been an estate owner of the land.[6] The certificate will only show entries made during the period specified.

(iii) For the same reason care must be taken to state correctly the name (and any former name) of the county in which the land is situate.

If, unusually, the address of the property is included in the application, entries affecting other land will be excluded from the certificate.

(c) The official certificate of search

An application for an official search can, in addition to post, be made by fax or telephone. In the case of telephone the results of the search can normally be read out over the telephone. But in all cases it is the official certificate sent by the Registry to the applicant which gives the protection of an official search.

The conclusiveness of an official search (as opposed to personal search) has been mentioned.

An official search certificate gives a protection period of 15 working days (the expiry of which is shown on the certificate, although not in law to be relied upon) during which completion can take place in reliance on the official certificate; that is, under s.11(5) of the 1972 Act, a purchaser will not be affected by any entry put on the register subsequent to the certificate of search (unless pursuant to a priority notice then on the register).

If for any reason completion does not take place during the protection period, a new search will have to be done against the present estate owners.

If the certificate shows no subsisting entries against a name, then there is no need for further investigation. If there are entries against the name for the period and county searched, the certificate will give the class of entry - e.g. class F - the date of registration and the registration number and, frequently, the postal address of the land affected. In this case further investigation will be necessary. If the entry clearly does refer to the land being purchased, an office copy of the entry should be applied for on Form K 19 unless available from the vendor. If there is a mere possibility that it affects the land, the vendor's solicitor may be in a position to certify that it does not; failing this, an office copy of the entry will probably have to be obtained. If and when it has been ascertained that an entry does affect the land, there are two possibilities: First, that it relates to a matter

---

[6]   There are conceivable situations in which an effective entry may have been made against the estate owner before or after this period and so there is an argument that the search should be for a period going back to 1925 against each name; in practice this is not done.

disclosed in the contract subject to which the land is expressly being sold – for example, disclosed restrictive covenants. Such entries will of course be expected. Secondly, the entry may relate to an undisclosed matter. This may be one which is removable by the vendor and which she is expecting to remove before completion – for example, a puisne mortgage.

In any event, the vendor must remove any undisclosed charge before completion (or provide a proper solicitor's undertaking to do so) or provide a proper application for cancellation, failing which she will be in breach of contract.

An entry can be cancelled by application on Form K 11[7] and must be signed by the person who made the registration in the first place or her authorised solicitor,[8]: or sufficient evidence of title to the charge of the person signing the application must be produced.

A class F land charge is removed by application on Form K 13. Section 4 of the Matrimonial Homes Act 1983 provides that a contract for the sale of a dwelling-house with vacant possession is subject to an implied term that the vendor will procure the cancellation of any class F land charge. But quite apart from this provision, and whether or not the sale is with vacant possession, the vendor is under a duty to remove any undisclosed land charges[9] (whether entered before or after exchange of contract). Provided the purchaser gets an application signed by the spouse (or authorised solicitor) to cancel the entry then she (the purchaser) will be protected by her official certificate of search against any danger of the spouse re-registering her statutory right at the last moment in place of the one cancelled.[10]

BANKRUPTCY 13.7

Bankruptcy of vendor

One of the matters which may be revealed by a search is bankruptcy proceedings against the vendor (or an earlier estate owner). This may affect the validity of a conveyance by the bankrupt and should be investigated.

13.7.1

---

[7]   Land Charges Rules 1974, rr. 9-13.

[8]   See *Holmes v. Kennard* (1984) 49 P.& C.R. 202, a land registry case where the purchaser's solicitor was held negligent for accepting the wrong form of cancellation of an entry on the register signed by the vendor's wife's solicitor without her authority.

[9]   See Emmett, para.11.028.

[10]   Even if registered, the spouse's statutory right will not necessarily be allowed by the court to prevail over a purchaser; see *Kaur v. Gill* [1988] 3 W.L.R. 39.

Bankruptcy is now governed mainly by the Insolvency Act 1986. It arises from the inability of a person to pay her debts. Legally it begins with a bankruptcy petition presented by a creditor or the debtor herself. If successful this leads to a bankruptcy order when the Official Receiver takes control of the bankrupt's property. A trustee in bankruptcy is appointed and at that point the bankrupt's property vests automatically in the trustee. Petitions and orders are registrable under the Land Charges Act 1972 in the register of pending actions and of writs and orders affecting land respectively.

The crucial question here is whether a purchaser can safely deal with a person who might have gone bankrupt. *Prima facie*, s.284 of the Act makes any disposition after presentation of a petition (if leading to an order) void except under order of the court. However, the effect of s.284(4) of the 1986 Act and ss.5 and 6 of the Land Charges Act 1972 is that a purchaser in good faith for money or money's worth will get good title provided there is no current bankruptcy petition or order on the register against the vendor's name. (A registration is only effective for five years when it will have to be renewed).

In practice there is little likelihood of a petition or order not being registered, since the court and the official receiver respectively are under a duty to give notice of them to the Chief Land Registrar.

Bankruptcy of a vendor does not put an end to the contract; it means that the purchaser will have to deal with the trustee in bankruptcy. The trustee does have a right to disclaim unprofitable contracts under s.315 of the 1986 Act which is not likely to be exercised; and a person interested (the purchaser here) can give the trustee 28 days notice within which to elect whether or not to disclaim. Subject to this, both trustee and purchaser will be bound by the contract as made. If the trustee fails to complete on time and time is of the essence, or made of the essence by notice to complete, the purchaser can treat the contract as repudiated.[11] But any claim by the purchaser to damages or to recover a deposit held by the vendor or her agent (as opposed to stakeholder) will have to be proved in the bankruptcy and have no preference over other creditors.

If completion is to take place, the purchaser will need proof of passing of title to the trustee in the form of proof of the adjudication order and certificate of appointment of the trustee in bankruptcy. In addition it is important in this case that the bankruptcy order has been registered to protect the title of the trustee under s.6(5) and (6) of the Land Charges Act 1972.

Bankruptcy severs a joint tenancy in equity; and the bankrupt's equitable interest will vest in the trustee in bankruptcy. But it cannot

---

11 *Jenning's Trustee v. King* [1952] 1 Ch. 899.

sever a joint tenancy of the legal title which will remain in the joint tenants as trustees; and on sale the equitable interests will be overreached. Thus, in the common case where the legal estate is vested in a person now bankrupt and another jointly for the benefit of themselves jointly or in common there is no good reason to insist on the trustee in bankruptcy joining in the conveyance.[12]

Bankruptcy of the purchaser

Section 284(4) of the 1986 Act applies to money as it does to land, so **13.7.2** that if the vendor completes in good faith and without notice of the presentation of any petition she will get good title to the money.

As on the bankruptcy of the vendor, the bankruptcy of the purchaser does not affect the validity of the contract, subject to the right of the trustee to disclaim. If the purchaser is found to be bankrupt the vendor will have to deal with her trustee who will have to prove her title to complete the contract. If the trustee disclaims the vendor can forfeit the deposit and prove in the bankruptcy for any further damages.

Avoidance of voluntary dispositions

A purchaser may have to consider another hazard in relation to **13.7.3** bankruptcy. Under s.339 of the 1986 Act a transaction entered into *before* bankruptcy may be voidable. If a transaction is at an 'undervalue' and the transferor becomes bankrupt within two years, the trustee can apply to court and have the transaction avoided. If the bankruptcy occurs between the second and fifth years after the transaction, the trustee can have it set aside unless the transferor can be shown to have been solvent at the time of the transaction; and there is a presumption of insolvency. A transaction is at an undervalue if by way of gift, where the consideration is marriage and where the consideration received is 'significantly' less in value than that given. 'Insolvency' under s.341(3) of the 1986 Act means the inability to pay debts as they fall due or having assets of less value than liabilities.

Thus, where there is a gift (or other transaction at an undervalue) on the title, the danger of avoidance has to be considered. The likely situation is that Donor has transferred the land to Donee by deed of gift; Donee is now selling to Purchaser. Under s.342 of the 1986 Act a purchaser is protected if in good faith and without notice of the circumstances giving rise to the right to avoid the gift.

---

[12]   See *Re McCarthy* [1975] 1 W.L.R. 807; and Emmett, para.10.037.

If more than five years have elapsed since Donee acquired the property, there is no problem. A land charges search should be done against the Donor (even if one was done at the time of the gift). The search in the register of pending actions and writs and orders is not limited by period. If the search is clear in this respect for the five years subsequent to the gift, the title is safe. If there were a bankruptcy entry, the title would be defective and the trustee in bankruptcy would have to be joined in the conveyance to transfer good title.

If two years has not elapsed since the gift, the danger is that subsequent to the purchase, Donor will become bankrupt within the two year period. The transaction will be voidable; Purchaser will not be protected because having notice from the title of the making of the gift, she will have notice of the possible voidability of the transaction. In the absence of suitable title insurance, the title should not be accepted in such circumstances.

If more than two but less than five years have passed since the gift, Purchaser will be protected (if Donor goes bankrupt before the five year period expires) if on acquiring the property she did not have notice that the transaction was a gift and that Donor was (if she was) insolvent. In this situation the Purchaser is probably safe to complete is there is available a statutory declaration of solvency made by Donor at the time of the gift.[13]

13.7.4   There are three related matters that can be considered here. Under s.340 of the 1986 Act a trustee in bankruptcy can (within specified time limits) apply to court to have a transaction set aside if intended to give preference to one creditor over others. A purchaser will be protected under s.342(2) if without notice of the circumstances giving rise to the right to avoid - i.e. that the transaction was a preference. Evidence of a preference is not likely to appear on the title; and the purchaser, unless happening to have knowledge, will be protected.

Section 423 of the 1986 Act allows a person prejudiced to avoid a transaction at an undervalue intended to put assets beyond the reach of creditors. Under s.425 protection is given to a purchaser (not from the debtor) without notice of the relevant circumstances - i.e. the just mentioned intention. Again, therefore unless a purchaser happens to know of such intention she can safely ignore this rule.

Finally, under s.37 of the Matrimonial Causes Act 1973 a transaction can be set aside if made by a spouse with the intention of defeating the other spouse's claim to financial relief under the Act. A purchaser is protected if in good faith and without notice of the intention. In *Kemmis v. Kemmis*,[14] a registered land case with the same rules applicable, a company

---

13   See Emmett, para.10.050.
14   [1988] 1 W.L.R. 1307.

controlled by the husband mortgaged the house to a bank. It was held that the husband did have the intention; and that the bank knew almost as much about the family's financial and personal affairs as the husband did and should have been put on enquiry. However, so it was held, as such enquiries would not have revealed the intention of the husband, the bank did not have notice.[15]

In relation to the three provisions just referred to, it should be added that it is not the purchaser's notice of bankruptcy which is in issue; therefore bankruptcy searches are not relevant here.

SEARCH IN THE COMPANIES REGISTER

Where the vendor is a company or a company appears on the title as a   **13.8**
previous owner of the property, a search in the Companies Register may be necessary.[16] The search is necessary to reveal any fixed or floating charge on the land created by the company before 1 January 1970; and any floating charge created since then.[17]

If a floating charge is revealed evidence is needed of non-crystallisation at the time of sale by the company. Properly, this should be in the form of a certificate by the chargee; though in practice a certificate signed by an officer of the company itself is commonly accepted.

There is no procedure for official searches in the Companies Register and no period of protection given by any search. In the case of previous company owners of the land, the necessary company search and other evidence mentioned above should hopefully be available with the deeds and abstracted by the vendor. If any such search is not available it will have to be carried out by the purchaser's solicitor before completion; together with one against the vendor if it is a company

The search in the Companies Register is normally carried out by agents (who advertise their services in the legal press). They must be given proper, detailed instructions as to the company to be searched against, and the information sought. The search can be made in the Register either in Cardiff or London; and, of course, the result can be faxed or telephoned if necessary.

---

[15] The bank failed to get possession because the wife's mother who had contributed to the purchase price was in actual occupation at the time of the mortgage and so had an overriding interest.

[16] To be incorporated a company must be registered under the Companies Act 1985.

[17] Fixed charges created before 1 January 1970 could effectively be registered under the Land Charges Act 1925 or in the Companies Register. To bind a mortgagee, registration is still also, additionally necessary in the Companies Register.

In addition to charges, the purchaser may need to check:

(i) That the company had capacity to enter into the transaction - i.e. that the transaction was *intra vires* the company. Since the enactment of s.35(1) of the Companies Act 1985 as substituted by s.108(1) of the Companies Act 1989, 'the validity of an act done by a company shall not be called into question on the ground of lack of capacity by reason of anything in the company's memorandum'. Even before this, although an extract from the company's memorandum and articles showing the power ought to have been abstracted, memoranda were (and are) invariably drawn in such wide terms that any sale or purchase of land transaction would almost certainly be within its powers.

(ii) In a transaction negotiated with the directors, that the directors were authorised to act on behalf of the company. Under s.35 of the 1985 Act substituted by s.108(1) of the 1989 Act, 'in favour of a person dealing with the company in good faith, the power of the board of directors to bind the company, or authorise others to do so, shall be deemed to be free of any limitation under the company's constitution'. Lack of good faith is defined so narrowly that a purchaser has no need to investigate or seek proof (either from the memorandum of association or resolution of the company) that the directors are authorised.

(iii) Insolvency. Under s.522 of the Companies Act 1985, any disposition of a company's property will be void if made after the commencement of a winding up by the court - that is when the petition for winding up is presented to the court or, if this is preceded by such, with the resolution of the company for a voluntary winding up (s.524). Petitions have to be advertised in the London Gazette. Winding up orders must be filed with the Registrar of Companies. If there is any reason to suspect insolvency a search as to these matters should be instructed.

FURTHER SEARCH IN THE REGISTER OF LOCAL LAND CHARGES

13.9 It is sometimes suggested that a fresh local search should be done if there has been a long delay between contract and completion.

A local land charge search will (or should) have been done prior to contract - since standard conditions of sale invariably negative the vendor's duty of disclosure in this respect (para.4.5.3).

Local land charges affecting the property may arise between contract and completion at any time. They cannot in general be removed by the vendor and will bind the purchaser on completion. In general, they will be covered by the principle that on exchange of contract the risk of supervening events passes to the purchaser. In general, therefore, there is no legal point in doing a new search (or indeed a first one!) between contract and completion however long that period is.

It is possible that any such intervening charge arises from the neglect or default of the vendor or makes the vendor unable to fulfil her obligation to give vacant possession – either of which would put the vendor in breach and so should be discovered before completion. If there is any possibility of such a charge, a pre-completion search would be merited.

Standard Conditions 3.1.4 and 3.1.5 do require the vendor to inform the purchaser of any 'new public requirement' affecting the property which she learns about post-contract, but puts the burden of the cost of complying with any public requirement on the purchaser.

INSPECTION OF THE PROPERTY

It is important to inspect the property before completion. It is rare for the purchaser's solicitor to inspect, but at least the purchaser should be aware of what to look for. Where the solicitor is acting for both the purchaser and the lender on a purchase-linked mortgage, it is important in this context to distinguish the two roles.

13.10

(a) The purchaser will be concerned, before completing and handing over the purchase money, to check that the property is as it should be under the contract, that boundary fences have not been moved, damage not done, that vacant possession will be given, without a cellar full of rancid junk or a sitting granny. All such matters are equally important, though the books tend to have a fixation on the grannies and other 'dangerous persons'.

A few points need to be made. Any person left in occupation at completion will be a derogation by the vendor of her obligation to give vacant possession, whether there by right enforceable only against the vendor, against the purchaser if she completes, or without right at all (the squatter). Subject to the terms of the contract it is the duty of the vendor to see to the removal of any such person.

If such a person does have a right enforceable against the purchaser it is clearly a more serious matter. Whether or not there is such a right depends on the nature of the right of occupation and familiar (hopefully) principles of land law. For example, if the person has a legal, weekly tenancy, that will be binding on the purchaser regardless of notice.

If the person (the granny case) has an equitable interest in the property (for example, by virtue of contribution to the vendor's purchase) her interest will be overreached if the sale is by two or more trustees – but the vendor will still be under an obligation to actually get her out before completion whether by negotiation or in the back of the removal van. If not overreached, the purchaser will be bound unless a bona fide purchaser for value without notice of the equitable interest. It is notice at the moment of transfer of the legal estate that matters. The question is whether the purchaser had notice at that moment, not whether the equitable beneficiary was in actual occupation. The concept of actual occupation relates to registered title; actual occupation is likely to give rise to notice; but there could well be notice of such an interest without occupation.[18] As already emphasised, the vendor should have dealt with any such possible adverse claims or *de facto* occupations before exchanging contracts – either by making the sale subject to them, as on sale of a property with a sitting tenant; or taken steps to ensure that the occupation would be terminated in time for completion.

(b) Inspection and the purchase-linked mortgagee The principles just mentioned in (a) apply equally to such a mortgagee who is lending part of the purchase price. The security of the mortgagee's title stems from the security of the purchaser's title.

In addition however there is the spectre of the contributing granny, not refusing to leave, but arriving in the *purchaser's* pantechnicon; that is the fear that the purchaser will create adverse interests of this sort binding on the lender. Institutional lenders do make a point in their mortgage application forms and instructions to solicitors of checking for the possibility of such occupants.

One is talking here of equitable interests arising under a trust of the legal estate held by the purchaser. In principle, the mortgagee, being classified in law as a purchaser, will be bound by any such interest unless it is overreached or the mortgagee can claim to be a bona fide purchaser of the legal estate without notice of the interest.

In fact, lenders have little to worry about, since the courts have judicially erected an almost impregnable barrier in their defence which makes the doctrine of notice unimportant in this context. In particular:

(i) if the mortgage is executed in joint names, any such interests will be overreached. (This is of course a statutory provision). And note that lenders, unlike purchasers, are concerned with the right to possession if and when they need to enforce their security. Who is actually in occupation at completion is of no great concern;

(ii) if the beneficiary under the trust knew that money would to be raised to finance the purchase, she will normally be taken to have

---

[18]   Consider *Kingsnorth Trust Ltd. v. Tizard* [1986] 2 All E.R. 54. How should this have been decided had it been a registered land case?

authorised the creation of the mortgage in priority to her own interest,[19] even if (unbeknown to her) more money than necessary was raised in this way;

(iii) In *Abbey National Building Society v. Cann*[20] the House of Lords rationalised this type of transaction in the following way:

'The reality is that the purchaser of the land who relies upon a building society or bank loan for the completion of his purchase never in fact acquires anything but an equity of redemption, for the land is, from the very inception, charged with the amount of the loan without which it could never have been transferred at all and it was never intended that it should be otherwise.'

This means that in the purchase-linked mortgage situation, the mortgagee will take priority over any interest created by the purchaser – at least an interest under a trust. It is not clear what effect this reasoning would have if applied to interests registrable under the Land Charges Act 1972. Logically it would seem to mean that the mortgagee would not be bound by any registrable interest created by the purchaser even though protected by a priority notice. This might be significant where, for example, the purchase is of part of the land in a title with restrictive covenants being imposed for the benefit of the part retained. Presumably, applying point (ii) above in reverse, the mortgagee could be taken to have authorised them having seen the documentation for the purchase.

Institutional lenders do frequently require a consent form of some sort signed by anyone who is going to occupy with the borrower. In so far as it is not otiose, such a consent form would be effective to postpone any interest of the person signing on the principle of estoppel or as amounting to an authorisation within the principle in (ii) above.

In this situation the possibility of conflict of interest has to be kept in mind; that is a conflict between the interest of the purchaser and that of the mortgagee, where the same solicitor is acting for both. There is also the possibility of conflict between the interest of the purchaser and any relative or other person being asked to postpone a possible interest in the property.

It is convenient to deal here also with the situation where the purchaser, now the owner, subsequently raises a loan secured by a mortgage of the property, i.e where the loan is not being used to finance the purchase. In such a case in relation to the borrower, the mortgagee is in the same position as a purchaser. In relation to adverse interests under a trust, principles (i) and (ii) above are still applicable; (iii) would not be.

---

[19] This principle applies even in favour of a subsequent mortgagee whose loan is used to pay off the original loan. *Equity & Law Home Loan v. Prestidge* [1991] 1 W.L.R. 137; noted, [1992] Conv. 206, M.P. Thompson; and see J. Greed, 'Mortgagees and Contributors,' (1992) 142 N.L.J. 539.
[20] [1991] 1 A.C. 56.

THE PURCHASE-LINKED MORTGAGE

13.11   Where the same solicitor is acting for the purchaser and lender, all the above steps will have to be carried out on behalf of and with a duty to both of them. On behalf of the lender, the special factors in relation to adverse occupants have been mentioned. The need for a full search of the Central Land Charges Register has been mentioned; also the need to search in the name of the purchaser, securing her title which thus gives consequential security to the mortgagee's title. Where the mortgagee-lender is represented by a separate solicitor it will be the latter's duty either to take the above steps or to be satisfied that they have been taken satisfactorily by the purchaser's solicitor; and the evidence, such as search certificates, produced.

B REGISTERED TITLE

SEARCH IN THE DISTRICT LAND REGISTRY

13.12   The purchaser's starting point in investigating the vendor's title is either an office copy of the entries on the register and of the title plan; or access to the Land Certificate (para.11.2.1). Both have the same evidential value as the entries on the register itself.

Under s.110(1) of the Land Registration Act 1925, the vendor is obliged, if required, and notwithstanding any stipulation to the contrary in the contract, to provide copies (not office copies) of entries on the register and any filed plan. Standard Condition 4.2. requires the vendor to supply office copies.

If only supplied with copies (e.g. photocopies taken from the Land Certificate), the purchaser's solicitor must obtain her own office copies from the Registry (printed Form 109)or rely on production of the Land Certificate (probably at completion) to confirm the accuracy of her (non-office) copies. Both the Land Certificate and the office copy can be relied on as showing the state of the register at the date indicated by the Registry on them (when the Certificate was last brought up to date with the register; or the office copy made).

The purpose of the pre-completion search is to check that nothing adverse has been registered since that date which would affect the purchaser - i.e. to check that the title which the purchaser will obtain and be registered with will be free of any adverse interests not disclosed in the contract.

Procedure

An application for an official search is made on printed Form 94 A   **13.12.1**
(purchase of the whole title) or 94 B (purchase of part of the land in the
vendor's title) to the District Registry for the area in which the land is
situate. Under the Land Registration Act 1988 (and see Land Registration
(Open Register) Rules 1991, S.I. 1992 No.122), the Register is now
public; and the vendor's authority to search is not required. The
application must specify the date of commencement of the search - i.e.
the date of the office copy or the date when the Land Certificate was
brought up to date.

If it is a search of part, a plan in duplicate will have to accompany the
Form 94 B application to identify the relevant part, unless it can be clearly
identified by reference to the title plan, or it is a plot on a new building
estate which can be identified by reference to a plot number on an
approved layout plan (para.7.11.2(a)). In the last case, the date of approval
will have to be obtained from the vendor (in the requisitions on title or
otherwise) and supplied to the Registry.

Where the vendor's own application for first registration is still
pending at the Registry, an official search can be made, giving the same
protection as when the title is already registered, using printed Form 94A
or, in the case of part of the land being registered, 94B(FR).

The conventional method to search is by post and receive the
certificate back by post. Now, under Rules 3 and 14 of the 1990 Land
Registration (Official Searches) Rules, the Chief Land Registrar can
provide for the transmission of applications and results of official searches
by other means - including telephone and fax. As from 24 May 1993 a
telephone application for an official search can be made from anywhere in
the country against the whole of the land in a title or the whole of the
land subject to an pending application for first registration. The result can
be given informally on the telephone with the official result with priority
being posted normally the following day.

The official certificate of search

The official search certificate will show what if any entries have been   **13.12.2**
made on the register between the date mentioned above and the date of
the search. It will also show any pending applications affecting the title;
and any other unexpired official searches. The protection given by an
official search is twofold. First, unlike a search in the Central Land
Charges Registry, the certificate of search is not conclusive. The rights
protected on the register will not be affected by an error in the search;
but under the Land Registration Act 1925, s.83(3) a purchaser who

suffers loss will be entitled to indemnity from public funds. Secondly, if the purchaser completes and delivers her application to register to the proper Registry within the priority period, she will not be bound by any supervening entries or applications affecting the title. If the application is not made in time a new search can be done, but it will give a new period, not an extension of the old.

The priority period is 30 working days (i.e. when the Registry is working) from the date of the search. The application must be in order and received by the proper Registry before 9.30 am on the 30th working day after the search application is deemed to have been delivered at the Registry. An application received at the Registry after 9.30 am on any day is deemed to have been delivered immediately before 9.30 am on the following day. The certificate is stamped to show the 30th working day, though legally this cannot be relied on.

Under Rule 8 of the 1990 Rules, the priority between search applications deemed to have been delivered at the same time is as the parties agree or, failing agreement, as determined by the Chief Land Registrar under Rule 298 of the Land Registration Rules 1925 as amended. This fixing of priority of search applications is crucial since, through the mechanism of the priority period it can determine the order of priority of entries on the Register.

Since completion, stamping if necessary and submission for registration have to take place within the priority period, the search should be made as close to completion as possible.

Under Rule 6 of the 1990 Rules a search can only be made to give protection to an applicant who is a purchaser - that is a person (including a lessee or chargee) who in good faith and for valuable consideration acquires or intends to acquire a legal estate in the land.

It is not clear what good faith means in this context.[21] The danger is that it will be used to import the doctrine of notice back into registered conveyancing and undermine the principle (which is by no means inviolate anyway) that a purchaser should be able to rely on the conclusiveness of the register. What can perhaps be said is that a purchaser does not have to go 'looking for trouble'. If she does not know of any adverse, off-the-register, claim she does not have to query whether there might not be one. Even knowledge of an off-the-register claim would not by itself be a reason not to complete. But if there was knowledge of an undoubtedly valid (apart from non-registration) claim, it might be risky, on the present state of the authorities, to complete without getting the matter resolved.

---

[21]   See *Smith v. Morrison* [1974] 1 All E.R. 957 where Plowman J. defined it in terms of honesty, lack of ulterior motive - which does not take the matter much further.

Search by purchase-linked mortgagee

Where there is a purchase-linked mortgage, the mortgagee being a **13.12.3** purchaser will need the protection of an official search. Rule 6 of the 1990 Rules provides in effect that where a purchase (i.e. here, the mortgage) is dependent on a prior dealing (here, the purchase itself) a search by the subsequent purchaser will give the benefit of the protection period to both the transactions. In short, if (as where the same solicitor is acting for both) only one search is done it should be done on behalf of the mortgagee; and its protection will extend to the purchaser.

Bankruptcy

Subject to what is now said the same principles apply as in the case of **13.12.4** unregistered title. On appointment title to registered land vests automatically in the trustee without registration. This is an exception to the fundamental principle of registered title that the legal owner is the person shown as proprietor on the register.

Bankruptcy petitions and adjudication orders are automatically registered in the central Land Charges Register whether or not the bankrupt is known to own unregistered or registered land. This registration does not affect the title to any registered land and there is no need whatsoever for a purchaser of registered land to search in the central Land Charges Register.

Where the bankrupt does own registered land the Registrar is required to protect the petition by means of a creditor's notice in the proprietorship register and subsequently to protect the adjudication order by means of a bankruptcy inhibition, again in the proprietorship register of any land which appears to be affected.

Under s.61(1) of the Land Registration Act 1925, the effect of entry of a creditor's notice (which remains effective until cancelled) is that any dealing with the land by the proprietor will be subject to the rights of the creditors protected by the notice.

Under s.61(4) the effect of entry of a bankruptcy inhibition is that the only dealing that will be registered is the registration of the trustee in bankruptcy as proprietor (who will then be able to deal with the land).

Provided no creditor's notice or bankruptcy inhibition is entered on the register, a purchaser in good faith for money or money's worth from the proprietor will acquire a good title (s.61(6) as amended). The section goes on to provide that a purchaser who has 'notice' of a (unprotected) bankruptcy petition or order at the time of the transfer will not be in good faith; but that this does not impose on her any obligation to search in the Central Land Charges Register. What this means is that the purchaser is not fixed with notice of any bankruptcy entry on the Land Charges register; but if she does in fact know of the bankruptcy or actually knows of something which ought to have put her to further enquiry or has wilfully abstained from enquiry to avoid notice,[22] she will have notice, not be in good faith and her title will be defective. (As to bankruptcy search by a mortgagee see below, para.13.14).

Joint proprietors

Where one of two joint proprietors goes bankrupt, the position is exactly the same as in the case of unregistered title.[23] The bankrupt proprietor cannot be divested of her legal title (since this would involve the impossibility of severing the legal joint tenancy). Thus a creditor's notice or bankruptcy inhibition will not be entered. The interests of the creditors can be protected by restriction (if the joint tenancy is not already subject to one against dealings by the survivor) or a caution.

Dealing with the trustee

Where the bankruptcy does come to light, the purchaser will have to deal with the trustee. The effect on the contract is essentially the same as in the case of unregistered title. If the vendor becomes bankrupt, the purchase will have to be completed or enforced against the trustee in the same way. The trustee will prove title either by getting herself registered as proprietor or (if the purchaser agrees) deal with the land without being registered. In this case, the purchaser will have the bankrupt proprietor's title proved in the usual way; and in addition will require an office copy of the bankruptcy order, a certificate signed by the trustee that the land is included in the trustee's estate, and a certified copy of the certificate of appointment of the trustee.

If the purchaser goes bankrupt the position is the same as in the case of unregistered title.

Voluntary dispositions

13.12.5   Registered title can be the subject matter of a gift in the same way as unregistered (printed Form 19 being adapted to commence: 'In consideration of my natural love and affection'). It has to be adjudicated by the stamp office before registration (Stamp Act 1891, s.17) in effect to confirm that no duty is payable. The donee will be registered as proprietor and not being a transferee for value will hold subject to any

---

[22] See Farwell J. in *Hunt v. Luck* [1901] 1 Ch. 45, p.52, quoted in *Kemmis v. Kemmis* [1988] 1 W.L.R. 1307.

[23] Ruoff & Roper, para.28.09.

minor interests (even though not on the register) subject to which the donor held the land (Land Registration Act 1925, s.20(4)) and will be liable to have her title upset if the donor becomes bankrupt, in accordance with the rules under the 1986 Act mentioned above. This potential liability of the donee to have her title upset is not shown on the register. If the donee disposes of the land the ordinary rules of registered conveyancing apply. A transferee for value will not be affected by such liability unless protected on the register (if for example proceedings to set the gift aside have been commenced and protected on the register).

Dispositions intended to give a preference, those intended to defraud creditors and those intended to defeat a spouse's claim for relief under the Matrimonial Causes Act 1973 are subject to the same principles as in the case of unregistered land (para.13.7.3). And, in the case of a claim under s.37(4) of the Matrimonial Causes Act 1973 at least, the transaction will be set aside against a disponee with notice even though registered as proprietor.[24]

FURTHER SEARCH IN THE REGISTER OF LOCAL LAND CHARGES

13.13 What has been said above in relation to unregistered title applies in exactly the same way in relation to registered title. Local land charges, being overriding interests will not be revealed by the search of the title register.

CENTRAL LAND CHARGES SEARCH

13.14 A search is not necessary in the central Register of Land Charges on behalf of the purchaser. The Land Charges Act 1972 does not apply to charges affecting registered land.[25] Nevertheless, institutional mortgage lenders do habitually require bankruptcy only searches against the borrower. The value of this exercise is open to question.

It is quite clear from s.61(6) of the Land Registration Act 1925 that the mere fact of registration of a bankruptcy petition or adjudication order in the Central Land Charges Register will not affect the lender with notice of it so as to avoid the mortgage against the trustee in bankruptcy and that there is no obligation on the lender to search there. On the other hand, it is possible that if the lender does choose to search and does discover such an entry, she will be affected by notice, so will not be a

---

24 See *Kemmis v. Kemmis* [1988] 1 W.L.R. 1307.

25 Land Charges Act 1972, s.14(1).

purchaser in good faith, and so (if completing the mortgage) will have a mortgage void against the trustee in bankruptcy.[26] It is not clear why the lender, being protected in relation to bankruptcy by not making a search, should choose to make one.

It is commonly said that the search is concerned with the financial status of the borrower rather than her legal title; that, as petitions and orders are first automatically registered in the Central Land Charges Registry, the search might show a bankruptcy which had not yet got onto the register of title. Institutional lenders have every opportunity to and do check the financial status of borrowers before making a mortgage offer. Moreover, it is the long term likelihood of being able to keep up repayment instalments that really concern the lender. And it may well be that only a very small proportion of the mortgage defaulters and repossessed are ever actually made bankrupt. Generally, it is not worth bankrupting the poor. Indeed, it is unlikely to be bankruptcy that prevents a borrower from making repayment instalments. Section 310 of the 1986 Insolvency Act provides that the court can make an order for part of the bankrupt's income to be paid over to the trustee in bankruptcy, but is not to make one 'the effect of which would be to reduce the income of the bankrupt below what appears to the court to be necessary for meeting the reasonable domestic needs of the bankrupt and his family'.

INSPECTION OF THE PROPERTY

13.15   The distinction noted above is equally relevant here; that is between the concern of the purchaser and that of the purchase-related mortgagee. In general the principles discussed in relation to unregistered title apply. The difference is that which determines whether any interest of a person contributing to the purchase price will bind a purchaser is not the doctrine of notice but whether the person is in actual occupation and has an overriding interest under the Land Registration Act 1925, s.70(1)(g). Only a few points need to be made here in a relation to a subject that should have been fully rehearsed in earlier study of land law. The crucial moment at which actual occupation must exist to bind a purchaser is the moment of completion not registration of the purchase. This gives the purchase-linked mortgagee yet one more string to her bow; the contributing granny is not likely to have been installed by the moment of completion. As decided in *Cann*[27] acts preparatory to occupation are not the same as actual occupation. More is required than getting the carpets in and giving the workmen their first cup of tea.

---

[26] See Ruoff & Roper, para.28.15.
[27] [1990] 2 W.L.R. 832.

CHAPTER 14

COMPLETION[1]

FRIDAY MORNING, 19 MARCH. A TRANSFORMATION? TIMOTHY GETS IT RIGHT!

The dawn of Timothy's first completion has broken - in fact, three **14.1** completions; the Obebe sale and purchase and the Goldberg sale. The peak of his conveyancing dream; though Timothy, whose poetry consists of a few ill-digested and ill-forgotten lines of schoolboy Shakespeare, and an endless collection of rugby songs, does not see it with quite such poetic vision (and what conveyancer would?). But he is now trying very hard; and we are going to imagine (whether or not an idle fancy) that today he gets things more or less right. Old Jarndyce hopes that this is a sign of real progress. He is happy enough to have preserved the reputation of the firm so far, in the face of Timothy's bumbling onslaughts, in the eyes of clients, potential clients and potential *ex*-clients.

Timothy takes out the Goldberg file. The following is the file copy of the completion statement sent to the Singhs' solicitor.

---

[1] For what, exactly, the term means, see D.G.Barnsley, 'Completion of a Contract for the Sale and Purchase of Land: Taming a Variable Beast' [1991] Conv. 15, 81, 185. For the difficulty, and possible importance, of establishing the exact time at which completion has taken place, see *Abbey National Building Society v. Cann* [1990] 2 W.L.R. 832.

Document 14.2 Goldberg Sale: Letter to Purchasers' Solicitor

Jarndyce & Jarndyce
Solicitors

24, The Strand, Ledchester LR2 3JF Tel: (2350) 002244 Fax: (2350) 123765 Dx: Ledchester Park Square 14709

To: Messrs.Moriarty & Co

Date: 16 March 1993

Goldberg to Singh
Land at Fell view, Koppax
Your ref: MM/PC

Further to our phone conversation this morning, we confirm
that we are now ready to complete and that we have your
instructions to act as your agents in accordance with the
Law Society's Code for postal completion.
If you will give us a ring on Friday morning when you have
arranged for the transfer of funds we will finalise matters.
We confirm that we have your written instructions on matters
you wish us to deal with.
We will require a letter releasing the deposit held by us as
stakeholders.
The amount required for completion will be £8,987 made up as
follows:

Purchase price	£10,000
Less deposit paid to us	
as stakeholders	<u>1,000</u>
	<u>9,000</u>
Less Interest on deposit	
[Standard Condition 2.2.3.]	
@5%, 1st March to 14th March	2
Less Interest on purchase	
price 14th to 19th March	
[Standard Condition 7.3.]	
- 5 days at 8% (contract rate)	11
	<u>£8,987</u>

Yours faithfully,

Jarndyce & Jarndyce

Jarndyce & Jarndyce

Partners: J.J. Jarndyce, Thomas Trippit, Trevor Trippit, Barry Bopper, Henry Oxbridge. **Consultant:** Edward Trippit

14.3   The letter of instructions from Moriarties to act as their agents to complete contains the following:

> 'We enclose the epitome and copy documents; please kindly mark as examined against the originals for return to us. Please endorse memorandum of the present conveyance on the conveyance to your clients dated 24 June as per our requisition on title. Please supply original death certificate of Mrs Goldberg as agreed and deed appointing Miss Goldberg trustee to convey. Please check that the conveyance has been duly executed by Mr Goldberg, Miss Goldberg and the building society and insert date of completion.'

14.4   The day has not dawned for Mrs Goldberg. She died suddenly two days before completion was due to take place. Her humble but worthy dream of a mortgage-free Fell View (and this is the stuff that conveyancing dreams are made of) was not to be fully realised. At least, and in fairness, it has to be said that Timothy's conveyancing practices did not in any way contribute to her premature demise. Fortunately, conveyancers are not doctors.

Her death does explain the delay in completion and item of £11 for interest deducted in the completion statement sent to Moriarties (above). On the Obebe sale and purchase, Miss Obebe was on the phone to Timothy yesterday. Her sister already has a set of keys. Miss Obebe's removal van is due to arrive at 11 o'clock this morning to start loading. Her sister is moving in with the help of friends later today. Miss Mixford moved out yesterday and has left the keys with a neighbour to be picked up by Miss Obebe after completion. Timothy will ring the neighbour as soon as completion has taken place.

All three solicitors involved in the sale and purchase have agreed to use the Law Society's Code for completion by post.

Note: Timothy decided, with a little help from Old Jarndyce, not to act for Miss Obebe's sister as well (para.9.3).

Question Suppose that Miss Obebe arrives with her pantechnicon to find Miss Mixford's rather elderly and rather obdurate sister in occupation. The sister is claiming that the mother appointed Miss Mixford as her personal representative, but left the house to her (the sister). Miss Mixford, so says the sister, was living with the mother at the time, and refused to move out or transfer the property to the sister. Knowing that Miss Mixford was moving and having a set of keys, last night the sister left her flat and moved in. She now slams the door in Miss Obebe's face. Miss Obebe, in some panic, rings Timothy.

Consider the legal position of the sister, Miss Obebe and Miss Mixford. What steps should Timothy advise on the assumption that he (a) has or (b) has not completed the purchase when Miss Obebe rings?

Fortunately, the above scenario has not arisen. Miss Mixford's sister has not moved in. Timothy goes through his check list (which he now assiduously keeps for every transaction, his shopping and his social life). Everything is in order. Necessary funds from the building society and Miss Obebe have been received and cleared through the client account (below, para.14.8.2).

Timothy completes on the sale and then immediately on the purchase. All goes without a hitch. Even Old Jarndyce is not unhappy.

Question Spell out in chronological order each step that you would expect to be taken by each of the solicitors involved in the Obebe sale and purchase on the day of completion using the Law Society's Code for Completion by Post (Appendix 5).

Question List the documents which Timothy should receive from Miss Mixford's solicitor on completion of the purchase. Remember that Miss Mixford is not the registered proprietor (para.4.1.1).

Timothy turns back to the Goldberg sale. He rings Mary Moriarty at Moriarties who confirms that she is just about to instruct their bank to transfer funds to Jarndyce's account. Half an hour later, in accordance with their instructions, Pennyworth Bank plc (where Jarndyces bank) rings Timothy and confirms that they now hold the £8,9875 to the credit of Jarndyce & Jarndyce in their client account.

Timothy takes the file and gets the deeds sent up from the strong-room. He checks the epitome and copies against the originals and marks each copy as examined. 'Examined against the original, 19 March 1993, Jarndyce & Jarndyce, Solicitors, Ledchester.' He checks that the conveyance to the Singhs has been signed and witnessed by Mr Goldberg and Miss Goldberg, the building society and the Singhs; and enters the date. He has already had a memorandum of the sale endorsed on the conveyance to the Goldbergs which he completes in the following terms:

'By a conveyance dated the 19 day of March 1993 made between Larry Goldberg and Sonia Goldberg (1) and Balraj and Jinder Singh (2) part of the land conveyed by the within conveyance was conveyed to the said B. and J. Singh.'

Note: As to the need to keep a copy of the conveyance on a sale of part, see para.14.10 below.

He makes a file note of the completion, rings Moriarties to confirm that completion has taken place; and dictates a letter to Mr Goldberg and his sister enclosing a statement of account of the transaction and bill of costs.

Question Produce the statement of account and bill of costs. Assume that Jarndyces' costs on the sale were £200 plus Vat with an extra £50 plus VAT for the documentation in connection with the death of Mrs Goldberg. (For illustration see paras.14.8.2(a) and 14.8.2(b) below).

Timothy also dictates a letter to the Ledchester & Bongley Building Society with a copy of the statement of account and a cheque drawn on client account for the balance of the proceeds of sale.

OLD JARNDYCE COMMENTS

14.5   The division of topics between this and the last chapter is one that is conventional but artificial. Both deal with matters which have to be dealt with at some point between contract and completion. It is not possible to give a universally applicable time chart. The time at which any particular step needs to be taken may depend on the circumstances - for example, how long it is likely to take to get necessary funds from the client herself.

The timing of some steps is governed by the contract - for example, the steps in deducing and investigating title. The timing of some is governed by general law - for example, when application for an official Land Registry search must be made to have the benefit of its protection prior to registration.

What is important is to have a checklist of steps to be taken between contract and completion (possibly part of a checklist for the whole transaction, with space to enter the date when each step should be taken, and space to indicate, when such is the case, that a step has been completed and a properly organised diary system to ensure that each step is in fact taken at the right time.

Some of the steps leading from contract to completion do remain to be commented on. What follows applies equally to registered and unregistered title, unless the contrary is indicated. After that matters relating to completion itself will be considered.

A COUNTDOWN TO COMPLETION

VACANT POSSESSION

14.6   Subject to the terms of the contract the vendor is obliged to give the purchaser vacant possession at completion.

The most likely case where the contract will provide otherwise, is where the property is expressly sold subject to an existing tenancy of the whole of part of the property. In such a case, in respect of that whole or part, the purchaser is buying the reversion. Here, the following points should be noted. Both under an open contract and the Standard Conditions (6.3.) the rental income for the period current at the time of completion will have to be apportioned; and the purchaser will have to be put into possession of the right to receive the rent by providing her with a letter directing the tenant to pay future rents (and other payments due under the lease) to the purchaser.

Under s.3 of the Landlord and Tenant Act 1985, the new landlord of a dwelling must give notice in writing of the assignment and of her name and address to the tenant not later than the next day on which rent is payable under the tenancy (or within two months if that is later). Failure to comply without reasonable excuse in a summary offence.[2] Under s.3A of the same Act, introduced by s.50 of the Landlord and Tenant Act 1987, the assignor will continue to be liable on the landlord's covenants until notice has been given, either by the new landlord or the assignor.

Vacant possession connotes both a physical fact and a legal right. Physically, it means empty of both objects and persons; whether any such person is there without right (for example, a squatter who has entered before completion) or under some right capable of binding the purchaser (for example, a spouse of the vendor with a statutory right of occupation under the Matrimonial Homes Act 1983. Legally, it means free from the right of anyone else to take possession as against the purchaser.[3]

The contractual obligation to give vacant possession on completion is an exception to the principle that the contract merges with the conveyance (para.5.7) and so the purchaser can sue for failure to give vacant possession even after completion has taken place.

DEATH BETWEEN CONTRACT AND COMPLETION

As would be expected in a mature property-owning democracy, **14.7** death has no vitiating effect on a contract for the sale of land! It may be a tragedy; but in conveyancing it is just a matter of title. On death, the rights and obligations under the contract of the deceased will pass to her personal representatives as administrators of her estate. In order to be able to complete, the personal representatives will have to prove their title to the property.

---

2 And see s.48 of the same Act requiring a landlord to give the tenant notice of an address in England and Wales for the service of notices.

3 See, e.g. *Wroth v. Tyler* [1974] Ch. 30; and see para.3.5.4.

The proving personal representative(s) will have to replace the deceased in the conveyance and will be expressed to convey in the capacity of personal representative(s) (para.5.7).

Death of sole vendor: Unregistered title

14.7.1   A purchaser will be concerned with a number of matters.

Firstly, that the title has properly passed from the deceased to the personal representative(s). This will be proved by production of the grant of probate or letters of administration. The vendor should supply a copy to the purchaser and produce the original for inspection.

At this point a distinction should be noted between the original grant sealed by the Registry which contains a copy of the will within it and an office copy of the grant. This is a copy of the grant without a copy of the will but sealed by the Registry and equally admissible in evidence. Any number of such copies can be obtained from the Registry on payment of a fee. It is, of course, possible to have photo or other unofficial copies of the grant. Any necessary memoranda must be made and looked for on the original grant.

The purchaser will not receive the original on completion since it will relate to the whole of the deceased's estate; and should, as with all the title deeds, mark her copy as examined against the original. In addition, she should ensure that an acknowledgement for production of the original grant is drafted into the conveyance (para.12.4.3(c)).

The purchaser will need to check that all the personal representatives proving the will (and no one else) are party to the conveyance. A sole personal representative (i.e. if there is only one personal representative) acting as such can give a good title.[4] This will not apply if the personal representative has ceased to hold as such on conclusion of the administration and is holding as trustee; or if the property has come from the deceased as trust property.

Secondly, the purchaser must check that the personal representative has not already disposed of the land elsewhere.

A personal representative can do one of two things with the land of the deceased. First, she may assent it to a beneficiary, who might be herself; or, if it is to be held on trust, she may assent it to the trustee; and, if she is trustee as well as personal representative she will have to assent it from herself as personal representative to herself as trustee. Under s.36(4) of the Administration of Estates Act 1925, an assent must be in writing and signed by the assentor and name the person in whose favour it is

---

[4]   Law of Property Act 1925, ss.2(1)(iii), 27(2).

given. For reasons given below, the assentee should (as she is entitled to under s.36(5) of this Act) ensure that a memorandum of the assent is endorsed on the original grant of probate or administration.

Alternatively, the personal representative may sell the property. From a purchaser's point of view, the danger is that the personal representative has already vested the estate in someone else by assent and so has no title to pass to the purchaser. Such an event is unlikely since the assentee would normally have obtained the title deeds to the property.

In any case, a purchaser in good faith for money or money's worth is protected under s.36(6) of the Administration of Estates Act 1925 and will get good title (thus depriving any previous assentee of the title) if two conditions are satisfied. First, there must be no memorandum of any previous assent endorsed on the grant. This explains why the assentee should get such a memorandum of her own assent endorsed. Secondly, the personal representative must make a statement in writing that she has 'not given or made an assent or conveyance in respect of the legal estate'. This statement is invariably made in the conveyance to the purchaser itself (generally in the form of a recital). If the personal representative has herself died the statement can be made by the person who takes over as personal representative of the (original) deceased.

This provision protects the purchaser against the possibility of an earlier assent; it cannot upset the title of an earlier purchaser for money or money's worth. This of course is the normal situation of any purchaser. As already said, this is unlikely to happen; additionally it is a criminal offence for a personal representative to make a false s.36 statement. Further, this protection only operates in favour of a purchaser. If a personal representative makes an assent to B having already made an assent to A, A's title will not be disturbed whether or not she has had a memorandum endorsed on the grant.

Where the personal representative assents to the property, rather than selling it, it is common to have a s.36 statement included in the assent. This will not give the assentee protection. It has also been said that it will not protect a subsequent purchaser from the assentee, because the statement has not been made to the purchaser by the personal representative. But it is difficult to see why, under the section, it should not be relied on by such a subsequent purchaser

It follows from the above, that wherever a purchaser takes from a personal representative and wherever there is the death of a sole owner on the title, the purchaser should check the grant; check that there were no adverse memoranda on the grant at the time of conveyance; and that a s.36 statement by the personal representative was or will be made.

The third point of concern will be the interests of the beneficiaries. Being aware, as she will be, that the land is held by a personal representative, a purchaser will in principle have notice of the existence of the beneficial interests and be affected by any breach of obligation to them by the personal representative - if, for example, the personal representative has assented the property in favour of the wrong person.

However, in accordance with the underlying philosophy of the 1925 legislation to keep all equitable interests off the title, a purchaser is not required to concern herself with them. First, on a proper sale their interest will be overreached. Secondly, the purchaser is not in general concerned with whether the personal representative has acted properly. Section 36(7) of the Administration of Estates Act 1925 provides that the assent in itself is sufficient evidence that it was made to the right persons provided no adverse memorandum has been endorsed on the grant. Further, under the Trustee Act 1925, s.17, a purchaser is not concerned to investigate the reasons for the sale, or the use to which the sale money is put. And by s.36(8) of the Administration of Estates Act 1925 her title will not be upset even if she happens to know that all the estate's debts have been paid (i.e. that there might be no cause to sell).

Death of joint owner: unregistered title

14.7.2   Where the deceased was one of two joint tenants (as in the case of the Goldbergs) the vendors will necessarily have held as trustees. They may, as likely in the common case of co-ownership of the matrimonial home by spouses, have held in trust just for themselves as joint tenants or tenants in common in equity. On the other hand they may have been holding in trust for others (in addition or not to themselves). Either way, on a sale by both of them, the purchaser would not be concerned to investigate such beneficial interests because of the overreaching machinery provisions of the Law of Property Act 1925, ss.2(1) and 27.

The death of one of them will automatically vest the legal title in the survivor(s). If the purchaser takes a conveyance from a sole survivor she will get legal title; but she will have notice that there is a trust (if only because there has been a conveyance to more than one person) and, not paying the money to at least two trustees or a trust corporation, will not be protected by the overreaching machinery. Therefore, unless the Law of Property (Joint Tenants) Act 1964 can be resorted to, it will be necessary to have a second, new trustee appointed to join in the conveyance to receive the capital money and trigger the overreaching machinery. Under s.36 of the Trustee Act 1925, the surviving trustee will normally be the one with power to appoint a new trustee. The appointment can be made in writing. In addition the legal title to the property will have to be vested in the existing and new trustee so that it can be conveyed to the purchaser. Under s.40 of the Trustee Act 1925 if the appointment is made by deed and contains a suitable vesting declaration, the single deed will be sufficient both to make the appointment and to vest the property. The purchaser would need to be supplied with a copy of this deed and production of the original for examination and either receive the original or an acknowledgement for its production. Commonly, the appointment and vesting is included in the conveyance to the purchaser itself.

In the common case - i.e. beneficial joint owning spouses - the legal and equitable title will be held in joint tenancy. On the death of one of the two the survivor will automatically become sole beneficial owner and able to convey the same to a purchaser. The purchaser, however, will not know that this is the case without investigating the equitable ownership (which might involve the difficulty of proving a negative - for example, that an original equitable joint tenancy had not at some point in time been severed). And, in any case, the object of modern conveyancing is to keep equities off the title, to avoid this sort of investigation. Without special provision the purchaser would have to do this; or to have a new second trustee appointed as described above.

The Law of Property (Joint Tenants) Act 1964 is intended to deal with this situation. It provides that if certain conditions are satisfied the survivor is 'deemed' to be solely and beneficially entitled; and can therefore give (and can insist on giving) good title without the appointment of a new trustee. The conditions are that:

(a) The original conveyance must have been to the joint tenants as joint tenants in equity as well as law (or at least, it seems, not have contained anything to suggest that they were not such). Thus an initial conveyance to A and B without any mention of the equitable ownership at all would be within the protection of the Act.

(b) No memorandum of severance of the joint tenancy must have been endorsed on the initial conveyance to the joint tenants.

(c) No bankruptcy petition or receiving order must have been registered against either of the joint tenants. This would cause automatic severance.

(d) The survivor must convey to a purchaser as beneficial owner or the conveyance contain a statement that she is so entitled. If the survivor has died, s.1(2) provides that the same principle will apply with necessary modification to a conveyance by the personal representative of the survivor.

Whether or not the Act can be relied on, the purchaser will need to see an official copy of the death certificate. Production of a grant is not necessary; since the legal title passes automatically to the survivor simply by virtue of the death.

Where the Act cannot be relied on, the purchaser can insist on the appointment of a second trustee. Section 42 of the Law of Property Act 1925, provides, in effect, that any stipulation in a contract shall be void if it requires a purchaser under a trust for sale to take title with the concurrence of any equitable beneficiary instead of by the appointment of a second trustee.

The Act should also be viewed from the perspective of the person with an interest in the property as tenant in common in equity. The Act adds to the importance of expressly declaring the allocation of equitable ownership in the conveyance, whether or not those interested are to share in holding the legal title.

Question Explain why and in what probable capacity Sonia Goldberg has been made a party to the conveyance to the Singhs. See the memorandum endorsed by Timothy on the conveyance (para.14.4) and the conveyance to Mr and Mrs Goldberg (Document 5.2(b)).

In the question in para.12.3.1 you were asked to draft the conveyance on the Goldberg sale. Using that as a basis, now draft the amendments you think necessary in the light of Mrs Goldberg's death and Sonia's involvement. See Encyclopedia, Vol. 36, Form 84.

Question Suppose that A and B are the joint beneficial owners of Blackacre. A dies not having severed the equitable joint tenancy. B then dies and his personal representative executes an assent vesting the property in nephew C. The assent contains no statement under s.36(6) of the Law of Property Act 1925 (see above). C is now negotiating to sell the property to D. Consider whether C give good title to D without joining anyone else in the conveyance. If not, who should be joined in as a party and for what purpose?

Delay caused by death

14.7.3   As indicated above, death of the vendor has no effect on the obligation to complete the contract according to its terms. But delay, which may be substantial, is likely to be caused if, for example, a grant of representation has to be obtained. Any delay will be a breach of contract. Under the Standard Conditions, Standard Condition 7 will operate making the vendor's estate liable to pay at least compensation measured at the contract rate for the period of delay. This is what has happened in the Goldberg case and explains the £11 allowed to the Singhs in the completion statement (above, Document 14.2) Equally, the purchaser may choose, if there is delay, to serve a completion notice making time of the essence if not already so.

Registered title

The effect of the death of a sole proprietor or of one of joint proprietors has already been considered (paras.11.3.4 and 11.3.5). As to acknowledgements for production, see para.12.9(d).   **14.7.4**

Question Blackacre was transferred on purchase to Joshua Tetley and John Smith some years ago by a transfer dated 24 June 1984 from Larry Agelout. The transfer (and consequently the register) contained the usual restriction that the survivor could not give a valid receipt for capital monies. Joshua died (of alcohol poisoning) six months ago. John is negotiating to sell the property. What steps must he take to give good title to a purchaser. Draft any necessary document(s) (making up any additional facts which you think it necessary to have).

Death of the purchaser

As on the death of the vendor the contractual rights and liabilities of the deceased purchaser are assumed by her personal representatives as managers of her estate. Whether the title is registered or unregistered, the obligation to complete in accordance with the contract will continue, with consequences parallel to those mentioned above in the event of delay. On completion, the vendor will need proof of the title of the personal representatives (normally in the form of production of the grant) to receive a conveyance/transfer of the property under the contract.   **14.7.5**

MONEY   14.8

The vendor's solicitor

The vendor's solicitor will have to send the purchaser's solicitor a completion statement showing how much is required from the purchaser to complete. (See Document 14 above.) The purchaser's solicitor needs to check this to see whether it is agreed.   **14.8.1**

In addition to the purchase price, items which may have to be included as credits or debits include:

(a) Apportionments of outgoings and income

Any periodic sums recoverable from the owner for the time being of the estate being purchased (leasehold or freehold) will need to be apportioned for the period encompassing completion. If already paid by the vendor for the period extending beyond completion, the purchaser will be debited with that amount. If unpaid for the period prior to completion, the purchaser will be credited with the amount due for that period. The same principle is applied to any periodic income from the property.

Under an open contract such sums are apportioned as at the contractual date for completion, whether or not completion takes place on that date. Standard Condition 6.3. deals with apportionment. In two cases (Standard Condition 6.3.2.) the relevant date is the date of actual completion. In particular, this is so where, as is the usual case, the whole of the property is being sold with vacant possession.

Debts and credits which are personal to the vendor are not apportioned and if adjustment is necessary it will be made directly between the payer and payee. For example, if the vendor has paid telephone rental or electricity standing charges for the period after completion, she will claim the rebate from the company. To some extent it is a matter of practice and convenience which payments are apportioned. Rent (including ground rent) is apportioned whether as income due to the purchaser of the reversion or as an outgoing on purchase of the lease. Water and drainage rates are apportionable (though commonly now these are left to be adjusted directly by the client with the company). Council tax is left to be adjusted directly between the client and the local authority.

The vendor's solicitor should warn her client to inform all service suppliers of the intended cessation of ownership; and arrange to have any meters read. Failure to give notice may leave the vendor liable to pay for services enjoyed by the purchaser. For example, under s.144 of the Water Industry Act 1991, the occupier will continue to be liable unless she informs the water and sewerage company at least two days before the cessation of occupation.[5]

Where payments are apportioned the vendor's solicitor should send the relevant receipts/demands to the purchaser's solicitor or at least have them available for inspection at completion.

---

[5]   As to Council Tax, see Local Government Finance Act 1992, Schedule 2. And see TransAction Protocol, para.8.4.

(b) The deposit

Where the deposit is held by a stakeholder, the vendor's solicitor will require at completion a written authority from the purchaser's solicitor authorising its release. Although Timothy has asked for such authority, it is not usual to bother with one where the deposit is being held by the vendor's solicitor as stakeholder. No doubt the act of completing amounts to an implied authority.

(c) Chattels

(See para.4.4.2.)

(d) Compensation for late completion

This is dealt with in chapter 16.

(e) Other sums

There may be other amounts to be credited or debited in this final reckoning. For example, if under TranAction Protocol the vendor's solicitor has supplied pre-contract searches the cost of these will have to be re-imbursed by the purchaser. If this has not been done (as it should have been after exchange under para.6.3 of the Protocol) an adjustment can be made in the completion statement.

The vendor's solicitor will need to send the vendor a final statement of account (completion statement) and bill of costs. The principles are the same as for the statement sent by the purchaser's solicitor to her client (see below). In the case of a sale with no related purchase, the statement is likely to be sent to the client after completion with a cheque for the balance due to the client.

The purchaser's solicitor

The purchaser's solicitor will have to collect together the funds **14.8.2** needed to complete. These are likely to be coming from the mortgage-lender, proceeds of a related sale and/or the purchaser direct.

Any payment by cheque should be received in time for the cheque to be cleared through the client account before being drawn on for completion. If payment is made against a cheque paid into the client account which is not met, this is a breach of the Solicitors' Accounts Rules 1991, rr. 7 and 8; and the solicitor will at once have to pay the appropriate amount from her own resources into the account (*Guide*, para.27.30).

As in the case of the vendor's solicitor a statement of account (completion statement) and bill of costs should be sent to the purchaser. A solicitor cannot draw money from a client account for payment of her own costs unless 'there has been delivered to the client a bill of costs or other written intimation of the amount of costs incurred and it has thereby or otherwise in writing been made clear to the client that money held for him is being or will be applied towards or in satisfaction of such costs' (Solicitors' Accounts Rules 1991, Rule 7).

Further points of professional conduct relating to costs should be noted here.

'Unless a solicitor has, at the outset of the retainer, required the client to make a payment or payments on account of costs, the solicitor should not refuse to complete a transaction for the client if the sole reason for that refusal is that the client has not made such a payment.' (*Guide*, para.24.14).

This principle does not apply in the case of non-payment of disbursements by the client.

As a matter of law as well as conduct in a non-contentious matter

'... a solicitor may not sue the client until the expiration of one month from he delivery of the bill. Further, a solicitor must not sue or threaten to sue unless he or she has first informed the client in writing of the right to require a remuneration certificate and of the right to seek taxation of the bill.' (*Guide*, para.14.06).

If money is needed from the client to complete, the account will be sent before completion with request for payment of the amount due.

The following is a copy of the bill of costs and the statement of account sent to Fancy French and Sam Saunders.

Document 14.8.2(a) French/Saunders Purchase: Bill of Costs Sent to Clients

Jarndyce & Jarndyce

Solicitors

24, The Strand, Ledchester LR2 3JF Tel: (2350) 002244 Fax: (2350) 123765 Dx: Ledchester Park Square 14709

DATE: 10 March 1993 No: 402461/2   **INVOICE**

Mr. S. Saunders, Ms F. French, 22 Backup Lane, Ledchester

Re: Your purchase	CHARGES	DISBURSE-MENTS	V.A.T.
To: Provision of legal services in this matter; including taking instructions on purchase and acting therein; making local searches; drafting conveyance; attendance and correspondence; and all necessary steps to complete. Also acting on mortgage advance from Ledchester & Bongley Building Society.	300.00		52.50
Disbursements			
Local search fee		75.00	
HM Land Charges Search		4.00	
Bank telegraph fee		20.00	
HM Land Registry fee:		160.00	
Total	300.00		
Disbursements	259.00		
Total VAT	52.50		
TOTAL	611.50		

RECEIVED WITH THANKS
WITH COMPLIMENTS

Partners: J.J. Jarndyce, Thomas Trippit, Trevor Trippit, Barry Bopper, Henry Oxbridge. Consultant: Edward Trippit
Regulated by the Law Society in the conduct of investment business.
VAT Registration No: 482 0861 42

Document 14.8.2(b) French/Saunders Purchase: Statement of Account Sent to Clients

Mr. S. Saunders & M/s F. French   402461/2
COMPLETION STATEMENT
Purchase: 24 De Lucy Mount, Ledchester

Purchase price		£75,000.00	
ADD: Stamp Duty		£ 750.00	
Debit paid to Dream Homes	£ 1,000.00		
paid to us	£ 6,500.00		
OUR COSTS (as per attached bill)		£ 611.50	
Advance from: Ledchester & Bongley B.S.	£65,000.00		
Balance due from you	£ 3,861.50		
	£76,361.50	£76,361.50	

E. & O.E

429

The statement should show clearly the detail and amount required to complete, including the purchase price less any deposit paid and additional sums payable to the vendor less any advance on mortgage received and the total shown by the completion statement. The bill of costs will show the solicitor's professional fee with VAT shown separately and disbursements.. The costs may include as separate items the costs of acting on sale, redemption of mortgages on the property sold, the purchase, on a new mortgage (possibly for acting for the lender as well as the borrower) and giving financial advice covered by the Financial Services Act 1986. It is sometimes the practice to send a single account incorporating both the bill of costs and the completion statement.

It may be that the funds for completion of a purchase will not be available until after completion is due; for example, where a related sale is not scheduled to be completed until after completion of the purchase (of course, if the sale proceeds of an existing property are essential and there is no contract to sell yet in existence, the whole project is risky) or where perhaps there has been retention by a mortgagee-lender pending the completion of works on the property. In such a case the client may look to a bridging loan from a bank or other financier and her solicitor may be asked to give a professional undertaking to pay the proceeds of sale when received to the bridging financier. What has already been said about professional undertakings (para.5.13) applies fully to any such undertaking.

Question Compile a bill of costs and statement of account for the Obebe purchase and sale (see Appendix 2 for location of information). Assume that she sold to her sister for the price she was going to get from the Headcases and that the figure for redemption of the mortgage on 14 Hardcastle Drive is correct. Research and include correct figures for search fees. Where figures are not given or discoverable, compose them.

B COMPLETION

MATTERS TO BE ATTENDED TO AT COMPLETION

14.9   It should be noted that some of these matters require some attention before actual completion.

Payment

14.9.1   The money due to the vendor as shown by the completion statement will be paid over. Under Standard Condition 6.7. payment may be made in one of the following forms:

'(a) legal tender;

(b) a banker's draft (see para.2.3);

(c) a direct credit to a bank account nominated by the seller's solicitor;

(d) an unconditional release of a deposit held by a stakeholder.'

A solicitor would be acting negligently in accepting a cheque which was subsequently dishonoured.

The title documents

(a) Unregistered title

There are two matters to consider: examination of the title deeds (verification) and the handing over of the deeds to the purchaser.   **14.9.2**

Prior to completion (as part of the process of proving title) the purchaser will have received an abstract or epitome and copies of the title deeds. It remains (and for convenience this is normally done on the occasion of completion itself) to examine the original deeds themselves and check that they correspond with the abstract or copies. This process is commonly referred to as verification. The abstract or copy of each document should be marked in the margin indicating that it has been 'examined with the original' with the date, name, address and signature of the firm. The examined abstract or copy can then be placed with the title deeds. Verifying and marking the abstract or copy is particularly important in relation to documents which are going to be retained by the vendor. The marked abstract or copy will be the only immediate evidence held by the purchaser of her title; and will be necessary to gain registration.

In general the purchaser will be entitled to receive and keep all the original title deeds themselves relating to the property. Under the Law of Property Act 1925, s.45(9) the vendor is entitled to retain documents of title which relate to land being retained by her (i.e. on the sale of part of the land in a title) and any document containing a still subsisting trust – for example, the original of a grant of probate or letters of administration.[6]

Neither the vendor nor her mortgagee may have the originals of all or some of the title deeds. This will be the case if before the present ownership there has been a grant of probate or administration on the title, or if before then the land was split off on sale from a larger holding. If the conveyancing on previous transactions has been done competently, the

---

[6] See *Re Lehmann and Walker's Contract* [1906] 2 Ch. 640; vendor of part entitled to retain deed showing the extinguishment of a right of way over the retained land.

vendor will have the benefit of an acknowledgement for the production of such documents. And under an open contract, by virtue of the Law of Property Act 1925, s.45(4) the purchaser is entitled at her own expense to require the actual production of such original documents. In practice this is never done. What the vendor should have available with the title deeds is a marked abstract or copy of any such originals made and placed with the deeds at the time of the previous transactions as described above. At least, if the marking shows that the verification against the originals took place at the same time as completion of the sale off, this is acceptable. If it took place at an earlier date it is conceivable (though a lot less than likely) that, for example, adverse memoranda were added to the originals between the date of examination and completion of the sale off.

Standard Condition 4.2.3. expressly allows the vendor to produce, instead of the original of a relevant document: 'an abstract, epitome or copy with an original marking by a solicitor of examination either against the original or against an examined abstract or against an examined copy.'

Thus, before transferring the money the purchaser's solicitor should have examined either the originals of all the title deeds or marked copies as described in Standard Condition 4.2.3. Upon completing, in relation to each document of the title, she should be in possession of the original, an abstract or copy marked by a solicitor on a previous dealing with the land or an abstract or copy marked by herself. In relation to any original which she does not receive, there should be an acknowledgement for its production given either in an earlier conveyance or in the present conveyance to the purchaser.

Before completion, the vendor's solicitor should prepare in duplicate a schedule of the documents to be handed over. The purchaser's solicitor should check this with what she is receiving and, if correct, sign one of the copies to be retained by the vendor's solicitor (and see para.12.4.3).

(b) Registered title

On a sale with absolute title there will not be title deeds to examine. The purchaser's solicitor will have office copies of the register and have made an official, pre-completion search (para.13.12). On the sale of the whole property in the title, the vendor will have to produce and hand over the land certificate; or, if the property is subject to subsisting mortgage, the charge certificate for each charge (the land certificate being held at the Registry). It is simply necessary to check that the land or charge certificate is the right one.

On a sale of part, the certificate relating to the whole will not be handed over. Instead there should be a special condition in the contract requiring the vendor to place the land certificate (or for the mortgagee to deposit the charge certificate if the part being sold is to be released from a subsisting mortgage) at the Registry and to supply the purchaser with the deposit number. After completion the purchaser's solicitor will then be in a position to complete the registration of the new title to the part purchased.

Occasionally, documents other than the land or charge certificate relating to the title will be necessary (for example, where a personal representative is selling without first getting herself registered as proprietor) and, subject to the terms of the contract, will need to be produced by the vendor at completion and handed over.

Discharge of outstanding mortgages

The vendor will be under a duty to discharge any subsisting **14.9.3** mortgages prior to completion unless, in the unusual case, the contract is to buy subject to an existing mortgage.

A mortgagor generally has a right in equity to redeem her mortgage at any time on giving reasonable notice. Some lending institutions do require notice of, maybe, a month of intended redemption or payment of interest in lieu. The vendor's solicitor should check this at the time of taking instructions and see that any necessary notice is given.

(a) Unregistered title

In the case of unregistered title the vendor's solicitor should produce the mortgage with proper evidence of its discharge. The normal method is by receipt endorsed on the mortgage itself. Section 115 of the Law of Property Act 1925 provides that

'A receipt endorsed on, written at the foot of, or annexed to, a mortgage for all money thereby secured, which states the name of the person who pays the money and is executed by the chargee by way of legal mortgage or the person in whom the mortgaged property is vested and who is legally entitled to give a receipt for the mortgage money shall operate ... as a discharge of the mortgaged property.'

The receipt should, though it seems that it is not essential to its effectiveness, state the name of the payer and be executed as a deed.[7] Where the receipt shows that the money was paid by someone other than the person entitled to the immediate equity of redemption the receipt will operate not as a discharge of the mortgage but as a transfer vesting it in the person paying off (s.115(2)). Thus, for example, if a first mortgage is shown by the receipt to have been paid by a second mortgagee, this would operate as a transfer of the mortgage to the second mortgage.

---

[7] See *Edwards v. Marshall-Lee* (1975) 235 E.G. 901; *Simpson v. Geoghegan* [1934] W.N. 232.

There will be no transfer (unless expressed to be intended) under sub-section (2) if the receipt indicates an intention to discharge the mortgage, or if it is paid off by a personal representative or trustee.

A statutory form of the receipt envisaged by s.115 is provided in the Third Schedule to the Act. Its use is optional and the form of wording can be altered. It is as follows:

> 'I [name] hereby acknowledge that I have this [date] received the sum of [amount] representing the balance remaining owing in respect of the principal money secured by the within written mortgage, together with all interest and costs, the payment having been made by [name of payer].
>
> As witness, etc.'

Where part of the land in a title is being sold free of a mortgage affecting the whole, the part will be released either (as is usual) by the mortgagee joining in the conveyance for that purpose or by the mortgagee executing a separate deed of release. The vendor will have to obtain the agreement of the mortgagee to release the part before committing herself to the contract of sale.

Building societies can, but do not normally, use the s.115 for proof of receipt. They normally use the alternative form provided by the Building Societies Act 1986, Schedule 4, para.2(1). This form, which should be followed strictly, is as follows:

> 'The [name] Building Society hereby acknowledge to have received all monies intended to be secured by the ['above written' or 'within written' or 'annexed'] deed. [Attestation and execution].'

The completed form should be sealed and counter-signed by a person acting under the authority of the Board of Directors. Such a receipt is different from the s.115 receipt in that it does not name the payer and cannot operate as a transfer of the mortgage.

Undertakings

Commonly the vendor will be expecting and will only be able to redeem subsisting mortgages out of the proceeds of sale. In principle, a purchaser is entitled to have any mortgages redeemed before completing. In practice the purchaser's solicitor will normally accept a professional undertaking from the vendor's solicitor to pay the necessary redemption money to the mortgagee and forward the receipted mortgage to her. The purchaser's solicitor should be informed beforehand, in replies to requisitions on title, or otherwise that such an undertaking is to be offered. Though it is normally stated that the 'usual' undertaking will be given, the form of wording should ideally be agreed.

The Law Society has recommended the following form of undertaking to discharge a building society mortgage (*Guide*, p.454):

'In consideration of your today completing the purchase of ... WE HEREBY UNDERTAKE forthwith to pay over to the ... Building Society the money required to redeem the mortgage/legal charge dated ... and to forward the receipted mortgage/legal charge to you as soon as it is received by use from the ... Building Society.'

The principles relating to the giving of professional undertakings have been discussed (para.5.13) and apply here. Note that the undertaking does not commit the solicitor to redeem the mortgage or have it receipted or anything else not within her control; but simply to forward the money and hand over the receipted mortgage when it is received. Note also that the undertaking should relate to a specified mortgage or mortgages; not to mortgages on the property in general.

(b) Registered title

When a registered charge is discharged it will be deleted from the register. The Registry will require production of the charge certificate together with a proper form of receipt.

Section 115 has no application to registered land (see s.115(10)). The proper form of receipt is printed form 53 (or 53(Co) if the lender is a company, corporation or a building society). This is as follows:

'County, District ...

Title no ...

Property ...

Date ...

... hereby admits that the charge dated ... and registered on ... of which he is the proprietor has been discharged.'

The form should be executed as a deed. Use of Form 53 is not obligatory and the Registrar will act upon any other satisfactory evidence of discharge.

The same form is also applicable where part of the land in a title is being released from a charge i.e. on a sale of part. In this case the following words are added to the above wording:

'... as to the land shown and edged with red on the accompanying plan executed by the said proprietor, being part of the land comprised in the title above referred to.'

The plan must be properly executed by the chargee and securely attached to the form. Here, with the use of Form 53, there will be no need for the mortgagee to join in the transfer to release the part sold, though its pre-contract consent will be necessary.

Building societies normally use Form 53 (Co), though they can use any other proof of discharge which is acceptable to the Registrar - such as the Schedule 4 form (above). Form 53 (Co) should be executed in accordance with Rule 152 of the Land Registration Rules as amended; that is, it should bear the seal of the society affixed by order of the Board of Directors and be countersigned by the secretary and a director or other authorised officers.

A professional undertaking to discharge a registered charge is subject to the same principles as one to discharge an unregistered charge. The reference to the receipted charge in the form quoted above will be amended to refer instead to Land Registry Form 53 or 53 (Co) duly executed. In addition to registered charges, the removal of any other entries on the register which are to be removed by the vendor should be checked.

Delivery of the conveyance or transfer

14.9.4 The most important matter from the purchaser's point of view is to take delivery of the conveyance or transfer. This transfers title to the purchaser (subject to registration in the case of registered title). It is crucial, before handing over the purchase money, to check that the document has been properly executed by the vendor and any other parties. The date which will have been left blank should be inserted.

14.10 MATTERS ARISING ON A SALE OF PART

Unregistered title

(See further as to dating and execution of the deed, para.12.4.4).

There are three matters, associated with traditional conveyancing practice, to mention. What has to be remembered is that today, on a conveyance on sale of the freehold, the title of the purchaser will have to be registered.

(i) The retention of the title deeds by the vendor, the importance of obtaining a marked abstract or copies of those retained and an acknowledgement for their production has been considered (above, para.14.9.2; as to acknowledgements, see para.12.4.3).

(ii) Endorsing a memorandum of the sale. It has always been customary for the purchaser to require a memorandum of her conveyance to be endorsed on the last conveyance of the whole. Section 200 of the Law of Property Act 1935 gives her a right, where the conveyance to her contains provisions imposing restrictions on or rights over the retained land, notwithstanding any stipulation to the contrary, to have such a memorandum giving notice of any such provision. The first edition of the Standard Conditions (Standard Condition 4.6.5.) imposed an obligation on the vendor (on a sale of part) to endorse a memorandum of the sale on the last document of title. This condition has been omitted from the second edition.

Failure to have a memorandum endorsed does not affect the title of the purchaser in any way. It is designed to warn any possible subsequent purchaser from the owner of the retained land that there has been a sale off – a matter of conveyancing politeness to save her from suffering a double conveyance. In addition, it would draw the attention of such a purchaser to the possibility that easements or covenants might have been imposed on the land sold or the land retained. The endorsement of such a memorandum does not obviate the need to register restrictive covenants.

(iii) It has also always been customary and advisable for the vendor to retain a copy of the conveyance to be kept with the title deeds of the retained land. This would provide the detailed evidence (and in practice the endorsed memorandum would rarely do more than record the bare fact and date of the sale off) of any rights granted or retained in relation to the part sold off and affecting the part retained. It has to be remembered that the owner of the retained land would not have the benefit of any acknowledgement for production of the actual conveyance itself.

The question to consider, briefly, is how these practices are affected by the now universality of compulsory registration on a sale of freehold. The purchaser will have to register the title of the part purchased. The title to the part retained will remain unregistered until it too is sold. A subsequent purchaser of any part of the retained land will, or should, do a public index map search. This will show if any part of what is now being bought has been sold off before and registered – the danger of a double conveyance will not threaten a reasonably competent conveyancer. But without an endorsed memorandum the subsequent purchaser may well not know that there has been a previous sale off of adjoining land with the possible creation of easements or covenants affecting the part retained and now being sold. If she does know, and inspects (as there is now a public right to do) the register of title of the part sold, this will show the benefit and burden of easements expressly created on the sale off, and the burden of covenants. But it is unlikely to show the benefit of covenants creating a burden on the retained land – though the actual existence of such covenants should be shown on the central Land Charges Register against an estate owner of the retained land.

For these reasons it seems sensible that the practice of endorsing a memorandum of sale on the last conveyance of the common title, and keeping a copy of the conveyance with the deeds, should continue. But it is not really the concern of the purchaser of part and there seems no need to have a term in the contract requiring a memorandum to be endorsed. It is really a question of good house (or rather title) keeping by the vendor's solicitor, so that when the retained land is sold there is a clear, available picture of what rights benefit or burden the land.

Registered title

Where the sale is part of an already registered title, the purchaser will again have to have a new title to the part registered. The existing register of title of the retained land will be amended to show the sale off. The title plan will identify the land which has been taken out of the title. A subsequent purchaser of the retained land can easily see if she is being offered a double conveyance. She can see that there has been a previous sale off which might have created or reserved easements or restrictive covenants. There is no place for endorsing a memorandum of the sale; and indeed no place to endorse it. Land and charge certificates include a printed warning against adding to, altering or tampering with them. The benefit and burden of any easements and the burden of any restrictive covenants expressly created by the transfer will be shown on the register of the title of the retained land she is buying. However, as already indicated, the benefit of appurtenant covenants is not likely to be shown – though they will be shown (as burdens) on the register of the title sold off. For this reason, when a transfer of part does take restrictive covenants from the purchaser, a certified copy of the transfer should be kept with the certificate and other documents relating to the title. The transfer itself is kept at the Registry which will not, in general, supply copies of it. As a matter of discretion, copies will be supplied to the parties to the transfer.

Question Refer back to Chapter 12, and question 5 (sale of Horseacre) after Document 12.2. List the documents which you would expect to be handed over by the vendor's solicitor to the purchaser's solicitor in that transaction. Similarly, list the documents which you would expect to be handed over on completion of the French/Saunders purchase.

THE MECHANICS OF COMPLETION

14.11   The detailed arrangements for completion will have to be agreed between the respective solicitors, either in the course of making and replying to requisitions or separately.

Date and time of completion

This has already been dealt with (para.9.2). On a related sale and purchase it may be important to ensure that completion on the sale takes place before the purchase and in time to have the proceeds available for the purchase. If necessary a special condition should have been put in the contract providing a completion time to allow this.

Place

Standard Condition 6.2. provides that 'Completion is to take place in England and Wales, either at the seller's solicitor's office or at some other place which the seller reasonably specifies'.

If there is an outstanding mortgage to be redeemed, and the vendor's solicitor is also acting for the lender, completion is likely to be at the vendor's solicitor's office. Where the lender is separately represented, it may have to take place at the lender's solicitor's office.

Method of completion

Completion can take place by personal attendance by the purchaser's solicitor, which may still happen where the offices are near each other. Where there is no such proximity, the purchaser's solicitor can appoint another firm which is sufficiently close to attend and complete as her agent. In such a case, the agent must be given detailed instructions as to exactly what is required to be done. This practice is even less likely to be encountered today than personal attendance.

By far the most usual practice is for the parties to complete by a combination of post and telephone, following the Law Society's Code for Completion by Post (*Guide*, p.466). A copy of the Code is contained in Appendix 5.

It is a recommended practice which will only apply where the respective solicitors have specifically agreed to use it. If it is adopted, any variation must be agreed in writing beforehand. The Code is incorporated into TransAction Protocol. It is important to note that it does involve the giving of professional undertakings.

The essence of the code is that the purchaser's solicitor appoints the vendor's solicitor to act as her agent (unpaid) to complete. Thus, the vendor's solicitor completes with herself acting as both vendor's solicitor and purchaser's solicitor's agent. The Law Society are able to take the view that acting for both vendor and purchaser to this extent does not necessarily involve a conflict of interest. If, during the completion process, a conflict did materialise the vendor's solicitor would have to halt matters and contact the purchaser's solicitor at once.

It is important that the purchaser's solicitor gives the vendor's solicitor detailed instructions as to what must be done on her behalf. The purchaser's solicitor will send the completion monies to the vendor's solicitor. This can be by banker's draft but is more likely to be by telegraphic transfer of funds between their respective banks.[8] The vendor's solicitor's bank will be instructed, by her, to inform her when the money arrives, whereupon it will be held by her to the order of the purchaser's solicitor pending completion. The vendor's solicitor can then complete, attending to all the matters instructed by the purchaser's solicitor, whereupon she will have at her own disposal the purchase monies (for use in a related purchase, for example) and will hold the conveyance or transfer and the other title documents as agent for the purchaser's solicitor. Confirmation that completion has taken place should be given immediately to the purchaser's solicitor.

TransAction Protocol provides:

'8.1. If completion is to be by post, the Law Society's Code for Completion shall be used, unless otherwise agreed.

8.2. As soon as practicable and not later than the morning of completion, the buyer's solicitor shall advise the seller's solicitor of the manner of transmission of the purchase money and of the steps taken to dispatch it.

On being satisfied as to the receipt of the balance of the purchase money, the seller's solicitor shall authorise release of the keys and notify the buyer's solicitor of release.'

One criticism of the Code which has been made is that it does not deal with the danger highlighted in *Edward Wong Finance Co. Ltd. v. Johnson, Stokes and Masters*[9]; that is that where completion takes place on the basis that part of the purchase money is to be passed on by the vendor's solicitor to the mortgagee in redemption of an outstanding mortgage, it does not guarantee that the vendor's solicitor has authority of the mortgagee to receive the money. It follows that if the vendor's solicitor absconds with the money the loss will be borne by the purchaser. Indeed, this risk exists whenever a purchaser's solicitor accepts the vendor's solicitor's undertaking to pay off an outstanding mortgage out of the proceeds of sale – it is not peculiar to the use of the Code; and it does not seem to be peculiar to Hong Kong conveyancing as the court saw it in *Wong*. To protect against the possibility of a negligence claim for allowing this to happen and to protect the client's money, there is not

---

[8]   For comment on possible delays under CHAPS (Clearing Houses Automatic Payment System) – important in the case of chain transactions – and recommendations of the Conveyancing Standing Committee of the Law Commission, see [1990] Conv. 145, (H.W. Wilkinson).

[9]   [1984] A.C. 296.

much point in asking (as recommended by the Code) the vendor's solicitor to confirm that she is the authorised agent of the outstanding mortgagee to receive the redemption money. A solicitor who is about to abscond with the money will hardly answer in the negative. The purchaser's solicitor should really either require the written authority of the lender to pay to the vendor's solicitor; or pay the part of the purchase money needed for redemption by draft in favour of the lender. The loss would then borne by the lender.

Question Suppose that the same solicitors (Moriarties) were acting for both Miss Obebe's purchaser and her vendor. Explain the steps by which postal completion using the Code would be effected.

Question Suppose that you are acting for the vendor of Blackacre and in the middle of completing under the Code. The purchasers, for whose solicitor you are acting as agent to complete under the Code, are Miss Highland and Mr Lowland. You suddenly notice that the transfer has not been executed by either of the purchasers. Does this matter? If it does, what should be done?

COMPLETION OF PURCHASE-RELATED MORTGAGE

Where the purchase is being financed in part by a mortgage of the new property, this new mortgage will have to be completed.   **14.12**

Where the same solicitor is acting for both purchaser/borrower and lender, as will normally be the case on a building society mortgage, she will be carrying out the steps already described on behalf of and with a duty to both. In addition, the following matters will need attending to either prior to or at completion:

Prior to completion she should have:

(a) sent a report on title to the lender and received the advance cheque (the amount of the advance less any deduction in respect of any retention, insurance premiums payable, etc) in time to clear it through the client account ready for completion;

(b) prepared the mortgage deed and arranged for the borrower to execute it;

(c) if it is an endowment mortgage, checked that the policy is in force, the insurers at risk, prepared (if required) an assignment of the policy to the lender and had it executed by the borrower and prepared a notice of assignment of the policy in duplicate to be sent to the insurance company after completion.

At completion:

(d) she should date the mortgage deed and any assignment of an endowment policy. The date will be the same as on the conveyance of the property.

All the matters attended to at completion on behalf of the purchaser will now be done on behalf of both the purchaser and the lender. The mortgagee needs to be satisfied that the title of the purchaser is secure so that, in turn, her own title as mortgagee will be secure.

The conveyance or transfer and the other title documents handed over by the vendor will be received on behalf of the mortgagee (in whose name the application for registration will be made). The executed mortgage will now be held on behalf of the mortgagee.

If the mortgagee is separately represented, the mortgagee's solicitor will have to send to the purchaser's solicitor, before completion, a completion statement showing the net amount of the advance that will be available. This will be the amount of the advance less any retention, insurance premiums and less the mortgagees solicitor's costs and disbursements. The latter will include the fees for registration and any stamp duty which matters will be attended to by the mortgagee's solicitor. The purchaser's solicitor will then have to obtain the balance necessary to complete as described above.

The mortgagee's solicitor may attend completion in person or appoint an agent, or ask the vendor's solicitor to act as agent to complete the mortgage under the Code for completion by post. Where the vendor or other agent acts as agent the advance money will have to be made available by draft or telegraphic transfer and detailed instructions given as to what is required. All the matters dealt with on behalf of the purchaser will have to be attended to on behalf of the mortgagee. The title documents and the mortgage (checked to see that it is in order and dated) will be handed to the mortgagee's solicitor.

CHAPTER 15

POST-COMPLETION STEPS

TIMOTHY RELAPSES

Timothy has completed on the Obebe sale. 'Plenty of time to register', he tells himself, feeling that such a momentous achievement entitles him to a few days off. 'Two months, otherwise the legal estate will revert to the vendor', he intones, fondly thinking that he is quoting his conveyancing lecturer. He is about to put the file away. 'Oh. Better do something about stamping. Let's see. What's the purchase price? £88,500 plus £1,500 for chattels. That's £90,000. Its beyond the £30,000 exemption. So that makes stamp duty at 1% on an excess of £60,000 – just £600. And a PD stamp. 'The thought of PD stamping brings another thought to his muddled mind. 'Ah! I remember. Nowadays, the Land Registry does the stamping when it gets the documents for registration. Might as well get the papers off. He puts all the documents in a bundle, including the transfer, a letter of undertaking from Miss Mixford's solicitor to discharge an outstanding mortgage on the property and a printed form 1A (much of which, not seeming terribly applicable, he leaves blank); and gives instructions for them to be sent off to the Registry with a cheque for the Land Registry fee and stamp duty. And leaves the office, thinking that the noise, rather like an exasperated cat, is the pigeon which is wont to perch outside his window.

OLD JARNDYCE (THE EXASPERATED CAT)

Timothy will have to go. Porterhouse tie or not. There is more to post completion tasks than putting away the file and transferring costs from client account to the office account. Indeed in relation to registered title, the term 'completion' is a misnomer; the title of the purchaser is only completed by registration. What follows looks first at the possible duties of the vendor's solicitor and then at those of the purchaser's solicitor. Where there is a distinction between registered and unregistered land transactions this is pointed out.

Question Once again, what has Timothy done wrong? What should he have done in relation to stamping and registration? What stamp duty is payable on this transaction? Which Land Registry form should Timothy have used? List all the documents which should be sent to the Registry in this case.

15.1

15.2

15.3   DUTIES OF THE VENDOR'S SOLICITOR

Undertakings

15.3.1   The vendor's solicitor should comply with any undertakings given to discharge outstanding mortgages out of the proceeds of sale. After checking that it has been properly executed, each receipted mortgage or Form 53 should be forwarded to the vendor's solicitor; and an acknowledgement received in return to show that the undertaking has been fulfilled.

There may also be other undertakings as to the purchase monies. For example, a bridging loan may have been made by the client's bank or other lender to finance payment of the deposit or the completion of a purchase taking place before completion of a related sale. To cover such a loan the vendor's solicitor may have given a professional undertaking to forward the net proceeds of sale, if and when received, to the lender (Document 5.1.1.). The money now having been received, the solicitor should, after deducting all costs and disbursements, honour the undertaking according to its terms, again requiring a receipt.

Redemption of mortgage of endowment policy

15.3.2   The purchaser is not concerned with the mortgage of the policy (as opposed to the mortgage of the land – though they may be contained in the same deed and have to be redeemed together). The vendor's solicitor should take the necessary steps to see that the mortgage of the policy is properly redeemed; the policy reassigned to the client if the mortgage was created by assignment; and that notice of the discharge is given to and acknowledged by the insurance company (para.2.5.(1)(b)).

The client may be buying a new property also with the aid of an endowment mortgage using the same endowment policy. In this case, before completion, it will have been necessary to prepare a new assignment of the policy if required by the lender on the new property and notice of the new assignment to the insurance company. If the policy is not required for a new mortgage it will be sent to the client.

Estate agent's fees

15.3.3   A solicitor does not have implied authority of the client to pay the estate agent's fees out of the proceeds of sale. If, as is common, the agent submits her bill to the vendor's solicitor, the latter should take instructions from the client before paying it.

Cancellation and registration of central Land Charges registrations

This only applies to a conveyance of unregistered title. There may be entries on the register against the name of the vendor (or a previous title owner) which will have to be cleared by the vendor to give the purchaser the title to which she is entitled under the contract. Such entries should have been cancelled before completion, or the purchaser given an application for cancellation signed by the person who created the charge, or accompanied by sufficient evidence of the applicant's title to have the charge removed. In the case of a spouse's right of occupation under the Matrimonial Homes Act 1983 the appropriate form is form K 13. In any other case, application is made on form K 11.

15.3.4

Registration of a charge does not make valid interests which are otherwise invalid. But defunct entries can create problems when the purchaser comes to sell or (as will now be the usual case) to apply for registration of title. The purchaser should ensure that all such entries are cancelled. If mortgages have been registered (puisne mortgages or general equitable charges) the mortgagee should be required to sign an application for cancellation when the mortgage is redeemed.

Conversely, a sale of part may give rise to charges in favour of the vendor which (under the unregistered title system) should be registered against the purchaser. In particular, this applies to restrictive covenants reserved over the part purchased in favour of the part retained. It would also apply for example if the contract gave an option to repurchase the land. These should have had their place on the register booked, as it were, by registration of a priority notice before completion and be actually registered pursuant to the priority notice immediately after completion (para.13.6).

In practice, this will only now apply in the relatively few cases where the transaction does not lead to compulsory first registration of title – for example, on the grant or a lease for not more than 21 years or the assignment of such a lease; or on a gift of the land. For the position where it does lead to compulsory first registration, see below, para.15.4.2(c).

Accounting to the client

The client should be informed immediately that completion has taken place. If not already done, a statement of account (para.14.8.2) should be sent to her together with a cheque for any monies payable to her. The amount due from her to the firm by way of costs or disbursements will then be transferred from client account to the office account.

15.3.5

15.4   DUTIES OF THE PURCHASER'S SOLICITOR:
                                    UNREGISTERED TITLE

Stamping

15.4.1   This has been dealt with (para.10.7.1).

Registration

15.4.2   (See also para.7.5.1.) On a conveyance on sale of the freehold the
purchaser's solicitor will now have to apply for first registration of title.
First registration by the purchaser is now compulsory on a purchase of an
unregistered freehold, within two months of the conveyance.

(a) Procedure

Application is on printed form 1B when made by a solicitor or
licensed conveyancer (1A if made by the applicant in person). The form
must state what class of title is sought; normally this will be absolute.
Form 1B includes a lengthy certificate to be signed by the solicitor as to
the soundness of the title, stating, where application follows from a
purchase, that she has investigated the title in the usual way and made all
necessary searches: setting out all incumbrances not mentioned in the
deed inducing registration (in the present context the conveyance); the
capacity of the applicant (beneficial owner or whatever other); confirming
that she is not aware of any doubt or question affecting the title or
adverse claim; and stating that she believes the applicant to be in
undisputed possession.

The form must also, in the case of joint purchasers, state whether the
survivor can give a receipt for capital monies (para.7.7(c)).

> 'A title should always be prepared for registration as if it were
> being prepared for examination by a purchaser, with full
> information on any points on which a well advised purchaser
> would raise requisitions.'[1]

The following documents should accompany the application:

- The completed application form.

- All the original deeds and documents of title (including a normal
examined abstract or epitome and marked copies) which the applicant
has in her possession or under her control, including the contract,

---

[1]   Ruoff & Roper, para.12-04.

preliminary enquiries, requisitions, replies and searches and the conveyance to the applicant.

– A copy of the conveyance including any plan, each being certified as a true copy of the original.

– Sufficient particulars, by plan or otherwise, to enable the Registry to identify the property on the ordnance survey map.

– If the applicant is a company, certified copies of its certificate of incorporation, memorandum and articles of association and particulars of other charges and debentures it has created. In practice the Registry accepts a certificate by the solicitor as to these matters.

– If the land has been mortgaged by the applicant, the original mortgage or charge and a certified copy.

– A list in triplicate of all the documents delivered with the application. The first is returned to the applicant's solicitor by way of acknowledgement of receipt; the second is filed at the Registry; the third is returned on completion of registration to show which documents have been retained in the Registry and which are being returned to the applicant.

– A completed P. D. form where no *ad valorem* stamp duty is payable.

– A cheque for the fee drawn in favour of H.M. Land Registry.

The Registry will examine the title contained in the application and, if necessary raise requisitions. When the Registrar is satisfied with the title, she will register it, with its own register, unique title number and title plan and whatever class of title is found to be appropriate. The new register of title is designed to reflect, in registered title format, the state of the unregistered title at its last moment of existence.

The land certificate for the title will be prepared and, if there is no mortgage, sent to the applicant's solicitor. If there is a mortgage, the land certificate will be retained in the Registry and a charge certificate prepared for that charge and sent to the chargee. A slightly modified charge certificate will be prepared for each of any second or subsequent mortgage and sent to the chargee.

The Registry will return all those documents not to be retained in the Registry to the applicant's solicitor having first, as a guard against fraud, placed its official stamp on the conveyance to the purchaser. Since a search of the public index register by a future purchaser (being sold the land as unregistered) would reveal that the land was then registered, fraud would be difficult in the face of a competent lawyer.

Under Land Registration Rules 1925, Rule 42, the registration, when completed, takes effect as at the date of the lodging of the application. This is therefore a crucial date. From that moment, on the assumption that the title is accepted for registration by the Registry, the land in effect becomes registered and ceases to be unregistered land.

(b) Mortgage financed purchases

Where the purchase is financed in part by a mortgage of the purchased property, the purchaser will be mortgaging unregistered land, although at a time when it is, by reason of the purchase, due to be registered. The title of the mortgagee will in the first instance be governed by unregistered title principles, but affected by the rules governing first registration.

In this situation the purchaser cannot apply for registration since the title deeds will have been taken by the mortgagee to complete its security (although the same solicitor is likely to be acting for both of them). The application for registration of both the purchase and the mortgage will therefore be made in the name of the mortgagee accompanied by all the documents listed above. Where the mortgagee is separately represented all these documents will have to be handed over to the mortgagee at completion (if not before).

Rule 72 of the Land Registration Rules[2] provides that any person who has the right to apply for registration as first proprietor can deal with the land before she herself is registered as proprietor in the manner and subject to the conditions which would be applicable if she were in fact registered proprietor. At least until an application for registration has been lodged, the land is still unregistered and in general subject to unregistered rules; but from the completion of the purchase giving rise to first registration, it can in general be dealt with as though it were already registered. An application to register any dealing by the presumptive first proprietor cannot be accepted by the Registry until the application to register the first proprietor has been received. However, under Rule 73(3) a chargee can lodge an application to register the proper applicant for first registration – i.e. the purchaser. Thus it is that the mortgagee's solicitor will apply to register both the title of the purchaser and the mortgage.

(c) Other interests created before first registration

The principles just mentioned apply to any transaction by the purchaser prior to first registration of title. In effect the system allows the purchaser to exercise all the rights of ownership in the period between completion of the purchase and registration and for any such transaction to be incorporated into the new register. For example, purchaser P1, after completion of her purchase but before registration, might want to sub-sell the land to P2. The sub-sale transaction will proceed in the same way as an ordinary unregistered sale of land transaction (which it is) with investigation of title as such down to P1's application to register (which

---

2   Made under Land Registration Act 1925, s.123(2).

should be required by special condition in the contract, if not then already lodged). The transfer to P2 may be in the form of an unregistered conveyance or, under Rule 72, in the form of a registered land transfer at the option of the purchaser (who drafts the conveyance subject to any provision in the contract). P2 will need to have clear searches in the Central Land Charges Registry down to the date of P1's application to register. An official Land Registry search should be made to cover the period from the lodging of the application to register. This search is applied for on printed form 94A (94B(FR) if in respect of part of the land in a pending first registration) and gives the same protection and priority as a search against a title already registered. Upon completion of her purchase, P2 will apply to be registered sending the transfer to herself to the Registry and, in fact, by virtue of Rule 72(3), will be deemed to be the applicant for first registration and, on registration, will be registered as first proprietor.

On such a sub-sale, the vendor will not be able to produce the original documents of title (being at the Registry), and a special condition may have to be drafted into the contract in something like the following terms:

'The vendor has made application to H.M. Land Registry for the registration of herself as proprietor of the property on first registration of title thereto. The vendor will deduce title by producing to the purchaser copies of all documents which are part of the title each with an original marking by a solicitor of examination against the original together with a schedule of such documents receipted by the H.M. Land Registry. The purchaser will not be entitled to production or delivery of the originals of such documents nor any acknowledgement whatsoever in respect thereof.'

Question If the Standard Conditions are being used, to what extent, if at all, is there any need for adding a special condition such as the above? Consider particularly, Standard Conditions 4.2.3 and 6.5. (and para.15.5.2 below).

Of course, if for any reason P1's title proves unacceptable to the Registry or is given a less than absolute title, P2's title will suffer the same fate. If P2 wishes to protect her contract prior to completion and registration she will have, P1's application having been lodged, to register a caution at the Land Registry.

Where a sub-sale takes place without any conveyance to the sub-vendor, (i.e. if the conveyance is made direct from the original vendor to the sub-purchaser) then P2 will in fact be the one to apply for first registration. Until that conveyance there will be no event giving rise to compulsory registration.

Similar principles would apply if, for example, P1, prior to her registration, created a second mortgage of the property.

As mentioned earlier, on a sale of part, the conveyance may contain restrictive covenants imposed on the part sold (due therefore for first registration) for the benefit of the part retained. These cannot be registered as land charges under the Land Charges Act 1972 which does not apply to a land charge created by an instrument giving rise to compulsory first registration (s.14(3)). On registration of the land, the burden of the covenants will automatically be entered on the charges register of the new registered title. Prior to application for registration of the conveyance they would presumably be protected (against the purchase-linked mortgagee for example) by the doctrine of notice.

Central Land Charges Register

15.4.3   If the title is unregistered, the purchaser may have registered charges on behalf of the purchaser – in particular an estate contract to protect the purchaser's contract and a purchaser's lien for the deposit if held by an agent for the vendor – class Ciii land charge. These should be cancelled.

On a sale of part, new charges may have been created by the conveyance for the benefit of the purchaser over the vendor's retained land – particularly restrictive covenants. As the title of the part retained will normally remain unregistered such charges will have to be registered in the Central Land Charges Register against the vendor's name. The protection of interests burdening the part sold (which will be subject to first registration) for the benefit of the part retained has been considered.

Custody of title documents

15.4.4   Normally, the process of first registration of title, already described, will have to be pursued. If it is not, if for example, the transaction is a gift of the land, then after stamping if necessary, the instructions of the client (donee in the case of a gift) should be sought as to custody; the client being warned if necessary of the importance of keeping them in safe custody. If the client is simultaneously mortgaging the land, the mortgagee, as first mortgagee, will be entitled to possession of the title deeds. The solicitor holding them for the mortgagee should forward them to the mortgagee or otherwise deal with them as instructed. Where the title is subject to first registration, the land or charge certificate will be dealt with as in the case of an already registered title (below). Deeds should only be released against a schedule, a copy of the schedule being receipted and returned by the recipient.

Endowment mortgage

If there is a mortgage of an endowment policy related to the purchase, notice of the mortgage of the policy in duplicate should be sent to the insurance company for one copy of the notice to be receipted and returned to be placed with the title documents. **15.4.5**

Registration at Companies Registry

If the purchaser is a company buying with the aid of a loan secured whether by fixed or floating charge on land, the particulars of the charge must be delivered to the Registrar of companies for registration within 21 days on form 47. This is in addition to any registration at the Land Registry or Land Charges Registry. Failure to register with the Registrar of companies makes the lender an unsecured creditor for the debt in the event of liquidation. The company's solicitor should either deliver the particulars or arrange for them to be delivered by the lender's solicitor. **15.4.6**

Notice to tenants

If the property is subject to tenancies, notice of the change of landlord should be given to the tenants. This is particularly important in the case of residential tenancies to comply with s.3 of the Landlord and Tenant Act 1985 (para.14.6). **15.4.7**

Reporting and accounting to the client

The solicitor should immediately report to the client that completion has taken place. If not already done, a statement of account should be sent to the client. **15.4.8**

DUTIES OF PURCHASER'S SOLICITOR: REGISTERED TITLE

15.5

Stamping

On a transfer of registered title there is a fairly tight time schedule. The transfer has to be stamped within 30 days of execution. Application for registration needs to be made within the 30 working days priority period from the date of the pre-completion official search. If stamp duty on any document requires adjudication (and in any case of doubt the **15.5.1**

Registrar will insist on adjudication) and this is likely to take a long time, the document and a certified copy of it should be sent to the Registry with the application and a request to return the original immediately, and an undertaking to return it to the Registry after being stamped. The application will then be entered and held over until the stamped document has been returned.

Registration of dealings with registered land

15.5.2   Any disposition of registered land capable of substantive registration must be completed by registration.[3] Thus, any transfer of the freehold (not just on sale), leases if registrable, mortgages and the express grant of easements must be registered in the appropriate way.

There is no time limit, although until registration the disponee will not acquire the legal estate and will have only a minor interest, though this may be protected as overriding if coupled with actual occupation. In this sense, in relation to registered land, the term 'completion' is a misnomer. It is a stage in the transfer of title to the purchaser. Moreover, if the application to register is not made within the 30 working day protection period of an official search of the register, protection of the search will be lost. A new search can be done, but it will not prolong the protection period of the original search.

(a) Procedure

The purchaser must make an application for registration to the appropriate District Registry accompanied by the following documents:

– The transfer and its plan, if any, and also, if it imposes restrictive covenants, a certified copy of both.

– The land certificate or alternatively (if there are any outstanding charges) the charge certificate for any registered charge. If the land certificate is on deposit at the Registry – for example, if it is a sale of part of the land in a title – its deposit number, obtained from the vendor, must be quoted.

– A form 53 or other proper discharge of any registered charge.

– Documentation to remove any other adverse entries on the register which are to be removed – for example, an application by a spouse to cancel a notice under the Matrimonial Homes Act 1983 (form 202).

– Application in printed form A4 (if a transfer of the whole land in the title); or printed form A5 (if a transfer of part of the land in a title).

---

3   Land Registration Act 1925, ss.18, 19.

- A cheque for the Land Registry fee.

- If no *ad valorem* stamp duty is payable, a completed PD form.

If the application has to be sent off before receipt of a form 53 from the vendor's solicitor in discharge of a charge pursuant to that solicitor's undertaking, the application should be sent with a copy of the undertaking, to preserve the transferee's priority and the form 53 forwarded when received.

Assuming that the documents are in order, the transferee will be entered on the register as the new proprietor, the land certificate amended and brought up to date and sent to the proprietor. If there is a charge the land certificate will be retained in the Registry and an up-to-date charge certificate issued to the chargee.

On a sale of part of the land in a title, the land sold will be removed from the vendor's title and an amended certificate sent to her (or charge certificate to the chargee). The property register of the retained land will contain a note that the land edged green on the filed plan has been removed from the title and registered under a new title whose title number is shown in green on the filed plan. A new title will be created for the purchaser and the land or charge certificate issued as above.

(b) Purchase-linked mortgage

The legal estate is not vested in the purchaser until she is registered as proprietor; although once this does happen it is deemed to be effective as from the date on which the application was delivered to the Registry.[4] This by itself would make it difficult for the purchaser to deal with the land between completion of the transfer and registration. However, s.37(1) and (2) of the Land Registration Act 1925 provides that a person who has become entitled to be registered as proprietor of the registered land (or a charge) by reason of death of the proprietor or a disposition by the proprietor, can deal with the land as if she were registered. A disposition made in such a case will, by subsection (2) have the same effect as if made by a registered proprietor. (Compare the position of a person entitled to be registered as first proprietor - para.7.5.2.)

This means that the purchaser can, immediately upon taking a transfer of the land, effectively execute a mortgage, as happens in an unregistered transaction. The difference is that the mortgagee will not actually get legal title until the purchase and the mortgage have in fact been registered; and if the purchase were not to be registered for any reason then the mortgagee would not get legal title. The application for registration will

---

[4]   Land Registration Rules 1925 as amended, Rule 83(2).

be made by the mortgagee's solicitor (who may in fact be the same person as the purchaser's solicitor) who will have received the transfer, the mortgage and the other documents of title on completion of the purchase and mortgage. The Registry will enter the new mortgage in the charges register and issue the charge certificate to the mortgagee. Other dealings can be carried out by the purchaser prior to completion of her registration, in a similar way. But there are two points to consider.

If the purchaser wishes to deal with the land by, for example, sub-selling, after application for, but before registration of, her title, she will not be able to produce the transfer to herself (which will be at the Registry) to the sub-purchaser. There will, of course, be no problem about producing office copies; but they will show the purchaser's own vendor and not the purchaser as proprietor. Further, s.110(5) of the Land Registration Act 1925 provides that notwithstanding any stipulation to the contrary in the contract, the purchaser can insist on the vendor getting herself registered or procuring a transfer from the registered proprietor.

It will therefore be necessary to deal with these points by special condition in the contract. For example:

'The seller has made application to HM Land Registry for the registration of himself as proprietor. If the seller's title to the property is not registered before completion then the title shall consist of office copy Land Registry entries and a copy of the transfer from the registered proprietor to the seller with an original marking by a solicitor of examination against the original. If the buyer requires the seller's title to be registered before completion then the buyer shall pay interest to the seller on the balance of the purchase price at the contract rate from the contractual completion rate until the date of actual completion.'[5]

As the title is registered, the sub-purchaser will have no problem in making an official search against the title.

Registered land: cancellation of entries and new entries

15.5.3   The purchaser's solicitor may have protected the interest of the purchaser against the vendor by entries on the register prior to completion - for example, the estate contract or the purchaser's lien for the deposit where held by an agent for the vendor. These will be defunct on completion. Their cancellation by the purchaser's solicitor will be dealt with in the purchaser's application for registration of the transfer.

---

5   See F. Silverman, *Standard Conditions of Sale* (4th ed.) p.231.

If, on a sale of part, the transfer creates incumbrances over the part retained for the benefit of the part sold, these will be noted automatically against the register of the retained land. On a sale of part the purchaser will need a special condition in the contract that the land certificate will be placed on deposit at the Registry and the deposit number supplied to the purchaser.

Custody of title documents

Where the title is already registered or becomes registered as a result **15.5.4** of the transaction, and there is no mortgage, a land certificate will be received from the Registry by the purchaser's solicitor. After checking, the instructions of the client should be ascertained as to custody, again warning, if necessary, of the importance of safe custody. If there is a related mortgage, the charge certificate will be received by the solicitor acting for the chargee. After checking, this should be forwarded to the chargee or otherwise dealt with in accordance with her instructions.

In all these cases, whether registered or unregistered title, there may be additional documents, not title documents as such, which should be kept with the title documents – for example, the NHBC documentation in the case of a newly built house.

Again in all cases, a schedule of the title documents and any other documents being held with them should be prepared in duplicate. Whoever they are handed over to should be required to receipt and return one copy of the schedule to be placed on the file.

Endowment mortgages; registration at Companies Registry; reporting and accounting to client

With these matters, the position is the same as for unregistered title. **15.5.5**

CHAPTER 16

REMEDIES

OLD JARNDYCE AWAKENS

Timothy has vanished, dematerialised. Just as well. He was about to learn about remedies; the post on his desk includes four writs for professional negligence, two notices to complete and a letter from an angry Fancy French (abandoned by Sam) who had just been served with a compulsory purchase order on 24 De Lucy Mount.

16.1

Miss Pinky is back at her desk in the corner so all is well with the conveyancing department and post-feminism. As Old Jarndyce nods off again – and we will follow his dreams no further – Mr Perky will talk about remedies. Miss Pinky will nod in agreement.

THE GENERAL PRINCIPLES

In general, although the terminology tends to be different, and as a result of more recent cases and the intervention of statute[1], a breach of contract for the sale of land is subject to the same principles as any breach of contract. Unless stated otherwise, what follows applies equally to unregistered and registered land and, although for convenience generally viewing the purchaser as the aggrieved party, applies equally to both vendor and purchaser. A purchaser (more so than a vendor, who in general is only concerned to get the money on time and has ample security for performance in the deposit) may have complaint for many reasons. The property may not be as it was described in negotiations or the contract; the vendor may not be ready to complete on time or unable or unwilling to complete at all; a defect in the title may be discovered; the purchaser may find the cellar full of junk, or a granny (her again!) left behind in the attic; she may find a neighbour claiming ownership of the ancient yew hedge which finally persuaded her to buy the property; or that the vendor has uprooted the hedge and taken it away; and so on.

16.2

---

[1] Note particularly, the abolition of the Rule in *Bain v. Fothergill* by s.3 of the Law of Property (Miscellaneous Provisions) Act 1989; *Johnson v. Agnew* [1980] A.C. 367; and *Raineri v. Miles* [1979] 3 All E.R. 763.

The following is the basic framework of principles which will determine the legal position.

(a) The purchaser may have a remedy for misrepresentation; that is a statement of fact outside but inducing the contract. This has been dealt with (para.4.4.1).

(b) There may have been a breach of contract. A breach may be breach of an express term or of an implied term. If the special conditions provide for completion on 5 January and the vendor fails to complete on that date, that is a breach of express term. If a binding restrictive covenant is discovered, which has not been disclosed in the contract, that is breach of the implied contractual obligation to convey the property free of latent incumbrances other than those disclosed in the contract.[2]

A misrepresentation may be incorporated as a term into the contract, in which case the purchaser will have claim for both misrepresentation and breach.

(c) To decide whether there has been a breach of contract you have to first decide what the terms of the contract are; what those terms mean; and then whether or not there has been a breach.

(d) Although the language of the books, the courts and, indeed, the Standard Conditions persists in the confusion, a distinction needs to be made between two meanings of the word 'rescission':

(i) The right to rescind (generally for misrepresentation) being the right of the innocent party to treat the contract as void *ab initio*; and, consequentially, for each party to be restored as far as possible to their pre-contract position (*restitutio in integrum*). The vendor will recover any documents handed over; the purchaser any deposit paid. The right to rescind does not itself give any right to damages for loss of bargain; although, distinctly, the purchaser may be able to claim damages for fraud or under the Misrepresentation Act 1967.

(ii) The right to treat the contract as discharged for repudiatory breach by the other party – in conventional contract law language, for breach of condition. As with the right to rescind, this is a right, not an obligation. The innocent party can accept the repudiation putting an end to the contract or choose to keep it alive and seek specific performance. In either case she will be entitled to damages for loss of bargain for the breach.

---

2   If, as under Standard Condition 3.1.1., the contract states the property to be free from incumbrances, the breach is of an express term.

(e) Any breach of contract will fall into one of two categories:

(i) A repudiatory breach as just described.

(ii) Any other breach – in conventional contract language, a breach of warranty – which will entitle the innocent party to damages but not entitle her to treat the contract as at an end. She can still be forced by an action for specific performance to complete.

Although all the terms of a contract (as with the Standard Conditions of Sale) are commonly referred to as conditions, in relation to remedies, they may have to be classified as conditions or warranties; that is the court may have to decide whether or not the breach of any particular 'condition' is a repudiatory breach.

It needs to be noted, and is often demonstrated in the reports, that, when applied to any particular situation, these principles may face the innocent party with a difficult and risky choice. V is in breach of contract. P decides that V's breach is serious enough to be repudiatory; accepts the repudiation, giving notice that she is treating the contract as discharged; and refuses to complete. If the court subsequently decides that V's breach was not repudiatory, P will have committed a repudiatory breach by refusing to complete and will have made herself liable to pay damages.

(f) In the case of a repudiatory breach the innocent party will be entitled to treat the contract as discharged and claim damages. Alternatively, she can refuse to accept the repudiation, and seek specific performance with an appropriate reduction in the purchase price. Specific performance, being a discretionary remedy, may be refused by the court (for example, where it would cause hardship to the defendant). In this case the plaintiff will have to be satisfied with damages.

(g) The above rights and remedies are subject to any express terms of the contract. However, equity can override the terms of the contract in that it can and may refuse to order specific performance against a party even though the terms of the contract require that party to complete. And in such a case, there is statutory power to order the return of a deposit to the purchaser; though it cannot award damages against the terms of the contract (see para.10.5.1).

TWO RECENT CASES

Some of the above principles are illustrated by two recent cases. In *Kelsie Graham v. Lurline Eugenie Pitkin*[3] V and her husband agreed in May

16.3

---

[3]   [1992] 1 W.L.R. 403 (P.C.).

1980 to sell property to P. The contract contained a condition stating that the contract was subject to P obtaining a mortgage from a specified building society for $19,000.

The building society agreed to lend $16,000 subject to survey and title. Breaches of restrictive covenants affecting the property were discovered by the building society which refused to make the advance unless these were condoned by the dominant owner or rectified.

In March 1981 V (her husband having died) informed P that she (V) was not prepared to rectify the breaches of covenant and that P must decide whether she wanted to proceed or to treat the contract as rescinded by mutual consent. P responded that she was still anxious to acquire the property and would write further within seven days. She did not; and, on July 9, V (without serving any notice to complete - as to which see below) purported to rescind the contract. On July 23, P stated that she wanted to complete, served 14 days notice to complete on V, and sued for specific performance.

Question   Assuming that the Standard Conditions applied to the above contract, would the discovery of breaches of restrictive covenants affecting the property amount to a breach of contract by V? Note that this is not a case of discovery of undisclosed restrictive covenants, but of breaches of known covenants.

In deciding for P, the court applied the following principles:

(a) The condition as to a mortgage was a term of the contract. It was not a condition precedent. A condition precedent is a specified event the happening (or non-happening as the case may be) of which automatically puts an end to the contract. It will be as if the contract had never been made. On the other hand a condition, in the sense of a term of the contract, which is solely for the benefit of one party can be waived by that party. P had waived this condition.

(b) A contract can be rescinded (i.e. terminated) by mutual agreement; but it cannot be terminated unilaterally by one party in the absence of misrepresentation, breach, etc by the other party. P had not agreed to V's suggestion to treat the contract as rescinded by mutual consent.

(c) V had purported to treat the contract as discharged for P's delay in completing. There had been delay. P had failed to complete at the contractual completion date and was therefore in breach of contract. The issue was whether this breach by delay was a repudiatory breach entitling V to treat the contract as discharged. It was held that it was not (see below). P was therefore entitled to specific performance.

In *Newbery v. Turngiant*[4] there was a contract dated 8 December 1987 for the sale of agricultural land by the plaintiff vendors to the defendant purchasers. Clause 5 of the contract provided that the Law Society's general conditions of sale (1984 revision) [one of the precursors of the Standard Conditions] were to apply 'so far as not inconsistent with the terms of the agreement'. (Compare printed special condition 1(a) of the agreement incorporating the Standard Conditions (para.5.1.6).) Condition 22 of the Law Society's general conditions provided that in the event of late completion 'the party in default' would be liable to pay compensation calculated at the 'contract rate' as defined in those conditions.

Clause 8 of the agreement provided that at the date fixed for completion (December 5, 1988) 'the balance of the purchase monies shall be paid and if not so paid shall bear interest at the rate of 5% above the base lending rate from time to time of Lloyds Bank plc'. Clearly, on the face of it this was much harsher to the purchasers, making them liable to pay interest regardless of whose fault the delay was.

A pre-completion search in the Land Charges Register by the purchasers (it being unregistered title) revealed two estate contracts (Civ's) and a general equitable charge (Ciii) registered against the vendors. What then happened is an interesting illustration of such a conveyancing situation. Office copies of the entries were obtained. One of the estate contracts was clearly defunct and cancellation by those who had originally entered it was obtained without difficulty. This does however emphasise the need to keep the Register (whether of land charges or the register of title in the case of registered land) clear of defunct entries. The office copies showed the other estate contract and the general equitable charge to have been registered by an Exeter firm of solicitors on behalf of a company called Bayswater. The Exeter firm, on being contacted, indicated that the partner who had initialled the application for the charges to be registered had retired; they no longer had the file; and no one in the office knew anything about the matter. A search against Bayswater in the Companies Registry revealed that Bayswater had been dissolved in 1986. The vendors' solicitors offered to complete on the basis of their undertaking to 'to use their best endeavours to get the entries removed'. This was (understandably) not acceptable to the purchasers' solicitors who wanted an unconditional undertaking to get them cancelled. Finally, the company being dissolved, the Registry was persuaded to cancel the entries (Note: there was the possibility, which concerned the Registry, that the company had assigned the benefit of these interests before its dissolution). Completion then took place on January 20 1989, 46 days late.

---

[4]   (1991) 63 P. & C.R. 458.

The vendors were claiming that interest was payable to them for the period of delay under clause 8 of the agreement. The purchasers were claiming that condition 22 of the Law Society's conditions, incorporated by clause 5 of the agreement applied, which entitled them to compensation for the period of delay because it was due to the vendor's default.

The Court of Appeal decided the following points, finding for the vendors:

(a) Although clause 8 of the agreement was on the face of it absolute, it had to be construed in the light of equitable rules to mean that interest would be payable by the purchasers if the delay was the purchasers' fault or no one's fault, but not if the fault was the vendors'. To this extent clause 8 was inconsistent and prevailed over clause 5 and the Law Society's condition 22, in that the latter did not make the purchasers liable to pay for the delay in a no-fault situation.

(b) The vendors were not at fault. They had acted promptly to get the offending entries cancelled once they had learnt from the purchasers of their existence on the register.

(c) The last point indicates that the vendors' solicitors had not checked the land charges Register before drafting the contract. However, the court decided, under the rule in *Bain v. Fothergill* (which still applied as the events occurred before abolition of the rule by the Law of Property (Miscellaneous Provisions) Act 1989 taking effect on 26 September 1989 – see below) a vendor is not at fault if the failure to complete is due to a defect in title.

(d) It followed that since the delay was not due to the vendors' fault, they were entitled to interest under clause 8 of the agreement.

This case concerned the consequences of delay in completion and of defects in title. We will now turn to these and other specific breaches that might occur.

BREACH DUE TO DEFECT IN TITLE

16.4   If the vendor is not able, at the contractual completion date, to convey (or require someone else to convey) the property with the title agreed in the contract (subject only to patent defects) she will be in breach of contract. As with any breach of contract the fact that the vendor did not know of a defect or (on learning of it) made every effort to get it removed, is no defence to a claim for breach of contract. This is subject, as always, to any express terms in the contract. Note here, in particular, Standard Condition 3.1.2(c) under which the property is sold subject to any incumbrance which 'the seller does not and could not know about'. The emphasis here must be on 'could not'. This condition does not relieve the vendor of the obligation to make a proper check on her title before drafting the contract.

If the defect is substantial so as to deprive the purchaser substantially of the title agreed under the contract, the breach will be a repudiatory one and the purchaser entitled to treat the contract as discharged and claim damages. It should be stressed that the purchaser does not have to serve notice to complete in such a case before taking this step and, indeed, it seems that she can treat the contract as discharged even before the completion date if it is clear that the vendor will or will not be able to cure the defect by that date.

If the title defect is not substantial, the purchaser will be obliged to complete and will only be entitled to damages in respect of the defect. No doubt if the facts show that the defect can be cured, though only in time for late completion, this will normally mean that the defect is not substantial; the purchaser will have to complete and claim compensation for the delay. It will be otherwise if time for completion is of the essence (see below) in which case the title must be in order by the completion date.

In the light of the discussion of *Newbery* above, mention needs to be made of the rule in *Bain v. Fothergill*. This rule was abolished by s.3 of the Law of Property (Miscellaneous Provisions) Act 1989. It supposedly arose from the difficulties, prior to the simplification of conveyancing, of a vendor knowing the state of her title. What it provided (as Old Jarndyce understands it - or would if he were not again snoring in his chair) was that if the vendor's breach consisted of a title defect, the purchaser could not recover damages for loss of bargain, but could only recover any deposit paid with interest and her costs of investigating title. In other words it limited the damages recoverable but did not annul the breach or make the vendor without fault. If this is correct, it means that the court in *Newbery* misapplied the rule; the vendors were in 'default'; the purchasers therefore not obliged to pay interest under clause 8; and the vendors should have paid compensation under clause 5 and the Law Society's general conditions (which to that extent were *not* inconsistent with clause 8).

However, the rule has been abolished. Whatever the position before its abolition, it means now that, in the words of Dillon L.J. in *Newbery* (p.470):

'... the vendor will be in default if he fails to clear before the contractual completion date any defect in his title which becomes apparent between contract and completion, of which he has been unaware at the date of the contract, however reasonable his conduct may have been. Any prudent vendor will therefore have, in his own interests, to search in the land charges register for unexpected registrations against his title before he exchanges contracts of sale.'

It should be added that a vendor will also need to be satisfied that adverse charges are not going to be registered between contract and completion – the possibility of a non-owning spouse registering a right of occupation may be relevant here. This, of course, underlines what has been stressed earlier in this book; that is, the need for the vendor's solicitor to check title before drafting the contract. And it is in line with the modern trend for the vendor to provide the proof of title including searches at the time of submitting a draft contract.

MISDESCRIPTION

16.5   A misdescription is a false statement of fact as to the property contained in the contract. It is to be distinguished from a misrepresentation which is a false statement of fact outside but inducing the contract. A common example is where the area of the property given in the contract is incorrect. Another example, from a well known case, is where the property was described as having a 'valuable prospective building element' whereas an underground culvert created a substantial drawback to building.[5]

Any misdescription is a breach of contract. The contract is, in effect, giving a contractual guarantee that the description is correct.

Traditionally and judicially, misdescription has been treated separately from other breaches such as title defects. Traditionally, the standard contract was divided into two parts: the Particulars of Sale containing the legal and physical description of the property and the Conditions of Sale dealing with proof of title and all the other matters. This is not now usual. Another reason for drawing the distinction was the application of the rule in *Bain v. Fothergill* to title defects but not misdescription and also because at least at common law a misdescription, however insubstantial, entitled the purchaser to withdraw from the contract.

It is probably true to say that now there is no reason for making a general distinction between misdescription and other breaches of contract. As with a title defect, if the misdescription is substantial it will be a repudiatory breach entitling the purchaser to treat the contract as discharged and claim damages. If it is not substantial, the purchaser will be entitled to damages only. Of course, if the terms of the contract deal expressly with misdescription, the meaning of those terms may have to be identified. In this context, it is convenient to turn to the provisions of the Standard Conditions dealing with remedies.

---

5   *Re Puckett & Smith's Contract* [1902] 2 Ch. 258.

Standard Conditions 7.1. and 7.2. are set out in Appendix 3. The following points should be noted.

(a) The condition applies to both misrepresentation and to misdescription or any other misleading or inaccurate plan or statement within the contract.

(b) Although it refers to 'omissions' it seems that this only covers what in conventional contract language is known as a half-truth; that is where something actually said is rendered inaccurate by something not said.

(c) Insofar as it relates to misrepresentation, it is subject to s.3 of the Misrepresentation Act 1967 and the test of reasonableness in s.11 of that Act. The 1967 Act does not apply to statements which are within the contract. But the rule in *Flight v. Booth*[6] does apply. This is that the courts will not allow a term in the contract to deprive the purchaser of the right to treat the contract as discharged where completion would force on her to take a property subject to a substantial misdescription or other defect. Standard Condition 7.1.3. does not attempt to do this and would not fall foul of the rule.

(d) In dealing with the remedial consequences of error or omission, Standard Condition 7.1.2. creates some confusion by dealing with misrepresentation and misdescription as one. To take them, here, separately:

(i) Misrepresentation. Standard Condition 7.1.2. gives a right to damages where the difference between the description or value of the property as represented and as it is in fact, is 'material'. A person claiming for misrepresentation has in any case to show that the misrepresentation was material. Under the common law and the Misrepresentation Act 1967, damages can only be claimed for fraudulent or negligent misrepresentation. Standard Condition 7.1.2. contains no such limitation and would seem to allow damages even for entirely innocent misrepresentation.

On the other hand, Standard Condition 7.1.3. limits the right to rescind to cases of fraud and recklessness and cases where the property is in fact 'substantially' different from the property as represented. Apart from provision in the contract, a party can rescind for any material misrepresentation (subject to being awarded damages in lieu under the 1967 Act) and does not have to show that it was fraudulent, reckless or substantial. To this extent, the Standard Conditions restrict the right of the injured party. As stated above, such a clause is subject to the test of reasonableness under the 1967 Act.

---

6   (1834) 1 Bing. NC 370.

(ii) Misdescription. As already explained, if any plan or statement within the contract is misleading or inaccurate, this will be a breach of contract, entitling the injured party to damages, at least. Depending on what 'material' is taken to mean (and it is not defined in the Standard Conditions) Standard Condition 7.1.2. may exclude the right of the injured party to damages in some cases. If it means simply 'not trivial' it probably does not have much, if any, effect on the open contract position.

Where the claim is for misdescription or other breach of contract, the term 'rescission' in Standard Condition 7.1.3. would seem to mean 'the right to treat the contract as repudiated for breach'. Even in the absence of Standard Condition 7.1.3. the injured party would only be entitled to treat the contract as discharged for substantial breach. Standard Condition 7.1.3. seems, in effect, therefore simply to reflect the open contract position.

(e) Where a party has a right, but has not yet exercised that right, to rescind the contract (in either sense), the general principle is that the contract remains alive for the benefit of both parties.[7]

LATE COMPLETION

16.6   Under an open contract any delay in completion is a breach of contract and entitles the innocent party to damages – that is compensation for loss caused by the delay. This may entail identifying the time within which the contract requires each step to be taken and deciding who is responsible for the delay. If, for example, the vendor delays in approving the draft conveyance which delay, by knock-on effect, prevents the purchaser from engrossing and executing the conveyance in time for the agreed completion date, the delay is clearly to be laid at the vendor's door. Of course, even if all pre-completion steps have been taken on time, one of the parties may still for some reason fail to complete on time.

In practice, both parties may be guilty of delay in taking a step towards completion in the time allowed for it by the express or implied terms of the contract. Any such delay will be a breach and potentially give the one party a claim for damages against the other.

---

[7]   See *McGrath v. Shah* (1987) 57 P.& C.R. 452. Compare *Foran v. Wight* (1989) C.L.R. (High Court of Australia), where a statement by the vendors prior to the completion date (time being of the essence) that they would not be able to complete on time estopped them from later claiming that the purchasers themselves, who only rescinded two days after the completion date, would not have been able to complete on time.

Section 7.3. (Appendix 3) deals with the situation where completion is late. The effect is that if the delay is solely attributable to the time-default of one party, that party will have to pay compensation to the other for the period between contractual and actual completion date. Under Standard Condition 7.3.2. compensation is calculated at the contract rate (as defined in the Standard Conditions) on the purchase price (less any deposit paid if the purchaser is the paying party).

Where both parties have been guilty of time-default during the transaction, the party guilty of the longer total period of default will pay compensation to the other for the excess period. If the delay between contractual and actual completion date is less than the period of default – i.e. if lost time has been made up – compensation will only be paid for the lesser period.

Question Suppose a contract is made on 1 May by V to sell to P subject to the Standard Conditions of Sale. The agreed completion date is 1 June. The price is £95,000 and a 10% deposit is paid to a stakeholder. The contract rate is fixed in the contract at 10%. V delivers the evidence of title to P three weeks after exchange of contracts. P delivers requisitions on title to V 14 days after receiving the evidence of title. V replies immediately stating that the requisitions are out of time, but that, as a matter of courtesy and without in any way prejudicing her position, she will answer them. Ten days after this V does reply to them. Immediately on receipt of these replies P sends a draft conveyance to V for approval. V returns this approved to P by return of post. Five days after receipt of the approved draft, P sends the engrossment, executed by P, to V The day after receipt, V phones P to say that she is ready to complete and completion takes place the same day – 1 July.

Consider who is liable to pay compensation for the delay and how much. If you think it necessary to assume facts not given, state what facts you are assuming.

DELAY CAUSING DISCHARGE OF THE CONTRACT

The general principle is that, although delay is a breach of contract, it does not of itself entitle the innocent party to treat the contract as discharged. Failure to complete may of course be caused by some other factor such as a substantial title defect which is itself a repudiatory breach.

The innocent party can only treat the contract as discharged where time is, or has been made, of the essence. In a contract for the sale of land, time is presumed *not* to be of the essence. It will be of the essence from the start in two cases:

16.7

(a) By express declaration of the parties in the contract. The contract may actually state that time for completion is to be of the essence – or words to that effect. Or, a proper construction of the contract as a whole may show that the parties intended time to be of the essence. Conversely, it may show that time was not intended to be of the essence. For example, if there is provision that interest is to be paid for late completion, this will normally lead to the latter inference.

(b) By implication from the circumstances surrounding the contract. The circumstances surrounding the contract, rather than the language used by the parties in the contract, may lead to the conclusion that time was intended to be of the essence. Here, express provision would be needed to make time *not* of the essence. In the somewhat odd and somewhat old case of *Tilley v. Thomas*[8] time was held to be of the essence on the purchase of a house wanted for immediate occupation on the day possession was to be given under the contract. It would probably require very unusual circumstances for this to apply today. And Standard Condition 6.1.1. expressly makes time *not* of the essence until a completion notice has been served.

Where time is not of the essence by express provision or implication from the circumstances, it can be made of the essence by service of a notice to complete. Even in the absence of such notice one party may delay for so long, that the other is entitled to treat the contract as having been repudiated, not for the delay itself, but rather because delay is evidence of an intention not to perform the contract. 'Delay may be an ingredient in deciding whether a party in default does not intend to proceed and has repudiated the contract.'[9]

NOTICE TO COMPLETE

16.8   Under an open contract, if one of the parties fails to complete on time (time not being initially of the essence) the other party can serve notice to complete by a specified date.

Service of a notice makes time of the essence for both parties; so that if either party then fails to complete by the specified date, the other can treat the contract as discharged and claim damages.[10] For a notice to be valid, the following conditions must be satisfied:

---

[8]   (1867) 3 Ch. App. 61.

[9]   Lord Templeman in *Kelsie Graham v. Lurline Eugenie Pitkin* [1992] 1 W.L.R. 403, p.406; noted [1992] Conv. 234 (H.W. Wilkinson); and see C. Harpum, 'The Construction of Conditional Contracts and the Effect of Delay in Completion' [1992] Conv. 318.

[10]   As to whether the party served with the notice can insist on completing *before* the specified date, see *Oakdown Ltd. v. Bernstein & Co.* (1984) 49 P. & C.R. 282.

(a) The server must herself be ready, able and willing to complete. This is not taken to its literal extreme. But she must have satisfied herself on all matters of substance that she can go forward to complete. Having to finalise the administrative arrangements for completion is not a bar to serving a notice.[11] For example, the outstanding need to provide a completion statement, execute the conveyance, or to discharge an outstanding mortgage will normally be mere administrative matters.

(b) If, unusually, the contract does not fix any date for completion, there is no breach and so no right to serve a notice until there has been unreasonable delay in completing. Where, the usual case, the contract fixes the date for completion, the notice can be served immediately on failure to complete on that date.

(c) The period given by the notice must be reasonable in all the circumstances.

(d) The notice must not be ambiguous and must make clear what is required.

A similar notice can be served in relation to any step which under the contract is required to be taken within a particular time.

These principles are illustrated by *Behzadi v. Shaftesbury Hotels Ltd.*[12] This was an agreement for the sale of two hotels to the plaintiff. The title to each was registered separately when the vendor had bought earlier in the year, and, in the process of registering the vendor as the new proprietor, there was discussion with the Registry about consolidating the two under one title. At the time of the contract with the plaintiff, the documents were still at the Registry. Under the contract the vendor was to deduce title by supplying an office copy of the register not later than 11 working days after exchange of contracts. The contract stated this time limit not to be of the essence. Due to the delays by the Registry the vendor was not able to supply the office copy in time. The purchaser thereupon, immediately served the vendor with notice to supply the office copy within seven days. On its failure to do so, the purchaser purported to treat the contract as discharged and claimed the return of his deposit with interest. The vendor disputed the right of the purchaser to do this, and in turn claimed damages for wrongful repudiation. It was held that in the circumstances it was wholly unreasonable and unnecessary for the purchaser to require the title to be deduced within the seven days given; the notice was therefore not valid; and the

---

[11] See *Cole v. Rose* [1978] 3 All E.R. 1121, p.1128 (Mervyn Davies Q.C.). And see *Pinekerry Ltd. v. Needs Ltd.* (1992) 64 P. & C.R. 245.

[12] [1991] 2 W.L.R. 251.

purchaser therefore not entitled to treat the contract as discharged. The court, further, refused to order the return of his deposit under s.49(2) of the Law of Property Act 1925.

Once a valid notice has been served, the party serving it can extend the period specified without invalidating the notice, but if she shows an intention to waive time being of the essence – in effect to abandon the rights given by service of the notice – she will have to start all over again with a new notice.[13]

Standard Condition 6.8. deals with the service of notices to complete, reflecting in general the open contract position described above. It expressly provides that the seller will be deemed to be ready, able and willing to complete where the purchase money will be sufficient to redeem an outstanding mortgage on the property. Standard Condition 6.8.3. stipulates 10 working days, excluding the day on which the notice is given, for completion to take place. The notice must comply with the contract, but a period longer than specified in the standard conditions can be given without invalidating the notice.[14]

Standard Condition 6.8. only applies to completion. Making time for completing other steps of the essence is governed by the open contract rules (see Standard Condition 4.1.1.).

VACANT POSSESSION

16.9   The obligation of the vendor to give vacant possession has been dealt with (para.14.6). As with the other breaches discussed, the court will here distinguish between a repudiatory and non-repudiatory breach.[15]

COVENANTS FOR TITLE

16.10   The possibility of the vendor being liable on the covenants for title has been dealt with (para.5.7).

---

[13] As to the deadline for completion on the specified day, and whether it is midnight or the end of normal working hours, see [1991] Conv. 475; [1992] Conv. 148; and [1992] Conv. 402.

[14] *Delta Vale Properties Ltd. v. Mills* [1990] 1 W.L.R. 445.

[15] See *Cumberland Consolidated Holdings Ltd. v. Ireland* [1946] K.B. 254; plaintiff awarded £80 damages on account of rubbish left in the cellar.

LIENS

(a) Vendor's lien

A vendor has a lien over the property in respect of any unpaid purchase money following completion. The lien is an equitable charge on the property which can be enforced by the court setting the contract aside or ordering the sale of the property. It is enforceable against the purchaser even if the conveyance contains a receipt clause for the purchase price. In the case of unregistered land, it is registrable as a Ciii land charge under the Land Charges Act 1972 and as such will be void against a purchaser for value of any interest in the land if not registered.[16] In the case of registered land, the lien can be protected as a minor interest by notice or caution. If the vendor remains in occupation, the lien will be overriding under s.70(1)(g) of the Land Registration Act 1925.

(b) Purchaser's lien

If the purchaser becomes entitled to the return of her deposit (e.g. on lawfully rescinding the contract) she has a lien on the property to secure its recovery. This is only the case where the deposit is held by the vendor or the vendor's agent; not (when it should not be needed) when it is held by a stakeholder.

As with the vendor's lien, the purchaser's lien can be protected by registration as a class Ciii land charge or, in the case of registered land, by entry of a notice or caution.

RECTIFICATION AND INDEMNITY

This only applies to registered title, and is not a remedy in the conventional sense of a right against the other party to the contract. Rectification is the right, subject to the discretion of the Registrar or the court, to have a register of title amended in recognition of some unregistered interest. As such, it is a limit on the notion of the register of title being absolute and indefeasible. However, a person adversely affected by rectification may have a claim to indemnity under the statutory insurance scheme maintained by the Registry.

---

[16]   And see Law of Property Act 1925, s.68.

The grounds on which rectification can be ordered (in some cases only by the court; in others by the court or Registrar) are set out in s.82(1) of the Land Registration Act 1925. They are very wide, concluding with:

> '... any other case where, by reason of any error or omission in the register, or by reason of any entry made under a mistake, it may be deemed just to rectify the register.'

Under s.82(3), where rectification would affect the title of a proprietor in possession, it will only be made to give effect to an overriding interest or where the proprietor has caused, or substantially contributed to, the error or omission by fraud or lack of proper care, or where it would be unjust not to rectify the register against him.

The right to indemnity is governed by s.83 of the Land Registration Act 1925. The general principle is that a person can claim indemnity where she suffers loss as a result of rectification of the register, or where she suffers loss by reason of an error or omission in the register which is not rectified in her favour. In addition there are some other specific cases where indemnity is available. Indemnity is not available where the register is rectified to give effect to an overriding interest, nor where the applicant has caused or substantially contributed to the loss by fraud or lack of proper care.[17]

---

17   For a detailed treatment, see Ruoff & Roper, Part VI.

CHAPTER 17

LEASEHOLD CONVEYANCING

OLD JARNDYCE NODS OFF AGAIN.
MISS PINKY EXPOUNDS

This Chapter will take a brief look at leasehold conveyancing, pointing out the ways in which it differs from freehold. As with freehold, registered and unregistered transactions should be carefully distinguished.

17.1

A UNREGISTERED TITLE

Introduction

There are two main transactions to mention: the grant of a new lease and the assignment of an existing lease. A lease may be granted out of the freehold (a head lease) or it may be granted out of another lease (a sub-lease or under-lease). Thus, F the legal freeholder can grant a lease to T for, say, 99 years; T can in turn grant a sub-lease to ST for, say, 21 years; who in turn can grant a sub-sub-lease to SST for, say, three years; and so on.

17.1.1

It is important to be clear that each of these persons has and continues to have a separate estate in the land. By the Law of Property Act 1925, s.205 (1)(xix), F's freehold (fee simple) will continue to be in possession by virtue of her right to receive the rents and so will continue to be a legal estate. T, ST and SST have terms of years absolute and, assuming the correct formalities have been observed, their estates too will be legal. SST will be the only one with physical possession of the land.

A leasehold estate can, in principle, be dealt with in the same way as F's or any other freehold estate - sold, mortgaged, gifted, settled, left by will or pass on intestacy, etc.; subject always to the limits of its life span and the terms of the lease held.

The terms 'landlord' and 'lessor' like the terms 'tenant' and 'lessee' are in law interchangeable. The same applies to the terms 'lease' and 'tenancy'. In practice, 'lessor/lessee' and 'lease' are used for long term leases. 'Ground rent' means the same as 'rent'; though it is usually used to refer to the low rent reserved on a long lease where a premium (capital sum) has been paid on the grant of the lease. The term 'tenancy agreement' is sometimes used to mean an informal legal lease within s.54(2) of the Law of Property Act 1925 and sometimes to mean an agreement for a lease, that is a contract to create a lease, which itself might be effective as a valid, equitable lease.

Positive covenants and the sale of flats

17.1.2   In law, the most distinctive feature of the leasehold, in contrast to the freehold, is that positive as well as restrictive covenants can run with the lease and with the reversion on that lease. If, in the above example, F sells her reversion (so called, though technically in possession) to F2 and T sells and assigns the lease to T2, then potentially the covenants in the lease whether positive or restrictive will be enforceable between F2 and T2. For this to happen the covenant must touch and concern the leasehold premises and there must be privity of estate between F2 and T2. There will not, for example, be privity between F2 and ST.

This attribute of leases is one of the main reasons why flats are almost invariably let on long leases rather than being sold freehold. There is nothing in law to prevent the sale of freehold flats; the freehold owner of a first floor flat, for example, would have what is commonly called a flying freehold – a cube of air surrounded by bricks, etc. Such a freehold is sometimes encountered with older properties (for example, where originally tenanted cottages have been sold off freehold), where maybe the first floor bathroom of one property extends over the kitchen of the next door property. In conveyancing with such a case, careful attention needs to be paid to identifying the property and its exact boundaries; to the existence of necessary easements of support, etc; and, to the extent that this is possible with freehold, to the existence of necessary obligations to keep interdependent parts in repair, etc.[1]

A number of points should be noted about the use of leasehold for flat ownership whether on the grant of a new lease or the purchase of an existing one.

In general, the ordinary principles of leasehold law and conveyancing apply. But, care must be taken that the physical description of the flat and its limits are accurately identified by plan. The exact location of your boundary when it is your bedroom floor is more crucial than when it is the hedge behind the dustbin.

---

1   For a recent case illustrating the problems, see *Rhone v. Stephens (Executrix), The Times*, 21 January 1993.

Careful attention must be paid to the existence of necessary easements of access over common parts, for passage and maintenance of service pipes and wires, of support, etc.

Equally, the proposed or existing positive and restrictive covenants should be examined with care whether designed to protect the interest of the landlord or the enjoyment of tenants. In general, restrictive covenants operate in the same way as in freehold conveyancing; though restrictive covenants contained in leases are not registrable as land charges under the Land Charges Act 1972; and in registered title will not be identified on the register. The landlord's reversion is capable of being the dominant property making the covenants enforceable for example against a sub-tenant where there is no privity. Similarly, they can be made directly enforceable between neighbouring flat owners by, for example, the creation of a building scheme.

As explained above, positive covenants can be made to run with the reversion and the lease. They are not enforceable directly between the landlord and a sub-tenant since there is no privity of estate; nor between neighbouring flat owners. The lessee's or assignee's solicitor should therefore be satisfied that:

(a) the leases of the other flats contain or will contain the covenants necessary to protect the client's enjoyment;

(b) the client's lease contains a covenant by the landlord to enforce the covenants in the other leases.

Quite commonly management of the flats (but not usually ownership of the reversion) will be taken over by a management company owned by the tenants. One arrangement is for the management company to be a party to each individual lease together with the tenant and the landlord. The service charge will be made payable to the management company which in return will covenant to carry out the landlord's obligations such as maintenance of common parts and structure, insurance, etc and to enforce the covenants entered into by each individual tenant. The ground rent will be payable to the landlord directly or through the agency of the management company. Alternatively, the landlord can grant a long lease of the block to the management company subject to and with the benefit of the individual leases, the rent being equal to the aggregate of rents on the individual leases. Such schemes give the tenants more direct control over management of the flats, common parts and the bringing to heel of anti-social tenants. On purchasing the lease of a flat in the scheme there will have to be a provision in the contract for the purchaser to have transferred to her the vendor's share in the management company.

It is, of course, possible for ownership of the reversion to be vested in a company owned by the tenants, creating a form of co-ownership.

A sub-lease has the same fragility of title as the head-lease out of which it is granted. This means, for example, that if the head-lease is forfeited the sub-lease will be destroyed with it, subject to any right to relief. The sub-lease should therefore contain a covenant by the sub-lessor to pay the rent reserved in the head-lease. Conversely, to protect the lessor, the covenants imposed on the sub-lessee should embrace those in the head-lease.

If forfeiture proceedings are taken against the head-lessee, the sub-lessee (including a mortgagee of the lease) will have a right to apply for relief under s.146(4) of the Law of Property Act 1925. Under the County Court Rules, Ord.6, r.3(1) and (2) a landlord taking forfeiture proceedings must file a copy of the particulars of claim to be served on any mortgagee of the land known to her. A mortgagee of a leasehold interest should therefore ensure that notice of the mortgage is given to the lessor, even if this is not required by the terms of the lease. Even more serious, by s.146 (9) and (10), the right to relief against forfeiture on bankruptcy is excluded altogether in some cases and limited in others. A sub-lessee or mortgagee of a leasehold is at risk if there is such a provision for forfeiture on bankruptcy in the lease and a mortgagee is unlikely to lend money.

Statutory regulation of leases

17.1.3   Leases and tenancies are subject to an extensive corpus of statutory regulation. Indeed, no leasehold transaction should be looked at without considering the possible application of this legislation. The matter is beyond the scope of this book, but, in brief, the following are the more important statutes applying to residential tenancies:

(a) The Housing Act 1985, Part IV. This gives security of tenure to public sector tenants ('secure tenancies').

(b) The Housing Act 1985, Part V, which gives secure tenants the right to buy.

(c) The Housing Associations Act 1985 which deals with housing association tenancies.

(d) The Protection From Eviction Act 1977 as amended by the Housing Act 1988, which is designed to protect residential occupiers from unlawful eviction and harassment.

(e) The Rent Act 1977, which applies to residential tenancies created before 15 January 1989, provides a scheme of security and rent control.

(f) The Housing Act 1988. This applies to residential tenancies created after 14 January 1989, and provides a limited degree of security to assured tenants and a scheme of assured shorthold tenancies under which, on expiry of the agreed term, the tenant has no security.

(g) The Landlord and Tenant Act 1985 which deals with disclosure of the landlord's identity, provision of rent books, statutory repairing obligations on landlords and control of service charges.

(h) The Landlord and Tenant Act 1927, s.19. This controls covenants which limit the right to assign or make improvements.

(i) The Landlord and Tenant Act 1988 is designed to force landlords to deal promptly with applications for licences to assign, etc.

(j) The Landlord and Tenant Act 1987. This gives the tenants of flats with long leases the right, in certain circumstances, to have a manager appointed, to have the terms of the lease varied and jointly to acquire the freehold reversion.

(k) The Leasehold Reform Act 1967 gives the tenant with a long lease of a house the right to purchase the freehold or extend her lease.

(l) Under the Housing and Urban Development Act 1993, long leasehold tenants of flats will have a collective right to purchase the freehold reversion from the landlord.

THE GRANT OF A RESIDENTIAL LEASE   **17.2**

The contract

It is common for a lease to be negotiated and granted without any   **17.2.1**
prior contract. In this case, the grant of the lease itself is the first and final legally binding expression of agreement.

If there is a contract a copy of the proposed lease will be annexed to and incorporated by reference into the contract (see Standard Condition 8.2.3.).

The Standard Conditions are intended to be applicable to the grant of a lease, the 'seller' in this case meaning the 'proposed landlord'; and the 'buyer' meaning the 'proposed tenant'.

The contract will need to contain words to the effect that the lessor (however identified in the contract) agrees to grant and the lessee agrees to take a lease in the form of the draft annexed.

No capacity will be stated for the lessor in the contract or lease (see below as to covenants for title). The consideration (possibly consisting of both a premium (capital payment) and rent, will be shown in the draft lease. The terms of the contract as to title depend on what is said next.

Investigation of title

17.2.2   The starting point is that, as curious as it may seem and being explained by the way in which land law developed, under an open contract the freehold grantor of a lease is under no obligation to prove her title (Law of Property Act 1925, s.44(2)). This means that the lessee will take subject to title defects affecting the freehold in the same way that a purchaser of the freehold would, but with no obligation on the lessor to show the freehold title, and no right for the tenant to investigate it. Thus, for example if a restrictive covenant affecting the land is registered in the Central Land Charges Register against a previous owner, the lessee will be bound by it, but, not having the names of the freehold estate owners, will not discover its existence. Further, it should be noted that the lessee does not have the right to public fund compensation which the purchaser of the freehold would have in respect of undiscovered land charges under s.25 of the Law of Property Act 1969 (para.13.6). On the other hand, by virtue of the Law of Property Act 1925, s.44(5), the lessee will not be affected by notice of non-registrable equitable interests which would have been discovered by investigation of the freehold title. As so few equitable interests are not registrable under the Land Charges Act 1972, this provision is of limited help. It also means that if any outstanding mortgage affects the freehold it will be binding on the lessee; and the mortgagee may not be bound by the lease. Under s.99 of the Law of Property Act 1925, a mortgagor in possession does have a statutory power to create certain leases binding on the mortgagee. But mortgages invariably exclude this power; and provide that the mortgagee's consent must be obtained to any lease by the mortgagor. If this consent is not obtained, the mortgagee will not be bound by the lease. If the lessor has no title to the property, neither will the lessee.

Wherever, at least, the lessee is paying a capital sum for the lease or security of tenure is important, she should insist on a stipulation in the contract that the lessor will deduce and prove the freehold title. Standard Condition 8.2.4. provides:

> 'If the term of the new lease will exceed 21 years, the seller is to deduce a title which will enable the buyer to register the lease at HM Land Registry with an absolute title.'

Since Standard Condition 3.1. will also apply this means that the lessor will, for a lease of more than 21 years, be under the same duty of disclosure and to prove title as on a sale of the freehold. It follows that pre–contract investigations and investigation of title itself will follow the same course as on a freehold sale. And TransAction Protocol can be used as on the sale of the freehold.

If the lease is to be for 21 years or less, the lessee will have no right to proof of title. It is not clear what effect Standard Condition 3.1. would have in such a case. As s c. 8.2.4. does not exclude Standard Condition 3.1. it would seem that the lessor would still have to show herself able to grant a lease free from incumbrances (apart from those listed in Standard Condition 3.1.2.) - which would involve showing the freehold title!

Without proof of the freehold title, the lessee may find it difficult to raise a loan on mortgage and will only obtain a good leasehold title on registration. If capital money is being paid for the lease or security important, the lessee will probably want to amend Standard Condition 8.2.4. perhaps by excluding the reference to 21 years. If the lessor is not going to prove the freehold title then presumably Standard Condition 3.1. should be removed.

Drafting the lease

The conventional practice, reflected in Standard Condition 8.2.3. is **17.2.3** for the lessor to draft the lease. By Standard Condition 8.2.6. the lessor will engross the lease and counterpart when agreed and send the counterpart to the lessee at least five working days before completion date. The counterpart is a duplicate of the lease, traditionally commencing with the words'This Counterpart Lease ...'. Alternatively, a simple copy of the lease may be used. The lessor will execute the lease itself to be delivered to the lessee and the lessee will execute the counterpart to be delivered to the lessor. It is important, even in the case of registered title (below) that each party retains an original copy of the lease executed by the other party.

Under the Costs of Leases Act 1958, reversing the traditional conveyancing presumption, the lessee will not have to pay the lessor's costs unless it is otherwise agreed in writing. The Standard Conditions do not provide otherwise.

The format of a lease is analogous to that of a freehold conveyance, though normally containing a great many more covenants. In brief, it will consist of the following parts:

(a) Introduction. Starting with the words 'This Lease ...' it will continue with the date, the names and addresses of the parties and possibly recitals. For example, in the case of a block of flats there may be a recital showing an intention to create a building scheme, somewhat as follows:

'Insofar as they have not already done so the Landlords intend to grant leases of the flats and garages on the Estate upon terms similar in all material respects to those contained in this Lease to the intent that the Landlords, the Management Company and any lessee for the time being of any of the flats and garages may be able to enforce at law or in equity the performance and observance of the obligations and restrictions so imposed by such leases.'[2]

(b) Operative part. Beginning with the consideration and receipt clause and the words of demise ('In consideration of the sum of £... [the premium] now paid by the Lessee to the Lessor (receipt whereof the Lessor hereby acknowledges) and of the covenants on the part of the Lessee herein contained the Lessor hereby demises All That ...' there follows the parcels clause which, on a lease of a flat, will need to be meticulous in detail and accuracy.

This will be followed, as in a freehold conveyance, by the grant of and exception and reservation of any agreed new easements, followed by the habendum setting out the term including its date of commencement (which may not be the same as the date of execution of the lease) and length;, followed in turn by the reddendum clause ('Yielding and Paying therefore ...') stating the rent, when it is to be paid and whether in advance or arrears.

(c) The covenants by the landlord and those by the tenant. These will be designed to suit the particular situation, though in the nature of things certain matters are dealt with in a more or less similar way in most leases. There are likely to be covenants allocating responsibility for repair and maintenance and redecoration, insurance, limiting the tenant's right to assign, etc or requiring notice of any assignment, etc by the landlord to give the tenant quiet enjoyment (below) and (in the case of flats) provide specified services;. There are also likely to be covenants controlling the tenant's use of the premises and her right to make improvements or alterations and giving the landlord a right to enter to view the state of the premises. Invariably there will be a forfeiture clause enabling the landlord to terminate the lease in the event of non-payment of rent or other breach of covenant by the tenant.

(d) Conclusion. There will be an attestation clause and execution by landlord and tenant of the lease and counterpart respectively as described above. The rules for the execution of deeds apply equally to a lease by deed as to a freehold conveyance (para.12.4.4).

Question Your client Phineas Frog is the freehold owner of a house, Tadpole End, Fishtown. He is shortly going to take up a two-year lecturing appointment in an Indian university, and then plans to spend a couple of years travelling around Asia. He wants to let the house for a four year term to a fellow lecturer, Jeremy Fisher (who will not accept a tenancy of less than four years).

---

2 See P.M. A'Court, *Estate Conveyancing*, Waterlow, 1984.

He does not mind Phineas assigning or sub-letting the house but he wants to be sure that any new tenant is financially sound and otherwise respectable. He would also like to ensure that any new tenant is a non-smoker and not Irish (his former wife was Irish and a heavy smoker).

Can he achieve these aims by suitable clauses in the lease? Can you properly, as a solicitor, assist him to achieve the last aim, if it can be achieved without breaking the law? If and so far as he can, draft relevant clause(s).

What advice would you give him and what steps should he take in view of the fact that he will be out of the country for most of the four years, especially given that he will be difficult to contact in the last two? Consider particularly the Landlord and Tenant Act 1988.

The covenant for quiet enjoyment

The grant of a lease does not include the implied covenants for title **17.2.4** which are included in the conveyance of the freehold (para.5.7). What, and all, the tenant does get is the covenant for quiet enjoyment (and an obligation not to derogate from grant). It is an implied, if not made express, term of a lease, arising out of the relationship of landlord and tenant, that the tenant will have quiet enjoyment of the premises. This protects the lessee against physical interference by the landlord and those lawfully claiming under her (i.e. those whose acts she has authorised). But it does not protect against the acts of strangers (where like any other landowner the lessee will have to rely on her own remedy in tort). More significantly, it does not protect against those with title paramount to the landlord, unless, which is unusual, the covenant is made absolute by express term in the lease. In other words, it gives no guarantee of the landlord's title to grant the lease or its freedom from incumbrances. This reflects the traditional, open contract principle that on the grant of a lease the landlord is not required to prove title.

Pre-contract and pre-completion steps

Where the freehold title is being deduced this will be done as on a **17.2.5** freehold sale. In the absence of any contractual obligation on the landlord to prove the freehold title, any investigation would have to take place before contract to serve much purpose (for example, a Central Land Charges search against the landlord would be possible) though if a defect did become known to the lessee after contract and before completion, equity would no doubt refuse to order specific performance and order the return of any deposit. As in the case of freehold, the lessor will in the absence of agreement to the contrary, be under an obligation to give vacant possession at completion.

Completion

17.2.6   The completion process will be much the same as on a freehold conveyance. The landlord's solicitor will receive the executed counterpart lease and the premium. In addition an apportioned part of the rent (if payable in advance) for the period spanning completion may have to be paid. The tenant's solicitor will receive the executed lease. If the freehold has been deduced this will be dealt with in the same way as on a freehold sale. The freehold title deeds will, of course, be retained by the landlord. The tenant's solicitor should examine them and mark her copies or abstract as examined against the originals.

Post-completion

17.2.7   The newly granted lease may require notice of dealings to be given to the landlord. This will have to be complied with in respect of any mortgage or sub-letting of the new lease. Notice should be given in duplicate for a receipted copy to be returned and placed with the deeds.

As on the purchase of freehold, stamping and first registration will have to be considered.

Stamping of leases

17.2.8   Particulars delivered stamping is required on the grant of a lease for a term of seven years or more and on the transfer on sale of any such lease. The term 'lease' includes sub-lease or any other tenancy.

Where a premium (i.e. a capital sum) is paid on the grant of a lease, stamp duty is charged on the premium at the same rates as on the consideration for a freehold conveyance. The duty payable on the document in respect of the rent element of the consideration depends on the length of the term and the amount of the rent.[3]

If the rent reserved is not more than £600 a year and the premium not more than £60,000, (if executed after 15 March 1993 and not stamped before 23 March 1993) and if the lease contains a certificate of value to that effect, it will exempt from stamp duty. A counterpart or duplicate lease still bears a fixed 50p deed duty (see also para.10.7.1).

Stamp duty on the assignment of an existing lease is the same as for a freehold conveyance.

---

[3]   For the details, see Finance Act 1891, Schedule 1, as amended by the Finance Act 1982, s.128(3); and now Finance Act 1993, s.201.

First registration

All areas now being compulsory, first registration will need to be applied for on the grant of a lease for a term of more than 21 years (Land Registration Act 1986).[4]

(a) Classes of title

Registration is possible with the same classes of title and with similar legal effect as freehold – that is, absolute, possessory and qualified leasehold.[5] In particular, under s.9 of the Land Registration Act 1925, the title of the proprietor with absolute leasehold will not be tainted by any defect affecting the reversion unless it is protected on the register of the leasehold title or overriding. The validity of the lease will be guaranteed. However, the title will be subject to the terms of the lease itself. Registration does not guarantee that the covenants and obligation in the lease have been performed to date or that the lease is not liable to be forfeited for breach of its terms.

In addition to these classes of title, registration with good leasehold title is possible and common. This will be granted where the freehold title has not been deduced and so cannot be proved to the Registry. Section 10 of the Land Registration Act provides that registration with good leasehold title

> 'shall not affect or prejudice the enforcement of any estate, right or interest affecting or in derogation of the title of the lessor to grant the lease, but, save as aforesaid, shall have the same effect as registration with absolute title.'

In short, a lessor can give no better title than she has and registration with good leasehold does not cure the lease of any resulting defect. The weakness of such a title as security for a loan has been mentioned.

Under s.77 of the Land Registration Act 1925, as substituted by the Land Registration Act 1986, a good leasehold title can be converted to absolute if the Registrar is satisfied as to the title to the freehold and any intermediate leasehold. This means that the Registrar will have to be satisfied that the original lessor had power to grant the lease and any incumbrances affecting the lease will have to be shown. If all superior titles are registered with absolute title there will be no difficulty in obtaining the conversion.

---

[4] If the lease is not registrable, being for 21 years or less, it will remain an unregistered lease subject to unregistered title rules. If the freehold comes to be registered, the lease will be overriding as far as the freehold is concerned.

[5] As to the conversion of these titles, see Land Registration Act 1925, s.77, as substituted by the Land Registration Act 1986.

(b) Procedure on registration

As with freehold, the application will have to be lodged within two months of completion.

Application will be made by the lessee's solicitor on printed Form 3B. It will need to be accompanied by:

The original lease with its plan;

copy of the lease and plan, both being certified as true copies of the original;

all other deeds and documents relating to the leasehold title which the applicant has;

if absolute title is being applied for, proof of the freehold title;

if it is a sub-lease, the evidence of title to the intermediate lease; sufficient particulars by plan or otherwise to identify the land.

The original deeds relating to the freehold will have been retained by the lessor and the Registry will accept examined abstract or copies. The proof of the freehold or superior leasehold will need to include, as well as the title itself, evidence of any necessary consent to the lease by a mortgagee and, in the case of a sub-lease, evidence of any necessary consent by the sub-lessor and evidence as to any incumbrances affecting the lease.

In addition, there must be included any mortgage of the new lease (which will be registered against the new leasehold title) with a certified copy, a list in triplicate of all documents sent and the necessary fee.

(c) The register of title

The register is in the same format as for freehold. The property register will state that the title is leasehold and will contain short particulars of the lease, namely:

the date of the lease;

the parties;

the length of the term and commencement date; and

the rent.

If the lease contains a prohibition or limit on the right to assign, sub-lease or charge, there will be a note on the property register to the following effect:

'There are excepted from the effect of registration all estates, rights, interests, powers and remedies under the lease at any time arising from any alienation prohibited or restricted by the lease.'

This means that when application is made to register a disposition of a registered lease the Registry does not investigate whether, and does not guarantee that, any necessary consent to an assignment, sub-lease or charge of the lease has been obtained (see below).

If applicable, there will also be a note of the number under which the lessor's title is registered. Where the freehold reversion is registered, the lease will be noted on the register of that title, thus making it binding on a purchaser of the reversion.

The proprietorship register will show the class of leasehold title., otherwise it, and the charges register, will be the same as in the case of freehold.

Grant of a sub-lease

Subject to what has been said and what is said below about title (para.17.3.2(f)) the principles governing the grant of a sub-lease are the same as for the grant of a lease. **17.2.10**

ASSIGNMENT OF AN UNREGISTERED LEASE

The sale of a lease resembles the sale of a freehold very closely. It is the disposition of an existing estate. Here, unless the land comprised in the lease is being split and only part being sold (which is quite possible, just as it is in the case of sale of part of a freehold title, but beyond the scope of this book) or the vendor happens to own other neighbouring land, there will be no scope for the creation of new appurtenant rights or burdens. The property will be sold with the benefit of whatever appurtenant rights and subject to whatever incumbrances are already attached to it. **17.3**

In what follows the term 'lease' is used to include an underlease/sub-lease (these latter two terms being synonymous) unless the contrary is indicated and what is said applies to the assignment of either. Subject to what is said the principles and procedures are as for a sale of the freehold.

Pre-contract investigations

These will, in general, be the same as on the purchase of freehold. The standard forms of Enquiries before Contract have additional standard questions relating to leasehold. Similarly, TransAction Protocol has an Additional Property Information Form for use in leasehold transactions. This includes questions aimed at providing information on such matters as the insurance arrangements, any management company, the amount of any service charge and the use to which it has been put, performance of the covenants in the lease by the seller, the neighbours and the landlord. **17.3.1**

The contract of sale

17.3.2   The following points should be noted.

(a) Legal description

The contract must state that the estate to be sold is a lease or, if such be the case, an underlease. Otherwise the greater estate is implied. Further, under an open contract, the vendor must disclose to the purchaser not only the existence of the lease, but any unusual covenants which it contains. This can be covered, as under Standard Condition 8.1.2., by supplying a copy of the lease itself with the contract.

(b) Physical description

The property can be described by reference to the lease. Thus, for example:

> 'Property: (Leasehold). All that land and house known as number 22 Eternal Drive, Heaventry, which is fully described in the lease ("the Lease") annexed hereto and dated the ... day of ... 1993 and made between Gabriel Smith (1) and Archie Angel (2) for the residue of the term of 99 years granted by the Lease.'

As to root of title, and incumbrances, see below para.17.3.2(f).

(c) Insurance

The lease is likely to contain terms allocating responsibility for insuring the premises (in which both lessee and lessor have an interest). Breach of such a term by the lessee might not only leave the property uninsured, but also make the lease being purchased liable to forfeiture.

The matter therefore cannot simply be left to be governed by Standard Condition 5.1.3. Accordingly, Standard Condition 8.1.3. requires the seller to comply with any lease obligation requiring the lessee (i.e. the vendor until completion) to insure the property. The buyer's solicitor should check, before exchange, what provisions as to insurance the lease contains and that these provisions have been complied with and that the insurance arrangements are effective to protect the purchaser's interest between contract and completion (see further, para.3.5).

(d) Capacity

The capacity of the vendor should be stated in the same way as on a freehold sale. On the sale (unlike the grant) of a lease the capacity does govern the covenants for title to be implied.

On an assignment for valuable consideration the four 'freehold' covenants discussed earlier will be implied (para.5.7) with the same effect in relation to the leasehold title. Under s.76 (1)(B) of the Law of Property Act 1925 two additional ones are implied, namely:

(i) That the lease is valid and subsisting; and

(ii) that the rent has been paid and the covenants in the lease duly performed.

On the purchase of a lease, the purchaser is concerned not only that the vendor owns the lease, but also that there has been no non-payment of rent or other breach of covenant making the lease liable to forfeiture in the hands of the purchaser.

These two additional covenants, like the first four, are qualified in that they only protect against the acts or omissions of the assignor and person through whom she derives title back to the last purchaser for value; that is, again, they do not protect against claims by title paramount.

In this context two points should be noted:

(i) In the absence of provision to the contrary in the contract, the vendor could be liable to the purchaser under these title covenants if, at the time of contracting, the state of disrepair of the premises constituted a breach of a lessee's repairing covenant in the lease. This would conflict with the *caveat emptor* principle reflected in Standard Condition 5.1.1. that the purchaser accepts the property in its physical state at the date of contract. Standard Condition 8.1.4. therefore limits the implied covenant for title to bring it into line with Standard Condition 5.1.1. and the *caveat emptor* principle. The point is that, without Standard Condition 8.1.4., the vendor would not be liable for the disrepair as such of the property at the date of contract, but for the fact that such disrepair (if a breach of a covenant in the lease) would make the lease liable to forfeiture and this liability to forfeiture would be a defect in the title caused by the act or omission of the vendor and so a breach of the title covenant.

(ii) Part of the vendor's duty in proving title to the lease is to show that there has been no breach up to the date of completion of any covenant in the lease making it liable to forfeiture. Even the purchaser's knowledge of a breach at the time of contracting would probably not deprive her of the right to object; since she would be entitled to assume that the vendor would remedy the breach before completion (at least if it were a remediable breach). Section 45(2) and (3) provide that, on the sale of a lease or under-lease, the purchaser must assume on production of the receipt for the last payment due for rent under the lease/under-lease before the date of actual completion, that unless the contrary appears, all the covenants and provisions of the lease/under-lease have been performed. This is likely to be satisfactory because if rent has been accepted by a landlord, knowing of a breach, the breach will be deemed to have been waived.

Standard Condition 6.6. requires the purchaser to assume that the person giving such a receipt is the person or the agent of the person entitled to receive the rent (i.e. the owner of the reversion). Where the freehold is being deduced this will normally make it clear that the person giving the receipt for rent is in fact the owner or her agent.

On a conveyance of a leasehold by a fiduciary, as similarly on a conveyance of a freehold, the only title covenant implied is that the fiduciary has not herself incumbered the land.

Question Your client John Purchaser is purchasing a leasehold property, Blackacre, from Jane Vendor. Draft a clause to put in the Assignment giving effect to Standard Condition 8.1.4. Would you need such a clause if the property were being sold and assigned jointly by Jane Vendor and her husband Joseph Vendor?

(e) Licence to assign

If, under an open contract, the lease requires the consent of the lessor to the proposed assignment (or other disposition) the vendor must obtain this. Failure to do so would make the lease to be assigned liable to forfeiture and would be a breach of contract by the vendor.[6]

Standard Condition 8.3.2. requires the vendor to apply for any such necessary consent and to use all reasonable efforts to obtain it. The purchaser is required to provide all information and references reasonably required. If consent has not been obtained within three working days of completion, either party (having complied with Standard Condition 8.3.2.) can rescind without being liable for breach of contract.

In practice, the purchaser is likely to want to be satisfied that the consent will be forthcoming before getting to the contract stage.

Where there are previous assignments of the lease, or other dealings requiring consent, on the title, the purchaser's solicitor should check that the necessary consents were obtained on those occasions (and they should be with the deeds), though any breach is likely to have been waived by subsequent acceptance of rent with knowledge of the breach. The same principle applies where the lease requires notice of dealings to be given to the lessor.

---

6   Unless the contract makes the existence of the contract conditional on consent being forthcoming (i.e. creates a conditional contract) in which case failure to obtain the consent (after properly attempting to obtain it) would simply put an end to the contract without liability. This is essentially the effect of Standard Condition 8.3.2.

(f) Title to be shown

In a sense a leasehold title contains two titles or layers of title. Firstly, it contains the title to the freehold reversion; that is the title of the freehold grantor of the lease to grant it and so creates a valid lease. Secondly, it contains the title to the lease itself; that is the evidence that the lease (assuming it to have been validly granted) has validly passed from the original lessee to the present vendor.

In the same way, a sub-lease consists of three layers: The title to the freehold reversion; the title to the lease; and the title to the sub-lease itself. For example, F4 grants a legal lease to T1. T1 grants a legal sub-lease to ST1. F4's title can be traced back to, say, F1. Subsequent to the grant of the lease it will continue and can pass from person to person like any freehold, subject always to the lease. Once the lease has been validly granted, assuming that it is a legal lease, nothing which happens to the freehold can effect it. This is because it is legal and in the case of unregistered land good against all the world. T1's lease can be dealt with and pass from person to person. Similarly, ST1's sub-lease can pass from person to person and be dealt with until it expires. And, again, if it is legal and was validly granted by T, nothing that subsequently happens to the freehold or the lease can affect it. Further, even if all the strands of the vendor's title to the lease are good, it has to be remembered that a lease is always vulnerable to destruction, particularly by forfeiture for breach of its terms.

To get a completely good title the purchaser needs to be satisfied as to each of the strands and that there has been no breach (which the landlord has not waived) making the lease liable to forfeiture. Taking the freehold and leasehold titles in turn:

(i) The freehold title. Under an open contract, by s.44 of the Law of Property Act 1925, the vendor is not obliged to prove the freehold title. There is no provision in the Standard Conditions for the sale of a lease equivalent to Standard Condition 8.2.4. (contrast the first edition of the Standard Conditions).

This means that the purchaser's title may only be as good as the original lease; it may be difficult to obtain a mortgage; and on first registration only good leasehold will be granted. The purchaser will have to consider whether to contract on these terms if a special condition cannot be agreed providing for proof of the freehold title.

The difficulty is that freehold title may not have been shown on the grant of the original lease (F4 to T1 in the example above). The present vendor, whether the original lessee or a subsequent assignee, will have no right to go back to the original lessor and require production of the freehold title. If the freehold title has at some stage been registered with absolute title there is no problem as the register is open to public inspection. If it is only registered with possessory title or still unregistered, the vendor may not be in a position to agree a term requiring the freehold to be proved unless the co-operation of the freeholder can be obtained.

(ii) The leasehold title. Proof of the leasehold title will show, on the assumption that the lease was validly granted in the first place, that it has been validly transmitted from the original lessee to the present vendor. Under an open contract and under the Standard Conditions the purchaser is entitled to production of the lease itself (however old it is) together with the title to the lease going back at least 15 years from the date of contract to a good root of title document dealing with the lease. If the lease is less than 15 years old, title will be traced back to the lease itself.

Investigation of a leasehold title is in general subject to the same rules and principles as investigation of the freehold, the rules of transmission being the same. For example, the Law of Property (Joint Tenants) Act 1964 applies. If there is an assignment of the lease by a surviving joint tenant on the title that assignment will be a satisfactory link in the title if the conditions imposed by the 1964 Act were complied with. Searches will be the same (only against the leasehold estate owners) as for freehold.

(iii)(a) Title on grant of a sub-lease. On the grant of a sub-lease (which it is convenient to mention here), the sub-lessee is entitled to proof of the leasehold title only, that is, production of the lease and any assignments for 15 years back from the date of the sub-lease; she is not entitled under an open contract to proof of the freehold title.

(iii)(b) Title on sale of sub-lease. On the sale of an existing sub-lease it seems that the purchaser is only entitled, under the Law of Property Act 1925, s.44 (3), to production of the sub-lease itself and assignments going back 15 years from the contract. She is not entitled to proof of the freehold nor the leasehold title. This makes the title of the purchaser of such a sub-lease twice as vulnerable as that of the purchaser of a lease. F4 in the example above may have had no title to grant the lease; even if she did, T1 may have had no power to grant the sub-lease (for example, may have granted it without the required consent of a mortgagee).

The Standard Conditions do not alter this open contract position relating to the sale of leases and sub-leases. Standard Condition 8.2.4. will apply on the grant of a sub-lease as on the grant of a lease. As discussed above, it may be possible in a transaction to negotiate a special condition increasing the obligation as to proof of title.

Drafting the Assignment

As on a sale of freehold the normal principle is that the purchaser will draft the assignment for approval by the vendor. Standard Condition 4, relating to the timetable for proving title and drafting the deed of transfer applies as on a sale of freehold.

The format of the Assignment (which must be by deed) will follow that of a conveyance of the freehold. The introduction, beginning 'This Assignment' and including the date, parties and any recitals, will be followed by the operative part. This will begin with a consideration and receipt clause and continue with something like the following:

'... the Vendor as beneficial owner [or trustee, etc] Hereby Assigns unto the Purchaser All That the property comprised in a lease (the "Lease") dated the 10th day of January 1943 and made Between Josephine Greasey of the one part and Jackie Turkey of the other part all which property is more particularly described in the schedule hereto To Hold the same unto the Purchaser for all the residue now unexpired of the term of years created by the Lease Subject to the rent reserved by and the lessee's covenants and the conditions contained in the Lease.'

Any incumbrances to which the lease is subject will follow as on a conveyance of freehold. Subject to what follows, the covenants and declarations will be as on a conveyance of freehold, including any joint purchaser clauses and certificate of value. Finally there will be the attestation clauses for execution by the vendor and, if necessary, the purchaser.

Special mention is needed of indemnity covenants. On an assignment for valuable consideration of a lease, s.77(1)(C) and Schedule 2, Part IX of the Law of Property Act 1925 imply a covenant by the assignee(s) that the assignee(s) and their successors in title will at all times pay the rent due under, and observe the covenants in, the lease and indemnify the assignor(s) for non-payment of rent or breach of any covenant in the lease.

Unless the wording of the covenant in the original lease provides otherwise, the original tenant will remain liable for any breach throughout the term, even after parting with the lease. Suppose L grants a lease to T who assigns to A and the same principles will apply if there are subsequent assignments. On the assignment by T the statutory covenant will be implied. On a breach of covenant by A, the landlord has a choice whether to sue the defaulting tenant, A, (liable by virtue of the privity of estate) or T, the original tenant (probably because A is not financially worth suing) with whom there will remain privity of contract. If sued, the original tenant will have to rely on the indemnity covenant to pass on liability to the next tenant in line, A (if she is worth suing). This continuing liability after parting with the lease is a risk of which a tenant needs to be warned when first taking a lease. One way of minimising the risk when assigning is to require a surety for the liability of the assignee. Further, unless special provision is made, T has no right to put an end to the lease and so to the default and has no right to force the landlord to do so. One way of avoiding this situation is for T to grant a sub-lease to A instead of assigning. On breach by A, T will then be able to forfeit the sub-lease and so put a stop to any further default.

Completion

17.3.4   Subject to what has been said about title, the steps leading to completion will be as for a freehold sale bearing in mind that searches will be necessary in relation to both any leasehold title involved and, if it is being proved, the freehold title. At completion the assignee's solicitor will expect to receive:

The assignment;

the lease;

the consent of the landlord to the assignment if required;

the title deeds relating to the leasehold title including any previous assignments;

consents to previous assignments and receipted duplicates of notices given to the landlord of previous assignments (where required by the terms of the lease) and any mortgages properly discharged or with undertakings to discharge;

if the freehold title has been deduced, an examined abstract or copies of the freehold title;

on the purchase of a sub-lease, if the leasehold title is being proved, an examined abstract of that title;

if there is a management company, a form of transfer of the vendor's share in the management company and share certificate;

the purchaser's solicitor will also need to see the receipt for the payment of rent last due.

The vendor's solicitor will expect to receive the balance of the purchase price and release of deposit if held by a stakeholder. The rent will probably have to be apportioned and the completion statement sent to the purchaser's solicitor adjusted accordingly.

Post-completion

17.3.5   Stamping has been dealt with (para.17.2.8 and 10.7.1).

The lease may require notice of any assignment, sub-letting or charging of the property to be given to the landlord. This should be sent in duplicate for a receipted copy to be returned and placed with the deeds. Any mortgage will be completed as in the case of freehold.

First registration

The assignment on sale of a lease with more than 21 years to run at the date of assignment is subject to first registration. Application should be made on printed Form 2B. If good leasehold is being applied for it should be accompanied by:

the lease itself if it is in the applicant's possession or control;

the previous assignments and any other documents relating to the leasehold title;

the assignment to the applicant together with a certified copy;

sufficient particulars to enable the land to be identified;

where the lease has been mortgaged by the assignee, the original mortgage and a certified copy (so that the mortgage will be registered at the same time);

a list of the documents submitted in triplicate; and

the appropriate fee.

Where absolute title is being applied for, the deeds and documents relating to the freehold and any intermediate lease will also have to be submitted.

B LEASES OF REGISTERED LAND

GRANT OF A LEASE OF REGISTERED LAND

Subject to what is said, it can be taken that the principles applicable to leases of unregistered land apply equally to registered land.

17.4

The grant of a lease out of the registered freehold is a disposition which, if for a term of more than 21 years, will have to be completed by registration for it to create a legal title.[7] If it is a legal lease for 21 years or less it will be overriding under the Land Registration Act 1925, s.70(1)(k).

As with a lease out of unregistered title, the steps taken and investigations made between negotiation and grant of the lease will depend on the term to be granted, whether the tenant is paying a

---

[7]   Land Registration Act 1925, ss.18, 19, 20.

premium and the degree of security of title needed. A student taking a one year assured shorthold of a term-time room will probably be more concerned with the Housing Act 1988 and the Protection From Eviction Act 1977 than with the possible existence of a tree preservation order on the old apple tree in the garden or Standard Condition 8.2.4.

In a formal transaction, pre-contract steps may include, as in the case of a freehold sale, a search of the Register of Local Land Charges and Additional Enquiries, Enquiries before Contract of the lessor, inspection of the property and the other possible investigations mentioned in para.4.12.6.

The Standard Conditions can be used for the grant of a lease out of registered title as for one out of unregistered title. The main difference lies in the title to be deduced.

The Land Registration Act 1925, s.110 does not apply to the grant of a lease. In the absence of express term in the contract, the lessee will not be entitled to proof of the freehold title. Under the Standard Conditions, Standard Condition 8.2.4. and 4.2. apply. It should be appreciated that if the lease is to be legal and for 21 years or less it will be overriding; but only to the extent that it is a valid lease. Designation as an overriding interest does not confer validity on an interest which is not otherwise valid. The argument for modifying Standard Condition 8.2.4. therefore applies equally here. Even without modification the lessor's registered title could be searched, the register now being open to public inspection. But, subject to the intervention of equity, discovery of a defect after contract, without modification of 8.2.4. would not give the lessee any contractual remedy. In this case the search would have to be made pre–contract.

Where the contract provides that the freehold title is to be proved it will be as provided under Standard Condition 4.2.1. and procedure will be as on purchase of a registered freehold. If the freehold is registered with less than absolute title the lessor will have, in the absence of special condition, to deduce the title not covered by the register as for unregistered title.

The deed of grant. A lease or sub-lease of registered land may be in any form which sufficiently refers, in the prescribed manner, to the registered land. It should be headed, as with a transfer of the freehold, with 'H.M. Land Registry: Land Registration Acts 1925 to 1988', then with the name of the county and district (or London borough), the title number of the freehold and a short description of the property. Subject to this it will be of the same format and content as a lease of unregistered land.

Proof and investigation of the freehold title, if it is to be proved, will be as on the sale of the freehold. If there is a subsisting charge which limits the right of the mortgagor to grant leases, this will, to be binding, need to have been protected by a restriction on the register (para.7.7(c)). If there is such a restriction, the consent of the chargee to the lease will have to be obtained and submitted to the Registry on registration of the lease.

On completion, the lessee's solicitor will need to receive the lease properly executed by the lessor. She will not receive the land or charge certificate. Production of the land certificate at the Registry will be needed to register the lease (if registrable) and note it against the freehold title. If the land certificate is not already held at the Registry (which it will be, for example, if there is a charge on the property) the lessor should be required to place it there on deposit and provide the deposit number. A special condition can be put in the contract to this effect, though it would seem in any case to be embraced by Standard Condition 8.2.4. If deposit has not been made before completion an undertaking should be required. In addition, she will need to receive any necessary consent of the lessor's mortgagee. The lessor will receive the counterpart lease, the balance of the purchase money and an apportioned part of the ground rent if payable in advance.

After completion, as with a lease out of unregistered title, stamping may have to be attended to and notice of any mortgage or sub-lease of the new lease may have to be given to the lessor. If for more than 21 years, the lease will have to be completed by registration within the priority period of the pre-completion official search of the register. This will be a new title. Short particulars of the lease will be shown on the register but the terms of the lease will not be and subsequently office copies of the lease itself will not normally be available from the Registry. The lease will be returned to the lessee and will remain a crucial document of title to be kept in safe custody with the land or charge certificate. The new lease will also be noted on the charges register of the title to the freehold reversion, for which purpose the land certificate of that title will be needed at the Registry (above). Application by the lessee's solicitor should be on printed Form 3B.

The land or charge certificate as the case may be, on issue by the Registry, should be dealt with as in the case of freehold land.

The grant of a sub-lease out of a registered lease is essentially the same as the grant of a lease.

TRANSFER OF A REGISTERED LEASE

Subject to what is said, the same principles apply as for the assignment **17.5**
of an unregistered lease.

(a) Pre-contract investigations will be the same as on the purchase of registered freehold, with the additional Enquiries Before Contract appropriate to leasehold purchases.

(b) The contract will be similar to that for the assignment of an unregistered lease. The points made about insurance and the capacity of the vendor are equally applicable. (For the significance of covenants for title in the case of registered land, see para.7.11(d).) Equally what has been said about the lessor's consent to assignment or other disposition is applicable. The Registry does not investigate whether any necessary consent to assign has been obtained (para.17.2.9).

The contract will have to include the title number and identify the property as leasehold and the class of title. For example:

'All that leasehold property known as 22 Heavenly Walk for the residue of the term granted by a lease ("the Lease") dated 2 October 1952 and made between Christopher Wren (1) and Robert Adams (2) and registered at HM Land Registry with absolute title under title number WYK 465798.'

A copy of the lease will be supplied with the contract.

(c) As to title to be shown. Section 110 of the Land Registration Act 1925 *does* apply to a transfer of an existing lease. Under both an open contract and the Standard Conditions the vendor will have to supply a copy (office copy under Standard Condition 4.2.1.) and title plan, together with a copy of the lease and any other documents required under s.110(2). If the title being sold is absolute leasehold, this will, of course, itself embrace a guarantee of the freehold. If the title being sold is only good leasehold the vendor will not, unless there is a special condition to the contrary, have to deduce evidence of the freehold.[8] If, in such a case, title to the freehold (that is the title of the grantor of the lease to grant the lease) is to be proved, it will be deduced and investigated as on a sale of freehold.

(d) The transfer will be drafted in the same way as a transfer of registered freehold and in practice the same printed form is usually adopted.

In addition to the indemnity covenant implied under s.77(1)(C) of the Law of Property Act 1925 (para.17.3.3) on an assignment for value, under s.24(1)(b) of the Land Registration Act 1925 an indemnity covenant by the transferee with similar effect is implied.

In relation to covenants for title, if the capacity of the transferor is stated in the transfer, the covenants for title will be implied under s.76 of the Law of Property Act 1925, as they would be in an unregistered assignment – that is either the six beneficial owner covenants or the fiduciary covenant. If no capacity is stated in the contract the vendor will be obliged, by Standard Condition 4.5.2., to transfer as beneficial owner.

---

8   Because, in the words of s.110, the purchaser would 'not have been entitled to it if the land had not been registered'.

In addition, under s.24(1)(a) of the Land Registration Act 1925 on the transfer of a lease, a covenant by the transferor is implied that

'the rent, covenants, and conditions reserved and contained by and in the registered lease, and on the part of the lessee to be paid, performed, and observed, have been so paid, performed, and observed up to the date of the transfer.'

This covenant is implied regardless of the capacity in which the transferor transfers and regardless of there being value. If the sale is by a trustee or other fiduciary, thought should be given to a special condition excluding the s.24(1)(a) covenant (if it is considered to be wider in effect than the s.76 fiduciary's covenant) leaving only the covenant under s.76 to be implied from transferring as fiduciary. As on an unregistered lease assignment, a declaration should be included in the transfer in accordance with Standard Condition 8.1.4.

(e) Pre-completion. As on the transfer of a registered freehold, an official search of the register of title will be needed giving priority. If the title is only good leasehold, unregistered title searches will have to be made against the freehold if it is being deduced.

(f) Completion. The purchaser's solicitor will expect to receive

the transfer properly executed;

the land certificate or, if there is an outstanding mortgage to be redeemed, the charge certificate with an executed Form 53 or undertaking;

the lease itself;

any necessary consent to assign or charge;

the transfer of the vendor's share in any management company and share certificate; and

if the title is good leasehold and the freehold is being deduced, an examined abstract or copies of the freehold title.

The ground rent and any service charge may have to be apportioned for the period covering completion; and the receipt for the last payment due of rent and any service charge produced for examination.

(g) Post-completion. Stamping will have to be attended to (para.17.2.8). Any necessary notice required by the terms of the lease of the transfer and any charge will have to be given to the landlord with a receipted duplicate being received back and put with the title documents.

The transfer will have to be completed by registration within the priority period of the pre-completion search. The transfer of a registered lease must be completed by registration even if 21 years or less is left unexpired. The application should be made on printed Form 2B accompanied, as in the case of a transfer of registered freehold, by:

the transfer (with a certified copy if new restrictive covenants are imposed – e.g. on the sale of part of the land in a leasehold title);

the Land (or Charge Certificate and Form 53 if there is an outstanding charge which is being discharged);

any new mortgage with a certified copy;

the Particulars Delivered form if no ad valorem duty is payable;

a list of documents in triplicate; and

the appropriate fee.

The land or charge certificate on receipt from the registry will be dealt with as in the case of registered freehold.

CHECKLIST OF STEPS IN SALE – PURCHASE/MORTGAGE TRANSACTION

Note: This checklist is intended to give an overall picture of the typical transaction. Whether or not some of the steps are necessary will depend on the circumstances of the particular transaction. Others, not mentioned, may need to be taken. To some extent a checklist has to be created for the particular transaction and to suit the style of the particular user. In format, it should be designed to show what steps have to be taken, to highlight those which have been satisfactorily dealt with and those which are still to be attended to. In addition there should be a proper diary system to ensure that steps are taken within the proper time.

The steps listed are based on traditional conveyancing procedure and can be compared with those given under TransAction Protocol (Appendix 4).

ACTING FOR PURCHASER AND LENDERS ON PURCHASE OF FREEHOLD

Note: The second column should be ticked when the step has been completed and marked N/A if not applicable to the transaction. The third column is for relevant dates to be noted and any other notes relating to a particular step. There is space for additional steps for a particular transaction to be added.

Question If you were acting for the purchaser with the lenders separately represented, how would you add to/amend the following checklist?

Question How would you amend/add to the following check list for acting on the purchase of a lease?

Question Draw up a checklist for use when acting for the vendor on the sale of freehold; and on the sale of leasehold.

	STEP TAKEN	Date for action; other notes
1 Instructions received		
2 Purchase details from agents		
3(a) Local search and additional enquiries sent		
3(b) Results satisfactory		
4(a) Draft contract received		
4(b) Approved		
5(a) Preliminary enquiries of vendor		
5(b) Replies satisfactory		
6(a) Search of index map		
6(b) Result satisfactory		
7(a) Commons search		
7(b) Result satisfactory		
8(a) British Coal search		
8(b) Result satisfactory		
9(a) Other searches, etc (Name)		
9(b) Results satisfactory		
10 Mortgage offer and instructions received		
11 Deposit arrangements satisfactory		
12 Deposit held/guarantee in place		
13 Financial arrangements satisfactory		
14(a) Undertaking re deposit given		
14(b) Undertaking performed		
15 Survey arrangements satisfactory		
16 Building insurance arrangements satisfactory		
17 Endowment policy – Insurers at risk		
18 Contract signed by clients		
19 NHBC documentation received/dealt with		
20 CONTRACTS EXCHANGED		
21 Epitome of title received		
22(a) Requisitions raised		
22(b) Replies to requisitions satisfactory		
23 Draft conveyance/transfer sent		
24 Draft approved		
25 Draft engrossed and signed by clients		
26 Engrossment sent to vendor's solicitor		

	STEP TAKEN	Date for action; other notes
27 Completion arrangements made		
28 Mortgage deed drawn		
29 Assignment of endowment policy drawn		
30 Mortgage and assignment signed by clients		
31 Notice of assignment to insurers drawn		
32(a) Completion statement from vendor's solicitor		
32(b) Completion statement approved		
33 Completion statement and bill sent to clients		
34 Funds received from clients		
35 Report on title and request for cheque to lenders		
36 Advance cheque received		
37(a) Search in Land Charges Register		
37(b) Result satisfactory		
38(a) Search in District Land Registry		
38(b) Result satisfactory		
39(a) Bankruptcy search		
39(b) Result satisfactory		
40 Vacant possession/keys arranged		
41 Funds received from related sale		
42 COMPLETION		
43 Report to client and lenders		
44(a) Notice of mortgage of policy to insurers		
44(b) Receipt of notice received		
45 Stamping attended to		
46 Registration applied for		
47 Title documents to lenders/clients		
48 Receipt for title documents received		
49 Costs transferred		
50 File closed		
ADDITIONAL MATTERS TO ATTEND TO		
1		
2		
3		
4		

APPENDIX 2

GUIDE TO TRANSACTIONS DEALT WITH IN TEXT

1. THE FRENCH/SAUNDERS PURCHASE

Fancy French and Sam Saunders are buying 24 De Lucy Mount, Ledchester, from Michel and Marie Melanie Rocard, with the aid of a mortgage loan from the Ledchester and Bongley Building Society. It is unregistered freehold title.

D. Copperfield & Co. of Bank Street, Ledchester are acting for the vendors.

Para.1.4 .... Taking instructions with copy instructions.

Documents 1.6.1, 1.6.2,
1.6.3 .... Letters to estate agents, vendors' solicitors and client care letter to Ms French.

Para.1.9.3............................ Can Timothy act for both Sam and Fancy?

Para.3.1 .... Fancy is worried about fire and things.

Document 4.1.8 .... Letter from vendors' solicitor.

Para.4.1.9............................ Timothy sends off Enquiries before Contract, Local land Charges search, Additional Enquiries of local authority, commons search, mining search, central land Charges search and inspects the property.

Documents 10.2 to 10.2.5...... Epitome of title and title documents of 24 De Lucy Mount.

Para.10.3............................. Requisitions on title.

Para.10.4............................. Reader asked to draft proper requisitions.

Document 12.2 .... Draft conveyance.

Document 13.2 .... Application for central Land Charges Registry search.

Documents 14.8.2(a),(b) .... Bill of costs and statment of account.

2. THE GOLDBERG SALE

Mr and Mrs Goldberg are selling part of their garden at Fell View, Koppax to Mr and Mrs Singh, with the benefit of planning permission to build one house. The whole of Fell View was originally part of Pit Mansion. The building society is going to join in the sale to release the part now being sold. Title is unregistered freehold.

Moriarty & Co. of Tumbledown House, The Bedrow, Ledchester are acting for the purchasers.

Document 5.1.1...................... Request to building society for the deeds and consent to join in sale to release part to be sold.

Document 5.1.3...................... Part of the instructions on sale.

Document 5.1.4...................... The sale plan of the property.

Document 5.1.6...................... The draft contract.

Documents 5.2(a), 5.2(b) .... The title to Fell View.

Document 6.2 .... The rest of the instructions on sale.

Para.6.2................................. Reader to draft rest of contract.

Document 9.2(a)................... Letter from vendors' solicitor re exchange.

Document 9.2(b) .... Memorandum of exchange by telephone.

Para.12.3.1............................ Reader asked to draft conveyance.

Document 14.2...................... Copy letter to purchasers' solicitor with completion statement.

Para.14.4............................... Death of Mrs Goldberg; Sonia Goldberg to join as trustee to convey.

Para.14.4............................... Completion. Reader to draft statement of account and bill of costs.

Para.14.7.2............................ Reader to draft conveyance to make Sonia a party to the conveyance.

3. THE OBEBE PURCHASE AND SALE

Miss Olive Obebe is selling 14 Harcastle Drive, on the Hardcastle Estate, part of a new developmennt built by Starrabs, from whom she bought about a year ago. She has agreed to sell to the Headcases. In its place she is buying 16 Winchester Avenue in Ledchester from Miss Mixford who inherited the property on the recent death of her uncle, Norman Mixford. The sale to the Headcases goes off at the last moment. Instead Miss Obebe sells to her sister. The title to both properties is registered freehold.

Moriarty & Co. are acting for Miss Mixford. Havisham & Co. are acting for the Headcases.

Purchase of 16 Winchester Avenue

Para.2.1 .... Miss Obebe worried about finance.

Document 4.1.1 .... Letter from vendor's solicitor. A contract race is started.

Document 4.1.2 .... Draft contract.

Document 4.1.3 .... Office copy entries and title plan.

Document 4.1.4 .... Property Information form with replies.

Document 4.1.5 .... Extract from Fixtures, Fittings and Contents list.

Document 4.1.6 .... Extract from Local Land Charges search form.

Document 4.1.7 .... Additional Enquiries of local authority.

Para.4.4.2 .... Miss Obebe's mother worried about the garden shed.

Para.9.3 .... Exchange of contracts.

Para.11.3.5 .... Reader asked to draft requisitions on the purchase.

Document 12.6 .... Draft transfer.

Document 13.3 .... Application for official search in Land Registry.

Document 13.4 .... Application for bankruptcy search.

Sale of 14 Hardcastle Drive

STANDARD CONDITIONS OF SALE (SECOND EDITION) (NATIONAL CONDITIONS OF SALE 22ND EDITION, LAW SOCIETY'S CONDITIONS OF SALE 1992)

1. GENERAL

1.1 Definitions

1.1.1 In these conditions:

(a) 'accrued interest' means:

(i) if money has been placed on deposit or in a building society share account, the interest actually earned

(ii) otherwise, the interest which might reasonably have been earned by depositing the money at interest on seven days' notice of withdrawal with a clearing bank less, in either case, any proper charges for handling the money

(b) 'agreement' means the contractual document which incorporates these conditions, with or without amendment

(c) 'banker's draft' means a draft drawn by and on a clearing bank

(d) 'clearing bank' means a bank which is a member of CHAPS and Town Clearing Company Limited

(e) 'completion date', unless defined in the agreement, has the meaning given in condition 6.1.1

(f) 'contract' means the bargain between the seller and the buyer of which these conditions, with or without amendment, form part

(g) 'contract rate', unless defined in the agreement, is the Law Society's interest rate from time to time in force

(h) 'lease' includes sub-lease, tenancy and agreement for a lease or sub-lease

(i) 'notice to complete' means a notice requiring completion of the contract in accordance with condition 6

(j) 'public requirement' means any notice, order or proposal given or made (whether before or after the date of the contract) by a body acting on statutory authority

(k) 'requisition' includes objection

(l) 'solicitor' includes barrister, duly certificated notary public, recognised licensed conveyancer and recognised body under sections 9 or 32 of the Administration of Justice Act 1985

(m) 'transfer' includes conveyance and assignment

(n) 'working day' means any day from Monday to Friday (inclusive) which is not Christmas Day, Good Friday or a statutory Bank Holiday.

1.1.2 When used in these conditions the terms 'absolute title' and 'office copies' have the special meanings given to them by the Land Registration Act 1925.

1.2 Joint parties
If there is more than one seller or more than one buyer, the obligations which they undertake can be enforced against them all jointly or against each individually.

1.3 Notices and documents
1.3.1 A notice required or authorised by the contract must be in writing.

1.3.2 Giving a notice or delivering a document to a party's solicitor has the same effect as giving or delivering it to that party.

1.3.3 Transmission by fax is a valid means of giving a notice or delivering a document where delivery of the original document is not essential.

1.3.4 Subject to conditions 1.3.5 to 1.3.7, a notice is given and a document delivered when it is received.

1.3.5 If a notice or document is received after 4.00pm on a working day, or on a day which is not a working day, it is to be treated as having been received on the next working day.

1.3.6 Unless the actual time of receipt is proved, a notice or document sent by the following means is to be treated as having been received before 4.00pm on the day shown below:

(a) by first-class post: two working days after posting

(b) by second-class post: three working days after posting

(c) through a document exchange: on the first working day after the day on which it would normally be available for collection by the addressee.

1.3.7 Where a notice or document is sent through a document exchange, then for the purposes of condition 1.3.6 the actual time of receipt is:

(a) the time when the addressee collects it from the document exchange or, if earlier

(b) 8.00am on the first working day on which it is available for collection at that time.

1.4 VAT

1.4.1 An obligation to pay money includes an obligation to pay any value added tax chargeable in respect of that payment.

1.4.2 All sums made payable by the contract are exclusive of value added tax.

2. FORMATION

2.1 Date

2.1.1 If the parties intend to make a contract by exchanging duplicate copies by post or through a document exchange, the contract is made when the last copy is posted or deposited at the document exchange.

2.1.2 If the parties' solicitors agree to treat exchange as taking place before duplicate copies are actually exchanged, the contract is made as so agreed.

2.2 Deposit

2.2.1 The buyer is to pay or send a deposit of 10 per cent of the purchase price no later than the date of the contract. Except on a sale by auction. payment is to be made by banker's draft or by a cheque drawn on a solicitors' clearing bank account.

2.2.2 If before completion date the seller agrees to buy another property in England and Wales for his residence, he may use all or any part of the deposit as a deposit in that transaction to be held on terms to the same effect as this condition and condition 2.2.3.

2.2.3 Any deposit or part of a deposit not being used in accordance with condition 2.2.2 is to be held by the seller's solicitor as stakeholder on terms that on completion it is paid to the seller with accrued interest.

2.2.4 If a cheque tendered in payment of all or part of the deposit is dishonoured when first presented, the seller may, within seven working days of being notified that the cheque has been dishonoured, give notice to the buyer that the contract is discharged by the buyer's breach.

2.3 Auctions

2.3.1 On a sale by auction the following conditions apply to the property and, if it is sold in lots, to each lot.

2.3.2 The sale is subject to a reserve price.

2.3.3 The seller, or a person on his behalf, may bid up to the reserve price.

2.3.4 The auctioneer may refuse any bid.

2.3.5 If there is a dispute about a bid, the auctioneer may resolve the dispute or restart the auction at the last undisputed bid.

3. MATTERS AFFECTING THE PROPERTY

3.1 Freedom from incumbrances

3.1.1 The seller is selling the property free from incumbrances, other than those mentioned in condition 3.1.2.

3.1.2 The incumbrances subject to which the property is sold are:

(a) those mentioned in the agreement

(b) those discoverable by inspection of the property before the contract

(c) those the seller does not and could not know about

(d) entries made before the date of the contract in any public register except those maintained by HM Land Registry or its Land Charges Department or by Companies House

(e) public requirements.

3.1.3 The buyer accepts the property in the physical state it is in at the date of the contract, unless the seller is building or converting it.

3.1.4 After the contract is made, the seller is to give the buyer written details without delay of any new public requirement and of anything in writing which he learns about concerning any incumbrances subject to which the property is sold.

3.1.5 The buyer is to bear the cost of complying with any outstanding public requirement and is to indemnify the seller against any liability resulting from a public requirement.

3.2 Leases affecting the property

3.2.1 The following provisions apply if the agreement states that any part of the property is sold subject to a lease.

(a) The seller having provided the buyer with full details of each lease or copies of the documents embodying the lease terms, the buyer is treated as entering into the contract knowing and fully accepting those terms

(b) The seller is to inform the buyer without delay if the lease ends or if the seller learns of any application by the tenant in connection with the lease, the seller is then to act as the buyer reasonably directs, and the buyer is to indemnify him against all consequent loss and expense

(c) The seller is not to agree to any proposal to change the lease terms without the consent of the buyer and is to inform the buyer without delay of any change which may be proposed or agreed

(d) The buyer is to indemnify the seller against all claims arising from the lease after actual completion; this includes claims which are unenforceable against a buyer for want of registration

(e) The seller takes no responsibility for what rent is lawfully recoverable, nor for whether or how any legislation affects the lease

(f) If the let land is not wholly within the property, the seller may apportion the rent.

3.3 Retained land

3.3.1 The following provisions apply where after the transfer the seller will be retaining land near the property.

3.3.2 The buyer will have no right of light or air over the retained land, but otherwise the seller and the buyer will each have the rights over the land of the other which they would have had if they were two separate buyers to whom the seller had made simultaneous transfers of the property and the retained land.

3.3.3 Either party may require that the transfer contain appropriate express terms.

4. TITLE AND TRANSFER
4.1 Timetable

4.1.1 The following are the steps for deducing and investigating the title to the property to be taken within the following time limits:

Step	Time Limit
1. The seller is to send the buyer evidence of title in accordance with condition 4.2	1. Immediately after making the contract
2. The buyer may raise written requisitions	2. Six working days after either the date of the contract or the date of delivery of the seller's evidence of title on which the requisitions are raised whichever is the later
3. The seller is to reply in writing to any requisitions raised	3. Four working days after receiving the requisitions
4. The buyer may make written observations on the seller's replies	4. Three working days after receiving the replies.

The time limit on the buyer's right to raise requisitions applies even where the seller supplies incomplete evidence of his title, but the buyer may, within six working days from delivery of any further evidence, raise further requisitions resulting from that evidence. On the expiry of the relevant time limit the buyer loses his right to raise requisitions or make observations.

4.1.2 The parties are to take the following steps to prepare and agree the transfer of the property within the following time limits:

Step	**Time Limit**
A. The buyer is to send the seller a draft transfer	A. At least twelve working days before completion date
B. The seller is to approve or revise that draft and either return it or retain it for use as the actual transfer	B. Four working days after delivery of the draft transfer
C. If the draft is returned the buyer is to send an engrossment to the seller	C. At least five working days before completion date

4.1.3 Periods of time under conditions 4.1.1 and 4.1.2 may run concurrently.

4.1.4 If the period between the date of the contract and completion date is less than 15 working days, the time limits in conditions 4.1.1 and 4.1.2 are to be reduced by the same proportion as that period bears to the period of 15 working days Fractions of a working day are to be rounded down except that the time limit to perform any step is not to be less than one working day.

4.2 Proof of title

4.2.1 The evidence of registered title is office copies of the items required to be furnished by section 110(1) of the Land Registration Act 1925 and the copies abstracts and evidence referred to in section 110(2)

4.2.2 The evidence of unregistered title is an abstract of the title, or an epitome of title with photocopies of the relevant documents.

4.2.3 Where the title to the property is unregistered, the seller is to produce to the buyer (without cost to the buyer):

(a) the original of every relevant document, or

(b) an abstract, epitome or copy with an original marking by a solicitor of examination either against the original or against an examined abstract or against an examined copy.

4.3 Defining the property

4.3.1 The seller need not:

(a) prove the exact boundaries of the property

(b) prove who owns fences, ditches, hedges or walls

(c) separately identify parts of the property with different titles further than he may be able to do from information in his possession.

4.3.2 The buyer may, if it is reasonable, require the seller to make or obtain, pay for and hand over a statutory declaration about facts relevant to the matters mentioned in condition 4.3.1. The form of the declaration is to be agreed by the buyer, who must not unreasonably withhold his agreement.

4.4 Rents and rentcharges

The fact that a rent or rentcharge, whether payable or receivable by the owner of the property, has been or will on completion be, informally apportioned is not to be regarded as a defect in title.

4.5 Transfer

4.5.1 The buyer does not prejudice his right to raise requisitions, or to require replies to any raised, by taking any steps in relation to the preparation or agreement of the transfer.

4.5.2 The seller is to transfer the property in the capacity specified in the agreement, or (if none is specified) as beneficial owner.

4.5.3 If after completion the seller will remain bound by any obligation affecting the property, but the law does not imply any covenant by the buyer to indemnify the seller against liability for future breaches of it:

(a) the buyer is to covenant in the transfer to indemnify the seller against liability for any future breach of the obligation and to perform it from then on, and

(b) if required by the seller, the buyer is to execute and deliver to the seller on completion a duplicate transfer prepared by the buyer

4.5.4 The seller is to arrange at his expense that, in relation to every document of title which the buyer does not receive on completion, the buyer is to have the benefit of:

(a) a written acknowledgement of his right to its production, and

(b) a written undertaking for its safe custody (except while it is held by a mortgagee or by someone in a fiduciary capacity).

5. PENDING COMPLETION

5.1 Responsibility for property

5.1.1 The seller will transfer the property in the same physical state as it was at the date of the contract (except for fair wear and tear), which means that the seller retains the risk until completion.

5.1.2 If at any time before completion the physical state of the property makes it unusable for its purpose at the date of the contract:

(a) the buyer may rescind the contract

(b) the seller may rescind the contract where the property has become unusable for that purpose as a result of damage against which the seller could not reasonably have insured, or which it is not legally possible for the seller to make good.

5.1.3 The seller is under no obligation to the buyer to insure the property.

5.1.4 Section 47 of the Law of Property Act 1925 does not apply.

5.2 Occupation by buyer

5.2.1 If the buyer is not already lawfully in the property, and the seller agrees to let him into occupation, the buyer occupies on the following terms.

5.2.2 The buyer is a licensee and not a tenant. The terms of the licence are that the buyer:

(a) cannot transfer it

(b) may permit members of his household to occupy the property

(c) is to pay or indemnify the seller against all outgoings and other expenses in respect of the property

(d) is to pay the seller a fee calculated at the contract rate on the purchase price (less any deposit paid) for the period of the licence

(e) is entitled to any rents and profits from any part of the property which he does not occupy

(f) is to keep the property in as good a state of repair as it was in when he went into occupation (except for fair wear and tear) and is not to alter it

(g) is to insure the property in a sum which is not less than the purchase price against all risks in respect of which comparable premises are normally insured

(h) is to quit the property when the licence ends.

5.2.3 On the creation of the buyer's licence, condition 5.1 ceases to apply, which means that the buyer then assumes the risk until completion.

5.2.4 The buyer is not in occupation for the purposes of this condition if he merely exercises rights of access given solely to do work agreed by the seller.

5.2.5 The buyer's licence ends on the earliest of: completion date, rescission of the contract or when five working days' notice given by one party to the other takes effect.

5.2.6 If the buyer is in occupation of the property after his licence has come to an end and the contract is subsequently completed he is to pay the seller compensation for his continued occupation calculated at the same rate as the fee mentioned in condition 5.2.2(d).

5.2.7 The buyer's right to raise requisitions is unaffected.

6. COMPLETION

6.1 Date

6.1.1 Completion date is twenty working days after the date of the contract but time is not of the essence of the contract unless a notice to complete has been served.

6.1.2 If the money due on completion is received after 2.00pm completion is to be treated, for the purposes only of conditions 6.3 and 7.3, as taking place on the next working day.

6.1.3 Condition 6.1.2 does not apply where the sale is with vacant possession of the property or any part and the seller has not vacated the property or that part by 2.00pm on the date of actual completion.

6.2 Place

Completion is to take place in England and Wales, either at the seller's solicitor's office or at some other place which the seller reasonably specifies.

6.3 Apportionments

6.3.1 Income and outgoings of the property are to be apportioned between the parties so far as the change of ownership on completion will affect entitlement to receive or liability to pay them.

6.3.2 If the whole property is sold with vacant possession or the seller exercises his option in condition 7.3.4, apportionment is to be made with effect from the date of actual completion; otherwise, it is to be made from completion date.

6.3.3 In apportioning any sum, it is to be assumed that the seller owns the property until the end of the day from which apportionment is made and that the sum accrues from day to day at the rate at which it is payable on that day.

6.3.4 For the purpose of apportioning income and outgoings, it is to be assumed that they accrue at an equal daily rate throughout the year.

6.3.5 When a sum to be apportioned is not known or easily ascertainable at completion, a provisional apportionment is to be made according to the best estimate available. As soon as the amount is known, a final apportionment is to be made and notified to the other party. Any resulting balance is to be paid no more than ten working days later, and if not then paid the balance is to bear interest at the contract rate from then until payment.

6.3.6 Compensation payable under condition 5.2.6 is not to be apportioned.

6.4 Amount payable

The amount payable by the buyer on completion is the purchase price (less any deposit already paid to the seller or his agent) adjusted to take account of:

(a) apportionments made under condition 6.3

(b) any compensation to be paid or allowed under condition 7.3.

6.5 Title deeds

6.5.1 The seller is not to retain the documents of title after the buyer has tendered the amount payable under condition 6.4.

6.5.2 Condition 6.5.1 does not apply to any documents of title relating to land being retained by the seller after completion.

6.6 Rent receipts

The buyer is to assume that whoever gave any receipt for a payment of rent or service charge which the seller produces was the person or the agent of the person then entitled to that rent or service charge.

6.7 Means of payment

The buyer is to pay the money due on completion in one or more of the following ways:

(a) legal tender

(b) a banker's draft

(c) a direct credit to a bank account nominated by the seller's solicitor

(d) an unconditional release of a deposit held by a stakeholder.

6.8 Notice to complete

6.8.1 At any time on or after completion date, a party who is ready able and willing to complete may give the other a notice to complete.

6.8.2 A party is ready able and willing:

(a) if he could be, but for the default of the other party, and

(b) in the case of the seller, even though a mortgage remains secured on the property, if the amount to be paid on completion enables the property to be transferred freed of all mortgages (except those to which the sale is expressly subject).

6.8.3 The parties are to complete the contract within ten working days of giving a notice to complete, excluding the day on which the notice is given. For this purpose, time is of the essence of the contract.

6.8.4 On receipt of a notice to complete:

(a) If the buyer paid no deposit, he is forthwith to pay a deposit of 10 per cent

(b) If the buyer paid a deposit of less than 10 per cent, he is forthwith to pay a further deposit equal to the balance of that 10 per cent.

7. REMEDIES

7.1 Errors and omissions

7.1.1 If any plan or statement in the contract, or in the negotiations leading to it, is or was misleading or inaccurate due to an error or omission, the remedies available are as follows:

7.1.2 When there is a material difference between the description or value of the property as represented and as it is, the injured party is entitled to damages.

7.1.3 An error or omission only entitles the injured party to rescind the contract:

(a) where it results from fraud or recklessness, or

(b) where he would be obliged, to his prejudice, to transfer or accept property differing substantially (in quantity, quality or tenure) from what the error or omission had led him to expect.

7.2 Rescission

If either party rescinds the contract:

(a) unless the rescission is a result of the buyer's breach of contract the deposit is to be repaid to the buyer with accrued interest

(b) the buyer is to return any documents he received from the seller and is to cancel any registration of the contract.

7.3 Late completion

7.3.1 If there is default by either or both of the parties in performing their obligations under the contract and completion is delayed, theparty whose total period of default is the greater is to pay compensation to the other party.

7.3.2 Compensation is calculated at the contract rate on the purchase price, or (where the buyer is the paying party) the purchase price less any deposit paid, for the period by which the paying party's default exceeds that of the receiving party or, if shorter, the period between completion date and actual completion.

7.3.3 Any claim for loss resulting from delayed completion is to be reduced by any compensation paid under this contract.

7.3.4 Where the buyer holds the property as tenant of the seller and completion is delayed, the seller may give notice to the buyer, before the date of actual completion, that he intends to take the net income from the property until completion. If he does so, he cannot claim compensation under condition 7.3.1 as well.

7.4 After completion

Completion does not cancel liability to perform any outstanding obligation under this contract.

7.5 Buyer's failure to comply with notice to complete

7.5.1 If the buyer fails to complete in accordance with a notice to complete, the following terms apply.

7.5.2 The seller may rescind the contract, and if he does so:

(a) he may

(i) forfeit and keep any deposit and accrued interest

(ii) resell the property

(iii) claim damages

(b) the buyer is to return any documents he received from the seller and is to cancel any registration of the contract.

7.5.3 The seller retains his other rights and remedies.

7.6 Seller's failure to comply with notice to complete

7.6.1 If the seller fails to complete in accordance with a notice to complete, the following terms apply.

7.6.2 The buyer may rescind the contract, and if he does so:

(a) the deposit is to be repaid to the buyer with accrued interest

(b) the buyer is to return any documents he received from the seller and is, at the seller's expense, to cancel any registration of the contract.

7.6.3 The buyer retains his other rights and remedies.

8. LEASEHOLD PROPERTY

8.1 Existing leases

8.1.1 The following provisions apply to a sale of leasehold land.

8.1.2 The seller having provided the buyer with copies of the documents embodying the lease terms, the buyer is treated as entering into the contract knowing and fully accepting those terms.

8.1.3 The seller is to comply with any lease obligations requiring the tenant to insure the property.

8.1.4 The transfer is to record that no covenant implied by statute makes the seller liable to the buyer for any breach of the lease terms about the condition of the property. This applies even if the seller is to transfer as beneficial owner.

8.2 New leases

8.2.1 The following provisions apply to a grant of a new lease.

8.2.2 The conditions apply so that:

'seller' means the proposed landlord

'buyer' means the proposed tenant

'purchase price' means the premium to be paid on the grant of a lease.

8.2.3 The lease is to be in the form of the draft attached to the agreement

8.2.4 If the term of the new lease will exceed 21 years, the seller is to deduce a title which will enable the buyer to register the lease at HM Land Registry with an absolute title.

8.2.5 The buyer is not entitled to transfer the benefit of the contract.

8.2.6 The seller is to engross the lease and a counterpart of it and is to send the counterpart to the buyer at least five working days before completion date.

8.2.7 The buyer is to execute the counterpart and deliver it to the seller on completion.

8.3 Landlord's consent

The following provisions apply if a consent to assign or sub-let is required to complete the contract.

(a) The seller is to apply for the consent at his expense, and to use all reasonable efforts to obtain it

(b) The buyer is to provide all information and references reasonably required.

8.3.3 The buyer is not entitled to transfer the benefit of the contract.

8.3.4 Unless he is in breach of his obligation under condition 8.3.2, either party may rescind the contract by notice to the other party if three working days before completion date:

(a) the consent has not been given or

(b) the consent has been given subject to a condition to which the buyer reasonably objects.

In that case, neither party is to be treated as in breach of contract and condition 7.2 applies.

9. CHATTELS

9.1 The following provisions apply to any chattels which are to be sold.

9.2 Whether or not a separate price is to be paid for the chattels, the contract takes effect as a contract for sale of goods.

9.3 Ownership of the chattels passes to the buyer on actual completion.

APPENDIX 4

GUIDANCE — THE LAW SOCIETY'S FORMU-
LAE FOR EXCHANGING CONTRACTS BY
TELEPHONE OR TELEX

FORMULAE A & B (1986)

Introduction

These formulae which solicitors are free to adopt were first published in 1980 ([1980] *Gazette* 13 February, 144), shortly after *Domb v Isoz* [1980] Ch. 548 which had suggested their creation. They have been republished twice: first in January 1984 unchanged ([1984] *Gazette* 18 January, 82), and again in July 1984 when they were extended to include document exchanges as a standard alternative means of communication ([1984] *Gazette,* 4 July, 1891). Although there is only minimal change in the wording of the formulae themselves from July 1984, this guidance has been revised to reflect some of the points that have come to light through experience of the use of the formulae. The one change in the wording of the formulae themselves is the reference to 'clients(s)' to emphasise that the solicitor warrants that all necessary parties have signed. **These formulae replace the earlier versions with effect from 31 July 1986.**

Experience has shown that to avoid the risk of misunderstandings, it is essential that an agreed memorandum of the details and in particular of any variations of the formula should be made at the time and retained in the file. This will be very important if any question on the exchange is raised subsequently. Moreover agreed variations should be confirmed in the subsequent correspondence. The serious risks of effecting exchange of contracts without a deposit were demonstrated in the case of *Morris v Duke Cohan & Co.* (1975) 1 19 S.J. 826.

As the persons involved in the exchange will bind their firms to the undertakings in the formula used, solicitors should carefully consider who is to be authorised to effect exchange of contracts by telephone or telex and should ensure that the use of the procedure is restricted to them. Because professional undertakings form the basis of the formulae they are only recommended for use between firms of solicitors.

Law Society Telephone/Telex Exchange — Formula A (1986)

(for use where one solicitor holds both signed parts of the contract):

A. A completion date of   19 is agreed. The solicitor holding both parts of the contract confirms that he holds the part signed by his client(s), which is identical to the part he is also holding signed by the other solicitor's client(s) and will forthwith insert the agreed completion date in each part.

Solicitors mutually agree that exchange shall take place from that moment and the solicitor holding both parts confirms that, as of that moment, he holds the part signed by his client(s) to the order of the other. He undertakes that day by first class post, or where the other solicitor is a member of a document exchange (as to which the inclusion of a reference thereto in the solicitor's letterhead shall be conclusive evidence) by delivery to that or any other affiliated exchange or by hand delivery direct to that .solicitor's office, to send his signed part of the contract to the other solicitor, together, where he is the purchaser's solicitor, with a banker's draft or a solicitor's client account cheque for the deposit amounting to £....

Law Society Telephone/Telex Exchange — Formula B (1986)

(for use where each solicitor holds his own client's signed part of the contract):

B. A completion date of   19 is agreed. Each solicitor confirms to the other that he holds a part contract in the agreed form signed by the client(s) and will forthwith insert the agreed completion date.

Each solicitor undertakes to the other thenceforth to hold the signed part of the contract to the other's order, so that contracts are exchanged at that moment. Each solicitor further undertakes that day by first class post, or, where the other solicitor is a member of a document exchange (as to which the inclusion of a reference thereto in the solicitor's letterhead shall be conclusive evidence) by delivery to that or any other affiliated exchange or by hand delivery direct to that solicitor's office, to send his signed part of the contract to the other together, in the case of a purchaser's solicitor, with a banker's draft or a solicitor's client account cheque for the deposit amounting to £....

Notes

1. A memorandum should be prepared, after use of a formula, recording:

(a) date and time of exchange;

(b) the formula used and exact wording of agreed variations;

(c) the completion date;

(d) the (balance) deposit to be paid;

(e) the identities of those involved in any conversation.

2. In formula B cases, those who are going to effect the exchange must first confirm the details in order to ensure that both parts are identical. This means in particular, that if either part of the contract has been amended since it was originally prepared, the solicitor who holds a part contract with the amendments must disclose them so that it can be confirmed that the other part is similarly amended.

9 July 1986 (updated January 1993)

FORMULA C

Introduction

Experience has shown the need for a further procedure in domestic conveyancing to cover cases where there is a chain of transactions when formulae A and B are not intended to be used. The Law Society's formula C for exchange of contract by telephone or telex has been drafted for use in this type of case.

Experience has shown that to avoid risk or misunderstanding, it is essential that an agreed memorandum of the details and, in particular, of any variations of the formula should be made at the time and retained in the file. This would be very important if any question on the exchange were raised subsequently. Moreover, agreed variation should be confirmed in writing. The serious risks of effecting exchange of contracts without a deposit, unless the full implications are explained to and accepted by the seller client, are demonstrated in *Morris v Duke-Cohan Co.* (1975) 119 S.J. 826.

As the persons involved in the exchange will bind their firms to the undertakings in the formula used, solicitors should carefully consider who is to be authorised to exchange contracts by telephone or telex and should ensure that the use of the procedure is restricted to them. Professional undertakings form the basis of the formulae so the undertakings are only recommended for use between firms of solicitors and licensed conveyancers.

The Council for Licensed Conveyancers have confirmed that they would regard any undertaking given by a licensed conveyancer under formula C as a professional undertaking. Accordingly, formula C and the accompanying introduction and notes may be read as substituting 'licensed conveyancer' for 'solicitor' where appropriate.

Formula C for exchange of contracts by telephone or telex is designed for cases of linked chains of transactions. It is in two stages: first, the solicitors confirm that they hold their own client's part of the contract duly signed, and the buyer's solicitor undertakes to exchange if — by an agreed time later that day (the time agreed should take account of the circumstances of the chain) — the seller's solicitor so requests; secondly, the seller's solicitor requests exchange, and the contract is binding. Both stages need to be recorded in the memoranda made by both solicitors. Special provisions apply to deposits (see below).

Formula C works like this. Assume a short chain: W sells to X, who sells to Y, who sells to Z.

10am: Z's solicitor telephones Y's solicitor: formula C, part I is agreed.

10.10am: Y's solicitor telephones X's solicitor: formula C, part I is agreed.

10.20am: X's solicitor telephones W's solicitor: formula B agreed — at the top of the chain, with part I of formula C in place further down the chain, an immediate exchange is possible.

10.30am: X's solicitor telephones Y's solicitor: formula C, part II activated — the X-Y contract is now binding.

10.40am: Y's solicitor telephones Z's solicitor: formula C, part II activated — the Y–Z contract is now binding.

Deposits

Formula C assumes that all the contracts in the chain require payment of a deposit on exchange. It allows for the case where some or all of the same money is used for all the deposits, because each seller uses the deposit received on the sale to pay the deposit on the purchase. To avoid delay on exchange of contract, formula C requires the deposit to be paid direct to the person who will ultimately hold it. The formula requires that the deposit under each contract is paid to the seller's solicitors as agents so that the deposit may be used to pay another deposit. The deposit must ultimately be held by a solicitor as stakeholder.

Arrangements for holding the deposit have to be made when the formula is used. To illustrate what happens, assume that the three-link chain used in the example above provides for 10% deposits, and W is selling to X for £60,000, X to Y for £50,000 and Y to Z for £40,000.

10am: when agreeing formula C part I, Y's solicitor requests Z's solicitor to pay the £4000 deposit to X's solicitor

10.10am: when agreeing formula C part I, X's solicitor requests Y's solicitor to pay, or arrange payment, of the £5000 deposit to W's solicitor.

10.20am: when agreeing formula B, X's solicitor stipulates (as a variation to formula B) that to make up the deposit of £6000, he or she will send £1000 to W's solicitor and will procure that £5000 is sent by solicitors further down the chain.

10.30am: nothing further is required when X's solicitors and Y's solicitor activate formula C part II. (The result of the 10.10am agreement is that Y's solicitor must remit £1000 to W's solicitor.)

10.40am When activating formula C part II, Y's solicitor amends the request to Z's solicitor. asking him or her to send the £4000 deposit to W's solicitor. W's solicitor will therefore receive the deposit of £6000 made up from: £4000 sent by Z's solicitor, £1000 sent by Y's solicitor and £1000 sent by X's solicitor.

Five points should be noted:

1. Formula C assumes the payment of a full contractual deposit (normally 10%). It is open to the parties to vary this but it is essential that negotiations to reduce the amount of the deposit should be undertaken at an early stage (for example, when raising enquiries before contract) and *not* when exchange of contracts is imminent as this can be extremely inconvenient and likely, at least temporarily, to cause the chain to break.

2. Obviously, when requesting all or part of a deposit to be paid to other solicitors, it is necessary to supply full details (name, address or DX number, reference and that solicitor's client's name). If particulars are given early in the transaction, it will be easier to guarantee a smooth exchange.

3. The contract term relating to the deposit must allow it to be passed on, with payment direct from payer to ultimate recipient, in the way in which the formula contemplates. The deposit must ultimately be held by a solicitor as stakeholder. Whilst some variation in the formula can be agreed this is a term of the formula which must *not* be varied, unless all the solicitors involved in the chain have agreed.

4. If a buyer proposes to use a deposit guarantee policy formula C will need substantial adaptation, It is essential that agreement on this, not only between the parties to the contract in question but also, so far as relevant, from the parties to the other contracts in the chain, is reached at an early stage in the transaction.

5. It is essential prior to agreeing part I of formula C that those who are going to effect the exchange must ensure that both parts of the contract are identical.

Solicitors' authority

Solicitors do not, automatically and as a matter of general law, have authority to exchange contracts on a formula C basis. To ensure that the formula works satisfactorily, and that solicitors do not become liable to their clients for a breach of professional duty, the solicitor should always ensure that he or she has the client's express authority to use formula C, preferably in writing. A suggested form of authority is set out below. It should be adapted to cover any special circumstances of the case.

Return calls

When part I of formula C is agreed, to avoid confusion and delay the buyer's solicitor should give the seller's solicitor the names of at least two people to whom the call to activate part II can be made. It is essential that there is somebody available in the buyer's solicitor's office up to the 'final time for exchange' to activate part II immediately the telephone call is received from the seller's solicitor and part I of the formula contains an undertaking to this effect.

Time for exchange

The contracts in a chain must be exchanged in the appropriate order. The 'final time for exchange' agreed in the case of each contract should be fixed with that in mind i.e. the times should be staggered to allow, before the end of the day, time to exchange the later contracts. Formula C assumes that contracts will be exchanged during the day on which it is initiated. Where part I has been agreed, but part II is not activated on the same day, the process must be started again, by agreeing part I on another day.

Solicitors' responsibility

Using formula C involves a solicitor in giving a number of professional undertakings. These must be performed precisely. Any failure will be a serious breach of professional discipline.

One of the undertakings may be to arrange that someone over whom the solicitor has no control will do something (i.e. to arrange for someone else to despatch the cheque or banker's draft in payment of the deposit) An undertaking is still binding even if it is to do something outside the solicitor's control (see Principle 19.03 in the Guide).

The Law Society accepts that solicitors can offer professional undertakings to, and accept professional undertakings from, licensed conveyancers in the same way as when dealing with solicitors.

Law Society Telephone/Telex Exchange — Formula C (1989)

(Incorporating amendments to include a reference to fax as stated in [1991] Gazette 11 December.)

Part I

The following is agreed:

Final time for exchange: pm

Completion date: 19

Deposit to be paid to:

Each solicitor confirms that he or she holds a part of the contract in the agreed form signed by his or her client, or, if there is more than one client, by all of them. Each solicitor undertakes to the other that:

(a) he or she will continue to hold that part of the contract until the final time for exchange on the date the formula is used, and

(b) if the vendor's solicitor so notifies the purchaser's solicitor by fax, telephone or telex (whichever was previously agreed) by that time, they will both comply with part II of the formula.

The purchaser's solicitor further undertakes that either he or some other named person in his office will be available up to the final time for exchange to activate part II of the formula on receipt of the telephone call, fax or telex from the vendor's solicitors.

Part II

Each solicitor undertakes to the other henceforth to hold the part of the contract in his possession to the other's order, so that contracts are exchanged at that moment, and to despatch it to the other on that day. The purchaser's solicitor further undertakes to the vendor's solicitor to despatch on that day, or to arrange for the despatch on that day of, a banker's draft or a solicitor's client account cheque for the full deposit specified in the agreed form of contract (divided as the vendor's solicitor may have specified) to the vendor's solicitor and/or to some other solicitor whom the vendor's solicitor nominates, to be held on formula C terms.

'To despatch' means to send by first class post, or, where the other solicitor is a member of a document exchange (as to which the inclusion of a reference thereto in the solicitor's letterhead is to be conclusive evidence) by delivery to that or any other affiliated exchange, or by hand delivery direct to the recipient solicitor's office. 'Formula C terms' means that the deposit is held as stakeholder, or as agent for the vendor with authority to part with it only for the purpose of passing it to another solicitor as deposit in a related property purchase transaction on these terms.

Notes
1. Two memoranda will be required when using formula C. One needs to record the use of part I, and a second needs to record the request of the vendor's solicitor to the purchaser's solicitor to activate part II.

2. The first memorandum should record:

(a) the date and time when it was agreed to use formula C;

(b) the exact wording of any agreed variations;

(c) the final time, later that day, for exchange;

(d) the completion date;

(e) the name of the solicitor to whom the deposit was to be paid, or details of amounts and names if it was to be split; and

(f) the identities of those involved in any conversation.

Authority from client to client's solicitor

I/We .... understand that my/our sale and purchase of .... are both part of a chain of linked property transactions, in which all parties want the security of contracts which become binding on the same day.

I/We agree that you should make arrangements with the other solicitors or licensed conveyancers involved to achieve this.

I/We understand that this involves each property-buyer offering, early on one day, to exchange contracts whenever, later that day, the seller so requests, and that the buyer's offer is on the basis that it cannot be withdrawn or varied during that day.

I/We agree that when I/we authorise you to exchange contracts, you may agree to exchange contracts on the above basis and give any necessary undertakings to the other parties involved in the chain and that my/our authority to you cannot be revoked throughout the day on which the offer to exchange contracts is made.

15 March 1989 (updated January 1993)

GUIDANCE — THE LAW SOCIETY'S CODE FOR COMPLETION BY POST

The Law Society's code for completion by post ('the code') was approved for publication by the Council's Non-Contentious Business Committee and is set out below. The attention of practitioners is drawn, in particular, to the notes that are published with it.

The Law Society's code for completion by post (1984 edition)

Preamble

The code provides a procedure for postal completion which practising solicitors may adopt by reference.

First, each solicitor must satisfy himself that no circumstances exist that are likely to give rise to a conflict between this code and the interest of his own client (including where applicable a mortgagee client).

The code, where adopted, will apply without variation except so far as recorded in writing beforehand.

The Code

1. Adoption hereof must be specifically agreed by all the solicitors concerned and preferably in writing.

2. On completion the vendor's solicitor will act as agent for the purchaser's solicitor without fee or disbursements.

3. The vendor's solicitor undertakes that on completion he:

(1) will have the vendor's authority to receive the purchase money; and

(2) will be the duly authorised agent of the proprietor of any charge upon the property to receive the part of the money paid to him which is needed to discharge such charge.

4. The purchaser's solicitor shall send to the vendor's solicitor instructions as to:

(1) documents to be examined and marked;

(2) memoranda to be endorsed;

(3) deeds, documents, undertakings and authorities relating to rents, deposits, keys, etc; and

(4) any other relevant matters.

In default of instructions, the vendor's solicitor shall not be under any duty to examine, mark or endorse any documents.

5. The purchaser's solicitor shall remit to the vendor's solicitor the balance due on completion specified in the vendor's solicitor's completion statement or with written notification; in default of either, the balance shown due by the contract. If the funds are remitted by transfer between banks, the vendor's solicitor shall instruct his bank to advise him by telephone immediately the funds are received. The vendor's solicitor shall hold such funds to the purchaser's solicitor's order pending completion.

6. The vendor's solicitor, having received the items specified in paras 4 and 5, shall forthwith, or at such later times as may have been agreed, complete. Thereupon he shall hold all documents and other items to be sent to the purchaser's solicitor as agent for such solicitor.

7. Once completion has taken place, the vendor's solicitor shall as soon as possible thereafter on the same day confirm the fact to the purchaser's solicitor by telephone or telex and shall also as soon as possible send by first class post or document exchange written confirmation to the purchaser's solicitor, together with the enclosures referred to in para 4 hereof. The vendor's solicitor shall ensure that such title deeds and any other items are correctly committed to the post or document exchange. Thereafter, they are at the risk of the purchaser's solicitor.

8. If either the authorities specified in para 3 or the instructions specified in para 4 or the funds specified in para 5 have not been received by

the vendor's solicitor by the agreed completion date and time, he shall forthwith notify the purchaser's solicitor and request further instructions.

9. Nothing herein shall override any rights and obligations of parties under the contract or otherwise.

10. Any dispute or difference which may arise between solicitors that is directly referable to a completion agreed to be carried out in accordance herewith, whether or not amended or supplemented in any way, shall be referred to an arbitrator to be agreed, within one month of any such dispute or difference arising between the solicitors who are party thereto, and, in the default of such agreement, on the application of any such solicitor, to an arbitrator to be appointed by the President of the Law Society.

11. Reference herein to vendor's solicitor and purchaser's solicitor shall, where appropriate, be deemed to include solicitors acting for parties other than vendor and purchaser.

Notes:

1. The object of the code is to provide solicitors with a convenient means for completion, on an agency basis, that can be adopted for use, where they so agree beforehand, in completions where a representative of the purchaser's solicitors is not attending at the office of the vendor's solicitors for the purpose.

2. As with the Law Society's formulae for exchange of contract by telephone/telex [see Annex 241 in the *Guide*], the code embodies professional undertakings and is, in consequence, only recommended for adoption between solicitors.

3. Cl 2 of the code expressly provides that the vendor's solicitor will act as agent for the purchaser's solicitor without fee or disbursements. It is envisaged that. in the usual case, the convenience of not having to make a specific appointment on the day of completion for the purchaser's solicitor to attend for the purpose will offset the agency work that the vendor's solicitor has to do and any postage he has to pay in completing under the code, and on the basis that most solicitors will from

time to time act both for the vendors and purchasers. If, nevertheless, a vendor's solicitor does consider that charges and/or disbursements are necessary in a particular case, as such an arrangement represents a variation in the code, it should be agreed in writing beforehand.

4. Having regard to the decision in *Edward Wong Finance Co. Ltd. v. Johnson, Stokes & Master* [1984] A.C. 1296, cl 3(2) of the code requires the vendor's solicitor to confirm, before he agrees to use the code, that he will be the duly authorised agent of the proprietor of any charge upon the property (typically but not exclusively the vendor's building society) to receive that part of the money paid to him which is needed to discharge such charge.

5. Cl 9 of the code expressly provides that nothing therein shall override any rights and obligations of parties under the contract or otherwise.

The above notes refer only to some of the points in the code that practitioners may wish to consider before agreeing to adopt it. It is emphasised that it is a matter for the solicitors concerned to read the code in full, so that they can decide beforehand whether they will make use of it as it stands or with any variations agreed in writing beforehand, whether or not they are referred to in the above notes, as the case may be.

THE NATIONAL CONVEYANCING PROTOCOL, 2ND EDITION ('TRANSACTION')

Council Statement

1. The Council recommend that solicitors follow the procedures set out in the Protocol in all domestic conveyancing transactions.

2. The procedures set out in the Protocol include the use of standardised documentation. This will simplify the checking of variables and will enable departures from the recommended format to be readily identified. The Protocol does not preclude the use of printed or typed contracts produced by firms themselves, although it may be thought desirable that the full text of the Conditions of Sale are reproduced rather than merely included by reference.

3. The introduction of a National Protocol is designed to streamline conveyancing procedures. Experience has shown that where local protocols have been implemented, these have speeded up the completion of pre-contract formalities and have improved communications between solicitors and their clients.

4 . The Protocol is a form of 'preferred practice' and its requirements should not be construed as undertakings. Nor are they intended to widen a solicitor's duty save as set out in the next paragraph. The Protocol must always be considered in the context of a solicitor's overriding duty to his or her own client's interests and where compliance with the Protocol would conflict with that duty, the client's wishes must always be paramount.

5. A solicitor acting in domestic conveyancing transactions should inform the solicitor acting for the other party at the outset of a transaction, whether or not he or she is proposing to act in accordance with the Protocol in full or in part. If the solicitor is using the Protocol he or she should give notice to the solicitor acting for the other party if during the course of the transaction it becomes necessary to depart from Protocol procedures.

6. A solicitor is, as a matter of professional conduct, under a duty to keep confidential client's business. The confidentiality continues until the client permits disclosure or waives the confidentiality (Principle 12.03 of *The Guide to the Professional Conduct of Solicitors* (1990)). With reference to paragraphs 4.5 and 5.3 of the National Protocol, the disclosure of information about a client's position is strictly subject to obtaining that client's authority to disclose. In the absence of such authority, a solicitor is not deemed to be departing from the terms of the Protocol and, as such, is not required to give notice as set out in paragraph 5 of this Statement.

The National Protocol (Second Edition)

Acting for the Seller

1. **The first step**

The seller should inform the solicitor as soon as it is intended to place the property on the market so that delay may be reduced after a prospective purchaser is found.

2. **Preparing the package: assembling the information**

On receipt of instructions, the solicitor shall then immediately take the following steps, at the seller's expense:

2.1   Locate the title deeds and, if not in the solicitor's custody, obtain them.

2.2   Obtain a copy of the O.S. Map, if necessary.

2.3   Make Local Search with the usual Part I Enquiries and any additional enquiries relevant to the property.

2.4   Make Village Green and Common Land searches if appropriate.

2.5   Make Mining Enquiries if appropriate and any other relevant searches.

Preparing the package: information from the seller

2.6   Obtain from the seller details to complete the Property Information Form or Seller's Property Information Form.

2.7   Obtain such original guarantees with the accompanying specification, planning decisions and building regulation approvals as are in the seller's possession and copies of any other planning consents revealed on the local search or details of any highway and sewerage agreements and bonds.

2.8   Give the seller the Fixtures, Fittings and Contents Form, with a copy to retain, to complete and return prior to the submission of the draft contract.

2.9   Obtain details of all mortgages and other financial charges of which the seller's solicitor has notice including where applicable improvement grants and discounts repayable to a local authority.

2.10 Ascertain the identity of all the people aged 18 or over living in the dwelling and ask about any financial contribution they or anyone else may have made towards its purchase or subsequent improvement.

2.11 In leasehold cases, ask the seller to produce, if possible:

   (1)   A receipt or evidence from the landlord of the last payment of rent.
   (2)   The maintenance charge accounts for the last three years, where appropriate, and evidence of payment.
   (3)   Details of the building's insurance policy.

If any of these are lacking, and are necessary for the transaction, the solicitor should obtain them from the landlord. At the same time investigate whether a licence to assign is required and if so enquire of the landlord what references are necessary and, in the case of some retirement schemes, if a charge is payable to the management company on change of ownership.

3. Preparing the package: the draft documents

As soon as the title deeds are available, the solicitor shall:

3.1 If the title is *unregistered:*

(1) Make a Land Charges Search against the seller and any other appropriate names.
(2) Make an Index Map Search in the Land Registry.
(3) Prepare an epitome of title. Mark copies or abstracts of all deeds which will not be passed to the buyer as examined against the original.
(4) Prepare and mark as examined against the originals copies of all deeds, or their abstracts, prior to the root of title containing covenants, easements etc., affecting the property.
(5) Check that all plans on copied documents are correctly coloured.

3.2 If the title is *registered,* obtain Office Copy entries of the register and copy documents incorporated into the land certificate.

3.3 Prepare the draft contract and Property Information Form or Seller's Property Information Form Part II using the standard forms.

4. A buyer's offer is accepted

When made aware that a buyer has been found the solicitor shall

4.1 Inform the buyer's solicitor in accordance with paragraph 5 of the Council Statement that the Protocol will be used.

4.2 Ascertain the buyer's position on any related sale and in the light of that reply, ask the seller for a completion date.

4.3 Send to the buyer's solicitor as soon as available:

(1) Draft contract.
(2) Office Copy entries, or a photocopy of the Land or Charge Certificate if they are not available, or the epitome of title (including details of any prior matters referred to

but not disclosed by the documents themselves).

(3) The Local Search, Index Map and other searches.

(4) The Property Information Form or Seller's Property Information Form with copies of all relevant planning decisions, guarantees etc.

(5) The completed Fixtures, Fittings and Contents Form. Where this is provided it will form part of the contract.

(6) In leasehold cases, a copy of the lease with all the information about maintenance charges and insurance which has so far been obtained and about the procedure (including references required) for obtaining the Landlord's consent to the sale.

(7) The seller's target date for completion.

4.4 Ask the buyer's solicitor if a 10% deposit will be paid and, if not, what arrangements are proposed.

4.5 If and to the extent that the seller consents to the disclosure, supply information about the position on the seller's own purchase and of any other transactions in the chain above, and thereafter, of any change in circumstances.

Acting for the buyer

5. The buyer's response

On receipt of instructions, the buyer's solicitor shall promptly:

5.1 Confirm to the seller's solicitor in accordance with paragraph 5 of the Council Statement that the Protocol will be used.

5.2 Ascertain the buyer's position on any related sale, mortgage arrangements and whether a 10% deposit will be provided.

5.3 If and to the extent that the buyer consents to the disclosure, inform the seller's solicitor about the position on the buyer's own sale, if any, and of any connected transactions, the general nature of the mortgage application, the amount of the deposit available and if the seller's target date for completion can be met, and thereafter, of any change in circumstances.

On receipt of draft documents:

5.4 Confirm approval of the draft contract and return it approved as soon as possible, having inserted the buyer's full names and address, subject to any outstanding matters.

5.5 At the same time ask only those specific additional enquiries which are required to elucidate some point arising out of the documents submitted or which are relevant to the particular nature or location of the property or which the buyer has expressly requested omitting any enquiry, including those about the structure of the building, which is capable of being ascertained by the buyer's own enquiries or survey or personal inspection. Additional duplicated standard forms should not be submitted; if they are, the seller is under no obligation to deal with them nor need answer any enquiry seeking opinions rather than facts.

5.6 Check the searches provided by the seller and

(a)   Confirm whether or not the searches (and any Search Validation Scheme Certificate) are accepted on behalf of the buyer and, if one or more are not

(b)   repeat the search, or searches, and/or make additional searches or consider use on behalf of the buyer of the Law Society's Search Validation Scheme.

5.7 Ensure that buildings insurance arrangements are in place.

6. Exchange of contracts

On exchange, the buyer's solicitor shall send or deliver to the seller's solicitor:

6.1 The signed contract with all names, dates and financial information completed.

6.2 The deposit provided in the manner prescribed in the contract. Under the Law Society's Formula C the deposit may have to be sent to another solicitor nominated by the seller's solicitor.

6.3 A cheque or cash to reimburse the cost of the searches and of a Search Validation Certificate provided by the seller, except those rejected by the buyer's solicitor when approving the draft contract.

6.4 If contracts are exchanged by telephone, the procedures laid down by the Law Society's Formulae A, B or C must be used and both solicitors must ensure (unless otherwise agreed) that the undertakings to send documents and pay the deposit on that day are strictly observed.

6.5 If contracts are exchanged in the post the seller's solicitor shall, once the buyer's signed contract and deposit are held unconditionally, having ensured that details of each contract are fully completed and identical, send the seller's signed contract on the day of exchange.

7. Between exchange and the day of completion

As soon as possible after exchange and in any case within the time limits contained in the contract:

7.1 The buyer's solicitor shall send to the seller's solicitor, in duplicate:

(1)   Requisitions on Title.
(2)   A draft conveyance, transfer or assignment.
(3)   Other documents e.g. draft receipt for fixtures, fittings and contents.

7.2 As soon as possible after receipt of these documents, the seller's solicitor shall send to the buyer's solicitor.

(1)   Replies to Requisitions on Title.
(2)   Draft conveyance, transfer or assignment approved.
(3)   If appropriate, completion statement supported by photocopy receipts or evidence of payment of apportionments claimed.
(4)   Copy of licence to assign obtained from the landlord if appropriate.

7.3 The buyer's solicitor shall then:

(1)   Engross the approved draft conveyance, transfer or assign-

ment, obtain the buyer's signature to it (if necessary) and send it to the seller's solicitor in time to enable the seller to sign it before completion without suffering inconvenience.

(2)   Take any steps necessary to ensure that the amount payable on completion will be available in time for completion.

(3)   Dispatch the Land Registry and Land Charges Searches and, if appropriate, a company search.

7.4 The seller's solicitor shall request redemption figures for all financial charges on the property revealed by the deeds/office copy entries.

8. Completion: the day of payment and removals

8.1 If completion is to be by post, the Law Society's Code for Completion shall be used, unless otherwise agreed.

8.2 As soon as practicable and not later than the morning of completion, the buyer's solicitor shall advise the seller's solicitor of the manner of transmission of the purchase money and of the steps taken to dispatch it.

8.3 On being satisfied as to the receipt of the balance of the purchase money, the seller's solicitor shall authorise release of the keys and notify the buyer's solicitor of release.

8.4 The seller's solicitor shall check that the seller is aware of the need to notify the local and water authorities of the change in ownership.

8.5 After completion, where appropriate, the buyer's solicitor shall give notice of assignment to the lessor.

9. Relationship with estate agents

Where the seller has instructed estate agents, the seller's solicitor shall take the following steps:

9.1 Inform them when draft contracts are submitted.

9.2 Inform them of any unexpected delays or difficulties likely to delay exchange of contracts.

9.3 Inform them when exchange has taken place and the date of completion.

9.4 On receipt of their commission account send a copy to the seller and obtain instructions as to arrangements for payment.

9.5 Inform them of completion and, if so instructed, pay the commission.

APPENDIX 7

LIST OF PRINTED FORMS

Note: The following is a selection of more commonly used forms for unregistered and registered conveyancing. For a full list see the catalogue published by the Solicitors' Law Stationery Society Ltd.

A. COMMON TO UNREGISTERED AND REGISTERED CONVEYANCING

SCS1 .... Standard Conditions of Sale (Second edition).

14E...................... Notice to complete under Standard Condition 6.

29 (Long)............. Enquiries before contract (Long form).

29 (Short) .... Enquiries before contract (Short form).

29 (CSC) .... Enquiries before contract (House).

LLC1 .... Application for search in Local Land Charges Register.

29 (1991) .... Enquiries of Local Authority (1991 Edition).

CR21 .... Requisition for official search of Registers of Common Land and Town or Village Greens.

29M...................... Coal mining search.

- .... Directory and Law Society's Guidance notes (coal mining).

27 .... Requisitions on title (Freehold).

28 .... Requisitions on title (Leasehold).

28A .... Requisitions on title (Leasehold or Freehold)(short form).

28B...................... Requisitions on title (Preliminary Enquiries having already been answered).

44 .... Memorandum of exchange of contracts by telephone.

58 .... Conveyancing check-list: Steps to be taken for vendor.

59 .... Conveyancing check-list: Steps to be taken for purchaser.

60 .... Conveyancing check-list: Steps to be taken when acting for building society but not borrower.

B. UNREGISTERED LAND

K1 .... Application for registration of land charge (except class F).

K2 .... Application for registration of class F land charge.

K6 .... Application for registration of priority notice.

K11 .... Application for cancellation of entry on register.

K13 .... Application for cancellation of class F land charge.

K14 .... Declaration in support of application.

K15 .... Official search in Land Charges Register.

K19 .... Application for office copy of entry in Land Charges Register.

C. REGISTERED LAND

96 .... Application for official search of index map.

13 .... Caution against first registration with statutory declaration in support.

16 .... Withdrawal of caution against first registration.

1B........................ Application by solicitor for first registration of freehold.

2B........................ Application by solicitor for first registration of leasehold on behalf of person other than original lessee (i.e. on assignment of unregistered lease).

3B........................ Application by solicitor for first registration of lease on behalf of original lessee (i.e. on grant of lease).

A13 .... List of documents.

109 .... Application for office copies of register and title plan.

110 .... Application for office copies of filed deeds.

94A .... Application by purchaser for official search with priority in respect of whole.

94B...................... Application by purchaser for official search with priority in respect of part.

94B(FR) .... Application by purchaser for official search with priority in respect of part of land in a pending first registration.

109 .... Application for certificate of inspection of title plan.

19 .... Transfer of whole (also obtainable in draft).

19(Co) .... Transfer of whole by company or corporation.

19(JP) .... Transfer of whole to joint proprietors.

19(r.72).................. Transfer of whole under Rule 72.

20 .... Transfer of part not imposing fresh restrictive covenants. Also obtainable in draft.

43 .... Transfer imposing fresh restrictive covenants. Also obtainable in draft.

34 .... Transfer of part of land in registered lease with apportionment of rent.

31 .... Transfer of whole in exercise of power of sale.

35 .... Transfer to a company or corporation.

53 .... Discharge of registered charge.

53(Co) .... Discharge of charge by by building society or other corporate body.

A4 .... Application for registration of dealing with whole.

A5 .... Application for registration of dealing with part.

A15 .... Documents deposited at Registry to await an application for registration.

A14 .... Documents deposited at Registry in connection with a pending registration.

6 .... Application for conversion of title.

56 .... Assent or appropriation.

82 .... Application to register the personal representative(s) of a deceased sole proprietor.

83 .... Application to register death of a joint proprietor.

63 .... Caution against dealings with statutory declaration in support.

71 .... Withdrawal of caution against dealings.

75 .... Application to register a restriction.

77 .... Application to withdraw or modify a restriction.

99 .... Application to register notice under Matrimonial Homes Act 1983.

202 .... Application to cancel notice under Matrimonial Homes Act 1983.

85A .... Notice of deposit of land or charge certificate.

86 .... Withdrawal of notice of deposit.

K16 .... Application for official search in Land Charges Register (Bankruptcy only).

APPENDIX 8

BIBLIOGRAPHY

TEXTS

Agency

Fridman's Law of Agency (6th ed., 1990, G. H. L. Fridman); Butterworths.

Bowstead on Agency (15th ed., 1985, F. M. B. Reynolds); Sweet & Maxwell.

Boundaries

C. F. Sara, *Boundaries and Easements*, (1991); Sweet & Maxwell.

Commons

G. D. Gadsden, *The Law of Commons*, (1988); Sweet & Maxwell.

R. Oswald, *Common Land and the Commons Registration Act 1965*, (1989); ESC Publishing.

Contract

Chitty on Contracts, (26th ed., A. G. Guest); Sweet & Maxwell.

K. Lewison, *The Interpretation of Contracts*, (1989); Sweet & Maxwell.

F. Silverman, *The Standard Conditions of Sale*, (4th ed., 1992); Fourmat.

F. Silverman, *Searches and Enquiries - A Conveyancer's Guide*, (2nd ed., 1992); Butterworths.

T. M. Aldridge, *Companion to the Standard Conditions of Sale (Second Edition)*, (2nd ed., 1992); Longman.

Conveyancing: registered and unregistered land

Sweet & Maxwell's Conveyancing Practice, (ed. P. H. Kenny and others); loose-leaf service.

J. F. Garner, *Local Land Charges*, (11th ed., 1992); Shaw.

J. F. Garner, *The Law of Sewers and Drains*, (7th ed., 1991); Shaw.

M. P. Thompson, *Investigation and Proof of Title*, (1991); Sweet & Maxwell.

T. M. Aldridge, *Companion to the Property Information Forms*, (2nd ed., 1990); Longman.

P. J. Palmer, *Housing Development Conveyancing*, (1991); Longman.

Barnsley's Land Options, (2nd ed., 1992, R. Castle); Butterworths.

Butterworths Property Law Service, Loose-leaf with up-dates.

K. Pugsley, *Enquiries of Local Authorities: A Practical Guide*, (2nd ed., 1991); Fourmat.

R. Annand and B. Cain, *Conveyancing Solutions 1: Enquiries Before Contract*, (1986); Sweet & Maxwell.

R. Annand and R. Whish, *Conveyancing Solutions 2: The Contract*, (1987); Sweet & Maxwell.

R. Annand and B. Cain, *Conveyancing Solutions 3: Remedies Under the Contract*, (1988); Sweet & Maxwell.

Fees, addresses, etc

Conveyancing Fees and Charges, (14th ed., 1992, Longman editorial); Longman.

Conveyancing Fees and Duties, (ed. Fourmat, 1993).

The Conveyancer's Directory; Fourmat.

Conveyancing: registered land

R. B. Roper and others, *The Law and Practice of Registered Conveyancing*, 6th ed.); loose-leaf service; Sweet & Maxwell. ('Ruoff & Roper').

T. B. F. Ruoff and E. J. Pryer, *Land Registration Handbook: Forms and Practice*, (1990); Sweet & Maxwell. ('Ruoff & Pryer').

Wontner's Guide to Land Registry Practice, (18th ed., 1991, P. J. Timothy), Longman. ('Wontner').

S. R. Coveney and A. J. Pain, *Interests in Land: A Practical Guide to Effective Protection at the Land Registry*, (1991); Fourmat.

Conveyancing: unregistered land

Emmett on Title, (19th ed., 1986, J. T. Farrand); loose-leaf with updates; Longman.

Easements

Gale's Easements, (15th ed., 1986, Spencer G. Maurice); Sweet & Maxwell.

Leasehold

G. Sheriff, *Service Charges in Leases*, (1989); Waterlow.

Handbook of Leasehold Reform, (ed. C. C. Hubbard and D. Williams); loose-leaf service; Sweet & Maxwell.

J. E. Martin, *Residential Security*, (1989); Sweet & Maxwell.

J. Warburton, *Sharing Residential Property*, (1990); Sweet & Maxwell.

Woodfall's Law of Landlord and Tenant, (ed. K. Lewison and others); loose-leaf service; Sweet & Maxwell.

Hill and Redman's Law of Landlord and Tenant, (ed. M. Barnes and others); loose-leaf work with service; Butterworths.

T. M. Aldridge, *Leasehold Law*, loose-leaf work; Longman.

T. M. Aldridge, *Law of Flats*, (2nd ed., 1989); Longman.

T. M. Aldridge, *Residential Lettings: Enfranchisement, Rent and Security*, (10th ed., 1993); Longman.

E. F. George & J. P. George, *The Sale of Flats,* (5th ed., 1984 with 1988 supplement); Sweet & Maxwell.

L. Crabb, *Leases, Covenants and Consents*, (1991); Sweet & Maxwell.

Litigation

The County Court Practice (the 'Green Book'); annual; ed. R. C. L. Gregory and others.

The Supreme Court Practice (The 'White Book'), (1991 with supplements); Sweet & Maxwell.

Mortgages

Fisher and Lightwood's Law of Mortgage (10th ed., 1988 with 1993 supplement, E. L. G. Tyler); Butterworths.

Planning

Butterworth's Planning Law Handbook, (3rd ed., 1992, B. Greenwood).

M. Grant, *Urban Planning Law*, (1982 with 1990 supplement); Sweet & Maxwell.

F. Bourne, *Enforcement of Planning Control,* (2nd ed., 1992); Sweet & Maxwell.

Encyclopedia of Compulsory Purchase and Compensation, (ed. C. Brand); loose-leaf service; Sweet & Maxwell.

Encyclopedia of Planning Law and Practice, (ed. M. Grant); loose-leaf service; Sweet & Maxwell.

M. Grant, *Permitted Development,* (1989); Sweet & Maxwell.

M. Grant, *Urban Planning Law,* (1982 with 1990 supplement); Sweet & Maxwell.

R. W. Suddards, *Listed Buildings,* (2nd ed., 1988).

Butterworths Planning Law Service; (ed. B. Greenwood and others); loose-leaf with service.

Professional conduct and negligence

Jackson & Powell on Professional Negligence, (3rd ed., 1992, R. Jackson & J. L. Powell); Sweet & Maxwell.

The Guide to the Professional Conduct of Solicitors, The Law Society, (6th ed., 1993). ('Guide').

Cordery's Law Relating to Solicitors, (8th ed., 1988 with 1991 supplement, T. T. Horne); Butterworths; ('Cordery').

P. M. K. Bird and others, *The Law, Practice and Conduct of Solicitors,* (1989); Waterlow.

Property law

Megarry & Wade, *The Law of Real Property,* (5th ed., 1984, Stevens); ('Megarry & Wade').

Cheshire & Burn's Modern Law of Real Property (14th ed., 1988, E. H. Burn); Butterworths.

M. P. Thompson, *Co-ownership,* (1988); Sweet & Maxwell.

J. Pugh-Smith, *Neighbours and the Law,* (2nd ed., 1993); Sweet & Maxwell.

A. J. Pain, *Adverse Possession: A Conveyancer's Guide,* (1992); Fourmat.

Restrictive covenants

Preston & Newsom's Restrictive Covenants Affecting Freehold Land, (8th ed., 1991, G. L. Newsom); Sweet & Maxwell.

Taxation and stamp duty

Whiteman on Capital Gains Tax, (4th ed., 1988 with 1992 supplement, P. Whiteman and others); Sweet & Maxwell.

Whiteman on Income Tax, (3rd ed., 1988 with 1992 supplement, P. Whiteman and others); Sweet & Maxwell.

R. Gregory, *Stamp Duty for Conveyancers*, (5th ed., 1990); Longman.

Tort

Clerk and Lindsell on Tort, (16th ed., 1989 with supplements to 1993, R. W. M. Dias and others; Sweet & Maxwell.

Charlesworth & Percy on Negligence, (8th ed., 1990, R. A. Percy); Sweet & Maxwell.

Wills, trusts and probate

The Probate Manual, (23rd ed., 1988, R. F. Yeldham and others); Waterlow.

Williams, Mortimer and Sunnucks on Executors, Administration and Probate, (17th ed., 1993, J. H. G. Sunnucks and others); Sweet & Maxwell.

Snell's Equity, (29th ed., 1990, P. V. Baker and P. St. J. Langan); Sweet & Maxwell.

PRECEDENTS AND DRAFTING

The Encyclopedia of Forms and Precedents, (5th ed., 1985 onwards); Butterworths. ('Encyclopedia').

Parker's Modern Conveyancing Precedents (2nd ed., 1989, E. Taylor); Butterworths. ('Parker').

T. M. Aldridge, *Practical Conveyancing Precedents*; loose-leaf; Longman.

Precedents for the Conveyancer, (ed. J. E. Adams); loose-leaf service.

T. M. Aldridge, *Practical Conveyancing Precedents*; loose-leaf; Longman.

C. Bennett, *Drafting Residential Leases*, (2nd ed., 1990); Longman.

T. M. Aldridge, *Practical Lease Precedents*; loose-leaf work; Longman.

D. Lush, *Cohabitation and Co-ownership Precedents*, (1993); Jordans.

Kelly's Draftsman, (16th ed., 1993, R. W. Ramage); Butterworths.

ARTICLES

Useful sources of articles on specific topics include:

The Legal Journals Index, (1986 continuing); Legal Information Resources Ltd. This covers English journals and is regularly updated.

Index to Legal Periodicals, with regular up-dates; H. W. Wilson & Co. Covers periodicals published in the U.S.A., Canada, Great Britain, Ireland, Australia and New Zealand.

Current Law. The annual volume includes a bibliography of books and articles published during the year. Monthly parts include books and articles under the appropriate headings.

RECENT CASES, LEGISLATION AND ORDERS

Current Law, published by Sweet & Maxwell, monthly with annual volumes includes recent cases, legislation and orders. Covers the U..K., Ireland and European Court of Justice cases. See also European Current Law first published in 1992.

The Digest, published by Butterworths with annual cumulative supplements; covers British, Commonwealth and European cases.

Halsbury's Statutory Instruments, published by Butterworths, includes a complete classification of all instruments in force of general application throughout England and Wales, with the full text of a selection.

Lexis includes cases (including a substantial number of unreported ones), statutes and statutory instruments.

Cases and articles of relevance to conveyancers will be found particularly in *The Conveyancer and Property Lawyer*.

INDEX